THE POWER
OF IDEOLOGY

By the same author

Marx's Theory of Alienation, Merlin Press 1970
Lukács's Concept of Dialectic, Merlin Press 1972
The Work of Sartre: Search for Freedom, Harvester Wheatsheaf 1979
Philosophy, Ideology and Social Science, Harvester Wheatsheaf 1986

THE POWER
OF IDEOLOGY

István Mészáros
Professor of Philosophy, University of Sussex

HARVESTER WHEATSHEAF
New York London Toronto Sydney Tokyo

First published 1989 by
Harvester Wheatsheaf,
66 Wood Lane End, Hemel Hempstead,
Hertfordshire, HP2 4RG
A division of
Simon & Schuster International Group

© I. Mészáros 1989

Printed and bound in Great Britain by
BPCC Wheatons Ltd, Exeter

British Library Cataloguing in Publication Data

Mészáros, István
   The power of ideology
   1. Ideology. Theories
   I. Title
   145

   ISBN 0-7450-0102-5

1 2 3 4 5   93 92 91 90 89

CONTENTS

PREFACE

I wish to draw the reader's attention to a volume of essays – *Philosophy, Ideology and Social Science* – which is complementary to the present study. In that volume, published by Harvester Wheatsheaf in 1986, four essays: 'Ideology and social science'; 'Contingent and necessary class consciousness'; 'Marx "philosopher"'; and 'Kant, Hegel, Marx: historical necessity and the standpoint of political economy' are directly relevant to some of the issues discussed in *The Power of Ideology*. Such issues are analyzed in these earlier essays, in their specific socio-historical context, in considerable detail. Thus, in order to avoid unnecessary repetition, I referred to the material which the interested reader can find in the volume on *Philosophy, Ideology and Social Science* only very briefly in the present study.

My apologies for the large number of notes and references; given the ramifications of the subject and the vast amount of literature that had to be critically examined in *The Power of Ideology*, it proved impossible to make convenient shortcuts. Nevertheless, in order to facilitate the assessment of the quoted literature, together with the additional theoretical material incorporated in the notes, I decided to use endnotes only and number them consecutively, in place of the frequently adopted, but from the point of view of the reader rather cumbersome, practice of splitting them up chapter by chapter. Hopefully, the ease with which the notes can now be consulted might help the reader to use the supporting evidence contained in them in conjunction with the text.

PART I

THE NECESSITY OF IDEOLOGY

Once upon a time a valiant fellow had the idea that men were drowned in water only because they were possessed with the *idea of gravity*. If they were to get this notion out of their heads, say by avowing it to be a superstitious, a religious concept, they would be sublimely proof against any danger from water. His whole life long he fought against the *illusion of gravity*, of whose harmful consequences all statistics brought him new and manifold evidence. This valiant fellow was the type of the new revolutionary philosophers in Germany.

Marx

CONSERVATIVE
dim, inconspicuous, quiet, restrained, subdued, tasteful, unassuming, un-obtrusive; canny, economical, frugal, provident, sparing, spartan, stewardly, thrifty, unwasteful; aloof, poised, reserved.

LIBERAL
advanced, broad, broad-minded, progressive, radical, tolerant, unbiased; bounteous, bountiful, free, generous, handsome, open-handed, unsparing; abounding, abundant, ample, copious, enough, galore, generous, overflowing, plentiful, plenty, prodigal, profuse, teeming.

REVOLUTIONARY
extreme, extremist, fanatic, fanatical, rabid, radical, ultra.

'Word Finder' Thesaurus of best-selling WordStar program.

1 · INTRODUCTORY

1.1 THE NATURE OF IDEOLOGY

1.1.1

What could be more objective than a dictionary? Indeed, what *should* be more objective and 'ideology-free' than a dictionary, be that a dictionary of synonyms? For, just like railway timetables, dictionaries are supposed to supply unadulterated factual information in order to fulfil their generally accepted function, instead of taking the unsuspecting passenger for a ride in a direction diametrically opposed to his or her chosen destination.

Yet, as we could observe on the preceding page, the *'Word Finder' Thesaurus* of one of the most popular word processor programs of all times, WordStar Professional,[1] heaps up with great generosity an astonishing range of positive characteristics on the 'Conservative' and the 'Liberal'; so much so in fact that one begins to wonder whether the adjectives 'heroic' and 'saintly' might not have been omitted by oversight. At the same time, the 'Revolutionary' receives an extremely short shrift – through which he would only qualify for treatment by the state judiciary and prison authorities – on account of being characterized as 'extreme, extremist, fanatic, fanatical, rabid, radical, and ultra'. This is what we get when the loudly proclaimed rules of 'objectivity' are applied to one side of the political spectrum, as against the other, even in as straightforward and 'ideology-free' a task as compiling a dictionary of synonyms.

All this may come as a surprise to many. Yet, the plain truth is that in our societies everything is 'soaked in ideology', whether we realize it or not. Moreover, in our liberal/conservative culture the socially established and dominant system of ideology can function in such a way as to present – and misrepresent – its own rules of selectivity, bias, discrimination, and even systematic distortion as 'normality', 'objectivity', and 'scientific detachment'.

In Western capitalist societies liberal/conservative ideological discourse dominates the assessment of all values to such an extent that very often we do not have the slightest suspicion that we are made to accept, quite unquestioningly, a particular set of values to which one could oppose a well founded alternative outlook, together with the commitments more or less implicit in it. For the very act of entering the framework of the dominant ideological discourse inevitably presents one with the pre-established 'rational' determination of: (a) how much (or how little) should be allowed to be considered contestable at all; (b) from what point of view, and (c) to which end in mind.

Naturally, those who take for granted the dominant ideology as the objective framework or 'rational' and 'scholarly' discourse reject as illegitimate all attempts that aim at identifying the hidden assumptions and implicit value-commitment of the ruling order. Thus, they have to disqualify the use of some vital categories of critical thought in the name of 'objectivity' and 'science'. For recognizing the legitimacy of such categories would mean consenting to submit to scrutiny the very assumptions that are being taken for granted, together with the conclusions that can be – and, of course, are – conveniently drawn from them.

A good example in this respect is provided by an Oxford Don who in a paper on economic exploitation of Africa insists that:

> *Exploitation*, like *imperialism*, is no word for *scholars* because it has long been confused by *ideological concepts*.[2]

As Harry Magdoff rightly comments:

> Scholars generally have had no trouble with emotionally laden words – such, for example, as murder, rape, or syphilis – even when the existing mores frowned on such usage in polite society. It is only a certain class of words, significantly enough, that over the years has raised the hackles of scholars. Thus, not only 'imperialism' and 'imperialist exploitation', but even such an important term in the socioeconomic lexicon as 'capitalism' is treated by academics with great circumspection.[3]

Once such concepts as 'exploitation' and 'imperialism' are expelled from any serious discussion of the relationship between the capitalistically advanced 'modern industrial' and 'post-industrial' societies and the economically dependent 'Third World' countries, the 'scholars' of self-complacent ideological consensus can go round in circles and successfully deduce from their assumed categorial matrix whatever suits the convenience of the ruling order and its hidden ideology. At the same time, the added benefit of this approach is that there is no need to pay the slightest attention to the arguments of the critical adversary, no matter how strong the theoretical and empirical evidence on his side. For he can be peremptorily dismissed on the strength of the assumed labelling device alone which rules 'out of bounds' his categories as 'confused ideological concepts', in the name of so-called 'objective scholarship' whose criteria are, again, circularly assumed as the self-evident standard of evaluation.

1.1.2

The dominant ideology of the established social system forcefully asserts itself at all levels, from the coarsest to the most refined. In fact there are many ways in which the various levels of ideological discourse intercommunicate. We may recall in this context that some of our most celebrated intellectuals in the postwar period argued in their books and academic studies that the 'antiquated' distinction between the political *Left* and *Right* made no sense whatsoever in our 'advanced' societies. As is well known, this wisdom has been eagerly embraced by the manipulators of public opinion and broadly diffused with the help of our cultural institutions, in the service of determinate ideological interests and values. Thanks to such interplay between the 'sophisticated' and the 'vulgar', it became customary to refer to the representatives of the *Right* as the *'moderates'*, while those on the *Left* were designated as *'extremists'*, *'fanatics'*, *'dogmatics'*, and the like.

Understandably, the ruling ideology has a great positional advantage in stipulating what may or may not be considered the legitimate criteria of conflict-evaluation, since it effectively controls the cultural and political institutions of society. It can misuse and abuse language quite openly, in that the danger of being publicly exposed is negligible; both because of the prevailing relation of forces and the *double standard* applied to the contested issues by the defenders of the established order.

To take only one recent example, the British government decided to force the jobless young people to join one of its 'Youth Opportunities' training schemes – which in reality provide very little training, if any, but have the primary purpose of 'massaging' the unemployment figures – by depriving them of their only livelihood, the social security benefits to which they are entitled by law. When the issue was debated in public, the government spokesmen declared with a straight face that there could be no question of *'forcing'* anybody; they only wanted to *'encourage'* the unemployed young people to take advantage of the 'opportunities' offered to them. (Just as they declared that the legal suppression of some BBC programmes – and even of some books – had nothing to do with *censorship*, but only with the 'government's duty of confidentiality'.) The question why the force of such an existentially hard-hitting law was chosen for the purpose of the pretended 'educational encouragement' of the young was, of course, left unanswered. As to the double standard practised by the same society, it is not too difficult to imagine how the state judiciary would respond if some of the young people who were deprived by the new law of their livelihood resorted to crime and tried to justify mugging their victims by saying that they did not 'force' anybody, but merely 'encouraged' people to hand over their money or other belongings.

Ideologically motivated and biased double standard is in evidence everywhere; even among those who take pride in their claim to represent 'the quality in life'. This could hardly be otherwise. For the ruling order must apply radically different criteria to itself than to those who must be kept in their subordinate position. Thus, the intellectual defenders of the *status quo* and 'neutral' guardians of its ideological orthodoxy can misrepresent their self-assured declarations of faith in their own wisdom, coupled with the most intemperate attacks on their adversaries, as undisputed 'scientific knowledge', without bothering to present in support of their claims the slightest proof from the dismissed theories.

In this spirit, John Maynard Keynes can write about Marx, amidst enthusiastic approval, in the most abusive fashion, using insults as 'evidence' both against his hated target and in favour of his own views. This is how he 'argues':

> How can I accept a doctrine which sets up as its bible, above and beyond criticism, an *obsolete economic textbook* which I know to be not only *scientifically* erroneous but *without interest or application for the modern world*? How can I adopt a creed which, *preferring the mud to the fish*, exalts the *boorish proletariat* above the bourgeois and the intelligentsia who, with whatever fault, are the *quality in life* and surely carry the seeds of all human advancement? Even if we need a religion, how can we find it in the *turbid rubbish of the Red bookshops*? It is hard for an *educated, decent, intelligent son of Western Europe* to find his ideals here, unless he has first suffered some *strange and horrid process of conversion* which has changed all his values.[4]

Evidently, it never occurs to Keynes that something might be wrong with, or problematical about, the exploitative values of the 'educated, decent, intelligent' – and blindly self-complacent – 'son of Western Europe'. Arguing from the standpoint and in the interest of the established socio-economic system, it seems to be enough to those who claim to 'carry the seeds of all human advancement' merely to *decree* the words of wisdom and the absolute unalterability of the values that sustain the powers in existence.

It goes without saying, if a socialist intellectual behaved in the same way and ventured to describe the Keynesian recipes of capitalist monetary manipulation as 'the pseudo-scientific rubbish of the blue bookshops', he would be instantly excommunicated by our vigilant 'scholars' and hounded out of the academic world without too much ceremony. Yet Keynes himself – whose ignorance of Marx's work is surpassed only by his boundless sense of superiority towards all those who produce everything that the 'quality in life' righteously expropriates to itself – can not only get away with such pompous and grossly 'unscholarly' tirades against his object of attack, but can be hailed at the same time as the great example of 'scientific objectivity' and the final refutation of Marx. Wishful thinking, obviously, knows neither shame nor boundaries.

1.1.3
Intellectuals in recent decades tended to shy away from admitting the class substance of their theories and ideological postures. Glancing at the dramatic change on the social map of the world between 1917 and 1949 – i.e. between the outbreak of the Russian and the victory of the Chinese

Revolution – they preferred to look for reconciliatory self-assurance in the direction of denying not only the existence of the (once admittedly contested but now happily superseded) phenomena of 'imperialism', 'exploitation', 'capitalism', etc., but even of 'classes' and 'class conflicts'.

Keynes himself had no use for such ideologically defensive stratagems. Utterly convinced that the ruling order would permanently maintain its control over everything that really mattered, he did not hesitate to declare with condescending self-confidence:

> When it comes to the *class struggle* as such, my local and personal patriotism, like those of everyone else, except certain unpleasant zealous ones, are attached to my own surroundings. I can be influenced by what seems to *me* to be justice and good sense; but the *class war* will find me on the side of the *educated bourgeoisie*.[5]

Thus, Keynes openly and defiantly assumed a highly partisan ideological position towards everything. If we now consider the orienting principles of his theory which Keynes formulates from such a firmly committed ideological standpoint, we find that despite the author's confident anticipations of a happy solution to the problems and difficulties whose existence he is forced to admit under the impact of the world economic crisis of 1929–33, his overall conception can lead us absolutely nowhere. For Keynes offers the most rigid and dogmatic separation of material/productive advancement ('the solution of the *economic problem*' in his terminology), and the betterment of the conditions of human existence in all respects, in accordance with the potentialities of consciously adopted objectives.

He describes the process of productive reproduction from the mechanical 'vulgar materialist' standpoint of what he himself calls 'the *economic machine*',[6] arguing with uninhibited optimism that science, technical efficiency and capital accumulation (and the latter thanks to 'the principle of compound interest,'[7] and not of indigenous and colonial exploitation) are well on their way to solving, '*gradually*' of course, 'humanity's economic problem'. A problem which, according to Keynes, should be considered 'a matter for *specialists* – like dentistry'.[8] If we are still experiencing troubles, like 'the prevailing world depression' and the 'anomaly of unemployment in a world full of wants',[9] that is only because:

> For the *moment* the very rapidity of these changes [in technical efficiency] is hurting us and bringing difficult problems to solve. Those countries are suffering relatively which are not in the *vanguard of progress*. We are being afflicted with a new disease ... namely, *technological unemployment*.... But this is only a *temporary phase of maladjustment*. All this means in the long run that *mankind is solving its economic problem*.[10]

As we can see, the sermon of ideological faith does not seem to have changed much, if anything, in all those years that separate us from the time when the lines just quoted were written. For our own growing unemployment is equally supposed to be no more serious than 'a temporary phase of maladjustment', due to the 'rapidity of changes in technological efficiency', all in the good cause of remaining in the 'vanguard of progress'.

The difference is that Keynes can still confidently anticipate – in 1930 – that 'mankind's economic problem' will be solved *within one hundred years* in the 'progressive countries'.[11] However, through his qualifications it transpires that for Keynes the concept of 'mankind' – which is declared to be in the process of solving the economic problem – is confined to the *'progressive countries'* and *'vanguards of progress'* (his codenames for the dominant imperialist countries). This, again, underlines the total unreality of his 'scientific' diagnosis.

Moreover, in agreement with the age-old postulate of bourgeois political economy, according to which nature itself implanted the 'money motive' into all human individuals, Keynes asserts that 'we have been expressly evolved by nature – with all our impulses and deepest instincts – *for the purpose of solving the economic problem*. If the economic problem is solved, mankind will be deprived of its traditional purpose.'[12] And yet, this is how he describes the coming positive change with regard to the self-same individuals who are said to be so deeply determined by *nature itself* in their innermost 'impulses and instincts':

> When the accumulation of wealth is no longer of high social importance, there will be great changes in the code of morals. . . . All kinds of social customs and economic practices, affecting the distribution of wealth and of economic rewards and penalties, which we now maintain at all costs, however distasteful and unjust they may be in themselves, because they are tremendously useful in promoting the accumulation of capital, we shall then be free, at last, to discard. . . . We shall honour those who can teach us how to pluck the hour and the day virtuously and well, the delightful people who are capable of taking direct enjoyment in things, the lilies of the field who toil not, neither do they spin.[13]

How touching; how poetic; and how appealing!

At a closer look, however, the Keynesian discourse on the miraculous conversion of nature's instinctual money-maker – a conversion which is here anticipated to occur a century or so after 1930 – turns out to be a totally gratuitous suggestion. For without any supporting ground, nay against his own arguments enunciated on the authority of 'nature' itself just a moment earlier, Keynes counterposes with wishful arbitrariness nothing but the impotent world of *'ought'* to the given reality of *'is'*, underlying their polarity also by the temporal abyss which he puts between them.

In any case, the hypostatized quasi-religious redemption is not the real purpose of the Keynesian discourse. He offers the moralizing/religious carrot of 'ultimate reward' to the individuals – for whom the promised land lies in the world of beyond, since in one hundred years they will all be dead – on condition that they trade in their quest for a possible radical change in the not so distant future for its *postponement* well beyond their feasible life-expectancy, accepting thereby with sanctified resignation the established order of things. Accordingly Keynes, immediately after the lines just quoted, takes us back to his own rather prosaic and utterly mystifying vision of reality. For this is how he continues his 'Essay in persuasion' after praising the lilies in the field:

> But beware! The time for all this is not yet. For at least another hundred years we must pretend to ourselves and to every one that fair is foul and foul is fair; for *foul is useful and fair is not*. Avarice and usury and precaution must be our gods for a little longer still. For only they can lead us out of the tunnel of *economic necessity* into daylight.[14]

Keynes mystifies his audience by deliberately conflating (and confusing) '*useful*' with *profitable* (the real operative term beneath his diversionary phraseology). He is convinced (or rather, he wants to convince *us*) that the problems of 'economic necessity' are *technical* problems, to be assigned to our '*specialists*' in usury-management and economic tooth-extraction. In this spirit, Keynes insists that the 'humble but competent' specialists recommended by him are destined to lead us out of 'the tunnel of economic necessity' to our own 'destination of economic bliss',[15] provided that we unconditionally entrust ourselves to them – just as no toothache sufferer in his or her right mind would query the wisdom of consigning themselves to the pain-relieving competence of dental specialists. In fact Keynes is so convinced of the validity of his dentist/specialist vision of the 'economic problem' that he concludes his essay with these words: 'If economists could manage to get themselves thought of as humble, competent people, on a level with dentists, that would be splendid.'[16]

Unfortunately, though, a mere 42 years from the deadline set by Keynes himself for reaching our promised destination of 'economic bliss', we are today much more distant from the mouth of the tunnel than 58 years ago, *despite* the tremendous advances in productivity accomplished in all these intervening decades.

The reason why this is so is that the 'economic problem' of which Keynes speaks is in reality not at all that of 'economc necessity' – which in his view is bound to be automatically eliminated in due course by the blissful 'accumulation of wealth' – but a profoundly *social* (or *socio*economic) problem. For no amount of accumulated wealth can do as much as even *begin* to remove the paralyzing constraints of the now imposed socio-economic determinations if the growing social wealth is poured down (as happens to be the case today) the bottomless pit of the military-industrial complex, as well as of other varieties of wasteful wealth-dissipation, instead of satisfying human need.

Similarly, despite the self-absolving (and in our own times precisely for that reason highly popular) Keynesian treatment of the problem, there is no such thing as *'technological unemployment'*. For mass unemployment – much greater today than in 1930, when Keynes promised us daylight 'before long' at the end of the tunnel – could be eliminated in principle virtually *overnight*. Not by the new job-creating miracles of a 'third' and 'fourth industrial revolution', but by a consciously adopted social strategy aimed at reducing the amount of labour-time undertaken by the members of society, in accord with the real needs and productive objectives of the available workforce.

Thus, the ideological interests which he unhesitatingly champions trap even such technically most competent economic tooth-extractors as Keynes in a hopeless position. For, given the necessary presuppositions of his social standpoint – presuppositions arising from the consciously and defiantly adopted aim to defend the vested interests of the 'educated bourgeoisie' – Keynes is prevented from noticing the obvious. Namely, that despite the assurances of his soothing economic sermon we cannot get any nearer to the promised daylight at the mouth of the tunnel even in a thousand years for the simple reason that we are moving in the *opposite* direction, pursuing *profit* under the pretext of 'usefulness', and destroying with reckless 'technical efficiency' the most precious human and material resources by conferring on capital's blind 'economic machine' the task of solving 'humanity's economic problem'.

1.1.4

Clearly, then, the power of ideology cannot be overstated. It affects no less those who wish to deny its existence than those who openly acknowledge the interests and values intrinsic to the various ideologies. It is utterly futile to pretend otherwise. To believe that one can get rid of ideology in our contemporary world – or indeed in the foreseeable future – is no more realistic than the idea of Marx's 'valiant fellow' who thought that men were drowned in water because they were possessed with the *idea of gravity*. Yet, we have witnessed many attempts, even in the very recent past, which followed the same path as this idealist 'valiant fellow', decreeing that ideology is no more than a superstitious, religious idea; a mere 'illusion', to be permanently disposed of by the good work of 'scientific objectivity' and by the acceptance of the proper intellectual procedures of 'value neutrality'.

In truth, however, ideology is not an illusion or a religious superstition of misdirected individuals, but a specific form of – materially anchored and sustained – social consciousness. As such, it is insurmountable in *class societies*. Its stubborn persistence is due to the fact that it happens to be objectively constituted (and constantly reconstituted) as the *inescapable practical consciousness of class societies*, concerned with the articulation of rival sets of values and strategies that aim at controlling the social metabolism under all its major aspects. The historically unfolding and *conflictually intertwined* social interests find their manifestations at the plane of social consciousness in the great diversity of relatively *autonomous* (but, of course, by no means *independent*) ideological discourse, with its powerful impact even on the most tangible material processes of the social metabolism.

Since the societies in question are themselves internally divided, the principal ideologies must define their respective positions both as '*totalizing*' in their explanatory claims, and as meaningful strategic *alternatives* to one another. Thus, the contending ideologies of any given historical period constitute the necessary practical consciousness in terms of which the major classes of society relate to, and indeed more or less openly confront, each other and articulate their vision of the right and proper social order as a comprehensive whole.

Understandably, the most fundamental conflict in the social arena concerns the social structure itself which provides the regulatory framework of any particular society's productive and distributive practices. And precisely because that conflict is so fundamental, it cannot be simply left to the blind mechanism of unaffordably wasteful and potentially lethal collisions. The less so, in fact, the higher the risk of actualizing the calamities implicit in the growing power of destruction at the disposal of the antagonists.

Nor can such conflict be resolved within the legislative domain of 'theoretical reason' alone, no matter how fashionable a name one may confer upon the latter. This is why the structurally most important conflict – whose object is to sustain, or, on the contrary, to negate the prevailing mode of control over the social metabolism within the confines of the established relations of production – finds its *necessary* manifestations in the *practice-oriented* 'ideological forms in which men become *conscious* of this conflict and *fight it out*'.[17]

In this sense, what determines the nature of ideology more than anything else is the imperative to become *practically conscious* of the fundamental social conflict – from the mutually exclusive standpoints of the hegemonic alternatives that face one another in the given social order – for the purpose of *fighting it out*. To put it in another way, the various ideological forms of social consciousness carry far-reaching (even if to varying degrees direct or indirect) practical implications in all their varieties, in art and literature no less than in philosophy and social theory, irrespective of their sociopolitical anchorage to progressive or conservative positions.

1.1.5

It is this practical orientation that defines also the type of rationality appropriate to ideological discourse. For the concerns of the latter must be articulated not as abstract theoretical propositions (from which nothing except some more of the same kind of abstract theoretical propositions follow), but as well grounded practical pointers and effective mobilizing inducements towards the socially viable actions of real collective subjects (and not artificially constructed 'ideal types').

Moreover, under the conditions of class society the social interests depicted and conceptualized by the rival ideologies are not only conflictually enmeshed (which undoubtedly they are), but done so in such a way that the *partial* issues are deeply affected by their location within the *overall* dynamics of the ongoing hegemonic conflict. Consequently, what might appear to be rational (or otherwise) on the very limited scale of a given partial issue, may very well turn out to be the exact opposite when inserted into its appropriate broader context, in accordance with the historically changing margin of action of the principal social agencies.

Thus, the question of ideological rationality is inseparable from recognizing the objective constraints within which the alternative strategies are formulated in favour of, or against, the continued reproduction of the given social order.

This is not a matter of conformity or non-conformity to some predetermined set of logical rules on account of which the particular thinkers should be praised or blamed, as the case might be. Rather, it is a question of understanding how the fundamental structural characteristics of a determinate social order assert themselves on the relevant scale and circumscribe the alternative modes of conceptualization of all the major practical issues. For the structural determinations in question offer significantly different vantage points to the rival social subjects according to their respective positions with regard to the available levers of social control. At the same time, the evaluation of the latter is subject to the important question of how enduring or transient the socioeconomic and cultural/political viability of the given levers of social control will turn out to be in terms of the irrepressible dynamics of the overall historical development.

It is the combination of the two – the adopted vantage point in its affirmative/supportive or critical/negating posture *vis à vis* the dominant instrumental/institutional network of social control, and the historically changing effectiveness and legitimacy of the available levers themselves – that defines the practice-oriented rationality of ideologies in relation to their age and, within it, in relation to the ascending or declining phases of development of the social forces whose interests they assert.

1.1.6

As a result of such inherently practical determinations (which can be clearly identified on a comprehensive temporal and social scale), the major ideologies bear the all-important mark of the *social formation* whose dominant productive practices (e.g. the value-orienting horizon of capitalistic private enterprise) they adopt as their ultimate frame of reference. The question of 'false consciousness' – which is so often one-sidedly misrepresented, so as to beg the question in favour of those who indulge in

it – is a *subordinate moment* of this epochally circumscribed practical consciousness. As such, it is subject to a multiplicity of qualifying conditions
which must be concretely assessed in their proper setting.

Ideologies are epochally circumscribed in a twofold sense.

First, in that the *conflictual* orientation of the various forms of practical social consciousness remains their prominent feature for as long as
societies are divided into classes. In other words, the practical social
consciousness of all such societies cannot help being ideological – i.e.
synonymous with ideology – because of the insuperably antagonistic character of their social structures. (The fact of such structurally determined
conflictual orientation of ideology is in no way contradicted by the pacificatory discourse of the ruling ideology. For the latter must appeal to
'unity' and 'moderation' – from the standpoint and in the interest of the
established hierarchical power relations – precisely in order to legitimate
its hegemonic claims in the name of the 'common interest' of society as
a whole.)

And *second*, that the *specific character* of the fundamental social conflict
which leaves its indelible mark on the contending ideologies in different
historical periods arises from the epochally – and not on a short-term
basis – changing character of society's productive and distributive practices
and from the corresponding need to subject to radical questioning the
continued imposition of the formerly viable mode of socioeconomic and
cultural/political intercourse as it becomes increasingly undermined in the
course of historical development. Accordingly, the limits of such questioning are set *epochally*, bringing to the fore new forms of ideological
challenge in close conjunction with the emergence of more advanced ways
of satisfying the fundamental requirements of the social metabolism.

Without recognizing the epochal determination of ideologies as the
practical social consciousness of class societies, their internal structure
remains thoroughly unintelligible.

We must differentiate, however, between three fundamentally different
ideological positions, with serious implications for the kinds of knowledge
compatible with each.

The first supports the given order with uncritical attitude, adopting
and glorifying the immediacy of the dominant system – no matter how
problematical and full of contradictions – as the *absolute horizon* of social
life itself.

The second, exemplified by radical thinkers like Rousseau, succeeds to
a significant extent in exposing the irrationalities of the *specific form* of
a rather anachronistic class society which it rejects from a new vantage
point. But its critique is vitiated by the contradictions of its own – equally
class-determined, even if historically more advanced – social position.

And the third, in contrast to the previous two, questions the continued
historical viability of the class horizon itself, anticipating as the objective

of its conscious practical intervention the supersession of all forms of class antagonism.

Naturally, in the history of thought all the way down to the present even the most positive varieties of becoming conscious of the fundamental social conflict could not help being affected by the structural limitations of class confrontation. Only the third type of ideology can even attempt to overcome the constraints associated with the production of practical knowledge within the horizon of divided social consciousness under the conditions of divided class society.

In this respect, it is important to bear in mind the Marxian insight that at the present juncture of historical development the question of 'transcendence' must be raised as the necessity to go *beyond class society as such*, and not merely beyond one *particular type* of class society in favour of yet another. But this proposition does not mean that one can escape the need to articulate social consciousness – oriented towards the strategic objective of reshaping society in accordance with the repressed productive potentialities of an identifiable collective agency – as a coherent and forceful *ideology*. For the relevant practical issue remains as before, namely, how to 'fight out' the fundamental conflict over the structural stake to control over the social metabolism as a whole.

Hence, to imagine that socialist theory could afford to be 'ideology free', and to stipulate that it should aim at defining its position in such – nowhere beyond the self-enclosed terrain of vacuous 'theoretical discourse' viable – terms, is in fact a self-disarming strategy. One which can only play into the hands of the adversary who has a very sound interest indeed in misrepresenting its own position as genuinely 'consensual', 'objective', 'scientific', and thoroughly 'free from ideological bias'. The point is not to oppose science to ideology in a positivistic dichotomy but to establish their practically viable unity from the new historical vantage point of the socialist project.

1.2 FROM 'MODERNITY' TO THE 'CRISIS OF POSTMODERNITY'

1.2.1
The categorial framework of theoretical discussions cannot be determined by arbitrary choices, even if apparent arbitrariness is often in evidence in the shifting claims of the dominant ideological/intellectual trends. However, looking at the self-definitions of such trends more closely, as a rule reveals a symptomatic pattern and objectivity, although by no means an unproblematical one. In contrast to the relatively high objectivity of the trends themselves, capriciousness and arbitrariness may very well pre-

dominate in the choices through which particular intellectuals embrace the dominant ideological orientation of a given period, jumping without very deep motivation in large numbers on the bandwagon of 'modernity', for instance. Yet, this phenomenon must be distinguished from the constitution of the bandwagon itself.

To explain why some individuals readily identify themselves with a dominant ideological/intellectual orientation, one needs no more objective motivation than the way in which the people concerned perceive their own location and role in the given academic establishment, for instance; or in relation to the highly tendentious projection of what might be termed 'important international cultural debates' by the media; or *vis à vis* the changing ownership patterns – the ongoing concentration of capital in the field of cultural production – which determine the state of the publishing industry; etc. In a sense it is 'axiomatic' that through such (more or less accidental) personal motivations the ultimately dominant ideological/ intellectual trends *become* dominant and broadly diffused.

However, the acknowledgement of this circumstance is not very helpful for the task of disclosing the inherent nature and ideological suitability of the trends themselves. For even if the power of the publishing industry (and of the media in general) explains the *mechanism* of the broad diffusion of the successfully adopted trends, this fact by itself reveals very little about the reasons why a *determinate* cultural/ideological trend (rather than some significant *alternative* to it) had been embraced in the first place for the purpose of general diffusion. It explains very little indeed, apart from the fairly obvious correlation that the trend in question must harmonize with the dominant material interests of the established order.

At any rate, precisely because of the imperative to produce a suitable match between the ruling interests and the adopted intellectual trends, the categorial framework of the dominant ideological strategies must be sustainable and 'consistent' on its own ground, no matter how frequent and extensive might be the shifts in self-characterization which we are offered in response to the various conjunctural changes. What is expected in this respect from the self-images of the ruling ideology is not the *truthful* reflection of the social world, with the objective representation of the principal social agencies and their hegemonic conflicts. Rather, they are called upon merely to supply a *plausible* account on the basis of which one should be able to project the *stability* of the given order.

This is why we find a tendency in the ruling ideology to produce a categorial framework that *attenuates* the ongoing conflicts and *eternalizes* the structural parameters of the established social world. Understandably, this characteristic is all the more pronounced the greater the importance of the stakes over which the principal social agencies antagonistically confront each other.

1.2.2

The category of 'modernity' is a striking example of this ideological tendency to ahistorical conflict-attenuation. To be sure, what is at issue here is not the straightforward chronological sense in which even the ideological self-conceptions of the late middle ages contrast themselves, as 'modern', to classical antiquity. Nor are we concerned here with the opposition between the *'ancien régime'* and the 'modern political formations' of the bourgeoisie which emerged victorious from such confrontation, liquidating with lasting effect the anachronistic remnants of the feudal order. (This is the sense in which Marx contrasts the historical anachronism of Germany with the conditions of the politically and economically up-to-date 'modern nations' of England and France.)

In sharp contrast to such fairly self-evident opposition, the problematical usage of the term 'modern' is characterized by a tendency to *obliterate* the sociohistorical dimension in the service of the dominant interests of the established order. True to this spirit, the required definitions of 'modernity' are constructed in such a way that the socioeconomic specificities are obfuscated or pushed into the background, so that the historical formation described as the 'modern society' in the various ideological discourses on 'modernity' should acquire a paradoxically *timeless* character in the direction of the *future*, on account of its uncritically overstated contrast with the more or less distant *past*.

Thus, undialectically, the moment of *discontinuity* and *'rupture'* tends to be exaggerated beyond recognition, tendentiously at the expense of some vitally important *continuities* – like, for instance, the insurmountably *class-exploitative* nature of capitalist society, no matter how 'modern' and 'advanced' – so as to be able to envisage imaginary 'universalities' and correspondingly fictitious 'solutions' to painfully real problems, which could only be resolved in reality through the practically fought out confrontations of society's major classes.

In accordance with this trend, already Hegel defines *'the principle of the modern world'* in such a way – by decreeing its identity with *'thought and the universal'*[18] – that he should be able to produce, at the ideologically opportune moment in history, the required sharp and undialectically drawn line of demarcation between the 'eternally present'[19] and the speculatively 'transcended' past. The meaning of such a tellingly undialectical move by a great dialectical thinker is to announce in relation to the present state of affairs (with the modern bourgeois state at its apex) the aprioristically anticipated 'reconciliation' of the World Spirit with itself, completing the ideological circle – praised by Hegel himself as 'the circle of circles'[20] – through the idealist glorification of the existent's 'rational actuality'. Thanks to this procedure, the exploitative partiality of the 'modern' *capitalist* order – preserved by Hegel in the practically untouched, yet fictitiously 'superseded' contradictions of bourgeois 'civil society' – is elevated to the noble status of the self-realization of both Reason and freedom in the state's postulated 'universality'. For in Hegel's view:

> the Universal is to be found in the State, in its laws, its *universal and rational* arrangements. The State is the *Divine Idea* as it exists on Earth.[21] ... The History of the World travels from East to West, for *Europe is absolutely the end of History*.[22]

Thus, the Hegelian conception of 'modernity' – defined as the 'rational universality' of the 'modern Germanic state' (i.e. of imperialistically dominant Europe)[23] that represents 'absolutely the end of history' – amounts to no more than the ideologically motivated eternalization of the ruling order, transforming thereby the historical dynamics of an open-ended process of development into the timeless closure of a frozen metaphysical entity, in the service of conflict-attenuation.

During the century that followed Hegel's death this tendency became ever more pervasive in the dominant ideological conceptions. The more so in fact the nearer we come to our own times. Indeed, if we look more closely at the ideological/theoretical debates of the postwar era, it becomes clear that the pursuit of conflict-attenuation constitutes one of their most important structuring principles.

For a while they evolve around the wishful rejection of the socialist project as *The Opium of the Intellectuals* (Raymond Aron), soon to be followed by the even more wishful celebration of the success of such an approach as *The End of Ideology* (Daniel Bell). This line of approach in its turn is succeeded by 'post-ideological' theorizations which want to remove even the possibility of the hegemonic conflict between capital and labour, talking instead about *The Industrial System* (Aron again) and *The New Industrial State* (John Kenneth Galbraith), postulating wishful 'convergences' – in accordance with the 'neutral' and in this scheme of things universally practicable strategy of 'modernization' and 'advancement' – that never materialize. Understandably, therefore, when the recommended 'universal modernization' (on the model of US capitalism) turns out to be a hollow fantasy, the next phase must try to get out of the newly emerging difficulties by talking about the '*post-industrial society*', offering the promise to transcend the still remaining contradictions of contemporary capitalism. And now that the expectations of the latter have been proved totally illusory, since the weighty problems at the roots of ideology stubbornly refuse to go away, we are presented with the refurbished ideologies of 'modernity and its discontents', and with the postulate of 'presentified postmodernity'. Indeed, to underline the extreme fragility of all these wishful 'supersessions', we are now offered theorizations of the latter's dissolution as well, shortly after it first appeared on the ideological stage, in headlines announcing 'The crisis of postmodernity'.[24]

Thus, while the contradictions of the social world become stronger than ever, manifesting themselves more and more in a way that approaches an all-engulfing global scale, they are repeatedly declared to be already 'left behind' – or just about to be 'superseded' – in an unending succession of ideological constructs that verbally metamorphose, under a new de-socialized 'post-' label, the same soothing rationalization as soon as its previous version loses its credibility.

1.2.3

Naturally, we cannot adequately explain these developments simply with reference to the postwar conjuncture of social conflict. For their intel-lectual roots reach back a great deal further; with regard to their most fashionable themes and categories to the first two decades of the century, and in their deeper theoretical foundations to the 'heroic phase' of the bourgeois world-view (i.e. the eighteenth and early nineteenth centuries) with which the accounts are now sceptically settled.

However, as regards our direct concern the crucial link is Max Weber. His influence – both methodologically and ideologically – cannot be un-derlined strongly enough. In Chapter 3 we shall consider in greater detail the role of Weber in postwar ideological developments. At this point we can only have a brief look at some of his fundamental methodological tenets on the basis of which 'modernity' is defined in its stipulated opposition to so-called 'traditional society'.

Weber recommends his 'typological scientific analysis' on the basis of its claimed 'convenience'.[25] Its scientificity is never established on other than purely definitional grounds. In fact the appearance of 'rigorous typological scientificity' arises from the 'watertight' and 'convenient' definitions with which Max Weber always embarks on the discussion of the selected prob-lems. He is the unrivalled master of circular definitions, justifying his own theoretical procedure in terms of the 'clarity and lack of ambiguity' of his 'ideal types', and of the 'convenience' they are said to offer. On the other hand, Weber never allows the reader to question the content of the definitions themselves, nor indeed the legitimacy and scientific validity of his method built on ideologically convenient assumptions and 'rigorously' self-sustaining circular definitions.

Take, for instance, the following Weberian claim as to what could – or, rather, what could not – be considered empirically (or historically) possible in accordance with the inherent nature of a 'traditional authority':

> It is impossible in the *pure type* of traditional authority for law or ad-ministrative rules to be *deliberately created by legislation*.[26]

Since, according to Weber, the 'pure type' of traditional authority is supposed to be distinguished from 'legal authority' by the absence of legislative legitimation, in that its mandate to authority, by definition, rests on 'traditions and the legitimacy of the status of those exercising authority',[27] the claim put forward by the author in the quoted passage is extremely problematical. Contrary to Weber's statement that his 'ideal types' have the virtue of clarity and 'lack of ambiguity', his way of categorically excluding the legislative potential of 'traditional authority' could not be, in fact, more ambiguous, since its empirical reference is totally devoid of content. The alleged 'impossibility' is valid only in terms of the original definitional tautology, inasmuch as the *pure type* of traditional authority, in consequence of the Weberian *definition* (and nothing else), is a priori incompatible with the type of legislation characteristic of the stipulated 'legislative authority' (another definitionally established 'pure type'). If, therefore, in historical reality we find counter-examples to the Weberian hypostatization, the author can easily reject them in the name of the universal escape-clause that they do not conform to his *pure* type'.

The same goes for Weber's treatment of 'modernity' in its circular linkages to the 'traditional' forms of society. The 'modern' establishes itself through its proclaimed definitional opposition to the 'traditional', and *vice versa*. Moreover, the Weberian method has the additional advantage that the author can quite arbitrarily choose the terms of his definitional assumptions in such a way that he should be able to be 'economical with the truth', more or less as he pleases. He tries to justify his choices in the name of 'convenience'. However, on closer inspection the latter turns out to be grounded not on objective criteria but merely on his own *ideological convenience*. Thus, in the case of 'rational capitalism', Weber's definition is constructed from constituents of the claimed 'rational calculability' of the capitalist process of production and distribution. In this sense Weber insists that 'a *rational capitalistic* establishment is one with *capital accounting*, ... an establishment which determines its income-yielding power by *calculation* according to the methods of *modern book-keeping*',[28] adding that:

A whole epoch can be designated as *typically* capitalistic only as the provision for wants is *capitalistically organized* to such a *predominant* degree that if we imagine this form of organization taken away the whole economic system must collapse.[29]

Thus, on the one hand, Weber offers us here the double tautology that defines 'typical' (i.e. his 'pure type' dominated by the assumed characteristics that exclude all the others) as 'predominant', and 'capitalistic' as 'capitalistically organized'. At the same time, on the other hand, the tendentious selectivity of the terms chosen by the author brings with it the ideologically convenient result that one of the most obvious characteristics of the far from harmoniously 'rational' capitalist system – its incurably *class-exploitative* and antagonistic structural determination – remains *conspicuously absent* from his 'typologically scientific analysis' of capitalism.

Ideologically determined selectivity and arbitrariness can thus rule supreme in the Weberian 'ideal typical' conceptual framework, misrepresenting itself as the paradigm of rationality. Since the definitional assumptions are simply enunciated, people are expected to take them for granted and treat them as the absolute standard of 'rational' analysis. That something might be *substantively* wrong with the proclaimed criteria of such 'typologically scientific analysis' and its assumed terms of evaluation, this question is a priori ruled out of bounds. Instead, we are expected to submit, without the slightest glimmer of doubt, to the self-evident soundness of the Weberian decree according to which:

> For example a *panic on the stock exchange* can be *most conveniently* analysed by attempting to determine first what the course of action would have been if it had not been influenced by *irrational affects*; it is then possible to introduce the irrational components as accounting for the observed *deviations* from this hypothetical course.[30]

It is indeed 'most convenient' to analyse a panic on the stock exchange in terms of 'irrationality', against the background of the Weberian definitional determination of capitalism as rational calculation. However, as we can see again, this 'convenience' is a purely ideological one. For Weber must treat all crisis-symptoms of the eternalized capitalist socioeconomic order as mere '*deviations*' from its intrinsic rationality as an overall system. It is a highly embarrassing (and utterly 'inconvenient') fact that 'a panic on the stock exchange' may very well be the direct result of the much idealized 'rational calculation' itself, whereby the 'wave to sell' simply anticipates – on capitalistically quite valid 'rational grounds' – the coming of a *recessionary* phase (a 'downward spiral'), bringing with it the rationally appropriate' action of the individual capitalists based on such anticipation, aimed at minimizing their likely losses. This fact cannot fit into the Weberian conceptual framework. For a truly critical analysis of the phenomenon of a 'panic on the stock exchange' would require not the 'convenient' and question-begging rejection of the 'irrationality' of individuals but, on the contrary, the radical questioning of the *structural limitations* of *capitalistic rationality* as such. And the latter would have to be questioned not only in relation to the type of 'reciprocity' manifest in the actions of the *particular* capitalist agents as situated in the – by Weber idealized – *market*, but also as regards the basic antagonisms of this 'modern society' as a *whole*. Instead, Weber treats his readers to the ideologically most convenient assumptions according to which:

> *Participation* in a market ... encourages *association* between the individual parties ... where they all agree on rules for the purpose of regulating transactions and of securing *favourable general conditions for all*. It may further be remarked that the market and the competitive economy resting on it form the most important type of the *reciprocal determination* of action in terms of *pure self-interest*, a type which is characteristic of *modern economic life*.[31]

Given such assumptions, there cannot be a meaningful critique of what happens within the idealized parameters of 'modern economic life'. All that one can do is to offer a generic condemnation of the types of action that can be labelled as 'irrational deviations' from the ideal reciprocity of 'pure self-interest'; a question-begging procedure that – through the definitional determination and simultaneous dismissal of capitalistic 'dysfunctions' as individualistic 'irrationality' – reaffirms, stronger than ever, the eternal validity of the 'modern' system as a whole in which the individuals' 'pure self-interest' on the one hand, and the 'favourable general conditions for all' on the other, find themselves in perfect harmony.

Characteristically, Chancellors of the Exchequer and various other political and intellectual defenders of capitalist 'modernity' respond in the same way as Max Weber to the encountered crisis symptoms, irrespective of whether they are his self-professed followers or, on the contrary, have never read one single line of his writings. Whenever they are called upon to explain something like 'a panic on the stock exchange' (e.g. 'Black Monday'), they invariably talk about the 'bull market' being transformed into a 'bear market' as a result of the 'deplorable irrational behaviour' (the 'sheer madness', etc.) of some individuals who misread the 'temporary fluctuations' of the international financial system. Thus, just like Molière's '*Bourgeois Gentilhomme*' who conversed 'in prose' without really knowing that he did so, all such defenders of the 'modern economic system' prove their fluency in the prosaic Weberian discourse of 'rationality versus irrationality' without being conscious of it. What ties them to Weber is not their familiarity with his 'typologically scientific discourse' (of which they may be totally ignorant), but the class-exploitative ideological interests which they fully share with him.

1.2.4

Weber proclaims that 'the primary effect of *traditional authority* on modes of economic activity is *usually in a very general way* to strengthen *traditional attitudes*.'[32] Naturally, he offers equally profound insights into the effect of the 'modern authority' and of the 'modern Occidental state'[33] on 'modern attitudes' to economic activity. And when he attempts to characterize 'modern capitalism' as such, he defines it – with tendentious ideological selectivity and ideal-typical circularity – as a 'culture' in which 'the governing principle is the investment of private capital'.[34]

Particularly important in this respect is the way in which the Weberian type of 'systematic' (definitional) approach to the historically specific contradictions of capitalist society *de-historizes* them, transforming the structural characteristics and explosive implications of an antagonistic social order into a categorial matrix in which 'modernity' (with its 'discontents') and 'rationalization' (said to be responsible for such discontents and 'disenchantments') occupy the central position. This is what turns out to be so influential after the two world wars not only in German 'critical theory', but in the development of European thought in general, with its ever-growing linkages to the ideological/intellectual trends (and institutions) of the United States.[35]

After the first world war, in *History and Class Consciousness*, Lukács, and to a certain extent under his influence Karl Korsch too, embrace some of Weber's theoretical concerns. At the same time, they go radically beyond Weber's way of assessing their implications as regards both theory and social practice. Whatever the limitations of *History and Class Consciousness*,[36] no one can deny that its author locates the problems of 'rationalization' in their appropriate, historically specific social context, focusing both on the tangible antagonisms of commodity society and on the diametrically opposed standpoints of the principal social agencies that offer alternative theoretical perspectives on the basis of which a solution to the identified contradictions may be envisaged.

Significantly, however, the impact of the Weberian influence on the Frankfurt School makes itself felt in the complete *reversal* of this sociohistorical concretization of the alienating contradictions of twentieth century capitalism by Lukács and others. Accordingly, not only is the Marxian social agency of the anticipated revolutionary transformation eliminated from the conceptual framework of 'critical theory' but, altogether, the problematic of '*reification*' is deprived of its social ground and redrafted in the abstract and ahistorical Weberian sense of 'rationalization'.

This is clearly in evidence in Habermas's account of his own encounter with Lukács and Korsch on the one hand, and Adorno and Max Weber on the other. As he puts it:

> Reading Adorno had given me the courage to take up *systematically* what Lukács and Korsch represented *historically*: the theory of *reification* as a theory of *rationalization*, in Max Weber's sense. Already at that time, my problem was a theory of *modernity*, a theory of the *pathology of modernity* from the viewpoint of the realization – the deformed realization – of reason in history.[37]

Thus, the 'critical theorist' decision to embark on a systematic project is conceived in the spirit of discarding historical specificity for the sake of a generic notion of 'modernity'. As a result, the Marxian problematic of 'reification' – with its revolutionary implications for the supersession of the capitalist social order – has to be abandoned altogether, in exchange for an idealist discourse on 'rationalization' and on the 'realization of reason in history'. Moreover, even that degree of objectivity and historicity which could be still contained, however unhappily, within the framework of the Hegelian discourse on modernity, is now liquidated. We are offered, instead, a return – via Max Weber – to a Kantian transcendental idealism deprived of its critical cutting edge.

The problems of 'modernity and its discontents' are defined in terms of the thoroughly idealist problematic concerning 'the deformed realization of reason in history', promising its fictitious transcendence through the good offices of an imaginary 'ideal communications community', as we shall see in Chapter 3. At the same time, the historically specific and objective contradictions of the capitalist social order as a global system recede into the background. Accordingly, Habermas declares not only that the category of *exploitation* is no longer applicable to the conditions of the 'advanced industrial societies' but, against painfully overwhelming evidence to the contrary, also that it has hardly any relevence even in the Third World.

In this respect, too, Weberian conservatism seems to be the model. For Max Weber decreed many years earlier that:

> the accumulation of wealth brought about through colonial trade has been of little significance for the development of *modern capitalism* – a fact which must be emphasized in opposition to Werner Sombart. It is true that the colonial trade made possible the accumulation of wealth to an enormous extent, but this did not further the *specifically occidental form* of the organization of labour, since colonial trade itself rested on the principle of *exploitation* and not that of securing an income through *market operations* . . . . The end of the capitalistic method of *exploiting colonies* coincides with the abolition of *slavery*.[38]

Again, as we can see, convenient definitional devices are used to settle the issue in favour of absolving 'modern capitalism' from the negative implications of its 'rationalized' exploitative practices. As if the '*market operations*' of the global capitalist system – which happen to be structurally prejudged both in the internal labour market and in the colonially (or, in our own times, neo-colonially) dominated territories in favour of 'advanced capital' – were incompatible with *exploitation*! Thus, the substitution of the category of 'rationalization' (and associated 'market operations') for the Marxian diagnosis of reification and exploitation seems to be able to explain away many ideologically inconvenient problems and contradictions of 'modern industrial society'.

1.2.5

In a recent interview Perry Anderson and Peter Dews asked Habermas an embarrassing question:

> The Frankfurt School tradition as a whole has concentrated its analyses upon the most advanced capitalist societies, at the comparative expense of any consideration of capitalism as a global system. In your view, do conceptions of socialism developed in the course of anti-imperialist and anti-capitalist struggles in the Third World have any bearing on the tasks of democratic socialism in the advanced capitalist world? Conversely, does your own analysis of advanced capitalism have any lessons for socialist forces in the Third World?[39]

This was all he could say in reply concerning an issue of the greatest theoretical and practical importance:

> I am tempted to say 'no' in both cases. I am aware of the fact that this is a eurocentrically limited view. I would rather pass the question.[40]

An answer that sounds like: 'stop the world, I want to get off'. What is particularly problematical here is that a thinker who claims to have articulated the 'reconstructive science of *universal* pragmatics'[41] should be able to envisage the realization of his project without paying the slightest attention to the predicament of 90 per cent of the world's population.

Contrary to the 'eurocentric' position of critical theory, what we are concerned with here is not a partial issue that could be safely neglected in a 'general theory'. For in view of the fact that the nature of capital's socioeconomic order is intelligible only in *global* terms, not much credence can be given to the conceptualization of the 'advanced capitalist world' itself from a perspective that consistently ignores the overwhelming majority of mankind and operates with categories that cannot pay attention to its actual conditions of existence.

Ignoring the far-reaching causal determinations and reciprocities through which the prospects of development in capitalistically advanced societies are inextricably tied to the chronically unsolved problems of the 'Third World' must produce extremely dubious theories even if they are consciously limited in their claims to the Western capitalist countries. But to claim that a 'universal pragmatics' can be derived from presuppositions grounded on the narrowly and tendentiously 'eurocentric' considerations of 'advanced capitalist' existence as such is a blatant contradiction in terms. It is therefore by no means accidental that in this kind of theorization there can be no room for the objective dynamics of global capitalist historical development from which it is quite impossible to exclude the burning issues of the 'underdeveloped world'.

Habermas's original conception bears the marks of the postwar period of 'consensus politics' in that it clearly displays at the time of its articulation a positive attitude towards the dominant tendencies of political accomodation and celebrates the 'post-Marxian' accomplishments of the prevailing socioeconomic and political order.[42]

In a later work, *The Theory of Communicative Action*, Habermas tries to shift his discourse to a more abstract plane, so as to be able to spell out and 'ground' consensus in terms of the 'universal pragmatics' of a transcendental opportunism. He does this at a time when in actuality the continuation of postwar consensus is no longer credible on the socioeconomic and political plane. Ironically, however, after having declared that the Marxian categories of *class, class consciousness, exploitation, forces and relations of production*, and several others, are applicable only to 'the phase of development of liberal capitalism, and not either before or after,'[43] Habermas is now compelled to take notice of the reemergence of social conflicts, if only as a possibility.

He takes this potentially critical step not just belatedly, but even under the more recent circumstances rather reluctantly, when in fact there are already abundant instances of serious social disturbances and confrontations in the everyday life of even the most privileged capitalist societies. However, Habermas's general theoretical framework does not allow him to admit clearly and unequivocally the objective implications of what he actually sees as a theoretically embarrassing and politically disturbing trend. On the contrary, given the background of his 'post-Marxian' theorizations, he must resist the idea that the now reluctantly admitted 'possibility' of renewed conflicts (even class conflicts) might be strategically significant. He argues, instead, in a somewhat peculiar fashion, that although the economic policies of a monetarist type government would lead to the dismantling of the welfare state, and thereby 'in turn could lead to a revival of traditional *class struggles*', nevertheless ' I presume such a government also would be smart enough to weigh such risks.'[44]

True to his general Weberian inspiration, Habermas presumes far too much on behalf of the rationality of the 'modern' bourgeois socioeconomic and political system. In any case, if the so-called 'old-fashioned' or 'traditional' class struggles are really, as earlier decreed by Habermas, the manifestations of merely 'nineteenth-century contradictions' (i.e. those of a strictly 'liberal capitalism'), how can they suddenly 're-emerge' (without the slightest self-criticism on Habermas's part), so as to disappear immediately on account of the postulated 'smartness' of the 'modern' capitalist governments involved? If it is true, as we were *categorically* assured at an earlier stage of Habermas's theory constructions, that 'in advanced capitalist society deprived and privileged groups no longer confront each other as socioeconomic classes',[45] what should we make of the concept of 'class-conflict-eliminating advanced capitalist society' itself under the anticipated new conjuncture, when '*traditional* class struggles' might revive again?

Since Habermas has no answers to such embarrassing questions, he must opt for the strange aprioristic postulate of the 'smartness of the modern capitalistic governments'. As a way out of his own theoretical contradictions, Habermas grants such a priori smartness to these governments not only in relation to their anticipated *perception* of the dangers of re-emerging class conflicts inherent in their policies but, even more problematically, also with regard to their postulated *ability* effectively to *control* the situation under the troublesome new circumstances.

1.2.6

Habermas's conception of 'modernity' is grounded on a theory of 'emancipatory critique', spelled out in terms of the postulated 'intersubjective communicative competences' which he derives from the 'speech acts' of analytical linguistic philosophy. It has been observed by one of Habermas's friendliest commentators that 'one reason why many critics, even sympathetic critics, of Habermas have been perplexed by his "linguistic turn" is because during the past *15 years* he has been more concerned with elaborating, justifying, and working out the details of this ambitious research programme of a theory of communicative action or universal pragmatics than with engaging in the *practice* of emancipatory critique.'[46]

The insurmountable difficulty here is that Habermas wants to offer a 'quasi-transcendentally grounded' theory of 'emancipatory critique' which he envisages to be in full agreement with the requirements of a *consensus* rooted in the 'universal species competence of communication'. In order to establish it, he has to project the fiction of 'unconstrained communication' as the aprioristic guarantee of success. In other words, he has to *presuppose* – in the form of a 'universal species competence' – what he has to *prove* to be a practically feasible strategy of emancipation from the crippling constraints of the established systems of domination. As Richard Rorty correctly argues, perceiving the contradiction between Habermas's inherently 'eurocentric' (or, more precisely, Western 'ethnocentric') position and his universalistic claims:

> Habermas's sympathetic American critics, such as Bernstein,[47] Geuss,[48] and McCarthy ...[49] ... doubt that studies of communicative competence can do what transcendental philosophy failed to do in the way of providing 'universalistic' criteria. They also doubt that universalism is as vital to the needs of liberal social thought as Habermas thinks it....
>
> Whereas Habermas compliments 'bourgeois ideals' by reference to the 'elements of reason' contained in them, it would be better just to compliment those untheoretical sorts of narrative discourse which make up the political speech of the Western democracies. It would be better to be *frankly ethnocentric*....[50]
>
> If one is ethnocentric in this sense, one will see what Habermas calls 'the *internal* theoretical dynamic which constantly propels the sciences ... beyond the creation of technologically exploitable knowledge' not as a *theoretical* dynamic, but as a *social practice*. One will see the reason why the modern science is more than engineering not as an ahistorical teleology – e.g. an evolutionary drive towards correspondence with reality, or the nature of language – but as a particularly good example of the social virtues of the European bourgeoisie.[51]

Indeed, Habermas is a genuine believer in the traditional virtues of bourgeois liberalism. And now that several 'Eurocommunist' parties have abandoned their radical principles, sympathy with their neo-social democratic stance can be safely advocated by Habermas, given the thoroughly discredited mainstream social democratic perspective manifest in his earlier advocacy of the so-called 'ideal communication community'.

The details of the latter are discussed later, in Chapter 3.4. What is directly relevant here is that Habermas's new found Eurocommunist sympathies equate 'liberalization' with 'normalization' and social advancement as such with the improvement of the prospects of a tiny intellectual elite within the framework of a '*liberal* political culture' (in his own words). It is in this spirit that Habermas advocates some liberalizing measures in the field of politics and culture.[52] The multi-billionaire boss of the Italian Fiat Company, Giovanni Agnelli, went a great deal further than that. He called for opening up the country's *government* itself for full participation by the Italian Communist Party. Yet, Agnelli does not picture himself as the radical champion of 'universal emancipation'.

In truth there is nothing radical about Habermas's eurocentric discourse on modernity, politics and ideology. If there was, he could hardly denounce the revolutionary aspirations of the German Left as 'Left-Fascism',[53] in much the same spirit as his mentor, Adorno.[54]

Habermas's motivations and theoretical interests are intelligible in terms of the long-standing demands and aspirations of the liberal/reformist discourse. To quote Rorty again:

> What links Habermas to the French thinkers he criticizes is the conviction that the story of modern philosophy (as successive reactions to Kant's diremptions) is an important part of the story of the democratic societies' attempts at self-assurance. But it may be that most of the latter story could be told as the history of *reformist politics*, without much reference to the kinds of theoretical backup which philosophers have provided for such politics. It is, after all, things like the formation of trade unions, the meritocratization of education, the expansion of the franchise, and cheap newspapers, which have figured most largely in the willingness of the citizens of the democracies to see themselves as part of a 'communicative community' – their continued willingness to say 'us' rather than 'them' when they speak of their respective countries.[55]

It is because Habermas, unlikely Rorty, cannot frankly admit that the aims and potentialities of all liberal/reformist 'ethnocentric' conceptions, including his own, are limited by their Western liberal-democratic standpoint, that he must end up with an extremely problematical theoretical framework which systematically ignores not only the actual predicament of the exploited in the 'Third World' but the sobering historical and structural constraints under which all communication must be carried on in class societies.

In this sense, Habermas must disregard the disconcerting fact that the well-entrenched socioeconomic and political *power relations* within which his idealized 'dialogue' takes place in class societies makes a mockery of all claims according to which one can consider such heavily constrained modality of communication a genuine *dialogue*. For, in view of the fact that the respective margins of action of the participating *class-individuals* – including the margins of their 'communicative action' – are *structurally prejudged* in favour of the *ruling order*, the likely outcome of the communicative interchanges of all individuals cannot be brought under the same model and reduced to an aprioristic common denominator.

The potentially consensual (or pseudo-consensual) nature of the ongoing communication in class societies varies according to whether the 'dialogue' in question takes place between individuals on the *same* side of the social divide, defending the *shared* interests of their class, or, in complete contrast, between individuals who identify themselves with antagonistically *opposed* classes.

In the latter case – when envisaging the possibility of an unconstrained dialogue is utterly idealistic – the individuals concerned must *contest* or *sustain*, within the established communicative framework and in further-ance of their mutually exclusive *hegemonic claims*, the power positions of the given social order. Considering the strategic importance of the issues at stake and the controlling power of the hierarchically articulated institutional complexes,[56] the kind of 'dialogue' that can take place within such boundaries must be in reality *structurally vitiated* against the possi-bility of an outcome that could objectively challenge the all-important structural parameters of the established social order. For the self-same parameters must (and do) *assign* their role to the participants – as class-individuals – in the prevailing mode of communicative action, thereby strengthening and enforcing the power of the materially and ideologically prejudged vicious circle, instead of opening it up in the form of a genuine dialogue.

Thus, as a result of such *necessarily* vitiated 'dialogue', what may *appear* to be a '*consensus*' is in fact the more or less one-sidedly enforced outcome of the dominant *power relations*, under the often deceptively unproblem-atical form of an 'agreement-producing' communicative interchange. The outcome happens to be enforced more or less one-sidedly (i.e. under its communicative aspect, more or less 'consensually'), depending on the 'incorporability'[57] or otherwise of the concessions made by the ruling classes, in accordance – in our own times – with the relative productive advantage which capital can squeeze out of the agreements concluded with its class adversary in terms of improved productivity and expanding 'relative surplus value'.

By the same token, periods of political consensus must give way to sharpened social confrontations – hence also to the increasing prominence of Habermas's curiously non-dialoguing 'cultural neo-conservatives',[58] as well as to the appearance of a bewildering variety of ideologies that aggressively proclaim and defend the 'non-negotiable' interests of the 'Radical Right' under the slogan: 'there is no alternative' – whenever the capitalist socioeconomic order has to cope with the complications arising from a major structural crisis. Under such historical circumstances, the postulated 'universal species competence' – which is supposed to result (strictly within the framework of a 'procedurally'[59] orientated discourse) in the redeeming fruits of Habermas's 'emancipatory communicative action', wishfully redressing thereby the negative consequences of the

Weberian 'disenchantment of the world', even though remaining within the social horizons of Weber's model of 'modernity' and 'rationalization' – demonstrates its utter vacuity. For its elusive 'quasi-transcendental' promises have no bearing whatsoever on the weighty existential problems which the real human agents have to overcome in their practical efforts aimed at emancipating themselves, not from the vaguely defined 'discontents of modernity', but from their subjection to the explotative power of capital.

1.2.7
Habermas tries to extricate himself from the contradictions of his consensual postulates by a number of dubious conceptual shifts. Thus, he attempts to hide the highly problematical character of the projected participation of the individuals in the hypostatized emancipatory communication communities by the introduction of the convenient escape clause that describes their membership as merely '*virtual*' or '*potential*',[60] which empties his original claim of any real content. For the positive/emancipatory significance of *potentiality* cannot be simply assumed or decreed. Before one can make anything of this category, it is necessary first to address oneself to the crucial issue, whether the potentiality in question is an '*abstract*' (hence vacuous) or a '*concrete*' or '*real potentiality*'. Without securing a positive answer on this score – by indicating the real trends of sociohistorical development through which the allegedly latent characteristics of 'universal species competence' are going to be *actualized* in an emancipatory way – it is pointless to look for reassurance in the direction of abstract potentiality. As it happens, Habermas fails to do this. Hence his use of the categories of 'virtual' and 'potential' is by no means less problematical than what we find in the writings of Adorno.[61]

In another respect, when Habermas has to admit that the Weberian 'three complexes of rationality, derived in formal-pragmatic terms from basic attitudes and world-concepts, point to just those three cultural value spheres that were differentiated out in *modern Europe*',[62] he adds immediately: 'but this is not in itself an objection against the systematic status of the schema'.[63] And this is how he justifies his assertion:

> According to Weber, *modern* structures of consciousness are the product of a *universal* historical process of *disenchantment* and thus do not merely reflect idiosyncratic traits of a *particular* culture.[64]

Thus, the validity of the dubious definitional characterization of modernity as 'universal' is established by simply reiterating the Weberian decree according to which the 'modern structures of consciousness' arise from a 'universal process of disenchantment', and as such, by definition, they cannot be subsumed under a 'particular culture'.

This eagerness to proclaim – on the shakiest possible ground – the 'universality' of Western modernity, is as revealing as its counterpart, the tendentious ignorance of the Third World in Habermas's theory. The underlying ideological motivation in relation to both happens to be the same. For Habermas wishes to elevate to universal theoretical significance an anti-Marxian claim according to which:

> in the *developed* capitalist societies there is no identifiable class, no clearly circumscribed social group which could be singled out as the representative of a general interest that has been violated.[65] . . . Correspondingly, the *concept of labour* has been purged of all normative content in industrial sociology and has been discharged from the role of an emancipatory driving force in social philosophy. If we add to this the trends towards shortening working time and towards a corresponding *devaluation of the relevance of labour within the life-world*, then it becomes evident that the historical development of industrial labour is cutting the ground from under the philosophy of Praxis.[66]

As we can see, Habermas's claim concerning 'the *developed* capitalist societies' in the above extract is itself of an extremely dubious (for strictly conjunctural) validity even in relation to the countries in question taken in isolation. Moreover, there is also the sobering fact that 'developed capitalism' is not an *island to itself*, but happens to be both in its privileged present-day actuality and problematical prospects of future development an integral part of the *antagonistically interdependent* capitalist world, whatever the illusions of Western 'critical' intellectuals. However, the function of Habermas's untenable claim is to make plausible the subsequent substantive assertion. In the course of developing this line of argument, we are witnessing a significant (and utterly fallacious) shift in Habermas's terms of reference. For by the time we reach the conclusion, the *limited* frame of reference – i.e. one confined to 'the *developed* capitalist societies' – becomes 'the concept of labour' *in general*, in order to be able to claim the 'devaluation of the relevance of labour within the life-world' as a vital supporting pillar of this 'universal pragmatics'. At the same time, the production of *mass unemployment* in 'advanced' capitalist societies – an undeniable *fact* in the last two decades – is just as fallaciously equated by Habermas with the *reduction in the labour-time* of those who remain in employment. For 'diminishing labour time', in the case of those who work, only marginally amounts to more than a well understandable *desideratum* or *demand* by the job-security oriented Western trade unions. A demand which capital stubbornly and tenaciously resists everywhere, with all power at its disposal, enforcing its own interests on the whole quite successfully also in this respect.

Obviously, to claim that labour-time is being substantially shortened as a *global* phenomenon, embracing within this trend also the super-exploited labour force of the 'Third World' (which constitutes the overwhelming majority of humankind), would be utterly absurd. But to add to such a claim that the trend in question automatically eliminates labour in general from historical development as an emancipatory force, this assertion would indeed require some theoretical underpinning even if the projection of universally decreasing labour-time was factually as true as it happens to be false. For one would still have to demonstrate the precise implications of the postulated 'devaluation of the relevance of labour within the life-world' for the future of capitalistic developments, and particularly for the contradictory capitalist *reproduction process* in which labour – not only as producer but also as consumer – plays the vital part, much to the 'chagrin' of capital and its ideological representatives. In other words, it would have to be demonstrated that there are no radical incompatibilities between the anticipated labour-eliminating developments in the production process and the crippling constraints of capitalist profit-accountancy.

The way it is articulated, Habermas's analysis does not stand up to critical scrutiny either in factual/historical terms, or as regards the author's theoretical conclusions. For, as a matter of fact, we are witnessing today, more than ever before, the negative impact of some powerful *counter-tendencies* to the alleged 'general trend' of decreasing labour-time, even in the capitalistically most advanced countries. No matter how contradictory all this is even from the standpoint of capital itself (which can only move in contradictions), one of these baffling counter-tendencies has been recently highlighted by the attempt of the management of British Coal to compel the miners of the country to work for *six days* per week, instead of the customary *five days*,[67] threatening to withhold investment–which is badly needed in the view of the labour force, in order to counter growing unemployment and the concomitant destruction of the mining communities – in case they refuse to comply with the management's blackmailing demand.

Thus, in defiance of the evidence supplied by actual sociohistorical development Habermas can only argue the way he does, shifting unjustifiably from the *partial* (and even in its partiality contradictory) experience of *Western* capitalism to the assertion of *general validity claims*. Since he cannot sustain the latter with reference to the *global* system of capital, as it is historically constituted and structured, he must give the *semblance* of plausibility to his *general* theoretical postulates – which assert with categorical and dogmatic finality nothing less than 'the devaluation of the *relevance of labour* within the life-world', simultaneously also dismissing the Marxian 'philosophy of praxis' as irrelevant for the cause of emancipation – by drawing '*universalistic*' conclusions from the factually badly assessed, and at any rate strictly limited (hence, without violating logic, *ungeneralizable*), *historical contingency* of 'developed capitalist' existence. Nor does he offer a factually and theoretically sustainable analysis of the historical *specificities* of contemporary capitalist developments (since that would undermine his *generic/aprioristic* theoretical claims). He prefers to deduce such developments – 'quasi-transcendentally' – from the category of 'modernity' and its 'life-world', disregarding at the same time all those facts and tendencies in the *real world* which point in a direction diametrically *opposed* to his own projections.

We find a similarly objectionable procedure in Habermas's use of the category of 'modernity' itself. This has a great deal to do with the ideologically convenient circularity for which Max Weber provided the model, as we have seen above. The point is that the opposition which Habermas sets up, following Weber, between the 'traditional' and the 'modern' is undialectically stretched to the point at which the role of the *traditional* constituents in the normative structures of society is almost completely obliterated with reference to present-day conditions. Such a procedure results in a theoretical construct that becomes 'rigorous' and 'watertight' by being locked into itself. By doing so, it prevents the required evaluation of the general validity claims of its discourse in terms other than what amounts to consenting to take for granted the presuppositions of this self-enclosed and aprioristically self-validating discourse on 'modernity'.

Yet, given the inseparably structural and historical determinations of the social order, the 'traditional' continues to play a crucially important role under all conceivable social formations, no matter how advanced. Indeed, in the dialectical relationship between *legally* articulated normativity and the *traditional* forms of socially effective normativity, the primacy belongs to the latter, and remains with it even under the conditions of capitalist 'modernity'.[68] Moreover, it is quite impossible to challenge critically the perverse socioeconomic structural hierarchies and corresponding legal and political framework of *class society* as such without recognizing the key role of 'customs' and 'tradition' as the predominant or *übergreifendes Moment* in this dialectic of *continuity* and *discontinuity*, on the basis of which the alienated normativity of the legal and political superstructure (as well as its institutionally articulated and reinforced linkages on the plane of morality and aesthetics) can be superseded by the self-constituting normativity of the associated producers. If, however, one follows Habermas in discarding not only the Marxian categories of 'base and superstructure', but also those of the 'forces and relations of production', replacing them, as he suggests, by the hopelessly abstract Parsonian pair of 'work and interaction',[69] in that case one must remain trapped within the self-referential categorial framework of 'modernity', devoid of any practical leverage that could facilitate a radical and effective intervention in the established order of structural hierarchies, instead of waiting for the Godot of the 'ideal communication community'.

Equally problematical is Habermas's characterization of 'symmetry' and 'reciprocity' within the framework of the postulated emancipatory communicative action. Their key role is aprioristically asserted by Habermas who declares at the same time that reliance on historical and socioeconomic experience is mistaken and suffers from what he calls the 'productivist bias'. And this is what his line of argument amounts to:

> I defend a cognitivist position ... namely, that there is a universal core of moral intuition in all times and in all societies.... These intuitions have the same origin. In the last analysis, they stem from the condition of *symmetry* and *reciprocal recognition* which are unavoidable *presuppositions* of communicative action....[70]
> The implicit connection of the theory of Marx with the *utopia of self-activity* – emancipation from heteronomous labour – suffered, I believe, from two mistakes. The first was the *productivist bias* which was built into this particular vision – as it was into all utopias from Thomas More onwards: namely, the idea that *scientific* control over *external* nature, and labour to transform it, is *in itself* liberating. The second error was more important, perhaps. It was not to realize that the only utopian perspectives in social theory which we can straightforwardly maintain are of a *procedural* nature.[71]

Several points must be made in relation to this quotation. First (this has been stressed by one of Habermas's sympathetic English critics), that the German critical theorist tends uncritically to '*assume* what must be shown, namely that orientation towards *understanding* is the basic aim of communication.'[72] Likewise, the 'symmetry' postulated by Habermas is no more than another unsubstantiated assumption, and a very problematical one at that. As the same critic pointed out:

> What Habermas's assumption of *symmetry* seems to neglect, and what his occasional allusions to the model of 'pure communicative action' do nothing to mitigate, is that the *constraints* which affect social life may operate in modes other than the restriction of access to speech-acts, for example by restricting access to *weapons, wealth or esteem*....[73] Habermas emphasizes that the application of the thesis of symmetry to representative and regulative speech-acts presupposes a reference to the organization of action contexts, and hence 'the emancipation of discourse from the constraints of action is possible only in the context of *pure communicative action*'.[74] This does not mitigate the problem because communicative action is defined so as to *exclude* considerations of *interest* and *strategy*, of *power* and *persuasion*; thus the latter are not thematized and suspended by the model of pure communicative action, but are *simply ignored*.[75]

Indeed, Habermas's 'pure communicative action' is a pure fiction. It is a notion hedged around with a whole range of circular escape-clauses, like '*possible* speech', instead of actually experienced or produced speech; 'we *contra-factually* proceed *as if* so and so' in such a 'possible speech'; '*competent* speakers' (i.e. speakers who obligingly conform to Habermas's definitional assumptions), as against real speakers; and 'the *idealizing proviso*: if only the argumentation could be conducted openly enough and continued long enough',[76] etc., etc. And it does not become any less of a fiction by calling it, as Habermas does, an *unavoidable fiction*'.[77] All the less since the powerful in the existing (and far from '*symmetrically*' structured and '*reciprocal recognition*'-oriented) historical world, who have ample wealth as well as the weapons of 'overkill' one-sidedly at *their* disposal, have no difficulty whatsoever in avoiding and ignoring *all* of the 'possible' emancipatory implications of Habermas's 'contra-factually possible ideal communications community'.

Another problematical aspect of Habermas's argument is the adoption of a *'procedural utopia'* as the only admissible ground of social criticism. This is why Marx must be described as guilty of the 'productivist bias' according to which 'control over *external nature*' is supposed to be *'in itself liberating'*. Yet, the truth of the matter is that Marx originated the idea of *'socialism or barbarism'* in the sharpest possible contrast to the simplistic 'productivist bias' attributed to him. This was followed by Engels and Rosa Luxemburg who diagnosed the relationship between productive developments and the destructive tendencies of capitalist 'advancement' in the same spirit. Marx had already insisted in 1845–46 that:

> In the development of productive forces there comes a stage when productive forces and means of intercourse are brought into being which, under the existing relations, only cause mischief, and are no longer *productive* but *destructive forces*....[78] These productive forces receive under the system of private property a *one-sided development* only, and for the majority they become *destructive forces*.[79] Thus things have now come to such a pass that the individuals must appropriate the existing totality of productive forces, not only to achieve self-activity, but, also, *merely to safeguard their very existence*.[80]

The explicitly *anti-utopian* and *anti-mechanistic* assessment of the relationship between productivity and destruction in the course of historical development could not be put more clearly. Marx even stresses that what is now at stake is the very survival of humanity, threatened by the inherently *destructive* forces of production which the *one-sided* capitalist process of productive advancement has brought to the fore. Yet, no matter how clearly and unequivocally these issues are treated in the writings of Marx throughout his life, Habermas adopts a rather peculiar mode of arguing. First he produces a *reductio ad absurdum*, 'reconstructing' his object of criticism in a way that suits his own conclusions, reducing the dialectical complexity of Marx's analyses to a simplistic mechanical view of the so-called *'scientific* control over *external nature'*, in place of the clearly envisaged (and by Marx *repeatedly* stated) requirement of an adequate *social control* over the totality of their life-activity by the associated producers, including what he calls their own *'second nature'*. Then Habermas proceeds, on the basis of his own complete misrepresentation of Marx – by now taken for granted as the self-evident truth – to ascribe to the object of his 'critical sublation' a totally caricaturistic position also at another level. In the present case Habermas does this a few lines after the last passage quoted from his interview by asserting that:

> What he [Marx] meant by socialism politically was just – we can say now after fifty years of Soviet history – *just* the abolition of the private ownership of the means of production.[81]

Anyone who takes the trouble to read as little as the few pages of Marx's *Critique of the Gotha Programme*, not to mention his much more detailed reflection on the subject in the *Grundrisse* and elsewhere, must realize what a caricaturistic distortion this is.

The reason why Habermas has to argue in this way is both ideological and methodological. Ideologically, in much the same spirit in which he once denounced the German radical left as catastrophe-inviting 'Left Fascism', Habermas now maintains that:

> *Systems theory* has sharpened our eye for the consequences of a – comparatively speaking – extremely heightened *social complexity*. Ideas of a total revision of existing social relations must today be measured against these risks. In highly complex societies *structural* alterations affect many elements at the same time and in unforeseen ways. Consequently the *status quo* has, not entirely without reason, settled into everyday intuition as an argument.... Still, the argument contains a kernel of truth that must make the *juste milieu* appear more and more worth preserving ... [For] with the *incalculability of interventions* into deep-seated structures of highly complex societies, the risk of *catastrophic alternatives* ensuing also grows.[82]

This is how the contradictions and inhumanities of *capitalist* society become the 'complexities' of a theory of 'modernity', preaching the perpetuation of the '*juste milieu*' – another 'unavoidable fiction' in view of its absence from the actuality of the globally exploitative capitalist system? – against the dangers of *structural alterations*, on the authority of 'systems theory'. Indeed, it is precisely this rejection of a radical *structural intervention* in the existing socioeconomic and political order – a rejection which aprioristically decrees the 'incalculability of interventions' on the sole ground of 'complexity', as postulated by Weber and systems theory – it is this fundamentally conservative ideological stance that makes the substance of Habermas's 'theory of modernity' totally incompatible with Marx.

The methodological principles corresponding to this ideological posture in Habermas's theory are centered around 'the *procedural* concept of communicative rationality'.[83] Marx is dismissed in the passage quoted from Habermas's interview as a naive utopian on account of mistakenly not realizing that only 'procedural rationality' can be the ground of social criticism. This cryptic remark becomes somewhat clearer when the idea of Marx's 'mistake' – or 'confusion' – is presented by Habermas in a more general form in his *Theory of Communicative Action*, arguing that 'it is only the *confusion* of a highly developed infrastructure of *possible* forms of life with the *concrete* historical totality of a *successful* form of life that is utopian'.[84] And he asserts elsewhere that the theory of 'procedural rationality':

> Has at its disposal *standards* for the critique of social relations that betray the promise to embody general interests which is given with the morality of legitimate orders and valid norms. But it *cannot judge the value of competing forms*

of life.... This perspective comprises *only* formal determinations of a
communicative infrastructure of *possible* forms of life and life-histories; it
does not extend to the *concrete* shape of an exemplary life-form or a paradig-
matic life-history .... The theory of social evolution permits no conclusions
about orders of happiness.[85]

However, the trouble with this methodology of 'procedural rationality' is
that its quasi-transcendentally produced 'standards' are so abstract and remote from actuality that the question of their *applicability* – not to mention
those questions that concern how could one demonstrate the *viability* and
efficacy of their *practical application* – does not appear even for a moment
in the considerations of their author. On the contrary, Habermas finds his
justification for this significant omission by declaring that his theory is
concerned only with '*formal* determinations', not with concrete historical
situations, and therefore has nothing to say on the comparative value of
'competing forms of life' or on the question of happiness.

Habermas grounds his theory of 'modernity' on a postulated '*semantic
potentiality*'.[86] And he insists that his own frame of reference – the 'communicative infrastructure of *possible* forms of life' – is the only one that is
'protected against the danger of dogmatically overstating its claims'.[87] In
truth, however, nothing could be more dogmatically overstated than a
'theory of communicative action' that claims to be the only viable theory of
emancipatory social criticism while simultaneously also denying the viability
of positive *structural intervention and alteration* in the established structure
of 'highly complex societies'. Thus, the Marxian critique of the established
order – concerned with the historically produced and likewise historically
transcendable *actuality* of the rule of capital – must give way to a 'procedurally' oriented abstract discourse on 'modernity', and the category of
actuality must be replaced by that of the '*contra-factually possible*'. The
consequence of this categorial shift is that Habermas's 'emancipatory promise' turns out to be quite hollow. For his discourse on 'modernity', not
merely in some of its details but in its entirety, cannot escape the weighty
objections to '*abstract potentiality*' raised against it ever since Hegel.

1.2.8
The controversy between 'modernity' and 'postmodernity' – understandably in self-commending confrontations – has been greatly exaggerated by
the interested parties. Siding with one or the other by taking their self-
characterizations at face value would be, thus, most misleading. Indeed,
what is quite significant here is that relatively small differences that separate the people involved are dramatically magnified in the polemics between
the advocates of 'modernity' and 'postmodernity', so as to assert the exclusive validity of their own position and transform what is in fact *complementary* into *incompatibilities*.

Since the disputes between these two currents have been much in the limelight in recent years, shifting the attention from substantive social and political issues to primarily methodological concerns (in which the ideological determinants that motivate the particular thinkers tend to remain hidden), it is worth looking at their respective claims, however briefly. It is necessary to do this in order to situate 'modernity' and 'postmodernity' not only in relation to one another, but also with regard to the role they have assumed and continue to play in the post-consensual articulation of 'the end of ideology'.

It is very interesting in this respect that one of the sharpest commentators on these controversies, the American Richard Rorty, wants to 'split the difference' between 'modernity' and 'postmodernity'. This is how Rorty diagnoses their rival positions, and attempts to reconcile their exaggerated differences:

> The thrust of Habermas's claim that thinkers like Foucault, Deleuze, and Lyotard are 'neoconservative' is that they offer us no 'theoretical' reason to move in one social direction rather than another. They take away the dynamic which *liberal social thought* (of the sort represented by Rawls in America and Habermas himself in Germany) has traditionally relied upon, viz., the need to be in touch with a reality *obscured by 'ideology'* and *disclosed by 'theory'*....[88]
> [But] Suppose, as I suggested above, one sees the wrong turn as having been taken with Kant (or better yet, with Descartes) rather than (like Habermas) with the young Hegel or the young Marx. Then one might see the canonical sequence of philosophers from Descartes to Nietzsche as a distraction from the history of concrete *social engineering* which made the contemporary *North Atlantic culture* what it is now, with all its glories and all its dangers. One could try to create a new canon – one in which the mark of a 'great philosopher' was awareness of new social and religious and institutional possibilities, as opposed to developing a new dialectical twist in metaphysics or epistemology. That would be a way of splitting the difference between Habermas and Lyotard, of having things both ways. We could agree with Lyotard that we need no more metanarratives, but with Habermas that we need less dryness. We could agree with Lyotard that studies of the communicative competence of a trans-historical subject are of little use in reinforcing our sense of identification with our community, while still insisting on the importance of that sense. If one had such a de-theoriticized sense of community, one could accept the claim that valuing 'undistorted communication' was of the essence of *liberal politics* without needing a theory of communicative competence as a backup.[89]

Whatever one may think of Rorty's own recommendations – which advocate the adoption of a Baconian perspective against Descartes, and a critical attitude to Kant and neo-Kantianism all the way down to the present, in the spirit of American pragmatism – his case for 'splitting the difference' and assuming a sceptical stance *vis à vis* the claims of both 'modernity' and 'postmodernity' must be considered sound. In fact it can be made much stronger if one extends criticism, as indeed one should, also to the ideology of *'social engineering'* in terms of which Rorty brings the two currents to a common denominator with which he can positively identify himself.

In assessing the relationship between 'modernity' and 'postmodernity', the first thing to stress is that *both* trends continue to assert that they go 'beyond ideology' while accusing the *other* of remaining within its confines. Thus, Habermas's self-commending claim that he offers the only valid alternative to 'ideologically distorted communication' and supersedes '*ideology*' by '*theory*', is coupled with the condemnation of 'postmodernity' as wedded to the ideological position of '*neo-conservatism*'. By the same token, however, Lyotard rejects the ideologies of 'modernity' – which in his view make 'an explicit appeal to some *grand narrative*, such as the dialectics of Spirit, the hermeneutics of meaning, the emancipation of the rational or working subject, or the creation of wealth'[90] – and he insists that the goal of 'universal consensus' pursued by Habermas:

> does violence to the heterogeneity of language games. [For] invention is always born of dissension. Postmodern knowledge is not simply a tool of the authorities; it refines our sensitivity to differences and reinforces our ability to tolerate the incommensurable. Its principle is not the expert's homology, but the inventor's paralogy.[91]

Accordingly, Lyotard recommends as his own model of non-ideological discourse what he calls – in obvious contrast to the ideologically guilty 'grand narrative' – the 'little narrative' [*petit récit*], describing it as 'the quintessential form of imaginative invention'.[92]

The gap thus seems to be unbridgeable in the eye of the contestants. Yet, a closer look reveals that much of their controversy is more imaginary than real. For the *consensus* advocated by Habermas is much more cautiously defined in recent years as regards its realizability under the conditions of 'modern industrial society' than at the height of the postwar political consensus, since he has been compelled to acknowledge the re-emergence of the once wishfully buried class conflicts even in the 'advanced industrial countries', as we have seen above. It is a consensus transcendentally predicated about a 'possible' future, in the name of the postulated 'universalistic principles of morality', i.e. an abstract *Sollen* (a mere 'ought to be'). As to the conditions of actuality, Habermas even subscribes to a *pluralist* perspective resembling that of Lyotard – if not by passion then by default – by saying that the 'common standard' which he hypostatizes for the assessment of the morality of legitimate orders 'cannot judge the value of competing forms of life' in concrete historical situations, since it is only concerned with the 'communicative infra structure of *possible* forms of life'.[93] On both counts, therefore, he is much closer to Lyotard than they seem to think. For Lyotard, too, can only offer an *ought* – even if he calls it a '*must* be'[94] – when it comes to demonstrating the viability of his model of postmodernity in relation to the actually existent.

Lyotard's advocacy of postmodern *particularism* is undoubtedly well in tune with the spirit of '*social engineering*'. He champions the virtues of '*little narrative*' (or 'little by little') against the 'totalitarianism' (or 'holism') of the '*grand narrative*'. However, Habermas is by no means very different from him also in this respect, as far as his assessment of the *real world* and of the right kind of conduct recommended in it are concerned. For he is extolling the virtues of the *juste milieu*, on the alleged justificatory ground of 'extremely heightened social *complexity*' and the concomitant 'incalculability of interventions', nay 'the risk of catastrophic alternatives', in case people attempt to introduce '*structural alterations* in highly complex societies', as we have seen in the previous section.[95]

Moreover, with regard to the most abstract regulative determinations both Habermas and Lyotard believe in the 'open system', no matter how problematical such claim might appear in relation to the established order. In Habermas's theory this belief is put forward by idealistically and idealizingly asserting that 'communicative reason does not simply encounter ready-made subjects and systems; rather, it takes part in structuring what is to be preserved.'[96] As to Lyotard's similarly idealizing procedure, he assumes much the same position as Habermas with reference to a curious conception of science that enables him to draw the conclusion required in favour of the advocated 'open system' by arguing that:

> To the extent that science is *differential*, its pragmatics provides the *antimodel* of a *stable system*. A statement is deemed worth retaining the moment it marks a difference from what is already known, and after an argument and proof in support of it has been found. Science is a *model* of an '*open system*', in which a statement becomes relevant if it 'generates ideas', that is, if it generates other statements and other game rules. Science possesses no general metalanguage in which all other languages can be transcribed and evaluated. This is what *prevents its identification with the system* and, all things considered, with terror. If the division between decision makers and executors exists in the scientific community (and it does), it is a fact of the *socioeconomic system* and *not of the pragmatics of science itself.*[97]

Thus, the idealized model of the 'open system' (just like that of the 'open society') is generated by definitionally excluding from it all that would clearly contradict its postulated image. In other words, what must be excluded in such discourse is precisely the *actuality* of science as it functions in the given society. For this purpose not only the 'decision makers' and the 'executors' are conveniently opposed to one another – as if that could make any sense with regard to the actual functioning of scientific research within the framework of the military/industrial complex – but, even more problematically, the self-contained 'pragmatics of science itself' is counterposed to the 'socioeconomic system' as such.[98]

In this way we acquire the 'model of an open system' which is simultaneously also the 'antimodel of a stable system'. But what can all this really amount to? Is this 'pragmatics' more realistic than Habermas's 'universal pragmatics' that cannot even *judge* the value of competing forms of life, let alone positively influence the outcome of the ongoing conflicts? Should not the author reflect on the rather inconvenient question concerning the viability of the 'pragmatics of science itself'? For if science itself, *despite* its claimed ideal pragmatics, cannot escape within its *limited* domain the massive negative impact of its own 'decision makers' and of the 'socioeconomic system' in general, how could it serve then as the – other than totally impotent – *universal model* of postmodern interchange in a materially and culturally articulated 'open system'?

It is highly significant that under the conditions of *post-consensual* capitalism the claims and arguments of both 'modernity' and 'postmodernity' must be spelled out in this 'quasi-transcendental' fashion. Naturally, the need of the system for consensus has not disappeared in the meantime, only receded into the background. Nevertheless, under the new circumstances the real operative model is imposed by the capitalist crisis itself. While the latter lasts, the rules that prevail are those of the most acute competition – going unashamedly for the jugular in the name of 'rationalization' – through which in the economic sphere the former independence of the overproduced units of capital (as autonomous 'actors') must be ruthlessly destroyed by being strictly subsumed under the most powerful and dynamic sectors. At the same time, the earlier relationship between capital and labour must also be fundamentally redefined and restructured, even if it involves the introduction of some openly repressive legal/political regulators, in accordance with the objective determinations and imperatives emanating from the changes that have taken place in the sphere of capital-accumulation and centralization. This is why the straightforward theories of 'consensus' and 'end of ideology' must be discarded under these circumstances in favour of those which formulate their 'models' and claims in such a way that they should not openly contradict the all too obvious evidence of sharpened conflictuality. To be sure, once the system is reconstituted and re-stabilized in accordance with the new power relations (on the side of both capital and labour), the need for soothing consensual ideologies can be pushed again into the foreground. However, this is a rather remote prospect at a time when the structural crisis of capital shows signs of intensifying, instead of being relieved by a new phase of undisturbed and for a meaningful period of time sustainable expansion.

Theories of 'modernity' and 'postmodernity' fulfil the ideological requirements of the conflictually sharpened circumstances. They both *retreat* from making their fundamental theoretical propositions on the ground of the historically given situation. References to the unfolding social processes appear more like occasional illustrative asides, rather than as an integral part of the theory itself. There is no inherent connection between the general theoretical discourse and the 'concrete life-world' of capital's historically given social order. Indeed, the radical separation of the two is often explicitly theorized, as we have seen in Habermas's opposition between the abstract 'possible' and the concrete 'actual'. As a result, there can be no feedback from the real world into the general theory either for strengthening it or with the effect of calling for a significant revision, since its primary validity claims are self-referential and self-enclosed. If the authors turn out to be wrong in their utterances about the actually existent and have cause to regret making them, they can carry on nonetheless as if nothing had happened. As we have seen above, Habermas can just as easily assert that 'in advanced capitalist society deprived and privileged groups no longer confront each other as socioeconomic classes' as its opposite. And, significantly, he can make such contradictory statements without modifying in the slightest his general theory. The 'non-ideological' ideology which theories of this kind present in the form of their discourses on 'modernity' and 'postmodernity' proves to be totally immune to the hazards of categorial reversals due to inevitable fluctuations and changes in the actual sociohistorical circumstances.

Given such (more or less openly theorized) retreat from the turmoil of the concrete historical world as the foundation of their discourse, the authors concerned contrast to the recognizably unstable social and cultural order – in the form of negative ideals or counter-images of one kind or another – their own models (or 'antimodels'). They are constructed in terms of some abstract discourse based on postulates of linguistic philosophical analysis, on the hypostatized 'universal communicative competences of the species', on aprioristic structural/functional determinations, on elements of game theory, on variously idealized conceptions of science, etc.

Furthermore, the nature of the link which they establish between the model-producing, highly abstract, core of their reflections and the given historical reality is that of a mere *ought* which, precisely for this reason, cannot effectively interfere with the ongoing socioeconomic and political processes, no matter how destructive they might appear even to the theoreticians in question.

This is clearly visible in Lyotard's argument about the constitution of 'the relationship between the antimodel of the pragmatics of science and society'.[99] As mentioned before, he substitutues *must* for *ought* and constructs his recommendations like this:

> Consensus has become an outmoded and suspect value. But *justice* as a value is neither outmoded nor suspect. We *must* thus arrive at an idea and practice of justice that is not linked to that of consensus. A recognition of the heteromorphous nature of language games is a first step in that direction.... The second step is the *principle* that any consensus on the rules defining a game and the 'moves' playable within it *must* be *local*, in other words, agreed on by its present players and subject to eventual cancellation. The orientation then favours a multiplicity of finite *meta-arguments*, by which I mean argumentation that concerns *metaprescriptives* and is limited in space and time.[100]

Curiously, though, we are not told who is going to turn the value *'justice'* – which is in fact a *highly suspect* value in our societies, in virtue of its constant violation in every respect and in every sphere – from an abstract moral postulate into a viable *social practice* that conforms to the model. Nor is it revealed who has the power to transform – i.e. radically restructure – the existing, highly centralized and bureaucratized, system of decision making into the ideal 'ought' (Lyotard's 'must be') of a fully democratic and genuinely participatory alternative.

This is all the more problematical (and unreal) since there is an obvious contradiction between the intrinsically *global* and *structural* character of the task itself (namely, how to wrench away power from the centralized system and its 'decision makers') and Lyotard's explicit denunciation of the idea of a radical structural intervention that would challenge the system itself. For the idea of such an intervention is exorcized by Lyotard as a 'grand narrative' that would necessarily result in terror. He imagines that the envisaged massive 'paradigm shift' from the dominant social practices to the 'politics of postmodernity' can be accomplished on the margin of the given system and by the grace of that system itself. He puts his faith, rather naively, in an imaginary tendency towards 'the temporary contract', which is supposed to be 'supplanting permanent institutions in the professional, emotional, sexual, cultural, family, and international domains, as well as in political affairs'[101] arguing that 'We should be happy that the tendency toward the temporary contract is ambiguous; it is not *totally* subordinated to the goal of the system, yet the system *tolerates* it.'[102]

Nevertheless, to characterize the position of Lyotard – or, for that matter, of Foucault and Derrida – summarily as 'neo-conservative' would be quite unjustified.[103] They are not at all more conservative (or 'neo-conservative') than Habermas himself, with his sermons about the *juste milieu* (the realm of the 'moderates') and the structural unalterability of the 'extremely complex system' of 'modern industrial society'. In fact Lyotard takes an activist stand on trying to open up computerized state secrecy. He does this both with a view to defend or extend civil liberties, and in order to put the acquired information to a positive use in his scheme of participatory democracy, insisting that this would:

> Aid groups discussing metaprescriptives by supplying them with the information they usually lack for making knowledgeable decisions. The line to follow for computerization . . . is, in principle, quite simple: give the public free access to the memory and data banks. Language games would then be games of perfect information at any given moment.[104]

All the same, the difficulty here is that, again, no indication is given how such objectives could be accomplished in the face of the unyielding opposition by the state authorities, often cynically enforced by them precisely under the pretext of protecting the values of 'liberty', 'democracy', and 'justice'. Lyotard's commending references to the computer practices of the municipality of Yverdon[105] are in this respect extremely naive, to say the least. No wonder, therefore, that as a final summation of his theory we are offered nothing but a rhetorical exhortation:

Let us wage a *war on totality*; let us be witnesses to the *unpresentable*; let us activate the *differences* and save the honour of the name.[106]

To anticipate nothing less than waging a successful 'war on *totality*' itself by means of the rather outdated local computer of Yverdon (installed in 1981, Lyotard tells us for the sake of 'perfect information'), must be surely of a tall order even for the most optimistic of all believers in 'the politics of postmodernity'!

But to do justice to Lyotard, the underlying difficulty is by no means an exclusive feature of his own version of postmodernity. He shares it with many other thinkers, irrespective of their self-identification with the position of 'modernity' or 'postmodernity'.

The ideological core of this problem can be pinpointed in the summarily negative attitude of the theoreticians concerned towards the emancipatory potential of labour. We have seen the formulation of this aprioristic rejection in Habermas's theory, both in the context of asserting that class conflicts, as a matter of historical fact, have disappeared from 'advanced capitalist society' (when they did nothing of the kind), and in claiming – in an even more general and categorical form – that the concept of labour has altogether lost its emancipatory relevance in social philosophy, due to its 'devaluation within the life-world' itself.

Paradoxically, Lyotard is by no means less categorical and dismissive in this respect than Habermas, although he believes that his position is radically different from that of 'modernity'. In reality, however, the *ideological substance* of his approach is basically the same. For even though he spells it out in the form of a categorical rejection of all kinds of '*metadiscourse*' (an unforgivable sin which he ascribes to 'the modern'), the substantive meaning of this rejection is the aprioristic disqualification of the very idea of 'the emancipation of the *working subject*'[107] on the ground that it is inextricably tied to the terroristic implications of metadiscourse.

The theoretical consequence of all this is that within the framework of both 'modernity' and 'postmodernity' there can be no room for a historically identifiable agency of emancipation, notwithstanding the fact that neither of them have explicitly abandoned their concern with the *possibility* of emancipation. This goes even for Adorno who confines his idea of emancipatory intervention in the present to throwing 'bottles with messages' into the sea, destined for a possible but totally unidentifiable future reader.

Thus, we are presented with general theories of one kind or another which are rather problematical even in their own terms of reference. For in their utter *negativity* they are parasitic on the rejected forms of emancipatory discourse,[108] without being able to indicate at the same time on the basis of the actual historical dynamics some feasible forces of individual and social emancipation, together with the modalities of their likely action through which the transcendence of the now prevailing conditions of (generically criticized) domination could be accomplished.

This failure – arising from the categorical rejection of labour as the emancipatory agency – brings with it far-reaching *methodological* consequences shared by the ideologists of 'modernity' and 'postmodernity' alike.

First, given their retreat from the actual sociohistorical context, coupled with the assertion of an abstract and generic emancipatory aspiration, their theoretical framework can only be articulated as a *metadiscourse* of some sort.

This happens to be the case even when they are trying to be critical of the latter, as Lyotard explicitly and programmatically claims to be. Yet, the only real content he can give to his idealized 'little narrative' is the discussion of the '*metaprescriptives*' to be adopted by the various groups (premissed by the absolute regulative principles of 'strict localism' and 'eventual cancellation'). At the same time, however, he avoids examining the viability of the postulated principles of *unconstrained particularism* (which is structurally not that different from Habermas's postulate of '*unconstrained communication*') in terms of the sobering but inescapable requirements of a *comprehensive* social intercourse.

Thus, Lyotard is caught between the devil and the deep blue sea. For, on the one hand, if he proceeded in a different way, attempting to establish the relevant global interconnections and mediations, he would be forced back to the tracks of reformulating another thematized 'metadiscourse' (or 'grand narrative'). On the other hand, however, the way he proposes to solve his dilemma, his general theory ends up not with a workable framework free from metadiscursive characteristics but, on the contrary, with a *second order metadiscourse* that exhausts itself in the discussion of rules of *structurally* dubious applicability. It is therefore by no means surprising that in the end the lines of demarcation between this conception of 'postmodernity' and 'modernity' are completely obliterated when Lyotard asks the question: 'What, then, is the postmodern?', and answers it in this way:

> It is undoubtedly a *part* of the modern.... A work can become *modern* only if it is *first postmodern*. Postmodernism thus understood is not modernism at its end but in the *nascent* state, and this state is *constant*.[109]

This conflation and confusion of the planes of historical temporality sounds almost like an empty sophistry. What is more important to notice, however, is that Lyotard is forced into this peculiar stance by the untenability of his original claim to supersede the 'metadiscourse' of Habermas's 'modernity' while retaining its motivational ground, the – 'post-Marxian' – ideological presuppositions of his theoretical adversary which reject the emancipatory potential of labour.

The *second* fundamental methodological corollary of the abandonment of the emancipatory social agency is that the necessary *mediation* between 'particularity' and 'universality' – which is absolutely essential for the

dialectical assessment of social complexes and trends of development –
cannot find a place in these theoretical conceptions.

In this respect it does not really matter whether 'universality' or 'particularity' dominates in the theories in question. In the end it comes to the
same thing. For the dominance of 'universalism' in 'modernity' can only
amount to *abstract universality*. And, by the same token, the cult of 'difference' and 'particularism' in 'postmodernity' remains constrained by the
inherent limitations of *abstract particularity*. In fact the theoretical consequence of the *missing mediations* – missing because they can be articulated only in relation to real social subjects and their concrete historical
situations – is that the categorial poles of particularity and universality must
be *directly* linked. This direct linkage must be established either through
explicit but undemonstrated postulates (Habermas) or by means of unspecified general assumptions (Lyotard), since in the final analysis neither
of the two approaches can afford to satisfy itself with remaining attached
exclusively to one of the two poles. 'Quasi-transcendental universalism'
must make its empirical relevance plausible by exemplifying its general
claims in relation to particularity, and diversity-oriented discourse must at
least imply the generalizability of its particularism in order to sustain its
claims as a legitimate and viable theoretical enterprise.

We have already seen that in Lyotard's 'postmodernity' the programmatically ungeneralized (anti-metadiscourse oriented) particularism cannot
be sustained. Paradoxically, therefore, in order to give it a proper theoretical status, the author is forced to rely on the category of *'metaprescriptives'*
which, however, cannot help being other than universalistic, even if it is
directly identified with the discursive practices of local groups. As to
Habermas's theory, we can observe in it the direct identification of the
postulated *universalistic* determinations with the predicament of *individuals*
when he asserts, for instance, that:

> The utopian perspective of reconciliation and freedom is *ingrained* in the con-
> ditions for the communicative sociation of *individuals*; it is built into the
> *linguistic mechanism* of the reproduction of the *species*.[110]

Marx criticized Feuerbach for abstractly defining 'human essence' – instead
of making it intelligible in terms of 'the ensemble of social relations' – 'only
as "species", as an *inner, mute, general character which unites the many individuals in a natural way*.'[111] Habermas is offering us the same kind of
solution, by implanting into the individuals the Feuerbachian 'mute generality' of a miraculous 'linguistic *mechanism*', by means of which the *species*
is supposed to emancipate the individuals, achieving reconciliation and
conquering freedom. Just as Lyotard expected great things from the
exemplarily operated computer at Yverdon – and not simply for the citizens
of Yverdon alone but for the 'post-grand-narrative' human species in

general – Habermas, too, finds his 'quasi-transcendental' equivalent to the Yverdon computer in the miraculous linguistic mechanism of the species as implanted in all individuals. The fact that it has not worked its miracles up to the present day, has no bearing, he would argue, on the matter. After all, the 'utopian perspective' he talks about is strictly *procedural*, concerned with *possible forms of life* only, from which one cannot draw 'conclusions about orders of happiness' in actual historical situations.

1.3 THE IDEOLOGICAL ARTICULATION OF SOCIAL NEEDS

1.3.1

Dominant intellectual trends and fashions – including the not so long ago highly-acclaimed rationalization of the established order in the name of 'the end of ideology' – have deeper roots, with much more complex ramifications than one would suspect.

It goes without saying, no one should deny, especially in the twentieth century, the power of the various cultural/ideological instruments and institutions to manipulate public opinion. By doing so, they can not only gravely distort the relative importance, but also artificially prolong the life-span of those manifestations which fall in line with the dominant material interests of the given society.

But even so, such distorting factors of institutionalized manipulation do not explain cultural/ideological change itself. While, undoubtedly, they may be able to prolong the life-span of the established intellectual movements when the latter lose their objective relevance, equally, they cannot do so at will and for an indefinite period of time. For precisely because what is at stake in these matters is the cultural articulation of the dominant material interests of the established order, the changing needs of the overall social complex and of its hegemonic class must assert themselves ultimately even against the institutionally best connected ideological groups, in case they are unable to turn the 'wind of change' of shifting social pressures to their own use.

Indeed, it is this strategy of harnessing the wind of change, despite the embarrassing 'u-turns' involved, which the representatives of the dominant intellectual trends as a rule try to pursue and, thanks to their privileged position in the structure of cultural/ideological production – which is always simultaneously also a form of ideological reproduction – they often succeed in without too much difficulty. Furthermore, the inherent requirements of the objective social structures themselves favour such ideological readjustments at the plane of the ruling personnel too. For the constant overturning of established ideological hierarchies, and the concomitant demolition of laboriously constructed intellectual reputations – be they real or imaginary – would be extremely wasteful and (on account not only of economic wastefulness but also of the resulting ideological instability) inadmissibly 'dysfunctional' to the system.

Thus, the strange 'conversions' and recantations of allegedly 'unattached intellectuals'[112] tell at least as much about the dominant, highly economical, and stability-oriented social mechanism of securing the continuity of cultural/ideological reproduction as about the strictly personal motivations and illuminations in terms of which such events are usually misrepresented by the interested parties.

Not surprisingly, in this sense, the same ideologists who so badly compromised themselves by proselytizing 'the end of ideology', succeeded very quickly in refloating their depleted intellectual stocks, notwithstanding the clamorous failure of their previous perspective. Under the changed circumstances of the growing social confrontations they reappeared again at the top of the cultural/ideological pyramid – as if nothing had happened to their past discourse – as the leading theoreticians of the 'post-industrial society', of its belatedly acknowledged 'malaise', and even of *The Cultural Contradictions of Capitalism*.[113] They could do this because their conflict-attenuating general approach to the fundamental practical issue of social antagonism was not simply a personal aberration. Rather, it was formulated in response to the fluctuating (but for that matter none the less objective) needs of a ruling class which retained its control over society after the previous ideological rationalization and legitimation of its hegemony lost its plausibility under the impact of the significantly sharpened social confrontations. Thus, although the *specific form* of conflict-attenuating ideology had to be changed under the new circumstances, the need to reproduce its *substance* in a suitably altered form persisted stronger than ever before.

This is how the multiple varieties of the new ideological discourse became fashionable, after the demise of the simplistic 'end of ideology' thesis, in virtue of their ability to focus attention on vaguely defined 'cultural' contradictions, when the stubborn persistence of ideology and the reappearance of unpalatable class conflicts could no longer be ignored or denied. In this way, the ideologies adapted to the changed circumstances could assume a mildly critical stance *vis à vis* the surface manifestations of the system in crisis, without subjecting to real criticism the ultimately explosive inner antagonisms of the established order.

As to how long lasting or ephemeral the contending intellectual products of a particular historical period might be, that question need not unduly worry us here. For what is at issue in the present context is the very nature of the relationship itself between the historically specific complex of social needs and the various cultural/ideological manifestations that arise on their foundation. This is a relationship of not one-sided mechanical but reciprocal dialectical determinations in the framework of which the competing cultural/ideological practices of the day *actively* respond to and help to articulate the needs with which society is pregnant. Through such a role they critically or apologetically intervene, with greater or less efficacy, in the unfolding historical developments and in the *actualization* of certain *potentialities* in preference to others.

1.3.2
In the ideological controversies of the postwar period some leading intellectual representatives of the United States came to occupy a growing importance. Their influence in Europe was, of course, by no means uniform. The militarily defeated and occupied Germany was, understandably, the first to be deeply affected by it, and France, arguably, the last. But be that as it may, in the end none of the countries of Western Europe could escape the impact of US hegemony manifest also in the field of culture and ideology.

This is how Habermas characterized the connection between the postwar political/intellectual developments of West Germany and the United States:

> The political culture of the Federal Republic would be worse today if it had not adopted impulses from American political culture during the first postwar decades. The Federal Republic opened itself for the first time to the West without reservations: we adopted the political theory of the Enlightenment, we grasped the pluralism which, first carried by religious sects, moulded the political mentality, and we became acquainted with the radical democratic spirit of the American pragmatism of Peirce, Mead, and Dewey.[114]

However, the influence of American politics and culture on European ideological developments was much more problematical than it might be thought on the basis of reading these lines. Nor was it indeed initiated in the postwar period. As a matter of fact, this relationship – reaching back to the mid-1930s – was (and remained ever since) particularly strong in the case of those who belonged to the Frankfurt Institute of Social Research. And it could hardly be considered a positively enlightening and democratizing connection. For in the orientation of the Frankfurt Institute one could witness from the very beginning the conservative impact of being integrated into the new political and intellectual setting when it was transplanted to the United States after Hitler's rise to power. (Marcuse, Leo Löwenthal, Erich Fromm, Franz Neumann, and a few others – who, significantly, became more and more peripheral to the activities of the Institute as time went by – constituted the notable exceptions in this respect.)

There was some heavy irony involved in this ideological reorientation of the Frankfurt Institute in accordance with the dominant political and intellectual climate of the United States; a reorientation which persisted also after the repatriation of the Institute to West Germany in 1949. For the Director of the Frankfurt Institute, Max Horkheimer, demonstrated already in the 1930s the 'post-Marxian' ideological opportunism of the new orientation by censoring the 'leftist' passages in the articles of their erstwhile friend and comrade, Walter Benjamin, and completed his intellectual accommodation after the war not only by suppressing some pre-war publications of the Institute but by censoring even his own writings.

Some of these developments are discussed in Chapter 3.4, in the context of Adorno's critical theory. Here it should suffice to recall the circumstances under which Walter Benjamin was censored:

> The original *Baudelaire* manuscript [by Benjamin] opens with a political discussion of Marx's assessment of professional revolutionary conspirators in the 1840s, contains constant allusions throughout to the proletarian struggles on the barricades of 19th century France, and closes with a moving evocation of Blanqui. It is unlikely to be an accident that all such passages disappeared from the essay eventually published in the *Zeitschrift für Sozialforschung*. If Benjamin in Paris was a too credulous believer in the thaumaturgical virtue of 'calling things by their names', his colleagues in New York certainly did not suffer from any trusting literalism: they were becoming too adept practitioners of the diplomatic art of euphemism and periphrasis, that *knowingly* does not call things by their name.
>
> This indirection had already been evident in the Institute's treatment of Benjamin's earlier essay, 'The Work of Art in the Age of Mechanical Reproduction', if on a lesser scale. The version printed in the *Zeitschrift* in *1936* was typically altered by such substitutions as '*totalitarian* doctrine' for '*Fascism*', 'constructive forces of mankind' for '*communism*', and '*modern* warfare' for '*imperialist* warfare'; while its preface, which directly invoked *Marx*, was *omitted altogether*.[115]

Understandably, this unforgivable interference with his work made a tragic impact on Walter Benjamin, since it was his profound dedication to the reassessment of some vital issues of modern capitalist political and cultural developments that kept his spirit alive in occupied France. As to Horkheimer's self-censorship, this was not a negligible tactical affair. It was not confined to smaller articles[116] but embraced even a major work, written jointly with Adorno, their *Dialectic of Enlightenment*.[117] For Horkheimer directly intervened on the occasion of the Italian publication of *Dialectic of Enlightenment*, asking the publisher, Giulio Einaudi, to depart from the original text and implement the specified cuts.[118]

As has been noted by commentators[119] (who reported also the serious misgivings of those members of the Frankfurt Institute who stayed behind in the United States), the repatriated Institute, first under Horkheimer's and later under Adorno's direction, played a dubious – not radically democratizing but actively Americanizing – role in the cultural developments of postwar Germany. What is, however, more significant in the present context, is that the international influence of its leading figures started relatively late. It coincided, in fact, with the triumph of the 'Atlanticist' perspective in Europe (which we have to consider later),[120] after overcoming a strong political and ideological resistance among the intellectuals in several European countries, especially in France.

Since the general perspective of the Frankfurt School – worked out to a large extent in the United States from the mid-1930s onwards – showed a

great affinity with the Atlanticist world view, there was very little chance of
the broad European diffusion of the influence of 'critical theory', so long as
the agenda for intellectual debates (not only in France but in Italy as well)
continued to be set by mass working class parties which openly professed
their allegiance to Marxism. For in France at first even Raymond Aron
could only be a rather isolated champion of this Atlanticist perspective,
constantly complaining about being 'persecuted' by the intellectuals of the
– for a considerable time after the war dominant – radical Left.

However, the objectively prevailing US hegemony in the economic and
political power relations of the West brought with it in due course the
corresponding adjustments on the plain of ideology as well. Sometimes
these changes took the form of clamorous reversals in the position of
important West European intellectuals who moved from a sharp and
sarcastic rejection of the Atlanticist political and ideological perspective
to a complete identification with it. As we shall see in Chapter 3.8, for a
number of years after the war Maurice Merleau-Ponty, for instance,
treated with utter contempt the formerly left-wing American intellectuals
(quite a few of them former Marxists)[121] who became the conservative
spokesmen of American cultural/ideological hegemony and of its highly
suspect institutional embodiments. He rejected at the same time, with
equal contempt, the Marshall plan as the economic vehicle of such hegemonic penetration into greatly weakened Europe. Paradoxically, however,
by the end of the 1950s, Merleau-Ponty's stance could not have been
more different from his once radical position, both with regard to the idea
of a 'Marshall plan' (which he now adopted as his model),[122] and even
in abandoning his earlier concern for the people of the 'colonies of
exploitation'.[123]

Changes of this kind, obviously, cannot be made intelligible in their
limited context, for they carry a meaning well beyond the immediate
motivations of the protagonists, be they (in Germany) the major representatives of 'critical theory', or (in France) Raymond Aron and Merleau-
Ponty. They show that the historically changing structural relations of
economy and politics sooner or later find their – at times most bewildering
– articulations in the domain of culture and ideology as well.

1.4 THE MAIN DETERMINANTS
OF CULTURAL/IDEOLOGICAL CHANGES

1.4.1

Considering the postwar ideological manifestations of the dominant social
interests from the distance of the by now established contrasting preoccu-
pations of a new historical situation, it might seem thoroughly astonishing,
if not altogether incomprehensible, that intellectuals should seriously

entertain even for a moment the idea that 'political philosophy is dead'[124] and that:

> the end of ideology closes the book on an era, the one of easy 'left' formulae for social change.... 'ideology' by now, and with good reason, is an *irretrievably* fallen word.[125]

Yet, the disconcerting fact is that for quite a long time philosophers, sociologists and political theorists in the West wholeheartedly embraced such notions, and they did so in very large numbers. Indeed, the prevailing intellectual climate for almost three decades after the second world war favoured the broad diffusion of the wishful thinking which greeted with enthusiasm 'the end of ideology'. But more than that, paradoxically it also succeeded in confusing and disarming the representatives of some intellectual currents even at the opposite end of the political spectrum, as we shall see in the course of this study.

To predicate 'the end of ideology', or to assign a one-sidedly *negative* connotation to all ideology, was always totally unrealistic, and it is bound to remain so for a long historical period ahead of us. For ideologies cannot conceivably 'wither away' by themselves – let alone can they be fictitiously 'superseded' within the self-enclosed domain of pseudo-scientific theoretical constructs – for as long as there are major social conflicts with which they are inextricably intertwined.

In truth, to proclaim 'the end of ideology' is itself a characteristic ideology. It implies either the adoption of a non-conflictual perspective of contemporary and future social developments (a position to which, as a matter of fact, the defenders of the ruling ideological interests committed themselves when they rather foolishly asserted 'the end of ideology in the West'[126]), or an attempt to transform the real life conflicts of ideological confrontations into the shadow-boxing of disorienting intellectual practices which imaginarily 'dissolve' the issues at stake by means of some claimed 'theoretical discovery'.

Such approaches are in their substance thoroughly idealistic, since they try to explain the changes in the dominant cultural/ideological climate in terms of some self-propelling theoretical dynamic of the ideas themselves. The representatives of the ruling ideology postulate this 'inner development' of ideas – which, by definition, could be controlled by the activity of the mind itself – because they cannot face up to the precarious *practical implications* of the unfolding social conflicts for the social interests with which they identify themselves. Already the young Marx argued against the illusions which wanted to retain for ideology this *'semblance of independence'*,[127] stressing at the same time that such views, even if they are coupled with verbal radicalism, are characteristic of 'the staunchest conservatives'.[128] He went on to say that the various ideologies and forms of consciousness corresponding to them have *no history* of their own, no self-contained dynamic of *development*[129] but must be understood in the closest conjunction with the developing material life processes of real individuals. The hypostatization of the inner dynamic and self-development of ideas and theoretical systems is only 'theoretical bubble-blowing'. In opposition to such misconceptions Marx concluded that 'the real, *practical* dissolution of these phrases, the removal of these notions from the consciousness of men, will be effected by *altered circumstances*, not by *theoretical deductions.*'[130]

However, just as the 'valiant fellow' refused to give up his idea that men were drowned in water only because they were 'possessed with the idea of gravity', in the same way, illusory belief in the 'semblance of independence' of ideological developments obstinately refused to give way to the overwhelming evidence to the contrary. Accordingly, in the recent past people continued to refer *ad nauseam* to the 'crisis of Marxism'. As if theories and ideologies could have a history of their own, and a self-contained inner dynamic of development, which could explain their 'crisis', or, for that matter, cure them of it. Yet, as Sartre rightly stressed, 'the "philosophical crisis" is the particular expression of a *social crisis*, and its immobility is conditioned by the contradictions which split the society. A so-called "revision" performed by "experts", would be, therefore, only an idealist mystification without real significance. It is the very movement of history, the struggle of men on all planes and on all levels of human activity, which will set free captive thought and permit it to attain its full development.'[131]

1.4.2

As far as Marxism is concerned, its tranformations (and 'crises') are inseparable from the development of the working-class movement. For Marxism is not an armchair philosophy that could be practised irrespective of the conditions prevailing in the international socialist movement. On the contrary, it is a world view which, right from its inception, consciously rejected the idea of a mere *interpretation* of the world and committed itself to the uphill struggle of *changing* it: a task whose realization is inconceivable without the successful implementation of suitable political strategies. Hence the actual state of the necessary strategic instruments of the working-class movement can never be a matter of indifference to Marxist theory.

In this sense, attempting to explain the problems at stake in terms of 'the crisis of Marxism' was a complete misdiagnosis. For this crisis primarily affected some working-class parties which once unreservedly adhered to the Marxian strategy. The way in which some of these parties disengaged themselves from their earlier strategies brought with it, in fact, rather disastrous consequences for them, precipitating thereby a crisis in perspective with which the Marxian theory and its originally envisaged application to emancipatory political practice had absolutely nothing to do. (It is enough to think in this respect of the sorry state of the French and Spanish Communist Parties today, among others.)

Thus, the problem in reality was not the inadequacy of the – objectively and consistently adaptable – Marxian strategic framework to the necessities of socialist struggle under the conditions of the 'modern industrial society' but, on the contrary, the unprincipled departure of the parties in question from it. When a once important historical force, the French Communist Party, reduces itself to the role of a fig leaf, in order to hide the non-existent endowments of François Mitterrand as a socialist,[132] no one should be surprised that a commensurate shrinkage takes place not only in its electoral fortunes but, more importantly, in its impact on the unfolding social developments. To ascribe such consequences to the 'crisis of Marxism' as their underlying cause is clearly an absurdity. In contrast to such pseudo-explanation, Sartre's warning addressed to the French Communist Party way back in February 1956 proved prophetic in this respect.[133] For he firmly underlined the dangers of a failure to find the right orientation and corresponding course of action against the false alternatives of a 'revolutionism emptied of its content' (and, of course, heavily tainted with Stalinism), and a 'reformism which will end up destroying the substance of the Party'.[134]

However, the matter is much more serious than the mere fact of the counter-productive reorientation of some European working-class parties by itself. It is discussed in this study both with reference to the fundamental strategic propositions of the Marxian theory,[135] and in relation to the organizational and political developments of the international socialist movement in the twentieth century.[136] In the present context the point is to emphasize the importance of the much neglected – and often even completely ignored – relationship between cultural/ideological changes and the *social movements* to which they are objectively linked.

France offers a particularly good example in this respect. For nowhere was the shift to the Right among intellectuals more dramatic in the last two decades than on the left bank of the river Seine in Paris. Many years ago, when Sartre lamented the French CP's failure to be the carrier of a 'living Marxism', he could simultaneously also underline that the leading intellectuals of the country, from the historian Georges Lefèbvre to the structural anthropologist Lévi-Strauss, were all '*marxisants*'.[137] And he could forcefully argue that:

> To the extent to which it is 'of the left', every intellectual, every group of intellectuals, every movement of ideas, define themselves – directly or indirectly – through their relationship to Marxism. Men of my age know very well that, even more than the two world wars, the great affair of their life has been their constant encounter with the working class and its ideology, which offered them an unchallengeable vision of the world and of themselves. For

us Marxism is not only a philosophy. It is the climate of our ideas, the environment in which they are nourished, the true manifestation of what Hegel called the Objective Spirit. We see in Marxism a cultural possession of the left; better: ever since the death of bourgeois thought Marxism is, alone, Culture; for it is the only one to enable us to understand men, work, and events.[138]

Indeed, in these years Sartre could confidently extend his conclusions about the importance of Marxism well beyond the boundaries of France, arguing that it was the only living philosophy for the whole epoch ahead of us, wherever we lived.[139] At the same time, in a rejoinder, the *'marxisant'* Lévi-Strauss wholeheartedly agreed with Sartre that 'in both our cases Marx is the point of departure of our thought'.[140] And in an important interview he admitted as late as March 1971[141] that the thought of Marx deeply marked his life, adding that his own intellectual contribution must be situated within the framework of the Marxian theory of ideology, particularly in relation to the categories of *'base and superstructure'*, since he always consciously aimed at a concrete elaboration of the second.[142] Thus, Lévi-Strauss could not turn against Marx – not even when the general political and intellectual climate started to become hostile to him – without devaluing simultaneously his own life-work.

Nevertheless, the tone and perspective of the 1971 interview was deeply pessimistic; talking of the 'disintegration of our civilization' and of the march of our world 'towards a cataclysm'; lamenting that our societies become 'enormous', which results in the triumph of 'sameness' and the loss of 'differences'; praising with nostalgia Gobineau's reactionary utopia while agreeing with the pessimistic judgement of its author about its unrealizability; and concluding that:

> Today the greater peril for humanity does not come from the activities of a regime, a party, a group, or a class. It comes from humanity itself in its entirety; a humanity which reveals itself to be its own worst enemy and, alas, at the same time, also the worst enemy of the rest of the creation. It is of this truth that one has to convince it, if there is to be any hope that one can save it.[143]

But who was going to do the convincing and saving of humanity? What kind of a vantage point could one adopt to stand outside humanity and castigate it as its own worst enemy, exempting at the same time the sociopolitical regimes, parties, groups, and classes of their responsibility? After all, when the Old Testament prophets thundered against sinful humanity, they claimed to have been ordered directly by God himself to do so. But now, where was to be found the social agency equal to the advocated task? How could one intervene in the actual process of transformation in order to counter the gloomily denounced trends of development, in the hope of realizing the desired objectives? There was not even a faint hint in Lévi-Strauss's interview how to answer these questions.

Admittedly, by the time Lévi-Strauss gave the interview quoted above, 'post-structuralism' was already in full swing. As he himself remarked with a touch of irony, 'since 1968 structuralism ceased to be fashionable'.[144] However, the world-views put forward by the leading intellectuals of the post-structuralist phase were by no means more reassuring than his pessimistic diagnosis of humanity's predicament. In fact, Michel Foucault painted an even more desolate picture:

> Throughout the nineteenth century, the end of philosophy and the promise of an approaching culture were no doubt one and the same thing as the thought of finitude and the appearance of man in the field of knowledge; in our day, the fact that philosophy is still – and again – in the process of coming to an end, and the fact that in it perhaps, though even more outside and against it, in literature as well as in formal reflection, the question of language is being posed, prove no doubt that *man is in the process of disappearing.*[145]
> As the archaeology of our thought easily shows, man is an invention of recent date. And one perhaps nearing its end. If those arrangements were to disappear as they appeared . . . then one can certainly wager that man would be *erased like a face drawn in the sand at the edge of the sea.*[146]

The last few lines were not a marginal note in Foucault's discourse but the emphatic concluding words of his book, indicating a deeply problematical perspective shared by many others as well. Only a short step separated such an orientation from saying explicitly 'Farewell to the working class':[147] a far cry indeed from Sartre's passionate pronouncement that for the intellectuals of his generation 'the great affair of their life has been their constant encounter with the working class and its ideology (Marxism), which offered them an unchallengeable vision of the world and of themselves.'

One of the principal factors behind these dramatic shifts in the perspective was undoubtedly the steadily worsening relationship between the French Communist Party and the intellectuals, both on account of the CP's failure to get rid of the Stalinist heritage and in connection with its dubious behaviour during the Algerian war of liberation. As the exasperated Sartre put it at the time of the Algerian war: 'Collaboration with the CP is both *necessary* and *impossible.*'[148] Naturally, this relationship became much worse as a result of May 1968 and its aftermath, bringing with it eventually a complete break between Sartre and the French Communist Party.

The consequences of these conflicts were far-reaching. For cultural/ideological discussions after the war in France were inescapably affected by working-class militancy in general and the CP's Resistance-enhanced active role in it in particular. The impact of Marxism, thus, reached well beyond the card-carrying intellectuals and the so-called 'fellow travellers'. Even those who had a hostile stance towards Marxism from the very beginning, like Raymond Aron, could not escape its gravitational pull and had to enter, in no matter how polemical a fashion, into the framework of the ongoing debates.

All this had significantly changed with the crisis of the CP and of the French working-class movement, to which one must also add the impact of the unfolding socioeconomic developments in the capitalistically advanced countries, in their problematical relationship to the rest of the world. As a result, the intellectuals have lost their orientation (irrespective of how unquestioning or critical it might have been towards the direct political forces and organizations of the working-class base), finding themselves on their own, with the temptation to withdraw into the domain of abstract theoretical discourses quite remote from identifiable practical issues. In a sense, therefore, the working class and its ideology have become 'super-fluous' in the eye of Western intellectuals. For they could not see a fundamental hegemonic challenge to the existing order emanating from the organized and politically conscious working-class movement.

It was in this radically changed ideological climate that the 'critical theory' of the Frankfurt School, too, seemed to acquire its broader inter-national relevance. For the leading ideologists of this school had for their target for many years the critique of 'working-class integration' as an incorrigible condition. They even provided the model for misdiagnosing the historically specific contradictions and crises of the Western working-class movement as the 'crisis of Marxism' from which there could be really no chance of recovery. As Hans-Jürgen Krahl correctly stated about Adorno's upside-down vision of these relations:

> The withering of the class struggle is mirrored in his critical theory as the *degeneration of the materialist conception of history*.[149]

The problems and their feasible solutions in reality are, therefore, twofold. On the one hand, they undoubtedly arise from the way in which particular intellectuals who articulate the various forms of ideological discourse engage in a critical confrontation with one another, pursuing their own answers to their logical conclusions and 'transcending' the adversary's discourse within their own theoretical framework. On the other hand, however, the demands inherent in the nature of the social movements of any particular historical period necessarily condition the theoretically arti-culated ideological discourses, even if by no means in a uniform way. As a rule, the stronger the objective dynamic of the *social confrontations* of the fundamental hegemonic forces of society, the more directly the cultural/ ideological conceptualizations bear their mark, and *vice versa*. In this sense, the self-oriented and predominantly abstract ideological discourse of a particular historical period – which attempts to solve its problems without any appeal to tangible sociohistorical forces, claiming to 'sublate' the previous attempts by its own 'post-' version of what was still yesterday the most up-to-date 'post-' solution – does not arise simply from ideology itself. It originates in the historically specific contradictions and crises of the potentially emancipatory social movements, and in the problematical relationship between the given social movements and the cultural/ideological agencies at work in society. This is why the promised theoretical/ideological solutions of the debated problems tend to be so elusive. For a so-called 'ideological crisis' is *never* ideological alone – in the sense that it could be done away with through ideological/theoretical discussions and clarifications – as we shall see on more than one occasion in the course of the present study. Since ideology is the practical consciousness of class societies, the solution of the problems generated in ideological confrontations cannot be made intelligible without identifying their materially as well as culturally effective practical dimension.

One day, when I asked Derrida, what was he hoping to achieve by 'deconstruction', he countered my scepticism by saying that the negativity of this venture was only the preparatory stage to the positive phase of *construction*, which will follow in due course. This was more than 12 years ago, and we are more deeply than ever entangled in the unrelieved negativity of 'preparatory deconstructions'. And no wonder. For positivity is not an *afterthought* that one could simply append to the groundwork of an inherently negative undertaking. However, it would be most unfair to blame Derrida for the non-arrival of the positive phase. For it is very difficult to be positive in an intellectual enterprise without the sustaining ground of an emancipatory social movement.

1.4.3
If we want to understand the dominant ideological themes of changing intellectual climates, we have to locate them within the framework of three fundamental sets of determinations:

1. The socioeconomic parameters of a given historical phase.
2. The principal political movements and their ideological/intellectual needs.
3. The prominent scientific theories and practices, as well as the various philosophies and self-reflections of science concerning the regulative significance of the latter in the overall complex of human activities.

Naturally, these three sets of determinations do not change at an even pace, nor indeed simultaneously. In the intellectual physiognomy of a certain period there may be 'discrepancies' or departures from the expected new pattern in the sense that some of the determinants brought into prominence at an earlier phase of historical development remain operational to a significant extent under the changed circumstances. As an example, we should remember how the sanguine social expectations arising from the nineteenth-century development of science and technology continued to characterize the ruling ideological trends well beyond the limited historical phase of their original socioeconomic, political and theoretical conjuncture, well into the long expansionary years of the postwar period.

However, overlaps and apparent contradictions of this kind do not alter the fact that across the complex trajectory of such continuities and discontinuities the intellectual physiognomy of particular historical phases is clearly discernible, since it is defined by the overall configuration of the three sets of determinations taken *together*, in their *specific* interrelatedness. Accordingly, continuities and overlaps are not simply *given*, as a self-contained entity, but must be constantly *reproduced* in the context of, and in relation to, the changing determinations.

It is precisely in virtue of this inescapably *context-bound reproduction* that the inherited continuities are not simply reasserted but simultaneously also modified. As a result, they acquire a meaning often significantly different – especially with regard to the relevant ideological functions – from the original one, even if on the face of it they appear to be identical to the earlier articulations of the same complex. This is why an apparently identical principle, correlation, or intellectual influence, brought into play under the contrasting circumstances of different historical situations, can mean radically different things at different times.

To take only one example here, Cartesianism as such fulfilled qualitatively different functions in the course of French historical developments, in accordance with the changing ideological needs of the French bourgeoisie, as Sartre rightly emphasized it.[150] In the same sense, the persistence or disappearance of various ideological trends and fashions is subject to much more objective determinations than might appear at first sight. Indeed, such phenomena can only be explained in terms of the *specific configuration* of all three fundamental sets of determinations mentioned above.

1.5 CONCLUSION

These are the problems, broadly speaking, which we have to address ourselves to in the present study. It will be necessary to situate them in their proper theoretical and historical setting, so as to be able to pinpoint the relevant material and cultural determinations at their roots, together with their practical implications for the future in the making in which the positive role of ideology cannot be overestimated.

Accordingly, Part One is dedicated to demonstrating not only the untenability of the various 'supra-ideological' claims, past as well as present, together with their clearly identifiable ideological motivations, but simultaneously also the vital active role which ideology plays in the social reproduction process.

Part Two, on the other hand, analyses the relationship between science, ideology and methodology, with particular reference to the much neglected practical dimension of each.

And finally, Part Three takes a closer look at the all-important connection between ideology and emancipation, reasserting the validity of a critical and self-critical socialist theory as the necessary strategic framework of emancipation.

2 · THE SOCIOECONOMIC PARAMETERS

2.1 POSTWAR EXPANSION AND 'POST-IDEOLOGY'

2.1.1

It is not too difficult to see that the dominance of anti-ideological ideologies for a considerable time after the second world war was quite inconceivable without the sustained expansionary phase of capitalistic developments in the same period as its material foundation. For many of the – nowadays laughable but at the time confidently preached – theses of our anti-ideological ideologists (from their views on the meaning of 'Left' and 'Right' mentioned in Note 126, to treating the concepts of 'class' and 'class conflict' as 'nineteenth-century anachronisms', etc.) acquired their plausibility in the context of the spectacular postwar economic expansion and of the promise of all-embracing material improvements and unimpeded social progress in the future.

As an ideological ancestor to all this, the founding father of capitalist 'scientific management', Frederick Winslow Taylor, was dreaming about the elimination of social conflicts as far back as the turn of the century in these terms:

> The great revolution that takes place in the mental attitude of the two parties under scientific management is that both sides *take their eyes off the division of the surplus* as the all-important matter, and together turn their attention toward increasing the size of the surplus until this surplus becomes *so large that it is unnecessary to quarrel over how it shall be divided*. They come to see that when they stop pulling against one another, and instead both turn and push shoulder to shoulder in the same direction, the size of the surplus created by their joint efforts is truly astounding. They both realize that when they *substitute friendly cooperation and mutual helpfulness for antagonism and strife* they are together able to make this surplus so enormously greater than it was in the past that there is ample room for a large increase in wages for the workmen and an equally great increase in profits for the manufacturer.[151]

In the heady days of postwar expansion, the conditions of Taylor's managerial utopia seemed to have been fully realized, transforming the contest over *social power relations* into the *technological/organizational* issue of how to maximize (or 'optimize'), under the authority of 'science', the production of surplus that should be destined to be unequally, yet – as far as the workers themselves were concerned – generously divided.

In his own days Taylor knew very well – just as his 'anti-ideological' followers did later on – that the social power relations of hierarchical domination and subordination were really at stake. Yet, with characteristic rhetorics, he enthused about 'the substitution of hearty brotherly coope-ration for contention and strife; of both pulling hard in the same direction instead of pulling apart; of replacing suspicious watchfulness with mutual confidence; of becoming friends instead of enemies', etc.[152] At the same time he was naive enough to spell out the real meaning of 'hearty brother-hood', 'mutual helpfulness', 'friendly cooperation', 'mutual confidence', etc., as seen from the point of view of capitalist 'scientific management':

> Now one of the very first requirements for a man who is fit to handle pig iron as a regular occupation is that he shall be so *stupid* and so phlegmatic that he more nearly *resembles in his mental make-up the ox* than any other type. The man who is mentally alert and intelligent is for this very reason entirely unsuited to what would, for him, be the grinding monotony of work of this character. Therefore the workman who is best suited to handling pig iron is *unable to understand the real science* of doing this class of work. *He is so stupid that the word 'percentage' has no meaning for him*, and he must consequently be trained by a man more intelligent than himself into the *habit of working in accordance with the laws of this science* before he can be successful.[153]

2.1.2

If we compare Taylor's way of looking at the relationship between capitalist working conditions and the 'mental make-up' of the workers with the approach to the same issue by the major representatives of the bourgeoisie in its ascendancy, we find a truly striking contrast. For people like Adam Ferguson – one of the outstanding figures of the Scottish Enlightenment – adopted a critical stance towards the unfolding socio-economic developments. Thus, they could still clearly distinguish the *causal* factors from their unavoidable *consequences*, instead of blinding themselves to the real nature of the relationship in question, in the interest of defending and idealizing the established order.

This is how Ferguson himself assessed, at the earliest phase of the industrial revolution, the inherently problematical character of the capita-listic productive practices (dictated in his view not simply by technical considerations but by the imperative of profit maximization) and their necessarily impoverishing impact on human beings:

> Every undertaker in manufacture finds that the more he can subdivide the tasks of his workmen, and the more hands he can employ on separate articles, the more are his expenses diminished, and his *profits increased*.... Nations of tradesmen come to consist of members who, beyond their own particular trade, are *ignorant of all human affairs*.... Many mechanical arts, indeed, *require no capacity*; they succeed best under a *total suppression of sentiment and reason*; and *ignorance* is the mother of industry as well as of superstition. Reflection and fancy are subject to err; but a *habit* of moving the hand, or the foot, is independent of either. Manufactures, accordingly, prosper most where

the *mind is least consulted*, and where the workshop may, without any great work of imagination, be considered as *an engine, the parts of which are men.*[154]

Taylor, in complete contrast, turned everything upside down, so that he should be able to find a convenient justification (and ideological rationalization) for the established mode of control of the working people within the framework of the 'scientifically managed' capitalist enterprise. Instead of taking any notice of the brutalizing and dehumanizing impact of the dominant productive practices, he transformed the necessary *consequences* of such practices on the 'mental make-up' of the workers into a pretended *original cause*. By doing so, he made the most callous treatment of the workers both entirely '*justified*' and 'scientifically sound'. For the people whose 'mental make-up resembled the ox' and who were destined by nature itself for tasks in accordance with their 'stupidity', did not deserve any better treatment. Nor were they indeed amenable to a different treatment, given the nature-determined limitations of their constitution.

Following this line of reasoning, the 'principles of scientific management' could claim to bring the organization of the capitalist system into full harmony with nature's own determinations, treating human beings as animals 'in accordance with the laws of the new science' as sanctioned not by the contingent order of society but by the unalterable lawfulness of nature itself. Compelling people to submit to the dictates of work performed as mechanical '*habit*' – dictates emanating from capital's relentless drive for profit – was for Adam Ferguson thoroughly reprehensible. By the time, however, when the Frederick Winslow Taylors composed the music soothing enough to the ear of the capitalist management of industry, absolute conformity to the same dictates of 'habit' was transformed into an unquestionable virtue.

Later representatives of this 'scientific management' have, of course, become far more sophisticated in the *presentation* of their recommendations. They have successfully added not only 'musak' to their music but also the 'science' of 'public relations', as well as the legally buttressed – unashamedly state-sponsored – 'art' of 'management consultancy' to their defensive arsenal. The substance of their apologetic wisdom, though, remained essentially the same, even if the more recent practitioners of 'scientific' managerial manipulation were careful enough not to champion publicly with the same brutish self-consciousness the cause of preserving the established power relations and the vested interests of the ruling class.

Naturally, the new 'anti-ideological' perspective, with its close links to long professed American ideologies and corresponding industrial practices, could not be successfully diffused in a deeply conflict-torn Europe in the immediate after-war years. The material circumstances of hardship, and at times even of starvation, were not exactly conducive to an unproblematical identification with the rosy idea of ever-improving affluence and technocratic integration of the European labour force in the 'American way of life'.

Only after the years of consolidation, accomplished under the tutelage and direct economic intervention of the dominant capitalist power and its 'Marshall plan', did matters change substantially in favour of the adoption of such a perspective. And, of course, even then one could by no means speak of a complete triumph of the 'anti-ideological' approach, since the latter itself had to continue to direct its fire-power against the *left* while preaching, with typical inconsistency, the 'irretrievable anachronism' of the traditional forms of division and conflict between 'Left' and 'Right'.

2.2 PREMATURE THEORIZATION OF 'THE END OF SCARCITY'

2.2.1

Nevertheless, the new creed, together with its institutionally promoted and safeguarded socioeconomic underpinning, became sufficiently dominant to induce even some leading figures of Marxism in the West – Lucien Goldmann, for instance – to talk of a successfully accomplished transition 'from *crisis capitalism* to *organized capitalism*', defining the latter like this:

> By the term 'organized capitalism', we mean the contemporary period which, through the creation of regulative mechanisms owing to state interventions, has made possible a continual economic growth and the diminution, not to say the total elimination, of internally generated social and political crises.[155]

The fact that the benefits of this 'continual economic growth' were confined to little more than 10 per cent of the world's population and, consequently, the whole edifice of 'organized capitalism' was being erected on very shaky foundations indeed, did not seem to carry much weight, if any, with the participants in the major ideological debates. This was partly because their political/intellectual horizon was, surprising as this may sound, confined to the problems of the 'advanced capitalist countries'. And partly because many of the thinkers who intended to offer a more critical approach to the problems of contemporary capitalism ended up, in fact, rather uncritically accepting the wishful thinking which asserted that 'the *conquest of scarcity* is now not only foreseeable but actually foreseen.'[156]

Thus, while in the real world millions of people continued to perish year by year as a result of malnutrition and starvation, the acceptance of the adversary's framework of discourse induced even some leading intellectuals of the Left in Western Europe and in North America to formulate thoroughly vague, if not altogether vacuous, strategies for the future. As we can see, for instance, in the following analysis of alleged trends and their implications according to which:

In the conditions of material scarcity that have always prevailed up to now, property has been a matter of a right to a material revenue. With the *conquest of scarcity* that is now foreseen, property must become rather a right to an *immaterial revenue*, a revenue of enjoyment of the *quality of life*. Such a revenue cannot be reckoned in *material quantities*. The right to such a revenue can only be reckoned as a *right to participate* in a satisfying set of social relations.[157]

The least one should object to this conception is, first, that the opposition between material and 'immaterial revenue' (whatever the latter might mean), just as the one between quantity and quality, is thoroughly undialectical. And second, that the cart is being put before the horse, in that it is the elementary *precondition* of any conceivable conquest of scarcity that the people should be able to strive for the realization of such a radically all-encompassing aim within the framework of an adequate set of social relations, rather than the other way round. Indeed the precondition in question requires not the somewhat hollow '*right to participate* in a satisfying set of social relations', but the fully *effective control*, by the associated producers, of the conditions of their own life – and in the first place, of their material conditions of production – for the sake of realizing the ends which they set themselves.

2.2.2
To conceptualize these matters in terms of abstract 'rights', asserting that under contemporary capitalism the main property of people 'is their *right to earn an income*, whether as self-employed persons or as wage or salary earners',[158] can produce nothing but disorientation. For, in truth, many millions of unemployed people do not have such rights even in the most 'advanced' capitalist societies, let alone in the rest of the capitalist world. And even if they did have those rights, which they do not and in such societies *cannot* possess, the rudely awakening fact is that there is an astronomical distance from the mere *possession of rights* to their meaningful and effective *implementation* through a whole network of materially sustained and socially viable practices of human gratification.

Ironically, thus, the dominant intellectual climate of postwar expansion, with its boundless promises for the future which seemed to be authenticated by some real advances in a limited part of the world, succeeded in distorting also the perspectives of some critical intellectuals who personally welcomed the possible end of capitalist exploitation. Under the conditions of apparently limitless growth and expansion, confidently advertised as the self-evident and final refutation of all dissenting views 'of nineteenth-century stamp', it was very difficult to challenge the ruling ideological images on their own terrain. To enter that terrain often meant adopting the categorial framework of a thoroughly vitiated form of discourse, with serious consequences for one's own position.

Unhappily, in this sense, there was a striking resemblance between the prominent Canadian Marxist Macpherson's just quoted categorization of 'changes in the concept of property' in the contemporary world, and the formalist structural-functionalist conceptualization of the same problems by the American conservative Talcott Parsons. For the American sociologist argued that 'there must be a property system which regulates *claims* to transferable entities, *material or immaterial*, and thereby *secures rights* in means of life and in the facilities which are necessary for the performance of functions.'[159] Paradoxically, however, while the apologetic intent of the Parsonian grand theorization could hardly be contested,[160] Macpherson became trapped by the same set of generic categories *despite* his honestly held and forcefully stated subjective emancipatory intentions.

2.3 THE FALLACY OF TECHNOLOGICAL SOLUTIONS TO SOCIAL PROBLEMS

2.3.1
In tune with the hustle and bustle of the strong expansionary trend, intellectuals went on enthusing about a whole series of alleged economic miracles: the German, Japanese, Italian, French and Brazilian 'miracles', to name but a few. They confidently anticipated the indefinite continuation of postwar expansion and, accordingly, produced a whole range of categories which presented their highly partisan and *prescriptive* conceptualizations of the ongoing developments as unobjectionably '*descriptive*' statements of fact. Thus, a multiplicity of *desiderata* appeared as either already accomplished, or well on the way to being accomplished. Nothing seemed to be unfit to be brought into the framework of this optimistic categorization.

In place of the contending *social* systems of capitalism and socialism, we were offered the *technologically* (as well as, of course, technocratically) defined 'new industrial state', the 'modern industrial system', the mythical 'technostructure', and the 'convergence'[161] of the rival 'industrial systems'. Similarly, on the model of some sort of 'internal convergence', the 'new reality' of rapid technological change was interpreted in terms of social relations as the producer of a 'new working class'[162] and of the necessary weakening, if not altogether the disappearance, of class conflict itself.[163] And perhaps best of all, the old social evil of mass unemployment was imaginarily transcended, thanks to some ideal postulates which were, again, characteristically misrepresented as irrefutable facts. On the one hand, with reference to the claimed 'technostructural transformations', Galbraith asserted that:

> The notion of unemployment, as traditionally held, is coming year by year to have less meaning. More and more, the figures on unemployment enumerate

those, who are *unemployable* in terms of *modern requirements of the industrial system*. This incapacity may coexist with *acute shortages of more highly qualified talent*.[164]

And on the other hand, Walt Rostow posited – on thoroughly fictitious yet unashamedly self-congratulatory political grounds, and with reference to some magic Keynesian 'technical tricks' – that the problem of unemployment would never bother us again. For now:

> There is *every reason* to believe, looking at the *sensitivity* of the political process to *even small pockets of unemployment* in modern democratic societies, that the sluggish and timid policies of the 1920s and 1930s with respect to the level of employment *will no longer be tolerated* in Western societies. And now the *technical tricks* of that trade – due to the *Keynesian revolution* – are widely understood. It should not be forgotten that Keynes set himself the task of defeating Marx's prognosis about the course of unemployment under capitalism; and he largely succeeded.[165]

Once captivated by the power of such 'certainties', there could be no limit to the flights of the imagination. Having disposed of unemployment with such ease in the present and in the future, there could be no reason why the same procedure should not be applied to the past as well, absolving capitalism as a social system of all its major problems with the help of the *counter-factual conditionals* and retrospective pseudo-explanations – of failures by failures due to failures – as exemplified by the following quotation:

> The relative inter-war stagnation in Western Europe was due not to long-run diminishing returns but to the *failure* of Western Europe to create a setting in which its national societies moved promptly into the age of *high mass-consumption*, yielding new leading sectors. And this *failure*, in turn, was due mainly to a *failure* to create *initial full employment* in the post-1920 setting of the terms of trade. Similarly the protracted depression of the United States in the 1930s was due not to long-run diminishing returns, but to a *failure* to create an *initial renewed setting of full employment*, through public policy, which *would have permitted* the new leading sectors of suburban housing, the diffusion of automobiles, durable consumer goods and services to roll forward beyond 1929.[166]

What was astonishing in all this was not simply that some well-established intellectuals should rationalize the far from unproblematical reality of capitalism in terms of such arbitrary rewriting of history with the help of counter-factual conditionals and through the retrospective superimposition of present structures on past realities. Rather, that their crude propaganda exercises[167] – which violated every rule of logic – were greeted in the prevailing ideological climate as the last word of scientifically inspired, objective wisdom.

The problem of poverty was explained away with similar dexterity, and the method employed was equally suspect. Starting out from the *particular* achievements of the globally dominant US economy, Galbraith's analysis soon culminated in *general* claims, insisting that:

> As a general affliction, [poverty] was ended by increased output which, however imperfectly it may have been distributed, nevertheless accrued in substantial amount to those who worked for a living. The result was to reduce poverty from the problem of a *majority* to that of a *minority*. It ceased to be a *general* case and became a *special* case. It is this which has put the problem of poverty into its peculiar *modern* form.[168]

This conception of *'modern poverty'* was self-complacent even with regard to the United States, not to mention the global dimension of the problem in which the US itself was – and more than ever still is – heavily implicated. It was further categorized as either *'case* poverty' (related merely 'to some characteristics of the *individuals* so afflicted,'[169] like drunkenness and mental deficiency), or *'insular* poverty, that which manifests itself as an "island" of poverty'.[170] The meaning of the latter was spelled out as follows:

> Insular poverty has something to do with the desire of a comparatively large number of people of spend their lives at or near the place of their birth. This *homing instinct* causes them to bar the solution, always open as an individual remedy in a country without barriers to emigration, to *escape the island of poverty* in which they were born.[171]

A few years ago the British Conservative Minister of Employment, Norman Tebbit, secured immortality for himself by advising well over three million unemployed people to get on their bikes (which they did not have) and look for a job (which they could not have). The numerous commentators who considered his remark totally mindless never suspected that he had such a sophisticated predecessor in the distinguished American professor quoted above.

2.3.2

Professor Galbraith declared already in his first widely acclaimed book *American Capitalism: The Concept of Countervailing Power*,[172] that the 'ancient' distinction between Left and Right has now become *useless*, primarily because of the association of the term 'Left' with the name of Marx. He proposed, therefore, to replace these compromised notions by the terms 'liberal' and 'conservative'.

This was in 1952. By 1958 – when the same author first published *The Affluent Society* – he felt that it was more appropriate not to confine the necessary correction merely to replacing 'Left' by 'liberal' but to speak in terms of *'modern* liberal politicians' and *'modern* trade union members'.[173] Every difficulty seemed to be amenable to an unproblematical solution by appending to it the 'modern' label, from 'modern poverty' to the 'modern economy' – the latter as characterized by its 'modern management' and

'modern trade union membership', and, of course, as benevolently relieved of its 'ancient' conflicts by the enlightened regulatory interventions
of 'modern government'. Even the characteristic change which we could
notice in the titles of Professor Galbraith's books reflected a suitable
adaptation to the prevailing ideological climate, moving from *American
Capitalism* and its still acknowledged conflicts through *The Great Crash
1929* (a book that celebrated, in 1954, the happy correction of the 'weaknesses in the economy' which, combined with the 'mood of speculation',
were said to have caused the crash) to *The Affluent Society* (1958) and
The New Industrial State (1967/1971). The last two books both took for
granted the permanence of the prevailing consensus, while the very last
also postulated the universal diffusion of the beneficial socioeconomic
practices of the 'new industrial state' as well as the inevitable 'convergence'
of the rival systems.

The 'concept of countervailing power' was introduced by Galbraith as a
most welcome innovation of the system and the lever with the help of
which the undisturbed expansion of the established order could be secured
with relative ease and stability. He praised the impact and positive social
significance of the 'countervailing power' like this:

> As a general though not invariable rule one finds the *strongest unions* in the
> United States where markets are served by *strong corporations*. And it is
> not an accident that the large automobile, steel, electrical, rubber, farm-
> machinery, and non-ferrous metal-mining and smelting companies all bargain
> with *powerful unions*.... By contrast there is not a single union of any
> consequence in American agriculture, the country's closest approach to the
> competitive model. The reason lies not in the difficulties of organization; these
> are considerable, but greater difficulties in organization have been overcome.
> The reason is that the farmer has not possessed any power over his labour
> force, and at least until recent times has not had any reward from market
> power which it was worth the while of a union to seek.[174]

This approach presented a highly idealized picture of the real state of
affairs even with regard to American trade unionism, considering its
violent history, not to mention its general applicability (for instance to
circumstances in which powerful US transnational corporations exploited
and repressed with everything at their disposal the Third World labour
force, unionized or not, instead of 'rewarding' it in accordance with their
own – often monopolistic – market power). The truth value of Galbraith's
assertions boiled down to the unilluminating truism that the rich and
powerful corporations have greater resources from which to 'reward' their
unionized labour than the weaker ones.

The facts remained, though, that such rewards (perhaps even more
substantial ones) were obtainable also by a non-unionized labour force
from highly profitable 'strong corporations' which possessed great market
power, like IBM, for instance. Besides, the difficulties of organization in
actual history are at times not only 'considerable' but downright prohibi-

tive; and not just when trade union organizers and militants are ruthlessly machine-gunned down by the paramilitary forces of 'strong corporations' (as they happened to be even in the United States at a certain time of its far from turbulent trade union history). It is, therefore, simply not good enough to declare that 'greater difficulties in organization have been overcome', without giving even one single example. Professor Galbraith, however, could always skate over such difficulties – both of the IBM non-unionization type (which he thought to have successfully covered in his reflections on the concept of 'countervailing power' by saying that his model represented 'the *general* though *not invariable* rule') and the aprioristic 'overcoming' of organizational difficulties, the proof of which never materialized in his book – with the agility of an ice-circus acrobat, witty pirouettes and all.

However, the fundamental weakness of Galbraith's concept of 'countervailing power' was twofold.

First, that the author (no doubt a man with genuine liberal social concerns and a theory fully consistent with them) took it seriously at all, believing that the power position of 'strongly unionized labour' – a notion which in Galbraith's definition necessarily implied as its material precondition the postulated permanence and undisturbed functioning of the most powerful and prosperous big corporations – could be considered truly substantive and irreversible within the contradictory/conflictual framework of the contemporary capitalist system. The *conditional/conjunctural* nature of the historically prevailing harmony of the two 'countervailing forces' in postwar American society (in which labour unionism, as far as its real achievements were concerned, was no more actually 'countervailing' than its narrow wage-bargaining orientation permitted it, and even in that strictly limited sense it was *partial* anyway, leaving out in the cold a very substantial part of the American labour force in Galbraith's own terms of analysis) was misdiagnosed by him as a permanent *structural* solution of the 'ancient' conflicts. As he wrote in 1954: 'An angry god may have endowed capitalism with *inherent contradictions*. But at least as an *afterthought* he was kind enough to make *social reform* surprisingly consistent with improved operations of the system.'[175] This may have been the case as things stood at the time of writing. Nevertheless, the real question was even then, how long can the effects of an 'afterthought' last in a *structurally defective* system. All the more since the system in question was itself only a small *part* – no matter how powerful in relative terms for the time being – of a structurally defective *global system* unable to rely in its entirety on the most unevenly distributed benefits of the angry god's afterthought.

The second fundamental weakness of the theory of 'countervailing power' was closely linked to the first, in that it wanted to turn the afterthought itself into the original structural design, so as to make the functioning of the established system stable and unassailable from now on ever after. This explained the oscillation (or ambiguity) in Galbraith's presentation of 'countervailing power' as both an objective socioeconomic and political development, one spontaneously arising out of the soil of 'modern' capitalist society, and the ideal regulatory device through which the 'modern government' of the enlightened liberal/capitalist state can remove the conflicts and contradictions of the socioeconomic system, replacing its potentially destructive mechanisms by a safe method of orderly expansion and universally desirable development.

In fact, it was the latter proposition that represented the real meaning of Galbraith's theorization. This is why the historical evidence had to be so scanty and painfully selective, with so many unfilled gaps, in strict subordination to the aprioristic conceptual requirements of the theory.

In Galbraith's case the whole theory of 'countervailing power' was built on the wishful assumption – spelled out at full length later, in *The Affluent Society* – that the real threat to the capitalist system came now from inflation and boom to which suitable regulatory devices could and should be counterposed. As he put it:

> I have argued that capitalism ... is an arrangement for getting a considerable decentralization in economic decision.... It is *inflation*, not *deflation* or *depression*, that will cause capitalism to be modified by extensive centralized decision.[176]

This is where, in Galbraith's view, 'countervailing power' was crucial in that it both preserved the original character of the system and brought it to terms with the necessary demands for regulation. For:

> The role of countervailing power in the economy marks out two broad problems in policy for the government. In all but conditions of inflationary demand, countervailing power performs a valuable – indeed an indispensable – *regulatory function in the modern economy*. Accordingly it is incumbent upon government to give it *freedom to develop* and to determine how it may best do so. The government also faces the question of where and how it will *affirmatively support the development of countervailing power*.[177]

The same consideration was directed at those concerned, i.e. at the representatives of 'spontaneous' countervailing power. For 'support to countervailing power is not endowed, *ad hoc*, by government. It *must be sought*.'[178] As a result of such consciously pursued strategies, an almost ideal situation could be created, according to Galbraith, which not even the conservatives should fear, since:

> A large part of the state's new activity – the farm legislation, labour legislation, minimum-wage legislation – is associated with the development of countervailing power. As such it is neither adventitious nor abnormal; the government action supports or supplements a normal economic process. Steps to strengthen countervailing power are not, in principle, different from steps to strengthen *competition*. Given the existence of private market power in the economy, the growth of countervailing power strengthens the capacity of the

economy for *autonomous self-regulation* and thereby *lessens* the amount of overall *government control or planning* that is required or sought.... It is some comfort that those who have worked most cohesively to develop countervailing power – the unions and the major farm organizations in particular – have so far comported themselves with some *restraint*.... It is only in light of history that our fear of the countervailing power of weaker groups dissolves, that their effort to establish their power in the market emerges as the stuff of which *economic progress* consists.[179]

Thus, Galbraith assumed that the Keynesian scenario[180] of economic development and progress was the unchallengeable model for the future. Not just for the immediate future, but the future in general. Anyway, he thought, managing the problems of American capitalism in this spirit was to the benefit of all, and there was no real alternative to it. Both 'self-restraining labour' and 'sensible conservatives' should be satisfied with the assurance that 'economic progress' would be the natural consequence of adopting the required policies, together with the caveat of *restraint*. As to the Liberals themselves, their reward would consist in running from enlightened government offices such an eminently rational and universally beneficial system.

Naturally, once the capitalist system was declared to be the absolute horizon of rationally viable economic activity, the only problems that could be acknowledged still to await solution were those that could be depicted as readily amenable to some *technical/technological* solution; technical in the domain of political/economic decision making, and technological in the field of production itself. Socialist alternatives to the capitalist system were aprioristically rejected by Galbraith in the name of another technical/managerial criterion: *administrative complexity*. Accordingly, the postwar history of '*nationalization*' in Britain by the Labour Party was fictionalized by him under the same heading, arbitrarily declaring that:

> After the Labour victory in 1945, it soon became evident that the rate at which industries would be taken into public ownership would be determined primarily by *administrative considerations*. A growing appreciation of the *scale and complexity of the administrative apparatus* required not only slowed the pace of nationalization but also, it would appear, tempered the enthusiasm of British socialists for the policy itself.[181]

The fact that the necessary restructuring and administration of nearly 800 privately owned coal mines in Britain represented the highest challenge in both 'scale and complexity', could not temper Professor Galbraith's enthusiasm for his naive belief in 'administrative complexity' as the ultimate saviour of capitalism. Instead, he managed to slip through the difficulty with astonishing speed and dexterity, by performing the acrobatic skating act again, mentioning just in passing – without the relevant figures which would have made people gasp at the sheer size of the problem that has been administratively overcome – that coal was 'an exception'.[182] This was again a case of the famous '*general* rule' that should not be considered '*invariable*'. In other words, when it suited the ideological preconception, the alleged fact of 'technical/administrative complexity' counted as irrefutable proof that there could be no alternative to the capitalist system; but when the actual historical example went against such eternalization of the established mode of production and distribution, suddenly it became an 'exception' which, without any further ado, simply confirmed the 'general rule'. In truth, though, if the 'exception' could be mastered in such an immense, run-down, and complex industry as coal-mining was in postwar Britain, why should it be a priori impossible to make such 'exceptions' succeed in other cases as well, or even as an 'invariable' general rule? Obviously, this question could not be raised within the ideological confines of Galbraith's theory.

The truth about British postwar nationalizations was, of course, much more prosaic than the heroic confrontation between 'administrative complexity' and its opposite might suggest. It concerned in fact the unavoidable and extremely painful issue of *bankruptcy* in key sectors of the economy. The latter simply *had* to be kept afloat, at an enormous cost to the taxpayer, in part as public utilities and, more importantly, as support bases to private capital (which could hardly be expected to survive without an energy industry, for instance). Indeed, it was precisely this prosaic consideration that motivated the 'enthusiasm' of even the Conservative Prime Minister, Edward Heath, for Labour's 'policy of nationalization', as he clearly demonstrated it when he nationalized one of the once most prestigious pillars of British capitalism, the bankrupt Rolls Royce company. By the same token, once the massive state subsidies (counted in tens of billions) turned the nationalized industries and companies into *profitable* entities (thanks to the give-away billions of 'taxpayers' money'), they have been duly 'denationalized' (or 'privatized') again, administrative complexity or not. As to Galbraith's counter-example, the consumer industry of automobiles,[183] unhappily it refuted his theory twice over. The first time, when the British government was *forced* to nationalize it in its hopelessly bankrupt state, notwithstanding its alleged 'administrative complexity'. And the second time, when despite all effort (and expenditure) to make it suitable again for profitable private capitalist 'administrative management', it continued to refuse to 'turn around' and respond positively to the government's crusading zeal of 'privatization'.

Thus, the real issue had precious little to do with administrative complexity as such. However, the need for ideological rationalization – in the name of technical competence and a priori administrative superiority – was overpowering. Accordingly, Galbraith had to conclude his argument in favour of what he termed 'the *modern case for capitalism*' by saying that whatever the problems it might encounter, capitalism 'survives because there isn't *anything administratively workable* to take its place.'[184]

The only difficulty that was acknowledged to remain was that the Keynesian techniques could not be applied to everything with equal success. But even in this respect, the necessary correctives could be envisaged, according to Galbraith, in much the same spirit. They could be articulated, in his view, in straightforward technical terms, like the application of 'a strong tax policy',[185] for instance. The meaning of such 'technicalities' (which were meant to be Keynesian correctives to Keynes, particularly with regard to the difficulties involved in the management of inflation and boom) was spelled out by Galbraith like this:

A strong tax policy works by reducing the pressure of production on capacity. But in different terms, this means that some plant and some labour *must be unemployed*. This does not happen in competitive industries, like agriculture, where a new equilibrium of supply and demand with full use of resources will promptly be found at a lower price. It is an absolute and inescapable requirement for *stability* in industries characterized by a generally developed *countervailing power*. Some *slack* in the economy is what keeps countervailing power from being converted into a *coalition against the public.* . . . unemployment and idle capacity necessary for stability is not probably of great consequence. Such unemployment is *not chronic*. It need not be great in amount, as we have now discovered. Those whom it affects, apart from the fact that they are now *protected* by social security and public welfare assistance, can normally expect *re-employment* in their regular occupation within a reasonably *short time*. They can as individuals, with reasonable *luck* and diligence, find re-employment in another occupation *at any time*.[186]

To turn in this way the human misery of unemployment into one of the technicalities of 'boom-management' was characteristic of the dominant ideological climate. The concept of countervailing power was an essential part of this ideology, for it postulated the permanent *integration* of labour – as 'self-restraining' labour – into the '*modern*' productive system. As Professor Galbraith put it, revealing the rationalizing secret of what was supposed to be an objective law of socioeconomic development: 'There is no other so satisfactory explanation of the great dynamic of labour organization in the *modern capitalist community* and none which so *sensibly integrates the union* into the theory of that society.'[187]

The real concern was, of course, the integration of the labour unions not merely into the 'theory' of capitalist society but into 'modern' capitalism as such. Inasmuch as it was feasible at all, the regulatory machinery required for its realization could be elevated to the noble status of a new 'natural law'[188] of social life, the law of 'countervailing power'. However, in crucial areas where the new-found 'objective law' refused to work, a new 'technical corrective' could be brought into play which, despite its splendid '*modern*' economic/scientific costume of '*slack*', suspiciously resembled the 'ancient' device of successfully depressing wages with the help of the 'industrial reserve army'. By the time Galbraith published *The Affluent Society*, in 1958, the advocated corrective has been turned into a major pillar of the whole theory. It was presented, with optimistic overtones, as follows:

> If the marginal urgency of goods is low, then so is the urgency of employ-
> ing the last man or the *last million men* in the labour force. By allowing
> ourselves some *slack*, in turn, we reduce the standards of economic perform-
> ance to a level more nearly consonant with the *controls* available for its
> management.... If our need for production is of such a low order of urgency
> that we can afford some *unemployment in the interest of stability* – a
> proposition, incidentally, of impeccably conservative antecedents – then we
> can afford to give those who are *unemployed* the goods that enable them to
> sustain their *accustomed standard of living*. If we don't need what the unem-
> ployed do not make, we can obviously afford them what they customarily *eat
> and wear*.[189]

At the same time, Galbraith's optimism was extended to the field of Extra
Sensory Perception as well, announcing the emergence of a '*New Class*',[190]
whose function was not only to counter Veblen's misgivings about the
'*leisure class*' but also to overcome in actuality the distinction between
manual and mental labour;[191] and all this while remaining firmly anchored
to the inner determinations and contradictions of the capitalist socioeconomic order. Technology, it seemed, could perform miracles on a
vast scale.

Galbraith's concept of the 'New Class' in *The Affluent Society* was already
a firm pointer to *The New Industrial State* and its equally miraculous
'technostructure'. The latter was not a *deus ex machina*; rather, it was a
machina without *deus*. It had no need for any, since it was said to be all-
powerful and eternal, here to stay with us to the end of time, wherever we
might look on earth. As Galbraith argued:

> The decisive power in *modern industrial society* is exercised not by capital but
> by organization, not by the capitalist but by the industrial bureaucrat. This
> is true in the Western industrial systems. It is true also of the socialist
> societies.... For organization – bureaucracy – is *inescapable in advanced
> industrial technology*.[192]

Thus, we have reached the end of the road where one could still talk about
'capitalism' in particular – like 'American Capitalism' – or in general. Such
terms have now been superseded with absolute finality by 'the modern
industrial society', 'the Western industrial system', 'the new industrial
state', etc. Inevitably (and ironically), however, with such a change the
object identified in Galbraith's subtitle to *American Capitalism – The
Concept of Countervailing Power* – also suffered an irreversible defeat.
After all that praise which the author heaped up on it in the past, the great
new law of 'countervailing power' turned out to be no law at all. In fact it
disappeared completely from *The New Industrial State*, and the author did
not feel the need to offer us any explanation why his curious earlier
attachment to it vanished without a trace. Instead, he presented us with

a new ideological rationalization of our new 'permanent' condition of existence, arguing that the loss of union membership was not the temporary result of a potentially reversible historical conjuncture but the manifestation of a *'permanent decline'*.[193]

As to the explanation of the alleged changes, Galbraith offered essentially technical/technological factors, like 'the shift in power from ownership and the entrepreneur to the technostructure [due to growth in scale and administrative complexity], technological advance, the regulation of markets and aggregate demand, and the imperative of price and wage regulation'.[194] Likewise, *'modern technology* opens the way for a massive shift from workers who are within the reach of unions to those who are not.'[195] All in all:

> The *industrial system*, it seems clear, is unfavourable to the union. Power passes to the *technostructure* and this lessens the *conflict* of interest between *employer* and *employee* which gave the union much of its reason for existence. Capital and technology allow the firm to substitute *white-collar workers and machines* that *cannot be organized* for blue-collar workers that can. The regulation of aggregate demand, the resulting high level of employment together with the general increase in well-being, all, on balance, make the union less necessary or less powerful or both. The conclusion seems *inevitable*. The union belongs to a *particular stage* in the development of the industrial system.[196]

The only point on which Galbraith's theoretical position remained rock-solid throughout his ideologically motivated and accommodating metamorphoses, concerned the assessment of *unemployment*. In this respect he remained consistent from *American Capitalism* all the way down to the revised edition of *The New Industrial State* (published as late as 1971, when the dark clouds of *structural and chronic unemployment*, despite his categorical assurances to the contrary, were already all too clearly in evidence on the horizon), insisting that in the 'modern industrial system' unemployment could only be 'marginal' and 'insular', as we have seen in Section 2.2.1. He had to remain faithful to his totally uncritical position because admitting the possibility of *depression* – when he repeatedly declared that the problem was, on the contrary, boom-management – would have made his whole theoretical edifice crumble.

Thus, in the end, his message to labour in *The New Industrial State* sharply contrasted with his fairly sympathetic treatment in *American Capitalism: The Concept of Countervailing Power*. Although he did not use the term, he made it amply clear in *The New Industrial State* that there was no longer any need for 'countervailing power'. For the 'ancient' conflict between capital and labour disappeared through the (rather mysterious) shift in power from capital and the capitalist to the East/West-embracing universal *'industrial bureaucrat'* – who was himself, poor devil, an *'employee'*, after all, and therefore, strictly speaking, one could and should not really talk any longer of a 'conflict of interest between *employer* and *employee*' either – leaving us with the task of drawing whatever conclusion we could (or wished to deduce) from the alleged fact that the 'interests that were once radically *opposed* are now much more nearly in *harmony*.'[197]

Galbraith's own conclusion announced as an irrefutable fact – instead of allowing at least a small question mark to hover over it, as far as the future was concerned, given the highly contentious character of the issue of *'integration'* – that 'the industrial system has now largely *encompassed* the labour movement',[198] identifying in the most cavalier fashion the bureaucratized right-wing labour unions with the labour movement as such.

But, of course, Galbraith could not end the chapter on such a serious note. He could not resist the temptation to sound witty, adding with customary frivolity and bad taste the last sentence, 'Such then is the present stage in the journey on from the Tolpuddle Martyrs'.[199] Not really, Professor Galbraith, not really.

2.4 THE CURE OF 'UNDERDEVELOPMENT' BY 'MODERNIZATION'

2.4.1

In the real world of global capitalism the relationship between wealth and poverty was the exact opposite to its conceptualization by Galbraith and others. What was, in fact, an 'island' was not the world of *poverty* but that of 'the affluent society'. Generalizing, however, from the *special case* of American capitalism turned everything upside down, transforming the hopelessly *general* into the manageably *'special'*, and thereby the *overwhelming majority* of humankind into a wishfully receding *'minority'*.

Naturally, the strategy adopted for dealing with the burning issues of the deprived majority was to place before it the mirage of an eventual approximation to the ideal model of American 'high mass-consumption'. Accordingly, the task of overcoming 'underdevelopment' in the 'Third World' was defined as plain *'modernization'* and convergence with the values of 'the democratic North': 'until the age of high mass-consumption becomes universal'.[200] At the same time, the socialist alternative was described, with 'scientific objectivity', as 'a kind of *disease* which can befall a transitional society if it fails to organize effectively those elements within it which are prepared to get on with the job of modernization.'[201]

'Scientific piecemeal social engineering' was opposed to dangerously tempting (Marxian) 'holism', and the beneficial arsenal of modernizing science was extended from 'scientific management' *tout court* to 'scientific demand management' as well. And more was still to come, in the shape of a whole series of 'revolutions'. It all started way back in the 1930s with the 'managerial revolution', to be followed by the 'Keynesian', 'technological', 'scientific', 'second industrial' – and according to some ideologists and politicians even the 'third industrial' – 'information', etc. revolutions. In fact, we have seen in this period postulated as already well in the process of unfolding the 'revolution' of almost anything under the sun. The 'only' thing studiously excluded from the legitimate range of revolutions was, of course, the revolutionary transformation of the prevailing social relations of production and distribution.

It must be added, though, for the sake of completeness, that the 'under-developed South' was not entirely left out of this crowded agenda of revolutions. It was, in fact, offered the great scientific promise of the 'Green Revolution', the true meaning of which has been clearly demonstrated by the massive poisonous gas leak – due primarily to substandard safety measures – at Union Carbide's antiquated and neglected Bhopal plant in India in 1984, killing 3,000 people, seriously injuring 50,000, and injuring with by no means negligible consequences another 250,000.[202]

Those who paint the fantasy-picture of 'the post-industrial society' fail to realize (or to mention) that the cynical policy of transferring the 'smoke-stack industries' to the 'Third World' does not make the global system of capitalist production any less industrial. Thus, the allegedly objective and scientific discourse on 'post-industrial society' demonstrates also in this respect its function of blatant ideological rationalization of the established exploitative relationships. For such 'technology transfers' only remove the most obnoxious productive practices, together with their highly pollutant consequences, from the 'advanced capitalist countries' and deposit them, often under the pretext of 'development aid', on the doorstep of the dependent countries.

An outstanding Filipino scholar, Renato Constantino, provided us in one of his recent books with a striking example of the practices involved. He wrote:

> In a country where foreign giant enterprises have been able to gain enough economic control and to influence the policies of the host government with the aid of global financial and banking institutions, the industrialization which takes place is one which is controlled by and serves the interests of inter-national capital. This type of development denies that country any possibility of establishing its own industrial complex for its own interests. Its economy becomes a mere appendage of the global giants, the whole country a sweat-shop with an unlimited supply of cheap labour. A case in point is the sintering plant acquired through the peculiar kindness of Japan's Kawasaki Steel Cor-poration. Residents of Chiba Prefecture in Japan, where Kawasaki has its steel mill, filed a lawsuit against the corporation demanding that it suspend construction of its new sintering plant. Pollution has been the plague of Chiba. The sea has a coffee colour and the air is a dirty violet smog. Residents have permanent sore throats and coughs. A company official of Kawasaki informed the court in September 1975 that the sintering plant would be transferred from Chiba to Mindanao. This is what he said:

Although a sintering plant is an indispensable part of a steel plant, it also produces more air-polluting materials than any other part of the plant. Therefore, we at Kawatetsu, Kawasaki Steel, have decided to build the new sintering plant which is needed for the 6th blast furnace in a foreign country, even though this involves overcoming difficulties connected with the loading, unloading and transportation to prevent pulverization of the sintered ore. The new sinter plant is now under construction in Mindanao, Philippines, as part of Japan's economic aid to that country.

The effects of Japan's 'economic aid' to the Philippines are already being felt. Some Filipino workers at the sintering plant are suffering from asthma. Dead fish have been found in the canal near the plant and fishermen in the area report that the volume of their catch has decreased considerably. Two thousand people comprising 110 households were evicted to make way for the construction of the plant; out of this number, Kawasaki employed only 75 persons. Economic projects designed to provide additional jobs have failed.... The sintering plant has been hailed as the initial step toward a local steel industry. Actually, the ore that is sintered is not for Philippine use but is exported to the main company in Chiba, Japan. Moreover, the ore comes from Australia and Brazil.[203]

Thus, the gap between reality and its ideological rationalization could not be greater. The establishment and operation of Kawasaki's Mindanao sintering plant – one among many similar enterprises – revealed the real meaning of the loudly announced 'revolutionary transformation' of the underdeveloped world by 'development aid' as practised by the decision makers of the 'advanced post-industrial societies'.

2.4.2

It goes without saying that to query the viability of the much advertised 'revolutions', on the basis of painfully conclusive evidence to the contrary from the 'Third World' itself – which showed that it was quite impossible to implement the scientific fruits of the *green* revolution without the necessary social groundwork of the *red* revolution – would have been greeted as an outrageously 'ideological attitude'. At the same time, the technocratic advocacy of the various miracle-remedies to the socially induced privations in the 'developing South' acquired the status of self-evident wisdom and was advocated as the paradigm of objectivity.

The reality was, of course, quite different. For, due to the power of the dominant material interests in the world of legal and political decision making, the *social foundation* of chronic inequalities had to remain untouched. As a consequence, even the potentially beneficial impact of the technological factors themselves had to be nullified by the determinations of the ruling social order. As has been rightly argued about the failure of agricultural modernization in India, after 40 years of independence from direct colonial rule, and after several decades of 'Green Revolution':

Some 300 million, out of a total *rural* population of 560 million (in 1985), *are net buyers of food grain*. These are the poorest of the poor, comprising landless labourers and marginal and small peasants, below the so-called 'absolute poverty line', which is defined by the World Bank as 'that income level below which a minimal nutritionally adequate diet plus essential non-food requirements is not affordable'. The purchasing power of those below this 'absolute poverty income level' (at present estimated to be about 1,400 rupees per capita per year in the rural areas, less than a tenth of a middle-class income) has *seriously declined over the last few decades*. The reason is that the price of coarse grains on which the poorest spend the bulk of their income has steadily increased (recall that there are no 'fair price' shops in the villages!). The *theoretical* net availability per capita per day of cereals remained the same, about 415 grams during the second period (1966–84), while that of legumes (the only regular protein source for the vast majority) has actually declined by a factor of one third from 60 grams in 1965 to 40 grams in 1985! . . .

Irrigation, fertilizers, pesticides, farm mechanization, and good storage facilities for grain are the essential technological ingredients in the high-yielding-variety (HYV) strategy of the Green Revolution. The essential economic ingredients are credit facilities and good support prices for the farmers. The unequal availability of these technological and economic ingredients has produced a *sharp worsening of existing disparities* between states and between different classes of farmers within the states. Irrigation-rich states where middle-level farmers constitute the bulk of the cultivators, like the Punjab, Haryana, and Uttar Pradesh, showed annual rates of growth in cereal production of 4.3 to 7.2 per cent, against an all-India average of 2.8 per cent during the period under consideration (1967–1985). Most of the Green Revolution has happened in these three states. Irrigation-poor states with small and marginal peasants and landless labourers making up the rural majority, like Bihar, Orissa, and Madhya Pradesh, have recorded very poor cereals growth rates of between 1 and 1.7 per cent. Broadly speaking, not more than half a dozen of India's 22 states (excluding the nine union territories) have benefited so far from the HYV strategy, and within them the benefits have gone in the main to *middle and large farmers*.[204]

In the end all this could hardly be considered surprising. For only the middle and large farmers had benefited from the timid social reforms introduced in the countryside by the 'colour-blind' post-colonial governments which tried to substitute for the unavoidable social revolution the elusive, technologically inspired and confined, 'Green Revolution':

> For the rest, however, *the so-called land reform was a total sham*. Of the massive amount of legislation on paper, the one thing of any significance to be implemented was the expropriation of absentee landlords, whose lands became the property of their former middle and large tenant farmers. Landless labourers and marginal and small peasants got virtually nothing out of it. Over the last four decades *less than 0.6 per cent* of the total cultivated area has actually been distributed among the landless.[205]

2.4.3
The incorporation of the former colonial empires in the ideological perspectives of 'development' towards the 'universality of high mass-consumption' corresponded, of course, to the distinctly new form of global integration and domination[206] under the radically changed postwar relation

of forces among the major capitalist countries. The emergence of the
United States from the war as the unrivalled hegemonic power in the West
enabled the US to embark on the realization of its long-standing aspiration to institute a more dynamic socioeconomic order 'by international
economic readjustment.'[207]

In practical terms this meant the opening up of the British and French
Empires to 'normal trade', and the replacement of the rather anachronistic
pre-war system of direct political/military domination in the colonies by
the incomparably more sophisticated and efficient exploitative practices of
neo-colonialism.

Naturally, the relative *political* emancipation of the 'Third World' did
not bring *economic* self-determination, since the new system of 'normal
trade' was operated within the framework of structural dependency and
'unequal exchange'.[208] Such trifle circumstance, however, could not matter
less at a time when the dominant ideology anticipated with great self-
assurance the supersession of 'underdevelopment' by the Taylorian method
of 'increasing the size of the surplus until this surplus becomes so large
that it is unnecessary to quarrel over how it shall be divided'.

This was, of course, nothing but self-serving ideological rationalization
and legitimation of the unjustifiable. Nevertheless, in its turn it helped to
generate and diffuse in broad intellectual circles (even on the Left in the
advanced capitalist countries) the illusion that 'the conquest of scarcity is
now not only foreseeable but actually foreseen', with all the disorienting
and disarming consequences of such a view.

Thus, for a long time everything seemed to fit perfectly well into the
postwar conception of 'anti-ideological' ideology as sustained by the universally welcomed economic expansion. The promised 'multiplication of
the surplus' was the main theme of ideological persuasion in the West. The
alleged 'convergence of the rival industrial systems' was supposed to solve
the problems of East-West relations; and the irresistible 'modernization'
of the 'Third World' was expected to deliver us from all evil in the still
somewhat unruly, nationalistically agitated 'Southern region'.

The internal collapse of the long expansionary dynamic and the eruption
of crises in the 1970s put an end to the ideological preponderance of this
approach. Under the circumstances of growing conflicts on *all planes* of
social life, less self-complacent and more flexible ideological conceptions
had to be found to explain the disturbing socioeconomic phenomena which
were not so long before declared to belong 'irretrievably to the past' and to
the outmoded discourse of 'irretrievably fallen ideology'.

This was indeed a 'U-turn' of such magnitude that the traditional forms
of ideological readjustment and the concomitant salvage of the ruling
personnel mentioned in Chapter 1 could not successfully bring it about
even up to the present day. In sharp contrast to the Golden Age of 'the
end of ideology', the 'tentative', rather eclectic, and at times thoroughly

insecure character of the ideologies that became dominant in the last decade indicates – notwithstanding the state-imposed monetarist dogmatism of the 'Radical Right' – an ideological vacuum which will be very difficult to fill in the foreseeable future.

3 · POLITICS AND IDEOLOGY

It is rather doubtful whether we shall ever see a return of the lost Golden Age of openly self-complacent supra-ideological ideology. For the latter was brought into life and nourished not only by the apparently crisis-free material foundations of postwar economic expansion but also by the corresponding insitutional framework of *'consensus politics'*.

Harold Wilson, the Labour Prime Minister of England for almost a decade, used to boast that the Labour Party was the 'natural party of government'. And he had a point. For capital could hardly find a more convenient arrangement than the one whereby the mass party of industrial labour was *in government* while capital itself remained, more entrenched than ever, *in power*.

3.1 MANAGERIAL IDEOLOGY AND THE STATE

3.1.1
Naturally, the idea of ruling society by some sort of 'consensus', rather than by ruthlessly enforcing the established power relations in order to subdue class-opposition, was nothing new. After all, even the far from liberal 'Iron Chancellor' of Germany, Bismarck himself, tried to apply the more subtle strategy of 'carrot and stick', instead of relying on the straight-forward police methods of state-repression alone, as some of the German 'National-Liberal' theoreticians advocated at the time. As a matter of fact, he would have liked to entice back to Germany from England Marx, the 'Red Doctor', in order to put him in charge of managing – and maybe even of 'scientifically managing' – the German working class, in preference to openly suppressing the latter by means of the 'Anti-Socialist Law' whose failure in the end was responsible for Bismarck's own downfall.

Here, again, a passage from F.W. Taylor's famous managerial utopia is instructive as regards the deep-seatedness of capitalistic consensual aspirations. The problem Taylor had to face concerned the socially pro-duced surplus and the conflicts generated by its blatantly unjust division. And this is how he saw the solution:

> Scientific management will mean, for the employers and the workmen who adopt it – and particularly for those who adopt it *first* – the elimination

of almost all causes for dispute and disagreement between them. What con-stitutes a *fair day's work* will be a question for *scientific investigation*, instead of a subject to be bargained and haggled over. *Soldiering will cease because the object for soldiering will no longer exist.*[209]

The disturbing problem of confrontation over the capitalist appropriation of surplus value haunted classical political economy virtually from the beginning, and its last great figure, Ricardo, made no attempt at hiding the irreconcilable contradictions involved. In sharp contrast, however, later developments – from 'neo-classical' economics to various theories of 'managerial revolution' and developmental 'modernization' – had as their chief concern how to conjure away the problem itself, since none of the advocated remedies seemed to work in reality, no matter how powerful the agencies that backed their application.

Situated well within the same line of approach, Taylor discovered a veritable 'philosophers' stone' by wanting to do away with 'soldiering' as such through the radical elimination of what he described as the 'object for soldiering'. In truth, however, his solution was based on a *mystifying conceptual shift* with regard to the contested object itself. For the real object for 'soldiering' and confrontation was (and untranscendably remains for as long as capital survives as the main regulator of the fundamental social metabolism): *who*, and on the basis of what criteria, *controls* the production and allocation of the *total social wealth*, and not the relative *size* of the *particular entrepreneurial product* whose claimed managerial provenance and imaginarily inflated magnitude *a priori* justifies its unques-tionable allocation *by capital* in its own favour? Without this mystifying, double conceptual shift – from the 'who?' to the 'how large?', and from the 'total social' to the ideologically question-begging 'particular entre-preneurial' – the plausibility of Taylor's 'scientific' solution would be absolute zero.

3.1.2

It is highly significant in this respect that the postwar development of the consensus-oriented capitalist state introduces a *practical corrective* to this fallacious conceptualization by directly intervening – in its professed capacity as both the collective sovereign and the humbly dedicated repre-sentative of the particular individuals – in the allocation of the overall social product. In other words, it claims to transcend the contradiction inherent in the *real* object for 'soldiering' – the stubbornly contested 'who?' – by ascribing the crucial role of arbitration not only in political but also in economic matters to itself, hence ruling the issue as such *'out of court'*. At the same time, in the framework of the 'Welfare State' and analogous (albeit with regard to their scope more limited) state practices, it takes upon itself the task of overruling *particular* capitalist interests which oppose such – for capital's overall reproduction necessary – practices, thereby apparently resolving the contradiction between the general/social and the vested/sectional interests.

To be sure, all these 'correctives' do not change in the slightest the established structure of society; nor do they minimally alter the hierarchical subordination of Taylor's 'workmen' to capital in the prevailing social division of labour. For in the postwar development of state practices we are presented, again, with a characteristically mystifying shift. Only on this occasion the shift is not from the 'who?' to the 'how large?', nor from the 'total social' to the 'particular entrepreneurial'. It is – much more sweepingly and confusingly – from the internally divided *socioeconomic* arena of class relations (often referred to as 'civil society') to the *pseudo-universality* of the *political sphere* itself. Through this shift, the structural contradictions of the *material base* are claimed to be 'resolved' within the framework of the legal and political *superstructure*, on the terrain of more or less powerfully manipulative state interventions.[210]

3.1.3

Of course, the very attempt to do away with the contradictions of the *material base* by means of *superstructural manipulation* is self-contradictory. Nevertheless, while it is obviously illusory to expect the supersession of society's basic material antagonisms through such measures, even though the eruption of the most acute contradictions may be successfully *postponed* for quite some time, it would be rather foolish to minimize the practical effectiveness of consensus-generating state-manipulation precisely in relation to ideological belief.

In this respect, the postwar configuration of politics and ideology represents a qualitatively more advanced solution from the point of view of capital than Taylor's managerial utopia and its more or less direct derivatives. For the state's effective intervention in the management of 'dysfunctions' and potentially devastating conflicts is an undeniable practical dimension of contemporary social reality which speaks loudly enough for itself. Within its framework, the politically/institutionally underpinned ideologies of consensus carry much greater weight and power of persuasion than even the most eloquent direct appeal – in the name of science or whatever else – to particular individuals and limited social groups 'to revolutionize their mental attitude' in the interest of 'friendly cooperation'. An appeal which, on its own, is bound to remain confined to the level of mere wishful thinking.

The same ideas, however, should sound incomparably more persuasive and serve much better their inherent ideological purpose if reformulated, with the appropriate correctives mentioned above, against the background of really existing, state-sponsored vehicles of potential practical implementation. Without this historically specific practical embeddedness in the institutional reality of the neo-capitalist state-formation, the 'scientific management' of capitalist competition could aspire, at best, only at producing some *local*[211] benefits. Through its insertion, however, into the emerging institutional forms, in accordance with the ideological needs of the new political trends, it gained a more general significance by complementing the political dimension of social transformations on the terrain of 'civil society'.

In fact, the two not only *complemented* one another but provided a *reciprocal authentication* too for the great social merits of each. The postwar state authenticated the world of managerial utopia by adopting the latter's 'consensual' aspirations as the model of its own political-economic interventions, conferring upon the adopted – in their substance highly partisan – aspirations the blessing of its pseudo-universality. At the same time, the adoption of the ideal aims of 'scientific management' (for overcoming 'soldiering' by eliminating the 'object for soldiering' itself, which remained elusive on the plane of managerial efforts alone) authenticated the neo-capitalist/interventionist state as the one and only practically feasible realization of society's universal objectives and values. Besides, the combined effect of this reciprocal authentication was meant to be the radical transformation of conflict-torn 'crisis capitalism' into conflict-less 'organized capitalism', hence the resolution not only of the antagonism *within* 'civil society' itself but also of the traditional contradiction *between* 'civil society' and the political state. Thus, it was by no means accidental that the old dreams of 'scientific management thinkers' met with the wholehearted intellectual approval as well as practical adhesion of such a broad ideological constituency as the one we have been witnessing in the postwar period of political consensus.

3.2 THE IDEOLOGICAL ROOTS OF POSTWAR 'ANTI-IDEOLOGY'

3.2.1

As regards the broader historical context of these developments, there was a curious 'criss-crossing' that extended across ideological, political and geographic frontiers, from Anglo-Saxon and French democracy to early twentieth-century Germany, and from the latter to American sociology and politics, only to be returned, with 'compound interest', to postwar Europe.

While there were some early ideological conceptions in the United States as well as in England which anticipated by half a century or more some major propositions of the postwar belief in the 'end of ideology', the systematic theoretical formulation of such line of reasoning could only be credited to Max Weber who remains by far the most influential of 'post- Marxian' ideologues. I have discussed elsewhere[212] some of Weber's seminal ideas, and the ideological impact of his methodology is considered in Section 6 of this chapter. What matters in the present context is to trace,

very briefly, the revealing trajectory of the just mentioned ideological/
political frontier-crossing.

This is how Lukács described German ideological developments at the
turn of the century and Max Weber's special place in them:

> Such influential sociological works as Hasbach's *Modern Democracy* were
> nothing more than scientifically puffed-up pamphlets attacking democracy.
> Just as earlier, the 'historical school' of German economics had glorified the
> Bismarck régime as a superior political and social form, so now German
> sociology was writing apologetics for Wilhelmine imperialism. Max Weber
> occupied a special position in this development. Admittedly, his method-
> ological foundations were very similar to those of his contemporaries; he too
> adopted the Western sociological criticism of modern democracy. But his
> attitude to it was totally reversed: despite all the criticism, he regarded
> democracy as the form most suited to the imperialist expansion of a major
> modern power. He saw the weakness of German imperialism as lying in its
> lack of internal democratic development. 'Only a *politically mature* people is a
> "master race" . . . *Only master races are called upon to intervene in the course
> of global developments.* If nations attempt it without possessing this quality,
> then not only will the *safe instinct* of the other *nations* protest, but they will
> also come to grief in the attempt internally . . . The will to powerlessness in
> home affairs that the writers preach is irreconcilable with the "will to power"
> abroad which has been so noisily trumpeted.'[213]
>
> Here the social derivation of Max Weber's democratism can be clearly
> grasped. He shared with the other German imperialists the view of the world-
> political (colonizing) mission of the '*master races*'. But he differed from them
> in that he not only failed to idealize German conditions under specious
> parliamentary government, but criticized them violently and passionately.
> Like the English or French, he thought, the Germans could become a 'master
> race' only in a democracy. Hence for the sake of attaining Germany's im-
> perialist aims, a democratization had to take place internally and go as far as
> was indispensable to the realization of these aims.[214]

What was perhaps the most remarkable in all this was that Max Weber,
who had an extremely conservative, Bonapartist-inclined conception of
democracy, should become in the course of twentieth-century political/
ideological developments the thinker revered all over the Atlantic world as
representing – with a theoretical rigour that must be considered exemplary
even by the most 'objective' of all social scientists – the ultimate values of
'liberal democracy' and of the 'free world'.

3.2.2

The secret of Weber's growing Atlantic influence was the favourable
conjunction between the characteristics of his own orientation and the
ideological needs of the changing international sociopolitical order. This is
why his authoritarian political inclinations could be so easily overlooked by
his Western followers, perhaps even secretly admired.

Lukács quoted a conversation that took place after the first world war
between Max Weber and the extreme right-wing figure, General Ludendorff, Hindenburg's Chief of Staff and one of Hitler's earliest champions.

These were Weber's words, as reported not by some hostile critic but by his widow, Marianne Weber:

> In a democracy the people elects as its leader a man it trusts. Then the man elected says, 'Now hold your tongues and obey!'. Neither the people nor the parties may contradict him. . . . Afterwards it is for the people to judge – if the leader has erred, then away to the gallows with him.

And Lukács rightly added: 'It is not surprising that Ludendorff said to this: "I like the sound of such a democracy!"'. Thus Weber's idea of democracy lapsed into a Bonapartist Caesarism.'[215]

Weber could be forgiven so many things, thanks to his impeccably anti-socialist but subtly articulated, and thus in similarly disposed liberal/democratic circles thoroughly respectable, ideological credentials. He was a 'man for all seasons', both as a result of his greatly adaptable methodology and in virtue of the key propositions of his theory, organically linked to his central methodological tenets. For he managed to formulate a critique of *bureaucracy* and *technological rationality* while simultaneously declaring them – and on their account capitalism as a socioeconomic and political order – to be fundamentally *untranscendable*.

Paradoxically, such a view suited not only the unashamed defenders of the established social system but also approaches like the Frankfurt School of 'critical theory', and similar conceptualizations of the contemporary world in France and elsewhere. For the latter, oriented exclusively towards the temporary opulence of a few 'advanced industrial societies', developed their conceptions of protest and opposition in a social vacuum, on the basis of self-defeating presuppositions (equivalent to the most pessimistic practical conclusions), like the alleged structural 'integration' of the working class into the world of 'organized capitalism'.

3.3 RAYMOND ARON'S WEBERIAN PERSPECTIVE

3.3.1

The sophisticated Weberian 'eternalization of the established social order' was bound to exercise a powerful influence at a time when that order itself seemed able to resist all conceivable assault by successfully integrating within the framework of consensus-politics the traditional forces of opposition. To the defenders of the capitalist system the Weberian categories came as manna from heaven, since in the name of 'rationalization', 'calculation', 'efficiency', 'technology' and the like, it was possible to prove a number of wishful notions as established facts. Thus, in the first place, the fundamental identity of capitalism and socialism:

> To the degree that *industrialization* leads to greater *rationalization*, business enterprises develop more and more common features. They must *calculate* expenses, receipts, profits, and taxes; the *calculations* must cover a certain

duration – since the production cycle itself requires time; all the elements of the balance-sheet must be translated into *comparable quantities* – and thus, no essential distinction can be established between the cost of manpower and that of material. Man is replaced by the machine when figures prove that this would be profitable. In this respect, not only *capitalist* society but *any society* treats man as if he were a *commodity* or as an *instrument of production*.[216]

Significantly, the question concerning the necessary basis or orienting framework of calculation is totally left out of consideration. Rather, 'calculation' as such is assumed to be the one and only conceivable 'rational' framework of orientation, which is simultaneously also its own justification. At a certain point, however, the real meaning of this 'neutral' and inescapable (absolute) 'calculation' is revealed when it is stated that 'man is replaced by the machine when *figures prove* that this would be *profitable*'.

This is, of course, both sheer nonsense and a typical ideological mystification elevated by decree to the status of self-evident wisdom. Nonsense, because – as even the most advanced capitalist countries can testify, not to mention many others – it takes a great deal more than merely having at hand some 'figures to prove' that it would be 'profitable to replace man by the machine' to actually proceed with the complicated and often contradictory process of such replacement itself. And mystification, because it arbitrarily equates *profit-orientation* with *rational calculation*.

Admittedly, by *assuming* the untranscendability of the capitalist mode of production, in the spirit of Weber, this equation sounds plausible, but only in virtue of the circular coincidence of the conclusion with the arbitrary assumption from which it is derived. The moment we submit the socially destructive *self-expansion of exchange value* and its 'profitability' to *critical scrutiny*, the whole issue of 'calculation' – as linked to a self-assuming pseudo-rationality – is blown wide open. For the answer to the question of how to orient the vitally necessary *social accountancy* of an alternative society – i.e. one opposed to the dehumanizing, irrationally profit-orientated monetary accountancy of commodity-society – cannot be deduced from the Weberian concepts of 'calculation' and 'rationalization'. Thus, the reduction and submission of social choices to the allegedly self-evident criteria and material dictates of balance-sheets in pursuit of profit – stipulated as absolutely inescapable by Aron – stands for a conception of 'rationality' which in its self-assuming circularity (and a priori exclusion of an alternative *social accountancy*) reveals an unmistakably biased ideological substance.

Moreover, one should also notice in the passage quoted above the subtle 'equation' according to which *any society* treats man as 'a *commodity or as an instrument of production*'. For while it is certainly true that in all societies men treat themselves *also* as instruments of production – and there is nothing wrong with that by itself – it is only under the rule of capital that man is treated as a *commodity*, which makes all the difference.

In other words, hammering a nail into a piece of timber quite appropriately involves treating our *arms and hands* as *instruments* of our self-controlled productive activity, but not as *commodities* which we *ourselves* inevitably become when we are compelled to work (as alien-controlled labour-power) in a capitalist factory. However, Aron's fallacious and confusing equation obliterates this fundamental difference and reduces everything to the untranscendable common denominator of the 'modern industrial society' in which such differences, by definition, cannot possibly matter.

3.3.2

The ideological partisanship of Aron's approach, adopted from Weber, appeared fairly transparent in another passage, even though it was put forward in the name of transcending ideology itself:

> Social institutions and mechanisms no longer lend themselves easily to trans-plantation, since the existing systems are becoming less and less 'pure' and *borrow from ideal-types* that, on the abstract level, are incompatible. Most important of all, the present trend of history illustrates both the power of *technology* when applied to the environment and the *resistance of human nature* and society to those whose ambition is to '*reconstruct*' *the social order.* What is more, events seem to show that the more fervently men believe in the *Promethean illusion* that they are shaping history, the more readily they submit to it; on the other hand, leaders who modestly approach problems as they occur are more likely to obtain results that correspond to their intentions. The *pragmatic* approach of the *social engineer*, not the vast ambition of the *ideologist*, is most in keeping with the spirit of *rationalism* and gives men the best opportunity, not to become 'masters and possessors of society', but to improve it while *accepting its rules*. In Europe, no one any longer denies that 'ideological syntheses' have lost their force. Observers of the European scene even tend to apply the term *depoliticization* to what is merely *indifference to traditional ideologies*.[217]

Within the categorial framework of such an approach, it was possible to blow at the same time hot and cold air from the same pipe. And more. For it was possible to maintain simultaneously that the rival socioeconomic systems of 'modern industrial society' were fundamentally the *same*, and that the private enterprise system was far *superior*. While it was often categorically stated that the crucial determinant was *technology* as such, when it suited the ideological interests championed by the 'post-ideological' ideologists, the argument could easily be shifted instead to the glorification of the profit motive, even if the case itself which was referred to clearly indicated the successful application of a more advanced form of technology. As, for instance, in arguing that 'the American telephone system, *by far the best* in the world, is operated *strictly along profit-making lines*.'[218]

Also, it was possible to maintain both that Western industrial societies succeeded in solving their material problems, and that those aspirations which implied some criticism of their achievements should not be con-

sidered other than illusory ideals or the irrational manifestations of 'anarchistic individualism'. This is how the first half of this 'non-ideological'
reasoning was presented:

> Reality has outstripped fiction. Both defenders and critics of the capitalism of
> fifty years ago would be astonished at the material results it has achieved.
> (These results are perhaps inferior to what *technological advance* has made
> possible, but no society has ever fully realized its own potential.) Even the
> theoretician of the Great Refusal[219] has little doubt that industrial societies
> are capable of gradually eliminating the *isolated patches of poverty* and
> undeserved misfortune that are still found in the midst of *opulence*.[220]

At the same time, the critical doubts were hushed aside – echoing not only
Max Weber but F.W. Taylor as well – like this:

> A *rationalized society* is a *graded* society in which the greatest number
> meekly accept their fate. If we start from the *utopian idea* that men, both
> singly and as a community, should choose their own destiny, modern society
> *appears* increasingly oppressive, authoritarian, and totalitarian as it *becomes
> more industrialized*. Within each business firm, there can be no relaxation
> of discipline, since more often than not the worker performs his duties
> *without realizing or understanding* the nature of the total entity to which he
> belongs.... *Freedom* in work will *always* be restricted by the demands
> imposed by *efficiency*, by the *inevitable authority of technical experts or
> directors*.... Whether we refer to work or to leisure pursuits, *self-determina-
> tion* is no more than an *ideal* ... we cannot arrange things so that an *industrial
> society* – that is, a *rationally administered* one – corresponds to the *impulses of
> anarchistic individualism*.[221]

Naturally, this kind of conceptualization of the problems that political
and social movements had to confront carried an extremely conservative
message, in the spirit of '*accepting the rules*' of the established order as the
one and only 'rational' way to proceed. At the same time it could reconcile
its 'anti-ideological' claims with the assumption of extreme ideological
positions. For just as Max Weber directed his 'value-neutral' fire against
socialism, which he definitionally identified with the *total bureaucratization*
of social life, so the theorists of the 'end of ideology' occasionally brought
out into the open the real political/ideological meaning of their efforts,
insisting that 'far from weakening the defenses of the West against Communism, *anti-ideology* (its degree of optimism or pessimism is immaterial)
provides it with the *best possible protection*.'[222] Since, however, settling
the accounts with the adversary by means of a global war was far too
horrendous to contemplate, the other side too had to be granted the status
of a 'rationalized and calculating' industrial society, even if only – of
necessity – an inferior one:

> The dialogue is now, essentially, between the *two versions of rationalist
> thought*, the Western and the Soviet. Now Western-type liberal democracy,
> once it ensures the development of the productive forces and the spread
> of material prosperity, possesses an *obvious superiority* (except in the eyes

of certain intellectuals) over the so-called popular democracy of the Soviet type.[223]

Given such perspective, the solution of the outstanding problems had to be expected by the ultimately unavoidable 'convergence' of the 'other rationalist system' towards its a priori superior counterpart:

> As the Revolution recedes into the past, revisionism gains ground, along with a more *middle-class mode of life*. The more men enjoy possession of a world they are in danger of losing, the less impatient they are to *change* that world.[224]

Thus, wishful thinking ruled the day, advertising itself as the self-evidently superior embodiment of pragmatic, efficiency and technology-oriented, non-utopian, modestly realistic, non-Promethean, gradualist, social-engineering, rational, and anti-ideological scientific wisdom. Its inconsistencies and self-contradictions would take far too long even to enumerate. Let it suffice to mention in conclusion that while its writings were peppered with constant polemics against the Marxian conception of history, in the name of an extreme form of scepticism – insisting that 'I do not know what the future for humanity will be, but *I do know that we do not know*'[225] – it did not hesitate to predict the subsumption of post-revolutionary developments under the superior Western-type 'industrial society' in which people adopt, and forever adapt themselves to, the 'middle-class mode of life' and wisely refuse to contemplate any significant *change*.

3.4 THE CRITICAL THEORY OF ADORNO AND HABERMAS

3.4.1
The alignment of 'critical theory' with the Weberian perspective was, on the face of it, much more surprising. Nevertheless, there were some important points of contact with it across the whole of the Frankfurt School, whatever the differences among its individual members.

To be sure, this School embraced a truly heterogeneous collection of thinkers. Its diversity ranged from Walter Benjamin's hopes for direct participation in left-wing political praxis[226] to Marcuse's 'outsider-oriented' political activism, and from Adorno's effective sociopolitical non-involvement all the way down to the extraordinary theoretical eclecticism[227] and, notwithstanding his verbal protests, technocratically-inspired political opportunism of Jürgen Habermas. There was some irony in the promotion of the intellectuals concerned to the status of a venerable cultural institution. For, to make a 'school' out of the great diversity of individuals who were eventually subsumed under the label of 'critical theory' had as much to do with the needs of the 'culture industry' and the 'manipulative mass media' – two of the most frequent targets of Adorno's scathing denunciations – as with the intellectual coherence of their ideas.

However, beyond the significant differences, the Weberian provenance of their critique of 'bureaucracy' and 'instrumental reason' – shared by virtually all members of the Frankfurt School – is fairly obvious. And more important still, we find a strong *élitist* tendency in the writings of all 'critical theorists', no matter at which particular point of the political spectrum they were situated.

With regard to Adorno, this has been stressed on numerous occasions. To quote a sympathetic analysis:

> Adorno's talk of the mediation between intellectual praxis and political praxis remained abstract and vague, with no explication of the social medium which might serve as a conduit for this mediation, once the role of the Party was rejected. The medium for Adorno's 'mediation' remained as mysterious as the medium between the spirits and the flesh of the world, and Hanns Eisler's criticism had an undeniable kernel of validity: 'This metaphysical blind belief in the "development of music". If Adorno would only once understand that music is made by people for people – and if it also develops, this development is not abstract but somehow can be connected with social relationships! – then he would not say this abstract nonsense.'[228] There was indeed something metaphysical in Adorno's stress on truth, and in his vision of the *intellectual élite* as the formulators of that truth.[229]

The problem was, in fact, even more complicated than indicated in this passage, in the sense that not only the 'social medium or conduit' of Adorno's programmatic 'mediation' was missing, but also its emancipatorily effective *terminus ad quem*. This carried with it the necessity of an intellectual self-orientation and withdrawal, articulating itself in the pessimistic perspective of a '*negative dialectic*' deliberately opposed to the adoption of a *social standpoint*, and yet envisaging a rather mysterious solution of the identified problems as a result of operating from the problematical ground of this desperate self-containment.

Perhaps because of the strongly felt practical hopelessness of this *negation without affirmation* from the perspective of an intellectual self-containment, forced upon Adorno by the inner logic of the missing '*conduit*' and *terminus ad quem*, he assumed some postures which seemed rather strange even in its own terms of reference. Thus, while postulating the abstract 'mediating' role of his élite, Adorno also used to idealize being immersed, in total silence, in reading the musical score – a practice obviously confined to the select few – as the only really adequate, 'unmediated' and 'unadulterated' enjoyment of music.[230] Sadly, in comparison to such conception of musical communication, the aristocratic statement of his idol, Schönberg – according to which the audience is only good for improving the acoustics of the concert hall – could sound like the manifestation of mass-oriented, democratic humanism.

Also, Adorno's romantic tirades against jazz betrayed his extreme élitism. He saw and abhorred in jazz 'the perennial gesture of *mass culture*,'[231] ridiculing its 'passionate devotees' for 'hardly being able to give an account, in *precise, technical musical concepts*, of whatever it is that so moves them'.[232] While condemning the inability of such 'primitives' to articulate their ideas on their object of admiration, Adorno volunteered his own view of what is really involved in performing and experiencing jazz, which sounded terribly profound. It went like this, 'The aim of jazz is the *mechanical reproduction of a regressive moment*, a *castration symbolism*.'[233] And that was not all. In addition we were offered another profundity as well, concerning the 'subject' of jazz. It was defined by Adorno in the following terms:

> The subject which expresses itself expresses precisely this: I am nothing, I am filth, no matter what they do to me, it serves me right. Potentially this subject has already become one of those Russians, accused of a crime, and who, although innocent, collaborates with the prosecutor from the beginning and is incapable of finding a punishment severe enough.[234]

As so often in the writings of Adorno, his arbitrary statements were 'substantiated' by nothing but equally arbitrary analogies. Of course, the unobjectionable, privileged subjects, who could formulate their accounts of their own musical experiences (uncorrupted by 'the culture industry') in 'precise technical musical concepts', and who were already fully tuned in on the proper wavelength of abstractly universe-negating (but concretely well accommodated) 'critical theory', would find no difficulty in accepting the two statements – on the one hand about the 'filth subject' of jazz, and on the other about 'those Russians' – on their face value, together with their combined illuminating relevance to understanding the nature of jazz which must have eluded lesser mortals. This was a procedure very similar to what one finds when two nouns are connected with an 'and' in book titles by their authors, in order to establish an 'organic' link between two fields which otherwise have nothing in common. But no matter how problematical such a procedure might be, those who shared Adorno's standpoint could not have had any objection to it. They, no doubt, would have also instantly appreciated that one of the most obvious indictments that one could level against 'primitively improvising' and 'monotonously syncopating' jazz was that it made very little use, if any, of *musical scores*.

All this, however, could not alter the fact that in the whole of Adorno's resentful and haughty attack on jazz one could not find *one single line* of musical analysis; neither in 'precise technical musical concepts' nor in any other form. Instead, the true meaning of jazz was described by Adorno like this:

> 'Give up your masculinity, let yourself be castrated,' the eunuchlike sound of the jazz band both mocks and proclaims, 'and you will be rewarded, accepted

into a fraternity which shares the mystery of impotence with you, a mystery revealed at the moment of the initiation rite.' If this interpretation of jazz – whose sexual implications are better understood by its shocked opponents than by its apologists – appear arbitrary and far-fetched, the fact remains that it can be substantiated in countless details of the music as well as of the song lyrics.[235]

Yet, despite the promise of substantiating 'in countless details' what he himself had to acknowledge to be amenable to the charge of arbitrary and far-fetched assertions, not one single work of jazz was even mentioned, let alone adequately analysed by Adorno in his crusading essay. Not even the names of a few jazz musicians were given as illustrative examples, except two – Mike Riley and Louis Armstrong. But even Riley and Armstrong were taken second hand from two American critical works quoted by Adorno.

The second hand reference to Louis Armstrong compared him to 'the great *castrati* of the eighteenth century,[236] without even noticing the obvious contradiction between the generic claims of Adorno's own theory about the nature of jazz in a 'totally integrated and reified mass society' and the eighteenth century; the latter not in the least troubled by 'planned production', 'mass culture', 'total reification', and the ubiquitous 'culture industry', yet having its – by no means only symbolically castrated – 'great *castrati*', who were nevertheless said to illuminate the baffling predicament of jazz and of the alleged castration complex of all those who participate in jazz. In Adorno's aphoristic framework of declarations and declamations it was quite sufficient merely to assert the author's ideological preconceptions and generic negations of 'society as such' without any real effort at substantiating them, while at the same time thundering in equally generic terms against ideology.

3.4.2
Once the great Russian revolutionary democrat Belinsky stated that the whole movement to which he belonged emerged from Gogol's '*Coat*'. One could find a similar connection between Lukács's *Theory of the Novel* as well as his *History and Class Consciousness* and the early representatives of the Frankfurt School. However, the main difference in this respect was equally striking. For unlike the Russian revolutionary democrats who represented a forcefully radicalizing trend in Russian intellectual history, linking up through Chernyshevsky even with Plekhanov and Lenin, the Frankfurt School moved in the opposite direction. As time went by, its members (with the exception of Walter Benjamin who died prematurely, and of Herbert Marcuse for a while, as we shall see in the next section) more and more disengaged themselves from the social agency of emancipation, opting instead for the most abstract and generic terms of opposition and negation whose target could hardly be identified.

Thus, Lukács could rightly point out in his 1962 Preface to *The Theory of the Novel* that the emulation of the mixture of 'left ethics with right epistemology and ontology' characteristic of that early work (written in 1914–15 and much idealized particularly by Adorno) conducted to an intellectual and political blind alley, producing in his German followers 'conformism disguised as non-conformism'.[237]

The Theory of the Novel was conceived by Lukács 'in a mood of permanent despair over the state of the world',[238] identifying its author's outlook with Fichte's definition of the present as 'the age of absolute sinfulness'.[239] This mood of intense cultural pessimism proved to be most influential in the West. Moreover, once the main points of Lukács's theory of *'reification'* in *History and Class Consciousness* were added to it, we could see emerging some of the most important 'Leitmotifs' of critical theory. The trouble was, though, that the genuine social criticism of Lukács's approach had been watered down beyond recognition by the addition of meaningless categories like 'absolute commodity'[240] and 'absolute reification'[241] which replaced socially tangible criticism by vacuous verbal radicalism.

Thus, the overwhelming majority of 'critical theory' became as critical as 'the great historical compromise' of Eurocommunism was 'great'. Lukács characterized very well this predicament by saying that:

> A considerable part of the leading German intelligentsia, including Adorno, have taken up residence in the 'Grand Hotel Abyss' which I described in connection with my critique of Schopenhauer as a beautiful hotel, equipped with every comfort, on the edge of an abyss, of nothingness, of absurdity. And the daily contemplation of the abyss between excellent meals or artistic entertainments, can only heighten the enjoyment of the subtle comforts offered.[242]

Naturally, political commitment had to be strictly banned from the Grand Hotel even retrospectively. In this sense Walter Benjamin had to be censured for his alleged '*naïveté*' in these words:

> In its close contact with material which was close at hand, in its affinity to that which is, his thought, despite all its strangeness and acumen, was always accompanied by a characteristic unconscious element, by a moment of *naïveté*. This *naïveté* enabled him at times to sympathize with groups in power-politics which, as he well knew, would have liquidated his own substance, unregimented intellectual experience.[243]

The same went for Picasso and Sartre,[244] as well as for Bertolt Brecht who, according to Adorno, only deluded himself if he thought that his political intentions could be brought to a fruition in literature. For:

> Brecht's work, intent as it was on change since the writing of *St Joan of the Stockyard* (1929), was probably *politically impotent*; ... His impact might be characterized as a form of *preaching to the converted*.[245]

Indeed, Adorno elevated to the level of a glorified philosophical/aesthetic principle – that of the mysteriously 'participatory politics' of apoliticity – his own accommodations by saying that art 'participates in politics even though it is *apolitical*'[246] and that 'the emphasis on the nexus between art and society is valid, *provided it avoids direct partisanship* such as we find it in what is nowadays called "*commitment*".'[247] Attempts of writers and artists to achieve social change through meaningful 'political interventions' were condemned by Adorno as 'dubious', insisting that they lead to being 'regularly enmeshed in a *false social consciousness* because they tend to oversimplify, selling out to a myopic praxis to which they contribute nothing but their own blindness'.[248]

Like '*ideology*', '*collectivity*', too, became a dirty word in Adorno's philosophy. The *age* itself was defined as 'the age of *repressive collectivity*', from which it seemed to follow according to the rules of Adorno's curious logic that 'the power of resistance to compact majorities resides in the *lonely, exposed producer of art*'.[249] The idea, that the constitution of *non-repressive collectivities* might be a better solution in this respect, simply could not enter Adorno's conceptual horizon. But, to be fair to him, if the 'age' itself was – by definition – identified with 'repressive collectivity' as such, then, of course, any attempt at countering its power through the agency of a 'non-repressive collectivity' had to be an absolute non-starter, and nothing but the manifestation of 'oversimplifying false social consciousness'.

However, the problem was precisely that so much had to be settled *by definition* and constant *re-definition* in the absence of a viable anchorage (of the postulated pseudo-agencies and of his personifications of abstract entities) in reality itself. Thus, we were told that '*by definition* art works are socially culpable.'[250] This was an assertion immediately followed by another one which stated: 'but the *worthy* ones among them try to *atone for their guilt*', which acquired its meaning, again by definition, with reference to the first definition. Similarly, it was categorically stated that 'it is one of the basic characteristics of *ideology* that nobody ever believes it entirely and that it advances from self-contempt to self-destruction':[251] another totally arbitrary assertion which ran away from the difficulties of offering the slightest evidence for a number of alleged – and, to say the least, extremely contentious – characteristics by simply imposing them on ideology (and on the unsuspecting reader) *by definition*.

Naturally, once the reader has become accustomed to Adorno's way of dealing with everything in terms of self-asserting definitions, he could be expected to accept almost anything, including the most bewildering propositions, like, for instance: '*empirical reality as such* ... has become a *self-duplicating ideology*'.[252] In this way anything that Adorno wanted to reject could be done away with on a grand scale, by definition, without worrying even about the violation of the relevant historical context. This is why it came as no surprise when we were told that 'actually, the [Aristotelian] doctrine of *catharsis* had already inaugurated, in principle [i.e. by Adorno-type definition], the *manipulative domination of art* that came into its own with the advent of the *culture industry*.'[253]

Adorno's method of settling issues by definition was coupled with a constant search for paradoxes and pointed phrases. This was well in tune with the ideological substance and sociopolitical evasiveness of his work. For if it was really true that the *age* itself was wedded to 'repressive collectivity'; that *'empirical reality as such'* has become a *'self-duplicating ideology'*; that 'social structure has become total and *completely melted together*';[254] that already the Aristotelian *catharsis* had inaugurated 'in principle' the society of 'total reification' and the concomitant manipulative domination of art by 'the culture industry'; that 'in the *administered world* neutralization becomes *universal*';[255] that 'totality is society as a thing-in-itself, with all the guilt of *reification*';[256] that 'the mutilation of man which is the present particularistic rationality is the stigma of the *total irrationality*';[257] that 'the calculated,, distributive apparatus of industry, the commercialization of culture culminates in absurdity. *Completely subdued, administered*, thoroughly "cultivated" in a sense, it *dies out*';[258] that 'the struggle against deceit works to the advantage of *naked terror*';[259] that *'life transforms itself* into the ideology of reification – a *death mask*';[260] that *'absolute reification* . . . is now preparing to *absorb the mind entirely*';[261] etc., in that case it would have been far too much to expect that 'the lonely, exposed producer of art' should be able to make even the slightest dent in the massive power of all these negativities.

Accordingly, the identified difficulties and contradictions had to be metamorphosed in the course of articulating Adorno's theory in such a way that the power of definitions (and suitable redefinitions), in conjunction with carefully designed and reworked paradoxes, should be able to offer the promise of a 'solution' where none could in fact be indicated in terms of actual sociohistorical developments.

This is why the reader was constantly presented by Adorno with verbal fireworks and a kind of 'conceptual tongue-twisting', giving him the *illusion* of a solution after insisting – in terms of the vague and generic negation of the various 'totalities' (total irrationality, reification, administration, calculation, integration, etc.) and 'absolutes' – that it was *impossible* to find a solution; and, indeed, that the very attempt to look for it would be hopelessly ideological: the manifestation of 'false social consciousness', deserving only an unqualified condemnation. Thus, the reader was spuriously reassured that 'by *rejecting* reality . . . art *vindicates* reality';[262] that 'the *irrationality* of art is becoming *rational*, . . . art *internalizes* the repressing principle, i.e. the unredeemed condition of the world (*Unheil*), instead of merely airing *futile protests* against it';[263] that 'works of art are *absolute commodities*; . . . An absolute commodity *rids itself* of the *ideology* inherent in the *commodity form*';[264] that art 'participates in politics even though it is *apolitical*';[265] that 'it is this *fetishism* – the blindness of the art work to the reality of which it is a part – that enables the work of art to break the spell of the *reality principle* and to become a *spiritual essence*';[266] that 'art is *semblance* even at its highest peaks; but its semblance ... is given to it by what is *not semblance.... Semblance* is a promise of *nonsemblance*';[267] etc., etc. Adorno even found a way of partially redeeming ideology (although he categorically rejected it as a rule) in the form of a 'must be', by saying, in the context where it suited him, that 'ideology is socially necessary illusion, which means that if it is necessary it *must be* a shape of *truth*, no matter how *distorted*.'[268]

It has been frequently pointed out that 'there can be little doubt that a lengthy journey through the thicket of Adorno's prose does give the impression of passing the same landmarks with uncomfortable frequency ... we find ourselves apparently going in circles, retracing the contours of a latent system, despite Adorno's protestations to the contrary'.[269] However, the attempt to justify this state of affairs by saying that 'the repetitive ever-sameness that Adorno so disliked in the modern world could not help but permeate his own thought'[270] does not sound in the least convincing. After all, many other intellectuals, too, lived in the same world without falling victim to its alleged 'repetitive ever-sameness'. Besides, there was a very good reason why Adorno had to proceed the way he did. For what was in fact characteristic of, and highly revealing about, Adorno's consistently apolitical method of definitional paradox-production, articulated by interminable and *non-cumulative* variations on recurring themes, with suitably *shifting* meaning in the sense we have seen above – which constituted the fundamental and more or less conscious structuring principle of his method – was that (in contrast to Marcuse) the 'social bite' had to be systematically taken out of the issues under his scrutiny, even when the author's 'negations' sounded 'total', 'absolute', and 'categorical'.

3.4.3
Given his conscious disengagement from any socially identifiable agency of negation and emancipation, with the exception of the far from convincing and viable 'lonely, exposed producer of art', Adorno condemned himself to looking for an alternative in the form of mythological substitutes. The only feasible social agencies of the necessary quest for emancipation have been summarily dismissed by him as 'repressive' and 'integrated', together with the 'age itself' that represented for him 'the unredeemed condition of the world' – a faint echo of the early Lukács's Fichtean 'age of absolute sinfulness'. At the same time, the romantic anti-capitalist aspirations of 'negating subjectivity' could not be abandoned. For that would have meant declaring totally useless the role of the intellectual. Nor could indeed the 'critical intellectual' be allowed simply to appear as in fact he was:

an isolated individual. For that would have made painfully obvious the rhetorical vacuity of his discourse on 'radical negation'.

This is why Adorno had to end up with 'subjects' and 'actors' depicted in the form of such generic entities as 'music' and its abstractly hypostatized 'development' (rightly condemned by Hanns Eisler as a 'metaphysical blind belief', as we have seen above); of 'art itself' under many of its strange permutations (including its mysterious embodiment as 'the absolute commodity'); of 'thought' and 'the autonomous mind' (which we shall see soon); of the 'age itself' and 'society as such', and many more like these. Even 'empirical reality as such' was converted into the pseudo-personality of 'self-duplicating ideology'. What remained, however, conspicuously absent from Adorno's major theoretical generalizations, yet speaking louder than anything else precisely through its studied absence, was the category or *combative/emancipatory social class* and the idea of non-repressive but *reciprocal-commitment-demanding collectivity*.

This was all the more telling since in limited contexts – when the target of Adorno's critique was not the antagonistic capitalist order but one of its well-established ideologists and his own intellectual rival, Karl Mannheim (with whom he had also a personal score to settle) – he could sharply focus on the incorrigible failure of the 'sociology of knowledge' due to its harmony-orientated social apologetics and the transformation of conflicting social classes into fictitious logical entities. This is how Adorno spelled out his damning objections in one of his finest critical analyses:

> The distortions of the sociology of knowledge arise from its method, which translates *dialectical* concepts into *classificatory* ones. Since in each case what is *socially contradictory* is absorbed into individual logical classes, *social classes* as such disappear and the picture of the whole becomes *harmonious*.[271]

In the light of these insights, it was almost incomprehensible to see Adorno's consistent evasion of the fundamental social antagonisms of capitalist society. At best, he could only bring himself to voice an 'even-handed condemnation' of the principal social agencies, assuming thereby a position that in the end amounted to the same complicity with the established order which he rightly rejected in Mannheim's sociology of knowledge. He was determined to stay away from the subject of *structural antagonisms*, with all their constituents and *dynamic* implications, preferring to talk, instead, about the 'administered society', with its 'total reification' coupled to the fictitiously commodification-transcending 'absolute commodity'.

In such emasculation of social criticism he was by no means on his own. All the other members of the Frankfurt Institute who returned with Adorno and Horkheimer to West Germany in 1949 participated in the same enterprise. In fact, notwithstanding their claimed critique of the 'administered' society and its mass-manipulating 'culture industry' (of which the United States constituted in their eyes the paradigm example), they willingly accepted the function to become in Germany the Trojan Horse of American cultural/ideological hegemony and the disseminator of its 'anti-ideological' (or 'supra-ideological') social science. As Martin Jay correctly reported:

> the returning members of the [Frankfurt] Institute were generally reticent about publicizing the Marxist aspects of their previous work. When they launched a new series of *Frankfurt Contributions to Sociology*, they deliberately chose not to include a translation of such Institute-sponsored projects as Franz Neumann's *Behemoth*, whose analysis of Nazism largely in terms of *monopoly capitalism* seemed too simplistic, (or too provocative in the Cold War atmosphere of the 1950s). Equally symptomatic, the Institute's collectively written volume in the series, *Aspects of Sociology*, included a chapter on the *masses*, but not one on *classes*. As early as 1951, members of the Institute who remained in America had noted a subtle change in its orientation. When Leo Lowenthal complained that the empirical research techniques Horkheimer was now so vigorously supporting were at odds with critical theory, the Institute director defensively replied, 'We stand here for the good things: for individual independence, the *idea of the Enlightenment*, science freed from blinders.' ... For the co-author of *Dialectic of Enlightenment* to assert his support for 'the idea of the Enlightenment' suggests how far the Institute had gone in moderating its earlier hostility to bourgeois values ... Horkheimer, in fact, steadfastly refused to allow ... the republication of his controversial essay of 1939 on 'The Jews and Europe', which contained the widely cited remark, 'He who does not wish to speak of *capitalism* should also be silent about *Fascism*.'[272]

Understandably, when even the concept of 'capitalism' had to be discarded, the Marxian category of 'classes' could no longer be entertained any longer in any meaningful sense of the term. The '*modern world*' – and 'modernity' in general, in an apparently inexhaustible number of combinations – was considered a much more palatable category than '*capitalism*', just as the category of the '*masses*' was much more readily amenable to the required ideological manipulation and distortion by 'critical theory' than the concept of antagonistic '*classes*'. Likewise, instead of critically assessing the contradictions of monopoly capitalism, not just in its historically defeated fascist form but as manifest in the contemporary reality as well, it was much more convenient to subsume the recent historical experience itself under the rubric of the '*authoritarian personality*' (which tended to metamorphose the problems at stake into a matter of individual psyche and family socialization), while at the same time exercising the most extreme form of *institutionalized authoritarianism* by suppressing Franz Neumann's book on fascism and monopoly capital, even though that book was the product of a member of the Institute at an earlier phase of its development. Thus, although in the *Dialectic of Enlightenment* Adorno and Horkheimer lamented the deadening obliteration of social memory and the triumph of reification in the form of 'forgetfulness', now they were themselves actively promoting the repressive obliteration of politico-intellectual memory – not only of others but of their own as well – in the rather naive belief that the contradictions of capitalism and their own integration within its system will disappear if one no longer talks about them, obliterating through institutionally enforced 'forgetfulness' even the most obvious historical connection between Nazism and monopoly capital.

In a characteristic way, Adorno succeeded in having it both ways also in relation to the concept of class. He retained for an occasional use the *word* 'class' and totally emptied it of its *critical content*. This he did by asserting that although the classes themselves remained in modern society the *class struggle* itself had ended.

There was nothing 'radical'[273] about using the word 'class' as such. For one can recognize the existence of classes in quite different ways, including the soothing approval of their 'proper place' in the social order, practised by those who ideologically reconciled and 'ended' the antagonisms of the given order even in slave-owning ancient society. Once, however, the actuality of the class struggle is denied, all claims to radicalism go with it. Even the explicit recognition of class contradictions can only become radical if it is coupled with realistic strategies about resolving such contradictions by intervening at the level of the fundamental structural determinations of society, with a view of actually overcoming the antagonism of class domination and subordination.

Hegel himself was, in fact, well aware of the pernicious actuality of class contradictions when he underlined the striking inequalities between the *alienated* conditions of existence of the dispossessed and those who ruled them. But he wanted to 'resolve' these contradictions by the imaginary 'second alienation of alienated existence' (a kind of 'negation of the negation') through the graphically described 'religious experience', whereby the pauper was meant to detach himself from his earthly existence. He described the transformation of the latter in the course of the religious experience as 'a speck of cloud' that disappears on the horizon, producing the feeling in the 'no longer alienated' (for 'de-objectified') pauper in the cathedral that he equals the prince ('*er ist dem Fürsten gleich*'). Naturally, when they both leave the cathedral, with their 'objectivity/alienation' dully reconstituted, they resume their actual existence in the real world exactly where they left it off before they entered the cathedral. Thus the order of society – with all its contradictions – remains totally unchanged.

The 'radicalism' of Adorno's acknowledgement of the existence of classes was not in the least more radical than the Hegelian 'second alienation of alienated existence'. Quite the contrary. For, on the one hand, Hegel acknowledged that the pauper, not the prince, was the suffering subject and envisaged the need for the 'second alienation' on his behalf, rather than putting an equal sign between the two classes by saying – in the name of 'universal reification' and its rhetorical negation – 'plague on both your houses'. At the same time, on the other hand, Hegel clearly perceived that the relationship between 'Lord' and 'Bondsman' (or 'Master' and 'Servant', etc.) was a *hierarchical* and unstable use of *domination* and *subordination*, hence potentially dynamic (materially contestable) and explosive, which worried him a great deal. By contrast, Adorno tried to transform this relationship into a *static symmetry*. (He did this, incidentally, with every single Hegelian category which he tried to redefine.) For instance:

> Within a *reified society*, nothing has a chance to survive which is not in turn *reified*. The concrete historical generality of *monopolistic capitalism* extends into the *monopoly of labour*, with all its implications. A relevant task for *empirical sociology* would be to analyse the intermediate members and to show *in detail* how the *adaptation* to the changed capitalist relations of production *includes* those whose objective interests conflict, in the long run, with this *adaptation*.'[274]

As we can see, in this passage 'monopolistic capitalism' and the somewhat mysterious 'monopoly of labour' were treated symmetrically, within the framework of a universally reified society in which everything had to suffer the condition of reification (by definition). Reference to 'monopolistic capitalism' itself was made only in the context of the alleged 'monopoly of labour', which in its turn remained totally undefined. Adorno's peremptory assertions concerning the permanence of universal reification and 'the monopoly of labour' were simply assumed as self-evident. The task for 'empirical sociology' was defined in terms of merely showing 'in detail' the (twice underlined) *adaptation* of labour to the unavoidable conditions of universal reification. There was nothing whatsoever to investigate about the nature and *structural contradictions* of monopolistic capitalism. All that Adorno demanded was the 'empirical' confirmation of his aprioristic thesis of labour's necessary adaptive integration. And we could also guess quite easily what conclusions were supposed to emerge from the 'analysis in detail of the intermediate members', since Adorno asserted on more than one occasion that the class struggle itself had ended.

3.4.4

To be sure, one could find a slightly – and often even sharply – different formulation to almost everything Adorno ever stated; sometimes even on the same page. The 'repetitive ever-sameness', with all its measured variations, was a necessary feature of Adorno's way of developing his ideas, arising from the conscious determination to define (and, whenever needed, opportunely redefine) his terms of reference, so that he should never be 'caught off guard'. The unavoidable abstractness and vagueness of his formulations – as a rule hidden behind the carefully constructed façade of conceptual tongue-twisting and 'striking' verbal embellishments – was the consequence of his ever-more-pronounced avoidance of sociohistorical specificities and of the disdainful rejection of all practical commitment. In the words of one of his most gifted students, his 'concept of negation moved further and further away from the historical necessity of an objective partisanship of thought'.[275] Thus, it came as no surprise to his – once highly sympathetic – followers that at the time of the Vietnam war and the social conflicts that erupted in conjunction with it in the US and in Europe, Adorno ended up sharing 'a *fatal complicity* ... with the ruling powers'.[276]

Adorno's celebrated aphorism 'the whole is the false'[277] *sounded* most impressive in its scathing rejection of Hegel. However, as soon as one started to ask the question, what exactly was the meaning of such a statement, the aphorism totally deflated itself. For, apart from its facile overturning of Hegel's profound (even if in his own use rather problematical) formula: 'the truth is the whole', it amounted to no more than a piece of rhetorical meaninglessness.

Staccato profundities like this anti-Hegelian jibe constituted the organizing principle of Adorno's writing. This is why his synthesizing works remained so utterly disorganized, no matter how much effort was dedicated to their orderly presentation. In fact Adorno's systematic books (like *Negative Dialectics* and *Aesthetic Theory*) fall to pieces in the sense that it does not matter where one starts to read them, in what order one continues, and at which particular point the reading is terminated. These books leave the reader with the impression of having gone through something not only *unfinished* but in a theoretical sense even *unbegun*. The earlier mentioned *non-cumulative* nature of Adorno's analyses and the *repetitive ever-sameness* of his generalizations is as characteristic of his synthesizing works as of his short essays and deliberately aphoristic volumes. The reason why one becomes much more conscious of these characteristics while reading Adorno's *Negative Dialectics* and *Aesthetic Theory* is that in such works, consciously planned as the rigorous sytematic elaboration and summation of his ideas, both the author and the reader would have expected (or hoped for) something qualitatively different and more coherent.

That things had turned out the way in which they did was neither accidental nor the consequence of some *formal* defect. Adorno's concern for formal accomplishment and linguistic refinement – almost to the point of a neurotic self-torturing – was legendary and well publicized. The weighty causes behind his 'disintegrative' theoretical composition were primarily ideological and political.

What paralysed him in a theoretical sense was that he wanted to achieve the impossible; namely, to offer a valid critical assessment of the fundamental issues of the capitalist socioeconomic and political order, projecting a way out of its destructive contradictions, while simultaneously also proclaiming the utter futility and even dangerously counter-productive (in his view fascism-provoking) character of all practical political negation of that order.

Moreover, even at the core of his theoretical enterprise one could find a fundamental contradiction which tended to paralyse him not only politically and ideologically but also intellectually. For while he accepted the Marxian theoretical framework (in the form in which he inherited it above all from Lukács's *History and Class Consciousness*, instead of appropriating it on the basis of a solid first-hand study) as a tool of *diagnosis* for grasping the general outlines of the capitalist age and its 'reification', he had to reject it in its historical specificity as the necessary *strategic framework of action* applicable to his own circumstances. He had to reject it because acceptance of the Marxian perspective in the second sense was radically incompatible with his own 'principled' rejection of both active political/ organizational involvement and ideological *commitment*, in favour of a generic form of 'criticism'.

These were monumental contradictions whose continued presence could only result in a theoretical *stalemate* and a concomitant *static* mode of conceptualization of all major issues. The rejection of the *practical* dimension of Marxian theory inevitably meant in his case that also its *diagnostic* categories had to be diluted to the point of utter meaninglessness, losing in the end both their historically illuminating power and their relevance to the contemporary age. As his highly gifted pupil, Hans-Jürgen Krahl had put it in his obituary of Adorno, one year before he also died prematurely, in a car accident:

> Adorno's negation of late capitalist society has remained *abstract*, closing itself to the need for the specificity of specific negation, i.e. the dialectical category to which he knew himself obligated by the tradition of Hegel and Marx. In his last work, *Negative Dialectics*, the concept of praxis is no longer questioned in terms of social change in its specific historical forms, i.e. the forms of bourgeois relations and proletarian organization. The withering of the *class struggle* is mirrored in his critical theory as the *degeneration of the materialist conception of history*.[278]

Thus, Adorno drew the logical conclusions with regard to what he considered to be the inadequacy of the Marxian theoretical framework to the problems of the 'advanced industrial society'. What he failed to notice, however, was that the formal consistency of his own logic was an utterly perverse one, arising from the ideological need to rationalize the contradictions of his own position which counterposed theoretical analysis and diagnosis to action, and 'resolved' the contradiction by rejecting also the Marxian theory that insisted on the necessary unity of theory and practice.

Although the negative/conservative consequences of Adorno's inner contradictions came to the fore with great abundance and clarity only in the last decade of his activity as a writer, they were already visible in various contexts many years earlier. Since the critical diagnosis of capitalist

society and the strategic framework of the feasible practical solutions to its
contradictions were radically separated from and opposed to one another
in Adorno's conception of 'Western Marxism', there could be no question
of locating in it a genuine historical subject which could indicate a way
out of the denounced conditions. Fictitious, quasi-mythological pseudo-
subjects had to assume the role of historical agency, like 'the spirit',
'music', 'art', 'society as such', etc., etc. Significantly, therefore, despite
the fact that Adorno's aim at the time of writing his essay on 'Cultural
criticism and society' was to articulate a *materialist* conception of critical
theory, he ended up with a fetishistic hypostatization of '*the mind*' (which
he criticized in others). Hegel himself, whose 'world-mind' (*Weltgeist*) was
defined in infinitely more coherent and realistic terms, would have, no
doubt, rejected Adorno's idealist hypostatization of 'the autonomous
mind', etc. as totally arbitrary. This is how Adorno formulated his critical
concerns:

> The notion of the free expression of opinion, indeed, that of intellectual
> freedom itself in bourgeois society, upon which cultural criticism is founded,
> has its own dialectic. For while *the mind extricated itself* from a theological–
> feudal tutelage, it has fallen increasingly under the anonymous sway of the
> status quo. This regimentation, the result of the progressive societalization
> of all human relations, did not simply confront *the mind* from without; it
> immigrated into its immanent consistency. It imposes itself as relentlessly on
> *the autonomous mind* as heteronomous orders were formerly *imposed on the
> mind* which was bound. Not only does *the mind mould itself* for the sake of its
> marketability, and thus reproduce the socially prevalent categories. Rather, it
> grows to resemble ever more closely the status quo even where it subjectively
> *refrains from making a commodity of itself.*[279]

But Adorno did not stop at that. For after recommending the 'immanent
method' as the proper way to deal with the situation, he went on in the
same work to describe the actual conditions of existence and the emerging
trends of development in just as unrealistic terms as he characterized 'the
mind' a few pages earlier, but this time in the key of absolute gloom and
doom. These were his words:

> The *sinister, integrated society of today* no longer tolerates even those rela-
> tively independent distinct moments to which the theory of the *causal
> dependence of superstructure on base* once referred. In the *open-air prison*
> which the world is becoming, it is *no longer so important to know what
> depends on what*, such is the extent to which *everything is one*. All phenomena
> rigidify, become insignias of the absolute rule of that which is. There are no
> more *ideologies* in the authentic sense of *false consciousness*, only advertise-
> ments for the world through its duplication and the provocative lie which does
> not seek belief but commands silence. . . . Of course, even the immanent
> method is eventually overtaken by this. It is *dragged into the abyss by its
> object.* . . . The more *total* society becomes, the greater the *reification of the
> mind* and the more *paradoxical* its effort to escape reification *on its own*. Even
> the most extreme consciousness of doom threatens to *degenerate into idle*

chatter. . . . Absolute reification, which presupposed intellectual progress as one of its elements, is now *preparing to absorb the mind entirely*.[280]

To say that 'the greater the reification of the *mind* the more *paradoxical* its effort to *escape* reification *on its own*' must have been, surely, the understatement of the week, even if totally unintended. From the panoramic window of 'Grand Hotel Abyss', Adorno caught a clear sight of 'absolute reification' as it was 'preparing to absorb the mind entirely', and painted its inexorable coming with shades of black on a black canvas. What remained incomprehensible, though, was the purpose of this gloomy denunciation of the 'sinister, integrated society', defined summarily as an *'open-air prison'*. What was the vantage point and the envisaged aim of Adorno's message? And who was the addressee of his discourse? Obviously, 'the mind itself' could not have been, since it was about to be absorbed entirely by 'absolute reification'. Collectivities, too, could not have been of any use, since they have been dismissed under the label of 'the age of repressive collectivity'. And, finally, the actually existing individuals, in their limited particularity, could not have constituted the addressee either, since their power was simply not commensurate to the size of the problem: that of total reification in a totally integrated society.

In any case, if 'even the immanent method' was in the process of being 'dragged into the abyss by its object', then the advocacy of its continued exercise as the road to salvation could amount to no more than either 'idle chatter' or self-contradiction. In reality, of course, the social world was not an 'open-air prison' but a dynamic whole characterized not only by fateful contradictions but also by practical possibilities and levers of intervention, amenable to countering the power of the destructive forces. To do so, however, it would have been all the *more* necessary *'to know what depends on what'* (as opposed to rhetorically denying its importance), so as to be able to envisage a *strategically effective intervention* in objective terms, instead of inflating the isolated intellectual into 'the mind' and ideologically justifying its self-oriented inactivity by the fictions of 'absolute reification' and 'total integration'.

The *addressee* of Adorno's discourse was problematical, thus, from the very beginning, since the socially viable historical *subject* was nowhere to be found in it. This in its turn inevitably affected both the *object* of his theoretical analysis (the sociohistorical diagnosis of the issues) and the *practical strategic implications* of the whole enterprise. For these four factors are always inextricably intertwined in social theory and philosophy.

He had an élitistic view not only of the 'masses' and 'mass culture' but also of the chosen few intellectuals, like himself, even if he tried to disguise his élitism by the category of 'stroke of luck', thinly coated with a moralistic *'Generaltunken'*.[281] As Martin Jay observed:

> In later years the Frankfurt School would come to believe that true consciousness rested in the minds of certain critical theorists who were able, for reasons they did not really explore, to avoid the gravitational pull of the prevailing

universe of discourse. Adorno argued: 'If a stroke of undeserved luck has kept the *mental composition* of some individuals not quite adjusted to the prevailing norms – a *stroke of luck* they have often enough to pay for in their relations with their environment – it is up to these individuals to make the moral and, as it were, representative effort to say what most of those for whom they say it cannot see or, to do justice to reality, *will not allow themselves to see*.'[282]

In his boundless negation of the world in which 'everything is one', Adorno defined the task of viable critical theory as 'throwing bottles into the sea', so that future addressees – whose identity could not possibly be known today – might one day be able to fish them out. There were two major difficulties intrinsic to this strategy. The first was that if we could know *nothing* about those future addressees, how could we assume that there *would* be any? And the second, perhaps an even greater one: how could we make sure that the message itself would survive the indefinite battering of the sea? For Adorno always considered the organizational/instrumental dimension of the task ahead of us – i.e. the job of 'instrumental rationality', like putting corks into the bottles – way beneath the 'critical' intellectuals who were chosen for their superior mission in our 'advanced industrial societies' by a 'stroke of luck'. Sadly, however, corkless bottles – no matter how noble the message buried in them – tend to sink very quickly even in unagitated waters, not to mention the stormy sea.

3.4.5
Adorno had a negative/one-sided, undialectically oversimplified, and tendentiously obfuscating conception of ideology. It consisted in lowering a thick metal shutter before the light-source, so that in the resulting proverbial darkness everything should become melancholy-black. Thus he stated that 'whether one can talk of *ideology* depends directly upon whether one can distinguish between *illusion and essence*',[283] and that '*ideology means society as appearance*',[284] He even decreed 'the *incompatibility of ideology and existence*',[285] and in his last work he diagnosed the predicament of 'the subject' like this:

> Tagging along behind its *reification*, the subject limits that reification through the mimetic vestige, the plenipotentiary of an integral life amid a damaged life where *the subject is being reduced to an ideology*.[286]

These were no accidental slips. Notwithstanding their rhetorical unreality, they represented a characteristic and in its own way consistent line of dealing with the problems at stake. Adorno manoeuvred himself into a position where he could not help drawing such an unremittingly desolate picture. For, given his élitistic posture towards the *masses*, he *had* to translate every Marxian proposition into his own, idealist discourse on the socially generic 'subject' and the equally generic 'mind', obliterating thereby also the *positive power* of ideology that could only arise out of the *materially felt emancipatory need* of the oppressed people.

We can see that the two thinkers were worlds apart if we compare Marx's original formulation of the dialectical relationship of reciprocity between radical theory (oriented towards a real historical agency, not a fictitious ideal 'subject') and the necessary material force of 'the class for itself' (the proletariat) with Adorno's confused and emasculating paraphrase of the Marxian idea. These were Marx's words:

> The weapon of criticism cannot replace *criticism by weapons*, material force must be overthrown by material force; but theory also becomes a *material force* as soon as it has *gripped the masses*. Theory is capable of gripping the masses as soon as it demonstrates *ad hominem*, and it demonstrates *ad hominem* as soon as it becomes radical. To be radical is to grasp the root of the matter.... Theory can be realized in a people only insofar as it is the realization of the *needs* of that people.... It is not enough for thought to strive for realization, *reality* must itself strive towards thought.... Only a revolution of *radical needs* can be a radical revolution ... As philosophy finds its *material weapons* in the *proletariat*, so the proletariat finds its spiritual weapons in philosophy.... Philosophy cannot be made a reality without the abolition of the proletariat, the proletariat cannot be abolished without philosophy being made a reality.[287]

And this is how Adorno transformed them – by turning his back on the radical needs of the oppressed people in favour of a vacuous denunciation of the existent in general, coupled with the rejection of any commitment to socially specific movements and struggles – in his own image:

> The fact that theory becomes real force when it moves men is founded in the objectivity of *the mind itself* which, through the fulfilment of its ideological function *must lose faith in ideology*. Prompted by the incompatibility of ideology and existence, *the mind*, in displaying its *blindness* also displays its effort to *free itself from ideology*. Disenchanted, *the mind* perceives naked existence in its nakedness and delivers it up to criticism. The mind either *damns the material base* ... or it becomes aware of its own questionable position, by virtue of its *incompatibility with the base*.... *Today* the definition of consciousness in terms of being [i.e. Marx] has become a means of dispensing with all consciousness which does not conform to existence.... As with many other elements of dialectical materialism, the notion of ideology has changed from an instrument of knowledge into its strait-jacket. In the name of the *dependence of superstructure on base*, all use of ideology is controlled instead of criticized. No one is concerned with the objective substance of an ideology as long as it is expedient.[288]

Thus, an utterly voluntaristic/idealist discourse had to be substituted for the Marxian dialectic of *base and superstructure*, quixotically opposing 'the mind' to the material base (at times even to 'causality' and 'empirical reality as such'), decreeing 'the mind's incompatibility with the base', so as to be able to declare the spurious freedom of the 'subject' on the edge of the 'abyss'. A freedom which seemed to be good only for contemplating the cosmic-goose-pimple-producing advancement of 'absolute reification' in its forward march to 'absorb the mind entirely'. The fact that, as a gratuitous reconciliatory gesture towards those who might have held on to the Marxian position, Adorno suggested that 'in this epoch of the sinister, integrated society' – when allegedly 'everything melted together' and became 'one' – it was no longer important to know what depended on what, and therefore the discourse on base and superstructure did not matter any longer anyhow, in either way, was quite meaningless as far as the substance of the theory was concerned. As a gesture without content it could only demonstrate that Adorno always had to have it in more ways than one.

However, his voluntaristic way of disposing of the Marxian dialectic of base and superstructure was by no means a matter of minor importance. On the contrary, it had far-reaching consequences for the whole theory. For, freed from the constraints of a coherent and objectively defined categorial framework, ideology could be swapped at will for practically everything under the sun, and in the purely spiritual realm as well. Thus, it could be substituted with the greatest ease for the 'subject' and the 'object'; for 'the spirit' as well as 'the mind'; for 'society as appearance' and for 'empirical reality as such'; for the advocacy of art[289] as well as for 'life' as such; for 'repressive collectivism' and for the 'administered world'; for conscious political praxis (condemned as 'dubious political interventions enmeshed in a false social consciousness') and for 'the culture industry'; and even for 'the material process of production'[290] in its entirety. Thus, the '*Ideologiekritik*' of Adorno's critical theory could 'negate' everything in general, without confronting within the strategic framework of a historically defined and organized mode of action anything in particular.

To be sure, in this rejection of the dialectic of base and superstructure Adorno was not on his own, even if in this respect his views were the most extreme. A curiously disoriented perspective prevailed in the writings of the Frankfurt School as a whole on the subject. The objective significance of the necessary operating conditions of the capitalist reproduction process (i.e. the historically specific – technology-embedding – relationship between the *capitalist state* and the productive practices of commodity society) tended to be ignored by all its members in favour of a vague discourse on 'instrumental rationality', producing as a result a thoroughly unrealistic assessment of capitalist technology and production as such. Moreover, since this major dimension of the dialectic of base and superstructure was left out of sight, the ideological critique of 'advanced industrial society' articulated by the representatives of this school suffered considerably, in that it could not point to any foundation for its criticism except itself. The moralizing negativity in evidence in so many works of 'critical theory' was the necessary consequence of such omission.

Adorno, for instance, defined the conditions of an emancipated society in terms of its being 'so organized as the productive forces would *directly permit it here and now*, and as the conditions of production *on either side*

relentlessly prevent it.'[291] Thus, the 'plague on both your houses' posture
(which wanted to 'equidistance' itself from everything, in the spirit of
Ranke suitably adapted by Adorno to his own purposes) produced the
vision of a paralysing stalemate. The weaknesses of this conception were
threefold.

First, the *global misery* upon which the apparently successful productive
forces were built in the contemporary capitalist system was not in the least
taken into account. Consequently, the vital question of how much or how
little *generalizable* (that is to say, without a massive social earthquake
globally diffusable) was the dominant productive technology – a question
which in the last analysis would decide whether it was viable at all, not to
mention its actual suitability to be the foundation of the necessary socialist
transformation – was not even raised.

Second, inasmuch as the available level of productive technology was
declared to be adequate also for the purposes of an emancipated society,
its deep-seated objective contradictions – inherent in the necessary operating conditions of the established mode of productive reproduction, which
steered it in a perilous direction and thereby constrained it in all major
respects, *'here and now'*, with ultimately explosive implications with regard
to its future development – escaped all criticism.

Third, since in the *capital/labour* relationship the responsibility for
'relentlessly preventing' the emergence of the envisaged emancipated
society on the already given foundations of productive technology was
ascribed as much to one side as to the other, the possibility of finding an
agency of emancipation equal to the task disappeared completely.

Once, however, the situation was diagnosed in such terms, Adorno was
forced into the dubious posture of a generic moral denunciation of the
existent from the point of view of his élitistically conceived 'negative
dialectic'. It could be therefore of no consolation whatsoever to postulate
that, 'In the lyric poem the subject negates both his naked, isolated
opposition to society as well as his mere functioning within rationally
organized society.'[292] How the 'subject' of the lyric poem could perform,
single-handed, such mind-boggling miracles was never revealed. Adorno's
discourse remained thoroughly desolate because the hypostatized subjective redemption could by itself not alter the *actual* relations of 'absolute
reification' and its concomitant ideology, one-sidedly and negatively defined by him even in its 'historical necessity' as *false consciousness*. It was
stated that 'ideology is untruth – *false consciousness*, a *lie*. It manifests
itself in the *failure* of art works, in their own *intrinsic falsehood*, and can be
uncovered by criticism.'[293] Against this, the function of successful art was
projected as a romantic counter-image:

> The greatness of works of art lies *solely* in their power to let those things
> be heard which *ideology conceals*. Whether intended or not, their success
> *transcends false consciousness*.[294]

Adorno did not seem to realize that by defining art in this way he made them parasitic on 'false consciousness' and its absolute perpetuation, having no *raison d'être* other than letting to be heard what ideology's function was to conceal. Furthermore, even if one could consider valid the assertion according to which by doing this art 'transcended ideology', that would still only apply to transcending ideology *in art*, without affecting in the least the actuality of reification and the manifold interchangeability of ideology, as depicted by Adorno himself, with almost everything in the world of productive reproduction and everyday social intercourse. The actual rule of reification and its concealment of everything substantive (or 'essential') under the veil of the degrading appearances of ideological 'false consciousness' would thus continue to assert itself as before, whatever the services that 'lyric poetry' (or art in general) might be able to render in its rare redemptive moments to the privileged few genuine 'subjects', but not to the hopelessly integrated and 'duped masses'.[295]

At the roots of Adorno's characterization of art (as a wishful antidote to what it could not really affect) one could find his categorically negating and unreal assessment of some fundamental material and human relations. There was something deeply wrong about Adorno's diagnosis of the real world if he could talk in terms like this:

> Art works are a *constant indictment* of the system of *practical activities* and *practical human beings*, who in turn are mere façades for the *barbaric appetite of the human species*. As long as they are ruled by this appetite, there will be no humankind, only domination.[296]

One could only wonder, in amazement, who on earth this disdainful 'subject' might be, and from what vantage point could he champion the constant indictment of the existent by 'autonomous art' while situating himself outside and above the 'barbarous human species'. On closer inspection, however, it transpired that anyone who could dismiss the human species as such on account of its alleged 'barbaric appetite', in the name of 'autonomous art', could only demonstrate his contemplative remoteness from both.

The 'system of practical activities and practical human beings' could be swept aside with such a rhetorical ease only in a conception quite incapable of differentiating between the strictly *conjunctural* and the *substantive* aspects of the dominant social relations of production, even though it continued to denounce *ideology as such* for being incurably tied to *appearance* (and to 'false appearance' at that). This is why Adorno had to end up castigating another one of his numerous pseudo-subjects – rhetorically personified but sociohistorically utterly vague 'society' as such – on account of what could be in fact no more than a *transient* moment in the development of postwar *capitalist* society, denouncing it in the most generic terms as the:

society that has intentionally put the ideal of *full employment* in the place of the abolition of labour ... the pernicious social trend to *deify means – production for production's sake, full employment*.[297]

Yet, well before he died, there had been already a sharp turn away from 'the ideal of full employment' – not to mention its *reality* – in our 'advanced industrial societies'. Adorno, however, refused to take any notice of that, since it went against his abstract preconceptions concerning 'instrumental reason' and the nature of the social world in which the 'practical activities of practical human beings' had to be pursed, even if it offended the refined taste of critical theorists.

In the same way as he dimissed the practical activities of practical human beings, Adorno also denounced the idea of *planning*[298] in the most scathing terms. Yet, he refused to pay the slightest attention to the sobering fact that a *rationally planned* mode of social production is the *absolute pre-requisite* for making any advancement in the direction of freeing human beings from the burden of even the most dehumanizing forms of labour, not to mention the complete 'abolition of labour'. As we shall see later, Marcuse fell under the spell of the same siren song of rhetorical unreality, even if not to the same extent.

Given his sweeping generic negation of the existent, devoid both of a historically viable subject and of a socially tangible object of negation, Adorno failed to notice not only that '*full employment*' was a strictly conjunctural phase in the socioeconomic order of 'advanced industrial society' (which 'cured' itself of this particular 'evil to be denounced' with devastating and lasting effects, it seems). Even more surprisingly, he remained blind also to the fact that the given mode of production was maintained in existence neither for the sake of '*deifying means*' (a grotesque mystifying notion), nor '*for production's* sake' (an even more grotesque one, given the real motive force of the established productive system), but for the much more prosaic (and socioeconomically quite tangible, even if by Adorno's 'critical theory' characteristically unnamed) purpose of *capitalist profit*. For he would only mention 'capital' when he could simultaneously blunt the edge of the necessary criticism by diluting its terms of reference in the spirit of the mindless 'marginal utility' theory and its '*consumer*', so as to make *labour* disappear altogether from the picture. Thus we were told that:

In its original economic setting, *novelty* is that characteristic of *consumer goods* through which they are supposed to set themselves off from the self-same aggregate supply, *stimulating consumer decisions* subject to the needs of capital. As soon as *capital does not expand*, or, in the language of circulation, as soon as *capital stops offering something new*, it is going to lose ground in the *competitive struggle*. Art has appropriated this economic category. The new in art is the *aesthetic counterpart* to the *expanding reproduction of capital in society*. Both hold out the promise of undiminished *plenitude*.[299]

If the denounced society was a 'mass consumer society', how could consumer goods 'set themselves off' (another personification) from aggregate supply for the purpose of stimulating individual 'consumer decisions', even if the latter were subject to the need of capital? To attempt to explain the contradictions of capital-expansion and competition – in an age dominated by *monopoly capital* – by subsuming them under the category of 'novelty' and its dysfunctions, was an astonishing example of *self-imposed* political-economic illiteracy, resulting in a total mystification. For the inner contradictions of capital-expansion manifest in the *inability* of the system to expand *no matter how new* the wares that capital in crisis has to offer to the individual or institutionalized consumer.

Another curious feature of this theory of capital-expanding 'novelty' was that, although Adorno continued to thunder against the 'reflection theory of art', he did not hesitate to offer as his own 'dialectical' counter-theory the crudest mechanical version of it, in the form of a *direct homology* (a distant echo of Lukács's theory of 'reification' and its impact on class consciousness, deprived of its social connotations). He seemed to assume that by turning *art* itself into a pseudo-subject ('art has appropriated this economic category') and by rebaptizing the process in question as 'the *aesthetic* counterpart' to capital-expansion, it would lose its mechanical/reflective character. (Adorno's favourite *methodological* device of peremptorily *personifying* things was frequently employed in the same way, in an attempt to transubstantiate mechanical notions into dialectical ideas. The idealistically treated 'subject' – in all its bewildering personified varieties – was supposed to be the self-evident authentication of the claimed dialectical character of this enterprise.)

Even marginal utility theory would not go in its absurd subjectivism as far as Adorno did when he attempted to subsume the motivation (or 'stimulation') of individual consumer demand under the category of 'novelty'. It had a much more plausible explanation of consumer choice by suggesting that the particular individuals allocated their resources between the available alternatives with a view for 'optimizing their marginal utilities'. This explanation, despite its total failure as the conceptualization of the *overall* process, made at least *some* sense, in relation to the individual consumer. By contrast, Adorno's shallow positivist – but romantically inflated – sociological concept of 'novelty' tried to turn the apologetic self-image of the advertizing industry (through which the latter rationalized and justified its parasitic appropriation of a not negligible portion of the available surplus value) into something frightfully profound, by decreeing it to be the key '*economic category*' that explained 'capital-expansion and the competitive struggle' on one side, and its 'aesthetic counterpart' on the other.

To make things even more vacuous, Adorno concluded his reasoning with a self-contradictory talk about 'the promise of undiminished *plenitude*' (in the context of 'novelty') as manifest in capitalist production as well as in the production and consumption of art. Yet, if there was anything at all that one could sensibly (even if somewhat tautologically) predicate about capitalistic 'novelty', it was precisely the spurious desirability of its *scarcity*-suggesting 'novelty value'. For by the time this 'novelty' became 'plenitude', of necessity it ceased to be 'novelty'. Thus, Adorno ended up by totally undermining his alleged 'economic category' of *novelty* in which mass-consumer-goods-producing capital – unlike *pseudo-novelty*-oriented Madison Avenue – could never be interested anyway.

Such was, then, Adorno's characterization of the economic laws which were said to rule the existent. All this was well in tune with the nature and spirit of his anticipations about the future. For, looking in the direction of the 'emancipated society' Adorno declared, in exactly the same vein of unreality, that 'a free society would situate itself beyond . . . the *means-end rationality of utility*.'[300] This assertion was perhaps the most surprising one to find in a 'critical theory' of the established social order and its 'utopian counterpart'. By making it, Adorno identified himself with the Keynesian mystification which *conflated profit with utility*, as we have seen above, denouncing thereby something that the 'human species' (whether indicted or not by art) could *never* conceivably do without, irrespective of how refined its 'barbaric' appetites might become. For the continued existence of human beings, in no matter how advanced and emancipated a society, depended on a meaningful and truly economic relationship to the 'means-end rationality of utility', beyond the alienating material imperatives and constraints of *capitalist profitability*. The problem, as Marx saw it, was that:

> In a future society, in which class antagonism will have ceased, in which there will no longer be any classes, *use* will no longer be determined by the *minimum time* of production; but the *time* of production will be determined by the degree of its *social utility*.[301]

The contrast between Marx's precise definition of the issue, together with its feasible solution, and Adorno's confused advocacy of the Keynesian 'utility-denouncing' wisdom, could not have been greater. It showed how defective was Adorno's grasp not only of the present socioeconomic order but also of the orienting parameters of the 'utopian' future society, which he liked to invoke in his abstract denunciations of the existent.

3.4.6

Commentators have noted the bleak sterility of Adorno's *Negative Dialectics*. His *Aesthetic Theory*, despite the greater familiarity and immediate attractiveness of its subject matter to the reader, was an even bleaker exercise of going round in circles and getting nowhere. Reading it from beginning to end was a truly frustrating effort, and when the painful task was finally over, one was left with a feeling of void. Not that one could not find in this work a variety of typically Adornoesque formulations. In fact, much like before, Adorno wrote in his last work many memorable *phrases* and a totally unmemorable *theory*.

As usual in Adorno's writings, the problem in his *Aesthetic Theory* was that the particular details refused to add up to a coherent whole. For the author's verbal fireworks were not designed to illuminate their object, in its manifold dialectical connections with the *whole* (which the author denounced a long time earlier as 'the false'), but to dazzle the reader. Adorno constructed them in such a way that he himself should be able to have it not merely in *both* ways, but in *every* way that suited him. Unhappily, as a result, his striking formulations and aphorisms *cancelled out each other* even in his last, consciously synthesizing, work.

Not surprisingly, therefore, Adorno had to rationalize his failure as a paradigm virtue and as the universally valid *model* for 'the age'. As the editors of his posthumous *Aesthetic Theory* – his widow Gretel Adorno and his pupil Rolf Tiedemann – reported in their epilogue to this unfinished work, Adorno argued:

> that 'the *fragmentary* quality of a work becomes part of its expression' (because it expresses the *criticism of totality and systematicity* which is so much a part of his philosophy) obviating the *illusion necessarily perpetrated by spirit*,[302]

adding elsewhere in the form of a characteristically self-justifying (but otherwise quite empty) paradox that 'for *systematic* theories to disclose their truth content they must *disintegrate* into fragments'.[303] And when even after completing the third draft of *Aesthetic Theory* he had to admit to himself that, notwithstanding his 'desperate efforts',[304] the interminable fragments of his long manuscript simply refused to add up to a properly integrated whole, Adorno made a virtue out of it again. He theorized the fiasco as the only truly authentic way of writing an aesthetic theory for the age and, indeed, for the first time ever in history, since in his view all previous attempts – from Aristotle to Kant, Hegel and others – had to fail inevitably.[305] Instead of evidence and theoretical proofs, he offered a few more or less colourful metaphors in self-justification:

> Interestingly the content of thoughts has, *for me*, a bearing on their form. I knew and expected this all along. But now that it has happened I am dumbfounded all the same. *My theorem* that there is no philosophical 'first thing' is *coming back to haunt me*. I cannot now proceed to construct a universe of reasoning in the usual orderly fashion. Instead I have to put together a *whole* from a series of partial complexes which are *concentrically* arranged and have the *same weight* and relevance. It is the *constellation*, not the succession one by one, of these partial complexes which has to make sense.... This book must be written *concentrically* such that the *paratactical parts* have the *same weight* and are arranged *around a centre of gravity* which they *express* through their *constellation*.[306]

This is how in the end Adorno's consistent ideological/political evasiveness and its concomitant generic discourse on 'totality' revenged themselves against their maker, concealing his defeat from Adorno himself behind a self-absolving and even self-mythologizing ideology.[307]

Adorno could write his best pieces when his undertaking consisted in a well-defined negation of a fairly concise object, where the framework of his own reflections was constituted by the theoretical propositions of his adversaries, as we have seen in the context of his critique of Mannheim's Sociology of Knowledge. The specificity of that kind of enterprise worked in his favour, in that his rejections had a clearly identifiable object and therefore did not have to suffer the consequences of remaining generic and abstractly moralizing.

Many of his shorter critical works, in this sense, could sustain themselves on the basis of what they were set out to oppose. Indeed, often his specific negations offered partial insights which he hoped to incorporate into a general theory. The latter, however, could never materialize. This was by no means accidental.

In fact, Adorno's attempts at formulating a general theory were self-contradictory. For the building blocks from which he wanted to construct eventually the comprehensive theoretical edifice resisted, by their very nature, such a project. Adorno shaped his building blocks from the two-fold negation of both the existent and its various conceptualizations. Thus he built around himself a cage from the 'absolute negations' of the 'absolute negativities' which he 'indicted' (usually in the name of 'autonomous modern art' whose only authentic spokesman he claimed to be) as we have seen above, denouncing the very possibility of positive identification with anything in the world of the existent, including all commitment to the project of its revolutionary transformation.

Paradoxically, therefore, Adorno barred his own way out of the self-imposed situation, carrying with him the partial, but inherently negative, results of his intellectual achievements – the would-be building blocks of his final synthesis – as a millstone around his neck. Thus, he was 'whistling in the dark' in order to encourage himself when he declared that the truth content of systematic theories can only be disclosed through their disintegration into fragments. For there is an intrinsic dialectical connection between the *parts* and the *whole* also in theory, in that the overall theory both reflects itself into, and helps to illuminate through their manifold interconnections whose framework of intelligibility it constitutes, the parts themselves; and, *vice versa*, the dialectically constituted – that is, 'microcosm-like' – parts through their very make-up call for, rather than resist being sythesized into, an overall theory. By the same token, it is quite impossible to build a coherent theory from *disintegrative parts* which tend to undermine themselves even in their limited partiality, instead of being suitable to become the building blocks of a theoretical synthesis.

The only solution Adorno could, therefore, offer in his synthesizing works, without disengaging himself from his accumulated boundless negativities, was to inflate his own inability to articulate positive ideas into the constitutive principle of the universe by decreeing that 'art is able to utter the unutterable, which is Utopia, through the medium of the *absolute negativity of the world*'.[308] Curiously, Adorno never ceased to castigate 'the undialectical'. Yet, nothing could be more undialectical than his own hypostatization of the 'absolute negativity of the world', together with a great many other 'absolutes' which he cast in the same mould. Alas, out of metaphysical entities like 'absolute negativity', 'absolute reification', and 'absolute negation', one could never constitute a coherent and comprehensive theory.

3.4.7

The reasons why Adorno's work had to remain inherently *fragmentary* can be identified in the closely interrelated terms of (a) politics and ideology, (b) theory, and (c) methodology.

With regard to *politics and ideology*, Adorno's denunciation of *commitment* was of utmost importance. It provided him with an automatic justification of all kinds of evasion and accommodation and, worse still, their transformation into virtues, thanks to the good services of ideological rationalization. Thus, in his scathing dismissal of Brecht (and Sartre too) Adorno declared that 'committed works look like pantomimes'[309] and that 'the notion of a "message" in art, even when politically radical, already contains an accommodation to the world.'[310] From such premises he could draw the most self-comforting conclusions and illusions (while castigating the 'comfort' of committed art):

> The feigning of a true politics here and now, the freezing of historical relations which nowhere seem ready to melt, oblige *the mind* to go where it need not degrade itself. . . . This is *not a time for political art*, but politics has migrated into *autonomous art*, and nowhere more so than where it seems to be *politically dead.*[311]

As some sympathetic commentators pointed out:

> The political assumptions of 'critical theory' have weathered rather less well than those of Sartre's libertarian existentialism. It should be added here that the notion of a residual transcendental subject was structurally essential to Adorno's thought, furnishing the only point of leverage in a putatively totalitarian social order (and founding the possibility of a thought that could indict it as such). No assessment of his aesthetics can overlook this *semi-miraculous* persistence of the subject in a conceptual schema that posits its *complete reification*. Sartre's belief in the efficacy of individual engagement seems much less questionable than a theory in which the production of '*autonomous*' works of art is little less than *magical*.[312]

To justify his own practical accommodations, projected as the very em-bodiment of 'the autonomous mind', Adorno was constantly trying to invent the most absurd 'common denominators' between his adversaries, directed on the whole against the left. Thus, he decreed the identity between 'a wide spectrum of people from *Hitler* ... to *leftist writers*, who are wary of the concept of aesthetic avant-gardism [e.g. Lukács] because of their *zealous desire to be politically avant-garde.*'[313] This line of 'argument' represented the worst kind of *demagoguery* whose purpose was to discredit the left without entering into the substance of the aesthetic controversy itself on its own ground. He found it much easier, instead, to claim for his own stance an automatic self-justification as the one and only true cus-todian of anti-fascism. (This was all the more dubious since it happened somewhat belatedly. Hannah Arendt, a refugee from Hitler's Germany, condemned Adorno in no uncertain terms for what she considered to be his 'almost collaborationist mentality' during the 1930s.[314]) Similarly to decreeing the unholy 'communality' between Hitler and the 'leftist writers' whom he wanted to denounce because of their sociopolitical commitment, Adorno brought to a peculiar common denominator, as we have seen above, the 'monopoly of capital' and the 'monopoly of labour'. He pro-duced such arbitrary equations in the interest of his double-sided self-distancing from the existent out of which he tried to make a virtue. Sometimes this attitude assumed the most surprising forms by ahistorically projecting twentieth-century concerns even to the circumstances of clas-sical antiquity. Thus, Adorno did not hesitate to assume, in his pursuit of ideologically motivated 'self-equidistancing' from everything, the most extreme anti-historical position, so as to be able to lash out in all directions by means of empty analogies. In this sense, he was able to 'discover' already in the Aristotelian principle of *catharsis* 'the manipulative domina-tion of art by the culture industry'; and he could even talk of '*Plato's embryonic state socialism*',[315] directing the sting of the latter 'insight' against the actually existing forms of socialism, of course.

Naturally, Adorno had to pursue the rationalization of his accommo-dations also in the form of projecting his wishful thinking as an objectively unfolding artistic trend. Thus he repeatedly dismissed Brecht (against whom he was full of resentment thoughout his life) as someone who is 'naive and rationalistic in the worst sense of the term' and went on to say: 'It may not be far-fetched therefore to *predict the end of his present fame.*'[316] At the same time, the total unreality of his self-perception enabled him to collaborate with the worst forces of oppression in the name of 'the autonomous mind'. This is how his sympathetic commentators reported the circumstances under which Adorno's utterly self-debasing attack on Lukács – who was under house arrest at the time in Hungary – was published first in the CIA journal of West Germany (*Der Monat*) and soon afterwards in the other CIA funded journals (like *Encounter*) all over the world:

When the Hungarian Revolt erupted in October 1956, Lukács – while lucidly assessing the probable chances of success of an essentially spontaneous social explosion – did not hesitate to cast his lot with the cause of the insurgent workers and students. Participating in the Nagy government, in which he presciently warned against withdrawal from the Warsaw Pact, he was seized by Russian troops during the Soviet intervention, and confined in Rumania. Released in March 1957, he completed his preface to the book he had been writing, and sent it abroad. *The Meaning of Contemporary Realism* was published in West Germany in 1958. When it appeared, Hungary was held fast in the grip of repression, and Lukács was silenced in his own country, subject to attacks of increasing vehemence. It was this book that Adorno was to review ...

Adorno had become, in the same year [1958], Director of the Institute of Social Research in Frankfurt. No two situations could have been more contrasted. Adorno, at the summit of his career, was free to write wherever he chose in the Federal Republic. In the event, his essay was published in *Der Monat*, a journal created by the US Army in West Germany and financed by the Central Intelligence Agency. Adorno's strictures on Lukács's mental 'chains' thus had their own irony: when he was writing, it was Lukács who was resisting police culture, while Adorno was unwittingly yielding to it.[317]

How 'unwittingly' Adorno yielded to the forces of oppression, need not concern us here too much. Jameson also suggested that 'it may be easy enough in retrospect to identify his repudiation of both Lukács and Brecht, on the grounds of their political praxis, as a characteristic example of an anti-communism now outmoded with the Cold War itself.'[318]

Clearly, such matters must be discussed in their proper setting. However, what is directly relevant in the present context is that Adorno defined his own ideological/political position in such a way that in the name of the 'autonomous mind' he should be able to license himself to make whatever accommodations might have suited him under the circumstances. Thus, he could feel free to indulge constantly in the most scathing and generic denunciation of 'institutions' and 'bureaucracy' as such, while assuming paradigm bureaucractic and institutional functions – like doctoring Walter Benjamin's heritage and 'censoring' even his own writings that belonged to a more radical period – first as Deputy Director and then as Director of the Frankfurt Institute of Social Research, recreated in West Germany after his return from the US 'with the benevolent approval of the Adenauer regime'.[319] But more than that, he could also feel free to denounce some of the most courageous manifestations of the struggle for a genuine socialist transformation, collaborating quite happily even with the professional enemies of socialism in the name of 'the autonomous mind'.

In Lukács's case, Adorno surprised his readers even with a strange about-turn. For in the past he used to pay compliments to the thinker regarded by Thomas Mann as the greatest living critic and to whose discourse 'on the great forms of epic literature' and on 'reification' Adorno himself owed so much. However, all this changed drastically when Lukács – as an act of open and perilous defiance of the powers that savagely attacked him in Hungary and elsewhere in Eastern Europe, suppressing his publications wherever they could – committed the unforgivable effrontery of publishing his book on *The Meaning of Contemporary Realism* in West Germany, where Adorno considered himself the unchallengeable cultural institution of 'critical thought'. Thus, he joined Lukács's attackers, using terms of abuse against the Hungarian philosopher which would have made even a gutter press baron and his obliging editors blush with shame.

Here is a sample of Adorno's 'ideology-free' pronouncements through which he tried to exorcize the intruder from what he regarded as his own sovereign territory. He called Lukács an 'officially licensed' undialectical thinker and an 'inquisitor'; someone who in the manner of 'a provincial Wilhelminian school inspector' writes 'the most threadbare clichés of conformism' and 'doggedly clings to a vulgar-materialist shibboleth', since he is 'paralysed from the outset by the consciousness of his own impotence'; a 'dogmatic professor who knows he cannot be interrupted'; 'no bearded Privy Councillor could pontificate about art in a manner more alien to it' than Lukács whose views are 'at once philistine and ideological'; a 'Cultural Comissar' and a 'wilful misinterpreter' who dons a 'dictatorial mantle' and 'issues decrees'; 'the pedantry of his general manner is matched by his slovenliness in matters of detail' and therefore he has 'no right at all to an opinion on literary matters'; someone whose work is characterized by 'a stylistic amalgam of pedantry and irresponsibility', whose 'abuse brings with it all the horrors of persecution and extermination, and not only in Russia'; Adorno accused Lukács of 'joining the chorus of censors' (no doubt in the inner comfort of his house arrest), of putting Kafka 'on his index', and of doing all this in a 'stentorian voice'; worse still, he likened Lukács to 'public prosecutors who call for the extermination of those unfit to live or who deviate from the norm'; also, he mysteriously dismissed Lukács's critical appraisal of Thomas Mann as a 'fulsome flattery which would have nauseated the great chronicler of decay' (mysteriously because Thomas Mann died two years before he could have been 'nauseated' by Lukács's 'flattery', though presumably he would have enjoyed instead Adorno's refined and purely descriptive judgement of being 'the great chronicler of decay'); he dismissed Lukács on account of having a 'stultified bureaucratic mind' and, moreover, of writing in a way which is 'at once abstract and childish'; and he added for good measure, 'Here is a man desperately tugging at his chains, imagining all the while that their clanking heralds the onward march of the world-spirit.'[320] These were the terms in which Adorno felt free to denounce in the internationally networked and unashamedly cold-war-mongering periodicals of the CIA 'culture industry' someone whose profound socialist commitment and lifelong struggle against the dehumanizing power of reification no one could seriously doubt, not even Adorno himself. At the same time when he was indulging in such an inherently problematical enterprise (to put it mildly), the German 'critical theorist' continued to imagine that his own ideological and political accommodations represented the paradigm of radical independence in a world of 'total reification', corresponding to the highest vantage point of 'the autonomous mind'. No theoretician could extricate himself from the negative determinations of such a contradiction.

The *theoretical consequences* of Adorno's ideological and political self-rationalizations were far reaching. As mentioned already, his political-economic illiteracy was self-imposed, in that it suited very well his own ideological and theoretical position to substitute the most superficial categories of American sociology (like 'the desire to keep up with the Joneses' as the question-begging 'explanation' of 'the masses' relation to art and their relation to real consumer goods',[321] for instance) for historically up-to-date and comprehensive Marxian socioeconomic analysis.

Indeed, the adoption of such categories was coupled with the totally unsustained claim that they actually 'superseded' the Marxian theoretical framework, in accordance with the changed conditions of 'consumer society'. It did not seem to matter that the banalities offered by the new categorial framework were tailored in their original inceptions to the conjunctural conditions of a few capitalistically advanced societies (above all to US capitalism), and therefore could not be elevated to the position of a general theory without first passing the test of a serious critical scrutiny. In its eagerness to throw overboard the Marxian heritage, 'critical theory' proved itself utterly uncritical in relation to its new-found sociological ally.

The Marxian conception was articulated by its originator as a *global* theory in which the trends of development and underdevelopment had to be assessed in their dialectical interconnectedness, judging the validity of Marx's particular propositions and anticipations on the same basis. Adorno's generically negating but concretely far too accommodatory theory found most embarrassing the explosive implications of such a global theory that pointed an accusing finger in the direction of the highly privileged advanced capitalist societies. It was therefore not in the least surprising that there could be no room in this 'critical theory' for the critical examination of the *exploitative* relationship exercised by the 'metropolitan centres' of capitalist advancement over their underdeveloped counterparts. The vague and shallow categories which Adorno borrowed from the American sociological literature, in 'supersession' of the disconcerting Marxian discourse concerning the global system of exploitation and its explosive antagonisms, came to the rescue. Thus, he could conveniently take notice of the 'underdeveloped nations' only when he could simultaneously also condemn them for wanting to keep up with the Joneses, lamenting over 'the regression which threatens to overshadow the *European mind* as a whole, a shadow cast over the *developed nations* by the *underdeveloped ones* which are already starting to *follow the example of the former*'.[322] Thus, the theatrical 'world-pain' (*Weltschmerz*) of the 'autonomous mind' – and indeed on this occasion of the autonomous 'European mind' – could only be used for the purpose of obliterating the very real pain caused by denying the satisfaction of even the most elementary needs of the exploited people in the 'underdeveloped nations'. This was an *actuality*, in the establishment and continued existence of which the 'European mind' had more than its fair share of responsibility. To metamorphose, therefore, something extremely problematical into an *ideal* the way in which Adorno did this, was a good indication of the 'radicalism' of his approach.

Understandably, Marx's fundamental tenets could not be fitted into such a line of 'critical' reasoning. He had to be discarded altogether as someone whose diagnosis had been proved wrong and whose hopes and ideas concerning the emancipatory power of human needs have no real points of contact with the contemporary world. For:

> The once confident hope that the *needs of the people*, along with the *growth of productive forces*, would raise the quality of the social whole to a new and higher level has *no substance any more*, ever since needs have been made subject to *integration* and falsification by *society*.[323]

Thus, just as Adorno earlier declared that the Marxian definition of the relationship between being and consciousness was no longer valid, nor did indeed matter according to him any longer to know 'what depended on what' in the relationship between base and superstructure, here we were told that the Marxian characterization of the needs of the people, together with his views on the nature and limitations of the unfolding capitalistic productive developments, had 'no substance any more'. But to make plausible the decreed 'supersession' of Marx, his views had to be distorted beyond recognition. For the Marxian proposition that:

> Theory can be realized in a people only insofar as it is the realization of the *needs* of that people.... It is not enough for thought to strive for realization, *reality* must itself strive towards thought.... Only a revolution of *radical needs* can be a radical revolution

was meant to emphasize the importance of social agency as the material embodiment of all meaningful social theory, as opposed to the grotesque self-referentiality of the 'autonomous mind', be it presented in its naked generality or dressed up in this or that geographical costume. Similarly, Marx never thought that there could be a mechanical 'growth of productive forces' as such. For he *explicitly* stated the necessary dialectical inter-relationship between the *forces* and the *relations* of production in virtue of which the crippled character of the prevailing (capitalistically limited) social relations can and *must* cripple also the development of the *forces* of production. The postulate of the 'growth of the productive forces' in and by themselves *never* had, and never *could* have, any substance whatsoever. Consequently, the attribution of such a view to Marx, made in order to be able to negate and discard it – and thereby to refute him altogether as someone whose 'confident hopes' have 'no substance *any more*' – was somewhat disingenuous and missed its target by a thousand miles.

This is the context in which the intrinsically conservative meaning of Adorno's 'critical theory' came to the fore with great clarity, together with the self-imposed limitations of his political-economic ideas. For Adorno's earlier quoted assertion according to which 'the productive forces would *directly permit here and now*' the realization of an ideal social order, carried no information whatsoever about the real world. It constituted merely a rhetorical device through which the author's opportunistically double-edged self-equidistancing from the existent could be accomplished.

In the same way, in the upside-down postulate of the 'growth of productive forces' and their alleged direct emancipatory implications which were said to have 'no substance any more', the point of Adorno's statement was not an invitation to undertake an adequate assessment of the actual dynamics of productive forces, human needs, and the prevailing (antagonistic) social relations of production. Instead, the meaning of his enterprise consisted in uttering again his abstract and generic laments about the 'integration and falsification of needs by *society*' as such, transforming thereby the explosive dynamics of antagonistic interrelations into the static stalemate of a fully 'integrated society' from which, as a matter of definitional necessity, there could be no escape. This is why Marx's original terms of reference *had* to be so grossly misrepresented by this 'critical theory'.

In all this, Adorno's self-imposed limitation through which he conflated *abstract* potentiality with *real or concrete* potentiality was a decisive moment. He could never come to grips with these important dialectical categories because doing so would have undermined his fundamental theoretical pronouncements. Instead, Adorno consistently obliterated the line of demarcation between abstract and concrete (or real) potentiality, in the service of his ideologically motivated self-equidistancing and tendentious self-commitment to the virtues of maligning and condemning actual sociopolitical commitment. This determination to obfuscate the necessary lines of demarcation transpired also in the passage where he asserted that:

Art is the true consciousness of an epoch in which Utopia – the belief that this earth *here, now and immediately* could, in virtue of the present *potential of the forces of production*, become a paradise – is *as real* a possibility as total catastrophic destruction.[324]

The sobering truth of the matter is, of course, that whereas 'paradise on earth', as postulated in relation to the given articulation of the forces of production, is an absurdly *unreal* and totally *abstract* potentiality, 'total catastrophic destruction' is, on the contrary, a thoroughly *real* possibility for which all the necessary means have been *actually produced* many times over, awaiting only a few buttons to be pushed for their sinister realization.

By simply equating the two potentialities, as Adorno does, one can only nullify one's awareness of the devastating actuality of the second, together with the urgency of the feasible and tangible tasks aimed at its prevention. If, in virtue of Adorno's anti-dialectical obliteration of the vital distinction between abstract and concrete potentiality, one is '*as real as the other*', then the only discourse that one can pursue is the impotent rhetorics of 'total irrationality' in a world of 'total reification', thanks to the frequently but in vain denounced 'instrumental rationality' (said to be inherent in the 'dialectic of enlightenment') for which 'humanity with its barbarous appetites' and unwillingness to listen to the noble sermons of 'the autonomous mind' can only blame itself.

The adoption of such a framework of discourse meant for Adorno that the targets of criticism had to be defined in a quixotic way, advocating an imaginary attack on causality, on the 'means-end rationality of utility', etc. as we have seen above. Naturally, the chances of success of the advocated confrontations were even less promising than those of Don Quixote's duel against the windmill. For the Spanish noble lord could at least physically charge his imaginary enemy, whereas Adorno's targets were so abstract and unreal that they had to remain totally beyond anybody's reach. At the same time, the real and feasible targets of emancipatory action – necessitating the actual social commitment of real historical agents – were a priori ruled out by the 'autonomous mind' as *capitulation* to the 'crudely heteronomous demands which [Brecht] desperately imposed upon himself'.[325]

Adorno tried to extricate himself from his contradictions by substituting for historically concrete *social determinations* the questions of *technique*. This is why the solutions he offered had to remain *verbal*, instead of being genuinely *theoretical*, often dissolving themselves in the quasi-sophistry of arbitrary definitions and declamations. In this sense, it could carry very little weight when Adorno simply decreed that:

> The phenomenon of the *métier* is the *agency* that limits creation and prevents art from becoming a 'bad infinite' in the sense of Hegel's *Logic*. *Métier* determines the *abstract possibility* of art, hence transforms it into a *concrete possibility*. This is why every true artist is obsessed with questions of *technique* and method. And this is also what is legitimate about *fetishism of means* that is so ubiquitous in art.[326]

To establish the relationship between abstract and concrete potentiality in art, it would take a great deal more than to subsume them *by definition* under the word '*métier*', not to mention the rest of Adorno's definitional subsumptions under the same term which sounded very much like begging the question. In fact the real meaning of Adorno's statement was contained in what he did *not* talk about, rather than in what he made explicit. For, by linking the individual artist directly to society in general – i.e. the 'abstract individual' to the 'abstract universal': both of them inherently *ahistorical* – and by defining him as the generic embodiment of the *'forces of production'* through his *'métier'* (while abstractly/generically negating the *relations* of production), Adorno escaped again from the difficult question of the *historically specific collective social agency* as the real subject also in art, in the form of being dialectically mediated through the particular artists' complex *class relations*, in their inseparability from their *social commitment* which the German critical theorist so categorically rejected. This is why Adorno, on the one hand, had to personify 'art' and 'society' in general, in order to be able to confer a spurious 'collective dimension' on the isolated individual artist. At the same time, on the other hand, he had to substitute for the sociohistorical specificity of manifold dialectical interdeterminations between the material base and cultural/ideological/political superstructure, as well as between the particular artists and their social setting, the question of *technique*.

Paradoxically, however, by opting for such a solution Adorno could only extricate himself from the 'bad infinity' mentioned with reference to Hegel's *Logic* by way of a *definitional assumption* which suddenly (and astonishingly) metamorphosed 'the abstract possibility of art' into 'concrete possibility'. Unfortunately the same considerations applied also to his assessment of the *emancipatory potentialities* of the capitalist forces of production. By treating them as purely technical/technological factors, he conferred upon them the *mythical infinity* and fictitiously boundless emancipatory power of an *abstract potentiality*, in order to be able to squeeze the gloom of absolute negation out of them on account of their failure to materialize in the 'totally integrated' and 'totally reified' society of 'both sides', dismissing at the same time Marx's allegedly 'confident hopes' to the contrary. Yet, as we have seen, this whole line of argument was a complete misrepresentation of the real state of affairs and their conceptualization by Marx, based on Adorno's own false identification of the abstract and concrete potentialities of the existent, coupled with an equally complete disregard for the specific sociohistorical determinations and characteristic social embeddedness of the dominant technology as the – far from 'concrete-potentially' emancipatory – *capitalist* technology of 'advanced industrial society'.

The *actuality* of this technology is the way we know it, which happens to be immensely *wasteful* and *destructive*, as well as being socially articulated in such a way as to *necessitate* the subordination and exploitation of the overwhelming majority of humankind. As to its *concrete possibilities*, the picture is even less promising. For, apart from its determinate productive potentialities that could – subject to the inherent limits and contradictions of capital – extend the material power of this technology, delivering some actual gains to a relatively small number of people while maintaining the ruthless exploitation of the overwhelming majority, it also has as its *concrete possibility*, within quite easy reach, the total destruction of man-kind. The *'bad infinity'* of the *abstract potentialities* open to science and technology is in fact cut down to a manageable size, and thus turned into their *concrete potentialities*, precisely by their socially determined orientation and practical articulation. In the case of capitalist technology, this could not be more problematical, instead of being amenable to idealization.

Thus, all talk about the emancipatory potential of productive technology, including Marx's discourse in the *Grundrisse* and in *Capital*, necessarily implies the *radical overthrow* of the capital system itself, together with its sociohistorically specific technology. Indeed, Marx's anticipation of a socialist system of production quoted above – one in which *use* (and 'legitimate' need) are no longer determined by the crippling constraints of *minimum time*, corresponding to the dictates of capitalist profitability, but the time dedicated to the consciously planned production of non-commodifiable goods is allocated to specific production targets in accord-ance with their *social utility* – foreshadows a radically different orientation of both science and technology.

The abstract potentiality of 'technology as such' is a pure fiction. For 'technological potentiality' to lose its fictional character – frequently postulated by Adorno and others in the form of the miraculous 'here and now' possibilities of the 'forces of production' – so as to become truly synonymous with *emancipatory potentiality*, it would first have to be con-verted into the concrete potentiality of a practically viable and historically well defined socialist project, through whatever intermediary steps might be required to make possible such a conversion. But then, of course, one could no longer talk about the emancipatory possibilities of the forces of production as we know them 'here and now'.

We have already seen in Section 3.4.6 some of the major *methodological* concomitants of Adorno's ideological and theoretical position. Here we may confine ourselves to the discussion of a few additional aspects.

With regard to negativity as a key structuring principle of Adorno's work, at first its deeply problematical implications could remain latent, insofar as the pointed *aphorisms* and *paradoxes* of *Minima Moralia* and the early essays had for their object the assessment of the phenomenal manifestations of some specific contradictions to which a purely negative response seemed appropriate. Some people argued on this basis that he should have stayed with partial tasks which seemed to suit so well his method of writing, instead of venturing into the field of comprehensive theory which he more than once declared to be futile in his essays.

Such an alternative, however, was not really open to Adorno. For the partial negativities of his short essays and aphorisms were formulated from the standpoint of a *totalizing negativity*, and therefore even their limited validity depended on their linkages among themselves within the overall framework of his categorical negations. Moreover, the negative methodo-logical constitutive principle of his work as a whole resulted in a peculiar kind of 'accumulation'. For, given Adorno's general approach, the exten-sion of the debated range of subjects brought with it the multiplication of the negative signposts on the author's map whose meaning was far from self-evident. The *non-cumulative* character of his explanatory framework mentioned earlier was the necessary consequence of this multiplication of Adorno's rather opaque negative assertions. In order to make them (as well as the inherent nature of the whole enterprise) intelligible, he had to show, *either*, the *positive* dimension of the specific dialectical intercon-nections that could be located within the antagonistic framework of the established order (which he *could not* do, because of his generic and aprioristic negation of the 'totally reified society' in which 'everything is one', etc.), *or*, he had to demonstrate that his methodological totalizing principle of *negative dialectics* was, despite everything, feasible as the intrinsically meaningful overall strategy of throwing corkless bottles (filled with categorical denunciations) into the raging sea.

The methodologically insurmountable difficulty for Adorno was that he tried to derive *dialectic* from an incorrigibly *static* and undialectical categorial framework which he imposed upon himself through a set of aprioristic negations. Solving the problem by calling his own approach 'negative dialectics' was of no help. For the chosen categories resisted being synthesized into a coherent and dynamic whole. His cult of the '*windowless monad*' was symptomatic of this self-imposed difficulty. The dialectic of the relationship between *part* and *whole* was replaced in Adorno's 'monadology' by a frozen and self-enclosed metaphysical entity whose relationship with the real world could only be rhetorically postulated, but never demonstrated. Moreover, having declared that the whole was 'the false', it became hardly intelligible why should one even attempt to relate the 'windowless monad' to anything outside itself, not to mention the complete mystery of declaring that 'the work [of art] is a windowless monad of society'[327] as such. This 'conclusion' was no more than the last member of a series of non-sequiturs in which Adorno tried to combine, by definition, *abstract subjectivity* with *abstract potentiality* as well as *abstract universality* in order to derive from them the semblance of sociohistorical specificity. This is how Adorno constructed his line of argument:

> That totality of abilities called *métier*, while merely *subjective* in appearance, is in fact *potential presence* in the art work of *society* defined in terms of its *productive forces*. Thus the work is a *windowless monad of society*.[328]

The failure to establish the sociohistorical character of the work of art, and the subsequent solution of the problem by predicating the somewhat mysterious relationship between art and society under the category of 'a windowless monad', was by no means accidental. For it is quite *impossible* to define society as a sociohistorical reality merely 'in terms of its *productive forces*', transforming thereby the dynamic and dialectical interrelationship between the forces and the relations of production into a static stalemate between an abstract generality and its metaphysically hypostatized reflection in a 'windowless monad'. Similarly, the vague generality of Adorno's category of '*modernity*' was the consequence of liquidating the sociohistorical character of the issue at stake. Thus, adding the adjective 'sophisticated' to two abstract and static generalities could not turn them into a genuine dialectical complex. For, after stating that 'modernity is not chronological at all', Adorno could only define it as 'the most advanced consciousness where *sophisticated technical* procedures and equally *sophisticated subjective* experiences interpenetrate.'[329] What was missing, again, was precisely the *social determination and mediation* through which the categories of 'technique' and 'subjectivity' could acquire their true historical dimension as well as their dialectical meaning. And the reason for this absence was not an oversight but an ideological, theoretical and methodological necessity. For Adorno's abstract determination of 'modernity' was well in tune with the abstractness and vagueness of his category of 'advanced industrial society' which appeared a couple of lines further down on the same page.

Adorno's treatment of historical time was very problematical. One of his favourite methods for claiming self-evident plausibility for his boundless negativity was to say '*today*' (*Heute*), followed by an assertion. It seemed to him that by categorically opposing the present to the past – by merely invoking the word 'today' – he could justify his own negative decrees (like 'today it matters no longer what depends on what', which simultaneously also justified his dismissal of all practically feasible and effective commitment), as well as his assertion that there is *objectively* no alternative to the 'total integrative power of absolute reification' (yet another self-justifying declaration), nor could there be, consequently, any alternative to conceptualizing the existent in a way contrasting to his own.

This procedure was inherently undialectical, even when it was made in the name of 'negative dialectics'. Adorno disrupted the dialectic of *continuity and discontinuity* by simply declaring the preponderant rule of *discontinuity* on the authority of 'today', without attempting to show either its ground or its implications. Also, it fitted in well with his generic condemnation of the 'reified world' and its 'humanity with its barbarous appetite' to define 'autonomous art' as '*gloomy objectivity*'.[330] At the same time, he had to admit to himself that the undialectical one-sidedness into which he turned the dialectical oppositions – between 'old' and 'new', 'continuity' and 'discontinuity', etc. – could not be consistently sustained, and he tried to introduce some correctives into his line of reasoning.

Unfortunately, however, Adorno's correctives often amounted to very little, since his aprioristic 'negative dialectics' undermined the possibility of recognizing the objective determinations and dynamically unfolding inter-connections of social dialectics. Accordingly, he had to content himself with the kind of answers which he gave to the question as to how the non-gloomy and actually enjoyable 'old continues to be possible', when in his peremptorily and frequently stated view 'autonomous art' was supposed to be 'radically new' and utterly 'gloomy'. His answer was that such possibility arose 'because of the new',[331] And he added to this rhetorical evasion another verbal decree, in place of a theoretical explanation, insisting that this curious persistence of the 'old' (exemplified by the music of Bruckner) 'takes the concrete *shape of modernity* while at the same time being the *antithesis of modernity*'.[332] Thus, the question received a pseudo-answer only, since the original problem reasserted itself more puzzling than ever in its metamorphosed form – namely: how was it possible for the 'antithesis of modernity' to assume the 'shape of modernity'? To which no answer was even attempted. This is why the reader could not help the feeling of being back at square one after 250 pages of directionless exhausting journey.

An even more serious consequence of Adorno's method of introducing correctives as a mere afterthought into the one-sided negativity of his general postulates was that they tended to undermine his original asser-tions. This was like trying to build a house by making the left hand remove the brick which the right hand had just deposited on the wall. Thus, in a section of his *Aesthetic Theory* entitled 'Black as an ideal' Adorno decreed:

> If works of art are to survive in the context of extremity and darkness, which *is social reality* ... they have to assimilate themselves to that reality. Radical art today is the same as dark art: its *background colour is black*. Much of contemporary art is irrelevant because it does not take note of this fact, continuing instead to take a childish delight in bright colours.[333]

However, a few lines after hypostatizing the necessary blackness of auto-nomous art, Adorno had to concede as an afterthought:

> All the same, black art has certain features which, if hypostatized, would perpetuate our historical despair. Therefore, as long as there is hope for change, these features may be regarded as *ephemeral, too*.

Yet, even this reversal was not the end of Adorno's peculiar method of house building. For a few lines further down the reader was presented with yet another undialectical reversal:

> There is more pleasure in *dissonance* than in *consonance* – a thought that metes out justice to hedonism, measure for measure.[334]

In this way, Adorno moved from afterthought to afterthought, changing constantly the ground of his arguments and tending to undermine the partial insights instead of integrating them into a comprehensive theory. As a result, the details of his writings could not cohere, forcing the author both to reiterate them and to contradict them, thereby making it necessary for him to start everything over and over again.

Since the omission of the crucial sociohistorical mediations compelled and condemned Adorno to make a fetish out of *technique*, he had to elevate fetishism itself to the status of a *representative paradox*. He argued that:

> *Fetishization* is the word that sums up the paradox of art in a state of general uncertainty. The paradox is this: how can art, a human artefact, exist for its own sake? This *paradox* is the *life blood* of modern art.
>
> Of necessity, the new is the product of the will.... The new *wills non-identity* but, by willing, inevitably *wills identity*. To put it differently, modern art is constantly *practising the impossible* trick of trying to *identify the non-identical*.[335]

The – conscious or unconscious – model for this line of reasoning was Hegel's critique of Kant's and Fichte's conception of the Will. With a significant difference. For, in Hegel's view, it was a 'bewildering contradiction' of his two great philosophical predecessors that their conception of the Will 'requires that its End should not be realized', because 'if the world were as it ought to be, the action of the Will would be at an end'.[336] Adorno, by contrast, could see nothing wrong with contradictions, not even with 'bewildering contradictions'. He renamed them, instead, as 'dialectical tensions' and 'paradoxes', leaving things at that in the name of 'the autonomous mind' and of 'the most advanced consciousness'. How could it be possible for the mind to be so 'autonomous', and for consciousness to be so 'advanced', under the totally reified conditions of 'advanced industrial society', was never revealed. It was merely postulated that 'art is truly modern when it has the capacity to *absorb the results of industrialization*';[337] a task defined largely in fetishistic technical terms. What became abundantly clear, however, was that such a conception of the mysteriously self-generating and self-sustaining 'most advanced consciousness' – which could contemplate its diametrical opposition to the existent – could not be reconciled with an alternative view that tried to understand and transform the world through the dialectical unity and dynamic interrelationship of *social being* and *social consciousness*. This is why there could be no place for Marx in this 'critical theory'.

3.4.8

The solutions offered by the politically more active Habermas were by no means less problematical. His 'ideal communications community' and 'ideal speaking situation' championed a view of social conflict and of its potential resolution which could be described at best as 'naive'. However, a less charitable assessment of their substance should not find it difficult to pinpoint the apologetic intent behind Habermas's *consensus-orientated* super-eclecticism which embraced everything that could fit into such an orientation, from Parsonian structural functionalism to systems theory, and from analytical linguistic philosophy to aprioristic armchair-anthropology.

Lukács's definition of class consciousness[338] (which greatly influenced the original members of the Frankfurt School, as mentioned before) was transmuted by Habermas into the vague and vacuous category of 'collectively and bindingly interpreted needs of the members of a social system', so as to be able to impose on 'anti-ideological' social theory as its fundamental terms of reference and evaluation the 'limiting conditions and functional imperatives of society',[339] i.e. the anti-historical straitjacket of systems theory.[340]

Since no specific social determinations were indicated by Habermas, and since the obvious ones – namely the existing class-determinations – were spirited away without trace, it remained a dense mystery, what on earth could and would turn those 'members of a social system' into a coherent *collective* force, capable of 'bindingly interpreting their needs', unless it was their 'adequate knowledge' – i.e. their blind acceptance – of the 'limiting conditions and functional imperatives' of their society. And, of course, the limiting conditions and functional imperatives of society apply, by definition, to *all* members of society.

Thus, the 'how?' of this anti-ideological 'critical theory' was a priori decided by circularly *assuming* the conclusion of 'limiting conditions and functional imperatives' as the necessarily orienting *premisses* of the collectively binding interpretation of the individuals' needs. And the criterion of adequacy for the correct interpretation of their needs by the 'members of a social system' in such a circularly consensual world was the recognition of the inescapable functional imperatives of their world.

According to Lukács's original formulation the 'thoughts and feelings appropriate to the objective situation [of the particular classes]' were articulated in such a way that they could enable and induce the parties concerned to fight out their class differences. In Habermas, by contrast, the objective situation itself became synonymous with the 'limiting conditions and functional imperatives of society' as such, which therefore could not be challenged if one possessed a non-ideological 'adequate knowledge' of the social world.

Having severed in this way all links with a historically identifiable social agency of emancipation, all that remained to Habermas were the arbitrary assumptions of a transcendental pseudo-anthropology, from a fictitious 'primordial urge to self-reflection' to explaining social development as such in terms of 'an automatic inability not to learn'.[341] To this, he added a circular and convoluted deduction about 'agreement' and 'consensus' (even 'contra-factual consensus'[342]) guaranteed by 'communicative competency',[343] concluding his discourse on the significance of the 'ideal speaking situation' in the 'ideal communications community' with the axiomatically self-reassuring but singularly unilluminating assertion that:

'Always, when we begin a discourse and carry it on long enough, a *con-sensus* would have to result which would be *per se* a *true consensus*.'[344]

Naturally, the 'emancipatory agents' engaged in the production of such 'true consensus' could only be the privileged élite – the various 'experts' and self-appointed specialists in communication – who would carry on 'long enough' their ideal discourse (while others worked long enough also on their behalf), so as to sort out and transcend (i.e. to dissolve and 'explain away', in the spirit of linguistic philosophy) the identified differences.

More important still, the social universe in which this consensus-generating ideal communication could be effective, had to be *for a start* an essentially *conflict-free* world, rendering thus the labour of our 'ideal speakers' *totally redundant*. For if the social antagonisms themselves persisted in the real world, beyond the artificial walls of the 'ideal communications community', in that case no matter how long our competent communicators went on arguing among themselves, they were not likely to achieve anything whatsoever, other than graphically display their own *impotence*. On the other hand, if the objective contradictions of society no longer existed, the role of those (redundant) ideal interlocutors had to be confined to rejoicing over the already instituted fundamental consensus, advertising – in the spirit of 'communication' treated as a public relations exercise – its virtues and ideal potentialities.

Thus, the real meaning of Habermas's communications theory could only be an *apologetic ideological* one, concealing the persistence of structural antagonisms in advanced capitalist society and fictitiously 'superseding' instead the deficiencies of 'distorted communication' by the vacuous procedures of his circularly self-anticipatory and self-fulfilling 'ideal communications community'.

Indeed, Habermas's main theoretical concern was to show that 'modern societies'[345] – the societies of '*organized, advanced capitalism*'[346] – have successfully resolved their structural problems through a 'growing interdependence of research and technology, which has turned the sciences into *the leading productive force* ... thereby eliminating the conditions relevant for the application of political economy in the version correctly formulated by Marx for *liberal capitalism*'.[347] Having thus paid to Marx a left-handed compliment, giving him a pat on the back that simultaneously relegated him to the irretrievably bygone age of 'liberal capitalism', Habermas proceeded to jettison *all* of Marx's fundamental tenets in the name of bringing Marxism 'up to date'.

3.4.9

The first to go was the labour theory of value, on the ground that 'technology and science become a leading productive force, rendering inoperative the conditions for Marx's labour theory of value.'[348]

It is worth quoting at some length this 'refutation' of Marx by Habermas's 'critical theory'. It sets out from an upside-down perception of modern capitalistic developments, described as 'the *scientization of technology*'[349] when, in fact, what we are witnessing is a very dangerous process that should be characterized, on the contrary, as the pernicious *technologization of science*, with far-reaching negative consequences for scientific development itself, as we shall see later on.

The next step consists in a totally uncritical assessment of the military/industrial complex and of its allegedly beneficial consequences for civilian production. It goes like this:

> With the advent of *large-scale industrial research*, science, technology, and industrial utilization were fused into a system. Since then, industrial research has been linked up with research under government contract, which primarily promotes *scientific and technical progress in the military sector*. From there *information flows back into the sectors of civilian production*.

The last sentence is immediately followed by Habermas's rejection of the Marxian theory of value, with a curious justification:

> *Thus* technology and science become a leading productive force, rendering inoperative the conditions for Marx's labour theory of value. It is no longer meaningful to calculate the amount of capital investment in research and development on the basis of the value of unskilled (simple) labour power, when scientific-technical progress has become an *independent* source of surplus value, in relation to which the *only* source of surplus value considered by Marx, namely the *labour power of the immediate producers*, plays an *ever smaller role*.

With regard to Habermas's reasoning let us see a passage from the essay by Müller and Neusüss referred to in Note 350. It makes the valid point that:

> More recent state socialist theories [like Habermas's] are no longer formulated in terms of the social praxis of the labour movement (and hence, they are no longer really revisionist). They present themselves primarily as socio-political theories relegating the analysis of the 'economy' to economic theories. From the latter, they lift out those statements that fit with their conceptions. Habermas thus relies on Joan Robinson for the 'refutation' of Marx's theory of value, Offe on Shonfield, and all of them on the Keynesian variety of bourgeois economics. They no longer understand that to postulate as absolute the particular segments of the totality of the capitalist mode of production is already implicit in the particular sciences and in their division of labour with respect to theory construction. Glueing together statements in the various segments cannot result in a conception of the whole. Since Bernstein, however, all revisionists share the position that the production process – even where it is explicitly discussed – cannot be seen as the contradictory unity of labour and capital realization. Rather, it appears as a mere labour process which is still identifiable as capitalist only because of its specific legal and organizational forms. Luxemburg already criticized Bernstein because 'by "capitalist" [he] does not mean a category of production but of property rights; not an economic unit but a fiscal unit ... By transferring the concept

of "capitalist" from the relations of production to property relations ... he moves the question of socialism from the realm of production into the realm of relations of fortune [or, in more recent terms, the "well off" and the "underprivileged"] – from the relation between capital and labour to the relation between rich and poor'.[350]

Rosa Luxemburg's criticisms directed against Bernstein apply to Habermas just as well. But in addition to the confusion created by the reductive transplantation of the category of capital to the sphere of political relations, so as to make plausible its radically new mode of operation under the sovereign authority of the (benevolent) interventionist state, the assertions concerning science and technology as the leading productive force are not only factually incorrect with reference to Marx but also thoroughly mystifying in their substance. To anticipate in one sentence what we shall see in more detail, a *contradictory tendency* of capital – 150 years ago identified by Marx himself as such – is taken for granted by Habermas as the *unproblematical reality* of present and future development of 'advanced, organized capitalism'.

For one thing, the statements claiming to establish this tendency as an unproblematical fact amount to no more than a mere *tautology*. To quote Marx:

> The fact that in the development of the productive powers of labour the objective conditions of labour, objectified labour, must grow relative to living labour – this is actually a *tautological statement*, for what else does growing productive power of labour mean than that *less immediate labour* is required to create a greater product, and that therefore social wealth expresses itself more and more in the conditions of labour created by labour itself?[351]

As regard Marx's allegedly narrow conception of the labour power of the immediate producers as the only source of surplus value, a few quotations from the *Grundrisse* speak for themselves. For, in sharp contrast to Habermas's total misrepresentation of his views, this is how Marx actually assessed these matters as far back as 1857:

> The theft of alien labour time, on which the present wealth is based, appears a *miserable foundation* in face of this new one, created by *large-scale industry* itself. As soon as *labour in the direct form* has ceased to be the great wellspring of wealth, *labour time ceases and must cease to be its measure*, and hence exchange value must cease to be the measure of use value.'[352]
>
> As the basis on which large industry rests, the appropriation of alien labour time, ceases, with its development, to make up or to create wealth, so does *direct labour as such cease to be the basis of production*, since, in one respect, it is transformed more into a *supervisory and regulatory activity*.[353]

3.4.10

The question, then, is not whether or not one sees this trend – for Marx clearly identified it a very long time before his 'critical sublators' were even born – but what one makes of it. There are two major considerations in this respect. The first concerns the genesis of science and technology on the material ground of a historically specific objectification of labour, as opposed to their question-begging 'self-development' out of the assumed, somewhat mysterious 'characteristics of advanced capitalism'. And the second, even more important question, is tied up with the evaluation of the trend itself in relation to living labour, in its *global* context, and not merely within the rather exceptional circumstances of the – again arbitrarily and wishfully generalized – 'advanced industrial societies'.

Clearly, with regard to both questions Habermas and Marx are worlds apart. The first issue is assessed by Marx as follows:

> The development of the means of labour into machinery is not an accidental moment of capital, but is rather the historical reshaping of the traditional, inherited means of labour into a form adequate to capital. The accumulation of knowledge and of skill, of the *general productive forces of the social brain*, is thus absorbed into capital, as opposed to labour, and hence appears as an *attribute of capital*, and more specifically of fixed capital, in so far as it enters into the production process as a means of production proper.... Further, in so far as machinery develops with the accumulation of *society's science*, of productive force generally, *general social labour* presents itself not in labour but in capital. The productive force of society is measured in fixed capital, exists there in its objective form; and, inversely, the productive force of capital grows with this general progress, which *capital appropriates free of charge*.[354]
>
> The entire production process appears as not subsumed under the direct skilfulness of the worker, but rather as the *technological application of science*. [It is] hence, the tendency of capital to give production a *scientific character*; direct labour [is] reduced to a mere moment of this process.[355] The transformation of the production process from the *simple labour process* into a *scientific process*, which subjugates the forces of nature and compels them to work in the service of human needs, appears as a quality of *fixed capital* in contrast to *living labour*; ... individual labour as such has ceased altogether to appear as productive, is productive, rather, only in these common labours which subordinate the forces of nature to themselves, and ... this elevation of direct labour into social labour appears as a reduction of *individual labour* to the level of *helplessness* in face of the *communality* [*Gemeinsamkeit*] represented by and concentrated in capital.[356]

Thus, as we can see, while there is no trace in Marx of the simplistic view attributed to him by Habermas – a view capable of recognizing the importance of 'simple labour power' only in the development of capitalism – equally, he has no use whatsoever for Habermas's apologetic fiction of '*independent*' science and technology as the 'leading productive force'. For living labour, in conjunction with science and technology, constitute a complex and contradictory unity under the conditions of capitalist developments, no matter how 'organized' and 'advanced'.

It is precisely this contradictory conjunction of living labour with science and technology which Habermas wants to replace by a fictitious consensual configuration. This is why he must reject the Marxian categories wholesale. For, according to Marx:

> Capital itself is the *moving contradiction*, [in] that it presses to reduce labour time to a minimum, while it posits labour time, on the other side, as sole measure and source of wealth. Hence it diminishes labour time in the *necessary* form so as to increase it in the *superfluous* form; hence *posits the superfluous in growing measure as a condition – question of life or death – for the necessary*. On the one side, then, it calls to life all the powers of science and of nature, as of social combination and of social intercourse, in order to make the creation of wealth *independent (relatively)* of the *labour time* employed on it. On the other side, it wants to use labour time as the *measuring rod* for the giant social forces thereby created, and to *confine them* within the limits required to maintain the already created value as value. Forces of production and social relations – two different sides of the development of the social individual – appear to capital as mere means, and are merely means for it *to produce on its limited foundation*. In fact, however, they are the material conditions to blow this foundation sky-high.[357]

Thus, the *tendency* of capital to give production a scientific character is *counteracted* by capital's innermost limitations: i.e. by the ultimately paralysing, anti-social requirements 'to maintain the already created value as value' so as to contain production within capital's *limited foundation*. This is why this contradictory tendency – taken for granted by Habermas as an unproblematical and irreversible process of productive self-actualization of 'independent science and technology' – cannot, in fact, unfold to anywhere near the point where (capitalistically confined) wealth becomes 'real wealth', i.e. 'the developed productive power of all individuals', at which point the measure of wealth is 'not any longer, in any way, *labour time*, but rather *disposable time*'.[358] Indeed:

> The development of fixed capital indicates to what degree *general social knowledge* has become a *direct force of production*, and to what degree, hence, the conditions of the process of social life itself have come *under the control of the general intellect* and been transformed in accordance with it. To what degree the powers of social production have been produced, not only in the form of knowledge, but also as *immediate organs of social practice*, of the real life process.[359]

However, precisely because capital is and remains 'the moving contradiction', it must remain at an astronomical distance from actually and fully turning *general social knowledge* into the *immediate organs of social practice*, in accordance with the immense positive potentialities for regulating society on the basis of *disposable time*.

This is where we can clearly see why Habermas must jettison the Marxian categories of 'forces and relations of production' and replace them by what he calls the 'more abstract' (i.e. practically meaningless, Parsonian-type) pair of 'work and interaction'. For the plausibility of his consensus-oriented approach depends on the elimination of not only 'nineteenth-century contradictions' (like 'old-fashioned class struggles') from the picture, but also of the likelihood of new ones arising out of the clash between the *necessarily constraining* requirements of self-expanding exchange value and the inner dynamics of productive development. Hence the latter must be – imaginarily – extricated from its capitalistic integument by denying the existence of the relationship itself, both with regard to the present and the future, as well as retrospectively, with the exception of the brief historical phase of 'liberal capitalism'.

As a result, thanks to Habermas's 'new formulation of historical materialism', science and technology acquire an 'independence' unconstrainable by social productive relations, (or their structural contradictions, which no longer exist), and enjoy their new-found status as the leading productive force of society forever, relegating the 'ever smaller role of the immediate producers' to practical insignificance. (Incidentally: on what ground can Habermas continue to speak of science and technology as 'the leading productive force' while dismissing the Marxian categories of 'productive forces' and 'relations of production' as historically obsolete, is a mystery whose solution is known only to Habermas himself.)

3.4.11
By eliminating the labour theory of value with reference to 'science as the leading productive force', Habermas assumed a position virtually indistinguishable from that of the most openly anti-Marxist 'post-ideologists'. (In fact Daniel Bell was quick to voice his wholehearted agreement, quoting Habermas and concluding that 'a post-industrial society is characterized not by a labour theory but by a knowledge theory of value'.[360]) But this was only the beginning. It was followed by the statement that 'two key categories of Marxian theory, namely *class struggle* and *ideology*, can no longer be employed',[361] not to mention 'exploitation and oppression'.[362] Furthermore, Habermas also stated that:

> If the relativization of the field of application of the concept of ideology and the theory of class be confirmed, then the category framework developed by Marx in the basic assumptions of historical materialism requires a new formulation. The model of *forces of production* and *relations of production* would have to be replaced by the more abstract one of *work* and *interaction*. The relations of production designate a level on which the institutional framework was anchored only during the phase of development of *liberal capitalism*, and not either *before* or *after*.[363]

Thus, the list of 'superseded' Marxian categories grew into a most impressive one. It ranged from the 'labour theory of value' to 'class struggle' and 'class conflict', from 'ideology' to 'exploitation' and 'oppression', and from the 'forces of production' to the 'relations of production'. And since at an earlier point the categories of 'base and superstructure'[364] had already been dismissed from the Marxian theoretical framework, one could only wonder, with some trepidation, what might have been eventually allowed to remain from the original conception of historical materialism by the time Habermas had succeeded in bringing to a conclusion his 'new formulation'.

Needless to say, proofs were never offered, only dogmatic assertions and circular deductions. We were simply told that 'state regulated capitalism, which emerged from reaction against the dangers to the system produced by open class antagonism, *suspends class conflict*',[365] and that 'in advanced capitalist society deprived and privileged groups no longer confront each other as socioeconomic classes'.[366] Habermas should have tried sometime to convince of this 'advanced capitalist wisdom' the British miners who endured the extreme hardship of a *one-year-long strike*, in direct confrontation with the capitalist state, and stubbornly continued to conceptualize their predicament in antiquated 'liberal capitalist' class terms.[367] Obviously, however, there could be no room for such considerations in Habermas's apologetic ideological 'new formulation of historical materialism', structured around the circularly interlocking categories of wishful thinking.

In Habermas's 'up-to-date' categorial framework the 'Third World', too, could only make the briefest possible appearance, in appendage to the perspective expressed in the last two quotes above. Accordingly, we were assured that 'this model seems applicable even to the relations between the industrially advanced nations and the formerly colonial areas of the Third World. Here, too, growing disparity leads to *a form of underprivilege* that in the future *surely will be less comprehensible through categories of exploitation.*'[368] And that was where the case for the emancipation of the 'Third World' was left to rest by Habermas who continues to profess a 'eurocentrically limited view' (in his own words) even in his latest pronouncements on the subject, as we saw in Chapter 1.

In truth, though, other emancipatory projects did not fare much better either. The movement for the emancipation of labour was declared to be obsolete on the ground that 'the capital–labour relation today, because of its linkage to a loyalty ensuring political distribution mechanism, no longer engenders uncorrected exploitation and oppression.'[369] Tellingly, the methodology inherent in this 'new formulation' of the 'modern' capital–labour relationship – as representing the historical supersession of '*uncorrected* exploitation and oppression' (whatever they might mean) – operated through a network of circular cross-references. First, on the model of traditional revisionism (criticized already by Rosa Luxemburg, as we have seen above) it transferred, with arbitrarily 'innovative' theoretical reductionism, the question of *distribution* – as contested by capital and labour – from the sphere of *production* to the directly state-controlled *political* sphere. And then it concluded, with triumphant circularity, that as a result of the historically new location of the capital–labour relation within the framework of the state-interventionist, 'conflict avoiding, loyalty ensuring political distributive mechanism' (postulated by Habermas's theory), the 'conflict still built into the structure of society in virtue of the private mode of capital utilization is the very area of conflict which has the greatest probability of remaining latent'.[370]

Explanations of political/ideological developments were often attempted with reference to scientific/technical changes – which, together with state-interventon, seemed to be able to explain virtually everything in Habermas's system – as their self-evident ground. For instance, it was claimed that 'the leading productive force – controlled scientific-technical progress itself – has now become the basis of legitimation. Yet this new form of legitimation has *cast off the old shape of ideology*.'[371] But, again, the whole explanatory framework was enmeshed in self-contradictions and circularity. The emergence of the large-scale scientific-technical complex was explained as inseparable from vast, *directly state-controlled*, primarily military-orientated 'research under government contract' and its 'feedback' into the sectors of civilian production. At the same time, the legitimating power of the state-interventionist 'modern social system' was explained with reference to the '*quasi-autonomous progress* of science and technology' considered 'as an *independent variable* on which the most important single *system variable*, namely economic growth, depends'.[372] Thus, the requirements and 'feedback-mechanism' of large-scale scientific/technological development postulated the necessity of state-intervention, which in turn postulated the unavoidability of the existing type of large-scale scientific/technological development, which in turn postulated the 'modern social system' as locked into itself and legitimating itself,[373] and so on.

Understandably, from the point of view of such technocratically conceived system, the emancipatory project of extricating social life from the dehumanizing and destructive determinations of *capitalistically embedded* science and technology had to be dismissed with undisguised contempt:

> The idea of a New Science will not stand up to *logical scrutiny* any more than that of a New Technology, *if indeed* science is to retain the meaning of *modern science* inherently orientated to possible *technical* control. For this function, as for *scientific-technical progress in general*, there is no more '*humane*' substitute.[374]

Of course, the words '*if indeed*' did not indicate here the acknowledgement of the problematical/contestable character of the preceding assertion. On the contrary, they were interjected so as to underline the incontestable self-evidence of the one and only tenable view of '*modern* science' (corresponding to the needs of '*modern* society') advocated by Habermas himself. Yet, curiously enough, Habermas was censuring his opponents for their alleged failure to stand up to the test of logical scrutiny.

The 'logical scrutiny' to which he wanted to submit those who argued in favour of a non-reified science and technology was a technocratic/behaviourist interpretation of science, adopted by him as the necessary premiss from which it could be proved, with 'conclusive' circularity, again, that there could be no other interpretations beside it:

> Arnold Gehlen has pointed out in what *seems to me conclusive* fashion that there is an *immanent* connection between the *technology known to us* and the *structure of purposive-rational action*. If we comprehend the *behavioural system* of action regulated by its own results as the conjunction of rational decision and instrumental action, then we can reconstruct the history of technology from the point of view of the step-by-step objectivation of the elements of that very system.... Technological development thus follows a logic that corresponds to the structure of purposive-rational action regulated by its own results, which is in fact the structure of work. Realizing this, it is impossible to envisage how, as long as the organization of *human nature* does not change and as long therefore as we have to achieve self-preservation through social labour and with the aid of means that substitute for work, we could renounce ... *our technology*, in favour of a qualitatively different one.[375]

Thus, the emancipatory concern of those who tried to focus attention on the *necessary social embeddedness* of all technology was technocratically swept aside in the name of a fictitiously unmediated 'technological development' which was said to correspond directly to the 'structure of purposive-rational action'. And since the nature of '*our technology*' was categorically identified with the 'organization of *human nature*' itself – and who in his right mind would have dared to argue against such a final authority in our universe of purposive-rational action conclusively in harmony with Arnold Gehlen's behavioural system of action? – there could be no question of challenging the 'modern social system' and its (capitalistically structured) large-scale technology.

The only thing that was difficult to understand was, why on earth should one be concerned at all with contemplating an 'ideal communications community'? Since '*our* technology' in its necessary linkage to the '*modern social system*' directly corresponded to the *immanent* requirements and determinations of *human nature* itself, what problem was there left to talk about 'long enough' with a view to resolve? After all, we lived, if not in the best *possible* world, at any rate in the best *practically feasible* one, enjoying the benefits of '*our* technology' as articulated in accordance with untranscendable human nature and with the transcendental/a priori structure of purposive-rational action. And, in the truest spirit of Voltaire's Pangloss, nothing could be more reassuring than that.

3.5 THE DILEMMAS OF MARCUSE'S 'GREAT REFUSAL'

3.5.1
Marcuse's approach to social criticism was, in many ways, fundamentally different. His hatred and denunciation of the suffocating domination exer-

cised by the prevailing social order was passionate and uncompromising. Thus, it was all the more paradoxical that – as a result of adopting the socio-political perspectives which predicated the socially unassailable integrative power of 'organized capitalism' – his conception too had to suffer the paralysing consequences of a negation devoid of socially tangible affirmation. The substitute agencies of negation which he tried to devise (from the 'outsider' to the rather mythical psychological and biological forces of liberation) could not extricate him from these difficulties.

Notwithstanding some major differences with Adorno on other counts, *negativity* was the orienting principle also of Marcuse's philosophy, from *Negations* to *One-Dimensional Man*, and from *An Essay on Liberation* to *Die Permanenz der Kunst*.[376]

His *Essay on Liberation*[377] was typical in this respect. For the inherent dialectic of the positive and negative dimensions of social development was disrupted – indeed liquidated – by the one-dimensional stress on negativity. To such vision of the prevailing order of things only a thoroughly utopian 'aesthetic dimension' could be counterposed, on the basis of the Kantian *categorical imperative* and its modification by Schiller, in the cult of the 'aesthetic form'. Accordingly, in Marcuse's words:

> The future ingresses into the present: in its *negativity*, the desublimating art and anti-art of today 'anticipate' a stage where society's capacity to produce may be akin to the creative capacity of art, and the construction of the world of art akin to the reconstruction of the real world – union of liberating art and liberating technology.... A utopian vision indeed, but realistic enough to animate the militant students of the Ecole des Beaux Arts in May 1968.[378]

Such a vision may have been 'realistic enough' to animate (for a brief historical moment, that is) Marcuse's *'new historical Subject of change*,'[379] as opposed to what he considered to be the *'integrated working class'*. But how realistic was this opposition itself in anticipating the desired outcome of remodelling society, in accordance with the 'aesthetic dimension', through 'desublimation' and negativity?

Marcuse himself was forced to admit that 'the notion of "aesthetic form" as the Form of a free society would indeed mean reversing the development of socialism *from scientific to utopian* unless we can point to certain tendencies in the infrastructure of *advanced industrial society* which may give this notion a realistic content'.[380] Yet, all we were offered in this *essay* was a set of categorical imperatives, linked to the wishful stipulation of a somewhat mythically growing 'biological sensitivity': another 'ought', in fact.

Since Marcuse had to realize that the students of the Ecole des Beaux Arts were a somewhat insufficient 'new historical Subject of change', he ascribed to them the function of being the carriers of the emerging new 'biological and aesthetic needs'[381] in conjunction to which he could then describe the future in these terms:

> The *life instincts* themselves strive for the unification and enhancement of life; in *nonrepressive sublimation* they would provide the libidinal energy for work on the development of a reality which no longer demands the exploitative repression of the Pleasure Principle. The 'incentives' would then be built into the *instinctual structure* of men. Their sensibility would register, as *biological reactions*, the difference between the ugly and the beautiful, between calm and noise, tenderness and brutality, intelligence and stupidity, joy and fun, and it would correlate this distinction with that between freedom and servitude.[382]

With such noble peroration Marcuse turned his back to the real world and, for a short period, he went on projecting with great enthusiasm the *utopian counter-image* of the existent, sustained only by the precarious ground of wishfully postulated 'biological determinations'.

3.5.2
The weakness of Marcuse's and Adorno's position had similar roots. For although Marcuse (unlike Adorno) had great sympathy for 'the wretched of the earth', his overall social perspective was based on much the same misdiagnosis of the capitalist system's inherent productive potentialities and accomplishments as Adorno's. He, too, tended to exaggerate the role of 'technological progress' and 'technical capacities' (as developed under capitalism) for human emancipation, understating their fateful social limitations not only with regard to their actuality but also to their potentiality. At the same time, one-sidedly and unhistorically generalizing from the given and necessarily transient conditions of a few, highly privileged countries, Marcuse, too, greatly overrated the ability of the *global* capitalist system to solve its deep-seated antagonisms by making reification totally dominant in the social world. In this spirit, disregarding the ultimately explosive implications of the contradictory *whole* also for its privileged *parts*, Marcuse asserted with gloomy unreality that as a result of 'the greater happiness and fun available to the *majority* of the population',[383] 'the working class ... has become a conservative, even *counter-revolutionary* force'.[384]

Marcuse's position could not have been more paradoxical. For he was quite willing to admit that he was trapped by 'the vicious circle: the rupture with the self-propelling conservative continuum of needs must *precede* the revolution which is to usher in a free society, but such rupture itself can be envisaged only in a revolution'.[385] Thus he could only offer an abstract moral imperative – the mysterious 'emergence of a morality which might precondition man for freedom'[386] – as a way out of his self-imposed 'vicious circle', advocating the strategy of 'passing from Marx to Fourier'[387] and even to Kant. (As Marcuse put it: 'Here too, Kant's aesthetic theory leads to *the most advanced notions*: the beautiful as "symbol" of the moral.')[388]

To make things worse for himself, Marcuse not only categorically asserted 'the integration of the organized (and not only the organized) labouring class into the system of advanced capitalism',[389] but even tried to offer a *biological* underpinning to the alleged structural integration by predicating that: 'It is precisely the *excessive adaptability of the human organism* which propels the perpetuation and extension of the *commodity form.*'[390] This was in sharp contradiction to the Marxian explanation of the prevailing – historically and socially qualified – form of 'false consciousness' in terms of the 'fetishism of commodity', although Marcuse took his original inspiration in this respect from Lukács's account of reification and commodity fetishism in *History and Class Consciousness*.

Furthermore, Marcuse also insisted that the 'utopian possibilities' which he advocated were 'inherent in the *technical and technological forces* of advanced capitalism' on the basis of which one could 'terminate poverty and *scarcity* within a very foreseeable future',[391] Just as Macpherson hypostatized, in a world full of starvation, suffering and exploitation, that the question of 'material revenue' was now obsolete and therefore we must concern ourselves, instead, with the difficulties of securing 'immaterial revenue', Marcuse too asserted that 'the question is no longer: how can the individual satisfy his own needs without hurting others, but rather: how can he satisfy his needs without hurting himself'.[392]

Given such assumptions, Marcuse ended up with a picture that closely resembled the technologically premissed postulates of John Maynard Keynes which we have seen above, in section 1.1.3, no matter how far he might have wished to distance himself from the Keynesian social values and ideological aspirations. These were Marcuse's words:

> Is such a change in the 'nature' of man conceivable? I believe so, because *technical progress* has reached a stage in which reality no longer need be defined by the debilitating competition for social survival and advancement. The more these *technical capacities* outgrow the framework of exploitation within which they continue to be confined and abused, the more *they propel* the drives and aspirations of men to a point at which the *necessities of life cease to demand* the aggressive performances of 'earning a living', and the 'non-necessary' becomes a vital need.[393]

Thus, similarly to the Keynesian diagnosis, a radical change in 'human nature' was postulated. And just like in Keynes, no indication was given how such change might actually come about. We were only told that 'this qualitative change *must* occur in the needs, in the infrastructure of man',[394] to the point that the stipulated moral 'ought' of 'the rebellion would then have taken root in the very nature, the "biology" of the individual',[395] establishing in the 'organism' itself 'the instinctual basis for freedom'[396] and 'the biological need for freedom'.[397]

3.5.3

Nearly ten years after writing his '*Essay on liberation*', in *Die Permanenz der Kunst*[398] the optimistic tone of Marcuse's utopian 'anticipations' had disappeared without trace, leaving us with an even more pronounced emphasis on the Kantian categorical imperative and Schiller's 'aesthetic dimension'. Accordingly, art was assigned a meta-social, permanent and autonomous function, in the service of this categorical imperative, postulating that 'art's autonomy contains the *categorical imperative*: it must be otherwise'.[399]

Understandably, since the working class was characterized by Marcuse as 'integrated', and since it had to be admitted that the 'new historical Subject of change' had not achieved much,[400] only the categorical imperative itself (as manifest in the sphere of rebellious subjectivity, said to be the meaning *par excellence* of the 'aesthetic dimension') could appear as the postulated guarantor of 'it must be otherwise'.

The function of art – with its frame of reference defined as individuality and subjectivity overshadowed by death to which, 'in contradiction to bad existentialism',[401] only art could give a meaning – was identified as the *negation of reality* and as the (deliberately) utopian anticipation of a better future. But even the utopian anticipations were rendered extremely problematical by the overall pessimism. For, in Marcuse's words, 'aggression and destruction might be put more and more at the service of Eros; but Eros itself works under the sign of suffering, of the past. The finality of enjoyment is achieved through the death of the individuals. And perhaps finality itself does not last very long. The world is not made for man, and it has not become more human.'[402] This passage summed up better than anything else the general orientation of Marcuse's aesthetic dimension. Given such orientation, the function of art could only be conceptualized as 'a *regulative idea* [Kant again] in the *struggle in despair* for the transformation of the world'.[403]

The emancipatory strategy of this 'negative thinking' was undermined by two fundamental contradictions:

1. Marcuse expected art to generate the kind of consciousness he approved of, in order to overcome the problems produced by the 'integration' of the masses. At the same time he insisted that the artist (or writer) 'is obliged to take his stand *against* the people: *he cannot speak its language. In this sense the concept of the élite* has a *radical meaning* today.'[404]

Marcuse's élitism was the most paradoxical of all. For it was coupled with the abstractly democratic postulate of 'universal human emancipation'. The latter, however, had to remain abstract, and ultimately rather vacuous, since no emancipation is feasible without its socially identifiable agency: one capable of practically accomplishing the postulated emancipation. Thus, whether one explicitly sets out from élitistic ontological and epistemological premises, or 'takes them on board' in the form of isolating onself from the practically feasible social agency of emancipation, it comes ultimately to the same thing. For, the chosen social standpoint asserts itself at all levels of conceptualization, penetrating the innermost core of theory and methodology, ideology and epistemology, meta-theory and ontology. That is why a sincerely democratic thinker like Marcuse finds himself in the end, against the original intentions of his own theory, in the curious predicament of sharing and actively advocating an aristocratic position with which he would otherwise strongly disagree on strictly philosophical grounds.

Marcuse was forced into this dubious position by his own scheme of things which took for inescapable the condition of working-class integration and its deadly impact on collective consciousness. And yet, paradoxically, he expected from art – which *could not* and, according to him, *should not* speak the language of the people – the production of the right kind of consciousness in the masses while it was *structurally incapable* of communicating with them.

2. At another level, Marcuse talked about the future society as a 'permanent revolution'. However, he defined the *raison d'être* of the same society as '*Stillstellung*' (staying still): '*Stillstellung* in the will to power, contentedness in enjoying the given,'[405] yet stipulating 'the abolition of work not worthy of man' (*die Abschaffung der menschenunwürdigen Arbeit*) which in fact *necessarily presupposed* the 'ever-improving productivity' (*die immer verbesserte Produktivität*: the alleged enemy of the idealized *Stillstellung*) that he so passionately (and romantically) rejected in the same sentence. Social praxis, in Marcuse's words, was thus turned into a 'fight *against the impossible*' (*ein Kampf gegen das Unmögliche*),[406] and art had to be situated accordingly: 'In reality *evil triumphs*; there are only *islands* of good to which one can *escape* for short periods of time.'[407]

Sadly, and despite his original intentions, Marcuse ended up with a far from inspiring orientation for art – or indeed for any other form of human praxis.

The trouble with all such 'negations of reality' – in the name of the 'categorical imperative', the 'regulative idea', the 'necessary rupture', the 'struggle against the impossible', the 'irruption of the superstructure into the basis' etc. – was indeed that, ironically but *necessarily*, they led to the perspective of 'delivering the world to the existent': to a 'reality' in which 'evil triumphed' and from which only shortlived *escapes* could be 'regulatively' devised, to more or less imaginary 'islands of good', for the benefit of the cultivated (and even openly élitistic) 'individualities and subjectivities', as opposed to the collective 'bad totality' of the one and only really existent social totality.

Since the challenging problem of reciprocally determining (or 'totalizing') interaction and mediation of individuals, groups and classes was systematically avoided, or summarily treated under the category of 'integration', Marcuse could not help ending up with an utterly desolate and timeless 'evil reality' from which there seemed to be no way out. Furthermore, since the individual defended by Marcuse was separated from his real social bonds, the possibility of hope could only arise through the rather mysterious agency of the pre-Hegelian 'categorical imperative' and its Schillerian transformation into the 'aesthetic dimension'.

Naturally, Marcuse could not expect the isolated individual, notwithstanding the claimed 'radical meaning' of its élitistic subjectivity, to accomplish single-handed the work of the categorical imperative. Thus, he had to provide his individual with a *'collective dimension'* – by idealistically drawing a *direct line* of emancipatory connection between the *isolated individual* and the *human species* – that regulatively transcended the evil class-reality of organized capitalism. Hence Marcuse's idealization of 'instinctual rebellion', of 'the life instincts', of the claimed emergence of new 'biological and aesthetic needs', of 'incentives built into the instinctual structure', of choosing between values and disvalues as a matter of 'biological reactions', etc.

Understandably, the social effectiveness of such negation, grounded in nothing more secure than the abstract postulates of the categorical imperative and the dubious expectations of an 'instinctual rebellion' emanating from humanity's 'instinctual structure', had to remain rather remote. Thus Raymond Aron put his finger on a major weakness in Marcuse's approach when, from a position diametrically opposed to the latter's emancipatory intent, he noted that:

> It is not without irony that a critique of society obviously deriving from Marx should have as its supreme aim the pacification of human relations, while admitting its inability to achieve this. 'The critical theory of society possesses no concepts which could bridge the gap between the present and its future; holding no promise and showing no success it remains negative. Thus it wants to remain loyal to those who, without hope, have given and give their life to the Great Refusal.'[408] I am not sure that there is such an enormous difference between the Great Refusal, which is without hope and impossible to realize, and universal resignation.[409]

There was another irony as well in all this. Namely, that such diverse figures as Adorno, Aron, Habermas, Horkheimer, Marcuse, Popper, etc. – with ideologies ranging from the open complicity of 'piecemeal social engineering' with the given order to the desperate self-orientation of the 'negative dialectic without a standpoint', and from the apologetic transcendentalism of the 'ideal communications community' to the passionate denunciatory radicalism of the 'Great Refusal' – should find their unsuspected common denominator, notwithstanding their very different personal and political motivations, in their postwar conceptualizations of 'universal resignation'.

3.6 THE MAN FOR ALL SEASONS: WEBERIAN
THOUGHT AND ITS POSTWAR REVIVAL

3.6.1

Curiously, this resignation at times assumed – in the writings of those who championed 'the end of ideology' – forms that came very close to utter cynicism. As, for instance, in the case of Aron himself who categorically asserted, in sharp contrast to his radical scepticism with regard to his opponents' claims to knowledge, that:

> *I know* (and who does not?) that human history advances *blindly* upon the ruins of civilizations and over the dead bodies of the innocent. States are *built by violence* and are *maintained by force* that has become an institution, a *camouflage of violence* that is henceforth unperceived even by those who suffer it.[410]

The rhetorical 'and who does not?' – immediately contradicted by the reference to those who only *suffer* 'camouflaged violence', without *perceiving* even its existence, not to mention its provenance from the state – was, of course, in no way an invitation to voice an alternative view. On the contrary, it was an attempt at a priori ruling out the possibility of any (legitimate) disagreement with Aron's position. Moreover, by lumping together the first sentence with the second, Aron in his usual way presented the reader with a 'package deal' of acknowledging the undeniable – the state's self-maintenance by open or camouflaged force – on condition that one does not wish to do anything about it, since the diagnosed evil is supposed to be inherent in the necessarily 'blind' movement of history. Accordingly, one's resignation and capitulation to the 'endless renewal of alienation' – as contrasted with capitalistic (not-quite?) 'alienation', put in inverted commas – could be advocated as an 'anti-ideological' virtue:

> *Anti-ideology* as I conceived it ten years ago and as I still see it today means ... being resigned, not to present forms of 'alienation', but to the *endless renewal of alienation* in some form or other.[411]

How assertions like the ones contained in the last two quotes could be reconciled with talking about 'the end of ideology', is totally incomprehensible. What is clear, though, is that only the views of those who wanted to introduce major socioeconomic and political changes qualified as 'ideological'; just like only those who had a less cynical view of historical development and of the possibilities for a better future than the ones propounded by Aron and his ideological comrades in arms had to be dismissed as being hopelessly trapped by a preconceived 'philosophy of history'. The considerations, in terms of which the 'irretrievably anachronistic left' had to be curtly relegated to oblivion, apparently did not apply to the 'post-ideological' judges themselves. Not even when they were peremptorily reiterating the pessimistic clichés of a 'philosophy of history' reminiscent of Spengler and Arnold Toynbee.

Max Weber's influence in this respect was an indirect and rather complicated one. For, on the one hand, he had an incomparably more subtle conception of history than Spengler and his followers. And yet, on the other hand, his overall perspective was no less pessimistic than theirs, even if the underlying desolation was presented in an intellectually more palatable form. As Lukács noted:

> In his eyes, after all, the democratizing of Germany was only a technical step towards a better functioning imperialism, only an alignment of Germany's social structure with that of the Western European democracies. And these, he perceived clearly, were equally subject to the problems of "disenchantment", etc. in respect of their essential social life. Hence, when he began looking at the essence of the life of society, he saw nothing but general gloom all around.[412]

Weber could become the 'man for all seasons' of twentieth-century capitalism because he drew some ingenious lines of demarcation that suited the new intellectual needs of the epoch, as they were emerging in tune with the changing circumstances. As we all know, Kant had to find *'room for faith'* before he could become the universal philosopher and the unsurpassed model of dichotomous bourgeois thought, in contrast to the necessarily *episodic* influence of even Hegel, for instance. In the same vein, and more or less consciously bringing the Kantian approach up to date, Weber attempted to produce a new model of *reconciliation*, under the circumstances of incomparably sharper social antagonisms and – no longer deniable – explosive contradictions.

Thus, the magnitude of Weber's task was defined as the *reconciliation of the irreconcilable*: i.e. finding *'room for faith'* for the acceptance of a perspective that was gloomily acknowledged to be devoid of perspective. This he tried to achieve with two – complementary – intellectual strategies. The first consisted in an extreme *relativization of values*, coupled with the glorification of arbitrary *subjectivity* and of its dubious accommodations to the 'demand of the day', as required by the established order. In this sense, after sneering – with a scepticism verging on cynicism – at 'the many people today who are awaiting new prophets and saviours', Weber spelled out his credo in unmistakably relativist and subjectivist terms:

> Let us act differently, let us go to our work and satisfy the 'demand of the day' – on the human as much as the professional level. That demand, however, is plain and simple if each of us finds and *obeys the demon* holding the threads of *his* life.[413]

The same glorification of relativism and subjective arbitrariness was expressed by Weber a few pages earlier:

One thing is the Devil and the other God as far as the individual is concerned, and the individual must decide which, *for him*, is God and which the Devil. And this is so throughout the orders of life.[414]

As to the *ground* on which the individual himself could make *his decision*, that question was a priori ruled out of order; just like in Indian mythology, where the elephant was supposed to carry the world on its back while standing on the back of the cosmic turtle, and no one was expected to ask questions about the supporting ground of the mythical turtle itself.

All the same, the matter could not be allowed to rest at that. For even if in Weber's view the value-oriented choices could not be objectively justified, since 'the various *value spheres* of the world stand in *irreconcilable conflict* with each other',[415] a way had to be found to sustain the scientific enterprise itself. The latter had to be rescued from the disastrous implications of extreme relativism and subjectivism, stipulated as the orienting principles for the constitution of 'world-views' under the 'disenchanted' circumstances of the modern epoch. For this reason, the Weberian 'room for faith' had to be extended to embrace the totality of *science* as well.

This was the other side of our philosopher's Kantian coin. Accordingly, it had to be established both that those who chose science as their 'vocation' could – while being *incorrigibly subjective* with regard to their '*ultimate standpoint*' – nevertheless be *rigorously objective* in their scientific pursuit, and, at the same time, that the objective conditions of scientific activity as such enabled them to do so.

This solution had to be attempted, since the imperatives of self-expanding exchange value presented science and technology – on a scale never even imagined before – with their unavoidable *practical demands*. They were pressing for *objective guarantees* as regards the realization of those demands under the circumstances of a necessarily *longer time scale* – requiring capitalistic 'planning' and factually supported 'foresight' – for the productive as well as scientific/technological practices involved, in response to the ever-growing global interconnections and the new complications and contradictions arising from them. Understandably, therefore, it was quite inadmissible to apply to science the same criteria of orientation which produced with regard to the 'various value spheres' the relativism and subjectivism which we have seen above.

And this is where Weber's second ideological/intellectual strategy had to be brought into play. It was articulated as a methodology for radically opposing to one another the constitution of 'world-views' and the realm of 'factual knowledge'. A position exemplified in a passage enthusiastically quoted by Merleau-Ponty:

It is the *destiny of a cultural epoch* which has tasted of the tree of knowledge to know that we *cannot decipher* the meaning of world events, regardless of how completely we may study them. We must, rather, be prepared to create them ourselves and to know that *world-views* can never be the product of *factual knowledge*.[416]

Thus, Weber's message – echoed later by Raymond Aron and others – was that 'we only know that we do not and cannot know', as far as the historical unfolding of world events are concerned. Accordingly, we had to conceptualize the latter in terms of 'world-views' based on subjective choices, *'weltanschauliche* positions',[417] 'irreconcilable attitudes',[418] and 'value judgements about which nothing can be said in the lecture-room'.[419] However, the world of science could be rescued from the throes of this universal scepticism and relativism, provided that we adopted the up-to-date, Weberian/Kantian dichotomy of 'value spheres' and 'factual knowledge'. And since the radical exclusion of value judgements had been laid down as the necessary *and sufficient* orienting principle of scientific objectivity, even history and the social world could be made accessible to rigorous enquiry, on condition that such enterprise was guided by the aim of constructing 'ideal types', in accordance with the requirements of 'value neutrality'.[420]

By drawing in this way the lines of demarcation, Weber produced a solution that appeared to satisfy the demands for 'scientific exactitude' in the domain of untranscendable capitalistic 'rationality' and 'calculation', without interfering with the isolated individual's longing for subjective self-orientation and sovereignty in the sphere of values. Like the Kantian framework, the 'new universality' of Weber's solution offered to intellectuals many points of access and rejoinder, 'for all seasons' of the capitalist reality that went on renewing itself despite its contradictions. For Weber did not try crudely to deny the existence of the latter. Instead, he attempted the come to terms with them in an intellectually respectable form. On the one hand he advocated, as we have seen above, one's unquestioning submission to the 'demand of the day'. At the same time, on the other hand, he tried to introduce a critical distance by saying that:

> The *fate of our times* is characterized by *rationalization* and *intellectualization* and, above all, by the 'disenchantment of the world'. Precisely the *ultimate and most sublime values* have retreated from public life either into the transcendental realm of *mystic life* or into the *brotherliness* of direct and personal human relations.[421]

What a criticism! We cannot help feeling the deepest compassion for the plight of poor Don Carlos, born-again into the fateful cultural epoch of rationalizing and intellectualizing modern industrial society. For he has been condemned to the transcendental realm of the mystic life offered to him by the Grand Inquisitor – after being cruelly deprived of the brotherliness of the Marquis de Posa, as well as of the more tender personal contacts with his father's young wife – not because of the unfavourable socio-historical conjuncture with respect to the social struggle for collective emancipation, but because the 'fate of our times' had made the ultimate and most sublime values 'retreat from public life', in tune with the un-challengeable 'disenchantment of the world' that assumed 'the form of impersonal forces'.

3.6.2

Characteristically, the methodological precept – concerning the strictly subjective grounding of value claims – was violated by Weber himself every time the opportunity presented itself. For in the last quoted passage Weber was talking about values as if they belonged to a fetishistically given set of existents, arranged in relation to one another in accordance with the determinations of some absolute metaphysical hierarchy; as if on the basis of the latter one could refer objectively, and in the most generalized terms, to 'the ultimate and most sublime values', presumably in contradistinction to some lesser ones. Yet, if every individual could really find his 'personal demon', and in this way choose or define the values as it pleased him, constituting for himself as 'god' the same 'value sphere' that was defined as 'devil' by someone else, in that case talking about 'the ultimate and most sublime values' which have objectively 'retreated from public life' had to be totally meaningless or self-contradictory.

Naturally, such talk was introduced by Weber because it suited in the given context his generic, shallow, and socially vacuous 'critical' posture. Hence, the passage continued like this:

> It is not accidental that our greatest art is intimate and not monumental ...
> If we attempt to force and to 'invent' a monumental style in art, such miserable monstrosities are produced as the many monuments of the last twenty years.[422]

Such 'radicalism' must have, surely, more than satisfied every *bel esprit*.

Moreover, this fetishistic autonomization of values – as divorced from the deliberations of both individuals and social groups, while simultaneously superimposed upon them in an irrationalistic/mystifying fashion – had another function as well. For, in case someone started to have ideas about taking control over the 'disenchanted' conditions of society – ruled at present by the 'impersonal forces' acknowledged by Weber – he had to be badly disappointed. There was nothing much one could do about the world's 'disenchantment'. If the ultimate and most sublime values had 'retreated from public life, that was just too bad. The methodology of ascribing values to the 'eternal struggle of independent gods' served its apologetic purpose well. No identifiable human agency was indicated as responsible for the hypostatized 'retreat', let alone as capable of inter-vening practically in the process in question, with the aim of reversing it so as to render our social world less reified, less 'disenchanted', and less impersonal. The only appropriate attitude to the change in values described by Weber was to acknowledge that it had taken place, and to refrain from producing in art 'monumental monstrosities'.

Weberian criticism, thus, revealed itself as the ultimate form of accommodation. By declaring that 'world-views' – necessarily linked to irreconcilable sets of values – can 'never be the product of factual knowledge', he deprived them of any possible ground of *justification*, other than a purely subjective and thoroughly arbitrary one. (As we have seen, the Weberian criteria for choices had to make 'subjective sense'[423] only.) And by locating the whole discourse over values in the sphere of *isolated subjectivity*, he a priori excluded the possibility of a coherent and objectively viable articulation of 'world-views' and associated values on a *collective* and *socially effective* basis. But that was, precisely, the fundamental ideological meaning, as well as the structuring core, of the monumental, and with respect to its ideological/intellectual power of attraction in many ways even today unsurpassed, Weberian undertaking.

3.6.3

Significantly, while Weber was influential only in select intellectual circles during the first half of the century, the postwar period produced dramatic changes in this respect. It is true that some of his main works have been published in various languages, including English, well before the war. But they appeared in small editions, read by very few people, making no more than a strictly academic impact. After the war, by contrast, his earlier published works were reprinted, again and again, in quick succession, and formerly unpublished works too, together with popularizing selections from a cross section of his writings, appeared all over the Western world. As a result, within the space of a few years after the second world war, Max Weber – the far from easy to read 'intellectual of intellectuals' – acquired a mass readership on both sides of the Atlantic. Indeed, his work became the principal ideological and methodological inspiration for those who tried to elaborate an Atlanticist[424] sociopolitical 'world-view'.

Thus, Weber's growing postwar popularity was undoubtedly linked to a favourable historical conjuncture. Not in the sense that the postwar set of needs and circumstances should have constituted the one and only situation of great receptivity for the Weberian conception. Outstanding ideological conceptualizations of historically predominant social interests covering a longer time-scale are much more flexible than that. Like Nietzsche another 'man for all seasons' – Weber articulated his thought with socialism as the main adversary in mind. And that is what constitutes in this respect the *übergreifendes Moment*: the 'factor of overriding importance'. For so long as the fundamental lines of confrontation remain drawn, in a world historical sense, between capitalism and socialism, his influence is likely to maintain its vitality, or surface again if it goes out of fashion for some time, provided that certain specific historical conditions call for the Weberian type of 'reasoned' engagement – described by Raymond Aron as 'the politics of the understanding' and approvingly quoted,[425] with a qualification stressing even more strongly the reasoned and self-questioning element, by Merleau-Ponty[426] – rather than an immediate frontal assault of life or death, to be pursued to the bitter end.

As it happened, in the postwar period socialism had to be treated as an *interlocutor*, in the aftermath of the still all too obvious failure of the Nazi/Fascist attempt to *outlaw*[427] and violently repress it. This was particularly true in France, where disengagement from the crumbling Empire[428] had to be accomplished in the presence of a strong Marxist party. Accordingly, the usefulness of Weber – as an 'understanding' interlocutor and, at the same time, as a subtle ideological/intellectual enemy and 'sublator' of the Marxist position – could not be missed. Merleau-Ponty, in fact, described it in the following terms:

> Weber is not a revolutionary. It is true that he writes that Marxism is 'the most important instance of the construction of *ideal types*' and that all those who have employed its concepts know how fruitful they are – on condition that they take as *meanings* what Marx describes as *forces*. But for him this transposition is incompatible with both Marxist theory and practice. As historical materialism, Marxism is a *causal explanation* through economics; and in its revolutionary practices Weber never sees the fundamental choice of the proletariat appear. It thus happens that *this great mind* judges the revolutionary movements which he witnessed in Germany after 1918 as if he were a provincial, bourgeois German.... [He] never sees a new historical significance in the revolutions after 1917. He is against the revolution because *he does not consider it to be a revolution* – that is to say, the *creation of a historical whole.*[429]

Characteristically, what Merleau-Ponty was trying to do was to rescue the Weberian theory from its contradictions by suggesting that the embodiment of 'this great mind' in a 'provincial bourgeois' body was not a necessary connection; that his 'failure is perhaps only of Weber the man';[430] and that his blatantly anti-socialist blind spots were of no consequence because 'one can seek to read the present more attentively than Weber did, to perceive "elective affinities" that escaped him.'[431]

In truth, however, Weber laid down conditions which were radically incompatible not only with historical materialism as a causal explanatory system (i.e. asking it to turn its categories – defined by Marx as social *Daseinsformen*, 'forms of social being' – into vacuous 'ideal types'), but also with socialism and revolution. He never imagined for a moment that a socialist revolution could 'create a historical whole', for the simple reason that he considered capitalism – with its necessary 'calculation', 'rationalization', 'bureaucracy', etc. – fatefully *untranscendable*. It was, therefore, rather disingenuous of Merleau-Ponty to suggest that the structural incompatibilities and necessary ideological bias of Weber's conception could be removed by a 'more attentive reading' in the Weberian key – of those somewhat mysterious 'elective affinities' in the present. Sadly, in the end – as a result of an intellectual development perhaps not entirely free from *causal* connections with the social struggles of the epoch – Merleau-Ponty's 'self-doubting politics of the understanding' took him very far indeed from the originally anticipated fruits of Weberian politics and rationality: to the world of desolate mysticism and pessimistic isolation, at an astronomical distance from a socially meaningful engagement with the present.

3.6.4

The growing Weberian influence in the postwar period had a great deal to do with the way in which his work could be inserted in the unfolding confrontation with Marxist oriented socialism under the new historical circumstances. Both in a *substantive* sense, by opposing to it, like Aron and others did, the Weberian 'untranscendability' of capitalism (as the necessarily calculating and rationalizing, bureaucratic and authoritarian[432] 'modern industrial' society), and by adopting the *methodology* of the 'ideal types' in the name of which everything could be *relativized* and the very idea of objective laws and trends of historical development discredited, as we shall see later on.

But there was an equally important condition which favoured the diffusion of Weber's influence on both sides of the Atlantic. It was the suitability of the Weberian approach to provide the framework for the articulation of a 'world-view' needed by the radically changed postwar relation of forces – under the hegemonic power of the not only militarily but also economically victorious United States – which relegated British and French imperialism to a minor role. Of course, it was necessary to make some adjustments to the Weberian system before it could fulfil its new ideological role. Nonetheless, the required adjustments could be made, without too many difficulties, on the basis of real 'elective affinities'. This is how Weber rose to the intellectual prominence coupled with an otherwise incomprehensible broad diffusion which we have witnessed in the postwar period.

Having just emerged from the most destructive strife ever known to man, the 'world-view' of the new hegemonic power had to be eminently 'reasonable', promising a strife-free social order in place of the historically antiquated and discredited traditional imperialism. Also, the embarrassing fact that two European imperialist powers had to be unceremoniously supplanted by the new dominant power in the former colonies had to be made as palatable as possible by some common ideological frame of reference, so as to counter the accusation that the much advertised 'American way of life', in this 'American century' of ours, was merely the reimposition, despite its novel form, of imperialist domination and exploitation. Accordingly, the new world order was defined as releasing the positive potentialities of the 'modern industrial society', both in the advanced countries themselves and in the newly independent nations: in the former, by way of bringing to an end *class struggle* as such, and by simultaneously diffusing the benefits of growing prosperity; and in the 'underdeveloped countries', by extending to them the financial and technological resources required for '*modernization*', with an aim to raising them ultimately to the level of the very model of all modern industrial societies, the United States of America.

As already mentioned, the adoption of Weber as the leading social theorist and methodological inspiration (the 'meta-theorist' *par excellence*) of this period, and the adaptation of his system to the ideological needs of the 'new world order', involved repeated crossings backwards and forwards over intellectual and geographic frontiers. The theoretician who was presented in the writings of the 'post-ideological' ideologues – Raymond Aron and Daniel Bell, for instance – was by no means necessarily the 'historical Weber', but one made suitable to the ideological purposes for which he was expected to supply the ultimate intellectual authority. The influence of Talcott Parsons as a mediator of Weber to Europeans, from a characteristically American standpoint, was highly relevant in this respect. There is no need here for a detailed discussion of such mediations and modifications, interesting and revealing though they might be in their proper place. What directly matters in the present context is to stress that there was more than enough common ground between the new ideological needs and the original Weberian theory to make the postwar revival feasible and effective in its specific Atlanticist orientation.

On the face of it, this is contradicted by Weber's undeniable German imperial aspirations. However, one should not forget that he linked such aspirations to the question of an *internally stable* social order, on the model of the *Western democracies* which he wholeheartedly accepted, together with their 'disenchanted' conditions. Moreover, he sharply opposed *nationalism*, in the name of the same rationality of development and capitalistically inspired 'rational attitude' to social practices which fitted perfectly well the requirements of the neo-imperialist postwar world-view. The fact that this anti-nationalist and pro-Western 'democratic/imperial' conception was coupled with a doctrine predicating the necessary failure of socialism in the face of the untranscendability of capitalism, and that all this grew out of the European soil – hence had to be a priori absolved from any conceivable accusation of American cultural/political imperialism – could only enhance the representative significance of the Weberian outlook with regard to the dominant ideological needs of the epoch.

3.7 WESTERN 'UNIVERSALISM' VERSUS 'THIRD WORLD NATIONALISM'

3.7.1

The new ideological perspectives were not suspended in the thin air of ideology itself. On the contrary, they received a very firm institutional underpinning through a variety of 'universalistic' readjustments to the network of international relations, from the establishment of NATO to bringing together the unruly and often antagonistically opposed countries of Western Europe in the framework of the European Economic Community. Such institutions openly, and with far-reaching practical efficacy, challenged the traditional notions of national sovereignty as representing the chief obstacle to the realization of the new world order. The postulate of 'universalism' – a favourite theme of Weberian thought,[433] and even more so of its reformulation in accordance with the needs of the present by Talcott Parsons[434] – had to be asserted and defended both with respect to the evaluation of the established socioeconomic order itself, and in relation to ideology. (With regard to the latter, by sharply opposing the universalistic claims of 'post-ideology' to the narrow partiality of the adversary's ideology only, of course.) Thus, Raymond Aron insisted that 'a *universal* society is coming into being. . . . The West is dying as a separate "culture", but it has a future as the *centre of a universal society*.'[435] At the same time Merleau-Ponty advocated the establishment of a '*new universalism*' by way of escaping from 'the *conception of ideologies*'.[436]

It goes without saying, there could be no uniformity as to how intellectuals, who had set out from different directions in pursuit of different sociopolitical aims, would fit into the overall framework of the dominant postwar political/ideological perspectives. Some tried to reject it outright, formulating an alternative view, whereas others accepted it with a combination of apologetic enthusiasm and resignation. And others still – like Marcuse, for instance – found themselves in the awkward predicament of arguing within its framework not because they cherished the dehumanizing Atlanticist perspective of 'organized capitalism', but because they could not envisage any social agency to go beyond it, as we have seen above. What was impossible was to opt out or to ignore it. For the dominant self-reproductive needs of the overall sociopolitical framework – as articulated through historically specific state practices which correspond to the prevailing material relation of forces, in their *global* socioeconomic setting – set the margin of freedom within which, for or against, different ideological/intellectual images of social intercourse can arise and compete with each other.

Thus, it was a matter of paramount importance how the various intellectuals conceptualized the global interrelationship between the 'advanced' and the 'developing' countries. The more or less complete *absence* of this

POLITICS AND IDEOLOGY   157

problematic (like, for instance, in the case of the Frankfurt School) spoke just as loud as its openly pro-Western treatment, negatively affecting the viability of the whole conception. Not that one would have expected the advocacy of some romantic 'Third Worldism' as a substitute for the negating action of the working class allegedly integrated into the structure of 'organized capitalism'. Obviously, the social contradictions of the 'advanced industrial societies' could only be solved by their own forces of radical opposition, and not by some outside agency *for*, or *in place of*, them. Nevertheless, for an adequate formulation of the overall perspectives of development, it was necessary to take fully into account, already at the *given* stage of global interchanges, the inescapable practical implications – for the beneficiary Western countries – of the ongoing 'development of underdevelopment', not to mention the more distant repercussions of a potential blockage in the international pipeline of exploitation, with the unfolding of the inherent contradictions of capital in their global context.

Aron was a major representative of those who engaged in the most enthusiastic advocacy of the Atlanticist perspective, contemptuously rejecting all criticism of it as 'megalomania, anti-Americanism, the political "progressiveness" typical of Latin intellectuals whether they are on the banks of the Seine, in Havana, or in Rio de Janeiro'.[437] In pursuance of his aims, Aron introduced a fairly transparent ideological 'corrective', replacing *'capitalism'* by *'all modern societies'*,[438] so as to be able to assert that 'in the age of *industrial society*, there is *no contradiction* between the interests of underdeveloped countries and those of advanced countries',[439] and that 'the state of high development of some countries is neither a cause nor a condition of the underdevelopment of other countries'.[440]

The arguments used by Aron to support his totally uncritical position were at times truly astounding even by his own standard. Like, for instance, the following:

> The belief that the conqueror is responsible for the prosperity of the vanquished is quite a novel one. A century ago, the English ruling class did not feel any such obligation toward its subject peoples.[441]

Was the fact that the English ruling class had no scruples in its colonial ventures supposed to dispose of the case against the pernicious past and present practices of imperialist exploitation? Or was Aron's example merely to illustrate why he preferred Anglo-Saxon 'maturity' to the hotheaded and 'megalomaniac anti-Americanism' of Latin intellectuals?

Be that as it may, there could be no doubt as to the ideological meaning of the intellectual strategies adopted by Aron. On the one hand, he revived the 'scientific' idea of the ever-expanding – hence forever *strife-superseding* – surplus, postulated by F.W. Taylor, by saying that 'a *modern society* is in a state of constant change as well as of *constant expansion*',[442] and that 'the volume of wealth is no longer a fixed quantity; it *expands* with the increase in that fraction of mankind capable of applying *science* to industry'.[443] With this, the apologetic wisdom of Taylor's 'scientific discovery' was generalized and transferred from its original setting – concerned with the supersession of *internal* class antagonisms – to the international arena of 'enlightened' neo-imperialist class and state relations, redefining the Atlanticist social order as the post-ideological, aid and trade-oriented society of boundless expansion and modernization.

On this score alone the advanced capitalist countries had to be absolved from all responsibility with regard to the past and the present, while, of course, the existence of structural contradictions had to be relegated to the past for good, together with the 'anachronistic ideologies' that tried critically to conceptualize them in the present.

But Aron was not satisfied with offering merely this science and growth-oriented 'strife-free' solution. He added to it, on the other hand, an argument which wanted to justify – in the name of the massive regional inequalities generated by a gravely distorted neo-colonial development, under the tutelage of US capitalism – his thesis that there could be no contradiction between the interests of developed and underdeveloped countries, since all depended on science and efficiency.

3.7.3
Even this kind of rationalizing argument was not enough. For after asserting that in *the age of industrial society* there is no contradiction between the interests of underdeveloped countries and those of advanced countries, Aron continued:

> The former can make progress without the latter losing ground. What is more, progress in one quarter helps progress in the others (*at any rate, as long as raw materials are abundant* and the area available is capable of accommodating and *feeding the population*). And if these statements seem surprising to Brazilians, say, let them think a moment about the contrast between the different regions of Brazil. Can it be said that the poverty of the barren Northeast is attributable to the development of comparative wealth at São Paulo? Can it be said that the development of the Northeast would be impossible but for the corresponding impoverishment of São Paulo? The answer is obviously no. The Brazilians of the Northeast may think that São Paulo does not make a large enough contribution to the improvement of the poor states of the Federation; the taxpayers of São Paulo, on the other hand, may be of the opinion that too great a proportion of their taxes is spent on Brasilia and Recife. But no Brazilian, I think, would conclude that the development of the Northeast involves the impoverishment of São Paulo. And indeed, since true wealth depends on *efficiency*, why should mankind imagine itself to be involved in a *struggle* to the death when *there is no lack of natural resources* and all men can be taught to take advantage of them, even if some do not yet know how to do so?[444]

On closer inspection of this passage it is impossible to avoid the conclusion that we are offered in it a very strange mode of reasoning indeed. For the objectively *non-symmetrical* socioeconomic and political relations of domination and subordination are arbitrarily misrepresented by Aron – in order to reach the rationalizing conclusion prefigured right from the beginning[445] – as if such relations could be switched around in reality itself at will. As if one wanted to argue – which no one ever did – that helping to develop the desperately poor and ruthlessly exploited regions of the world would have to pauperize the United States of America.

Most certainly, however, capitalist developments in São Paulo had a great deal to do with the exploitation of the Northeast and the use of its 'surplus' population as a most convenient industrial reserve army. Just as the type of socioeconomic development we have witnessed in Brazil as a whole had a great deal to do with the interests of powerful capitalist groups in Britain, Germany, Japan, and above all the United States.[446] But, of course, no one in his right mind would think that this relationship also worked the other way round, or that it could be capriciously reversed. Raymond Aron's attempt to discredit the concern with dependency and exploitation by way of a *reductio ad absurdum* thus speaks for the colour of its 'post-ideological' position in no uncertain fashion. His method of trying to divert attention from the objective merits of the case itself by speculating about the Brazilian regional consciousness of some mythical 'taxpayers' reveals, of course, the same ideological interests.

Another characteristic of Aron's approach must also be noted. For there is an obvious contradiction between the beginning and the end of our quotation. And it is by no means an accidental slip. At the end he categorically states that '*there is no lack of natural resources*', in order to prove that there is no need whatsoever for strife and struggle. Clearly, this proposition is a necessary part of the promised solution through an 'ever-expanding and constantly growing' surplus in 'modern industrial society' which makes the social strife over the distribution of wealth historically 'antiquated', just as it was for F.W. Taylor. And yet, at the beginning Aron had to qualify his assertion that 'progress in one quarter helps progress in the others' – which is by no means self-evident – by adding that 'at any rate, *as long as raw materials are abundant* and the area available is capable of accommodating and *feeding the population*'.

The trouble is that the qualification, which obviously contradicts Aron's conclusion, is an equally necessary part of his conception as a whole. For he is well aware of the fundamental conflict of interest involved in the choice between appropriating by the developing countries, for themselves, their resources and the fruits of their own labour, or transferring the lion's share of it all, as they do at present, to the 'advanced industrial societies'. A conflict which can only intensify under the pressure of the unfolding social contradictions and demographic determinations. Since, however, the existence of fundamental social contradictions has been ruled out as far as the 'modern industrial society' is concerned, Aron can only acknowledge the 'demographic danger'. Even with regard to the colonial past he can only admit to a 'discrepancy between the increase in population and economic growth',[447] said to be the result of introducing the 'natives' to the fruits of 'Western science and culture'.[448]

Thus, from the point of view of Aron's Atlanticist approach the solution is seen as combating the danger of a 'population explosion'[449] – and its concomitant 'moral and material disaster' – which he puts on a par with that of a 'thermonuclear war'.[450] This is why the contradiction between the beginning and the end of the quotation here discussed is a *necessary* one. For the two irreconcilable propositions are structurally intertwined ideological articulations of the same class interests.

3.7.4

This line of reasoning had to constitute the ultimate proof for the validity of Aron's approach, as well as the last word in the polemics against the critics of neo-colonialism. For its double rationalization removed all blame not only from the governmental policies and from the giant transnational corporations of the dominant neo-colonial power,[451] but also from its repressive client régimes which tended to implement the 'democratic' developmental idea of 'modernization' in the form of the most brutal military dictatorships.

Understandably, from the point of view of this Atlanticist rationalization *nationalism* had to be condemned and opposed wherever it appeared. In the 'Third World' it was said to be advocated by those 'anti-American' intellectuals who nourished the 'impulse towards irrational and foolish hope'[452] that aimed at progressing in the direction of a 'radiant future', beyond the constraints of neo-colonial domination, that is. We have seen with what sarcasm and contempt Aron treated them in his jibes against their 'megalomaniac' unruliness.

But Western European varieties of nationalism had to be rejected just as emphatically. Of course, the argument used by Aron had nothing whatever to do with the merits of the case, defended in terms of political sovereignty and a demand for equality in inter-state relations by his adversaries. He presented an 'economic' argument, uncritically describing the prevailing relation of forces (dominated by the American military/industrial complex) in a way which implied that there was nothing one could or should do about it. He asked the rhetorical question: 'how can one get excited about the temporal grandeur of a collectivity which is incapable of manufacturing its own arms?', and gave the answer like this:

> The *American defence budget* represents three-quarters of the total military expenditure of the Atlantic alliance.... In our century, a *second-class nation-state* is not an adequate framework for full human expression.[453]

According to this logic, so long as France was a full-blown imperialist power – a 'first-class nation-state'; a 'politically mature master-race' in terms of the Weberian 'politics of the understanding' – everything was perfectly in order. Whereas now, presumably, submitting to the hegemonic internationalist political logic of the American military/industrial complex, as well as to the economic imperatives arising from the defence budget of the all-powerful ally, constituted the one and only adequate framework for full human expression in the Atlantic world. Granted the premiss of the prevailing relation of forces as the unchallengeable framework of our life, who could argue with that? And, especially, who could argue that alternative strategies, which dared to question such wisdom – by critically re-examining its premisses and pressing for a comprehensive *disarmament* as a way out of its false dilemmas – should be considered other than a Quixotic ideological relic from the past, if not much worse?

3.8 MERLEAU-PONTY AND THE 'LEAGUE OF ABANDONED HOPE'

3.8.1

Compared with Raymond Aron's unwavering liberal-conservatism, in Merleau-Ponty's case we could witness a very strange transformation over the years. In the immediate postwar period his 'world-view' contrasted rather sharply with Aron's conservative posture. As Sartre's friend and perhaps closest collaborator at the time – one of the co-founders of *Les Temps Modernes* and its political editor until their clamorous public break – Merleau-Ponty identified himself with the causes of the left and on several occasions strongly defended '*marxisant*', if not altogether Marxist, positions. In this sense, the trajectory of his intellectual development was all the more revealing. For by the early 1950s – i.e. the years of consolidation of the Atlanticist perspective, on the ground of the material and political/ideological support which it received from a wide range of powerful institutions, from NATO to the budding EEC, as mentioned before – his position was virtually indistinguishable from that of Raymond Aron. Thus, in 1954, when he wrote *Adventures of the Dialectic* – the same year in which Aron wrote the book that established his world fame: *The Opium of the Intellectuals* – they shared not only their intellectual hero, Max Weber (who figured prominently in both works), but also a thoroughly sceptical and conservative approach to the great social issues of the contemporary world.

To understand the nature and magnitude of Merleau-Ponty's ideological metamorphosis, we have to recall that in July 1948 – in a polemic against the American C.L. Sulzberger, a special correspondent of the *New York Times* – he was still quoting with full approval the Fourth International's condemnation of Burnham, Eastman, Sidney Hook, Schachtman, Victor Serge and Souvarine as 'intellectuals in retreat' who belonged to the 'league of abandoned hope' and constituted a 'brotherhood of renegades'.[454] At the same time he strongly criticized General de Gaulle's chief adviser, the former communist André Malraux, for the interview he had given to Sulzberger and for an article which culminated with the assertion that 'the guarantee of freedom is the force of the state in the service of all its citizens.'[455] Merleau-Ponty retorted with undisguised irony:

> This ambiguity of intentions which oscillate between creative freedom and the force of the State corresponds to that of a movement which brings together a handful of ex-Communists (in its headquarters) and militants who, as the elections show, are for the most part *conservatives*. Giving way to the passion for doing something at any cost, Malraux consents to see his movement only through his own past; he implies that he remains the same, that his Gaullism of today is his Trotskyism of yesterday. (Only one question here: in case Trotsky had won out over Stalin, would General de Gaulle have been a Trotskyist too?) We are right in the middle of an individual fog. But at just this moment, and just to the extent he gives way to the vertigo of self, Malraux stops being a political cause and lets himself be sucked in by the wave Sulzberger speaks about.[456] Through complacency towards himself, he becomes a thing and a tool.[457]

By the time the General was reinstalled in power by the French Right, in 1958, the irony towards him and his movement had been replaced by Merleau-Ponty's assurances, given in an interview, that 'it would take a lot to rob me of the respect I bear for General de Gaulle.'[458] In the same interview, Merleau-Ponty complained that 'we are living on the leftovers of eighteenth-century thought, and it has to be reconstructed from top to bottom'.[459] And the direction of the 'reconstruction' which he advocated under the circumstances of an extreme political crisis was reminiscent of Weber's conversation with the proto-Fascist General Ludendorff on 'democracy'. For, according to Merleau-Ponty:

> Fifty years ago Alain could still define the Republic by checks and balances and the *citizen's permanent polemic* against those in power. But what do checks and balances mean when there is no longer any action to check and balance? The only task, in 1900 as two centuries before, was to organize *criticism*. Today it is necessary, in continuing the criticism, to *reorganize the power*. Many stupid things are said against '*personal power*' or '*strong power*': it is genuine *strength and personality* which those in power during the Fourth Republic lacked.... There is *no freedom* in submission to each *shiver of opinion*. As Hegel said, freedom requires something *substantial*; it requires a *State*, which bears it and which it gives life to.[460]

Ironically, therefore, the Weberian '*self-doubting* politics of the understanding' (in the name of which he criticized Alain in *Adventures of the Dialectic*) turned out to be the advocacy of a strong state, with more than one trait of Bonapartism. Malraux had been censured in 1948 for an 'ambiguity of intentions' with regard to the possibility of such a strong state. By 1958, the concern with that question had disappeared in that Merleau-Ponty, without ambiguity, adopted the position which he had so forcefully opposed a few years earlier.

3.8.2

With that, Merleau-Ponty's long and tortuous journey from his proximity to Marxism to an unreserved identification with the most problematical, indeed reactionary, dimension of the Hegelian system, under the sign of 'the owl of Minerva [that] spreads its wings only with the falling of the dusk',[461] had been brought to an end. Naturally, Merleau-Ponty could not simply become a Gaullist militant. His intellectual formation, and some of the ideological commitments of his past, to which he remained faithful despite the major changes which had occurred since the early 1950s in other respects, did not allow him to take that step. In any case, by the time of de Gaulle's return to power Merleau-Ponty had lost all interest in an active involvement in politics. Thus, his journey had to end in resignation. Not surprisingly, thus, the final words of his interview raised a rather desperate question to which, of course, he did not expect an answer. These were his words: 'The officers prophesy; the professors sharpen their pens. Where are the counsellors of the people, and have they nothing they can offer us but their regrets?'[462]

In 1948 Merleau-Ponty added the names of Malraux, Koestler and Thierry Maulnier to the 'league of abandoned hope and the intellectuals in retreat', accusing them of having 'acquiesced to chaos', and dismissing at the same time what he termed the manoeuvres of 'Americanism'.[463] Even as late as 1950, in a sharp critique of formerly left-wing American intellectuals, he still insisted that the revelations about Stalin's labour camps should not divert one from a Marxian inspired, global and not 'social engineering'-type, socialist perspective:

> For along with Stalinism and Trotskyism, they [the intellectuals in question] have jettisoned every kind of *Marxist criticism*, every kind of *radical temper*. The facts of *exploitation throughout the world* present them with only *scattered* problems which must be examined and solved *one by one*. They no longer have any political ideas. As for the United States, they say with a straight face, '*we do not have class struggle here*,' forgetting fifty years and more of American history. 'Participate in American prosperity', such were at least the words of one of them. Seated, as if on the world's axis, on American prosperity, which has felt many shocks and, judging by the decline of Marshall Plan policies and plans for world re-equilibrium, is in the process of feeling new ones, they ask to make an *absolute* of it. And when we explain to them that they are in the process of sacrificing all political evaluation to this uncertain fact, and that *all things considered* the recognition of man by man and the *classless society* are less vague as principles of a world politics than American prosperity, that the *historical mission of the proletariat* is in the last analysis a *more precise* idea than the *historical mission of the United States*, we

are told, as Sidney Hook put it in *Partisan Review*, that it is urgent to send a few masters of thought of his caliber to France.[464]

On the basis of these considerations, Merleau-Ponty warned – with words of passionate commitment – the European followers of such ideological/ political strategies that they might 'end up, like so many American intellectuals, who have gone beyond everything, at *political nothingness*', challenging them to declare where they stood with regard to the condemnation or acceptance of '*compromises with colonial and social oppression*'.[465]

Ironically, a few years later Sidney Hook's idea, treated with sarcasm by Merleau-Ponty, was institutionally implemented in Europe through the agency of the 'Congress for Cultural Freedom' and its CIA-sponsored 'post-ideological' periodicals, and the former scourge of the 'league of abandoned hope' became one of the intellectual heroes of this new crusade against 'antiquated socialism' and Marxism. By the second half of the 1950s Merleau-Ponty's earlier rejection of compromises with colonial oppression had given way to castigating radical intellectuals – Aron's 'progressives' – for what he described as a 'moralizing' failure[466] in that 'they do not envisage any *compromise in colonial policy*'.[467] Similarly, the defence of 'Marxist criticism and radical temper' was replaced by his rejection of 'the Marxist philosophy of history' in the same spirit that we find in Walt Rostow's ludicrous theory of 'modernization'. Thus, exchanging Marx for a view identical to that of the crudest apology of American global domination, Merleau-Ponty argued that even if 'all the newly independent colonial countries ended up militarizing themselves and realizing a sort of communism, this would not mean that the Marxist philosophy of history is true, but that an authoritarian and non-bourgeois régime is the only possible outcome when political independence precedes *economic maturity*'.[468] Equally, the perspective of a 'classless society', to be realized through the 'historical mission of the proletariat', was abandoned by him with the excuse that '*the very idea of a proletarian power has become problematical*',[469] Thus, very little remained of the erstwhile political commitments of Merleau-Ponty – the intellectual who once passionately denounced all those formerly left-wing 'intellectuals in retreat' – after he had brought to its resignatory conclusion his own ideological retreat.

3.8.3
Perhaps the most obvious and – in their implications for repressive/exploitative state and class practices, as well as for the articulation of the intellectual's 'world-view' in support of them – the most important of Merleau-Ponty's recantations concerned the attitude to the former colonial territories. For in the immediate postwar years he did not hesitate to condemn François Mauriac in the sharpest possible terms, describing his

approach as nothing short of '*scandalous*'.[470] On that occasion, again, Merleau-Ponty used with great effectiveness the weapon of irony, saying that 'Mauriac repudiates colonialism "as it was practised in the nineteenth century" (*as if it had changed so much since then*)',[471] and he identified himself with the words of a Vietnamese who described the hypocritical 'division of labour' in colonial systems between the 'colonialists', and the 'administrators, writers and journalists', like this: 'The former act, the latter speak and are the former's moral guarantee. Thus principles are saved – and *colonization remains in fact just what it has always been*.'[472] By contrast, in the 1958 interview he described 'French public investment in the countries south of the Sahara' in the decade between 1946–56 as 'an *African Marshall Plan*',[473] insisting that 'we can no longer say that the system is made for exploitation; there is no longer, as it used to be called, any "colony of exploitation".'[474]

Following on from such premises to the question of what kind of policies ought to be pursued with regard to future developments, Merleau-Ponty produced a most incredible argument for denying independence to the colonies in the name of safeguarding world peace:

> I do not want Algeria, Black Africa, and Madagascar to become *independent* countries without delay; because *political* independence, which does not solve the problems of accelerated *development*, would give them on the other hand the means for *permanent agitation on a world scale*, and would *aggravate the tension between the USSR and America* without either one being able to bring a solution to the problems of underdevelopment as long as they continue their arms race.[475]

The openly apologetic character of this rationalization of colonial interests, which only to Merleau-Ponty was not transparent, became even more obvious in the next sentence when he got involved in a twofold self-contradiction. First, when – after insisting that *politics alone* could not solve the urgent demands of socioeconomic development – he advocated in place of granting independence to the colonies the concession of a *limited* '*internal autonomy*' and 'the means of *political expression* so that their affairs [i.e. the affairs of the colonial peoples] may become *really theirs*, and their representatives may obtain from France the maximum it can do in the direction of a "handout economy"'.[476] (In other words, since politics as such – even the politics of full independence – could not possibly bring about the necessary development, let us give them just a little 'internally autonomous' politics, carefully controlled by us and linked to some economic 'handout', and that should be sufficient and adequate to the job.) And second, when he had to admit that 'the difficulties are evident'[477] as regards the chances of success of the policy he advocated. Not surprisingly, therefore, Merleau-Ponty had to try to escape from this double contradiction into the idealization of an 'enlightened' colonial order (which did not sound that different from the 'white man's burden'). In this respect, again, the contrast with his earlier position was really striking. As we have seen, in his confrontation with Mauriac he sided with the Vietnamese who expressed his condemnation of the rationalizing role of 'administrators, writers and journalists' in no uncertain fashion. This time Merleau-Ponty completely reversed the positions and took the side of the 'Frenchmen, I should say administrators': 'One of them said to me: "We are teaching them to do without us." He was right. That is indeed *the mission of French administrators* under an *internally autonomous* régime.'[478] How utterly convincing. Just like the claim that '400,000 Algerian workers are working in France and feeding two million Algerians in Algeria itself . . . confirming the *fact* that this relation between Algeria and France [in 1958!] has *nothing to do with colonialism*.'[479] This defence of the established order was much worse than the earlier emphatically condemned '*compromise* with colonial and social oppression'. For it represented an attempt to *perpetuate* colonial and social oppression by pretending that they no longer even *existed*. In the end, by seriously advocating a position which tried to solve the debated problems by 'explaining them *away*', together with the fundamental social contradictions to which they referred, Merleau-Ponty did not seem to have noticed the ironical meaning of his own personal journey. Namely, that 'all things considered', the historical mission of the proletariat is a more precise idea than the historical mission not only of the United States, but also – and even more so – of enlightened colonial administrators, no matter to which country they might owe their allegiance.

But the most revealing statements of Merleau-Ponty's 1958 interview came towards the end, in response to the question why he opposed France's withdrawal from Africa. First he gave the moralizing rationalization – of which he was utterly contemptuous in his polemics against Mauriac and others in the immediate postwar years – by saying that 'because I think she was able to and still is able to do some *good* there'. And then he added immediately – in the spirit of Weber's 'master races, called upon to intervene in the course of global developments' – that 'because I would rather be a part of a country which *does something in history* than of a country which *submits to it*.'[480]

Now which were the countries that 'submitted to *history*' (not to the armies of big powers, imperialist invaders, and colonial exploiters)? Naturally, the small countries and the colonial peoples. And which were the countries that 'did *something* in history'? Obviously, the dominant powers; Aron's 'first-class nation-states': those which could 'manufacture the arms' needed for imposing their will on others; the mighty who did not hesitate for a moment to use their weapons, together with the required brutal methods, in order to impose on the smaller nations their vested interests. The magnitude of the oppression inseparable from Merleau-Ponty's 'doing something in history' was considered irrelevant. For Merleau-Ponty categorically stated on the same page, in undisguised justification of the established power relations – in accordance with Hegel's dictum: '*What is rational is actual and what is actual is rational.*'[481] – that 'I cannot consider this [colonial] encounter an evil. *In any case, it is something settled.*'

In the end Merleau-Ponty's answer to the suggestion: 'You seem to believe that our values, the values of Western civilizations, are *superior* to those of the underdeveloped countries' – came as no surprise. He agreed by saying that they were superior '*in respect of their historical value*'.[482] And that completed Merleau-Ponty's radical reversal of his earlier position on all major issues.

3.9 THE POWER AND ACTIVE ROLE OF IDEOLOGY

3.9.1

All these developments unmistakably displayed the heavy imprint of the postwar world. And there was nothing really surprising about that. For, as not the historical materialist Marx but Hegel himself had put it: 'It is just as absurd to fancy that a philosophy can transcend its contemporary world as it is to fancy that an individual can overleap his own age, jump over Rhodes.'[483] However, what Hegel omitted to say in his scathing dismissal of the views opposed to his own 'science of the state'[484] as mere 'opinions' – a justification of the *status quo* gratefully adopted by the no longer '*marxisant*' but '*de Gaullisant*' Merleau-Ponty – was that so long as the age in question continued to be torn asunder by deep-seated social antagonisms, it was totally unreal to expect the solution of the issues at stake by an incontestable 'science of the state', to the exclusion of the rival ideological/political conceptions.

Indeed, in the postwar period, too, the dominant ideological tendency of 'anti-ideology' had to develop and consolidate its positions in constant confrontations with competing tendencies and diametrically opposed views. Raymond Aron's never-ending polemics against 'Marxist-Leninists', 'progressives', 'Latin intellectuals', 'the new Holy Family of Althusserians', Sartre, and many others, were by no means exceptional in this respect. For the ideology of the established order becomes the ruling ideology precisely by demonstrating its ability to defend the prevailing material and political interests against those who question their viability as regards the essential requirements of the overall social metabolism and attempt to put forward a radical alternative.

Clearly, the dominant ideologies of the given social order enjoy an important *positional advantage* over against all varieties of 'counter-consciousness'. Since they assume a positive attitude towards the prevailing relations of production, as well as towards the fundamental self-reproductive mechanisms of society, they can count in their ideological confrontations on being supported by all the major economic, cultural and political institutions of the whole system. At the same time, since they identify themselves 'from the inside', so to speak, with the ongoing processes of socioeconomic and political/ideological reproduction, they can stipulate *'practicality'* as the *absolute prerequisite* for assessing the seriousness or categorical inadmissibility of criticism and the legitimacy of social change. Thus, it is by no means accidental that ruling ideologies insist on the insuperable virtues of *'pragmatism'* and *'piecemeal social engineering'*, dismissing (more often than not merely by the application of some exorcizing label) all forms of 'total synthesis' or 'holism', – i.e. in the self-assured words of one of their representative figures, any conception of the social order *'radically different from the established one'*.[485]

Furthermore, given their privileged position in the prevailing social order, they can dictate the general conditions and rules of the ideological discourse itself. This tends to bring with it serious consequences for the intellectuals who try to articulate some form of *counter-consciousness*. For the latter are compelled to react to the conditions imposed upon them, on a terrain chosen by their adversaries. Understandably, therefore, they often suffer the negative impact of being trapped by the framework and problematic of the dominant ideological discourse, as we have seen above on more than one occasion.

The necessary positional disadvantage of critical ideologies is manifest in two major respects, unfavourably affecting their conceptualizations of the negated social system and of the margin of meaningful intervention. On the one hand, in reaction against the pressure of presenting *practicable* alternatives – and 'practicality' is always defined, of course, from the point of view of the ruling interests – they tend to assume a thoroughly *negative* stance in relation to the contested issues. And on the other hand, in opposition to the dominant institutional network of the established order – the much hated 'system' – they often refuse to link their criticism to specific institutional structures, attacking *institutions as such*, and thereby exposing themselves to accusations of championing 'the impulses of *anarchistic individualism'*.[486]

Unfortunately, however, the negativity of their response in both respects tends to result in an *inner* weakness of the assumed critical position. First, because the *dialectic of negation and affirmation* is broken in favour of a one-sided negation which necessarily remains *dependent on the negated object* for its self-definition. And second, because the challenge of articulating the alternative theory comprehensively – on the plane of *individual* as well as *collective* action, together with all the necessary *instrumental and institutional* complexes required for its practical implementation – ultimately cannot be avoided. The radical critique of the social status quo must define its *'praxis'* (i.e. the practically feasible strategy of a revolutionary transformation) with reference to *its own*, inherently *positive*, ground.

In the final analysis, the question of radical criticism is inseparable from that of a *social agency* in relation to which it is feasible to envisage a *structural alternative* to the given social order. In other words, it is not possible to articulate the content of a radical social criticism in terms of the necessary institutional and instrumental complexes – i.e. with a fairly precise indication of its practicability on the appropriate historical time-scale – without the identification of an adequate social force capable of becoming the *hegemonic alternative*[487] to the ruling class (or classes) of the established order.

From this follows that one cannot point at will to just *any* agency of negation – the somewhat mythical 'outsider' of Camus or Marcuse, for instance – in expectation of the desired solution. The irremediably negative character of a theory is not a matter of arbitrary intellectual choice (let alone the result of some 'philosophical mistake'), but the necessary manifestation of its structuring core: the kind of agency (or 'the Subject', in traditional philosophical terms) to which it refers for the realization of the advocated perspective.

Accordingly, radical negations of the prevailing social order cannot free themselves from their dependency on the negated object and from the power of the ruling ideology which they try to compete with unless they can indicate a historically identifiable potential hegemonic force as their supporting ground. And since ideologies are – directly or indirectly, but nonetheless inherently – enmeshed with politics, operating within the inescapable confines of the state which institutionally regulates and controls the social metabolism as a whole (so long as states exist), critical ideologies and forms of 'counter-consciousness' cannot help being partial and one-sidedly negative in their self-definition unless they can offer a viable hegemonic alternative to the prevailing practices under the given state-formation on all planes of social life.

3.9.2

Naturally, such hegemonic alternative – which foreshadows as the condition of its realization the creation of a radically different structure of society (a priori ruled out by Aron and others) – calls for a very special agency indeed. Since, however, agencies with the power of constituting a genuine hegemonic alternative to the social order which they oppose very seldom arise in history, inasmuch as they do they necessarily determine the character of materially feasible and effective negations for an entire historical epoch. Consequently, it would be absurd to expect the appearance of fundamentally different revolutionary theories parallel to every conjunctural change – or even periodic crises – in that the time-scale of development of the social agency in terms of which radical theories must conceptualize the situation is measured in centuries, rather than in decades.

In this sense, asserting the historical validity of Marxism as the – for the foreseeable future – untranscendable revolutionary conceptualization of the globally unfolding structural transformations is not simply the acknowledgement of a great intellectual achievement but, more importantly, the necessary recognition of the broad epochal limits within which such theories and practical strategies of radical negation are bound to operate. This in turn also means that the *positive* dimension of radical negation, concerning the institutional and instrumental complexes required for its implementation, cannot be spelled out in terms of and as a direct response to the immediacy of the established order. Not even if the institutions of the latter are mirrored in the strategies of radical negation in an inverted form, with their meaning completely reversed. For that would still preserve the dependency of the socialist counter-consciousness on the negated object, intolerably restraining the possibilities of its own practical articulation. Instead, the radical negation of the ruling order must retain as its framework of reference – in the midst of all contingent sociological and temporal fluctuations – the broad epochal orientation from which it derives its ethos, as required by and appropriate to the historical margin of action (and freedom) of the alternative hegemonic force to which the theory itself is inseparably linked.

At the same time, the potential hegemonic agency in question – within the class determinations of the capitalist order: the working class, as far as the historical perspectives of socialism are concerned – is not an abstract theoretical invention but a tangible social reality, with its needs and conditions of existence that must be constantly reproduced, in accordance with the available means and possibilities. To say, therefore, that the working class is 'integrated' is either a truism or an absurdity. It is a truism in that the working class in necessarily 'integrated' insofar as it cannot help being an integral part of the society in which at any particular time (and place) it must reproduce itself while producing and reproducing the conditions of existence of the given society as a whole. And it is an absurdity, since the general category of *labour*, as the structural opposite and antagonist of *capital*, refers to the *totality* of labour of which only specific *parts* can be contingently 'integrated' into a particular society at a determinate point in history.

Likewise, to talk about the 'embryonic' state of the working class – in contrast to its anticipated radicalization and ensuing action for reshaping society, in tune with its inner determinations and objective requirements – refers to a historically *specific* condition, as manifest in some *particular* socioeconomic setting. Thus, the development of the working class as the hegemonic alternative to the established order can only mean the unfolding of capital's tendency of self-expansion to its point of saturation in a multiplicity of different social situations, together with the cumulative impact of the contradictions involved on a global scale. The maturation of capital's inner contradictions does not imply at all the emergence of a mythically homogeneous working class – with an equally mythical 'unified class consciousness' – somewhere well 'beyond the diversity' of its actual constitution, but 'merely' the intensification of the contradictions themselves at all structurally critical points of the sociohistorically evolving diversity itself. Only this dialectic of the global arising out of the multiplicity of the *tendentially* coherent specificities – as opposed to its superimposition upon the latter in an abstract/a priori fashion – can establish the validity of the overall theory within the framework of its *epochal* orientation. And by the same token, in view of its epochal orientation and criteria of self-assessment (call it 'verification' or falsification, or whatever else), particular instances of 'working-class integration' – as separated from and counterposed to the necessarily long-term global trends of development – can in no way undermine the fundamental validity of the socialist negation of the established order.

However, saying this does not mean in the least that one can ignore the complications, contradictions and setbacks that necessarily arise from the changing circumstances of the specific sociohistorical situations, deeply affecting the sociological articulation of the hegemonic force to which the socialist theory refers. Indeed, since it is always the locally/circumstantially defined *particular* social being of the working class which is inserted – as particular groups of people, with differents sets of very real interests of their own – into the overall dynamics of the world situation, the complex interaction of so diverse forces within the global framework of sociohistorical development can only be conceptualized as *uneven* development. Inevitably, such uneven development has varying impact on the particular social groups in question across time, bringing with it advances and relapses as well as major changes in the interests of the selfsame groups concerned. Consequently, insisting on the *epochal* validity of the Marxian theory is equivalent to acknowledging that its validity is *only* epochal. In other words, it means recognizing that while the general conceptual framework of this theory embraces the capitalist epoch in its entirety, it must be, nevertheless, constantly brought to life through specific reelaborations in response to the challenge of the necessarily shifting relation of forces in the *global* framework of *uneven development*.

3.9.3

Without the active intervention of a comprehensive ideology, the strategic potential of the more or less extensive changes that spontaneously are set in motion at different points of the social system cannot be articulated for want of a meaningful common focus which cumulatively retains and enhances their – separately very limited – significance. Accordingly, the particular changes devoid of a strategic frame of reference (which only a coherently defined ideology can provide) tend to be confined to the *immediacy* of their narrowly circumscribed potential impact.

This is where one can clearly see the fundamental methodological as well as substantive/theoretical difference between the apologetic ideologies of the established order and the radical forms of socialist counter-consciousness. For the former can safely afford to keep things within the confines of immediacy ('piecemeal social engineering' and the like) in that they already happen to be in *overall control* of the social order to which they a priori refuse to contemplate any radically different ('holistic') alternative. Thus, in such ideologies the vital methodological line of demarcation between immediacy and global orientation is blurred, indeed often completely obliterated. Moreover, their ideologically telling cult of immediacy is rationalized and elevated to the status of an ideal standard by their scornful denunciations of comprehensive socialist strategies – their polar opposites both methodologically and in a substantive sense – as 'totalitarianism', 'Marxist-Leninist philosophy of history', 'nineteenth-century ideology', etc. as we have seen above.

By contrast, radical socialist strategies cannot spell out even their most elementary objectives without challenging the power of immediacy at all levels and in all of its manifestations, from the mystificatory/ideological as well as repressive material/institutional complexes of the established state-formation to the 'internalization' of the unavoidable pressures of 'integrative' self-reproduction within working-class consciousness itself. At the same time, the radical negation of immediacy from the perspective of a social order radically different from the established one cannot satisfy itself with simply reiterating the epochal validity of its negation of the immediately given. Rather, it has to find the right course between the 'Scylla and Charybdis' of self-defeating compromises with the power of immediacy on the one hand (the all too well-known hallmark of 'revisionism'), and the abstract negativity of the categorical 'Great Refusal' on the other. In other words, the greatest positional disadvantage of all radical forms of socialist counter-consciousness consists in the immense difficulty of securing viable points of contact with the available social forces of practical negation, fully taking on board the objective requirements of the latter without abandoning their own epochal orientation which envisages the necessary transcendence of many of those immediately given – and in their generalized implications often undoubtedly very problematical – requirements.

The accusations of 'transcendentalism' and 'aprioristic philosophy of history' levelled against socialist strategies by establishment apologetics are, however, totally out of place here. For the radical negation of immediacy need not degenerate at all into transcendentalism simply as a result of retaining its epochal orientation from the point of view of which it can envisage the transcendence of the established order, as well as of its own limitations, of course, as tied to the particular determinations of that order at a specific time in history.

The whole issue hinges on the necessary *mediations* through which it becomes possible to establish the points of contact with the particular forces and conditions of potential negation without abandoning the epochal orientation of socialist strategy. The various forms of revisionism which define themselves through their manifold compromises with the power of immediacy – amounting in the end to a practical capitulation to it – do not need such mediations. Nor do the defenders of the established order have any need (or use) for *transcending mediations*. It is this revealing absence of the category of *mediation* from both approaches that establishes the far-reaching *methodological affinity* between revisionist 'reformism' and the 'piecemeal social engineering' of unashamed apologetics.

By contrast, socialist negations need not look for the necessary mediations in a vaguely anticipated *future* to which they directly link the theory itself. For that would certainly amount to no more than some sort of aprioristic transcendentalism. They can find the required intermediary connections between the negated immediacy, and the forces capable of historically superseding the ruling order, already in the antagonistically torn yet dynamically self-reproducing *present* itself.

Indeed, the category of 'transcending mediations' is meaningful only if its points of reference – i.e. the social forces and practices which can link the present to the future – are structurally operative, through the dynamics of their contradictions and reciprocal interchanges, in the prevailing order itself. The semblance of inertia, used by establishment apologetics to rule out a priori the possibility of a radical alternative to the given, can exercise its mystificatory power only so long as the particular social complexes and their manifestations are considered in *atomistic isolation*. It is, therefore, by no means accidental that such apologetics is as a rule philosophically wedded to *atomistic individualism* and radically opposes not only the idea of transcending mediations but also all *comprehensive* approaches that can fracture the carefully protected mystificatory shell of inertia.

3.9.4

In the sociohistorical reality there are, of course, no isolated facts but only reciprocally interacting social complexes. Consequently, the meaning of such complexes is always inherently dynamic, and it manifests itself through the complicated structural linkages which the particular instances of the prevailing immediacy have among themselves precisely in and through their interactive totality. And since the social complexes themselves are objectively structured in this way – namely within a historically changing structure of reciprocal interconnections – the real meaning and potential of any particular instance can only be grasped in a comprehensive theoretical framework: one capable of taking fully into account the dynamics of their shifts and internal transformations.

This is how the *practically viable mediations* can become visible in the historically given present. However, they cannot become visible unless the immediacy of the specific social interactions and confrontations is transcended through a 'totalizing' evaluation which brings to the fore their 'hidden meaning', as inherent in their overall structural connections on the one hand, and in the historical trajectory of the fundamental structures themselves on the other. The point is that – to take the most problematical case wth regard to the perspectives of a radical socialist transformation – even if by themselves, in their limited but for the time being highly privileged social setting, some local manifestations of labour may exhibit the signs of 'integration' (e.g. the US), the overall picture, as linked to the ultimately unavoidable question concerning the indefinite sustainability or otherwise of the existing privileges, tells a very different story. For, assessed in terms of their manifold interactions with other forces and situations, as integral parts of the *comprehensive* framework of global development, even the most bewildering manifestations of 'integration' indicate on a more distant time-scale the necessary eruption of the underlying contradictions, and thereby the *tendential transcendence* of the prevailing condition and circumstances.

In any case, the socialist *transcendence* of the prevailing order can only be envisaged as a *tendency*, since its practical manifestations always refer to *particular* social forces and their institutional practices, with the possibility of relapses and even major reversals. This must remain the case so long as the tendency in question is not successfully accomplished on a *global* scale; or at least so long as one cannot speak of such a radical breakthrough in the relation of forces between global capital and the totality of labour which unambiguously points in the direction of the effective fruition of the tendency within a relatively short period of time. The vital role of socialist ideology as the radical negation of the established order consists precisely in identifying and helping to activate through its comprehensive orientation all those potentially transcending and liberating mediations which, without its active intervention, would remain dormant and dominated by the power of isolating immediacy as managed and manipulated by the ruling ideology.

PART II

SCIENCE, IDEOLOGY
AND METHODOLOGY

If I were a young man again and had to decide how to make a living, I would not try to become a scientist or scholar or teacher. I would rather choose to be a plumber or a peddler, in the hope of finding that modest degree of independence still available under present circumstances.

Einstein

Every philosophy is *practical*, even the one which at first appears to be the most contemplative. Its *method* is a *social and political weapon*. The analytical, critical rationalism of the great Cartesians has survived them; born from conflict, it looked back to clarify the conflict. At the time when the bourgeoisie sought to undermine the institutions of the Ancien Régime, it attacked the outworn significations which tried to justify them. Later it gave service to liberalism, and it provided a doctrine for procedures that attempted to realize the 'atomization' of the Proletariat.

Sartre

4 · SCIENCE AS LEGITIMATOR OF IDEOLOGICAL INTERESTS

4.1 PLURALISM AND LEGITIMATION

Representatives of the ruling ideology never tire of extolling their 'pluralism'. Irrespective of the fairly obvious apologetic intent of such claim as counterposed to the alleged 'holism' and 'totalitarianism' of the adversary, there is a certain degree of truth in it, in the sense that several contrasting ideological approaches are compatible with the overall social imperatives of the established order.

To be sure, on capitalistic material foundations the pluralism in question cannot reach very far. For its absolute parameters are set by the a priori presupposition of the capitalistic material and institutional foundations of social life as such to which there can be no alternative. Nevertheless, it is inseparable from the very nature of capital to be constituted as the untranscendable *plurality of capitals*. Indeed, no amount of concentration and centralization of capital can radically alter this constitution. It can only increase the relative size of the constituent parts and thereby intensify the structural contradictions of capital itself on an ever-increasing scale.

This means on the one hand that the ideologically much advertised pluralism *radically excludes* the legitimacy of being contested from the point of view and in the interest of the structurally subordinated, alternative hegemonic class. Consequently, in terms of the truly meaningful criterion of whether or not this pluralism embraces the whole of society, it can only amount to a *sham pluralism* whose real class substance comes to the fore at times of major crises. As indeed twentieth-century history amply testifies: from the emergence of Fascism and Nazism out of the soil of liberal capitalist societies to the more recent rise of the 'radical Right' on neo-capitalist social foundations.

On the other hand, however, the untranscendable plurality of capitals within the confines of the capitalist social formation itself makes the periodically attempted totalitarian remedy a necessarily *transient* phenomenon (however long), operable only in *limited* areas (however extensive), but in no way a *permanent global solution*.

The principal function of the totalitarian interval is to *reconstitute* the overall framework of capitalist social metabolism and thus to prepare the ground for a return to the pluralistic mode of political/ideological legitimation. Accordingly, in the aftermath of the totalitarian interlude the

representatives of the ruling ideology tend to dissociate themselves demon-
stratively from the historically just superseded 'state of emergency' which
many of them had actively helped to bring about in the first place. Such
change of attitude should not be considered merely an opportunistic personal accomodation to the new circumstances, no matter how strong that
motivation might have been in some well known cases. The issue is, rather,
the pressure emanating from the plurality of capitals as regards their
objective requirements of functioning.

Thus, the permanence of a totalitarian system on a generalized scale –
i.e. a configuration implying a fully closed network of monopolies as its
material foundation – in conjunction with the effective plurality of capitals
in a self-regulating market society is a contradiction in terms. By contrast,
the more or less voluntary suspension of the relative autonomy of the
particular units of capitalistic decision making for the duration of the state
of emergency only (whose purpose is the reconstitution of the overall
conditions of capitalist self-regulation) is an entirely different matter. Our
historical experience abounds in examples of the latter, produced under a
variety of forms both in Europe and on other continents.

Under normal circumstances the diverse interests of competing capitals
not only allow but forcefully stipulate the pluralist mode of political/ideo-
logical legitimation of the established order, so as to secure the effective
manifestation and interplay of the alternative strategies that correspond to
the objective differences of interest within the ruling class itself. The
transition from 'Butskellism' to 'Thatcherism', or from Rooseveltian 'New
Deal' to 'Reaganomics' (and their equivalents in other countries) provides
some graphic illustrations of how broadly the spectrum of capitalist pluralism can extend.

In this limited sense then, as reflecting the structural interplay of the
plurality of capitals within the established social order, the pluralistic mode
of legitimation, far from being an empty sham, is in fact most effective not
only among the competing interest groups of the ruling class but simultaneously also as a powerful regulator of the socio-political metabolism as
a whole. For up to a certain point its historically well-tried mechanism can
accommodate initiatives coming from the 'opposite side' – hence the well-
known phenomenon of 'co-option' – so long as the criticism can be confined to 'piecemeal social engineering' and, at the political level, to the
strictly circumscribed margin of manoeuvre of the institutionalized 'official
opposition' (as even codified under names like 'Her Majesty's Opposition').

Furthermore, since the terms of reference of this pluralism are set by the
non-contestable presuppositions and a priori 'constitutional' imperatives of
the prevailing social order itself, the class character of pluralism is never
really questioned by the institutionalized oppositional forces. For they are
themselves constituted on the premiss of operating within the predetermined limits of the adversary's framework of political and ideological

legitimation. Indeed, the openly acknowledged and ritualistically reiterated acceptance of that framework, in the name of *pluralism* – which fails to recognize the effective linkage of the latter to the partial interests of competing capitals as opposed to those of the overwhelming majority of society – makes the established mode of pluralistic legitimation one of the most powerful weapons in the arsenal of the ruling ideology.

Thus, on the plane of ideology a multiplicity of approaches are brought into action, ranging from the apparent 'value neutrality' and political aloofness of formalistic structuralism to the open apologetics of the Raymond Arons and beyond, all the way down to former Marxists turned professional anti-Marxists as well as to highly inflated media-creations like 'the New French Philosophers' (who are very far from being new, let alone philosophers).[488] Since value commitments can be transposed to the methodological and 'meta-theoretical' level where they may acquire a highly mediated form, the fundamentally identical class substance of the pluralistically ruling ideologies often remains hidden and thereby can exercise all the more effectively its mystificatory function.

All that is required of the manifold pluralistic approaches to turn them into integral constituents of the ruling ideology is the acceptance of some fundamental methodological tenets as their common denominator. We have already seen in this respect the far-reaching ideological function of the methodological prescriptions of pragmatism and '*practicality*', of the cult of *immediacy*, of the idealization of the '*piecemeal*' in opposition to comprehensive strategies, etc. What needs to be underlined in the present context is that it is precisely thanks to their shared methodological presuppositions that ruling ideologies can afford to be pluralistic with regard to the explicitness or otherwise of major value commitments. For so long as the defence of the established order can be stipulated in the name of some elementary methodological precondition of all rational discourse – like the claimed self-evident superiority of 'little by little' and 'piecemeal social engineering' in opposition to 'holism' – not only is the value implicit in such recommendation effectively hidden but, at the same time and with the same stroke, the very possibility of counterposing to it another value as a radical alternative to the prevailing order is successfully dismissed as the manifestation of 'emotivism' and irrationality.

4.2 THE IDEOLOGICAL MAINSTREAM OF SCIENTISM

4.2.1

Perhaps the most effective of the ways in which partisan value commitments are presented with a claim to neutrality and unchallengeable objectivity is the appeal to the authority of science in the name of which the adoption of certain measures and courses of action is commended. This has become particularly pronounced in the twentieth century, although its roots go back a long way. To be more precise: they reach at least as far back as the rise of Positivism in the first half of the nineteenth century, and arguably even further than that.

What makes things rather complicated in this respect is that science itself can assume very different functions in intellectual and ideological confrontations, according to the changing social contexts. After all, one should not forget that a few decades prior to the emergence of positivism, the second half of the eighteenth century brought with it the climax of science's positive involvement in a major struggle of emancipation against the earlier forms of obscurantist ideological control and interference with the development of the productive forces. Through its active participation in the crucial ideological confrontations, science thus contributed in a big way to the victory of the movement of the Enlightenment, and to clearing the ground not merely towards its own future development, but simultaneously also to the practical unfolding of the Industrial Revolution. As a result, a new type of relationship came into being between science, technology and industry,[489] sustaining the actualization of society's productive potentialities to a formerly unimaginable extent.

Understandably, therefore, with this new relationship between science and production also a new mode of ideological legitimation appeared on the horizon; and it proved extremely powerful ever since. For one thing, obscurantist interference prior to the triumph of the Enlightenment was not a figment of some people's imagination but a very real brake on productive developments, and 'letting reason follow its own course' was demonstrably able to make major improvements possible in this respect. At the same time, the problems and contradictions of the established social order, with all its crying inequalities, could be depicted for the first time in history as strictly *transient* phenomena which the advancement of scientific knowledge and its systematic application to production would overcome as certainly as day follows night.

Even the most enlightened thinkers of the bourgeoisie in ascendancy, like Adam Smith, assumed a thoroughly uncritical position *vis à vis* the inexorable and ubiquitous advance of the capitalistic division of labour as linked to science, notwithstanding their willingness to acknowledge its harmful consequences as a marginal phenomenon. Not only did they not put forward any serious proposals to counter those harmful consequences but, on the contrary, they expected, somewhat naively, the elimination of all remaining problems and contradictions from the universal diffusion of the capitalistic mode of production and exchange with which they fully identified themselves. Thus, the fallacious expectation of removing structural social inequalities by means of the quantitative expansion of production – to be accomplished, as an unproblematical and unquestionable objective, thanks to the advancement of science and technology – which has been so predominant in the last few decades, goes back a long way in the capitalistic practice of ideological legitimation. (The fundamental difference between the position of the Adam Smiths of the eighteenth century and the apologists of our own times being that the intervening two centuries, with their painfully obvious failure to fulfil even minimally the original expectations, should have taught the latter a lesson or two.)

Another problem that must be mentioned here is that the socialist tradition in its entirety – i.e. irrespective of whether it became known as 'utopian' or 'scientific' – assumed a highly positive attitude towards the marriage of science and productive technology. In particular in the case of Marxian socialism it was forcefully stressed that there could be no point in envisaging the 'generalization of misery' as the self-defeating aim of 'egalitarian socialism'. Consequently, the development of the productive forces to the highest possible level – in conjunction with the unhindered application of the creative potentialities of science in a rationally planned and regulated social framework – constituted in Marx's view the necessary prerequisites to that 'free development of individualities'[490] which he considered the *raison d'être* of socialism.

Marx identified the potentialities of emancipation as *tendentially* inherent in capital itself, though of course deeply submerged beneath the latter's manifold contradictions. As he put it:

> There appears here the universalizing tendency of capital, which distinguishes it from all previous stages of production. Although limited by its very nature, it strives towards the *universal development* of the forces of production, and thus becomes the *presupposition* of a new mode of production, which is founded not on the development of the forces of production for the purpose of reproducing or at most expanding a given condition, but where the *free, unobstructed, progressive and universal development* of the forces of production is itself the *presupposition of society* and hence of its reproduction; where advance beyond the point of departure is the only presupposition.... The development of science, this ideal and at the same time practical wealth, is *only one aspect*, one form in which the development of the human productive forces, i.e. of wealth, appears. Considered ideally, the dissolution of a given form of consciousness sufficed to kill a whole epoch. In reality, this barrier to consciousness corresponds to a definite degree of development of the forces of material production and hence of wealth.... The barrier to capital is that this entire development proceeds in a contradictory way, and that the working out of the productive forces, of general wealth etc., knowledge etc., appears in such a way that the working individual *alienates himself* [*sich entäussert*]; relates to the conditions brought out of him by his labour as those not of his own but of an *alien* wealth and of his own poverty. But this antithetical form is itself fleeting, and produces the real conditions of its own suspension. The result is: the *tendentially and potentially* general development of the forces of production – of wealth as such – as a basis; likewise, the universality of intercourse, hence the world market as a basis. The basis as the possibility of the universal development of the individual, and the real development of the individuals from this basis as a constant suspension of its barrier, which is recognized as a barrier, not taken for a sacred limit. Not an ideal or imagined

universality of the individual, but the universality of his real and ideal relations. Hence also the grasping his *own history as a process*, and the recognition of nature (equally present as practical power over nature) as his real body. The process of development itself posited and known as the presupposition of the same. For this, however, necessary above all that the *full development* of the forces of production has become the *condition of production*; and not that specific conditions of production are posited as a limit to the development of the productive forces.[491]

Thus in the Marxian conception, in sharp contrast to its Althusserian positivist interpretation, for instance, the importance of science was put in perspective as 'only one aspect' of the overall complex of development. As such, it had to be considered as inevitably subject to the same contradictions which characterized capitalistic productive practices in their entirety. There could be no privileged position assigned to some idealized 'science' (in opposition to 'ideology' or whatever else) from the vantage point of which one could contemplate and adjudicate over the rest of the world. Since the existing forms and practices of science were themselves specific manifestations of the prevailing alienation and division of labour, the whole complex had to be radically questioned, in all its aspects, if one was to explain how the immense *creative potentialities* of the unfolding trends were turned on all planes – including that of science – into *destructive realities* by the structural contradictions of capital.

Given the positivistic misconceptions of science ascribed to Marx by the Althusserian school, it will be necessary to return to some of these problems shortly. What needs to be stressed at this point is that it was by no means accidental that Althusser's positivistic misreading of Marx's work (and not only of his *Capital*), undertaken in order to derive from it a fictitiously 'anti-ideological science', was coupled with a crusade against the 'ideological concept' of alienation, based on the totally unfounded claim (refuted by our last quote from the *Grundrisse*, as well as by countless other passages in the same work and in *Capital*, etc.) about the 'disappearance' of that concept from the 'mature Marx'.[492]

4.2.2

Marx was by no means the first to situate in a historical perspective the qualitatively new interaction of science and technolgy under the rule of capital. Rousseau attempted to do the same in his analyses of modern historical and productive developments, reaching in the end rather pessimistic conclusions as to the prospects for the future. While Rousseau's critical counterblasts against the ongoing trends and their accommodating conceptualizations represented a significant corrective to the 'uncritical positivism' of the political economists, his own social standpoint – defending the virtues of an idealized 'middle condition'[493] – prevented him from fully unravelling the implications of his powerful diagnosis of capitalistic alienation and dehumanization.

However, notwithstanding its limitations, Rousseau's attempt to treat science and its far-reaching impact on social transformations in a historical and critical manner was a major achievement, especially in the light of subsequent developments. For by the middle of the nineteenth century – which witnessed for the first time the treatment of Hegel as a 'dead dog'[494] – the historical approach originally associated with the bourgeoisie had become thoroughly marginal.

In its place, 'uncritical positivism' ruled the day, even if in most countries it did not call itself positivism as yet. Indeed, through the formulation of the doctrines of Auguste Comte and his followers, the 'uncritical positivism' inherent in many (at the time successful) theories in one way or in another, had been elevated to an ideal status, radically eliminating the historical dimension from the dominant world-view. The great success of positivism (and 'neo-positivism') ever since, under a great variety of forms, from its original version to the recently fashionable ideologies of structural functionalism and structuralism, owes more to this radical liquidation of the historical – and by implication critical – dimension than to anything else.

Thus ahistorical scientism became the common frame of reference for a multiplicity of different ideologies, deeply penetrating even the working-class movement and the writings of the leading figures of the Second International: a tradition paradoxically revived by Stalinism, in the guise of voluntaristic verbal radicalism, not only in Russia but also in France and elsewhere. This is how we came to witness the curious spectacle of Stalinists directing the same sort of strictures against Marx, on account of his alleged 'Hegelianism', as their politically denounced adversary Bernstein did a long time before them.[495]

Naturally, in the course of making the 'new orthodoxy' of positivistic scientism dominant, Hegel had to be killed and 'treated as a dead dog' on more than one occasion. To inject sophistication into Comtean crudity, the efforts of 'Hegel-exterminators' (not just critics) were often conducted on the lines of some kind of neo-Kantian revival. (In point of fact, there are as many varieties of 'scientific' neo-Kantianism as there are of positivism and neo-positivism.) Significantly, however, the burial of Hegelian philosophy as 'unscientific metaphysics'[496] was as a rule directed against precisely the most positive aspects of that philosophy: its historical aspirations, coupled with the principles of an objective dialectic which constituted the methodological underpinning of the Hegelian interpretation of development as irrepressibly dynamic in every sphere of human activity, including that of science.

No matter how strong one's reservations about Hegel's way of implementing his own philosophical programme – and we all know that Marx's reservations were strong enough – the relevant question presented itself like this: which one of two sharply opposed alternative attitudes should one adopt towards the Hegelian philosophy. The first, advocated by Marx, was to try to enhance the historical dimension and the objective dialectic inherent in it, whereas the second attempted the liquidation of both dialectics and historicity in view of their incompatibility with the aims of social apologetics, whether capitalistic or Stalinist.

It is important to stress here that the authority of science – in fact a veritable travesty of science: conceptualized as a thoroughly ahistorical construct – was used to camouflage the conservative social substance of the advocated views. Thus 'historicism' could be treated as self-evident sinfulness, to be exorcized with fire and brimstone on account of its alleged polarity to science. Likewise, *dialectics* became almost a term of abuse. True to form, Bernstein played a central role in the intellectual disorientation of the Second International also in this respect, arbitrarily and arrogantly dismissing not only the Hegelian but also the Marxian dialectic as sheer 'cant' and a 'useless plank' in the 'scaffolding' of a 'speculative theory', as we shall see in Chapter 8.5 below.

As far as the right and proper development of philosophy and socioeconomic theory was concerned, the fate of dialectics was supposed to have been 'definitvely' settled by the 'scientific solution' (i.e. agnostic dissolution) of its problems[497] provided in the Kantian *Critique of Pure Reason*, whereafter only 'irrationalists' or those who were 'confused' could talk of dialectical contradictions seriously. For the only 'dialectic' that could be considered legitimate by the defenders of the given social order was the ahistorically stipulated '*unending dialectic* between producing the same things better and in larger quantities and producing different things – between producing goods of the same kind in a different way and producing goods which had never been thought of before. The exact form that the satisfaction of an aspiration takes is the result of *scientific progress*, but the basic needs remain the same'.[498]

This conception of productive social interaction as an 'unending dialectic' confined to the permanent reproduction of the established productive practices on the basis of an eternally persistent set of 'basic needs', in accordance with the alleged dictates of nature itself, was of course diametrically opposed to the revolutionary implications of the Marxian dialectic. For Marx never ceased to insist on the fundamentally subversive and transforming potential of the unfolding historical process as the '*übergreifendes Moment*' of the dialectic of social interaction. Here, however, in the 'unending' pseudo-dialectic of Aron and others – modelled on the vicious circularity of self-reproducing and self-expanding exchange value – we were offered nothing but the idealization of conservative social inertia. As such, it could only envisage the quantitative expansion of the same processes of reified commodity production, but under no circumstances the possibility of a radical restructuring of the established mode of production and social interchange which it categorically rejected with revealing apriorism.

As it befits a theory which aimed at the 'eternalization of the prevailing social relations', the pseudo-dialectical notion of circularly self-reproducing commodity production was complemented by the hypostatization of a pseudo-natural order. And the latter was supposed to prescribe to society the repetitive reproduction of the 'same basic needs' which could be readily satisfied (at least for the time being) by commodity society as nature's obvious social equivalent. This view, again, was put forward in opposition to Marx, who characterized the historical dialectic from the very beginning as dynamically intervening in the production of *new needs*[499] beyond the naturally inherited ones, thus laying the foundations for a *qualitatively* different mode of productive human self-reproduction.

Equally significant was the function assigned to 'scientific progress' in this conception. For it was unashamedly used to help liquidate the historical and critical dimension of social theory in the guise of vacuous references to an abstract temporality, derived from the allegedly self-referential 'logic of scientific progress' as opposed to the historically unfolding dynamics of objective social processes and contradictions.

Since the established mode of production and its property relations had to be represented as untranscendable, hence timeless – an aim accomplished through the assertion of their ideal correspondence to the 'natural' order of satisfying and reproducing the postulated set of unchanging 'basic needs' – the only way in which time could be allowed to enter the picture was one that not only did not upset but, on the contrary, positively strengthened this arrangement.

Naturally, under the impact of capital's unprecedented power of self-expansion the fact of historical change – inevitably bringing with it new circumstances and formerly unimaginable types of social conflict and interaction – could not be denied even by the crudest form of apologetics. Nor was it indeed necessary to deny altogether the reality of the instituted socioeconomic and cultural changes; especially since the representatives of the ruling ideology wanted to ascribe in glowing terms the credit for the 'progressive' achievements of the new productive developments to the capitalist social system as such.

Nevertheless, they had to face and resolve a, by no means negligible, difficulty. For their ideological rationalization of the existent, if it was to be effective at all, had to be spelled out both as something *historically specific* – so as to be able to make the best of the claimed achievements – and at the same time *aprioristically timeless*, in order to exclude the possibility, not to mention the necessity, of a radical historical transformation. Thus, a way had to be found to secure the 'right kind of evaluation' of the undeniable changes which would not interfere with the ideology that insisted on the naturalness and untranscendability of the established order.

This is where the positivistic interpretation of science and 'scientific progress' turned out to be so useful. The premise on which such progress was postulated claimed, as we have seen, the existence of two 'natural' orders: that of 'the basic needs which remain the same', on the one hand, and the system of commodity-production ideally suited to their satisfaction on the other. Moreover, the way in which this relationship between the two pseudo-natural orders was described, simultaneously also implied and at times explicitly asserted their fundamental identity. Now with the introduction of (positivistically interpreted) science into the overall conception, a new relationship of identity could be stipulated. This was the identity between 'progress' – represented as 'scientific progress', the 'scientific spirit', etc. – and the capitalistic mode of production itself. For the latter was supposed to be not only the ideal productive equivalent of the natural determinations directly arising from the basic needs themselves. Also, it was said to be the one and only adequate embodiment of the 'scientific spirit' as such and of the self-evident benefits it bestows upon the people of the 'modern industrial society' – i.e. the society that truly corresponded to the inner requirements of the somewhat mythical 'scientific spirit' – in the form of never ending 'scientific progress'. To quote the exact words in which Raymond Aron put this conception of science as necessarily interlocking with 'progressive' commodity-production:

> A society is not truly industrialized until the actions of men and the operation of institutions are in harmony with the *spirit of industry*. Provisionally, we have called *the spirit of modern economy scientific*. Fundamentally, industrialized societies may be called scientific, in that both mechanization and productivity are the fruit of the *scientific spirit* and are the *ultimate causes* of both industrialization and *the progressive nature of the economy*.[500]

This solution had the all-important advantage of transforming the question of *historical temporality* into a totally elusive problem. In place of the social parameters of historical time we were offered the absolutization of the *immanence* of scientific development as a fictitious substitute. For while in reality science is always inextricably linked to the developments of the society on the soil of which it operates and without whose support its progress is totally inconceivable, here everything appeared upside down and the immanent development of science, arising from the mysterious determinations of 'the scientific spirit', was presented as '*the ultimate cause*' of social development itself.

Naturally, no one would wish to deny that the 'logic' of scientific development has its *relatively autonomous* aspect as an important *moment* of the overall complex of dialectical interdeterminations. However, acknowledging this can in no way amount to the absolutization of the immanent logic of scientific development on its own, and thereby to the tendentious ideological obliteration of the weighty and often highly problematical sociohistorical determinations. To absolutize the immanence of scientific progress and of its impact on social developments can only serve the purpose of social apologetics. As indeed we found it in the case of Aron himself who postulated the sovereign agency of 'the scientific spirit' as 'the ultimate cause' of socioeconomic developments in order to be able simultaneously to assert and legitimate in the name of 'scientific progress' the otherwise far from obviously *progressive nature of the economy*' of his 'modern industrial society' which he claimed to be in complete 'harmony with the spirit of industry'.[501]

4.2.3

The original conception of positivistic scientism was linked to the great expectations of a somewhat simple-minded evolutionist optimism. The repeated eruption of capitalist crises in the second half of the nineteenth century, understandably, put an end to all that. As a result one witnessed the recasting of the ideology of scientism in a deeply sceptical, if not altogether pessimistic mould. Its anti-historical approach to the problems encountered made it eminently suitable to the 'eternalization' and ideological legitimation of the established system, especially since it also provided the *illusion* of temporality: one directly emanating from science itself. At the same time, again in contrast to the sweeping improvements anticipated in the original conception, the elimination of the social ills, inasmuch as their existence was acknowledged at all, was confined to the 'gradual work of scientific progress' as the only possible (not to say admissible) solution.

The insistence on the exclusive rationality of 'little by little' revealed an astonishing logical inconsistency. For if the elimination of all social ills and inequalities was strictly a matter of scientific progress, and if the future development of science was unpredictable, as it was maintained, how could one also maintain, totally *prejudging* the issue, that the only conceivable development and improvement of the prevailing social conditions had to be accomplished 'little by little'? Why couldn't there be such a fundamental scientific revolution as a result of which one could envisage some all-embracing positive changes? All the more since there was no end of talk in the writings of the advocates of neo-positivistic scientism about the 'logic of scientific revolutions' and about the 'second industrial revolution': another revealing inconsistency.

To understand the curious logic of 'logical positivists' as well as of numerous intellectuals besides them from among other varieties of neo-positivism, one must look at the underlying social interests. For only the *conservative ideological motivations* at the roots of neo-positivistic scientism can explain the blatant logical inconsistencies with which even the writings of its most distinguished representatives abound.

It was primarily on account of its unrivalled efficacy for supplying the required rationalization in the service of the dominant socioeconomic and political interests that neo-positivistic scientism could acquire its prominence – despite its striking logical deficiency and irrationality – as the paradigm of rational social explanation and the mainstream of ideological legitimation.

In place of the historical dialectic of complex social interrelations it offered the fetishistic objectivity of crude material/instrumental determinations. And in opposition to all critical assessment of the hierarchical social division of labour it continued to misrepresent the latter as purely techno-logical/scientific, and thereby, of course, as necessarily permanent.

In both respects it was well in tune with the prevailing productive practices of commodity society and with their spontaneous conceptualizations at the level of everyday experience. For, as Marx argued, due to the fetishism of commodity in capitalist society:

> The mutual relations of the producers, within which the social character of their labour affirms itself, take the form of a social relation between the *products*.... There is a definite social relation between men, that assumes, in their eyes, the fantastic form of a *relation between things*.... Since the producers do not come into social contact with each other until they exchange their products, the specific social character of each producer's labour does not show itself except in the act of exchange. In other words, the labour of the individual asserts itself as a part of the labour of society, only by means of the relations which the act of exchange establishes *directly between the products*, and indirectly, through them, between the producers. To the latter, therefore, the relations connecting the labour of one individual with that of the rest appear, not as *direct social relations* between individuals at work, but as what they really are, *material [dinglich = thing-like]* relations between *persons* and *social* relations between *things*.... The character of having value, when once impressed upon products, obtains *fixity* only by reason of their acting and reacting upon each other as quantities of value. These quantities vary con-tinually, *independently* of the will, foresight and action of the producers. To them, their own social action takes the form of the *action of objects*, which *rule the producers* instead of being ruled by them.... Man's reflections on the forms of social life, and consequently, also, his scientific analysis of those forms, take a course directly opposite to that of their actual historical develop-ment. He begins, *post festum*, with the *results* of the process of development ready to hand before him. The characters that stamp products as commodities, and whose establishment is a necessary preliminary to the circulation of commodities, have already acquired the stability of natural, self-understood forms of social life, before man seeks to decipher, not their *historical character*, for in his eyes they are *immutable*, but their *meaning*.[502]

Neo-positivist scientism made a virtue out of the misery of this reification by taking all that was given 'ready to hand' ahistorically for granted and by reducing the dynamic complexity of social relations to the petrified fixity of 'relations between products' (at best: between 'competing products').

The attempt to eliminate social agency and collective consciousness from its mechanistic equations (from behaviourism to structuralism) was an integral part of the same willing submission to reification which could only make sense of relations between persons if they were '*thing-like*'. Hence the glorification of the capitalist 'contract' and exchange relations in every context, including even the most astonishing ones. One may recall in this respect the way in which structuralists and structural functionalists arbitrarily projected the dominant capitalistic institutional forms and practices upon the qualitatively different circumstances of so-called 'traditional societies', so as to be able to 'prove' the omnipresence and eternal validity of 'capital' and 'exchange'.

At the same time, quasi-mythical power was attributed to 'social relations between things' as they imposed themselves on society in the framework of the market, treating them as if they could never be challenged and brought under control. Not surprisingly, therefore, social problems had to be meta-morphosed into 'neutral' (or 'value free') technological/scientific issues, so as to be able to avoid the question of their dependence of (historically established) social relations, as well as to rule out of court all possible challenge to the latter.

In this way we were offered – in place of highly contested social realities – the illusion of purely instrumental solutions to the reluctantly acknowledged difficulties, as we have seen above on several occasions. And since under the circumstances of commodity fetishism and reification – which turned social relations into things and things into uncontrollable social relations – the *social* dimension of the prevailing division of labour happened to be and had to remain inextricably intertwined with *capitalistic technological/instrumental* determinations (as articulated in a socially enshrined and reinforced *hierarchical* order), the ideology of neo-positivistic scientism could rely on a very solid material foundation indeed to support its mystificatory *conflation*[503] of the *social* with the *technological*, in the service of legitimating the former in the name of the latter.

It was this close affinity of neo-positivistic scientism with the objective structures of reification which enabled it to become the mainstream of ideological legitimation: a condition likely to remain with us, in the form of no matter how many fashionably 'different' permutations, for as long as the capitalistic structures themselves survive.

Its methodology, making use almost *ad nauseam* of models, diagrams, formulas, twisted statistical 'evidence', 'mass-observations' and 'mass-interviews' (based on 'scientifically' devised – though in reality derisorily puny – 'representative samples'), etc., reflected a vital need and practical imperative of commodity society. Namely: to secure the reproduction of exchange value on a constantly enlarged scale by means of the wanton *manipulation* of the social processes in every sphere of activity, from material 'demands' generated by 'supply management' to grossly *influencing* public opinion while pretending to represent it objectively, and from cynically 'producing' artificial scarcities in a world of plenty to 'massaging' the facts in the service of eliciting the required ideological and political responses in a systematically miseducated public.

The ideology of neo-positivistic scientism, which continued to idealize a science subservient to the reified technological requirements of the prevailing mode of production, was most appropriate to assume the leading role in this process of manipulation, in that it could promise to stamp with the lofty authority of science writ large even the most prosaic of manipulative practices. Indeed, the ideology of scientism – to be sure, not simply on its own, but largely thanks to its inherent linkages to the dominant productive practices – was so powerful that it successfully penetrated not only the citadels of knowledge but virtually all facets of everyday life as well. Its manifestations ranged 'from the sublime to the ridiculous', so long as they could be quantified or turned into models, formulas and 'paradigms'. For a rare example of the 'sublime', we can think of Max Weber's ingenious system of 'value-free ideal types'. As to the ridiculous and often grotesque abuse of science in the service of manipulation, the examples are legion: from the 'Mortuary Science' (read: lucrative funeral undertaking) and 'Apiary Science' (that is: bee-keeping) Departments of some American Universities to the *'technology of the unified field'* of the Maharishi Mahesh Yogi and his meditating followers, with their 'scientifically quantifiable' mumbo-jumbo about the *'square root* of the world's population'.

4.2.4

Naturally, the ideology of neo-positivistic scientism, with its pretentious appropriation of the categories of 'verification' and 'falsification' – and, indeed, the generous use of the second, even if not in the professed sense – was ideally suited to conduct the assault on 'ideology' in the name of a fictitious 'science'. Its preponderant weight, materially and institutionally supported by the manipulative imperatives of commodity society, asserted itself with such a pressure than it succeeded in producing politically rather surprising results even among those who continued to state their allegiance to Marxism.

Thus Althusserians, for instance, became trapped within the confines of the dominant 'anti-ideological' discourse, pursuing imaginary 'ruptures' – on the uncritically adopted presuppositions of neo-positivistic scientism and structuralism – so as to be able to stipulate, in line with the fashionable 'end of ideology' theme, the categorical opposition between 'scientific concepts' and 'ideological concepts'.

Ironically, Althusser was repeating here, five to ten years after their publication, the neo-positivistic platitudes contained in an article of a right-wing Italian politician/intellectual, Mario Albertini: 'Una nuova cultura o una nuova politica?'[504] For in this article, Althusser's little suspected predecessor, Albertini, was thundering not only against the *'ideological language'* of the Marxian analysis of *alienation* but also against the *'delusory'* concept of a 'personality-protagonist of history', i.e. the 'collective subject' of the proletariat. Just as Althusser did in his denunciations of the young Marx's 'theoretical humanism' and 'Hegelianism' (until, that is, he finally discovered that the 'mature Marx', too, was guilty of the same sins) and in his summary elimination of the category of 'subject' from proper philosophical and theoretical discourse.[505]

As Cesare Cases wittily commented on Albertini's article: 'Here we are offered the economics and the ethics of the servant: don't speak of alienation, just sell yourself, and do it at the highest price.'[506] Granted that nothing could be further removed from Althusser's intentions than identifying himself with the practical implications of the 'anti-ideological' and 'anti-subject' views of his Italian counterpart, which had as its target the hegemonic aspirations of the working class. And yet he ended up with the same neo-positivistic 'discoveries' as the politician/intellectual of Olivetti's *Comunità* movement.

Naturally, the point is not to trace influences and settle claims to 'originality'. It is quite unimportant here, whether or not Althusser was aware of Albertini's article; in any event they both *must* have read Galvano della Volpe and other influential figures of neo-positivistic scientism. However, what does indeed matter in the present context is that the ruling ideological climate at the time made such 'anti-ideological' notions broadly diffused commonplaces. To enter with them in a fetishistically 'science-oriented' discourse thus meant situating oneself, knowingly or not, within the framework of a discourse favouring the ideological adversary and contributing thereby to the legitimation of its enterprise.

4.2.5

To add insult in injury, the mystifying 'reorientation' of socialist theory by the Althusserians was accomplished in the name of a 'Marxism' which did not hesitate to dismiss as 'Hegelian' the totality of even Marx's own theoretical work, exempting only the slender few pages of the *Critique of the Gotha Programme* and the 'Marginal notes on Wagner'. Thus the acceptance of the ideological adversary's framework of discourse resulted in a *de facto* capitulation to a false problematic, bringing with it the painfully disorienting consequences of a thoroughly idealist conception of so-called 'theoretical practice'. Whatever the original intentions of the actors involved, all this in the end significantly contributed to the emergence of the virulent anti-Marxism of the 'New French Philosophers' and to that 'crisis of Marxism' which Althusserians tried to conceptualize from the imaginary vantage point of their self-proclaimed 'scientific discourse', as if their own 'theoretical practice' of *wholesale revision* had nothing whatsoever to do with the crisis they talked about.

Admittedly, there is always more to these matters than the pressure of the dominant ideological discourse. As has been emphasized earlier, there is a substantive affinity between the inherently conservative aspirations of capitalist and Stalinist rationalization and legitimation which find their rather curious theoretical manifestations in such convergences.

In this respect it is by no means irrelevant that all leading figures of 'Marxist' neo-positivism – from Galvano della Volpe[507] and Althusser[508] to Colletti[509] – were at some stage more or less heavily tainted with Stalinist orthodoxy, whatever their later changes of position. In fact the earlier quoted Italian literary critic, Cesare Cases, did not exaggerate but, if any-thing, kindly understated the point when he wrote in 1958:

> Della Volpe maintains excellent relations with the shadow of Zhdanov that gives him lessons in logic and aesthetics and teaches him to treat Hegel and Lukács as old slippers [pezze da piedi].[510]

Similarly with Althusser who continued to speak, in Marxist theory and philosophy, of 'the great *classical tradition* of the Workers' Movement, from Marx to Lenin, *Stalin* and Mao'.[511] And it took him no less than 13 years from the XXth Congress of the Soviet Party (held in 1956) to insert into his wholesome praise of Stalin's philosophical perceptiveness of the problems of dialectics the mild qualifier: 'at least on this point',[512] when almost everybody else was well aware of the scholastic and dogmatic character of the treatment which dialectics had received from this 'great classic' of Marxism.

All these connections with Stalinism are, of course, undeniable and pertinent for understanding the emergence and original orientation of Marxist neo-positivism. No doubt, the intellectual formation of the indi-viduals concerned played an equally important part in this respect. (For instance, it is of no minor significance that Galvano della Volpe – the not always acknowledged pioneer of this trend of neo-positivistic scientism in the postwar development of Marxism – was for many years an accomplished *neo-Kantian*[513] philosopher before being converted to Marxism.) Never-theless, one cannot insist enough on the preponderant role which the dominant ideology can play in determining the orientation of the whole of society, successfully imposing its discourse even on its political adversaries if for whatever reason, including the reasons indicated on the last few pages, they are caught off guard. Indeed, this phenomenon represents one of the most obvious ways in which the *relative autonomy* of ideology – in the form of the dominant ideology *directly* affecting other ideologies – asserts itself with such effectiveness.

4.3 TECHNOLOGY, SCIENCE AND SOCIETY

4.3.1
Thanks to the power of the reifying social forces behind the success of positivism and neo-positivism, an extremely one-sided view of the 'auto-nomous' development of science and technology has become not the 'com-mon sense' but the mystifying *common place* of our times. Its advocates range from Nobel Prize winning philosophers, like Bertrand Russell,[514] to media pundits engaged in the popularization of religiously followed moonshots, and from science fiction writers to the well rewarded propa-gandists of the military-industrial complex.

The postwar period of consensus and its twin brother, the ideology of 'the end of ideology', particularly favoured the uncritical acceptance of such view. It became fashionable to talk about 'the rise of *technological society*, a *totally new kind of human society* in which *science and technology dictate* the dominant forms of thought and increasingly shape almost every aspect of our everyday life.'[515] Accordingly, the spectre of technology as the all-powerful, independent agent interfering with the established order and its values was painted with some alarm: 'Because technology increasingly shapes almost every realm of our everyday lives ... *it could transform or destroy the social foundations* of our most cherished human values.'[516]
In the same vein E.T. Chase was arguing that:

> At last there is a dawning realization that in the United States it is *rapid technological change* rather than *ideological strife* or even *economics* that is building up a fundamental political crisis.... What is happening is that *technology's effects* are suddenly calling into question the viability of our political institutions to a degree unknown at least since the Civil War.[517]

The ideological substance of this approach which claimed to stand above 'ideological strife' became transparent just a few lines further on, when the author contrasted his own position with 'what *doctrinaires*, obsessed with *dated rhetoric about socialism versus capitalism* have led us to expect'. According to Chase the only relevant issue in the contemporary world was the 'cumulative impact of technology, an impact that is *impersonal, non-ideological, relentless*, and possibly *overwhelming*'.[518] For under the circumstances of our 'modern industrial society' unemployment was '*technological unemployment*' and technology was bound to impose upon society its '*exponential* rate of change'.[519]
At the same time, tellingly, while not only ideology but 'even economics' was dismissed as irrelevant to assessing the political dimension of social developments, we were also told that the real dilemmas for society presented themselves like this:

> When *technological unemployment* in combination with *scientific medicine* produces a growing population of 'retired' elderly persons in an urbanized, wage-based industrial society, how will their heavy medical costs for the inevitable chronic ills of old age be financed? Or when an essential *public service* is threatened with extinction as a *paying proposition*, owing to *fatal competition* from *more advanced technology*, is the government helpless, as in the case of the New Haven Railroad, or will our political leaders devise some successful expedient without incurring a constitutional crisis?[520]

If these matters did not belong to the realm of 'economics' – indeed, to the 'ideologically suspect' realm of *political economy* at that – one wonders what on earth could possibly qualify in that respect.
In truth, declaring from an allegedly 'supra-ideological' standpoint that such problems – including that of 'fatal competition' – have arisen from the strictly instrumental logic of a 'more advanced technology', betrayed an

extreme ideological eagerness on the part of the author. For his fetishistic
technological references tried to discredit any attempt at formulating the
question of *meaningful social choices* – with regard to the emerging trend
of unemployment and other structural contradictions of 'the modern
industrial society' – in terms of a strategy conceived from the perspective of
a *radical social alternative*.

This is why the discussion of *socialism versus capitalism* had to be
condemned with contempt as the 'dated rhetoric' of a bygone age. A
rhetoric in which only 'doctrinaires obsessed with ideological strife' could
conceivably indulge. Thus, this vacuous discourse about technology was
meant simultaneously to confer on the established order its *a priori justification* – for who in his right mind other than Luddites (who are supposed to
have no mind at all) could question the promised benefits of our 'advanced
technology'[521] – and, at the same time, to lay to rest for ever the 'antiquated' ghost of socialism.

4.3.2

Blindness in intellectuals is not a natural calamity that simply befalls them
as a matter of unavoidable destiny but a self-induced condition. In this
respect nothing could illustrate better the total blindness produced by their
'anti-ideological' eagerness to transubstantiate social problems and challenges into merely technological difficulties – such that are either instrumentally solvable (which is fine from the point of view of capitalist
rationalization and legitimation), or insuperable in purely technological
terms (which is fine too, since the question of *social criticism* cannot be
raised in relation to them) – than the editor's presentation of C. Wright
Mills' essay on 'Liberal values in the modern world' in Jack Douglas's *The
Technological Threat*.

This presentation claimed nothing less than that:

> C. Wright Mills briefly outlines the fundamental changes that have taken
> place in Western society, largely as a result of *technological changes* in the last
> century. Most importantly, Mills argues that *technology* has undermined the
> primary basis of nineteenth-century liberalism, which in turn was the funda-
> mental basis of democratic political institutions and values. Above all, *science
> and technology* have led to an increasingly centralized and massive form of
> production and marketing which has undermined the old system of decentra-
> lized entrepreneurial work.[522]

Characteristically, this bewildering summary of the position of C. Wright
Mills was a *complete* misrepresentation. For Mills said *absolutely nothing*
about 'technological changes' undermining liberalism, nor of 'science and
technology' leading to centralization and undermining 'decentralized entrepreneurial work'. He was talking, instead, of *social power relations*,
emphatically rejecting the 'fashionable supposition that there is no ruling
class', and pointing to *structural conditions* as the necessary framework

of explanation. He did indeed briefly outline the relevant conditions and developments. But, in sharp contrast to what was claimed by the editor, this is how he summed up his conclusions: 'What goes on domestically may briefly be described in terms of the main drift toward a *permanent war economy in a garrison state.*' As to the *concentration* in question, he un-equivocally – and repeatedly – pointed a finger to 'concentrated *property*', to an 'enormous increase in the scale of *property units*', to 'the dominance of *huge-scale property*', and to 'a *lop-sided competition* between and among *dominant factions and midget interests*'. Not *one word* about technology and scientific/technological change, but a great deal about alarming socio-economic and political/institutional forces producing what he called '*mass incapability*': a condition which he would have liked to see radically altered. For, according to Mills:

> What has happened is *the fusion of several institutional orders*; the co-ordination of the major orders has become the contemporary reality. We see in the United States today an increased coincidence and *fusion of the economic, political, and military orders.*[523]

The scandalous overturning of the far from complicated meaning of 'Liberal values in the modern world' and thereby the complete emasculation of its *strikingly obvious* social criticism which we could witness in the presentation of Mills' views as *technological* concerns was by no means accidental. On the contrary, it exhibited, however crudely, the *necessary* limitations of all approaches that perceive the problems facing society, as well as the only admissible solution to them, from the standpoint of capital which they take for granted. For if the possibility of a radical social change is *a priori excluded,* in that case – no matter how 'sophisticated' the characterization of the difficulties that must be subjected to scrutiny – only *technological* improvements can be offered in the way of solutions. And by the same token, if under the pressure of the rising tensions it must be admitted that the identified problems are by no means minor ones, blame for their existence, from the standpoint of capital, can never be acknowl-edged to be inherent in the established socioeconomic system itself. Invariably, it will only be assigned, instead, to the 'little by little' corrigible *technological deficiencies*.

4.3.3

To say that our 'technological society' is a '*totally new kind of society*' in which '*science and technology dictate*' what happens to the social body, undermining on their own the established institutions and 'destroying the social foundations of the cherished values' is a complete mystification. There can be no such thing as a 'totally new kind of society' brought about by the allegedly uncontrollable, self-propelling mechanism of scientific discoveries and technological developments. For, in fact, science and technology are themselves always deeply embedded in the social structures and determinations of their time. Consequently they are in and by themselves neither more 'impersonal and non-ideological', nor more threatening than any other important productive practice of the society in question.

If the impact of science and technology on society appears to be 'relentless and possibly overwhelming', raising the spectre of a total paralysis and social disintegration watched in anguish by 'helpless governments', that is not on account of their intrinsic characteristics. Rather, it is because of the way in which the dominant social forces – including in a prominent position those described as 'helpless governments' – relate themselves to science and technology; either assuming responsibility for their control in the service of human ends or, on the contrary, using them as a convenient and foolproof *alibi* for their own abdication to the powers of alienation and destruction.

The idea that science follows an independent course of development from which technological applications emerge and impose themselves on society with an iron necessity is a crude, ideologically motivated, oversimplification. As has been forcefully argued:

> While the inner order of science is a necessary condition of a particular advance being made, so that molecular biology must be preceded by classical genetics and organic chemistry, this does not mean that this condition is sufficient as well as necessary.... even the most basic of science that we do is a product of our society. Certain types of society therefore do certain types of science; they ask particular questions of nature. Ancient Babylonian religion demanded the accurate prediction of heavenly events and Babylonian science was largely devoted to the intensive study of astronomy. The emergent capitalism of the industrial revolution in Britain required technological advances in power generation and physicists studied the laws of thermodynamics and conservation and transformation of energy. It is no accident that many of these fundamental advances in physics were made in Britain in the half-century 1810–1860, whilst in chemistry and physiology the major centres were in France and Germany.... But the negative corollary of this relationship between science and society holds true too; that is, that in certain societies certain types of science are *not* done. They become either unperformable or unthinkable.... It is neither avoidable nor wrong that such constraints should exist. The questions we have to ask, in the long run, must take cognisance of them. They are: what sort of science do we want? how much of it do we want? who should do it? how should they and their activities be controlled? But the fundamental question underlying all these is: *what sort of society do we want?*[524]

The real question, then, is twofold. On the one hand, it consists in asking what kind of social developments – in their dialectical *interaction* with the corresponding scientific and technological practices – were responsible for bringing about the present-day configuration of society/science/technology which gives people cause for the most profound concern with regard to their ultimate implications for the very survival of mankind. And on the other hand, one must also ask: how is it possible to reverse the perilously growing trend of uncontrollability and 'mass incapability', as C. Wright Mills fittingly put it, so as to bring the *totality* of social practices – i.e. by no means *exclusively* but *including* those of science and technology – under a fully adequate *social control*.

The great dilemma of modern science is that its development was always tied to the *contradictory dynamism* of capital itself. Moreover, the inseparability of modern science and technology from this perverse dynamism is bound to remain with us for as long as a conscious and socially viable attempt is not made to produce and sustain the necessary disjunction. Accordingly, no matter how popular the fiction of 'immanent scientific development' might be, modern science could not help being oriented towards the most effective possible implementation of the *objective imperatives* that define the nature and inherent limits of capital as well as its necessary mode of functioning under the most varied circumstances.

Thus, to blame science for the fatefully threatening implications of its products – which are in fact the products of the socially prevailing mode of production in its entirety – would be just as absurd as to imagine that the isolated action of enlightened scientists could reverse the ongoing process. Rosa Luxemburg's stark alternative – 'socialism or barbarism' – whose prophetic meaning we can much better appreciate today than when she first formulated it, well over 70 years ago, with reference to the emerging trend of militarization as a way of displacing capital's inner contradictions, concerns the *whole* of society.

Obviously, one cannot run away from such contradictions to some remote 'no-man's-land' while leaving the social world of capital intact. To bring about the much needed disjunction between science and destructive capitalist determinations is conceivable only if society as a whole successfully escapes from capital's orbit and provides a new ground – with different orienting principles – on which scientific practices can flourish in the service of human ends. Hence arises – at a time when science, too, is in danger of being obliterated, with the rest of humanity – the urgency of the basic question from the point of view and in the interest of science itself: 'What kind of society do we want?'. For a less fundamental question than that (e.g. 'How can we improve the productivity of science?', or 'How can we improve productivity in general through science?' – two characteristically capital-oriented questions frequently asked today) does not even scratch the surface of the contradictions that must be confronted.

With regard to science, the primary reason why the question: 'What kind of society do we want?' calls for 'a radically different society' as an answer is that the growing *structural crisis* of capital inevitably endangers the future development of science as well.

What is at stake here is not some *a priori* condition, with its equally aprioristic negative connotations, but the highly problematical *historical* climax of a set of complex determinations which in their *original* context were responsible both for the emancipation of science from an extraneous (theological) rule – *ancilla theologiae* – and for the truly 'exponential' growth of science over the last two centuries. For no social mode of production before the capitalist one could even remotely be compared – in terms of its material as well as intellectual impact favouring the spectacular articulation of the productive potentialities of science – with the dynamism of capitalism which we have witnessed at least since the industrial revolution, with its roots reaching back to the early capitalist developments in the fifteenth and sixteenth centuries.

Undoubtedly, the novel combination of science with an ever-expanding productive technology, coupled with a powerful mechanism of feedback asserting itself through the competitive determinations of the market, go a long way to explain the unprecedented speedy unfolding of this success story. And yet, they stop far short of a real explanation, since they do not make intelligible anything more than the functioning of the given *mechanism* itself, without even touching upon the question of its sociohistorical origin as well as its necessary limitations which the origin usually foreshadows, even if often in a rather paradoxical form.

Indeed, the great paradox of modern science – a technologically articulated 'experimental science' which grew out of the soil of capitalistic *'utilitarian'* foundations – is that it turned out to be far less utilitarian in *some* of its dimensions than the science of earlier ages. That is to say, less utilitarian in the sense of being less *directly* tied to rather narrow social determinations, be they tangibly material/instrumental or like Ancient Babylonian science – of the religious kind.

Strangely, then, an age of the most obvious and ubiquitous material determinations ended up producing so-called 'basic science' and 'pure science', in addition to and in contrast with 'applied science' which became diffused under an immense variety of highly specialized forms. How was this kind of development possible? Clearly, something needs to be explained here in relation to which any amount of talk about the historically specific *mechanism* of capitalistic production/market/science/technology – even if it takes fully into account the corresponding network of complicated reciprocal feedback – could only beg the question.

4.3.4

The social determinations at the roots of such developments fell into two main categories. The first concerned the conditions for producing the much more autonomous *individual* scientist by breaking the 'umbilical cord' which formerly tied the practitioners of science rather more narrowly to determinate social and instrumental complexes. An *analogous*, though by no means *identical* phenomenon in this respect was the emergence of the modern artist as an 'independent' practitioner of his art and craft, representing a very mixed blessing indeed in comparison to the creative artist's previous status in society.

The second, and in a way more important development (in that it provided the material dynamism behind the 'individualization' of art and science) was the radical disengagement of production from the *constraints of direct use*. It was this latter that put productivity in all its aspects, including those concerning science and technology, on a radically different and qualitatively higher footing, thereby activating that precipitously accelerating pace of economic expansion which characterizes the history of capitalism up to the present.

However, the same socioeconomic determination of structural disjunction between use (corresponding to human need) and exchange-value-oriented production, which was responsible for setting into motion in the first place the prodigious productive advances of capital, also foreshadowed, right from the beginning, the future complications and, as time went by, increasingly asserted itself as an extremely problematical and ultimately destructive/self-destructive force. For the production of *use value* became ruthlessly *subordinated* to the imperatives of ever-expanding *exchange value*, progressively transforming the latter into a self-sustaining power. As such it became not merely *indifferent* to human need but actively and diametrically *opposed* to it, appropriating to itself, irrespective of the consequences, the available finite material and intellectual resources of society in its capacity of *necessarily* self-oriented and self-perpetuating *anti-use value*.

Thus, the motive power of these developments, right from the beginning, was *socioeconomic* in its substance, and not *technological/instrumental*, as apologetic misrepresentations of the prevailing state of affairs would have it. To be sure, science and technology were inevitably sucked into the process of alienated material articulation of capital's perverse logic. Indeed, the productive structures and technological/instrumental complexes created with the most active participation of science on the basis of the capitalist socioeconomic determinations acquired a character in accordance with and in furtherance of capital's inner logic. As a result science greatly contributed to the speedy unfolding of both the positive and the destructive potentialities of this social formation.

However, there is absolutely nothing in the nature of science and technology from which one could derive the structural subordination of use value to exchange value, with all its ultimately unavoidable destructive consequences. By contrast, the historical articulation of science and technology, the way in which they shape our lives today is *totally unintelligible* without fully acknowledging their deep embeddedness in capital's socioeconomic determinations, both on a temporal scale and in relation to the dominant contemporary structures. Without wishing to deny the dialectic of reciprocal interactions and unavoidable feedback, in the relationship between science and technology on the one hand, and the socioeconomic determinants – like the structurally dominant role of exchange value – on the other, the *'übergreifendes Moment'* happens to be the latter.

Modern science did not end up with the kind of research orientation and results about which many scientists are deeply worried today on account of its own 'immanent logic', but because of the inseparability of its development from the objective requirements of the capitalistic production process as such. It could never even dream about setting its own production targets in some social vacuum, following nothing but the 'immanent' determinations of an 'ideal' research situation. On the contrary, throughout its development modern science was compelled to serve with every means at its disposal the expansion of exchange value, within the framework of a market-oriented production system which itself was subjected to the dictates emanating from the concentration and centralization of capital, as well as to the absolute necessity of profitability under the conditions of the inexorably worsening organic composition of capital from the point of view of easy profitability. Accordingly, the *overall research orientation* imposed upon science by the imperatives of capital-expansion had to consist in *helping to displace* the ultimately explosive contradictions inherent in the growing concentration/centralization and worsening organic composition of capital. In this sense C. Wright Mills' anguished characterization of our 'permanent war economy in a garrison state' – which is inconceivable without the most active contribution of science, in response to the prevailing socioeconomic and political determinations – only underlines the fact that the science we have is not some atemporal entity operating within the framework of its own 'immanent' set of rules, but the science of a historically specific social order.

It is equally important to stress that the illusion of science's 'non-ideological' self-determination and corresponding 'neutrality' is itself the result of the historical process of capitalistic alienation and division of labour. It is not a 'mistake' or 'confusion' that could be done away with through the work of 'philosophical enlightenment', as logical positivists and analytical philosophers conceptualize these matters. Rather, it is a *necessary* illusion, with its roots firmly set in the social soil of commodity production and constantly reproducing itself on that basis, within the structural framework of alienated 'second order mediations'.[525] For as a consequence of the social division of labour, science is in fact alienated from (and deprived of) the social determination of the objectives of its own activity which it receives 'ready made', in the form of material dictates and production targets, from the reified organ of control of the social metabolism as a whole, namely capital.

Thus, operating within the confines of objective *premisses* – dense with *values* – which are categorically/unchallengeably superimposed upon it by the structural framework of the prevailing social division of labour itself, fragmented and divided science is directed to address itself to *'thing-like'* tasks and problems, producing *'thing-like'* results and solutions. As a result, science becomes not just *de facto* but *of necessity*, in virtue of its objective constitution under the given social relations, *ignorant* as well as *uncaring* about the social implications of its far-reaching practical intervention in the process of expanded social reproduction. And since in its 'normal' operation science, by its own constitution, is cut off from the social struggle that decides its tacitly assumed values, the uncritical reflection of the given *immediacy* of science's fragmented everyday practice generates and maintains in existence the broadly diffused illusion of its 'non-ideological self-determination' and 'unrelatedness' to values.

This is why all concern with social values becomes a mere *'afterthought'*, confined to the 'individual conscience' of isolated scientists, or in the best of cases of the aggregate conscience of a limited group of them who endeavour to raise the question of the 'social responsibility of science' (which they can only do outside the framework of their productive practices), and necessarily condemned to impotence by the inherently alienated structure of effective decision making under the rule of capital.

4.3.5
An essay by Norbert Wiener brings to the fore very clearly some insoluble dilemmas generated by being condemned to operate within the vicious circle imposed upon science by capital. Entitled: 'Some moral and technical consequences of automation',[526] this essay is written with a concern and commitment whose authenticity and validity no one should doubt. It is, therefore, all the more revealing that even a scientist of Wiener's stature and dedication to the cause of awakening the social responsibility of science should reach the kind of conclusions which he does.

This is how Norbert Wiener sums up the practical implications of his reflections:

> We have seen that one of the chief causes of the danger of disastrous consequences in the use of the learning machines is that man and machine operate on *two distinct time scales*, so that the machine is much faster than man and the two do not gear together without serious difficulties. Problems of the same sort arise whenever two control operators on very different time scales act together, irrespective of which system is the faster and which system is the slower. This leaves us the much more directly moral question: What are the *moral problems* when man as an *individual* operates in connection with the controlled process of a much *slower time scale*, such as *a portion of political history* or – our main subject of inquiry – the *development of science*?
>
> Let it be noted that the development of science is a *control and communication process* for the *long-term* understanding and control of *matter*. In this process *50 years are as a day in the life of the individual*. For this reason the individual scientist must work as a part of a process whose time scale is so long that *he himself can only contemplate a very limited sector of it*. Here, too,

communication between the two parts of a double machine is difficult and limited. Even when the individual believes that science contributes to the human ends which he has at heart, his belief needs a continual scanning and reevaluation which is only partly possible. For the *individual scientist*, even the partial appraisal of this liaison between the man and the process requires an *imaginative forward glance at history* which is difficult, exacting and only *limitedly achievable*. And if we adhere simply to the creed of the scientist, that an incomplete knowledge of the world and of ourselves is better than no knowledge, we can still by no means always justify the naive assumption that *the faster we rush ahead* to employ the new powers for action which are opened up to us, *the better it will be*. We must always exert the *full strength of our imagination* to examine where the full use of our new modalities may lead us.[527]

The greatest weakness of Wiener's train of thought is that he accepts the same framework of discourse against the disastrous consequences of which he sounds his noble warning. What is painfully missing from his considerations is their *social dimension*, even when the case he himself presents would be incomparably stronger if he tried to put the relevant social connections into relief. An obvious example is when he suggests, indeed somewhat naively, that the practical adoption of the maxim 'the faster we rush ahead the better it will be' is the result of a *'naive assumption'* on the part of some *individual scientists* who do not use 'the full strength of their imagination', while in reality it is the *necessary* consequence of capital's objective structural determinations as manifest in a ruthlessly *competitive-advantage-oriented* logic.

In truth, there are no moral problems attached to automation *as such* but only to its practical implementation in a determinate way in any *particular type of society*. Equally, while one can readily agree that science is itself a 'control and communication process', it is far too narrow a definition to suggest that its objective is 'the *long-term* control and understanding of *matter*'. It is narrow for two reasons. First, because science is simultaneously concerned with the problems of *short-term* control as well from which its *immediate* determinations arise. And second, because science has to address itself to much more than the understanding and control of 'matter' if it is to have any chance at all of successfully accomplishing its overall objectives which embrace social life under all its aspects, including the most complex moral and intellectual ones. Besides, by narrowly and one-sidedly defining science as the control of *matter*, the illusion is being created that the self-conscious agency of science is itself in control of its own practices, whereas in reality the alienated determination and control of its objectives by capital is the gravest issue facing science as much as society in general, with the potentially most dangerous and disastrous practical implications for the future.

Furthermore, difference in *speed alone* does not establish a separate scale of *temporality*. If it could do so, human society would be fragmented into an *infinite* number of scales of temporality even at a particular point in time, not to mention its all-embracing historical totality, with an *a priori impossibility* for understanding, communication, and control. Nor is it the case that 'the machine' has a temporality of its own. In reality there is no such thing as 'the machine', nor can there be; only *particular machines*. And even if, as undoubtedly happens to be the case, some machines are incomparably faster in their operation than man, that does not prove in the slightest that they have a temporality of their own. For man, in principle, can devise other machines in order to catch up with and overtake one that earlier seemed to run away from him, thus tangibly demonstrating the validity of his own temporality in the order of nature and men who all belong, of course, to the same order of nature and share fundamentally the same scale of temporality.

Admittedly, *fragmentation* with regard to the requirements of *control* to which Wiener refers confronts us with 'the danger of disastrous conse- quences' about which he is deeply and rightly troubled. However, this is by no means the result of the individual scientist's time scale conflicting with the long-term temporality of science as a whole, which is in any case an *a priori incorrigible* condition at the level of isolated individuality. For the fundamental issue is not that the individual scientist – confined in his life- span to no more than 'one day in the history of science' that itself embraces the whole of human development – 'can only *contemplate* a very limited sector' of science's historical totality. It is, rather, the disconcerting fact that even at the particular point in time when he is active, he is uncere- moniously confined to an almost infinitesimal *fragment of the fragment* on account of the prevailing division of labour.

To make matters worse still, the scientist can indeed only *contemplate*, with utmost frustration as Wiener himself did in his own field of activity, the fragmented structure and 'limited sector' of the science to which he contributes, without being able to influence significantly the vital sociopoli- tical determinations and decisions that directly or indirectly affect the given objectives as well as the future development of science in its inescapable social setting.

The structurally insurmountable problem is that the objective contradic- tions of a determinate, capitalistically structured *social being* – contradic- tions which assert themselves through the fragmented and reified mode of functioning of science, too, under the rule of capital – cannot be remedied by way of *individual self-reorientation*, however imaginative, enlightened and positive in its intent. This is why Wiener's dilemma addressed to individual scientists must prove insoluble.

At the plane of temporality itself the contradiction between the 'time scales' of the individual scientist and science as a whole can disappear only in the transhistorical unity of mankind to which all individuals belong. Such a solution, however, remains an *abstract postulate*, in the spirit of the dying

Faust as depicted with self-tormenting ambiguity and irony by Goethe, so long as the *present-day reality* of mankind does not exhibit the *actual unity* of the individual and collective subjects able to plan and regulate, in the 'short-term' as well as on a 'long-term' basis, the complex modalities of social intercourse, including that of science.

Thus the issue at stake concerns the practical articulation of radically different social complexes, with the necessary restructuring of the existing constitution of science as well, extricating it by means of collective social action from its present-day subjection to the alien ends of capital along with the rest of society. And no amount of 'imaginative forward glance at history' by isolated individual scientists – not even if they exercise to the utmost their creative imagination – can provide a viable substitute for that.

5 · SCIENCE UNDER THE SHADOW OF THE MILITARY/ INDUSTRIAL COMPLEX

The world that emerged from the 'Great Depression' of the 1930s and from the second world war closely connected with it had to face a new situation, with tensions and constraints of a very different kind as compared to the inter-war years. The 'isolationism' of the United States – which was consciously opposed by Roosevelt from the moment of his inaugural address – was irrevocably relegated to the past, and the active intervention of the most powerful country of the capitalist world in international affairs became the forcefully pursued official policy, while the former British and French Empires were replaced by new forms of 'neo-colonial' rule. At the same time, in the aftermath of the second world war the Soviet Union, too, appeared on the international stage as an incomparably more active world power than before the war, followed in 1949 by the victory of the Chinese Revolution: developments which significantly altered the earlier relation of forces.

Understandably, in the euphoria of postwar reconstruction and expansion very little attention was paid to the internal problems and contradictions of the capitalist system. Given the economic and political power of some industrial enterprises which gained an immensely strong foothold during the war years in the American economy through military production, a way had to be found to safeguard their continued profitability and expansion under the changed circumstances, by enlisting the good services of the state both in the home economy and for the creation of the kind of international relations which favoured the consolidation and growth of such forces.

As to the first dimension, the US Federal Employment Act of 1946 signalled a major departure from earlier practices. It pledged the full backing of the state for maintaining and financially supporting the highest level of economic activity through the policy of *full employment*, rationalizing and legitimating the audacity of state intervention in the idealized 'free enterprise system' by insisting that in an age of 'technological disruption' it was necessary to 'supplement' the market system by political action, so as to secure the 'rational allocation' of resources and the 'satisfaction of public need'. With regard to the international conditions which greatly benefited the peace-time expansion of military production, the same year of 1946 brought with it the eruption of the cold war – marked by Churchill's Fulton speech and by numerous moves to set up a new Western military alliance – which has been maintained at varying degrees of intensity, at times even threatening to erupt into a full-scale real war, ever since.

In the course of postwar developments, the economy has been quietly but radically restructured, so as to be able to meet the needs – euphemistically described as 'the public needs' – of the dominant socioeconomic forces. Naturally, science played a major role in these transformations. Given the sheer size of the productive forces involved as well as their capital-intensive technological articulation, the success of this enterprise would have been simply inconceivable without the most intensive participation of science. At the same time, in view of the very nature of such undertaking, science itself had to suffer the consequences of the developments to which it contributed so much. As a result, the control of science by the state has grown to such an extent that its present-day situation bears no comparison in this respect to past stages of historical development. Ironically, however, the ideology of 'scientism' and the illusions connected with the alleged autonomy and objectivity of the scientist's enterprise as the model for all never flourished more than under the postwar climate of 'the end of ideology'. Yet, in reality, we were witnesses to extremely problematical transformations, with far-reaching implications both for science itself and for society as a whole.

5.1 EINSTEIN'S POSTWAR STRUGGLE AGAINST THE MILITARIZATION OF SCIENCE

5.1.1

Towards the end of 1945, Einstein drafted a message to be read at a National Congress of Scientists, scheduled for January 10–12, 1946. Here are the main points of this message:

> I am sincerely gratified that *the great majority of scientists are fully conscious of their responsibilities* as scholars and world citizens; and that they have not fallen victim to the widespread hysteria that threatens our future and that of our children. . . . It is horrifying to realize that the poison of *militarism and imperialism* threatens to bring about undesirable changes in the political attitude of the United States at the very moment when this country ought to assume a position of leadership in establishing international security. . . . What we see at work here is not an expression of the sentiments of the American people; rather, it reflects the will of a *powerful minority* which *uses its economic power to control the organs of political life*. . . . Should the government pursue this fateful course, we scientists must refuse to submit to its immoral demands, even if they are backed by legal machinery. There is an unwritten law, that of our own conscience, which is far more binding than any bills that may be devised in Washington. And there are, of course, even for us, the ultimate weapons: *non-cooperation and strike*.

We justifiably blame German intellectuals for having unconditionally sur-
rendered themselves to the control of an unworthy government. It is right to
punish them for the crimes which they committed even though they claim that
they were legally compelled to act as they did. I am hopeful that our own
intellectuals are determined to avoid similar wrongdoing; the attitude they
have thus far adopted justifies such hope.[528]

As things turned out, Einstein's hopes were immediately dashed. The
projected National Congress of concerned scientists never materialized
and therefore Einstein's message could never reach its intended destination, remaining locked up in his drawers until it could see the light of day in
a posthumous publication of their author's contributions to the peace
movement.

To be sure, Einstein continued to raise his voice against the new
imperialism of American economic interests and against the militarization
of science under the pressure of the same economic determinations. He
defended Norbert Wiener – who condemned 'the massacre of Nagasaki'[529]
and courageously refused to work on a US Navy sponsored computer-
project which he feared might well be used for mass slaughter – by
categorically stating that '*Non-cooperation in military matters should be an
essential moral principle for all true scientists*'.[530] And at the time when
President Truman announced an all-out effort to develop the H-bomb,
Einstein expressed his alarm, in a television programme conducted by Mrs
Eleanor Roosevelt, in no uncertain terms:

The belief that it is possible to achieve security through armaments on a
national scale is, in the present state of military technology, a *disastrous
illusion*.... Every action related to foreign policy is governed by one single
consideration: How should we act in order to achieve the utmost superiority
over the enemy in the event of war? The answer has been: Outside the United
States, we must establish *military bases* at every possible, strategically important point of the globe as well as arm and strengthen economically our
potential allies. And inside the United States, *tremendous financial power is
being concentrated in the hands of the military*; youth is being militarized; and
the loyalty of citizens, particularly civil servants, is carefully supervised by a
police force growing more powerful every day. People of independent political
thought are harassed. The public is subtly *indoctrinated by the radio, the press,
the schools*. Under the *pressure of military secrecy*, the range of public information is increasingly restricted.... The weird aspect of this development lies
in its *apparently inexorable character*. Each step appears as the inevitable
consequence of the one that went before. And at the end, looming ever
clearer, lies *general annihilation*.[531]

What made things even more anguishing for Einstein was his growing
realization that:

While it proved eventually possible, at an exceedingly heavy cost, to defeat
the Germans, the dear Americans have vigorously assumed their place....
The German calamity of years ago repeats itself: *people acquiesce without
resistance* and align themselves with the forces for evil. And one stands by,
powerless.[532]

However, no matter how powerless he felt, Einstein never ceased to protest against such acquiescence. Fittingly, the last signature of his life was appended to a dramatic statement of scientists against the threat of nuclear annihilation. At the same time, he tried to understand the causes of one's powerlessness, and summed up his conclusions with great clarity in a letter addressed to an old friend – the remarkable Queen Mother of Belgium – just a few months before his death:

> When I look at mankind today, nothing astonishes me quite so much as the shortness of man's memory with regard to political developments. Yesterday the Nuremberg trials, today the all-out effort to rearm Germany. In seeking for some kind of explanation, I cannot rid myself of the thought that this, the last of my fatherlands has invented for its own use a *new kind of colonialism*, one that is less conspicuous than the colonialism of old Europe. It achieves *domination· of other countries by investing American capital abroad*, which makes those countries *firmly dependent* on the United States. Anyone who opposes this policy or its implications is treated as an *enemy of the United States*. It is within this general context that I try to understand the present-day policies of Europe, including England. I tend to believe that these policies are less the result of a *planned* course of action than the natural consequences of *objective conditions*.[533]

By 'natural consequences' Einstein meant, of course, the vitiating impact of the objective conditions of the capitalist socioeconomic system which inevitably superimpose themselves on conscious human pursuit as a 'quasi-natural law', frustrating the endeavours of individuals and nullifying their plans to check the anarchy of the prevailing social order.[534] It was the 'apparently inexorable character' of this anarchy and deadly objectivity which he found at times totally paralysing. Thus, he exclaimed with despair in reply to a question of *The Reporter* concerning the situation of the scientists in America:

> If I were a young man again and had to decide how to make a living, I would not try to become a scientist or scholar or teacher. I would rather choose to be a plumber or a peddler, in the hope of finding that modest degree of independence still available under present circumstances.[535]

5.1.2

The weakness of Einstein's position was not the result of *personal* failure, either in the sense of theoretical limitations or on account of some pretended political and moral 'neutrality'. On the contrary, his stature as one of the intellectual giants of the century was organically complemented by a profound commitment to the values of a socialist society whose realization he considered absolutely vital for the very survival of mankind. Thus, he was in fact a living refutation of J.L. Austin's grotesque notion of great scientists as producers of fundamental discoveries by way of 'pottering on one side and another with their instruments' and 'stumbling on something really important, rather than by saying one fine day: let us attack some great problem'.[536] For Einstein constantly tried to 'attack some great problem', in the comprehensive framework of its proper setting.

Moreover, being the most highly acclaimed and publicly celebrated physicist of the century, receiving grateful recognition for his achievements in a 'non-controversial field' from all over the world, he had unparalleled access to heads of governments as well as to the mass media. Indeed, he could command the full attention of the public whenever he wanted and on any subject of his choice, including the most controversial ones, thanks to the authority conferred upon him by innumerable awards – from the Nobel Prize to the Honorary Membership of the American Plumbers' Union – as well as by constant praise verging on distasteful (and by Einstein greatly resented) adulation as 'the Monarch of the Intellect'. It was therefore all the more significant in its implications for the position of science and scientists under the domination of the military/industrial complex that he had to feel not simply threatened, in the midst of aggressive political denunciations,[537] but intellectually and politically betrayed, isolated and so completely powerless that he could not help crying out, in agonizing and somewhat misanthropic resignation – a posture thoroughly alien to his positive and combative character – that: '*In the end men will get what they deserve.*'[538]

Einstein knew very well and clearly stated that 'men have never freed themselves from intolerable bondage, *frozen into law*, except by *revolutionary action.*'[539] This is why he insisted that: 'Deeds, not words are needed; mere words get pacifists nowhere. They must initiate action and begin with what can be achieved now.'[540] Thus the practical question confronting Einstein was twofold: (a) what kind of action was actually feasible under the prevailing circumstances in order to face up to the tasks inherent in the diagnosed problem? and (b) to what extent could the envisaged action be considered adequate to achieving the advocated end?

Inevitably, there had to be an important 'tactical' consideration, spelled out by Einstein in 1949 in the context of formulating a militant, uncompromisingly 'non-cooperationist' position. Defending an article written in the same spirit by Herbert Jehle, he added, in a letter to the editor who had rejected Jehle's article with transparent excuses concerning the 'rigour' of its logic:

> since this [i.e. the open advocacy of militant non-cooperation] *cannot be said in so many plain words*, any pronouncement about these issues will, of necessity, become defective logically. And, after all, *to speak more frankly would merely outrage the conformist crowd.*[541]

Many years earlier, Einstein had addressed himself with essentially the same considerations to the question of how to connect the objectives of socialism and pacifism. This is how he summed up his position in March

1931, in reply to a question by Norman Thomas who was at the time the leader of American socialists:

> It is easier to win over people to pacifism than to socialism. Social and economic problems have become much more complex, and it is necessary that men and women first reach the point where they actually believe in the possibility of peaceful solutions. Once this has been accomplished, they may be expected to approach economic and political problems in a spirit of co-operation. I would say that we should work *first for pacifism*, and *only later for socialism*.[542]

No doubt, to put the relationship between peace and socialism in such terms was extremely problematical. For, given the contradictions of society and the immense power of the materially as well as culturally dominant vested interests, there could be no guarantee whatsoever that the 'first phase' of pacifist enlightenment and understanding would be successfully completed, so as to be followed by the much needed 'second phase' of socialist cooperation.

Nevertheless, it would be quite wrong to see this issue in terms of the facile contrast between the 'correct' and the 'mistaken perspective'. For whatever the merits of the case, in reality there can be no way escaping the burden of articulating even the theoretically best strategy in relation to the material and ideological limitations of the available social agencies. In other words, the question that reveals the complete vacuity of all talk about some a priori 'correct perspective' is this: what kind of action could one envisage under the prevailing circumstances in case one adopted it. If, therefore, the adoption of the abstractly 'ideal' strategy offers no possibility for action, that can only demonstrate the theoretical absurdity and well deserved practical impotence of envisaging 'solutions' from *outside* the framework of the unavoidable – subjective as well as objective – sociohistorical constraints.

In truth, it was the great difficulty of locating a historically viable social agency of action which made Einstein's discourse at times so problematical, notwithstanding his profound theoretical insights coupled with the unshakable intensity of his moral and political commitments.

Nothing displays this more clearly than the rather ambiguous position which he assumed in his assessments of the power of reason. For, on the one hand, he was well aware of its limitations and expressed his scepticism[543] – indeed, at times even his utter pessimism[544] – with regard to its effectiveness. And yet, on the other hand, he was constantly forced to appeal to 'the best minds'[545] and to the sense of responsibility of those 'influential intellectuals'[546] whose active involvement in the realization of the advocated ends he considered absolutely essential as well as the only practically feasible strategy under the negative constraints of the prevailing circumstances. Unlike Romain Rolland, his friend and comrade-in-arms in the cause of militant pacifism, who worked in France in a social setting of growing mass movements, Einstein could not appeal to '*organized action on a large scale*' in the interest of a '*social revolution* as the only method for abolishing the system that begets war'.[547] He had to build on the foundations available to him, by activating the energies of concerned and influential fellow-scientists against the lethal menace of militarization in situations where sustainable mass action was, sadly, nowhere in sight.

In the end the contest proved to be a most uneven one, however great Einstein's moral and intellectual stature by any standard, let alone by comparison to his adversaries, from Congressmen like Rankin to 'the hired hacks of an accommodating press',[548] not to forget the countless accommodating and compromising members of the scientific community itself. His hope that 'the *great majority* of scientists are *fully conscious* of their responsibilities' turned sour as the 'inexorable' advance of the military/industrial complex made a mockery of 'the ultimate weapons: non-cooperation and strike', depriving him even of some of his closest earlier allies, as the practical capitulation of his own brainchild, the formerly loyal *Bulletin of the Atomic Scientists*, proved, among many other disappointments.

Having to contend with desperately uneven odds, against the advancing integration of science into the *perniciously* practical framework of the military/industrial complex, forced Einstein into a theoretically untenable position by his own earlier standard, when he declared in the spirit of a false dichotomy, in defence of the scientist's moral right to non-cooperation in the face of a threatening witch-hunt, that 'the progress of science originates from man's quest for *knowledge*, and rarely from his pursuit of *practical* objectives. *Science will stagnate if it is made to serve practical goals.*'[549] Thus, one of the greatest scientists who ever lived and who always proudly proclaimed the ineradicable social provenance as well as the necessary social destination of science[550] was forced into a corner in which he had to conduct his rearguard action on behalf and in the name of 'basic research' *vis à vis* 'practical goals' when in reality *both* had become surbordinated to and dominated by the *destructive practical objectives* of the military/industrial complex.

Since 'the ultimate weapon' – the scientists' strike – could not even be contemplated under the circumstances of an almost complete social isolation and its counterpart, the adversary's ever-increasing power, the only course of action that remained to Einstein, too, was to assume a posture very similar to Wiener's '*imaginative forward glance at history*', even if, paradoxically, formulated as a retrospective 'counter-factual conditional'. Thus, less than one month before his death Einstein wrote in a letter to his old friend, Max von Laue:

> My action concerning the atomic bomb and Roosevelt consisted merely in the fact that, because of the danger that Hitler might be the first to have the bomb, I signed a letter to the President which had been drafted by Szilárd. *Had I known* that that fear was not justified, I, no more than Szilárd, would

have participated in *opening this Pandora's box*. For my distrust of governments was not limited to Germany.[551]

The tragic fact, however, is not so much that Pandora's box has become
wide open, for future generations to confront with growing anxiety, so long
as they have the chance to do so, but that the scientists – even the greatest
among those who were involved in opening the box – had very little
alternative, if any, retrospectively or with an imaginative forward glance at
history, to do or not to do so, not to mention their utter powerlessness
to undo their fateful deed. For only a concerted and co-ordinated social
action, with all concerned scientists as an integral part of such undertaking, can conceivably match up to this unparalleled historical challenge
and to the corresponding magnitude of the tasks involved.

5.2 THE OBJECTIVE CONSTRAINTS
OF SCIENTIFIC RESEARCH

5.2.1
The great difficulty is that the obstacles to be surmounted arise on the
objective foundations of contradictory material determinations which
oppose anyone who tries to interfere with the material dictates of their
logic. To say that 'in the end men will get what they deserve' would imply
the intervention of a most peculiar, self-destructive divine justice, since the
overwhelming majority of men are one way or another deprived of the
power of decision making, and therefore do not really 'deserve' what they
get on account of the decisions of a tiny minority: a circumstance that turns
into its diametrical opposite the very notion of 'divine justice'. And in any
case, when former Prime Ministers and Federal Chancellors – like Edward
Heath and Willie Brandt – confess in a curious way the complete powerlessness of their high office, in the belated manifestations of their retrospective, even if quite genuine, good will (in the *Brandt Reports* which
are as totally ignored by their successors as the authors of these Reports
themselves underestimated the importance of the now acknowledged burning issues at stake while they held Prime Ministerial office); and when
former American Presidents, like Jimmy Carter, weep in front of television
cameras, openly admitting the failure of their policies and defending
themselves at the same time by saying that their presidential decisions
counted for nothing ('the President is completely powerless', as Jimmy
Carter put it), one wonders who really has the power of decision making in
contemporary society.

It was another American President, the former Supreme Commander of
the Allied Forces, General Eisenhower who – way back in 1961 – warned
against the growing influence of what he aptly termed the '*military/
industrial complex*'. He also recognized that the operation of that complex

was inseparable from 'a scientific-technological élite' which was geared to the self-propelling interests of the military/industrial complex, and he voiced his fears that public policy as a whole might become a *captive* to the forces whose pernicious influence he declared to be visible – already in 1961 – in every city, every state house, and every office of the Federal Government.

Of course, the roots of such developments go back to a much earlier historical phase, to the very beginning of the twentieth century, as we have seen with reference to Rosa Luxemburg. However, what matters in the present context is to stress that the sinister forces which frightened even some American Presidents are the manifestations of objective *structural* conditions – and contradictions – of the rule of capital at its 'advanced' stage of development. This is why the contest between the *objective structural determinations* of society and the *conscience* of limited numbers of concerned scientists of even Einstein's stature turns out to be such an uneven one. For what we can see in reality is not that 'men get what they deserve' but that the material forces corresponding to the fundamental structural determinations of society produce the *'men they need'* in every walk of life, including science, through the agency of which they can impose their destructive structural imperatives on society as a whole, irrespective of the consequences. This is why under the prevailing structural determinations the advocated 'non-cooperation and strike' of concerned scientists *necessarily* assumes the sobering and rather disconcerting form of the retrospective counter-factual conditionals – the tragically impotent 'had I known that . . .' – of even the Einsteins.

It is symbolic of our age that the highest intellectual achievements are rewarded with a large sum of money attached to a prize – the Nobel Prize – which represents the lucrative investment of the fortune amassed by the inventor of the greatest force of destruction known to man prior to the atom bomb. Moreover, the obscenity of glorifying the powers of destruction in the framework of world acclaim assumes an even more openly cynical form by honouring with the 'Nobel Peace Prize' some public figures who in virtue of their high office were directly responsible for major crimes against humanity in the form of saturation bombing and other acts of genocide against defenseless peoples. This is how the power of the military/industrial complex succeeds in turning everything into its opposite, reshaping in its own image, in the interest of its self-legitimation, even the scale of values in terms of which such acts could be brought to account, while – as Einstein wrote to the Queen Mother of Belgium – 'one stands by, powerless'.

One of the most stubborn illusions with regard to the natural sciences concerns their alleged 'objectivity' and 'neutrality', ascribed to them on account of their experimental and instrumental character, in contrast to the socially more involved and compromised character of the 'human sciences'. However, a closer examination shows not only that the claimed objectivity and neutrality is no more than a legend but that in reality the *opposite* happens to be the case.

Lukács used to say that philosophers are prone to imagine that the world is two-dimensional because the medium in which they produce their ideas is the two-dimensional surface of the paper in front of them. Admittedly, the natural scientists oriented towards the experimental confirmation of their ideas are most unlikely to be guilty of the same sin. But the reason why they can more easily escape this particular form of self-deception is precisely also the reason why they can afford to be far less detached from – let alone opposed to – the dominant productive structures of their society than the intellectuals active in the humanities and in the social sciences. What is at issue here is that since natural scientists must operate within the framework of tangible (as well as costly) instrumental complexes and supporting structures, they have to secure incomparably more substantial material resources as the elementary condition of their activity than their counterparts on the 'arts' side of the universities and in society at large.

It is a matter of common knowledge how much more expensive it is to set up and continue to fund science faculties in universities than numerically comparable arts faculties: a discrepancy that, striking though it is, discloses only a small part of the overall allocation of society's resources to science. To put things really in perspective, one must remember that *large numbers* of scientists in contemporary society can only function on the necessary *material premiss* of funds which far exceed, *annually and on average*, the Nobel Prize accorded to an *insignificantly* limited number of them *once in a lifetime*.

Thus natural scientists are even less '*freischwebend*' (i.e. 'free-floating' or 'unattached', in Mannheim's sense) than their intellectual counterparts in the humanities and social sciences. Sociologists and philosophers can continue to write books critical of the established social order irrespective of how many 'blacklists' contain their names. Obviously, however, the same condition does not apply to natural scientists who lose the necessary instrumental and institutional prerequisites of their activity if they dare to be critical of the threat to human survival represented by the military/ industrial complex, as the tribulations of even such outstanding figures as Oppenheimer, Wiener and others testify. No doubt, such a difference in the objective conditions of intellectual production puts into relief the measure of society's debt towards the scientists who raise their voice against the dangers they perceive, defiant of the consequences. At the same time, it also helps to explain why *on average* – in universities and elsewhere – natural scientists tend to assume a considerably more conservative posture than their colleagues on the arts side, rather than being more objective, more neutral, more independent, and therefore potentially more critical, as the legend suggests.

What we are concerned with here is a set of major constraints and determinations which point in a direction opposed to that of emancipation, despite the claims to the contrary by the ideologists of the established order. To be sure, the resources appropriated by science in its present-day social setting are truly prodigious. But precisely because they happen to be so forbidding, they are only affordable by a very few 'advanced' societies, thereby helping to *perpetuate* the historically established system of inequalities and exploitation on a global scale, instead of actively contributing to its removal, as the myths of 'modernization', 'transfer of technology', 'green revolution' and the like would have it.

To see, therefore, in the growth of contemporary science the new agency of social emancipation – counterposed to the 'historically obsolete' emancipatory force: the working class – asserting that thanks to 'The new class structure of post-industrial society'[552] the growing army of scientists can 'rival the dominant voice of the past, the business community', is to indulge in the 'post-ideological' fantasies of social apologetics. For such claim omits to mention that the science in question is not a materially and politically self-sustaining sovereign agency, but one inseparable from and subordinated to – or if one prefers President Eisenhower's expression: 'geared to' – the dominant voice of the present: 'the business community' of the military/industrial complex. Accordingly, to predicate the solution of capital's explosive contradictions by the mythical 'new class of scientists' (or by its equivalent: Galbraith's 'technostructure') is as realistic as expecting the abolition of racial discrimination and the full emancipation of all coloured people in South Africa – or, for that matter, even in the United States of America – by the much heralded but little visible 'development of black capitalism'.

5.2.2

In truth the facts at our disposal as evidenced by the last few decades of real development tell a rather discouraging story about the situation of science in contemporary society, notwithstanding the sheer size of the resources allocated to science and technology within the framework of the dominant socioeconomic structures. For the sums involved are directly or indirectly controlled by the military/industrial complex to an almost unbelievable extent, while the ideologies of legitimation and rationalization continue to eulogize the 'fierce spirit of independence' and the 'operational autonomy' of scientific research under the 'free enterprise system'. Since, however, more than 70 per cent of all scientific research in the United States is controlled by the military/industrial complex, while in Britain the equivalent figure is in excess of 50 per cent, and in both cases still rising, one wonders *whose* freedom and autonomy they are talking about in praising the established and – of course – best possible arrangements, within the confines of the given structures.

In Britain what is projected as the ideal for the academic world is an institution under the firm managerial rule of its head: 'Sir Henry Chilver, Vice-Chancellor and creator of the Cranfield Institute of Technology, Mrs Thatcher's automatic choice as a government troubleshooter.'[553] According to the full page hagiography published in the prestigious paper of the British establishment, *The Times*: 'There are few spokes in the information technology revolution that do not lead to Cranfield, Chilver or Chilver-inspired plans.'[554] Sir Henry's institution was:

> Re-formed as a degree-granting college in the late 1960s from a training school set up by the *aircraft manufacturers* [Cranfield – hence its name] ... Built around a Bedfordshire airfield, Cranfield expanded to take over the National Agricultural Engineering College at nearby Silsoe; earlier this year it *linked with the Royal Military College of Science* at Shrivenham.
>
> True, it has no faculty of arts. It is outside the University Grants Committee's ambit and deals directly with government which pays about one quarter of its income.... Cranfield's management style [means that] each department has to break even on its own by going out and drumming up research and sponsorship ... [According to Sir Henry] There is no subject – including sociology and the humanities – which cannot attract private money in order to support research; research which does not interest the external world does not deserve support.[555]

Since the funds of working class organizations and communities do not exactly match the fortunes of the Rockefellers, the GECs, the General Dynamics and the Texas Instruments of this world, one does not really need three guesses to figure out what kind of finance would be feasible under this prescription for the purposes of 'objective research'.

We are told that Sir Henry 'maintains that the Cranfield lessons can be applied elsewhere, disruptive though they would be for the sociologists and English teachers.'[556] But why should one worry about a little disruption if it can be counterbalanced by the benefits of freeing the academics in the humanities of the illusion of belonging to the 'unattached intelligentsia', bringing them fully in line with their colleagues in the natural sciences and technology by directly subordinating them to the purse-string controlled 'rationality' of the dominant socioeconomic structures? For even though – as a minor oversight – we are not told how many airfields, aircraft manufacturer training schools and Royal Military Colleges of Science can be found in the immediate vicinity of all the other British universities and institutions of higher education, the 'Cranfield lessons' and the 'Cranfield philosophy' are said to be fully generalizable as the model for the future. As the article adds:

> All this is, or ought to be, music to the ears of Sir Keith Joseph [the Tory Minister of Education at the time], but it would be wrong to convict Sir Henry of *ideology*. His knighthood, after all, came from the Callaghan era.[557]

Thus, characteristically, what qualifies as being 'above ideology' is the bipartisan/consensual adoption of the ideals which correspond to the interests of the 'dominant voice of the present: the business community' and its complementary state formation.

In the capitalistically advanced countries all branches of science and technology are brought into play in furtherance of the aims of the powerful economic and political/organizational structures. The traditional lines of demarcation between 'pure' and 'applied science' – as well as between business and the increasingly more contemptuously referred to world of the 'academe' – are radically redrawn so as to mould all forms of intellectual production to the needs of the military/industrial complex.

That the knowledge required for manufacturing a vast range of products even remotely connected with the lucrative business of military hardware is necessarily channelled into these grooves goes without saying. What is at first sight somewhat more surprising is that there seems to be no escape from the immense material pull – be it 70 or 50 per cent plus – of these developments, whether one works in genetic engineering or on the less tangible problems belonging to the realm of artificial intelligence. As a recent article emphasized: 'In one of those mysterious shifts of opinion which signals that an idea's time has come, hardboiled industrialists, cautious civil servants and military brass hats woke up to what artificial intelligence was doing.'[558] And no wonder. For:

> Both the pace and the complexity of modern war have left the human nervous system behind. The US Department of Defense is one of the main sources of funds for AI research. It is an *uncomfortable fact* that AI research was kept healthy in the US through the 1970s by a military establishment which, unlike business, can afford a few failures. Computers have become indispensable in the planning and management of war. Also, an awful lot of software goes into military hardware these days. Speech recognition, machine vision and other forms of pattern analysis, as applied to radar signals for example, are of particular interest to the armed forces, and this interest has benefited others. For example, the cruise missile's Tercom guidance system, which matches hills and valleys with an internal map, is reportedly unreliable. But companies believed to have worked on the system are now profiting from their experience by marketing industrial vision systems.[559]

It is indeed most uncomfortable to think not only that the 'healthy state' of an important field of enquiry should depend on the questionable handouts of the military; but also that the subordination of knowledge to the needs and interests of the military/industrial complex should be rationalized and legitimated by the well-established practice of business enterprises taking highly profitable piggyback rides on potentially apocalyptic military ventures and failures.

As to the healthy or unhealthy state of research in genetic engineering pursued under the control of the military, concerned scientists recently started to raise the alarm about the dangers for the future. They point to two deadly probabilities. One concerns the longer term prospect of the total extinction of life on this planet, as a result of a global conflagration of which the lethal contribution of biological weapons would be an integral part. The second, they say, is much nearer to hand: realizable practically tomorrow. It would consist in combining the clandestine dissemination of some already available and most virulent biological agents of destruction with the inherent weaknesses – in some cases amounting to an almost complete absence – of a viable health and hygiene infrastructure in the countries of the 'Third World'. And that would represent the 'final solution' to the problem of so-called 'population explosion' about which the military/industrial complex seems to be so deeply troubled.

5.3 THE APPLIED SCIENCE OF THE MILITARY/INDUSTRIAL COMPLEX

5.3.1

In one of his public addresses Einstein once stated that 'this is the century of applied science, and America is its fatherland', and he continued:

> Why does applied science, which is so magnificent, saves work and makes life easier, bring us so little happiness? The simple answer is that we have not yet learned to make proper use of it.[560]

Naturally, he knew very well that the 'learning' in question was not simply a deficiency in theoretical knowledge but concerned the apparently insurmountable *practical* obstacles represented by the way in which science and technology were embedded in the prevailing mode of production under the rule of capital. Later, when the pressures became more acute through the expansion of the military/industrial complex, Einstein protested in vain against the impending 'stagnation of science' as a result of its subordination to the 'practical goals' of the ongoing developments. His dramatic appeals in defence of 'true science' or 'basic research' against the imposition of extremely restrictive and damaging practical goals had to fall on deaf ears. For the very concepts of 'pure science' and 'fundamental research' were being *practically* redefined in a spirit which stipulated their close integration into the state-sponsored productive practices of the military/industrial complex.

Inevitably, such perverse practical redefinition of science and fundamental research under the emerging constraints turned many things upside down, so as to be able to realign the aspirations and values of science in accord with the new requirements. This is well illustrated by the story of how the 'father of the hydrogen bomb' – Edward Teller – first communicated to an audience of scientists his ideas about how one should proceed:

> Teller stood up and explained his new plan for a thermonuclear explosion, illustrating it with figures on the blackboard. Now the attention of the

scientists in the audience was riveted. They were carried away by the ingenuity of the idea. This was *not a new concept of the order of nature*, one of those intellectual revelations that can be, for the scientist, an expericence of an almost religious quality. But it was a *cunning trick to bend nature* to Man's will. 'It's cute,' exclaimed one scientist, 'it's beautifully cute!'[561]

Compared to Einstein who offered 'new concepts of the order of nature', Teller is nothing but a 'cute technician' who deals in 'cunning tricks to bend nature'. Moreover, since his enterprise is severed from its comprehensive human perspective, the 'cunning trick' in question bends nature in reality not 'to Man's will' but, in its ultimate implications, catastrophically *against mankind* in the most insane of all conceivable equations, which sees in the unlimited expansion of the dehumanizaing and necessarily destructive power of the military/industrial complex, despite the prospects of 'general annihilation looming ever clearer', the elementary conditions of human progress. Hegel used to refer to the objective dialectic manifest in the 'cunning of Reason' as the paradoxical but benevolent agency of historical development towards the realization of freedom. As it turned out, actual historical development produced the far from benevolent material agency of the military/industrial complex and the 'cunning tricks' of 'cute technicians' through which the 'cunning of Reason' seems to be well on the way to irrevocably *outwitting itself*, thereby assuming the form of *total Unreason* and, instead of realizing freedom in history, putting a radical end to history itself.

The real tragedy is that the transformation of science into the trade of 'cute technicians' is not a marginal problem but one affecting the contemporary development of knowledge in its entirety. This is why the Tellers of this world must be preferred to the Einsteins and Oppenheimers who must end their intellectual careers, no matter how great their stature, as desperately isolated and even witch-hunted figures. And this is why the production of knowledge as a whole must be reconstituted around the 'cute technicians' who are proclaimed great scientists in virtue of their unqualified willingness to champion the destructive and ultimately self-destructive interests of the military/industrial complex.

5.3.2

To understand this shift in the orientation of science it is necessary to identify without ceremony the powerful socioeconomic and political determinants of the ongoing process. Failure to do so leads to vacuous conclusions with regard to the *causes* and possible *remedies*, even if some of the *symptoms* are correctly described. A case in point is Popper's treatment of the problem. It is assessed by him in the following terms:

> The growth of normal science, which is linked to the growth of Big Science, is likely to prevent, or even to destroy, the growth of knowledge, the growth of great science. I regard the situation as tragic if not desperate; and the present

trend in the so-called empirical investigations into the sociology of the natural sciences is likely to contribute to the decay of science. Superimposed upon this danger is another danger, created by Big Science: its urgent need for scientific technicians. More and more PhD candidates receive a merely technical training, a training in certain techniques of measurement; they are not initiated into the scientific tradition, the critical tradition of questioning, of being tempted and guided by great and apparently insoluble riddles rather than by the solubility of little puzzles. True, these technicians, these specialists, are usually aware of their limitations. They call themselves specialists and reject any claim to authority outside their specialities. Yet they do so proudly, and proclaim that specialization is a necessity. But this means flying in the face of the facts which show that great advances still come from those with a wide range of interests. If the many, the specialists, gain the day, it will be the end of science as we know it – of great science. It will be a spiritual catastrophe comparable in its consequences to nuclear armament.[562]

The trouble with Popper's analysis is that he fails to notice the vital *complementarities* inherent in the diagnosed process – as rooted in a set of deep-seated *social determinations* – and therefore ends up with hollow oppositions and *disjunctives*, coupled with a *romantic élitism* and a disdainfully superior attitude with regard to what is going on in the world of science and its setting. Nor is it accidental that Popper fails to notice the complementarity, indeed the causal connection, between nuclear armaments and the emerging 'spiritual catastrophe' in the field of knowledge. For, given his profoundly conservative stance and the mythology of 'little by little' as the only admissible social corrective, he must compress everything so as to fit into the grooves of his a priori ideological disjunction, spelled out as the programmatic title of his article: 'Reason *or* revolution?'.

This is why we are offered by Popper the aprioristic rejection of all attempts that aim at critically assessing the social setting of science, coupled with the totally unsustained declaration and logical *non sequitur* that they are 'likely to contribute to the decay of science'. Also, this is why we are offered the sterile opposition between 'great science' and 'Big Science', as well as that between the specialized 'many' on the one hand and the elected wide-ranging 'few' on the other.

But, of course, what must be most bewildering to Popper is that his abstract appeal to reason and to the integrity of scientific knowledge is shipwrecked on the reality of science itself as it is reconstituted in the contemporary world. Moreover, it must be doubly disheartening that the earlier idealized methodology of the *social engineer's* 'little by little' should rebound on its ideological champion with a vengeance, forcing him to denounce it as the intolerable myopia of the '*scientific technician*' devoid of a comprehensive vision. After which nothing remains to the author except to lament over the misconceived orientation of 'Big Science' (a theoretically and socially vacuous concept) as well as to dismiss the foolishness of all those who prefer 'Big Science' to the intellectually superior credentials of 'great science'.

In reality, though, the problem is not that *science* is 'Big' (a sheer mystification) and that there are too many PhD students who pursue 'little puzzles'. It is, rather, that the dominant voice of the present – the 'business community' of the military/industrial complex – is far too big, and on the increase without an end in sight, subordinating the development of science to the reified imperatives of its own cancerous growth. And who could seriously suggest that one can reverse such trend 'little by little'? Not even Popper.

The shift visible in the postwar reconstitution of science is indeed most disturbing, and potentially catastrophic. But not on account of science itself being responsible for producing, on its own, an 'intellectual catastrophe' for which no other force in society could be blamed. The issue is not 'Big Science' versus 'great science'; not even 'pure science' or 'basic research' versus 'applied science'. It is, rather, that *science in general* is being transformed and degraded into the *'applied science' of the military/ industrial complex.*

Inevitably, an issue of this kind concerns the fundamental structural matrix of society and the alternative perspectives of its contending classes. Accordingly, the reversal of the identified trends in the postwar development of the conditions of knowledge is inconceivable without a major intervention at the plane of the social structure itself from which the destructive determinations of science and technology arise.

5.4 THE EQUIVALENCE OF CONSUMPTION AND DESTRUCTION IN CAPITAL'S LOGIC

5.4.1

The main reason why the 'non-cooperation and strike' of concerned scientists advocated by Einstein never had a chance to halt the growing domination of all fields and branches of knowledge by the military/industrial complex resides in the conditions of production of knowledge itself under the capitalistic organization and division of labour. Three major aspects of the relationship are relevant in this respect:

1. The partiality and fragmentation of individual intellectual production.
2. Differentials of talent and motivation, as well as a tendency to competition associated with them.
3. A historically specific social antagonism, articulated in a network of hierarchical social complexes which integrate into their framework the – in and by themselves as yet undefined – tendencies of the first two, giving them a direction in accordance with their own structural determinations and imperatives.

Defenders of the established order (ever since the early representatives of 'the standpoint of political economy') like to absolutize the first two. Indeed, they like to inflate them into 'natural laws' on the basis of which they can either completely *ignore* the third, or – when the contradictions of society erupt with too great an intensity to be ignored – *justify* the existing structural hierarchies, despite all their destructive manifestations, as *unchangeable* on account of their claimed correspondence to the order of nature.

Yet, the truth is that the individualistic articulation and organization of the conditions of labour is itself a historically established *social* condition. 'Competition', likewise, can assume a multiplicity of extremely diverse, even diametrically opposed forms and functions, in tune with its specific social setting. And in any case, there is nothing wrong with individual motivation and competition *as such*, but only with their socially divisive and paralysing articulation as *fragmentation, isolation,* and antagonistic *super- and sub-ordination*, which in fact condemns the allegedly 'sovereign' individuals to powerlessness, notwithstanding their 'good intentions'. To put it in another way, by using an analogy: it is the 'high explosive' of social antagonism and its twin brother, the corresponding hierarchical social division of labour – i.e. the third condition mentioned above – which fuse the by themselves harmless halves of 'uranium 235', representing the first two conditions, into the 'critical mass' of the bomb responsible for the nuclear explosion.

Thus, the socially determined fragmentation of intellectual production, and the structurally secured denial of control to the scientists over the conditions of their activity, make it virtually impossible to envisage large-scale 'non-cooperation and strike' within the framework of the prevailing socioeconomic system. For the domain of science does not constitute an autonomous force, with a self-supporting material ground, And even if it did, 'non-cooperation and strike' would still be well beyond the realistically feasible range of strategies, since it would represent a direct challenge to the established mode of social control in its entirety, rather than being confined to the specific concerns and issues of science.

Likewise, the 'non-cooperation and strike' of even the workers of the industrial enterprises – who undoubtedly possess a materially grounded power of opposition and the potentiality of embarking on the establishment of a radical social alternative – is not a viable strategy under the circumstances, short of becoming a *general strike* whose sociopolitical objective would be the overthrow of the capitalist system. For the fragmentation and lack of overall control inherent in the prevailing social division of labour applies to the working classes no less than to the individuals engaged in intellectual production. The military/industrial complex embraces a vast area of production and social reproduction, and its enterprises represent the conditions of *work* (and livelihood) for the people employed in them. Accordingly, given the internal and international links and reciprocal determinations in the contemporary framework of capitalist production, no *isolated action* can go beyond the objective of modifying to a limited extent the local conditions of work and pay. By contrast, envisaging an *alternative* – on the required scale – to the type of productive activity pursued within the confines of the military/industrial complex would in fact imply the inescapability of restructuring the overall production system and the mode of social control necessarily associated with it.

5.4.2

In view of all this, it is important to identify the sociohistorical *specificity* of the forces behind the spectacular postwar advance of the military/industrial complex, so as to be able to locate the required agencies of a radical social critique and an adequate margin for action. Equally, it is necessary to put into relief the *socioeconomic substance* of the criticized forces, since concentrating merely on some of the *political manifestations* of their activity leaves them a great deal of room for adjustments without seriously affecting their disastrous impact on contemporary social developments.

To illustrate this problem, let us see a passage from a manifesto signed by Einstein and others, entitled 'Militarism and civilization', in protest against what they called 'The militarization of America':

> Arnold J. Toynbee in his monumental *Study of History* points out that militarism 'has been by far the commonest cause of the breakdown of civilizations'. The present trend toward military control over American life and institutions should, therefore, be of the deepest concern to every patriotic American. It would be fatuous and suicidal for us to assume that we can adopt ways which have corrupted and destroyed other civilizations, and that we can ourselves escape the same fate. Militarism leads both to war and to loss of freedom. And there are subtle as well as obvious dangers to a nation which yields its civil functions to military control. The spirit of initiative and inquiry may be sapped even where some of the external trappings of regimentation do not appear. If, for example, the right to differ from the military is not vigorously exercised because of the increased prestige of military men, the theoretical or formal existence of the right will not profit or save our free society.[563]

The problem, though, is that Toynbee's vague notion of 'militarism' falls far short of explaining the destructive antagonisms of even past social formations, let alone of adequately grasping the historical novelty of postwar socioeconomic and political developments under the domination of the military/industrial complex. For neither the 'military control of civil functions', nor the McCarthyite violations of civil liberties could be considered *necessary* requirements for enforcing the dominant interests here referred to under all conditions, irrespective of the given margin for political adjustments under the changing circumstances.

To concentrate on the aspect of *militarism* tends to underscore the vital importance of the specific *industrial* articulation of capital at its present stage of historical development. Such articulation consists of a unique 'symbiotic' relationship whose principal objective is to secure the necessary funds for highly profitable military/industrial projects on a continuous basis and on an ever-expanding scale, and not the exercise of a direct military/ political control over the social body.

The political methods employed in this process entirely depend on whether or not the realization of such objective encounters an effective resistance. Hence, not surprisingly, British capitalism in the postwar period of consensus politics was in fact able to operate a far more restrictive 'Official Secrets Act' than the United States – through so-called 'Gentlemen's agreements', 'D-notices', etc. – without any need to engage in the open violation of civil liberties. When things change in this respect for the worse, as evidenced by the repressive anti-trade union legislation of the Thatcher government, that is not the result of the direct intervention by the military in politics. Rather, in its obvious *class content* it reflects the growing structural crisis of capital and the intensification of the fundamental social antagonism at the roots of it.

It is the latter that determines the margin of manoeuvre of the capitalist state formation at the level of political rights and civil liberties. Furthermore, since one of the major factors in the ideological legitimation of the interests of the military/industrial complex happens to be the claimed opposition – as a matter of principle – to 'regimentation' and 'totalitarianism', in the name of an uncompromising defence of the fundamental values of democracy and freedom, the open adoption of a militaristic way of running the *internal* [564] matters of advanced capitalistic societies, under an economically rather wasteful state of emergency, would be admissible only in the last resort.

In this sense, the 'militarism' of the military/industrial complex is of a type never encountered before in human history, since neither its mode of functioning inside the capitalistically advanced countries, nor its fundamental purpose are properly encapsulated by the traditional manifestations of that phenomenon. Thus, the issue that needs to be addressed is: what are the specific characteristics and structural determinations of this historically unique social complex, considered under all its major aspects, which define it as the dominant socioeconomic, political and ideological manifestation of contemporary capitalism. In other words, the relevant question concerns the representative significance of this social complex with regard to the historical dynamics of capital as the *overall controlling force* of society, rather than merely the more or less transient modifications of the political and military spheres in accordance with the available margin of manoeuvre ultimately circumscribed by capital's structural limits.

5.4.3
Given the inherently contradictory framework of determinations in which these problems themselves arise, we are often presented with pseudo-solutions which take the existing system for granted and uncritically reflect

its reified dictates as the latest word of creative wisdom. A representative case in point is provided by the reflections and recommendations of Charles J. Hitch, once Chairman of the Research Council of the RAND corporation and later, most appropriately, Assistant Secretary of Defense in the US government. At a conference concerned with politics and technology, he asked the question directly relevant to the interests of the military/industrial complex: 'To what extent should government finance or subsidize industrial research in general?', justifying his enthusiastic advocacy of such subsidies by saying that *relatively small* [sic!] expenditures for deliberately planned research and development in the military sector have been staggeringly, alarmingly, *productive*'. And he added: 'I have tried to think of any reasons why the military area should be unique in this respect; I can think of none.'[565]

Thus, the astonishing inability (if not the cynical refusal) to understand the *qualitative* difference between the difficulties involved in demolishing a building as compared to those of erecting one, or between thermonuclear destruction and the still elusive production of 'fusion power' for creative purposes even on a minute laboratory scale, or between causing cancer by nuclear radiation and finding a way to cure it, etc., seems to be the ultimate qualifier for ministerial office in the service of the military/industrial complex. The obvious 'counter-selection' manifest in bringing thereby the management and control of scientific research under a personnel happy with such 'guiding principles' serves, of course, the practical purpose of reorienting productive activity in all its dimensions towards the uncritically adopted aims of that complex. As to the doubts that might arise, they are handled with the rhetoric and sophistry of mentioning in passing – as a concession to 'critical awareness' – that military research and development has been *'staggeringly, alarmingly* productive', before recommending, nonetheless, its *general* adoption as the *model* to aim at in the pursuit of productive achievements.

However, it must be stressed again, we are not dealing with merely personal aberrations and conceptual confusions. Rather, the mystifications which we encounter – i.e. whose function is to conflate and conceptually 'reconcile' some categories which refer in reality to irreconcilable social conflicts and divergences of interest – are themselves the manifestations of deep-seated structural imperatives, reflecting the objective needs of the established mode of social reproduction and control at the present stage of historical development. The prominence of *relativism* under a great variety of its forms in twentieth-century intellectual history, and the popularity of the self-proclaimed 'revolutionary' method of 'dissolving' real life problems by vacuous *semantic* devices in philosophy and social theory, belong to the same trend.

We have to consider presently some of the 'categorial confusions' necessarily produced by the bewildering process of *practical confounding* that characterizes capital as the controlling force of social interchange and reproduction. But first it is necessary to discuss, even if only very briefly, one of the crucial determinations at the roots of modern capitalist developments: the dynamic but ultimately devastating tendential law of the decreasing rate of utilization. A law inseparable from the capitalist tendency for overproduction and the crises associated with it.

For a detailed discussion of these tendencies and of their unfolding impact, the interested reader is referred to my book on *The Crisis of Development*. In the present context the relevant point is that since the decreasing rate of utilization opens up new possibilities for capital-expansion, it acquires a very special role in the realization process of 'advanced' capitalism.

In the first place, in virtue of its ability to deal with the pressures arising from the interaction between production and consumption due to the constraining limits of circulation, the decreasing rate of utilization functions as the irreplaceable *means* to accomplish the required reproduction on an *enlarged* scale while artificially holding back the tendency to enlarge the consuming circle itself. Subsequently, however, the greater the dependency of the overall process of reproduction on the decreasing rate of utilization, the more obviously the latter becomes an *end in itself* in that it promises the possibility of *unlimited* expansion, on the assumption that the rate itself can be lowered without ultimate hindrance.

No matter how absurd this assumption might be in its final implications, the productive practices associated with it provide a powerful operational base for capitalist developments under circumstances when alternative courses of action (e.g. enlarging the consuming circle) could only intensify capital's contradictions. The aim and orienting principle of production thus becomes how to secure *maximum* expansion (and corresponding profitability) on the basis of the *minimum* rate of utilization that guarantees the *continuity* of enlarged reproduction.

Naturally, the adoption of such an aim favours the emergence and growth of those types of economic enterprise which can match up to the necessary requirements of this process with the greatest dynamism and efficacy. Thus, under the impact of these determinations, it is not the enlargement of the periphery of circulation that constitutes an inexorable trend of capitalistic developments but, on the contrary, the artificial restriction of the consuming circle and the exclusion of the 'underprivileged' masses from it not only in the 'Third World' but even in the capitalistically advanced countries of the West.

The agency willing and able to cut the Gordian knot of how to combine maximum feasible expansion with the minimum rate of utilization presented itself for capital in the shape of the military/industrial complex, following a number of failed attempts to deal with the problems of overproduction after the world economic crisis of 1929–33. While the first steps towards a solution to overproduction through militarist production were taken already before the first world war, its *general* adoption occurred only after the second.

The great innovation of the military/industrial complex for capitalistic developments was to obliterate the literally vital distinction between *consumption* and *destruction*. The reason why such change is feasible at all is because consumption and destruction happen to be *functional equivalents* from the perverse standpoint of the capitalistic '*realization process*': the only thing in which capital is really interested. Thus, the question as to whether normal consumption – i.e. the human consumption of *use-values* corresponding to need – or '*consumption*' *through destruction* will prevail, is decided on the ground of the comparatively better suitability of one or the other to satisfy the overall requirements of capital's self-reproduction under the changing circumstances.

This 'innovation' (which consists in relativizing and ultimately obliterating the difference between consumption and destruction) offered a sweeping solution to a contradiction inherent in self-positing value in all its forms, even though the contradiction in question became acute only under the conditions of contemporary capitalism. The contradiction here referred to arises from the restrictive *barriers* of self-expanding wealth which must be transcended at all costs if value as an independent operational force is to realize itself in accordance with its objective nature. This is why in imperial Rome, as Marx noted, alienated and independent value as consumption-orientated wealth 'appears as *limitless waste* which logically attempts to raise consumption to an imaginary boundlessness by *gulping down salad of pearls*, etc.'.[566]

The problem at stake is really twofold. First, it concerns society's *limited resources* and hence the necessity of *legitimating* their allocation. And second, it has to do with the actual *consumer* himself; that is to say, with all the natural and socioeconomic as well as cultural *limitations of his appetites*.

As it happens, the military/industrial complex successfully addresses itself to both of these fundamental constraints. For, with regard to the first dimension, contemplating the act of 'gulping down salad of pearls', the conclusion as to its decadent gratuitousness is irresistible, whereas the truly limitless waste of 'gulping down' resources equivalent to billions of such salads of pearls over the years – while countless millions of human beings have to put up with starvation as their inescapable 'fate', and so many of them perish daily in the process – succeeds in legitimating itself as unquestionable patriotic duty.

Similarly, in relation to the second vital aspect, the military/industrial complex succeeds in removing the traditional constraints of the consuming circle as defined by the limitations of the consumers' appetites. In this respect it solves the problem by restructuring the framework of production in such a way as to remove for all intents and purposes the need for real consumption. In other words, it allocates a massive and ever-increasing portion of society's material and human resources to a parasitic and *self-consuming* form of production which is so radically divorced from, and indeed opposed to, actual human need and corresponding consumption that it can envisage as its own rationale and ultimate end nothing less self-contradictory and inhuman than the total destruction of mankind.

5.4.4

Capitalism as a mode of social reproduction is characterized by the irreconcilable contradiction between production for *use* (corresponding to need) and production for *exchange* which at a certain stage of development becomes an end in itself which subordinates all considerations of human use to its own, utterly perverse logic of alienating self-reproduction. And since the expansion of exchange value is the overriding concern of this society, every form of mystification is used to pretend that the production of an ever-increasing quantity of exchange value, no matter how obviously wasteful, is in full agreement with the best principles of 'economic rationality', corresponding with great efficacy to some 'real demand'.

Accordingly, the question of *real use* is conjured away as part of the *practical confounding* process earlier referred to, and the mere act of *commercial transaction* becomes the only relevant criterion of 'consumption', thereby characteristically conflating the concepts of *use* and *exchange*. Thus, just as we can witness in other contexts the self–serving and totally mystifying equation of the '*producer*' with the *capitalist*, so as to eliminate the embarrassing real producer – the worker – from the stage, here we are presented with the tendentious identification of the *purchaser* with the '*consumer*' so-called.

Thanks to this latter mystification, two delicate problems are conveniently solved at one stroke. First, the question whether there is some *real consumption* – corresponding to *human need* – subsequent to the necessary preliminary step of '*contractual*' *transaction*, cannot even arise, since the very act of transferring the commodity to the new owner, in exchange for money to be reinvested, completes capital's circuit of enlarged self-reproduction. And second, commodities can now be *heaped up* without any difficulty of justification on both sides of the *exchange relation*, since the *act of purchase* itself can, in principle, 'consume' an *unlimited* quantity of goods (without consuming in reality *anything at all*) in view of the fact that it is not tied to the necessarily limited appetites of real human beings.

The military/industrial complex not only perfects the ways in which capital can now deal with all these structural limitations and contradictions, but also makes a 'quantum leap' in the sense that the scope and the sheer size of its profitable operations becomes incomparably larger than could be conceived at earlier stages of development. This quantum leap creates formerly unimaginable outlets, qualitatively modifying thereby the relation of forces in capital's favour for a period directly proportional to the size of the newly created productive outlets themselves.

Naturally, this new modality of production calls for the appropriate categorial adjustments so as to be able to match – for the vital purposes of ideological rationalization and legitimation – the dominant practices of capital's restructured order. Accordingly, if a major portion of the available resources is openly allocated for *waste production*, equating the production of the means of destruction with *production* full stop, all this must take place, of course, strictly for the unobjectionable purpose of 'providing much needed jobs'. Nor need one reckon any more with the difficulties due to the constraints of human appetites and personal income. For the '*consumer*' so-called is no longer just the available aggregate of limited individuals. Indeed, thanks to the major transformation of the dominant productive structures of postwar society, coupled with the corresponding realignment of their relationship to the capitalist state (both for economic purposes and for securing the necessary ideological/political legitimation), from now on the mythically fused *producer/purchaser/consumer* is nothing less than 'the nation' itself.

This happens to be another fundamental innovation of the military/industrial complex. For while the earlier misrepresentation of the *purchaser* as the *consumer* could only push aside the embarrassing question of human appetites and the traditional requirement of producing goods with real use corresponding to such appetites, it was not suitable to offer solutions with regard to the financial constraints attached to individual 'consumer sovereignty' which frustrated the alienated expansionary needs of the capitalist realization process itself. Only 'the nation' could promise to satisfy the dual requirements of providing an *inexhaustible purse* (for a while) on the one hand, in order to make possible capital's enlarged self-reproduction, and a *bottomless pit*, on the other, to swallow up all the resulting waste.

True, waste and destruction of productive assets has been associated with capitalistic practices now for a very long time. It manifested itself in the past primarily through the cyclic/periodic destruction of overproduced capital at times of major economic difficulties. However, the innovation of 'advanced' capitalism and of its military/industrial complex is that now the earlier practice – catering for the exceptional and emergency requirements of crises – is *generalized* and turned into the *model of normality* for the everyday life of the whole system orientated towards *production for destruction* as a matter of course, in conformity with the decreasing rate of utilization tending towards the *zero rate*.

This new-found normality of the capitalist system enables it to displace (but, of course, not to eliminate) the fundamental contradiction of developed capital: overproduction. For, thanks to the ability of the military/industrial complex to *impose* its needs on society, the age-old wishful thinking of bourgeois political economy – the claimed identity of *supply* and *demand* – is manipulatively realized for the time being within its framework.

Marx rightly took to task the classical political economists who tried to conjure away the contradiction between production and consumption by wishfully stipulating that 'supply and demand are . . . identical, and should therefore necessarily correspond. *Supply*, namely, is allegedly *a demand measured by its own amount.*'[567]

Now, what the political economists could only dream about is successfully implemented *by decree* of the all-powerful military/industrial complex acting in unison with the capitalist state. Thus both supply and demand are cynically *relativized*, so as to enable the legitimation of *actual supply* by *fictitious 'demand'*. As a result, the supply in question – no matter how wasteful, dangerous, unwanted and destructive – is forcibly imposed upon society by unchallengeable legal devices and becomes the supreme *'demand of the nation'*, truly and effectively *'measured by its own amount'* and protected by the obliging state aganst the limitations of even capitalistic criteria of 'rational cost-accounting' by inflation-proof annual military budget increases, at the expense of all social services and real human need.

Similarly with regard to the development of science and the transformation of productive practices in accord with its inherent potentialities which were meant to favour the expansion of use value and the dialectical interaction of progressively expanding use value with the unfolding of human needs. For, as a result of capital's new requirements and determinations, science is diverted from its positive objectives and assigned the role of helping to multiply the forces and modalities of destruction, both directly, on the payroll of the ubiquitous and catastrophically wasteful military/industrial complex, and indirectly, in the service of 'planned obsolescence' and other ingenious manipulative practices, devised for the purpose of keeping the wolves of overproduction from the door in the consumer industries.

5.4.5

To understand these bewildering characteristics of contemporary capitalism, a vital distinction must be drawn between *production* and *self-reproduction*. The reason why this distinction is so important is because capital is not in the least concerned with production as such, but only with *self-reproduction*. Likewise, capital's 'irresistible drive towards universality' (put into relief by Marx) only concerns the interests of self-reproduction, and not those of production itself.

Naturally, under determinate historical circumstances the two can in a positive sense *coincide*; and while they do, capital can increase the productive powers of society and spur on, up to the point both dictated and permitted by its own interests, the emergence of 'general industriousness'.

However, the necessary conditions of genuine production, and those of capital's enlarged self-reproduction, not only need not always coincide but, on the contrary, may even diametrically oppose one another.

In sharp contrast to the predominantly productive social articulation of capital in Marx's lifetime, contemporary capitalism has reached the stage where the *radical disjunction* of genuine production and capital's self-reproduction is no longer some remote possibility but a cruel reality, with the most devastating implications for the future. For the barriers to capitalist production today are overcome by capital itself in the form of securing its own reproduction – to an already large and constantly growing extent – in the form of *destructive self-reproduction*, in antagonistic opposition to genuine *production*.

In this sense, capital's limits can no longer be conceptualized as merely the material obstacles to a greater increase in productivity and social wealth, and thus as a *brake* on development, but as the direct challenge to the very survival of mankind. And in another sense, the limits of capital can turn against capital itself as the overpowering controller of the social metabolism not when its interests collide with the general social interest of increasing the powers of genuine production, but only when capital is no longer able to secure, by whatever means at its disposal, the conditions of its *destructive self-reproduction* and thereby causes the breakdown of the overall social metabolism.

The domination of science by the military/industrial complex is an integral part of capital's destructive self-reproduction. This is why the stakes for asserting the social responsibility of science, in the interest of emancipation, are today particularly high.

6 · METHODOLOGY AND IDEOLOGY

6.1 THE IDEOLOGY OF METHODOLOGICAL NEUTRALITY

6.1.1

Nowhere is the myth of ideological neutrality – the self-proclaimed *Wert-freiheit* or value neutrality of so-called 'rigorous social science' – stronger than in the field of methodology. Indeed, we are often presented with the claim that the adoption of the advocated methodological framework would automatically exempt one from all controversy about values, since they are systematically excluded (or suitably 'bracketed out') by the scientifically adequate method itself, thereby saving one from unnecessary complications and securing the desired objectivity and uncontestable outcome.

Claims and procedures of this kind are, of course, extremely problematical. For they circularly *assume* that their enthusiasm for the virtues of 'methodological neutrality' is bound to yield 'value neutral' solutions with regard to highly contested issues, without first examining the all-important question as to the conditions of *possibility* – or otherwise – of the postulated systematic neutrality at the plane of methodology itself. The unchallengeable validity of the recommended procedure is supposed to be *self-evident* on account of its *purely methodological* character.

In reality, of course, this approach to methodology is heavily loaded with a conservative ideological substance. Since, however, the plane of *methodology* (and 'meta-theory') is said to be *in principle* separated from that of the *substantive* issues, the methodological circle can be conveniently closed. Whereupon the mere insistence on the purely methodological character of the criteria laid down is supposed to establish the claim according to which the approach in question is neutral because everybody can adopt it as the common frame of reference of 'rational discourse'.

Yet, curiously enough, the proposed methodological tenets are so defined that vast areas of vital social concern are *a priori* excluded from this rational discourse as 'metaphysical', 'ideological', etc. The effect of circumscribing in this way the scope of the one and only admissible approach is that it automatically disqualifies, in the name of *methodology* itself, all those who do not fit into the stipulated framework of discourse. As a result, the propounders of the 'right method' are spared the difficulties that go with acknowledging the real divisions and incompatibilities as they necessarily arise from the contending social interests at the roots of alternative approaches and the rival sets of values associated with them.

This is where we can see more clearly the social orientation implicit in the whole procedure. For – far from offering an adequate scope for critical enquiry – the advocated general adoption of the allegedly neutral methodological framework is equivalent, in fact, to consenting not even to raise the issues that really matter. Instead, the stipulated 'common' methodological procedure succeeds in transforming the enterprise of 'rational discourse' into the dubious practice of producing *methodology for the sake of methodology*: a tendency more pronounced in the twentieth century than ever before. This practice consists in sharpening the recommended methodological knife until nothing but the bare handle is left, at which point a new knife is adopted for the same purpose. For the ideal methodological knife is not meant for cutting, only for sharpening, thereby interposing itself between the critical intent and the real objects of criticism which it can obliterate for as long as the pseudo-critical activity of knife-sharpening for its own sake continues to be pursued. And that happens to be precisely its inherent ideological purpose.

6.1.2
Naturally, to speak of a 'common' methodological framework in which one can resolve the problems of a society torn by irreconcilable social interests and ensuing antagonistic confrontations is delusory, at best, notwithstanding all talk about 'ideal communication communities'. But to define the methodological tenets of all rational discourse by way of transubstantiating into 'ideal types' (or by putting into methodological 'brackets') the discussion of contending social values reveals the ideological colour as well as the extreme fallaciousness of the claimed rationality. For such treatment of the major areas of conflict, under a great variety of forms – from the Viennese version of 'logical positivism' to Wittgenstein's famous ladder that must be 'thrown away' at the point of confronting the question of values, and from the advocacy of the Popperian principle of 'little by little' to the 'emotivist' theory of value – inevitably always favours the established order. And it does so by declaring the fundamental structural parameters of the given society 'out of bounds' to the potential contestants, on the authority of the ideally 'common' methodology.

However, even on a cursory inspection of the issues at stake it ought to be fairly obvious that to consent *not* to question the fundamental structural framework of the established order is *radically* different according to whether one does so as the beneficiary of that order or from the standpoint of those who find themselves at the receiving end, exploited and oppressed by the overall determinations (and not just by some limited and more or less easily corrigible detail) of that order. Consequently, to establish the 'commn' identity of the two, opposed sides of a structurally safeguarded hierarchical order – by means of the reduction of the people who belong to the contending social forces into fictitious 'rational interlocutors', extracted from their divided real world and transplanted into a beneficially shared universe of ideal discourse – would be nothing short of a methodological miracle.

Contrary to the wishful thinking hypostatized as a timeless and socially unspecified rational communality, the elementary condition of a truly rational discourse would be to acknowledge the legitimacy of contesting the given order of society in *substantive* terms. This would imply the articulation of the relevant problems not on the plane of self-referential theory and methodology, but as inherently *practical* issues whose conditions of solution point towards the necessity of radical structural changes. In other words, it would require the explicit rejection of all fiction of methodological and meta-theoretical neutrality. But, of course, this would be far too much to expect precisely because the society in which we live is a deeply divided society. This is why through the dichotomies of 'fact and value', 'theory and practice', 'formal and substantive rationality', etc., the conflict-transcending methodological miracle is constantly stipulated as the necessary regulative framework of 'rational discourse' in the humanities and social sciences, in the interest of the *ruling ideology*.

What makes this approach particularly difficult to challenge is that its value-commitments are *mediated* by methodological precepts to such a degree that it is virtually impossible to bring them into the focus of discussion without openly contesting the framework as a whole. For the conservative sets of values at the roots of such orientation remain several steps removed from the ostensible subject of dispute as defined in logico/methodological, formal/structural, and semantic/analytical terms. And who would suspect of ideological bias the impeccable – methodologically sanctioned – credentials of 'procedural rules', 'models' and 'paradigms'?

Once, though, such rules and paradigms are adopted as the common frame of reference of what may or may not be allowed to be considered the legitimate subject of debate, everything that enters into the accepted parameters is necessarily constrained not only by the scope of the overall framework, but simultaneously also by the inexplicit ideological assumptions on the basis of which the methodological principles themselves were in the first place constituted. This is why the allegedly 'non-ideological' ideologies which so successfully conceal and exercise their apologetic function in the guise of neutral methodology are doubly mystifying.

Twentieth-century currents of thought are dominated by approaches that tend to articulate the social interests and values of the ruling order through complicated – at times completely bewildering – mediations, on the methodological plane. Thus, more than ever before, the task of ideological demystification is inseparable from the investigation of the complex dialectical interrelationship between methods and values which no social theory or philosophy can escape.

6.2 THE REPRODUCTION OF REPRESENTATIVE THEORETICAL SYSTEMS

In his discussion of *The Problem of Method* Sartre opposed philosophy to ideology and made the point that:

> The periods of philosophical creation are rare. Between the seventeenth century and the twentieth, I see three such periods, which I would designate by the names of the men who dominated them: there is the 'moment' of Descartes and Locke, that of Kant and Hegel, finally that of Marx. These three philosophies become, each in its turn, the humus of every particular thought and the horizon of all culture; there is no going beyond them so long as man has not gone beyond the historical moment which they express. I have often remarked on the fact that an 'anti-Marxist' argument is only the apparent rejuvenation of a pre-Marxist idea. A so-called 'going beyond' Marxism will be at worst only a return to pre-Marxism; at best, only the rediscovery of a thought already contained in the philosophy which one believes he has gone beyond.[568]

Sartre had his own reasons for drawing the lines of demarcation between philosophy and ideology the way he did at the time of writing these lines. For this was the time when he was trying to bring about a synthesis between existentialism and Marxism within the framework of the latter. Accordingly, he designated the rare 'totalizing' systems by the name philosophy and reserved the term 'ideology' for the more limited enterprises which in his view cannot escape, no matter how hard they might try, from the gravitational field of the historically dominant, all-comprehensive system of their age. As Sartre put it, referring to the creators of such partial systems:

> These *relative* men I propose to call 'ideologists'. And since I am to speak of existentialism, let it be understood that I take it to be an 'ideology'. It is a parasitical system living on the margin of Knowledge, which at first it opposed but into which today it seeks to be integrated.[569]

There can be no doubt that this opposition of philosophy to ideology (of which the Althusserian counterposing of 'theory' to 'ideology' was an unacknowledged variant) is highly problematical. For every philosophy is simultaneously also an ideology. However, we are not concerned here with the historical and ideological determinants of the Sartrean position. What matters in the present context is his fundamentally valid proposition that closely links the great philosophies of the past and present to the particular social setting – grasped in its comprehensiveness embracing an entire historical epoch – which positively defines as well as negatively limits their conceptual horizon.

To situate the various philosophies in their historical/epochal setting is essential also for understanding the specific, value-laden meaning of their apparently *abstract*, often with regard to their explicit claims *timeless*, method. For:

Every philosophy is *practical*, even the one which at first appears to be the most contemplative. Its *method* is a *social and political weapon*. The analytical, *critical rationalism* of the great Cartesians has survived them; born from conflict, it looked back to clarify the conflict. At the time when the bourgeoisie sought to undermine the institutions of the Ancien Régime, it attacked the outworn significations which tried to justify them.[570] Later it gave service to *liberalism*, and it provided a doctrine for procedures that attempted to realize the 'atomization' of the Proletariat.[571]

Thus, the – no matter how abstract and mediated – methods of competing philosophies are inseparable from the *practical concerns* which they champion in their own way. They originate on the soil of such concerns and they can accommodate within their framework the epochally-defined interests of the social forces with whose standpoint the thinkers who conceptually articulate such interests happen to identify themselves more or less consciously.

As rival methods engaged in a practical struggle, they have a significant margin of manoeuvre, precisely because their tenets are spelled out in terms of the broadest outlines and general regulative principles of a methodology, rather than as highly specific propositions, enunciated with respect to circumstances of only partial structural significance. Propositions of the latter kind, by contrast, represent the more or less 'tactical' adaptation of the general principles themselves to the constantly shifting and changing circumstances, on the basis of a 'feedback' whose scope is flexibly but inescapably circumscribed by the 'totalizing' method as such. Indeed, in accordance with the historically changing determinations of the social classes whose fundamental interests they articulate, they may even change their central function from a dynamically progressive one (like the 'critical rationalism' of various forms of Cartesianism over a long historical period) to one that exhausts itself in the 'liberal' practice of social manipulation and apologetic rationalization of the established order. What they cannot possibly do, however, is to get rid of the specific social determinations and practical tasks which necessarily set the limits to the conceptual structure, and circumscribe the relative historical validity, of any methodology.

6.3 LIVING PHILOSOPHIES AND COMPETING METHODS

Two important questions arise in this context. The first concerns the conditions under which the various philosophical systems – with their specific methodological rules and models as to the 'correct procedure' – *originate* and successfully assert themselves as the comprehensive orienting framework of the thought of their epoch. And the second, equally important question is related to the continued *reproduction* of their relevance, in one form or another, to their epoch. For without the effective reassertion of the validity of their central tenets they would not possess the *representative significance* which they undoubtedly do precisely in virtue of such reproduction, whether we think of the Cartesian and Kantian philosophies or of the Marxian approach.

If we do not pursue these questions, then the complex determinations behind both the original articulation and the sociohistorically concrete transformations of the major philosophical systems are bound to remain elusive. As a result, we are either expected to ascribe their success to the more or less idealistically conceived 'discoveries' of great individuals, or to terminate the enquiry (as Sartre does) at the generic, even if in its genericity correct, affirmation that the systems in question give expression to the general movement of their society. Moreover, we are also expected to subscribe to the greatly oversimplifying view according to which 'you would never find at the same time more than *one* living philosophy'.[572]

Yet, the matter of how living or dead a particular philosophy might or might not be under the given circumstances is not decided by enlightened intellectuals with reference to the theoretically more advanced standard of another philosophy, be that the most up-to-date and progressive one. It is determined, less reassuringly, by the ability of the philosophy concerned to reproduce its own theoretical and practical relevance to some fundamental social force of the epoch.

In this respect it is of no importance how problematical (or even reactionary) that force – and, by implication, the corresponding theoretical substance of the philosophy in question – might be if viewed from a much broader historical perspective. For as long as it can successfully reproduce itself in the context of an ongoing social antagonism, nothing more is needed to sustain its claims to vitality than its power to fight its adversary with efficacy on the relevant planes of social and intellectual life. If, however, we separate ideology from philosophy, then talking about the 'ideological forms in which men become conscious of their social conflicts and fight them out', as Marx does, becomes rather pointless in that the confrontation involved is more like shadow boxing than a real struggle. For the issue at stake is automatically settled, by definition, in favour of the 'living philosophy' when the more recent period of 'philosophical creation' – the 'moment of Marx' for instance, as opposed to that of Kant and Hegel, not to mention others before them – consigns to the realm of the dead the philosophies which prior to the arrival of the new moment were still alive.

Curiously enough, the Sartrean assertion that we can never find at the same time more than one living philosophy is preceded by the reformulation of a typically Kantian idea, even if Sartre himself may not be aware of it. As he puts it: 'In our view *Philosophy does not exist*. In whatever form we consider it, this shadow of science, this Grey Eminence of humanity, is only a hypostatized abstraction. Actually, there are *philosophies*.'[573] And this is how essentially the same proposition appears in Kant's *Critique of Pure Reason*:

> *Philosophy* is the system of all philosophical cognition . . . the standard by which all subjective *philosophies* are to be judged. In this sense, philosophy is merely the idea of a possible science, which *does not exist in concreto.*[574]

Indeed, Kant goes as far as to deny existence even to the philosopher, considered as 'the ideal teacher who employs [mathematics, the natural sciences and logic] as instruments for the advancement of the essential aims of human reason. Him alone can we call philosopher; but he *nowhere exists.*'[575]

Naturally, the Kantian inspiration of a great deal of Sartre's philosophy goes much deeper than the reproduction of such ideas. The most important connections in this respect are to be found in Sartre's conception of morality and in his *Critique of Dialectical Reason*. However, the point that directly concerns us here is that philosophies whose original 'moment' goes back a long way (even as much as several centuries) into the past can gain a new vitality through their suitable reproduction under, and in accordance with, the changed sociohistorical circumstances. In this sense the Kantian philosophy, for instance, not only continued to exercise, to our own days, an influence which is incomparably more widespread than that of any other philosophy, but it succeeded in penetrating even into a variety of Marxist approaches, from Bernstein and Kautsky to Austro-Marxism, not to forget, in more recent times, Galvano della Volpe and his followers (Colletti, for instance).

But well beyond influences of this kind, even a much earlier system (e.g. the philosophy of Descartes) could come to life again and again in the twentieth century, exercising a major influence in the form in which it has been revitalized and adapted to the requirements of the new conditions. Husserl's *Cartesian Meditations* and the development of phenomenology in general – and, indeed, Sartre's own philosophy, in all its phases of development – bear witness to this.

6.4 THE NECESSITY OF METHODOLOGICAL SELF-RENEWAL

The same considerations apply to the assessment of the Marxian philosophy, notwithstanding its representative significance with regard to the intellectual embodiment of a more advanced phase of historical development. Its claims to being the most comprehensive living system of thought are not decided on the basis of the historical novelty of its central tenets, as first articulated in the work of its originator. They are settled primarily on account of its continued ability to offer – despite the numerous social setbacks, reversals and corresponding theoretical revisions – a framework for radical criticism aimed at a fundamental restructuring of society in its entirety.

The methodological radicalism of the Marxian approach and its relevance to the age in which it originated is determined by the profound crisis of a social order whose problems are not amenable to a solution other than a radical restructuring of the social order itself in all its fundamental dimensions. Short of such a solution, one can merely manipulate, 'little by little', the given socioeconomic contradictions and their ideological manifestations, thereby temporarily *postponing* the eruption of the impending crisis, without, however, instituting an adequate structural remedy.

Naturally, the realization of the task of a radical restructuring of society is inconceivable as a sudden and irreversible 'event'. It must be viewed, instead, as a self-renewing *process*, sustained for as long a historical period as the need for it persists in relation to *determinate* tasks and well recognizable ideological adversaries. Once the need for this radical restructuring 'from top to bottom the whole of society' no longer exists, inevitably the Marxian approach, too, loses its relevance and significance as an irrespressible 'living philosophy', and becomes the monumental historical document of a bygone age, as other great 'totalizing' systems before it.

Thus, paradoxically, the Marxian conception can only become victorious on condition that it puts itself 'out of business' and ceases to be the living philosophy – i.e. the comprehensive orienting framework – of the most progressive forces of the epoch.

This may sound disturbing to those who are captivated by the ideology of scientism and wish to transcend, in an imaginary fashion, all ideology. However, the consequences of adopting their point of view are not only that the origin as well as the inherent characteristics of the Marxian approach have to be distorted, so as to fit the scientistic preconception, but also that the subsequent developments of the original theory by Marx's followers become totally incomprehensible. They must be considered 'mistaken interpretations', 'ideological deviations', 'social betrayals', and the like. The trouble, though, is that characterizations of this kind, even when descriptively correct, merely put *labels* on the developments in question, without even attempting to understand their complex social determinants and functions in the living context of their changing historical setting.

In reality the Marxian framework – both in its origins and later transformations – is quite unintelligible without fully acknowledging the vital ideological role which it always had (and has) to fulfil *vis à vis* other ideologies. Accordingly, one should never forget that the 'three sources of Marxism' – classical German philosophy, English political economy and utopian socialism – were not just *sources* that had to be positively appropriated by Marxism. They were, simultaneously, also the three principal ideological adversaries of the new conception at the time of its original formulation by Marx.

They had to be assigned such a key position within the new conceptual framework not because they represented – since they did not – the other extreme of the ideological spectrum. Rather, and in addition to their intrinsic merits, because they happened to exercise a most disorienting influence on the developing working-class movement from which the latter had to be emancipated. In other words, they were identified as the most relevant ideological interlocutors and adversaries not in abstraction, as the representatives of a theoretically feasible polar opposite to Marxism, but precisely as *living* systems of thought whose tangible impact on the socialist movement could not be left unchallenged. Subsequent shifts in the assessment of these 'three sources' already in Marx's lifetime, not to mention the development of Marxist approaches towards the end of the nineteenth as well as in the twentieth century, become meaningful only in terms of the changing ideological requirements of the international labour movement, rather than as fictitious 'theoretical discoveries'.

It is instructive to recall in this respect the significant change in Marx's assessment of Proudhon, from warm sympathy to complete hostility. Similarly, the importance of a critical dialogue with utopian socialism greatly receded already in the early 1850s. Indeed, later, in the aftermath of a practical confrontation with Proudhon's followers who 'babble about science and know nothing', who 'actually preach the ordinary *bourgeois science*, only Proudhonistically idealized',[576] Marx summed up his position towards the outstanding figures of French and German utopian thought – in contrast to Proudhon whom he dismissed in the same context as 'a philistine utopian' – by saying that 'in the utopias of a Fourier, an Owen, etc. there is the presentiment and imaginative expression of a new world'.[577]

Even with regard to Hegel, the change – in a direction diametrically opposed to what we have witnessed *vis à vis* Proudhon, from a rather summary negative assessment in the early works to the highly positive evaluation in Marx's *Grundrisse* and *Capital*, notwithstanding some completely unfounded legends to the contrary – is inseparable from some 'internal' ideological controversies against Lange and others. For Lange, the author of *The Labour Question: Its Significance for the Present and Future* (1865), who assumed the role of a 'conciliator' in the German labour movement – and who, according to Marx, 'flirts with all sides'[578] – exercised a by no means negligible influence on the German working-class movement, spreading a dogmatically anti-Hegelian and anti-dialectical position (the two are often wedded together). As Marx wrote later:

> Herr Lange sings my praises loudly, but with the object of making himself important.... What the same Lange says about the Hegelian method and my application of it is really childish. First of all, he understands nothing about Hegel's method and secondly, as a consequence, far less, even, about my critical application of it.... Herr Lange wonders that Engels, I, etc., take the dead dog Hegel seriously when Büchner, Lange, Dr Dühring, Fechner, etc., are agreed that they – poor dear – have buried him long ago.[579]

Examples of this kind could be multiplied, from the historically determined ideological context of *The Holy Family, The German Ideology* and
The Poverty of Philosophy to Engels' *Anti-Dühring*. As far as the last work
was concerned, Engels himself made it quite clear that it was not the intellectual substance of Dr Dühring's book that induced him to write his extensive critical refutation of it, but the fact that people were 'preparing to
spread this doctrine in a popularized form among the workers'.[580]

Bearing in mind theoretical and political/intellectual developments like
these, it becomes clear that while the broad methodological parameters
of all major systems of thought are set for an entire historical epoch, they
must, nonetheless, constantly redefine themselves as living systems in
accordance with the practical requirements of their changing ideological
functions. They must enter into a critical dialogue with each other and, by
doing so, inevitably take on board the sociohistorically specific – indeed,
in principle 'alien' – problematic of their ideological adversaries, even
if only in order to 'overcome' them both in theory and on the practical/
organizational terrain of actual social confrontations.

6.5 METHODOLOGICAL RADICALISM AND IDEOLOGICAL COMMITMENT

6.5.1

A historical epoch always offers several, and to varying degrees viable,
practical alternatives – within the overall limits of its objective determinations – to the contending social forces. Accordingly, the realization of an
unfolding historical *trend* – and realistically one can never speak of
historical necessities in any other way than in terms of changing, often
disconcertingly 'flexible', and up to a significant point reversible, *trends* – is
decided on the basis of which particular alternatives, out of the available
ones, are chosen by the social forces involved in the course of their
objectively conditioned *inter*-actions. As a result, they are presented with
the necessity of making quite fundamental *reciprocal* adjustments and
readjustments in their strategies, so as to bring them in line with the
modifications of their objective possibilities of action.

To be sure, the fundamental *structural constraints*, corresponding to the
inherent characteristics of the forces in question, *ultimately* assert themselves, and cumulatively even tend to narrow down the feasible margin of
action of the competing social forces in relation to one another. Nevertheless, the unavoidable *choice* of *one specific alternative*, in preference to
others, carries with it an equally unavoidable *ideological commitment* to a
determinate position. Moreover, such choice also carries with it the necessity to realign one's overall perspective, in tune with the practically adopted
course of action implicit in the chosen alternative, thereby dismissing not

only the adversary but even the rival possibilities that might arise on the *same* side of the fundamental social confrontation. This is why every major system of thought, including the Marxian orientation of social criticism, is simultaneously and 'incorrigibly' also an ideology.

6.5.2

To illustrate this, it is enough to refer to the role which the concept of capital – defined as a global system that asserts its power through the world market – plays in the Marxian framework. In its origin it is linked to the Hegelian conception of 'world history' (the domain of the World Spirit's self-activity) to which the Marxian approach counterposes a set of tangible, empirically identifiable events and developments.

This is how Marx formulates his materialist counter-image to the Hegelian conception:

> The further the separate spheres, which act on one another, extend in the course of this development and the more the original isolation of the separate nationalities is destroyed by the advanced mode of production, by intercourse and by the natural division of labour between various nations arising as a result, the more *history becomes world history*. Thus, for instance, if in England a machine is invented which deprives countless workers of bread in India and China, and overturns the whole form of existence of these empires, this invention becomes a *world-historical fact*. . . . From this it follows that this transformation of history into world history is by no means a mere abstract act on the part of 'self-consciousness', the world spirit, or of any other metaphysical spectre, but a quite material, empirically verifiable act, an act the proof of which every individual furnishes as he comes and goes, eats, drinks and clothes himself. In history up to the present it is certainly likewise an empirical fact that separate individuals have, with the broadening of their activity into *world-historical activity*, become more and more enslaved under *a power alien to them* (a pressure which they have conceived of as a dirty trick on the part of the so-called world spirit, etc.), a power which has become more and more enormous and, in the last instance, turns out to be the *world market*.[581]

Naturally, this view of world history, conceived as the universal unfolding of the most advanced mode of production in the framework of a fully developed world market, carried with it a corresponding vision of the way out of the destructive antagonisms of the given social order. For it envisaged, as the necessary conditions of its realization, on the one hand, the highest possible level of productivity (which implied the transcendence of the local and national barriers and contradictions, as well as the all-round beneficial integration and co-operative rationalization of material and intellectual production on a global scale). And, on the other hand, it anticipated, as the necessary corollary to the global character of the identified task, the concerted action of the industrially most powerful nations, so as to bring about the new – in its objective mode of functioning 'universal' and in its spirit consciously internationalist – social order. To quote Marx again:

this development of productive forces (which at the same time implies the actual empirical existence of men in their *world-historical*, instead of local, being) is an absolutely necessary practical premise, because without it privation, want is merely made general, and with want the struggle for necessities would begin again, and all the old filthy business would necessarily be restored; and furthermore, because only with this *universal development* of productive forces is a *universal intercourse* between men established, which on the one side produces *in all nations* simultaneously the phenomenon of the 'propertyless' mass (universal competition), making *each nation dependent on the revolutions of the others*, and finally puts *world-historical, empirically universal individuals* in place of local ones.... Empirically, communism is only possible as the *act of the dominant peoples 'all at once' and simultaneously*, which presupposes the universal development of the productive forces and the *world intercourse* bound up with them.[582]

This is where we can clearly identify not only the superiority of the materialist conception of history to its idealist counterparts, including the Hegelian vision, but also the great difficulties that go with the adoption of the Marxian approach. For as far as idealist philosophies are concerned, the burden of material proof in relation to the practical realization of historical trends – grasped as they assert themselves in the objective circumstances of actually living individuals who pursue their aims within the network of complex social determinations – does not and cannot exist. This makes it all the more understandable why the first monumental conception of world history – the Hegelian one – had to be articulated as an idealist system. For, as such, it could easily bypass, without conceptual inconsistency, the immense complications involved in demonstrating the contradictory unfolding of an actually (i.e. in a socially tangible way) integrated historical totality on a global scale, under the rule of capital. Operating within the idealist conceptual framework enabled the philosophers concerned to substitute for the required material proofs the conveniently malleable and ultimately circular abstractions of 'self-alienating' and 'self-realizing' World Spirit.

Marx's difficulties, by contrast, were inseparable from the adoption of the materialist orienting principles and the corresponding historical and dialectical method. The problematical aspect of the vision displayed in the last two quotations was not its relevance to the new historical epoch as a whole – which could be hardly contested, except from an aprioristically hostile point of view – but its relation to the actual state of affairs in the greater part of the world at the time of its conception. For even today, 143 years later, the 'actual empirical existence of men in their world-historical, instead of local, being' is far from being a fully accomplished reality, in that the 'universal development of the productive forces and the world intercourse bound up with them' is still in the – rather contradictory – process of unfolding, with major controversies affecting the evaluation of both its feasible *time-scale* and *modalities* of practical realization.

Similarly, the assertion that 'communism is only possible as the act of the dominant peoples "all at once" and simultaneously' remains plausible as the 'absolutely necessary practical premise' and stipulative characterization of the conditions of a successful transition from the capitalist epoch to the new social order on a scale no longer vulnerable to external intervention and overthrow. Obviously, however, the same assertion becomes very problematical if one tries to read it either as a predictive statement about the specific forms of capital's breakdown, or as a guide to strategy with regard to the *necessarily partial* mediatory steps towards the future.

Understandably, Marx had to make a conscious choice as to the strategy to advocate, and he had to identify himself with the chosen alternative with a passionate ideological commitment. He was constantly looking, with anxious anticipation, for the signs of the coming crisis,[583] even under the circumstances of – at times quite unbearable – personal hardship and adversity.[584] As he once confessed in a letter:

> I had to use every moment in which I was capable of work in order that I might finish the task to which I have sacrificed my health, my happiness in life and my family.... I laugh at the so-called 'practical' men and their wisdom. If one chose to be an ox one could of course turn one's back on the agonies of mankind and look after one's own skin. But I should really have regarded myself as unpractical if I had pegged out without completely finishing my book, at least in manuscript.[585]

It goes without saying, the prospect of becoming a 'practical man' was rejected by Marx with contempt, despite the weighty personal dilemmas which his 'hardened' attitude necessarily carried with it. But even when the doubt about the implications of the globally still *ascending* development of capital entered his horizon,[586] he refused to shift his position. Considering the possible strategic pitfalls of those implications for the adoption of a demobilizing perspective by the working-class movement, he refused to make allowances for the capitalist order's margin of manoeuvre to *displace*, even if not to *supersede*, its inner contradictions. Quite the contrary, he continued to concentrate on those signals which pointed in the direction of a dynamic, early breakthrough. Examples in this respect range from the way in which he greeted the movement of the slaves in America and of the serfs in Russia[587] to his attempt at theorizing, in his correspondence with Vera Zasulich, the positive potentialities of a socialist transformation being initiated on the soil of capitalistically backward Russia.

6.6 THE METHODOLOGICAL UNITY OF SCIENCE AND IDEOLOGY

6.6.1

Inevitably, thus, Marx's *'proletarian* science', consciously opposed to the 'ordinary *bourgeois* science'[588] of Proudhon and his followers – or, for that matter, to anybody else who might imagine that scientific social theory can be divorced from and artificially counterposed to ideology, as plain 'science' – represented the sociohistorically attainable *dialectical unity* of theoretical acquisitions and value-determinations. Marx treated with sarcasm the pseudo-scientific posture of 'the representatives of "young France" (non-workers)' who summarily rejected the views of their opponents as 'antiquated prejudices', expecting salvation, with characteristic intellectual arrogance, from the emergence of an all-round conformity to their 'Proudhonized Stirnerism'.[589] And he made fun of their position by saying that they behaved as if in the meantime:

> history comes to a stop in all other countries and the whole world waits until the French are ripe for a social revolution. They will then perform the experiment before our eyes, and the rest of the world, overcome by the force of their example, will do the same. Just what Fourier expected of his model phalanstery. Moreover, everyone who encumbers the 'social' question with the 'superstitions' of the world is 'reactionary'.[590]

Marx has thus no use whatsoever for any notion of science that could be divorced even for a moment from a practically viable social commitment.

In this sense, the inextricable unity of science and ideology in the Marxian life-work, far from being a drawback to theoretical insight, constituted its personal motivation as well as its practical relevance and justification. Moreover, in terms of methodology, the explicit acknowledgement (and conscious acceptance) of the unavoidable ideological determinations at work in the constitution of *any* representative theoretical synthesis, enabled Marx, on the one hand, to grasp *critically* the true character and *inner structure* of past conceptions. And on the other, it made possible for him to assume an incomparably more *self-critical* position with regard to his own work – explained within and in relation to its specific social setting – than anyone else before him. Indeed, he elevated *self-criticism* to the status of the highest methodological principle precisely on account of its key role both for producing theoretical insights and for enabling the social movement of the proletariat to overcome the inevitable contradictions and defects of its practical undertaking.

Inasmuch as Marx's choice of the specific alternative – the orienting principle of the world-view and strategy advocated by him – dismissed, because of its potentially demobilizing implications, capital's *global ascendancy*, looking for radical openings in a direction firmly opposed to such prospects, his theory represented, of course, a 'short cut' towards a state of society which even today is still very far from its realization.

However, acknowledging this does not imply questioning the *epochal validity* of his vision. For it is an important methodological characteristic of the theoretical syntheses representative of a whole epoch that they tend to concentrate their efforts on drawing the fundamental lines of demarcation, hence they cannot articulate their own approach without *anticipations* and *short cuts*. By contrast, the actual historical trends themselves cannot obligingly conform to any model, 'classical' or otherwise, no matter how carefully formulated they might be from even the historically most advanced vantage point. Indeed, it cannot be stressed enough, at no particular point in time is it conceivable to anticipate in detail, way ahead in the future yet to be made, the unavoidable reciprocal impact of the various forces interacting with one another, together with the resulting 'deviations' from an earlier perceived and pursued course of action.

From all this it follows that theoretical (and practical) complications – manifest also on the methodological plane – not simply *can* but *must* arise according to the specific circumstances, limitations and contradictions of the movements associated with the Marxian perspective, even before the conquest of power. Naturally, this is much more the case after the breakthrough, when a particular 'road to socialism' is embarked upon, with its own strategy of development that tends to elevate to the status of a general model the 'force of circumstance' and the available, historically constrained and constraining, margin of action. This is why – in place of an unproblematical continuity in the development of some ideal *Marxism* in the abstract – history in fact produces a multiplicity of *Marxisms* competing, and at times in a most hostile fashion even clashing, with one another.

6.6.2
But no matter how significant the theoretical and practical departures from the originally anticipated course of development, two vital conditions remain operative in the midst of the most diverse ideological determinations. (Without them, extreme relativism would rule – and paralyse – the movements whose strategies the rival trends of Marxism attempt to articulate.)

First, that the various Marxist approaches (inasmuch as they are really committed to the Marxian perspective, rather than just pay lip-service to it, for whatever historical or tactical reason) must retain both the *central tenets* and the corresponding *methodological principles* of the original conception.

In this respect it is by no means accidental that the opportunistic social-democratization of the working-class movement was coupled on the plane of methodology with a mechanistically quantity-oriented 'evolutionism' and 'scientism', as well as with their corollary: the rejection of the *dialectic* of objective contradictions and qualitative (revolutionary) changes. As Engels rightly stressed, 'Marx and I were pretty well the only people to rescue conscious dialectics from German idealist philosophy and apply it in the materialist conception of nature and history.'[591] Thus, to take only one example, describing the dialectical principle of 'the negation of the negation' – which appears in Marx's writing in numerous contexts – as 'verbal juggling', in the manner of Dr Dühring, or as an 'inadmissible intrusion of Hegelianism into scientific materialism', in more recently fashionable phraseology, were manifestations of the same '*positivist rot*' against which already Marx complained.[592]

Characteristically, one of the ways in which people tried to jettison the objectivity of dialectical determinations from Marxism was to assert that it was an invention of Engels who talked about dialectics not only in *history* but, *horribile dictu*, also in *nature*. This, they insisted, must be rejected as incompatible with Marx's own writings. However, the facts themselves, again, speak otherwise. If anybody is 'guilty' in this respect, surely it must be Marx. For he wrote to Engels nearly *ten years* before the latter even *began* writing his *Dialectics of Nature*:

> You will also see from the conclusion of my chapter III [of *Capital*], where the transformation of the handicraft-master into a capitalist – as a result of purely quantitative changes – is touched upon, that in the text I refer to the law Hegel discovered, of purely *quantitative* changes turning into *qualitative* changes, as *holding good alike in history and natural science*.[593]

The *second* vital condition that remains operative despite everything, sustaining and justifying also the first condition discussed above, concerns the actual historical end of capital's global ascendancy. For it is the latter that ultimately decides the issue, by activating the structural contradictions of capital's iniquitous and wasteful productive system and universally dehumanizing mode of social control.

With regard to theory such overall determination presents an important practical qualifier. Undoubtedly, the particular varieties of Marxism are closely linked in their mediatory functions to their specific sociohistorical setting, not only necessarily reflecting the practical constraints of their situation but *ipso facto* also taking on board the ideological problematic of their adversary, in the form of major compromises. Nevertheless, no matter how understandable the particular determinations and mediatory requirements arising from the given historical contingency, the epochally oriented original conception of the 'new historic form' – which precisely as such cannot conceivably accommodate within its framework compromises with the old social order – must ultimately assert itself.

As to the truly unavoidable 'historical compromises', what is at issue here is not the rather ill-conceived and ill-fated strategy of 'Eurocommunism' which consciously aimed at bringing about what it called 'the great historical compromise', but the necessity of reciprocal adjustments in the actions of the major contending forces in their actual confrontations. For, whatever the immediate aims of the parties involved, their adjustments *vis à vis* each other *de facto* cannot be other than historical compromises, if viewed from the Marxian perspective that points towards a radical socialist transformation of the given social order in its entirety.

The inescapable constraints of such adjustments and compromises are, of course, determined by the prevailing historical circumstances and changing relation of forces. Given certain overriding pressures, such as the perilous state of the arms race, or extreme difficulties in securing the material conditions of 'original accumulation' (be it called 'capital-accumulation' or 'socialist accumulation') on the required scale, for instance, it is in principle conceivable that the Marxian approach, with its radically uncompromising attitude as regards the only feasible – genuinely socialist – *solution* to the structural antagonisms of society, has to be set aside for a significant period of time even in countries which claim to be involved in building socialism.

However, to see *permanent* solutions in *temporary* adjustments and compromises, no matter how necessary they might be under the prevailing circumstances, would be as naive as to imagine that the modernizing intent of the present Chinese leadership can transform the whole of China into a king-size Hong Kong. One should not confuse the necessarily varied *time-scale* and *modalities* of socialist transformation in *particular* areas with the *terminus ad quem* – the overall outcome – of the *globally* unfolding social process. For 'historical compromises' do not *eliminate* the underlying contradictions, only modify their conditions of eruption and eventual resolution.

In the end there can be no 'half-way house' between the rule of capital and the socialist transformation of society on a global scale. And that in its turn necessarily implies that capital's inherent antagonisms must be 'fought out' to an irreversible, structurally safeguarded conclusion. This is inescapable, even if the way in which the process of 'fighting out' unfolds, over a long and sustained historical period, can only be envisaged as a genuine transcendence (*Aufhebung*) produced through the complex interdeterminations of 'continuity in discontinuity and discontinuity in continuity', in the sense indicated by the dialectic of 'quantitative changes turning into qualitative changes', as we have seen above. That is to say, an objective dialectic of reciprocities which the socialist 'living philosophy' of the epoch must reflect both in its methodological complexity and in its ideologically sustained (and constantly reinforced) theoretical orientation towards the *terminus ad quem* of the journey.

It is in this sense that the Marxian vision, notwithstanding its fluctuating fortunes under the weight of the various 'historical compromises', remains methodologically and theoretically valid for the entire historical epoch of transition from the rule of capital to the new social order, thanks to the ideological vitality and scientific insight manifest in it in a dialectical unity.

6.7   SOCIAL ANTAGONISMS AND METHODOLOGICAL DISPUTES

6.7.1
Intense preoccupation with problems of method is particularly pronounced in historical periods of crisis and transition. At such times, when the

formerly preponderant ideology of the ruling classes can no longer ignore or simply brush aside its adversary, the hegemonic claims of *both* sides must be formulated in such a way that the most comprehensive meta-theoretical and methodological principles of the rival systems are made explicit. This happens precisely in order to reinforce the mutually exclusive aspirations of the contending parties to occupy the theoretically as well as practically dominant position in society.

In the case of the old ideology, usually this means the adoption of some form of *scholasticism* (or methodology for the sake of methodology) with the help of which – in the name of the stipulated *formal* rules, models and paradigms – the alternative approaches can be *a priori* discredited and banished from the legitimate framework of discourse. Of course, in reality they must be rejected on account of the challenging novelty of their *contents* and *corresponding* methods. For ideological reasons, however, the real motivations cannot be openly admitted. Consequently, the indictment must be formulated in such a way that it should appear to be concerned with nothing but the alleged violation of some universally valid rule of logic.

Since the old system must embody and defend the fundamental interests of the established order, it cannot renew itself under the conditions of social retrogression – no matter how successfully it reproduces itself as the 'living philosophy' of the ruling forces – in terms of significant, comprehensively valid contents, notwithstanding its universalistic claims. Hence the general tendency to *methodological formalism* (used to shore up the rather hollow claims to 'universality') and to methodology for the sake of methodology: features particularly prominent in the twentieth century, but by no means confined to it.

Thus, since the arguments of the socially challenging adversary cannot be met at the level of *substantive* propositions, the method of 'refutation' assumes an inherently *fallacious* form, in that some arbitrarily assumed *formal* criteria are used to dismiss categorically the essential *contents* of the rival system – by declaring them to be methodologically illegitimate. The 'end of ideology' approach – as well as theories of the same kind, both before and after the appearance of this particular form of ideology – display in their mode of reasoning this fallacious methodological formalism and apriorism. For they deduce from the adversary's alleged departure from a merely stipulated but never established generic rule (of 'scientific objectivity', 'value neutrality', 'freedom from ideological interest', etc.) the radical untenability of its specific *substantive propositions*. Thus, they formally disqualify, with the help of circularly self-exempting definitional criteria, the ideas and practical strategies of the other side which should be concretely analysed and assessed in terms of their determinate contents in the light of the available evidence. Paradoxically, therefore, the excessive methodological orientation of such approaches, though ostensively 'anti-ideological' in aim, manifests, in fact, a much closer ideological adhesion – characteristic of times of sharpened social conflict – to the structural imperatives and values of the established order. Closer and more class-conscious adhesion, that is, than what we can witness as a rule under less polarized historical circumstances.

6.7.2

At the same time, the ideologies of the ascending social forces, too, must spell out the significance of their position by drawing with great clarity the methodological lines of demarcation through which the differences with the attacked adversary can be presented in the most striking way. In fact, their claims to radical novelty and general validity simply cannot be articulated without the most rigorous formulation of the new approach in explicit methodological terms. For the very nature of the enterprise, and the inevitably 'premature' conditions under which its implementation must be at first attempted, mean that *anticipations* of the future appear in it as a matter of course. Consequently, in the absence of other proofs for the viability of the advocated framework, the ascending forces must assert and sustain their claims by demonstrating the theoretical coherence and liberating potential of their new approach in terms of its methodological radicalism and all-embracing universality. This is not less true of Bacon and Descartes (who continue to share in important ways the presuppositions of their scholastic adversaries) than of Kant's 'Copernican revolution'; and of the Hegelian dialectic as much as of the radical reorientation of philosophy by Marx.[594]

6.8 THE MEANING OF LUKÁCS'S 'METHODOLOGICAL GUARANTEE'

6.8.1

There are times when, due to some historical setback, a direct appeal to the orienting significance of the new methodology appears to be the *only* way of reasserting the continued validity of the overall perspectives of the theory in question in the face of the highly unfavourable historical circumstances.

A graphic example in this respect is Lukács's *History and Class Consciousness:* written against the background of the military defeat of the Hungarian Council Republic and the restoration of capital's international dominance and stability, after the short revolutionary interlude initiated by the Russian Revolution.

When Lukács insisted in this work that 'the Party is assigned the sublime role of bearer of the class consciousness of the proletariat and the conscience of its historical vocation', he did this in open defiance of 'the superficially more active and "more realistic" view [which] allocates to the party tasks concerned predominantly or even exclusively with organisation'.[595] In this defiant evaluation of the prevailing historical conditions, the working class – notwithstanding its internally divisive stratification and accommodating submission to the power of capital – was *ascribed* its totalizing class consciousness, and the Party was *assigned* the role of being the actual bearer of that consciousness, despite the clearly identifiable and highly disturbing tendencies of narrow 'realism' and bureaucratization in the international communist movement.

Thus, in the absence of the required objective conditions, the idea of a conscious totalization of the manifold conflicting social processs in the direction of a radical socialist transformation became extremely problematical. It had to be turned into a methodological postulate, to be kept alive for the future, and a theory had to be devised which was capable of asserting and reasserting its own validity in the face of whatever defeats and disappointments the emerging actual future might still have had in store for the beleaguered socialist movement.

Against the overwhelmingly negative circumstances which prevailed at the time, Lukács could not simply offer *likely* and *partial* improvements. He had to predicate the *certainty* of an *all-embracing* and irreversible revolutionary breakthrough in order to counterbalance all evidence pointing in the opposite direction. For nothing could be allowed to put under the shadow of doubt *'the certainty that capitalism is doomed* and that – ultimately – the proletariat will be victorious'.[596] However, since the international working class showed no convincing signs of 'bridging the gap between its *ascribed* and *psychological* class consciousness',[597] and since Lukács himself had to condemn the bureaucratic tendencies of the party that occupied the central position in his own strategic scheme, his discourse had to be transferred to the methodological plane. For, under the circumstances, the validity of the distant positive perspectives which he was defiantly reasserting could only be established – against all visible and (as he argued) conceivable evidence to the contrary – in terms of a primarily methodological discourse. The way Lukács himself put it, in immediate continuation of the passage just quoted about the certainty of capitalist doom and proletarian victory: 'There can be no "material" guarantee of this certitude. It can be *guaranteed methodologically* – by the dialectical method.'[598] In this spirit, an important point raised by Franz Mehring, for instance, was bypassed by Lukács in the name of method, turning a serious gap in Marx's theory into a virtue. For, as he argued:

> Mehring's question about the extent to which Marx overestimated the consciousness of the Weavers' Uprising does not concern us here. *Methodologically* [Lukács's italics] he has provided a *perfect* description of the development of revolutionary class consciousness in the proletariat.[599]

Such opposition of method and content was intended, of course, to remove the contingent factors from the theory, establishing thus its perspectives on foundations free from empirical and temporal fluctuations. However, in his attempt to provide a secure defence – in terms of the long-term temporality of a dialectical methodology – against the ideologically often exploited immediacy of daily political and economic confrontations, Lukács ended up with an extreme paradox:

> Let us assume for the sake of argument that recent research had disproved once and for all every one of Marx's individual theses. Even if this were to be proved, every serious 'orthodox' Marxist would still be able to accept all such modern findings without reservation and hence dismiss all of Marx's theses *in toto* – without having to renounce his orthodoxy for a single moment. Orthodox Marxism, therefore, does not imply the uncritical acceptance of the results of Marx's investigations. It is not the 'belief' in this or that thesis, nor the exegesis of a 'sacred' book. On the contrary, orthodoxy refers exclusively to *method*.[600]

6.8.2

The need to provide firm guarantees with regard to the 'certainty of the final victory', coupled with the difficulties of finding from his perspective other than purely 'methodological guarantees' for positive developments under the prevailing historical circumstances, produced a theoretical approach that remained with Lukács for the rest of his life.

In his essay on 'Class structure and social consciousness', Tom Bottomore expressed his surprise 'that Lukács should repeat, with great approval, in his new preface of 1967' the passage which opposed method to content in the opening essay of *History and Class Consciousness*,[601] originally published in 1923.

Bottomore's concern was, *prima facie*, fully justified. If, however, we situate the problems at issue in relation to the function which the idea of a 'methodological guarantee' played in Lukács's thought, as we have just seen, then the positive reassertion of the validity of his concept of method in 1967 can be considered far from surprising. In fact Lukács's constant polemics in defence of the dialectical method against 'vulgar Marxism' and against 'mechanistic fatalism ... the normal concomitant of reflection theory in mechanistic materialism', in his eyes simultaneously also fulfilled an important political/ideological function, in the struggle against 'sectarianism' and its undialectical cult of immediacy.

The long line of works in this respect went from Lukács's critique of Bukharin's *Historical Materialism* through his essay on 'Moses Hess and the problems of idealist dialectic' to *The Young Hegel, The Destruction of Reason*, and, ultimately, to *The Ontology of Social Being*. Indeed, as the conditions of open ideological and political debate disappeared with the consolidation of Stalinism, the discourse on how to overcome the proletariat's 'ideological crisis' became more and more confined to arguing in favour of the dialectical method as such, expressing, thus, in the 'Aesopic language' of philosophical methodology, Lukács's greatly mediated political aspirations. *The Young Hegel* was perhaps the most important document of this 'Aesopic phase' in Lukács's development.

Another important aspect of this problem was Lukács's insistence throughout his life that there could be only one 'true Marxism' (i.e what he called Marxist 'orthodoxy'; set by Lukács in inverted commas, in order to contrast it with institutionally imposed orthodoxy). At the same time, in accordance with the innermost character of his discourse – centred on the notions of the 'ideological crisis' and the 'responsibility of intellectuals' to pave the way out of that crisis – he was deeply concerned about enlarging the intellectual influence of Marxism.

These political/ideological determinations came together in Lukács's *methodological definition* of 'true Marxism'. On the one hand, such a definition had to be able to exercise a critical/excluding function against 'Stalinist dogmatism', 'mechanical materialism', 'vulgar Marxism', etc., without frontally attacking the powerful institutional objects of this criticism with regard to political/economic issues and theses. And on the other hand, the Lukácsian definition of Marxism had to be flexible enough to embrace in a 'non-sectarian' way, from a fairly broad political spectrum, all serious scholars and intellectuals who were willing to take the positive step towards Marxism. (The latter concern was, of course, one of the main reasons for Lukács's considerable influence among intellectuals.)

Both these aspects were clearly visible in a lecture delivered by Lukács in Italy in June 1956 – *The Cultural Struggle between Progress and Reaction Today*[602] – when for the first time after three long decades, in the aftermath of the XXth Congress of the Soviet Party, he could openly challenge his ideological adversaries. He insisted that in the interest of the 'clarifying propaganda of true Marxism',[603] aimed at exercising 'ideological influence ... to lead in a new direction the non-Marxist intellectuals'[604] and thus 'to influence the ideological ferment and development of the world',[605] it was necessary 'to break definitively with sectarianism and dogmatism'.[606]

The rejected 'Stalinist dogmatism'[607] was defined, again, primarily in methodological terms: as the 'absence of *mediation*',[608] the reifying 'confusion of *tendency* with accomplished *fact*',[609] the '*mechanical* subordination of the *part* to the *whole*',[610] the assertion of an 'immediate relationship between the *fundamental* tenets of the theory and the problems of the day',[611] the 'dogmatic restriction of dialectical materialism'[612] and, most importantly, as the misconceived belief that '*Marxism was a collection of dogmas*'.[613] He also stated categorically that the only way to exercise ideological influence was through '*immanent* critique'[614] which put the methodological issues into the foreground.

It was in the same spirit that he praised in the 1967 Preface to *History and Class Consciousness* his old methodological definition of 'orthodoxy in

Marxism which I now think not only objectively correct but also capable of exerting a considerable influence even today when we are on the eve of a Marxist renaissance'.[615]

6.9 CONCLUSION

As we can see, then, historical periods of crisis and transition, when the latent social antagonisms come to the fore with great intensity, tend to be accompanied by sharp 'methodological disputes'. The latter are by no means intelligible in strictly methodological terms but must be referred to the rival hegemonic claims of the parties involved. Thus, notwithstanding frequently held views to the contrary, the increased preoccupation of the major contending forces with deceptively abstract methodological issues happens to be the proof of much more, rather than less, pronounced ideological deteminations in shaping – intellectually and politically – their strategic orientation, irrespective of whether or not they themselves are conscious of being motivated by such factors.

PART III

IDEOLOGY AND EMANCIPATION

Socialism will not be and cannot be inaugurated by decree; it cannot be established by any government, however admirably socialistic. Socialism must be created by the masses, must be made by every proletarian. Where the chains of capitalism are forged, there must the chains be broken. That only is socialism, and thus only can socialism be brought into being. The masses must learn how to use power by using power. There is no other way.

Rosa Luxemburg

7 · SOCIAL REVOLUTION AND THE DIVISION OF LABOUR

Since ideology is the inescapable practical consciousness of class societies, articulated in characteristic forms in which the members of the opposing social forces can become conscious of their materially grounded conflicts and fight them out, the truly important question is this: will the individuals, armed with the ideology of the class to which they belong, side with the historically unfolding cause of emancipation or line up against it. For ideology can (and indeed does) serve both sides with its means and methods of mobilizing the individuals who, irrespective of how clearly they realize this, necessarily participate in the ongoing struggle.

The established socioeconomic order must constantly adjust itself to the changing conditions of domination if it is to prove its continued viability. Throughout history known to us, ideology played an important role in this process of structural readjustments. For the successful reproduction of the conditions of domination could not take place without the most active intervention of powerful ideological factors on the side of maintaining the order in existence.

Naturally, the ruling ideology has a vested interest in the preservation of the *status quo* in which even the most glaring inequalities are already *structurally* entrenched and safeguarded. Hence it can afford to proclaim the virtues of 'consensual' arrangements, of 'organic unity' and self-serving 'participation', claiming thereby also the self-evident reasonableness of (*ruling*) 'moderation'. Yet in reality the social order which it champions is, of necessity, torn by internal contradictions and antagonisms, no matter how successful the reproduction of the hierarchical structural framework of super- and sub-ordination and the *semblance* of 'organic communality' and 'mutually shared interests' across the ages.

The myth of 'organic unity' dominated ideological discourse ever since social intercourse had to conform to the material imperatives of securing the continuity of production within the potentially explosive framework of the hierarchical social division of labour that repeatedly changed its forms in the course of history but not its exploitative substance.

This correlation between pacificatory ideology and hierarchical social structure is perfectly understandable. For no matter how deeply divided and antagonistically torn all class societies are in their basic structural relationships, they must, nevertheless, be able to function under normal circumstances as *integrated wholes* (and in that sense 'organic systems'); with the exception, that is, of those periods of *explosion* which tend to draw the historical line of demarcation between one social formation and another.

The plausibility and spontaneous influence of the dominant ideological discourse well beyond the ranks of its true beneficiaries resides precisely in its soothing appeal to 'unity' and associated concerns, from 'observing the rules of objectivity' to finding the right 'balance' in the necessary – but because of the normally prevailing unequal relation of forces quite iniquitous – 'reciprocal adjustments' of the conflicting social forces. The necessary cementing function of the ruling ideology becomes all the more evident (and significant) if we recall that even its more aggressive variants – from chauvinism to Nazism and to the most recent ideologies of the 'Radical Right' – must claim to represent the overwhelming majority of the population, against the outside 'enemy', the 'racially inferior' minorities, the so-called 'mere handful of trouble-makers' who are supposed to be the cause of strikes and social unrest ('the enemy within' in Mrs Thatcher's parlance), etc.

From the standpoint of the ruling ideology, the ongoing hegemonic conflict can never be allowed to be depicted as one between potential equals. For that would *ipso facto* throw wide open the question of legitimacy and confer historical rationality on the adversary. It is therefore a matter of insuperable structural determination that the ruling ideology – in view of its aprioristic legitimatory aspirations – cannot function at all without misrepresenting its self-interest, no matter how narrow, as the 'general interest' of society. But precisely for the same reason, the ideological discourse of the ruling order must maintain its cult of 'unity' and 'proper balance', even if – particularly at times of major crises – this amounts to no more than empty rhetorics when set against the real operative principle of *divide and rule*.

Naturally, very different constraints apply to critical ideologies. For all those who try to articulate the interests of the subordinate classes have to assume – again as a matter of insuperable structural determination – a negating posture not only with regard to the pretended 'organicity' of the established order but also in relation to its objective determinations and institutions of socioeconomic and political/cultural control.

However, it must be also recognized that the story cannot end at the point of sheer negativity. For no social force can put forward its claims as a *hegemonic alternative* without also indicating, at least in its broad outlines, the positive/affirmative dimension of its radical negation. This is true of thousands of years of history, not only of the last few centuries. Ideologies which exhaust themselves in pure negation as a rule fizzle out within a very short time and thus fail to assert any real claim to constitute a viable alternative.

Moreover, somewhat paradoxically, it is a characteristic feature of none but the ruling ideologies that once the declining phase in the development of the social forces whose interests they express is reached, they are unable to offer other than a thoroughly negative conceptual framework, notwithstanding their 'uncritical positivism', i.e. their 'positive' identification with the *status quo*. For their affirmative dimension is really quite *mechanical/determinist* – as well exemplified in the frequently repeated dictum: '*there is no alternative*', which self-contradictorily claims to be the defence of 'freedom', 'liberty', 'individual sovereignty', etc. – and all their active concern is directed at dismissing their adversary with an *aprioristic negativity*, remaining thus entirely dependent (i.e. intellectually parasitic) on the arguments which they reject from the ground of their mechanical 'no alternative' preconception.

The socialist project, by contrast, sets out from the premiss that *there is an alternative*. It defines the conditions of bringing about that alternative – the practical conditions of emancipation – as a form of action in which the moment of negation acquires its meaning through the positive objectives which it entails. This is why the socialist project cannot content itself with the negativity of the *political* revolution, however necessary, but must strive for the intrinsically positive *social* revolution in the course of which the associated individuals can 'change from top to bottom the conditions of their industrial and political existence, and consequently their whole manner of being' (Marx). And this is why it must insist, with Rosa Luxemburg, that 'socialism will not be and cannot be inaugurated by decree; it cannot be established by any government, however admirably socialistic. Socialism must be created by the masses, must be made by *every* proletarian.'

Evidently, such objectives cannot be realized without the work of emancipatory ideology through which the necessary motivational framework of transforming the social individuals' 'whole manner of being' is defined and constantly redefined. Not from above but as a matter of consciously pursued self-activity.

To be sure, this perspective is not without its problems. Envisaging the kind of social transformation anticipated by the Marxian vision has to reckon not only with the difficulties inherent in the sheer magnitude of the tasks to be accomplished. But equally, one must be able to face up to the complications that inevitably arise from the shifting sociohistorical contingencies in the light of which the basic propositions of the original theory must be reexamined and, if necessary, adapted to the changing circumstances. This is what we have to concern ourselves with on the pages that follow.

7.1 THE STRUCTURAL FOUNDATION OF CLASS DETERMINATIONS

7.1.1

According to Marx, the class – including the 'class for-itself' – is necessarily confined to *pre-history*. Consequently, so long as the objective ground of class determinations survives, the idea of 'conscious collective totalization' (i.e. the conscious and fully adequate control of their conditions of existence by the totality of self-determining and mutually interacting individuals who form the 'universal class') is and remains a paradoxical concept, notwithstanding the *qualitative* differences between capital and labour as hegemonic social alternatives. For in attempting to assess the nature of even the most advanced class and its relationship to what Marx calls 'true history' (in opposition to 'pre-history'), we are confronted by the difficult problem that the class as such is both the *necessary* and the inherently *problematical* agent of emancipation. This happens to be the case for two principal reasons:

1. No matter how broadly based, the class is by definition an *exclusive* social force in that it cannot embrace other than its own members.
2. The relationship between the individuals and their class is itself subject to weighty critical qualifications, since its practical articulation *necessarily* raises the question of representation, hierarchy and domination.

It is for these reasons that even the 'class for-itself' is in Marx's view consigned to pre-history. He always insists on the necessity to transcend *all* classes as the fundamental condition of making 'real history'. For 'collective totalization' – even if it is centred around the interests of the historically most advanced class – under the determinations of pre-history necessarily involves a somewhat uncontrollable constituent. This is due to the fact that the antagonistic contradictions of capitalist society '*must be fought out*' by all available means and forms of confrontation, including those which happen to be more or less directly determined by the moves of the *adversary*. Naturally, the role of ideology is paramount in this process.

The idea of a fully conscious collective totalization through the agency of the class, without the self-determined participation of its individual members, is a dubious proposition. Equally, the objective limitations arising from the given sociohistorical circumstances (with regard to the institutional self-definition of the class itself, in accordance with its own basic aims as well as in response to the strategies and institutional realities of the contested forces) introduce serious question marks as to the possible *degree* of conscious collective interaction on the basis of self-determined individual involvement in any class society, including the various societies of transition towards socialism. Hence the class as such must be critically assessed under the following aspects:

7.1.2 Class versus individual

As it is painfully obvious, the class necessarily subsumes under itself all its individual members. Consequently, the individuals can only define their own position in society starting out from certain presuppositions which are inescapably imposed upon them in virtue of their mere belonging to their antagonistically poised social class. Marx is emphatically clear and firm on this point, linking the question of emancipation to the need for superseding the domination of individuals also by their own class, together with their liberation from the paralysing constraints of the historically established social division of labour of which the class itself is the necessary structural articulation. He writes in *The German Ideology:*

> the class in its turn assumes an *independent existence as against the individuals*, so that the latter find their conditions of life *predetermined*, and have their position in life and hence their personal development *assigned to them by their class*, thus becoming *subsumed under it*. This is the same phenomenon as the subjection of the separate individuals to the *division of labour* and can only be removed by the *abolition of private property and of labour itself.*[616]

Thus the class is, paradoxically, both the necessary vehicle and active *agent* of the historical task of socialist emancipation and, at the same time, also a fundamental *obstacle* to its accomplishment.

7.1.3 Class versus class

The confrontation between classes inevitably carries with it *reciprocal determinations* for all parties concerned. The struggle for hegemony requires the coordinated and disciplined mobilization of the total resources of the competing classes, imposing on their members a more or less rigid *command structure* in accordance with the intensity of the conflicts and the overall practical implications of the issues at stake.

Furthermore, the means and methods at the disposal of one side inevitably imply the adoption by the other side of appropriate strategic moves and counter-measures, with all their institutional corollaries. The characteristics of such moves and corresponding institutional complexes are designed, to a highly significant extent, so as to be able to *match* the adversary on its own terrain. This must be the case even if it means being deflected for some considerable time from the inherent positive aims of the class in question. Naturally, such reciprocal determinations have serious implications for the autonomy and margin of initiative available to the individual members of the opposing classes.

7.1.4 Stratification and unity

Modern classes are by no means homogeneous entities; nor could the process of global industrial development – with its complex interdeterminations and manifold divisions of interest – ever turn them into homogeneous social forces. Yet, the conditions of struggle for hegemony raise the question of *unity*, particularly at times of acute confrontations: a requirement which is much easier to postulate than to achieve in practice, as far as the subordinate class is concerned.

Regrettably, the problems of stratification belong to the most neglected part of the Marxist theory of classes. For even if Marx rightly stresses that the 'subsuming of individuals under definite classes cannot be abolished until a class has evolved which has no longer any particular class interest to assert against a ruling class',[617] this in itself by no means constitutes the solution of the thorny issues at stake, contrary to how it is often assumed to be the case. All it does is to define the *general conditions* under which a solution to the underlying contradictions may be envisaged. As such the Marxian definition of the necessary line of action does not suggest in the slightest that the practical problems and difficulties of proletarian class strategy automatically disappear with the complicated unfolding – with all its 'inadequacies, weaknesses and paltriness' (Marx), resulting in 'inter-ruptions' and relapses – of an objective *historical challenge* which is in principle *capable* of superseding capital's inner antagonisms.

To misrepresent the Marxian characterization of a *historical precondition* as a *ready-made solution* is nothing but a caricature of Marx, usually linked to attributing to him a primitive theory of 'proletarian immiseration', disregarding all evidence to the contrary in his writing. Stratification is a vitally important aspect of the reality of the class. One cannot deal with the problems arising from it by treating them in one-sidedly negative terms and thereby wishfully theorizing them out of existence. On the contrary, an adequate approach to stratification involves the elaboration and practical implementation of viable strategies which fully recognize the dynamic com-plexities of collective totalization as based on the self-activity of multi-faceted social forces, with objective interests of their own. The *socialist* common denominator of such diverse interests can articulate itself only through this self-activity itself, and not through the arbitrary imposition of some abstract 'unitary' postulate. Demands and postulates of 'unity' are often not only unrealistic; they also tend to be formulated from the standpoint of the dominant reformist-opportunist wing of the labour movement against the *Left* which is always blamed for 'rocking the boat' of electoral success with its radical demands.

Obviously with regard to the question of unity one cannot speak of a *symmetry* between the two fundamental classes contesting hegemony in capitalist society. For the ruling class has massive and self-evidently *real* vested interests to defend, which act as a powerful unifying force among its various strata. In complete contrast, the internal stratification of the subordinate class tends to intensify the contradiction between *immediate* and *long-term* interests, defining the latter as merely *potential* (anticipated, hypothetical, etc.) whose conditions of realization necessarily escape the immediate situation. Hence arises the need for an inherently *critical* attitude towards the requirement of unity in the subordinate class, implying the *practical* articulation of modes and means of action in order to positively mobilize and *coordinate* the diverse forces of its numerous strata, without superimposing on them a separate bureaucratic structure of 'unification' from above which tends to defeat its original purpose.

7.1.5 Class interest and institutional inertia

Understandably, the effective assertion of class interest (irrespective of which particular class we take as an example) is unthinkable without its own instrumentality and institutional framework. It is equally clear that the nature of the required institutional complexes cannot be isolated from the stakes and conditions of the ongoing struggle.

The trouble is, though, that the typical institutions aimed at successfully asserting class interest, because of their *dual* character – i.e. the required ability to *confront* the class antagonist on the one hand, and to *control* (or 'subsume') their own members under their objectively dictated determinations on the other – tend to strengthen their own material/institutional structure even at the expense of their supporters. Thus, the 'danger of ossification' (noted by Lukács in *History and Class Consciousness*) happens to be an intrinsic *structural* problem – a function of the *necessary duality* of the very nature and inner determination of any class institution as such – and can only be countermanded by conscious and *sustained* countermeasures, coupled with the required, truly democratic, institutional guarantees which positively involve the individual members of the class.

7.1.6 Hierarchy, domination, and participatory representation

Evidently, the thorny issues of social hierarchy are inherent in all four aspects of the relationship between individual and class mentioned so far. Taken together, they heavily underline the ambivalent character of the class as the unavoidable agency of emancipation. But well beyond the more or less burdensome contingencies of all such relations, hierarchy – as well as domination and repression that go with enforced hierarchy – constitutes a fundamental *structural* determination of class existence as such, irrespective of the personnel directly involved in the exercise of class rule at any particular time in history.

This means that the question of class domination and subordination does not simply arise with regard to the relationship of one class to another (i.e. as affecting the multiplicity of individuals who constitute the opposing sides of the given antagonistic class relations) but, more importantly, in virtue of the objective location of the major classes of society in the historically established structure of production. In other words, classes are dominated not only by the *personnel* of the other class but also by the *objective structural imperatives* of the historically given system of production and division of labour.

Indeed, in this relationship the *übergreifendes Moment* is, undoubtedly, the stubborn *persistence* of the relevant structural imperative that objectively sustains the personnel of a determinate class rule or, conversely, its disappearance with the changing of historical cicumstances. This is why the aristocracy as the ruling class of the feudal system becomes a 'superfluous class' – indeed a parasitic-obstructionist force – from the point of view of societal reproduction in the course of the objective restructuring that characterizes the socioeconomic process of the 'ancien régime' in its last phase of development, prior to the French Revolution.

The transition from the rule of capital to a socialist order of society, by contrast, brings with it some major structural differences in this respect, in the sense that the very notion of *structural hierarchy* itself is being radically challenged by the 'new historic form' of the classless society. Such differences must be realistically assessed – from the point of view of the social metabolism as a whole – also in terms of the complex dialectical relationship between the personnel assigned to carrying out determinate social functions and the objective structural imperative of the required functions themselves.

The unavoidable negative implications of the objective structural imperatives mentioned above surface with brutal suddenness and far-reaching consequences under historical circumstances when the ruling class is politically overthrown while the overall framework of production and the inherited – *hierarchical* – structural/functional division of labour remain fundamentally intact, as indeed for the initial phases in the development of a transitional social formation they must do so. The sharp contradiction which we experienced between the original theorizations of the dictatorship of the proletariat by Marx and Lenin, and the historical realization of such dictatorship in the twentieth century, had a great deal to do with the neglect of this crucial dimension of the problem.

It was originally anticipated that 'smashing the bourgeois state apparatus' on the one hand, and instituting in its place a system of *direct delegacy* – with 'compulsory mandate' and 'revocability of the mandate' as its regulating principles – would provide both the necessary safeguards against hierarchy, and at the same time, in positive terms, it would constitute the fully adequate instrumentality of the desired social emancipation. The question concerning the relationship between the mandate and the objective pressures – the weighty structural imperatives – of the inherited framework of production received no serious examination either in the context of the Paris Commune or in relation to later events. When Lenin (in November 1917, in the 'postscript to the first edition' of his *State and Revolution*) explained the unfinished character of this work, understandably he could still assert in an optimistic mood that: 'It is more pleasant and useful to go through the "experience of the revolution" than to write about it.'[618] Later on, however, he had to complain about unforeseen difficulties of insurmountable gravity and complexity at all levels of political and social life for which the proletarian revolution was neither theoretically nor practically prepared.

We may also recall in this context a letter by Marx to Joseph Weydemeyer[619] in which he talked about the *necessity* of the proletarian dictatorship as representing the *transitional* phase towards the transcendence (or supersession, not 'abolition') of classes (*Aufhebung der Klassen*). He closely linked in the same letter these propositions to their theoretical foundation, namely that the existence of the classes themselves is confined to 'determinate historical phases of the development of production' (*bestimmte Entwicklungsphasen der Produktion*).[620]

Thus, by implication, Marx's key concern was the necessarily inherited system of *production* in its objective socioeconomic determinations, as directly manifest through the class existence (or at least the class-like hierarchy-generating structural imperatives) of the prevailing social division of labour. Of the latter, the question of political/organizational forms can only constitute a specific *part* that in its turn must be always assessed in terms of the dynamically unfolding transformations of the production system of global capital itself. It is necessary to emphasize, however, that in this – both theoretically and practically vital – context the Marxian theory offers only indirect hints and implications. For, regrettably, Marx never reached the point in his original project where he could have started to sketch even the bare outlines of his theory of the state and of the state's relationship to the 'international relation of production; international division of labour; international exchange; the world market and crises',[621] although all this constituted an integral part of his overall theoretical framework.

The realities of class existence are inseparable from the overpowering material determinations of the social metabolism itself. These determinations are not radically altered by the removal of the formerly ruling personnel while the structure of production (for whatever reason) remains essentially the same as before. On the contrary, the vacuum created by the overthrow of the ruling class and of its political institutions must sooner or later be filled by what is customarily (and superficially) referred to as 'bureaucratization', in order to reconstitute the 'normal' (i.e. the inherited) functioning of the unrestructured social metabolism, in accordance with the prevailing social division of labour. For the latter, following the 'line of least resistance' in the aftermath of a major crisis, continues to supply the elementary requirements (thereby successfully responding to the objective structural imperatives) of this metabolism.

The subordinate class in its original constitution is, of necessity, hierarchically structured not primarily because of its confrontation with the ruling class but because of the vital metabolic functions which it must fulfil in the historically given system of social reproduction. The removal of the ruling personnel, and the overthrow of the specific institutional forms in which that personnel used to impose its mode of control on society as a whole, does not eliminate the need for the control of the given, materially/objectively hierarchical, structure of production. Even less does it remove the need for carrying on as undisturbed as possible with the vital metabolic functions – embedded in a most reified fashion in the inherited production structures themselves – upon which the livelihood of men and the continuity of social reproduction depend.

Thus, hierarchy and domination are painfully obvious material/structural imperatives of determinate forms of the division of labour on the basis of which they also articulate themselves, in like manner, at the political plane. This is why the proletariat can – and under certain conditions must – 'turn its dictatorship against itself'.[622] Consequently, postulating 'direct democracy' as the immediate remedy against hierarchy and domination is highly problematical not only on account of its doubtful feasibility – as forcefully argued by Norberto Bobbio[623] – but also in view of the fact that such an approach addresses itself to the problems at stake in fundamentally *political* terms alone, in opposition to capitalistic 'formal democracy' and its dubious practices of 'representation'. Nor is it possible to look for a solution in the form of some *moral postulate*, as Lukács tried to do in an essay[624] written not long before *History and Class Consciousness*.

Since the issue in question concerns the objective structural imperatives of the social metabolism as inherent in the established productive framework and division of labour, a realistic solution is inconceivable without a radical restructuring of the whole social framework, with all its vital material determinations and institutional manifestations. Naturally, the regulative principles of *socially anchored and controlled representation* (in contrast to merely parliamentary representation) and *direct participation* – which happen to be not only legitimate but also instrumentally vital concerns of any genuine socialist strategy – can only find their proper role and terrain of active intervention in the course of the selfsame process of radical structural transformations.

7.2 THE BURDEN OF HISTORICAL CONTINGENCY[625]

7.2.1

As we could observe it in the last section, Marx was well aware of the burden of class determinations which tend to subsume under their own logic the individuals who constitute society. Indeed, from his early writings to the *Grundrisse* and *Capital* he never stopped defining the task of emancipation as belonging to the social individual. Equally, he insisted on the necessity of the formation of a socialist *mass consciousness* as the inescapable requirement for activating the vast majority of individuals in their collective enterprise of self-emancipation.

Since Marx always maintained the primacy of social practice as the *'übergreifendes Moment'* in the dialectic of theory and practice, he could have no use whatsoever for abstract philosophical principles – like the Hegelian *'identity of the Subject and Object'* – to accomplish the work of actual history in an a priori fashion. Instead, he put the emphasis firmly on the maturation of certain objective conditions without which the 'solo song of the proletarian revolution', no matter how conscious, could only become 'a swan song in all peasant societies',[626] – that is to say, in by far the greater part of the world.

Thus, the two vital considerations of a genuine socialist transformation just mentioned – which focused on the necessary emancipation of social individuals from the constraints of their *own class* as a prerequisite to the construction of the 'new historic form' on a truly *mass basis* – were clearly identified by Marx from the very outset. Nor did he imagine that, no matter how radical, political measures alone could solve the immense problems confronting 'the *social* revolution of the nineteenth century'.[627] On the contrary, he insisted on the necessity of a fundamental structural transformation of society in its entirety.

Equally, he defined the conditions of the social revolution in inherently international terms already in *The German Ideology*,[628] and the revolutions of 1848–49, together with their painful aftermath, could only strengthen his belief that:

> Europe has taken on a form that makes every fresh proletarian upheaval in France directly coincide with a *world war*. The new French revolution is forced to leave its national soil forthwith and *conquer the European terrain*, on which alone the social revolution of the nineteenth century can be accomplished.[629]

According to this perspective, there could be no 'socialism in one country', let alone in an isolated and encircled peasant society in which the proletarian revolution had to face Marx's dilemma about its 'solo song' being turned by sociohistorical constraints into a 'swan song'.

7.2.2
Marx formulated his basic principles with regard to the conditions of a socialist transformation well before the burden of historical experience had deeply affected the political movement of the proletariat first through the accommodations of German Social Democracy, and then through the formation of the Leninist vanguard party after Marx's death. Understandably, therefore, the far-reaching implications of such developments had to remain beyond Marx's horizon, although the radical scepticism of his *'dixi et salvavi animam meam'* at the end of his *Critique of the Gotha Programme* bears witness to the feeling of unease with which he greeted the newly emerging trends of working-class involvement in the political arena. (More about such changes in the next chapter.)

In another respect, towards the end of his life – in a carefully drafted correspondence with Vera Zasulich – Marx addressed himself to the specific problems of peasant societies, concerning their potentialities for socialist development. However, he did not spell out in great detail his conclusions, nor did he modify his earlier strategic views as to the historical mandate of the proletarian revolution and its transitional state-formation: the dictatorship of the proletariat.

The possibilities of a much longer drawn-out development appeared on the margin of Marx's thought, formulated as a major dilemma – implying a great many unknown factors, with all their necessary theoretical consequences – in a letter to Engels:

> The historic task of bourgeois society is the establishment of the *world market*, at least in its basic outlines, and a mode of production that rests on its basis. Since the world is round, it seems that this has been accomplished with the colonization of California and Australia and with the annexation of China and Japan.
>
> For us the *difficult question* is this: the revolution on the Continent is imminent and its character will be at once socialist; will it not be *necessarily crushed* in this *little corner of the world*, since on a much larger terrain the development of bourgeois society is still in its *ascendancy*.[630]

In the same letter Marx also made it clear that the collapse of bourgeois society in the foreseeable future was only a *hope*, by no means a certainty: 'One cannot deny, bourgeois society lives its second sixteenth century which, I hope, will take it into the grave, just as the first one brought it into life.' The world situation had to be characterized like this precisely because of what Marx underlined as the undeniable *ascendancy* of capital on that 'much larger terrain' which necessarily put the European 'little corner of the world' into perspective.

As we can see, then, some key elements of a very different assessment of the coming socialist revolution appeared in Marx's thought after the 1848–49 uprisings, and they continued to surface in various contexts up to the end of his life. Such elements did not question the necessity of the socialist revolution, but they had far-reaching implications for its *time scale* and the potential *modality* of its unfolding. For it made a big difference, with regard to the feasible sociopolitical forms of transition, *where* and under what kind of *class relations* the socialist revolution broke out and had to attempt the radical restructuring of the given social metabolism, under the more or less heavily constraining degree of development (or underdevelopment) of the inherited production forces. And, of course, in their turn the unfolding forms of transition would necessarily affect the possibility of a truly self-determined integration of the individuals within the framework of conscious collective action, and thus their emancipation from blindly superimposed class determinations, as foreshadowed by the Marxian perspective of the emerging communist *mass consciousness*.

In this sense, the failure of the socialist revolution to break through in the European 'little corner of the world' – while its potential success was meant to block the development of the bourgeois order on the incomparably larger terrain of the rest of the world – carried some weighty implications for the maturation of capital's inner contradictions. Since the establishment of the anticipated new social order was said to be possible only as the 'act of the dominant peoples "all at once" and simultaneously', on the basis of the 'universal development of the productive forces and the world intercourse bound up with them', the possibility of developing capital's productive outlets ˉeverywhere where bourgeois society was still in its ascendancy was synonymous with the possibility of *displacing* for the duration of the selfsame historical ascendancy capital's inner contradictions. Until, that is, 'world intercourse' as a whole would become *saturated* by the dynamics of capital's inexorable self-expansion so as to drive the whole process to a halt through an ever-deepening structural crisis of the 'universally developed productive forces', on a truly global scale.

Naturally, Marx could not be primarily concerned with elaborating the manifold implications of this long-term perspective when he hoped – and explicitly said so – that 'the second sixteenth century of bourgeois society' would take the capitalist order into its grave as a result of the successful socialist revolutions of the proletariat in the advanced European countries. Thus, the briefly identified elements of such a perspective had to be confined to the margin of his conception, appearing there from time to time as somewhat isolated insights, but never fully integrated into his theory as a whole. Nevertheless, the very fact that such vital constituents of the alternative perspective appeared on the margin of Marx's thought at the initial phase of the growing European imperial drive which gave a new lease of life to capital, indicates that subsequent developments did not represent a radical departure from – or, as his adversaries argue, a refutation of – the Marxian theory, but the realization of some objective potentialities of development inherent in the complex sociohistorical factors of the age and already visible, at least to some extent, in Marx's lifetime.

7.3 THE GAPS IN MARX

As we all know today, bourgeois society was not taken to its grave by its second sixteenth century and by the social revolutions of the twentieth, let alone by those of the nineteenth. The successful exploitation by capital of the gigantic potential outlets of its global ascendancy in the peasant and underdeveloped societies presented the forces aspiring to socialist revolution with a new challenge. For while the 'dominant peoples' – the main beneficiaries of capital's renewed expansion and imperialist domination –

were held back by their vested interests from pursuing the road towards a socialist transformation, new types of contradiction appeared on the 'periphery' and at the 'weakest links' of the increasingly interdependent and saturated global system. At the same time, the eruption of revolutions in the underdeveloped periphery, and the successful consolidation of their (no matter how limited and problematical)[631] results, put the question of the *transition to socialism* on the historical agenda in a *hostile* global context; under conditions, that is, when even the most tentative first steps in the direction of the originally envisaged perspective of the state's '*withering away*' could not be seriously contemplated for a moment, in view of the prevailing relation of forces heavily dominated by the capitalist 'dominant peoples'.[632]

Thus, taking also 'hindsight' into account, the gaps in Marx's own approach to our problem are described in the following sections.

7.3.1

The problems of the *transition to socialism* were never discussed by Marx in any detail, apart from some brief general references to the fundamental contrast between the 'lower' and 'higher' phases of the envisaged future society in the *Critique of the Gotha Programme*, as dictated by the polemical context of the latter.

Admittedly the issue itself, with all its bewildering practical dimensions, was by no means an acute historical challenge in Marx's lifetime, given capital's newly won vitality on the ground of its imperialist expansion. Nevertheless, inasmuch as Marx contemplated the possibility that the 'dominant peoples' might not move 'all at once and simultaneously' in the direction of a socialist transformation, such consideration carried with it some weighty implications for future developments, especially with regard to the likely changes in the legal and political superstructure and their necessary impact on the material processes of society in general. For the fundamental requirements of the social metabolism assert themselves in very different ways under substantially different political circumstances, notwithstanding the primacy of the material base – 'in the last analysis' – in the overall structure of determinations and interchanges. This is why assessing the true significance and material inertia of the international division of labour *vis à vis* the societies of transition is inseperable from confronting the problems of the state in its global setting. (Clearly, the book Marx originally planned, on the state reciprocally integrated with the international relations of production and exchange, pinpoints a crucial missing dimension of Marx's undertaking in this respect.)

This factor is all the more important once the internal and international political parameters of the social metabolism (which are vital even under the most favourable circumstances) appear historically articulated as a set of *antagonistic inter-state relations*, in the aftermath of a socialist revolution at the 'weakest link' of the imperialist chain. Given such conditions, the inertial force of politics – defined as acting in response to the moves of a *hostile* outside world, under the banner of a besieged, hence greatly *strengthened* state, and not one that begins to show the first signs of 'withering away' – becomes overpowering.

7.3.2

The historical unfolding of the contradiction between *social production and private appropriation* was amenable to an alternative reading: one very different from that offered by Marx. As Paul Mattick rightly stressed:

> For Marx, capitalism was private-property capitalism, and where it seemed to lose its strictly private-enterprise nature, as in state-industries, and even in the joint stock companies, he saw it as a partial abolition of the capitalist mode of production within the capitalist mode of production; a sign of the decay of the capitalist system.[633]

In reality, however, a great variety of 'hybrid' combinations – all possible permutations of the mystifying 'mixed economy' – are thoroughly compatible with the continued survival (even temporary revitalization) of private capitalism, not to mention the ultimate limits of capital as such. Indeed, the fairly large-scale 'nationalization' of bankrupt industries which we have experienced in capitalist countries after the second world war – frequently followed by the profitable practice of denationalization in due course: after the imposition, that is, of the necessary, and by fragmented private capital unachievable, political/economic changes (with regard to Trade Union power, for instance) – represent a very welcome way of extending the manipulative rationality of the capitalist system.

In all such developments conscious collective self-activity of individuals does not advance one single step nearer to realization, since the control of the fundamental social/economic processes remains radically divorced from and opposed to the producers. The industry-wide, even transnational, integration of the production process does not make the producers any more 'associated producers' than they were in capitalist industrial enterprises of a more limited scale. For what really decides the issue is the successful transfer – from capital to the producers – of the *effective control* of the various units of production, whatever their size. And that is equivalent to a genuine *socialization* of the process of *production* in all its essential characteristics, well beyond the immediate problem of *ownership*, as opposed to its remote hierarchical mangement through '*statalization*' and '*nationalization*' – or, for that matter, through its growing transnational integration. In other words, the issue at stake is primarily political/social, requiring in the first place a qualitative political change for its realization. And the latter is by no means necessarily helped but may, on the contrary, be actually hindered by the unfolding of capital's centralization and concentration as an economic necessity so hopefully evaluated by Marx. For in the face of the massive power of capital's increasing concentration and centralization, the countervailing political force of labour must be on an equally large scale if it is to have any chance of success against its adversary.

7.3.3

Marx's optimistic evaluation of the Paris Commune as 'a Revolution not against this or that ... form of state power [but] a Revolution against the *State itself*'[634] was coupled with an equally optimistic characterization of the Bonapartist Second Empire as 'the last expression of that state power', the '*last possible form* of [bourgeois] class rule' and the '*last* triumph of a State separate from and independent of society'.[635]

This view was in marked contrast to his own way of linking in the same work[636] '*political superstructures*' to determinate '*social bodies*' which sustain them, talking about the 'withering away' of certain social bodies which make the continued existence of their political superstructures a historical anachronism. Also, in another passage[637] he stressed that the social soil that corresponds to the 'superstructure of a centralized state power' is the 'systematic and hierarchic division of labour', thereby indicating the strongest possible reciprocal determination and mutual support between the two.

The problem is, though, that the obvious and highly disturbing implications of such remarks undermine Marx's hopeful expectations about the 'last possible form' of a state power separate from and independent of society. For, so long as the social soil of the systematic and hierarchic division of labour exists – and indeed successfully renews and strengthens itself in conjunction with the ongoing transformation of the relevant social bodies of 'civil society' on an ever-extending scale, in the direction of an ultimate global integration – a corresponding restructuring of state-forms in the interest of continued class rule (both internally and at the level of inter-state relations) cannot be denied to the established system. Accordingly, even today we are still very far from the 'last form' of the capitalist state and its class rule, let alone at the time when Marx wrote the lines just quoted from his defence of the Commune.

7.3.4

The other side of the question of the state's continued domination of society and refusal to 'wither away' concerns the proletariat. For a working-class revolution – as Marx saw the Commune[638] – is only on a long-term historical scale *ipso facto* also a revolution 'against the State itself' (i.e. against the *state as such*). It is not so in terms of the really feasible impact of its inescapable immediate objectives.

Such a limitation is not simply the consequence of an isolated revolution and its ensuing 'encirclement', although, of course, the latter has a great deal to do with it in the sense that the *'harmonious national and international coordination'*[639] of social intercourse anticipated by Marx cannot be even dreamed about under such circumstances. Nevertheless, the painfully obvious historical delay in attacking the foundations of the state as such arises primarily from the very nature of the task itself: 'to work out the *economic emancipation* of labour' through the *'political form* at last discovered',[640] so that *'free and associated labour'* should assume the form of *'united co-operative societies'* in order 'to regulate *national* production upon a common plan'.[641]

Thus, in Marx's conception, the objective and subjective *requirements* of a socialist transformation – the full emancipation of labour from the prevailing social division of labour – stipulate a *political form* (the proletarian state) under which the advocated transition from the old to the new society should be accomplished, while this transitional state itself is called upon to act simultaneously as both master and servant of the long-drawn-out process of emancipation.[642] Such a state is said to have no interest of its own to defend, despite its unquestionably strategic function – as the *specific political form* of the necessary 'national coordination' of social life – in the division of labour whose continuation is unavoidable (even if progressively diminishing) for the whole period of radical restructuring. There seems to be no contradiction in asking the new *political form* to work out the *economic emancipation* of labour, since the working class is said to be in complete control of the political process in a social framework in which the interest of those who directly control the transitional state machinery and that of society as a whole fully coincide.

To be sure, Marx is well aware of the fact that the changes required for superseding the inherited division of labour can only result from a highly complex historical process of transformation. Indeed, he insists that the working class 'will have to pass through *long struggles*, through a series of historic processes, transforming *circumstances and men*.'[643] Yet, he has to resort to equivocation in order to reconcile the contradiction between the fact that the task of 'transforming circumstances and men' is far from accomplished, and the assumption that the communist consciousness of the working class is *already given*.

Communist consciousness was defined in *The German Ideology* as 'the consciousness of the necessity of a fundamental revolution'.[644] At the same time it was also stated: 'Both for the production on a mass scale of this communist consciousness, and for the success of the cause itself, the *alteration of men on a mass scale is necessary*.'[645]

The same ideas appear in the evaluation of the Commune, but this time ascribing to the working class *in the present* 'the *full consciousness* of their historic mission'.[646] Furthermore, it is also claimed that the working class possesses a practical determination to act in accordance with that consciousness – as well as the ability to do so without state-interference, 'in self-working and self-governing communes'.[647] Thus, beginning each sentence with: 'the working class knows', or 'they know',[648] Marx is able to turn some vital historical *imperatives* (whose realization depends on the full articulation of 'communist consciousness on a mass scale') into the *affirmatives* of already developed and effectively self-asserting social forces.

Similarly, in *The German Ideology* Marx stated that 'Communism is for us not . . . an ideal to which reality will have to adjust itself'.[649] Now the same idea is put forward in a significantly modified form, saying that: 'They [the working class] have no ideals to realize, but to set free the elements of the new society with which old collapsing bourgeois society itself is pregnant.'[650] The problem is not whether or not one should call the enterprise of 'setting free the elements of the new society' an 'ideal to realize'. What matters in the present context is the shift from '*for us*' – or from 'for the Communists' in some other writings[651] – to the *working class as a whole*, postulating, even if in an ambiguous form, the accomplished *actualization* of that communist mass consciousness whose *production* was presented in *The German Ideology* as a challenging historical task for the future.

This treatment of working-class consciousness is inextricably linked to Marx's reflections on proletarian political power. Indeed, we find a similar equivocation in refusing to call the proletarian state a state, describing it instead as 'the political form of social emancipation'[652] and as 'the Communal form of political organization'.[653] In praising the fact that under the Commune 'the state-functions [were] reduced to a few functions for general national purposes',[654] there is no hint that an extreme *state of emergency* – as the Paris Commune of necessity had to be – cannot be the model of the future development of the proletarian state and of its complex internal and international functions under normal circumstances. If the working class has the historic mission to work out through the 'new political form' the full emancipation of labour, and thus the emancipation of society as a whole from the social tyranny of the inherited division of labour, how could a task of such magnitude, intricacy, and long time-scale be carried out on the basis of the reduction of the state-functions to a simplified absolute minimum? This is so particularly in view of the fact that at the same time one has to achieve also that 'harmonious national and international coordination' of production and distribution – obviously representing a problem of the highest complexity – of which Marx spoke.

To be sure, the ultimate 'withering away' of the state is inconceivable without a progressive reduction and simplification of its tasks as much as feasible and their transfer to the 'self-working and self-governing' social body. To suggest, however, that this process of reduction and simplification at the political level can be accomplished by immediately substituting for the state as such an unproblematical 'new political form', whereafter difficulties remain only with regard to economically emancipating society from the division of labour, is to make ideal short cuts to the future. This is all the more problematical since the social soil of the 'systematic and hierarchic division of labour' is inseparable from the 'superstructure of a centralized state power', even if not of the capitalist type. In reality the state can only be laboriously 'dismantled' (in the process of the political 'de-alienation' and 'communalization' of society) to the extent to which the inherited social division of labour itself is correspondingly changed, and thus the social metabolism as a whole is effectively restructured.

The perspective of such short cuts – understandable in the context of the defence of the Paris Commune – brings with it also the stipulative characterization of working-class consciousness which we have just seen. Since the required social change is acknowledged to extend over a long historical process of confrontations and struggles, the power of 'communist consciousness on a mass scale' acquires particular importance in the Marxian conception. For, by virtue of its determination as *mass consciousness*, it protects the socialist forces involved in the struggle from internal divisions and from the establishment of new hierarchies, in contrast to Bakunin's élitist vision of the rule of society after the conquest of power by the self-appointed few who claim to know better.

Accordingly, if there is an identity of purpose among the vast majority of the population – an identity which, under the prevailing circumstances, only the working class's 'full consciousness of its historic mission and heroic resolve to act up to it'[655] can produce – in that case the *state* immediately becomes a fully controlled transitional 'political form' and a mere means to emancipatory action, since the difference between the rulers and the governed disappears by definition. This is why Marx can retort to Bakunin's question – 'The Germans number nearly 40 million. Will, for example, all 40 million be members of the government?' – with an emphatic '*Certainly*, for the thing *begins* with the *self-government* of the commune.'[656]

Another important aspect of communist mass consciousness in this perspective is that it can *bridge the gap* that separates the present conditions of hardship from the 'new historic form' aimed at. For through its orienting force it can guarantee the general direction of development that must be sustained, and minimize the danger of relapses and reversals under the pressure of the difficulties encountered. Indeed, under the unavoidably *premature* conditions of the advocated '*social* revolution' – when capitalism is acknowledged by Marx to be in its *ascendancy* on by far the greater part of the planet – only the stipulated communist mass consciousness can bridge this great historical gap and provide the desired guarantee for maintaining the impetus of the necessary struggle.

7.3.5
The final and most complex issue to consider here concerns Marx's evaluation of the working class's position in the existing *division of labour*. It is closely connected with his views on the post-revolutionary 'political form', with major implications for the development of class consciousness and for the articulation of socialist political strategies.

To anticipate the main point: in the Marxian perspective the *fragmentation* of the working class is greatly underestimated and the necessary political consequences of such fragmentation (and concomitant stratification) remain largely unexplored. The accent is on the proletariat constituting the '*universal class*', a characterization eminently suitable to underline the qualitative change from the old to the 'new historic form', but full of ambiguities and question marks as regards the practical constraints of the immediate future.

This is all the more remarkable since Marx insisted in *The German Ideology* that

> The division of labour implies from the outset the division of the conditions of labour, of tools and materials, and thus the fragmentation of accumulated capital among different owners, and thus, also, the fragmentation between capital and labour, and the different forms of property itself. The more the division of labour develops and accumulation grows, the further fragmentation develops. *Labour itself can only exist on the premiss of this fragmentation.*[657]

However, Marx never spells out what might be the consequences of labour existing 'on the premiss of the fragmentation' engendered by the capitalistic division of labour. On the contrary, a natural progression is stipulated from occasional and partial to permanent and comprehensive trade unionism, in accordance with the development of production on a world scale:

> combination has not ceased for an instant to go forward and grow with the development and growth of modern industry. It has now reached such a stage, that the *degree to which combination has developed in any country clearly marks the rank it occupies in the hierarchy of the world market*. England, whose industry has attained the highest degree of development, has the biggest and best organized combinations.[658]

At the same time it is also suggested that there is an irresistible movement from the defence of limited economic group-interests to the politically conscious assertion of the interests of universal emancipation,[659] accomplished by the united proletarian 'class for itself' through the abolition of all classes and through its own self-abolition.[660]

Significantly, Marx's early idea that the proletariat is 'victorious only by abolishing itself and its opposite'[661] is restated, again and again, throughout his life. For example, this is how Marx answers Bakunin's question, 'What is meant by the proletariat transformed into the ruling class?', in 1874:

It means that the proletariat, instead of fighting individually against the economically privileged classes, has gained sufficient strength and is sufficiently well organized to employ general means of compulsion in its struggle against these classes. It can, however, use only *economic* means designed to abolish its own distinctive trait as a wage-earner, and hence to *abolish itself as a class*. Its complete *victory* is consequently also the *end of its domination*, since its class character has disappeared.[662]

There is no hint in Marx that in addition to the fragmentation 'between capital and labour', etc., one must also face the fragmentation *within labour itself* as a major problem for the proletariat both before and after the conquest of political power. The process of emancipation in the aftermath of the revolution is conceived as an essentially *economic* problem (as we have seen on several occasions, including the last quoted passage). The proletariat's ability to act as a united force is predicated as a matter of course, in sharp contrast to the peasantry:

The small-holding peasants form a vast mass, the members of which live in similar conditions but without entering into manifold relations with one another. Their mode of production isolates them from one another, instead of bringing them into mutual intercourse.... . Insofar as millions of families live under economic conditions of existence that separate their mode of life, their interests and their culture from those of the other classes, and put them in hostile opposition to the latter, they form a class. Insofar as there is merely a local interconnection among these small-holding peasants, and the identity of their interests begets no community, no national bond and no political organization among them, they do not form a class. They are consequently *incapable of enforcing their class interests in their own name*, whether through a parliament or through a convention. *They cannot represent themselves, they must be represented.* Their representative must at the same time appear ... as an authority over them, as an unlimited governmental power that *protects them against the other classes* ... The political influence of the small-holding peasants, therefore, finds its final expression in the *executive power subordinating society to itself.*[663]

The problem is, however, that a great deal of what Marx says here about the peasantry is equally valid for the working class itself. Indeed, the united action and rule of the latter cannot be taken for granted without first confronting the difficult 'premiss of fragmentation' within the prevailing division of labour. For while the proletariat has the *potentiality* to overcome its own fragmentation and subordinate position in the existing division of labour, the *actualization* of this potentiality depends on the maturation of a number of objective conditions, including some major developments in the political organization and conscious collective self-determination of the individuals who constitute the class of 'freely associated producers'. Thus, to suggest that the 'degree of combination' of any particular country directly corresponds to 'the rank which it occupies in the hierarchy of the world market',[664] is to turn a historical *requirement* into a necessary *attainment*. Equally, to anticipate the global trade unionization and political articulation of the united working class, while the capitalistic division of labour – and the fragmentation of labour necessarily entailed by such division of labour – remains intact, is merely to restate the long-term potential of the 'universal class' for emancipating society from class rule, without indicating, however, the subjective and objective as well as the internal and international obstacles that must be overcome in the course of transition towards the end advocated.

There can be no disagreement with the proposition that the proletariat is 'victorious only by abolishing itself'. Also, considering the position of labour in maintaining the normal functioning of the social metabolism, it is impossible to disagree with Marx that the proletariat, on the one hand, 'cannot emancipate itself without abolishing the conditions of its life', and that, on the other hand, 'it cannot abolish the conditions of its own life without abolishing all the inhuman conditions of life of society today which are summed up in its own situation'.[665] However, saying this we only define the necessary *conditions* of a successful 'social revolution', but not the specific way in which this apparently vicious circle (making the victory of the particular enterprise depend on the successful solution of the problems of the whole, and vice versa) can and will be broken.

The vicious circle in question is not a *conceptual* one. Rather, it is the suffocating practical circularity of the prevailing social division of labour. For the latter assigns to labour itself the key role in sustaining the social metabolism, structurally constraining labour thereby with regard to its feasible margin of emancipatory and self-emancipatory action. This is why the Marxian conclusion is inescapable: the proletariat is 'victorious only by abolishing itself and its opposite', and labour's self-emancipation can only be accomplished to the extent to which society as a whole is emancipated. Thus the issue at stake concerns simultaneously both the division of labour as such, and the position of the proletariat (or labour) within it. In other words, the question is how to break the stranglehold of the social division of labour over labour, without jeopardizing at the same time the vital functions of the social metabolism itself.

Inevitably, in a question of such magnitude and complexity the subjective and objective, as well as the political and socioeconomic aspects are inextricably intertwined. *Subjectively*, only labour itself can accomplish the task in question 'for itself', which stipulates the necessary development of working-class consciousness. On the other hand, without demonstrating the *objective* determinations which actually propel the development of totalizing – as opposed to partial and narrowly self-interested – class consciousness, the necessity of the latter is only postulated, instead of being established as a social force adequate to its 'historic task'. Furthermore, while the *political* confrontation of labour with the capitalist state formation is the necessary point of departure (for which the appropriate institutional form must be· found), it can be no more than a point of departure. For the fundamental issue is the transcendence of the inherited social division of labour, which is conceivable only on the basis of the radical restructuring of the whole *socioeconomic* framework. Paradoxically, however, the latter implies that full political control of society remains for the duration of the entire process of restructuring. The various constituents of the social whole – including labour – must accommodate themselves to the available margin of action, under the guidance of the new 'political form'. Only the latter is in a position to supervise the overall process, although it was supposed to constitute merely the point of departue of the ongoing socialist transformation.

At this point we can see clearly perhaps the most acute of Marx's theoretical difficulties. He cannot really acknowledge labour's fragmentation and stratification, because that would greatly complicate, indeed ultimately undermine, his conception of the transitional 'political form'. For if the objective *partial interests* of the various groups of workers – inevitably arising on the basis of labour's structural fragmentation – are asserted in the form of conflicting claims, in that case the *'common interest'* defended and imposed by the new 'political form' is not as self-evident as it would appear on the assumption of *united labour*. Such an assumption, however, unjustifiably casts aside the unavoidable and earlier recognized 'premiss of labour's fragmentation'.

Thus, to give full weight to the necessary fragmentation of labour under the conditions of the inherited division of labour means, at the same time, to acknowledge the space left wide open for the exercise of *traditional* state functions for a whole historical epoch. That is to say, for as long as the fragmentation of labour is not effectively superseded – in material as well as in ideological and political terms – through the actual 'sublation' (*Aufhebung*/transcendence/radical restructuring) of the long-established social division of labour.

Naturally, this means that whatever might be the proletarian state's function in its *external* relations, internally it cannot be simply the defence of the proletariat against the former ruling class. Rather, the primary *internal* function of the proletarian state – after a relatively short period of time – is *arbitration* over a multiplicity of complicated, even contradictory, partial interests, on the basis of the continued social division of labour. This is why the proletariat can – and under such conditions indeed it must – 'turn its dictatorship against itself', and not because it fails to live up to the ideal dictates of some categorical moral imperative, as Lukács suggested in his essay on 'The role of morality in Communist production'.

Marx's theoretical difficulties are only in part due to his original linkage of the 'universal class' to 'the *categorical imperative to overthrow all relations* in which man is a debased, enslaved, forsaken, despicable being.'[666] He is, in fact, anxious to establish the world-historic role and task which the 'socialist writers *ascribe* to the . . . fully-formed proletariat'[667] on the basis of an objective sociohistorical necessity. This is why he insists that what decides the issue 'is not a question of what this or that proletarian, or even the whole proletariat, at the moment *regards* as its aim. It is a question of *what the proletariat is*, and what, in accordance with this *being*, it will historically be compelled to do.'[668]

However, in postulating the unfolding of a fully adequate proletarian class consciousness, in the face of the unavoidably *premature* character of the social revolution under the conditions of capital's *global ascendancy*, he is forced to claim that 'a large part of the English and French proletariat is *already conscious* of its historic task and is *constantly working* to develop that consciousness into *complete clarity*.'[669] Thus, he tends to anticipate a much less problematical course of events – just as he did in projecting a global trade unionization and corresponding political militancy – than the available historical evidence would actually support.

7.4 THE FUTURE OF LABOUR

The consequence of all this is that, on the one hand, a number of paradoxical and rather ambiguous propositions must fill the gap between the prevailing state of affairs and the long-term historical anticipations, and that, on the other hand, some important characteristics of working-class existence cannot be given their full weight in the Marxian perspective. In the first category it is enough to think of statements like 'the proletariat is victorious only by abolishing itself and its opposite', which is both incontestable in terms of its ultimate implications and full of riddles with regard to the necessary steps that must be taken towards its realization by the potentially 'universal and self-transcending' proletarian partiality. As to the second category, historical development provided us with far too abundant examples to need much discussion, from the 'social chauvinism' of working-class parties during the first world war to the 'integration' of the American working class and to the exploitative relationship of the Western working classes in general to the 'Third World'.

It is, therefore, very problematical to assert that 'with labour emancipated, every man becomes a working man, and productive labour ceases to be a class attribute.'[670] For such assertion merely stipulates that emancipation implies the universal sharing of work by all members of society, without defining at the same time the meaning of 'productive work' and, more important perhaps, ignoring an issue of utmost gravity with regard to the fragmentation and internal division of labour: the necessarily and precipitously growing *scarcity of labour-opportunities* within the framework of capitalist technological development.

The only context in which Marx addresses himself to this problem concerns the inherent inadequacy of capitalist accountancy to find outlets for the irresistibly growing productive potentiality of labour. He describes a process of development on the basis of 'large-scale industry' – treating it, in fact, rather ambiguously since it could never come about before a radical break with capital's constraining framework is effectively accomplished – as a result of which:

> Labour no longer appears so much to be included within the production process; rather, the human being comes to relate more as watchman and regulator to the production process itself. . . . [The worker] steps to the side of the production process instead of being its chief actor. In this transformation, it is neither the direct human labour he himself performs, nor the time during which he works, but rather the appropriation of his own general productive power, his understanding of nature and his mastery over it by virtue of his presence as a social body – it is, in a word, the development of the social individual which appears as the great foundation-stone of production and of wealth.[671]

At this point, Marx emphasizes again the irreconcilable contradictions involved in the developments he is concerned with, and concludes his line of reasoning with a number of powerful imperatives:

> The theft of alien labour time, on which the present wealth is based, appears a miserable foundation in face of this new one, *created by large-scale industry itself*. As soon as labour in the direct form has ceased to be the great well-spring of wealth, labour time ceases and *must cease* to be its measure, and hence exchange value *must cease* to be the measure of use value. The surplus labour of the mass has ceased to be the condition for the development of general wealth, just as the non-labour of the few, for the development of the general powers of the human head. With that, *production based on exchange value breaks down*, and the direct, material production process is stripped of the form of penury and antithesis. . . . Forces of production and social relations – two different sides of the development of the social individual – appear to capital as mere means, and are merely means for it to produce on its limited foundation. In fact, however, they are the material conditions *to blow this foundation sky high*.[672]

The difficulty here is that so long as the capitalistic determinations remain in control of society, labour – even if *ideally* it should – simply *cannot* cease to be the well-spring of wealth, nor labour time its measure. Equally, under such conditions, exchange value *cannot* cease to be the measure of use value, nor can we simply postulate that in virtue of the *ideal* implications of these relations – which turn the capitalist system into a *historical*, but by no means immediately visible and materially felt anachronism – the mode of production based on exchange value *actually* breaks down. Thus, as long as capital can find new outlets for expansion over the vast terrain of its global ascendancy, the non-realizability of the social individual remains only a *latent* contradiction of this society, instead of blowing its narrow foundations 'sky high'.

If, therefore, we consider the historically identifiable unfolding of capital's inherent tendency for the drastic reduction of necessary labour time, without postulating, *ipso facto*, the breakdown of the capitalist system (even if such breakdown is conceptually implied by the *long-term* and *full* articulation of this tendency), in that case it becomes clear that we have to face here a major *negative* force that sustains capital for a considerable time, rather than offering any comfort to labour in the foreseeable future. For the tendency in question in its immediate impact can only further divide and fragment labour, turning its various sections against one another, instead of positively contributing to the global 'unification' and homogenization of labour anticipated in the Marxian perspective.

7.5 THE DIVISION OF LABOUR

The fragmentation and hierarchical division of labour, thus, appears under the following main aspects, corresponding to significantly different objective divisions of interest:

1. Within any particular group or section of labour.
2. Among different groups of workers belonging to the same national community.
3. Between nationally different bodies of labour opposed to one another in the context of international capitalist competition, from the smallest to the most comprehensive scale, including the potential collision of interests in the form of wars.
4. The labour force of the advanced capitalist countries – the relative beneficiaries of the global capitalist division of labour – as opposed to the differentially far more exploited labour force of the 'Third World'.
5. Labour in employment, as separated from and opposed to the objectively different – and politically/organizationally in general unarticulated – interests of the 'unwaged' and unemployed, including the ever-multiplying victims of the 'second industrial revolution'.

The reason why such fragmentation and division of interests *within labour itself* matters so much is because it carries with it – both before and after the revolution – an inescapable reliance on the state, although in theory the latter is supposed to be the most obvious immediate target of the socialist revolution. Indeed, the bourgeois state finds its support among various groups of labour primarily on the ground of the 'protection' it provides in legally sustaining and safeguarding the objectively established framework of the division of labour. It is enough to recall the great variety of measures adopted by the state in this respect, from minimum wage and social security legislation to erecting protective tariffs and other national barriers, and from internally balancing the relation of forces against 'excesses', to embarking on international enterprises which secure the greatest advantage to the national ruling class, delivering at the same time some relative advantage also to the national labour force.

Naturally, the bourgeois state can perform its 'protective' function on behalf of the fragmented and divided groups of labour only to the extent to which the exercise of that function objectively corresponds to the interests of the ruling class as a whole. This condition happens to be, of course, also the basis upon which the state can overrule various fractional interests on its own side of the more or less latent social confrontation. Also, it cannot be stressed enough, we are not talking here about some negligible degree of shared interests, especially in the advanced capitalist countries. For precisely in view of the social division of labour that originates, reproduces and constantly reinforces labour's own fragmentation and internal division, labour itself has a major vested interest in continued *social stability* (hence the tendency to follow the 'line of least resistance') as the vital condition of its own self-reproduction.

Thus, under normal circumstances, internally divided and fragmented labour is at the mercy not only of the ruling class and its state, but also of the objective requirements of the prevailing social division of labour. Hence we see paradoxical and problematical manifestations of the interests which labour happens to share with its adversary within the compass of the materially and institutionally enforced (and to a large extent self-enforcing) social metabolism. Only at times of quite elemental crises – when the continued functioning of the fundamental social metabolism itself is called into question, in the midst of a massive economic collapse, or as a result of the bourgeois state's dramatic disintegration in the aftermath of a lost war, etc. – can labour temporarily extricate itself from these paralysing constraints.

It is under the circumstances of such elemental structural crises that labour can successfully assert its claims to being the only feasible *hegemonic alternative* to the established order in all its dimensions, from the basic material conditions of life to the most intricate political and ideological aspects of social interchange. The all-important question of submitting the state itself to labour's effective control, too, can only arise under the selfsame circumstances of a *hegemonic crisis* (i.e. the crisis of bourgeois hegemony).

However, while labour can successfully overthrow the bourgeois state and take over the control of the crucial political regulators of the social metabolism, thereby *initiating* the necessary process of radical *restructuring*, the 'workers' state' cannot conceivably *abolish* the inherited social division of labour, except insofar as it directly concerns the ownership of the means of production. Nor can the 'new political form' simply abolish the fragmentation and internal division of labour linked to and embedded in the inherited productive instruments and practices of society. For the required changes in question involve the whole process of restructuring itself, with all its objective and subjective constraints which escape the power of direct political intervention to a significant degree.

7.6 THE POST-REVOLUTIONARY STATE

This is where we can see the disconcerting 'new circularity' between the *post-revolutionary* 'civil society' and its division of labour on the one hand, and the proletarian state on the other. For the various sections of fragmented and internally divided labour need the protection of the state, for a long time after the revolution, not only against the former ruling classes but also against one another as situated within the framework of the still prevailing social division of labour.

Thus, paradoxically, they call into being and maintain in existence for the duration of the whole process of radical restructuring a *strong executive* over against themselves. This situation is not entirely unlike that of the French peasantry in its subjection to its own state-form under 'Napoleon le Petit' as a result of its fragmentation, since the latter enabled the Bonapartist executive power to subordinate society to itself, as we have seen in Marx's analysis.

At the same time, to complete the new vicious circle between the post-revolutionary civil society and its state, the latter is not merely the manifestation of the continuing division of labour but also the hierarchical apex of its system of decision making. Accordingly, it has a strong interest of its own to retain, indefinitely, the firmest possible grip over the ongoing process of transformation as a whole, thereby reinforcing, rather than undermining, the established social division of labour of which – in virtue of its strategic role – the post-revolutionary state itself happens to constitute the most privileged dimension. Here, again, we can see that the much disputed issue of 'bureaucratic privileges' is not simply a matter of the personnel involved but, above all, that of the retention of *objectively* 'privileged' – i.e. strategically vital – functions by the state in the overall social metabolism. The continued exercise of these, strategically privileged, functions by a separate body is bound to find in its turn its subjective equivalent at the plane of the 'bureaucratized state personnel' too, in the absence of some alternative form of social control based on ever-increasing and truly active mass-involvement.

The subordination of post-revolutionary civil society to the 'new political form' of a powerful executive in the early phases of transition is thus first and foremost the consequence of labour's own fragmentation and internal division as 'signed and sealed' by the inherited division of labour. This may be aggravated, of course, by some specific characteristics of structural underdevelopment – including so-called 'Asiatic backwardness' – on account of a particularly unfavourable relative position of a country's aggregate labour force in the international division of labour. However, the point to stress is that – in view of the objective structural conditions of the given social metabolism and the difficult material and institutional constraints of its restructuring – the politically 'top-heavy' conditions of development apply everywhere, even in the economically most advanced countries, with the longest historical tradition of liberal democracy. For the circumstances of more favourable economic developments and liberal democratic traditions, no matter how advantageous in some respects, do not eliminate the overwhelming negative determinant of labour's fragmentation and internal division. Consequently, on their own they do not support at all the anticipations of some theoreticians of the New Left, as well as of some leading politicians of the Labour Left, who see in them some sort of a priori historical guarantee with regard to the prospects of a democratic socialist transformation in advanced capitalist countries.

Furthermore, in accordance with the inherent necessities of structural transformations which cannot avoid attacking the foundations of the capitalist market economy, the liberal democratic measures that paradoxically arise out of the absolute material tyranny of the market, with no court of appeal, must be replaced by new types of political/administrative regulators, extending also over formerly 'unregulated' areas of social interaction. And in this respect it is of little comfort that the liberal democratic framework of relatively 'unregulated' regulation is feasible and affordable only because of the immense material discriminatory power of the capitalist market which minimizes the need for direct (political) interference with the everyday life of individuals under normal circumstances. For the fact remains that the socially necessary removal of the – no matter how blind and anarchistic – self-regulatory levers of liberal 'market-democracy' creates an institutional vacuum at the political level. Consequently, also in this respect, the less the post-revolutionary civil society succeeds in institutionally articulating and safeguarding the objective interests of its various groups on a truly cooperative basis, the greater the power of the state executive and its scope for the imposition of a *Stalinist type* 'political autonomy'.

Understandably, therefore, but by no means without some heavy 'irony of history', in the aftermath of the Stalinist abuse of power theories of '*market socialism*' appear, illusorily suggesting that it is possible to secure *socialist democracy* by reinstating the self-regulatory mechanisms of a modified capitalist market under 'state supervision'. Even if we disregard the incompatibilities necessarily involved in this course of action – tendencies towards the inadmissible wholesale restoration of capitalism on the one hand, and the reassertion of authoritarian political counter-measures to prevent the successful consummation of those tendencies, on the other –

the trouble with these theories is that nothing is really solved by the creation of such 'partially controlled markets'. Strategies of this kind can, at best, only *postpone* the all-important issue of radical *restructuring*, which is far from being only, or even primarily, an *'economic'* problem that could be tackled within the narrowly 'efficiency oriented' parameters of the idealized market. Curiously, the advocates of 'market socialism' seem to forget that the necessity of the socialist transformation itself arises in the first place out of the inescapable crisis of the socioeconomic order that brings to perfection and universal domination a structure of 'living contradictions': the self-regulatory market which they now want to rescue and use as the secure foundation of democratic socialist developments, disregarding (for the sake of a rather naive hope) the *certainty of mass unemployment* that goes with such a regulatory framework.

7.7 SOCIALIST CONSCIOUSNESS

Thus perhaps the greatest difficulty for socialist theory is this: how to envisage the transcendence of labour's fragmentation and internal division without reducing the problems at stake to some direct appeal to an idealized class consciousness, advocating *'unity'* as the desirable solution while neglecting the objective material basis of the existing fragmentation, inherent in the continued division of labour.

As we have seen above, Marx did not indulge in a direct appeal to an idealized proletarian class consciousness, except in the polemical context imposed on him by the need to defend the Paris Commune against a hostile press. Nevertheless, he firmly expected the emergence of what he called 'communist mass consciousness' – coupled with a fully adequate institutional articulation in the form of global trade unionism and corresponding political militancy – through the historical development of the capitalist social order, under the impact of the inexorable unfolding of the productive potentials as well as contradictions of that social order. Yet, it is not only thanks to the benefit of hindsight that we can see, today, that such expectations were rather problematical. In fact, some of the ambiguities of Marx's own analyses already pointed in the same direction, as we could witness on the last few pages.

To conclude then: given the helping hand in displacing its contradictions which global capital receives from the fragmenting and divisive impact of 'uneven development' and of the international division of labour, in their inseparability from the differential rate of exploitation of labour, some of the conditions for the socialization of production and the ensuing unification of labour anticipated by Marx are most unlikely to materialize within the confines and self-serving structural constraints of the capitalist social order itself.

Naturally, this does not decrease the importance of a socialist mass consciousness. On the contrary, it puts the vital sociohistorical function of such consciousness even more into relief. For the full realization of the socialist project is inconceivable without a successfully integrated and 'totalizing' (though, of course, not unmediated), conscious management of their problems by the associated producers, in a globally interlinked setting which is *'unconsciously'*[673] brought into being in the first place by the development of capitalism itself.

But precisely for the latter reason, one can realistically appeal to the increasing importance of a totalizing social consciousness only by calling at the same time for the necessary *material mediations* – aimed at transcending the given fragmentation of labour – through which the development of this consciousness first becomes possible.

Labour's fragmentation cannot be eliminated by the capitalistic 'socialization of production'. Neither can it be readily transcended – in view of the deeply embedded material structures of the inherited global division of labour – for a long time after the socialist political revolution. Hence the necessary *material mediations* in question, characterized by a vital capacity for bringing about a progressive reduction in the constraining role of the inherited *material determinations*, must remain the regulative framework of social life for the entire historical epoch of transition.

8 · THE CONSTITUTION
OF SOLIDARITY

8.1 HISTORICAL ILLUSIONS AND IDEOLOGICAL APPEALS

8.1.1

Even sixteen years after Marx wrote his critical comments on the Gotha Programme they could only be published amidst sharp controversy, forcing Engels to make it clear to the obstructionist leaders of the German Social Democratic Party that 'no party in any country can condemn me to silence if I am determined to speak'.[674] The reason for such controversy, notwithstanding the passing of time, was the painful reminder of how problematical the act of unification was right from the beginning.

Engels made it quite clear – after underlining that what was so objectionable in the first place was 'bartering away principles' – that the notion of unification represented a foreign intrusion into the socialist project. Referring to Wilhelm Liebknecht, the main author of the Gotha Programme, he wrote: 'From *bourgeois democracy* he has brought over and maintained a real *mania for unification*.'[675] And way back, at the time when the unification actually took place, Engels raised the vitally important point that the programme, on the basis of which the opportunistic manoeuvre of unification could be accomplished, also meant that 'the principle that the workers' movement is an *international* movement is, to all intents and purposes, *completely disavowed*'.[676] In the light of subsequent developments which cast their shadow to our own days no one can seriously doubt the validity of such insights.

Naturally, Marx (who also described what was going on in sarcastic terms as 'bargaining about principles'[677]) knew very well that 'the mere fact of unification is satisfying to the workers'.[678] But he also knew that 'it is a mistake to believe that this momentary success is not bought at *too high a price*.'[679] He suggested, as a practical and practicable alternative to the unprincipled act of unification, 'an agreement for action against the common enemy ... a programme of action or a plan of organization for common action'.[680]

As is well known, despite Marx's great prestige in the international working-class movement, his critical advice had to fall on deaf ears. Nor can one maintain that the eventual publication of his *Critique of the Gotha Programme* produced the results hoped for by Engels. For, in reality, the 'lessons of history' are not very easy to learn.

In this sense, it is not really surprising that Rosa Luxemburg had to complain in her last speech, more than four decades after Marx's *dixi et salvavi animam meam* (with which he concluded his *Critique of the Gotha Programme*, as mentioned above) and only sixteen days before she was assassinated:

> The weeks that have elapsed between November 9th and the present day have been weeks filled with multiform illusions. The primary illusion of the workers and soldiers who made the revolution was their belief in the possibility of *unity* under the banner of what passes by the name of socialism. What could be more characteristic of the internal weakness of the revolution of November 9th than the fact that at the very outset the leadership passed in no small part into the hands of the persons who a few hours before the revolution broke out had regarded it as their chief duty to issue warnings against revolution – to attempt to make revolution impossible – into the hands of such as Ebert, Scheidemann, and Haase. One of the leading ideas of the revolution of November 9th was that of *uniting* the various socialist trends. The union was to be affected by acclamation. This was an *illusion* which had to be bloodily avenged, and the events of the last few days have brought a *bitter awakening from our dreams*.[681]

Yet, whatever the lessons, the illusions continued to surface again and again, as if nothing had happened. Thus, three months after the bitter and bloody experience of Germany – which by the time counted among its victims, together with countless others, the two outstanding figures of the European socialist movement, Rosa Luxemburg and Karl Liebknecht, both brutally murdered by the right-wing military forces of 'law and order' under a social democratic government – in Hungary Lukács eulogized the unification of the Communist and the Social Democratic Parties in the most unrealistic terms. He wrote:

> The parties have ceased to exist – now there is a unified proletariat. [A logical *non-sequitur*.] That is the decisive theoretical significance of this union. No matter that it calls itself a party – the word party now means something quite new and different. . . . Today the party is the means by which the *unified will of the unified proletariat* expresses itself; it is the executive organ of the will that is developing in the new society from new sources of strength. The crisis of socialism, which found its expression in the dialectical antagonism between the party movements, has come to an end. The proletarian movement has definitely entered upon a new phase, the phase of proletarian power. The most prodigious achievement of the Hungarian proletariat has been to *lead the world revolution conclusively into this phase*. The Russian revolution has demonstrated that the proletariat is capable of seizing power and organizing a new society. The Hungarian revolution has demonstrated that this revolution is possible without fratricidal struggles among the proletariat itself. The world revolution is thereby carried another stage further. And it is to the lasting credit and honour of the Hungarian proletariat that it has been able to *draw from within itself the strength and the resources to assume this leading role*, to lead, not only its own leaders, but the proletarians of all countries.[682]

The prosaic reality of Colonel Vix's military ultimatum, representing the *Entente Cordiale's* non-negotiable (and by the ruling coalition unacceptable) demands, and the ensuing collapse of Count Károlyi's Liberal/Social Democratic regime was completely left out of account in Lukács's euphoric theorization of the events.

History repeated itself even in the sense that – just as the German Social Democratic enemies of the revolution referred to in Rosa Luxemburg's last speech quoted above – the Hungarian 'left social democrat' Vilmos Böhm, who later became the military chief of the 'unified will of the unified proletariat', two weeks before the unification (of which he was a major figure) was still pleading with Count Michael Károlyi, President of the shortlived Hungarian Republic, to let him 'free the country from the communists whose number according to him amounted to 1000': a request emphatically rejected by the sincere liberal/democrat Károlyi.[683] Suddenly, however, all such contradictions ceased to exist (or count) in the eyes of those who tried to conceptualize what they considered to be the fundamental characteristics and requirements of true or 'ascribed' – as opposed to 'false' or 'psychological' – proletarian class consciousness.

8.1.2

In Germany, in the aftermath of governmental blood-letting, Rosa Luxemburg pointed out that cure from illusion unfortunately involved 'that the people must be blooded.... The bloodshed in Chausseestrasse on December 6th, the massacre of December 24th, brought the truth home to the broad masses of the people.'[684] As a result, in Luxemburg's words, the German workers 'lost the illusion which had led them to believe that a union between Haase[685] and Ebert-Scheidemann[686] would amount to a socialist government.'[687]

Whatever the historical differences, greatly complicated by foreign military interventions and Allied ultimatums in Hungary, at the time of Lukács's optimistic reflections illusions were still rampant, manifesting in naive beliefs that the union of Béla Kún and Vilmos Böhm had actually produced the 'conclusive world-historical victory of the unified proletariat'. Thus, in the same spirit as he greeted the unification of the two working class parties, Lukács tried to overcome the immense material obstacles of the present – the precarious predicament of the Hungarian Council Republic under siege from all directions, internally as well as from abroad – by way of a moralizing direct appeal to proletarian class consciousness, arguing that:

> It is clear that the most oppressive phenomena of proletarian power – namely, scarcity of goods and high prices, of whose immediate consequences every proletarian has personal experience – are the direct consequences of the slackening of labour-discipline and the decline in production.... Help comes in two ways. Either the individuals who constitute the proletariat *realize* that

they can help themselves only by bringing about a voluntary strengthening of labour-discipline, and consequently a rise in production; or, if they are incapable of this, they create institutions which are capable of bringing about this necessary state of affairs. In the latter case, they create a legal system through which the proletariat *compels* its own individual members, the proletarians, to act in a way which corresponds to their class-interests: *the proletariat turns its dictatorship against itself.* This measure is necessary for the self-preservation of the proletariat when *correct recognition* of class interests and voluntary action in these interests do not exist.... Development would therefore proceed in a direction which endangered the appearance and realization of the ultimate aim.... It depends on the proletariat whether the real history of humanity begins – that is to say, *the power of morality over institutions and economics.*[688]

In truth, nothing could be more in need of a proper material foundation than the advocacy of 'the power of morality over institutions and economics'. Instead, Lukács could only offer his abstract appeal to the 'correct recognition of class interest' and to the 'realization' of the necessity of a greatly strengthened labour-discipline as the remedy. This he did notwithstanding the fact that the latter by themselves were devoid of a firm material anchorage and corresponding motivational force. He thereby completed the ideological circle from which there could be no way out.

And yet, the stubborn recurrence of illusions, which were supposed to have been left behind as a result of historical experience, calls for renewed caution. For it underlines the great difficulties involved in attempting to overcome the unreality of direct ideological appeals to an idealized class consciousness without abandoning at the same time the task of mobilizing and rendering self-conscious, in support of the advocated socialist objectives, the forces which are *objectively* in conflict (even if not immediately) with the interests of capital. The critique of idealistic appeals to 'unity and conformity to correct class consciousness' has no validity unless it can also indicate the road to the constitution of lasting *solidarity*, built on firm material ground, without which the socialist project itself is bound to remain unreal. In this sense even the most abstract direct ideological appeals which maintain their principled allegiance to socialist values are infinitely preferable to the '*Realpolitik*' – i.e. the opportunistic intellectual and political contortions – of many former Marxists today.

8.2 TENDENCIES AND COUNTER-TENDENCIES

8.2.1

The difficulties in drawing a valid line of demarcation between the rejection of abstract moralizing appeals on the one hand and ideological abdication, on the other, are truly daunting. Moreover, they seem to multiply, rather than diminish, parallel to the way in which the complex historical process brings to maturity capital's inner contradictions. As if the rules that regulate the fundamental social confrontation in actuality could be constantly rewritten and the 'goalposts' accordingly moved, so as to suit the convenience of the established order. For, in tune with the nature of more or less consciously pursued historical strategies and corresponding transformations, capital can adjust its defences to the moves of its adversary with all means at its disposal, which happen to be truly immense both on the economic plane and within the legal/political sphere. Thus, nothing could be more idealistic than to see in the problems and difficulties here encountered simply theoretical shortcomings, to be readily redressed by the appropriate – positive 'scientific' as opposed to negative 'ideological' – 'theoretical practice'.

As a matter of fact Marx offers an approach very different from and theoretically far superior to the one we have seen in Lukács's early writings, without however thereby disposing of the difficulties in question. This is how he describes the problem of 'unity' in *Capital*:

> That which is now to be expropriated is no longer the labourer working for himself, but the capitalist exploiting many labourers. This expropriation is accomplished by the action of the *immanent laws of capitalist production* itself, by the *centralization of capital*. One capitalist always kills many. Hand in hand with this centralization, or this expropriation of many capitalists by few, develop, on an ever-extending scale, the *cooperative* form of the labour-process, the conscious technical application of science, the methodical cultivation of the soil, the transformation of the instruments of labour into instruments of labour only usable in common, the *economizing* of all means of production by their use as the means of production of combined, socialized labour, the entanglement of all peoples in the net of the *world market*, and with this, the *international* character of the capitalistic regime.
>
> Along with the constantly diminishing number of the magnates of capital, who usurp and *monopolize* all advantages of this process of transformation, grows the mass of misery, oppression, slavery, degradation, exploitation; but with this too grows the revolt of the working class, *a class always increasing in numbers, and disciplined, united, organized by the very mechanism of the process of capitalist production itself*. The monopoly of capital becomes a fetter upon the mode of production, which has sprung up and flourished along with, and under it. *Centralization* of the means of production and *socialization* of labour at last reach a point where they become *incompatible with their capitalist integument*. Thus integument is burst asunder. The knell of *capitalist private property* sounds. The expropriators are expropriated.[689]

As we can see, the way in which here the historical constitution of *unity* is presented – in conjunction with the 'discipline' and 'organization' immanent in the capitalist labour process itself – has nothing in common with *subjective/political/ideological exhortations*. Instead, Marx insists on the *objective* material determinations with which 'capitalist production begets, with the *inexorability of a law of Nature*, its own negation'.[690]

All this is very important as far as the long-term prospects of socioeconomic development are concerned which progressively reduce the margin of manoeuvre compatible with capital's objective structural determinations.

However, we must always bear in mind that all economic laws are *tendential* laws. That is to say, they are in their innermost nature qualitatively different from the law of *gravity*, for instance. For the latter, as a material law of the physical universe, does not assert itself *tendentially* but with a categorical finality and predictability. This also means that in the context of economic laws we are talking about specific – and at least temporarily displaceable – *tendencies* which *in reality* itself cannot be separated from their *counter-tendencies*, although in the course of *theoretical analysis* it is unavoidable to treat them at times separately; whenever, that is, the accent must be put on one aspect as opposed to the other.

Every tendency is in fact necessarily counteracted – to a greater or lesser degree – by its contrary in the course of capitalist developments. This condition of complicated tendential interactions, which is generally applicable to the social sphere, is further enhanced (and in its implications for socialist strategies in the short run aggravated) as a result of the intrinsically contradictory nature of capital itself. (Whatever might be the immediately feasible corrective changes in this respect, the negative impact of the tendential and counter-tendential interactions inherited from the past remains a major problem, *mutatis mutandis*, for the postcapitalist phase too, at least for a considerable period of time.)

The final outcome of such interchanges is determined by the overall configuration of the various tendencies and counter-tendencies related to one another, on the basis of the objective characteristics of each. Theoretical relativism in this respect can be avoided only with reference to the irrepressible working of the *ultimate limits* (i.e. the immanent nature) of capital itself which determine the *global* (or 'totalizing') tendency of capital's most varied manifestations. This global tendency, in its turn, can only prevail – with its objective characteristics and determining force – through the manifold partial and conflicting interactions themselves. The latter in their historical specificity are of course subject to significant (and to a large extent consciously pursued) corrective feed-back within the material parameters of the *ultimately* insurmountable overall limits.

8.2.2

Accordingly, we can clearly identify in the present context a number of objective counter-tendencies in contrast to the tendencies enumerated by Marx. Thus, capital's irrepressible tendency to *monopoly* is effectively counteracted by *competition* (and vice versa);[691] likewise:

> *centralization* by *fragmentation*;
> *internationalization* by *national* and *regional particularism*;
> *economizing* by extreme *wastefulness*;

294 THE POWER OF IDEOLOGY

unification by *stratification*;
socialization by *privatization*;
equilibrium by the *breakdown of equilibrium*;[692]

the transformation of *cooperatively* usable productive instruments into paradoxically concentrated and thereby *atomistically* – but nonetheless with high productivity – usable ones (e.g. computers); etc.

Nor could we maintain, of course, that the objective tendencies of the economic process assert themselves in a self-contained fashion. So long as the social metabolism is articulated the way in which it happens to be, within the existing systems of 'civil society', the laws identified as emanating from, or centred upon, the 'economic sphere' as such, must be dialectically complemented and qualified in all theoretical assessments by the specifically *political dimension* with which the economic processes themselves unfold in actuality, within the sociopolitical confines of *state* and *inter-state* relations. Moreover, it must be also remembered that the state and inter-state relations in question are riddled with a multiplicity of contradictions of their own – some pointing in the direction of emancipation while others decidedly against it – which in their turn further complicate the picture.

8.3 RADICAL CHANGE IN THE ORIENTATION OF THE SOCIALIST MOVEMENT

8.3.1
In this regard it is important to put in perspective the ambivalent impact of the imperial expansion of the leading capitalist countries in the last third of the nineteenth century. Undoubtedly, in one sense this meant that the whole planet had been drawn into capital's orbit, thereby also highlighting the fact that the ultimate territorial limits cannot be further extended. At the same time, however, the negative consequences of such developments for the realization of socialist expectations came to the fore under two principal aspects.

First, the imperial expansion itself – which is by no means confined to the more or less remote past but embraces the whole line of development, from overt colonialism and imperialism to the more mystifying forms of domination of the 'periphery' by the 'metropolitan countries' (the latter forms customarily described as 'neo-colonialism' and 'neo-capitalism') – greatly strengthened (and still continues to underpin) the power of capital, postponing for a considerable time (for as long, in fact, as the globally diffused productive outlets can be sustained) the maturation of its immanent contradictions.

Second, the crucial organizations of the working class – its mass parties

and trade union movement – have become more and more closely tied to
the imperialist national state, maintaining their misplaced allegiance to the
latter even in extremely dubious ventures, as their capitulation to the most
chauvinistic forces of capital so clamorously demonstrated at the outbreak
of the first world war as well as subsequently. Rosa Luxemburg's account
of the behaviour of August Winnig – President of the German Bilders'
Union and plenipotentiary of the Social Democratic Ebert-Scheidemann
government in the peace negotiations with the British plenipotentiary – is
highly revealing in this respect.[693]

8.3.2
Thus, it was by no means accidental that the internal troubles of the *First
International* (still under Marx's intellectual and political leadership) became increasingly more pronounced in the late 1860s. By 1872 Marx was
forced to transfer its centre to New York, in the – soon to be disappointed
– hope of preserving its uncompromising internationalist orientation, not
to mention its bare existence.

The centrifugal force of national movements and of the national states to
which they were linked in the end proved far too much to withstand. The
First International itself fell to pieces as a result of such pressures and contradictions. The *Second International* which followed it – with the active
involvement of people like Wilhem Liebknecht: a deeply committed socialist
who played an important role also in the activities of the *First* – had
precious little to do with the revolutionary and consciously anti-state spirit
of its predecessor. Understandably, therefore, it practically disintegrated
through the intensification of national antagonisms and imperialist rivalries
(which eventually took the devastating form of the first world war), only to
be replaced by the *Third International*. But even the latter, in its turn,
became dominated by Stalinist strategies and state interests, and thereby
condemned itself to certain extinction very soon after its birth, although it
took some time for the act of formal dissolution to materialize.

There is a tendency to attribute these problems to 'ideological defects',
the 'rise of opportunism', the 'influence of labour aristocracy', the 'lack of
correct class consciousness', etc. Whatever we may think of such explanations, they all seem to beg the question in the sense of offering as causal
explanations phenomena whose appearance at a determinate time in history
is itself in need of explanation. In order to subscribe to explanatory hypo-
theses like 'labour aristocracy', etc., we would first have to equate people
like Wilhelm Liebknecht, Wilhelm Bracke and August Bebel – who were
all three imprisoned in 1870; for opposing the war and the annexation of
Alsace-Lorraine – with Ferdinand Lassalle and his closest followers who,
in complete contrast, were indeed scheming with the 'Iron Chancellor'
Otto von Bismarck behind the backs of their working class supporters.
(They unashamedly begged for Bismarck's secret political patronage and

financial favours, promising to deliver in exchange the German working class to his utterly reactionary cause.)

Marx had no use for such question-begging simplifications. In a circular letter of the General Council of the *First International* 'To the Federal Council of the Romance Switzerland', written by Marx in French at the beginning of January 1870, he forcefully defended Liebknecht's group (the 'Eisenachers', who later joined forces with the 'Lassalleans', within the 'unifying' framework of the *Gotha Programme*) against J.B. von Schweitzer's Lassallean 'General Association of German Workers', categorically stating that the latter's 'artificial, sectarian organization is opposed to the historical and spontaneous organization of the working class'.[694]

At the same time both Marx and Engels understood – even without full documentary evidence of Lassalle's secret dealings with Bismarck, which only came to light in 1928 – that some kind of an 'unholy alliance' had to lurk behind the public performance of the Lassalleans and their newspaper, the *Social Democrat*, edited by J.B. von Schweitzer. As Marx wrote in a letter to Engels: 'I regard Schweitzer as incorrigible (probably in secret understanding with Bismarck).'[695] Likewise, Engels correctly wrote to Marx that 'The worthy Lassalle is being gradually unmasked as just a common rogue after all',[696] speaking in the same letter of Baron Itzig's (i.e. Lassalle's) 'betrayal of the whole workers' movement to the Prussians'. The little they knew then that in a letter which Lassalle sent to Bismarck, together with the statutes of the recently formed General Association of the German Workers, he gave the following assurances to his dictatorially inclined political master and patron:

> [The statutes] will clearly convince you how true it is that the working class feels an instinctive inclination towards a dictatorship, if it can first be rightly persuaded that the dictatorship will be exercised in its interests; and how much, despite all republican views – or rather precisely because of them – it would therefore be inclined, as I told you only recently, to look upon the Crown, in opposition to the egoism of bourgeois society, as the natural representative of the social dictatorship, if the Crown for its part could ever make up its mind to the – certainly very improbable – step of striking out a really revolutionary line and transforming itself from the monarchy of the privileged orders into a social and revolutionary people's monarchy.[697]

Lassalle also argued, in another secret letter sent to Bismarck and written in the same spirit of arrogant paternalism towards the workers as the one just quoted (directly contradicting at the same time his own bombastic and vacuous remark about working class opposition to 'the egoism of bourgeois society'), that Bismarck should make his move before the planned Schleswig-Holstein war against the Danes (which Lassalle wholeheartedly supported), as follows:

> Why can you do anything you like in peace time? Why did I admit to you as long ago as last May that, so long as no external conflict arose, our country

would quietly acquiesce even in the most severe absolutism? In peace time the interests of private life completely predominate and reduce the mood of the people to one of indifference, whatever conditions may be.[698]

Obviously, thus, only the most myopic oversimplification (not to say complete ignorance) of the actual historical events could bring such diverse forces and motivations as we find manifest in the sociopolitical movements of Liebknecht/Bebel/Bracke and others like them on one side, and Lasalle, Schweitzer and their immediate followers on the other, to a simple common denominator, under the label of 'labour aristocracy' or whatever else.

8.3.3

However, despite the striking differences between the 'historical and spontaneous organization of the working class' and the 'artificial and sectarian organization' of Schweitzer, the contradictions of the unfolding sociohistorical process practically accomplished in 1875 the unification of the Eisenachers and the Lassalleans which only a few years earlier, in 1870, still seemed unthinkable. Furthermore, another of Marx's great hopes – mentioned in a letter to Engels in October 1869 and reaffirmed in the same circular of 'The General Council to the Federal Council of the Romance Switzerland' which gave total support to the Eisenachers in their principled opposition to the Lassalleans – came to a sad end very soon after its enunciation.

Marx's letter to Engels stated that 'one of the consequences of the Basle Congress must be the formation of the *Land and Labour League* (set up, incidentally, directly by the General Council), through which the workers' party is making a complete break with the bourgeoisie, and whose starting point is the nationalization land.'[699]

A few months later, the circular quoted above underlined the potential of the *Land and Labour League* to become a 'spontaneous movement of the English working class' while it opposed the appearance of purely *regionalistic* initiatives. Insisting on the high degree of '*maturity and universality*' of English capitalist developments, both on the plane of the economy and in the field of the class struggle (evidenced in the advanced trade-unionization of the working class), it asserted that 'the English possess all the necessary *material* conditions of the social revolution. What they are lacking in is the *spirit of generalization* and *revolutionary passion*,'[700] adding that only within the framework of the International could the exemplary potential of the English developments be brought to full realization, as opposed to the identifiable tendencies to regional separatism which surfaced in England at the time. And it concluded the whole line of argument by stressing that 'England should not be treated simply as one country among others, but as the *metropole of capital*.'[701]

Given these considerations, it is thoroughly unsatisfactory simply to assert, as the Moscow Institute of Marxism-Leninism's Preface to the

Documents of the First International does, that: 'because of the strong *reformist trend* in the British working-class movement represented by the *labour aristocracy*, and because of the *conciliatory* and *chauvinistic attitude* of trade union leaders, the League more and more came under *bourgeois influence* and gradually parted company with the International.'[702] For even if the *symptoms* are correctly described, they are naively and fallaciously put forward as if they were self-explanatory *causes*.

Lenin offered a qualitatively different explanation of the shift that came about in this period of working-class history, emphasizing that the *First International* 'made way for a period of a far greater development of the labour movement in all countries in the world, a period in which the movement grew in *scope*, and *mass* socialist working-class parties in *individual national states* were formed.'[703]

Moreover, with regard to the development of working-class consciousness Lenin drew a practically decisive conclusion from his evaluation of the new state of affairs. He summed it up by saying that under the prevailing circumstances only '*trade union consciousness*' could be produced on the basis of *spontaneous* class action, and therefore the role of formulating and implementing the necessary socialist strategies had to be assigned to the vanguard party.

8.4 THE CONSOLIDATION OF MUTUALLY EXCLUSIVE IDEOLOGICAL AND POLITICAL PERSPECTIVES

8.4.1

In practical terms all this amounted to a massive reorientation of the working-class movement, irrespective of how quickly and in what precise form the participants became conscious of it within the confines of their 'individual national states'. That is to say, within limits which in their turn were materially marked out by the different – and indeed more and more *structurally diverging* – socioeconomic positions of the particular national states in the historically unfolding global articulation of capital.

Quoting the statutes of the International Association, Marx's circular addressed to the Federal Council of the Romance Switzerland still insisted that 'the *economical emancipation* of the working classes is the great end to which every *political movement ought to be subordinate as a means*'.[704] From now on, however, in the bloody aftermath of the 1871 Paris Commune which demonstrated to participants and outsiders alike the awesome reality of bourgeois class consciousness,[705] two diametrically opposed strategies were adopted by the working-class movement, remaining with us ever since. They remained with us notwithstanding the naive enthusiasm with which the young Lukács greeted their 'world historical transcendence', praising the somewhat mysteriously emerged yet unproblematically 'correct ideological insight' manifest in the act of Hungarian party-unification.

The *first* strategy arose, not by accident – and by no means only in the country which Marx considered 'the metropole of capital' – in *all* capitalistically advanced societies. Under the banner of mainstream Social Democracy it advocated the *gradual* establishment of a *socialist* social order through the instrumentality of the *capitalist state* (a veritable contradiction in terms). Furthermore – a fact which forcefully underlines the historical significance of these developments – the perspective of labourist gradualism, despite well over one hundred years of failure to realize the once proudly announced social democratic programme, is more dominant today than ever before in the countries concerned. For, as a result of social and political realignments in Europe in the last two decades, today it counts among its supporters also a far from negligible number of its former antagonists on the Left, thanks to the social-democratization of even some of the important working-class parties (from the Italian Socialists to the Spanish Communists, etc.) which once belonged to the *Third International*. Only by now the original demands and expectations have been watered down almost beyond recognition, in accord with the defeats suffered in the long decades of historical disappointments.

The *second* perspective, by contrast, surfaced from deep-seated and it seems irrepressibly growing roots on the '*periphery*' of capital's global domination. It defined the fundamental task facing the movement in terms of the *revolutionary conquest* as well as the effective and *indefinite retention of state power* by the centrally disciplined *political vanguard* of the proletariat. While this perspective could never practically break through in capitalistically advanced countries, it nevertheless succeeded in realizing its central objective, in one form or another, in a significant part of the 'underdeveloped' world, directly regulating today the social interchange of at least fifteen hundred million people in Europe, Asia, Africa and – with the artificially isolated example of Cuba – even in the 'American hemisphere'.

The contrasts between these two perspectives have been sharply put into relief from the very beginning in the self-definitions of each, erupting at times in the form of the most acrimonious ideological confrontations and political struggles. It would be, however, theoretically quite wrong – and with regard to the necessary practical reconstitution of viable socialist strategies seriously misleading – to concentrate, as usually happens, only on their differences. For what was nevertheless common to them from the moment of their inception, notwithstanding their diametrical opposition on the plane of political action, was the fact that in *both* of them the original Marxian demand for the strict subordination of every political movement as a *means* to the central objective of the *economic emancipation* of the working classes – to be accomplished through the radical transformation of the historically established division of labour – was pushed into the background.

8.4.2

The obfuscation of this crucial fact (i.e. of their antagonistically common denominator) brought with it the onset of a selective ideological amnesia. This was in a sense perfectly understandable in the light of the socio-economic transformations that have actually taken place in the period when these mutually exclusive perspectives of working-class action in relation to political power were theorized and institutionally articulated. Unfortunately, however, the obfuscation of the underlying socioeconomic determinations inevitably also meant that the historically emerging and deepening *material/structural* changes of truly epochal significance had to be reduced to *ideological/political* differences, envisaging accordingly also their rectification, without any real chance of success, through the adoption of the appropriate ideological/political remedies.

The situation became even more complicated after the 1917 October Revolution and its reverberations in Germany, Hungary and elsewhere. For under the new circumstances the capital-labour antagonism inescapably also acquired the dimension of inter-state relations and conflicts, stretching from the immediate counter-revolutionary interventions of the capitalistically advanced countries in post-revolutionary Russia all the way down to the state rivalries and antagonisms of our own times. Nor did the contradictions of the Stalinist system help to alleviate the tendency towards growing ideological/political polarization and associated immobilism. On the contrary, they greatly contributed to such polarization, negatively affecting the chances of radical socialist movements in the West, movements which could not even begin to realize their sociopolitical potential – relatively weak though as it had to be in any event under the globally emerging and consolidating historical circumstances – without first extricating themselves from such compromising connections.

Thus, given the immobility of the prevailing historical situation, especially after the 1917–19 revolutionary wave had receded, it was almost inevitable that the problems and contradictions of multifaceted socio-historical movements, and of the social formations to which they belonged, should be conceptualized (not only by Lukács but also by many others on the radical wing of the socialist movement) as an 'ideological crisis'.

Naturally, from such a misdiagnosis of the complicated socioeconomic and political situation it also followed that the solution of the crisis in question, as they saw it, had to be envisaged through an uncompromising 'struggle for consciousness', postulating the replacement of 'false consciousness' by 'true consciousness'.[706] In the end the advocated ideological/political strategy culminated in the hopelessly one-sided and unrealistic proposition according to which the crisis of capitalist society was 'an *ideological crisis* which must be solved *before* a practical solution to the world's economic crisis can be found'.[707]

8.4.3

Two decades earlier – from the opposite perspective and in accord with the profoundly conservative motivation of reformist social democracy – Bernstein asserted that Marxism advocated '*political action* as the most important duty of the movement',[708] in direct contradiction to Marx's frequently repeated insistence that all political movement must be strictly subordinated to the *economic emancipation* of the proletariat, as we have seen above. Although with intentions and expectations diametrically opposed to those of the radical wing of the movement, represented by Rosa Luxemburg from the turn of the century until her assassination and by Lukács and others later, Bernstein went on to define the task of socialist emancipation in political/ideological/educational terms. The fairly obvious difference in orientation between them was that while Lukács advocated the revival of dialectics, with highly positive references to Hegel and in sharp opposition to Kant and his followers in the Second International, Bernstein called for a return to Kant (and to the neo-Kantian Lange) 'against the cant which sought to get a hold on the working-class movement and to which the *Hegelian dialectic* offers a comfortable refuge'.[709]

The diametrical opposition in intention and expectation between the two ideological perspectives became even more obvious when Bernstein argued that the task at hand consisted in rescuing the 'badly educated'[710] workers from the 'self-deception' and the '*misleading ideology*' of Marxian *materialism*,[711] so that they should acquire 'a high degree of mental independence'[712] and 'the high intellectual and moral standard which the organization and existence of a socialist community *presupposes*',[713] adding with patronizing arrogance well known in the social democratic movement ever since Lassalle: 'Just because I expect much of the working classes, *I censure* much more everything that tends to corrupt their *moral judgment*.'[714]

Naturally Lukács, in radical opposition to the spirit of the Second International, wanted the realization of the exact opposite of Bernstein's programme. He was fighting for the development and diffusion of both Marxian materialism and dialectics – in their inseparability from one another – as well as for the victory of the socialist forces on the ideological terrain from which he expected in due course the 'practical solution of the world's economic crisis'. All this, however, could not alter the fact that his discourse, too, remained locked into the rather unreal terms of reference of political/ideological confrontations which tended to abstract from the unfolding material determinations.

8.5 BERNSTEIN'S REPRESENTATIVE BLIND ALLEY

8.5.1

It must be stressed also in this context that the adoption of such a dubious position could not be simply ascribed to a theoretical failure on Lukács's part, just as the representative theoretical status which Eduard Bernstein acquired – and to our own days still retains[715] – could by no stretch of imagination be attributed to the theoretical excellence of his ideas. On the contrary, the intellectual substance of his *Evolutionary Socialism* is rather scanty, at best, as Rosa Luxemburg so clearly demonstrated already in the heat of the debates generated by Bernstein's work,[716] at the time of its first publication. And yet, she was quite unable to halt the growing influence of the tenets expressed in this little book, despite the intellectual rigour and clarity of her analysis, coupled with weighty historical and economic evidence which she had put forward in her demonstration of the shallowness, retrogressive character, and even logical fallaciousness of her adversary's conceptual framework and practical recommendations.

What is directly relevant to us here is that – no matter how vacuous were Bernstein's theoretical arguments and, more often than not, crudely distorting his accounts of the rejected Marxian propositions – it was by no means accidental that he should become a representative figure in the German and international social democratic movement, and indeed on that account *the* favourite Marxist (if not the *only* acceptable one) in the eyes of all liberal/bourgeois thinkers, including Max Weber.

It was not simply that he had put into words with great self-assurance what many people wanted to hear. Rather, the main reason for his success resides precisely in *why* they wanted to hear what he was so eager to say. For, even if in an upside-down fashion, his work reflected and ideologically rationalized the need for realigning the political strategies of the once internationally oriented movement, now deeply entrapped in its – imperialistically poised – national setting.

What was particularly welcome was that through the ideological rationalization supplied by Bernstein, the ongoing, extremely problematical and – with regard to the objective requirements of socialist emancipation – *counter-productive* tendency of socioeconomic and political development could be misrepresented not merely as one totally free from its, in reality *negative/destructive*, implications; worse, it could be also hailed as a great *positive* advance: the reassuring *evidence* for, as well as the *guarantee* of, the desired outcome.

8.5.2

To take one typical example – which displays both the extreme poverty of the alleged 'facts' and intellectual arguments marshalled by the author, and the conservative ideological/political tendency of the whole approach –

let us have a closer look at Bernstein's celebrated 'refutation' of Marx's analysis concerning the concentration and centralization of capital:

> To me the chapter [on the 'Historical tendency of capitalist accumulation' in Volume I of *Capital*] illustrates a *dualism* which runs through the whole monumental work of Marx ... a dualism which consists in the fact that the work aims at being a scientific inquiry and also at proving a theory laid down long before its drafting; a formula lies at the basis of it in which the result to which the exposition should lead is fixed beforehand. The return to the *Communist Manifesto* [which is quoted in a footnote in the chapter referred to] points here to a real residue of utopianism in the Marxist system.... as Marx approaches a point when that final aim [of striving for emancipation] enters seriously into question, he becomes uncertain and unreliable.... Contradictions then appear ... in the section on the movement of incomes in *modern society*. It thus appears that this great scientific spirit was, in the end, a *slave to a doctrine*....
>
> That the *number of the wealthy increases* and does not diminish is not an invention of bourgeois 'harmony exonomists', but a fact established by the *boards of assessment for taxes*, often to the *chagrin* of those concerned, a fact which can no longer be disputed. But what is the significance of this fact as regards the victory of socialism? Why should the realization of socialism depend on its refutation? Well, simply for this reason: because the dialectical scheme seems so to prescribe it; because a post threatens to fall out of the scaffolding if one admits that the *social surplus product* [mark it: not the exploitatively extracted *surplus-value*] is appropriated by an increasing instead of a decreasing number of *possessors*. But it is only the *speculative theory* that is affected by this matter; it does not at all affect the actual movement. Neither the struggle of the workers for *democracy in politics* nor their struggle for *democracy in industry* is touched by it. The prospects of this struggle do not depend on the theory of concentration of capital in the hands of a diminishing number of magnates, nor on the whole *dialectical scaffolding* of which this is a plank, but on the growth of *social wealth* and of the social productive forces, in conjunction with *general social progress*, and, particularly, in conjunction with the *intellectual and moral advance* of the working classes themselves.[717]

And this is supposed to be a theoretical 'classic', according to many well known intellectuals, from Max Weber to those who joined the 'league of abandoned hope'.

Let us see, then, what does this 'classic statement of democratic socialism'[718] really amount to?

In the first place, it makes a trivial chronological point: the indisputable fact that the *Communist Manifesto* historically preceded Volume I of *Capital*. (This is, by the way, the only indisputable thing in the long passage quoted above.) However, the claim attached to it is is very far from being indisputable. It is supposed to establish, with the force of self-evidence, that Marx was trying to prove 'a theory laid down long before its drafting'. Something that Bernstein considers thoroughly reprehensible because, in his view, 'the result to which the exposition should lead is *fixed beforehand*'. Thus, Bernstein's argument continues, preconceived utopianism dominates the 'dualistic' Marxian system, which therefore should be discarded – lock, stock and 'dialectical scaffolding'.

Unhappily, however, for Bernstein, the claimed substantive chronological point is completely the wrong way round. For the *Economic and Philosophical Manuscripts of 1844* – in which Marx first 'laid down' as well as 'drafted' in considerable detail his system – *preceded* by more than three years the drafting of the *Communist Manifesto*.

Not that one should make too much out of such facts either way. For theoretical claims and counter-claims must be established on their proper plane, through the use of demonstrable theoretical arguments, sustained by adequate material evidence from the real world. If, however, someone has at his disposal neither a proper theoretical framework, nor the required sociohistorical evidence, then, of course, not much else remains besides the elevation of some (by themselves in any case rather inconclusive, even when not completely upside-down) facts of chronology to the status of pseudo-theory.

The second characteristic of Bernstein's procedure: his ill-tempered denunciation of dialectics as 'cant' and useless 'speculative scaffolding', fits into the same pattern as his use of chronology; both offered as 'self-evident' substitutes in place of theoretical argument. For thanks to the insults heaped up against dialectics, this vital dimension of the Marxian theory can be apparently considered, without any further proof, to be fully discredited.

The logical structure of this kind of reasoning is: 'I hate you, therefore you are hateful'; which in itself proves nothing apart from its own utter fallaciousness. But in Bernstein's case there is somewhat more to it than just that. The real purpose of his logically fallacious and politically motivated – and in terms of its reformist social ground well buttressed – rejection of dialectics transpires only if we carefully observe what is actually happening as Bernstein's polemic unfolds. For behind the screen of the claimed demolition of Marx's 'dialectical scaffolding', unexpectedly a major theoretical shift is being brought about, without the slightest attempt at justifying it. All we are offered, instead, is the arbitrary declaration that the (both theoretically and practically quite fundamental) issue at stake: the inexorably growing centralization of capital, as described in Marx's *Capital*, is nothing but a useless plank of a superfluous scaffolding. It is simply decreed by Bernstein that such scaffolding matters only to the '*speculative theory*' which is itself devoid of any significance to the '*actual movement*'.

Thanks to this theoretical shift which not merely obliterates the objective trends of global socioeconomic development but denounces the very idea of concern with them as dialectical cant and speculative irrelevance, the 'actual movement' is, of course, radically severed from its overall perspective and strategic framework. What follows afterwards, Bernstein's programmatic statement, is not established either by theoretical argument or with reference to sociohistorical evidence on the required scale. It is simply (and categorically) stated to be *valid* in virtue of the categorically asserted *invalidity* of the *'speculative'* Marxian perspective.

We are told that the only things that really matter are: to watch, with an optimistic disposition, the growth of 'democracy in politics' (i.e. the increasing influence of Bernstein and his revisionist friends); the spread of 'democracy in industry' (i.e. the utopia of small workers' cooperatives triumphing over large-scale capitalist enterprise); the emergence of *'general* social progress' (i.e. the actualization of the ultimate utopia in which there is no more need, nor indeed any room, for social antagonism[719]), 'particularly in conjunction with the intellectual and moral advance of the working classes themselves'. For the latter, admittedly, we have to wait a long long time, perhaps forever, because the working classes, according to Bernstein, are 'immature and badly educated', and there is not much sign that the 'general social progress' is going to change that. In the meantime, therefore, the workers involved in the 'actual movement' must content themselves with Bernstein's patronizing assurances that one day they will become *worthy* of admittance to his utopia, in terms of the idealist Lange/Bernstein type *neo-Kantian moralism*. (And again, the virtues of the latter are not established in their own terms, on independent ground, but only through a categorical dismissal of the evil Hegelian/Marxist dialectic's 'hold on the working-class movement'.) In the end, what all this boils down to is this: the workers must appreciate that their morally and intellectually already fully developed leaders 'expect of them so much' and are therefore fully entitled to act on their behalf indefinitely, leading them in a direction diametrically opposed to Marx.

Moreover, since in the actually existing *capitalist* society the precious things enumerated by Bernstein cannot be honestly even daydreamed about, let alone actually obtained by the overwhelming majority of the workers – because the global tendency of centralization and concentration of capital (which he categorically ruled out of existence, despite all evidence to the contrary) stubbornly refuses to go away and continues to annihilate every day, with ruthless efficacy, the little havens of cooperative 'industrial democracy', etc. – all hope must be attached to 'the movement of incomes in *modern society*'. Thus Bernstein reveals himself, appropriately, as one of the intellectual ancestors of the recent theories of de-socialized 'modernity', and in that sense fully deserves his representative status. For in the same way as in the recent annals of modernity, his 'modern society' too, characterized by its promising 'movement of incomes', should not be considered any longer an iniquitous *capitalist* society by virtue of the explicitly stated claim that in this modern society the happily growing 'social surplus product' is appropriated by an ever-growing number of classless *'possessors'*.

8.5.3

Undertstandably, there can be no room for Marx within the framework of such a vision. However, in Bernstein's time Marx cannot be, as yet, simply dismissed as a hopelessly confused and old-fashioned 'nineteenth-century theorist', in view of the fact that he can still count on too many 'nineteenth-century followers' in the 'actual movement'. Thus, he is first given a wholesome pat on his back by Bernstein: he is said to have been '*a great scientific spirit*'. At the same time he also receives a massive kick in the teeth, in the same sentence, on account of being '*a slave to a doctrine*'. As to how someone, who is a 'slave to a doctrine', could be considered simultaneously also a 'great scientific spirit', remains a complete mystery.

What is, however, even more baffling than this piece of rather non-sensical diplomatic lip-service, dualistically wedded to a vilifying insult, is that Bernstein should accuse *Marx* of dualism, when it is in fact his own book which happens to be overcrowded with shallow dualistic propositions and crude mechanical dichotomies, as indeed fully befits someone who can see nothing but 'useless scaffolding' in the dialectic. Bernstein's dualisms range from the rigid opposition which he sets up between the '*final aim*' and the '*actual movement*' to the decreed antinomy between the '*reason*' of reform/legislation and the '*emotion*' of revolutionary interventions in the historical process, not to mention his vacuous/pedestrian and dualistic/opportunist 'wanting to have it both ways' method of arguing in terms of 'on one hand – on the other hand; yes – but; although – however; more – less; etc.',[720] – rightly taken to task on this score, as on many others, by Rosa Luxemburg.

But the most problematical – and at the same time the most representative and influential – aspect of Bernstein's work is the way in which he tries to prove that 'the number of the wealthy increases' in his 'modern society'. Obviously, to have any meaning at all, the author should first of all spell out the precise terms of reference within which the alleged proof itself could be assessed as to whether or not it really demonstrates the validity of his claims. In keeping with his customary procedure, however, Bernstein offers us nothing of the kind. Instead, he simply declares the 'indisputable fact' that the number of the wealthy increases is 'established by the boards of assessment for taxes', throwing in for good measure on top of his claimed indisputable fact another proposition, which he considers the self-evident and ultimate proof of the soundness of his own views, namely that all this happens 'often to the *chagrin* of those concerned'.

If now we ask, what exactly has been proved by Bernstein, we end up with the singularly unilluminating, even if 'self-evident', proposition: that the wealthy do not like being taxed, hence their 'chagrin'. To what extent are they *really* taxed, and to what extent can one consider *wealthy* the people who undoubtedly are being taxed, are, of course, highly relevant questions within their proper terms of reference. Bernstein, however, decides not to pay the sligtest attention to them. He prefers, instead, to divert *our* attention from such questions with his chagrin-ful remark about the existing boards of taxation, which must immediately strike a sympathetic chord with the heartfelt pocket of every self-respecting bourgeois, 'harmony-economist' or not. But what we are actually offered as 'new historical evidence' to build upon in order to secure the future of the movement amounts to no more than a handful of dry sand that quickly disappears between our fingers. It proves absolutely nothing besides the intellectual poverty of Bernstein's 'classic statement of democratic socialism'.

And yet, notwithstanding the vacuity of its theoretical substance and clumsiness of presentation, in the shape of this proposition and of its self-generating corollaries Bernstein bequeathed to the 'actual movement' a classical tenet of social democratic wishful thinking which remained with us ever since. In this sense, again, he can be considered a representative figure, in that he clearly identified the *blind alley* of gradual capitalist measures – among them, very high on the list of priorities, *capitalist taxation* – as the only really appropriate method of bringing about radical social change in a 'modern society'.

8.5.4

Naturally, the reality of such taxation turned out to be painfully different from the social democratic myth of '*progressive taxation*', as demonstrated with abundant empirical evidence even by some leading social scientists who professed genuine social democratic sympathies.[721] Thus Bernstein's attempt to use as irrefutable proof for the refutation of Marx's theory of the concentration and centralization of capital the 'movement of incomes in modern society', and the socially enlightened taxation of an increasingly larger number of wealthy people, turned out to be fatally flawed on account of being oblivious to several vital aspects of the issue at stake.

First, the quite elementary fact that the number of people to be taxed can be increased or diminished at will by the state legislative authorities, depending on the limits offered by the specific socioeconomic and historical circumstances which must be made explicit if one wants to ascribe any significance at all to the measures adopted, pointing in one direction rather than in the other. Short of such specification one can only end up with the grotesque idea that the taxation of everybody is 'irrefutable evidence' for the realization of the idealized 'social wealth and general social progress', whereas the absence of personal taxation, on the contrary, would have to be considered the clearest possible demonstration that the society in question is made up of untaxable paupers. Besides, the managers of the capitalist state understood a long time ago that universally imposed '*indirect taxation*' – as opposed to its *direct* variety – hits hardest precisely the poorest sections of the population, and that such indirect taxation can be conveniently combined with the declared policy of governments aimed at reducing the burden of taxation for those who badly need it, while in fact they do nothing of the kind.[722]

Second, Bernstein and his followers are oblivious to the most obvious, and even in straightforward statistical terms quite easily demonstrable, aspect of taxation. Not as a result of an accidental oversight, of course. For once the perspective of a radical structural intervention in the historical process is abandoned, the eagerness to assert that the 'actual movement' is moving towards the desired objectives, despite the reversal of direction, carries with it a congenital blindness to the rather unpalatable fact that the *burden of taxation* falls heavily on the shoulders of the *poor*, and not of the *rich*, contrary to what reformist wishful thinking must decree in order to make any sense at all of its gradualist future-oriented strategy.

One might perhaps wish to excuse Bernstein himself for predicting the happily unfolding condition of 'general social progress', etc., that did not materialize, absolving him on the ground that he did not have the empirical counter-evidence at his disposal, since we ourselves acquired it – in great abundance and in every single capitalist country – only as a result of many decades of disappointed expectations.

In truth, though, it would be quite wrong to suggest that the tendentious reformist misrepresentation of the burden of taxation can only be corrected 'in hindsight', on the basis of cumulative sociohistorical evidence. In any case, such empirical evidence, no matter how abundant and inexorably mounting, cannot conclusively undermine the expectations of gradualist wishful thinking, since there is always the possible excuse of *tomorrow*. Moreover, even the measure of actual achievements or failures can be changed, more or less arbitrarily – once the earlier adopted measure of 'general social progress' is deflated by historical evidence that clearly runs counter to yesterday's confident anticipations, and thereby fails to fulfil any longer its mystificatory function – in order to suit the one and only irreplaceable ideological constant: the a priori postulate that the 'actual movement' is on the right road.[723]

The basis on which Bernstein's upside-down conception of who actually does carry the necessary burden of taxation can be questioned, not 'in hindsight' but right from the moment of its first formulation, is the relevant theoretical framework itself; or rather its non-existence, as far as Bernstein himself is concerned. This is where we can see how the socially and ideologically conditioned jettisoning of the Marxian theoretical tenets as useless 'speculative scaffolding' acquires its perverse rationality and intellectual *raison d'être*. For in the absence of an adequate categorial framework anything and everything goes, enabling the reformist theore-ticians to substitute the most amazing fantasies for even the most obvious material factors.

They do this either by manipulating the temporal dimension of the disputed data (whenever the available evidence of the prevailing order of things contradicts their gratuitous postulates), or by attempting to discredit altogether – with empty rhetorical/exhortatory references to 'the spirit of the great Koenigsberg philosopher, the critic of pure reason'[724] and to the neo-Kantian 'social-political views of Friedrich Albert Lange',[725] etc. – the relevance of *material factors* for the constitution of viable sociopolitical strategies, with the excuse that they represent nothing but 'intolerably restrictive materialism' and 'misleading ideology'.

This is how they end up with the truly peculiar notion (pursued as perhaps the most important guiding principle in their entire practical programme) according to which they can succeed in taxing capital out of existence, in due course, provided that they continue long enough with their gradual efforts aimed at that objective. Moreover, they do not seem to question for a moment the realism of what they consider to be the only realistic strategy to pursue, despite the sobering – or rather, what *should be* sobering – circumstance that the anticipated fundamental transformation of society through progressive taxation is supposed to take place within the confines, and through the necessarily resistant instrumentality, of the *capitalist state*.

A serious theoretical analysis of the objective factors involved – i.e. of the intrinsic nature of capital and its necessary structural domination of labour, as regulated on the sociopolitical plane by the far from neutral capitalist state – could easily demonstrate to them, even within the categorial matrix of Adam Smith's political economy, the *inconceivability* of such an undertaking. But to proceed on those lines could only yield results which would be highly embarrassing for the whole approach. Hence their rejection of theory itself as 'speculative theory', which in its turn prevents them from noticing (irrespective of how many decades or even centuries might go by) that it is the poor who must be, and are indeed being, taxed; not out of existence[726] – because exploitation needs them also in the future – but simply to the bare bone. At the same time, in accord with the adopted socioeconomic objectives and corresponding practical strategies, the critique of *capitalist exploitation* must be replaced (in the kind of myopic theory which we are left with) by the praise of the all-promising '*movement of income in modern society*'; and the concept of the *capitalist state* on which critical attention can and must be focused, must be discarded in favour of the vague and wishful notion of '*democracy in politics*'.

The *third* major omission of Bernstein's sentence about the increasing number of wealthy tax subjects takes us to the heart of the matter. It can be clearly identified if we try to locate the *limits* – an undertaking of quite elementary importance whenever one has to deal with sociohistorical trends and economic as well as political tendencies – within which the numbers referred to can be taken seriously.

What we find in Bernstein's case is that the task of setting the limits is systematically evaded, combining instead the dubious factual claim of increasing numbers with an ahistorical projection of the hypostatized 'general social progress' into the future as a self-sustaining absolute. In truth, though, nothing could be more problematical than that. For the fetishistic appeal to numbers as a substitute for theory fails to situate the trend in question within its proper parameters, in relation to other relevant tendencies and counter-tendencies of the unfolding socioeconomic development. As a result, the relative significance of the historically specific expansion of social wealth in a limited number of capitalist societies is distorted beyond recognition, both in its *internal* and in its *international* aspects.

On the *internal* plane, the pedestrian/quantitative projection of numbers which abstracts from all *qualitative* considerations also ignores that there can be no question of an automatically self-sustaining expansion of wealth in any society, let alone under capitalism. For the claimed numbers themselves must be *causally* sustained from the margin of *productive material advancement*, instead of being miraculously pulled out of a bottomless top hat. In other words, the 'growth of social wealth and general social progress' in any particular capitalist country is credible only to the extent to which it is compatible with the untranscendable structural limits imposed by the need for *capital-expansion*. It is the persistence of such limits that prevents the realization of '*general* social progress' even at the peak of capital's ascendancy, and even in the most privileged of capitalist societies.

Thus, it is quite ficitious to hypostatize the growth of adequately distributed social wealth and general social progress when in reality even the richest capitalist societies are characterized by – not accidental and marginal but necessary and ubiquitous – *structural inequality*. An incorrigible inequality that emanates not from the wickedness or foolishness of unenlightened individuals (who in principle could be converted to the cause of the social reformer) but from capital's innermost determinations which must subordinate everything to the imperative of *profitable capital-expansion*, thereby negatively affecting by far the greater part of the working population even in the most privileged countries, and even under the most favourable circumstances. Consequently, the more or less conscious omission of the necessary historical qualifications (which must be defined in terms of and in relation to capital's inescapable structural determinations) makes it totally meaningless to attempt, as Bernstein and his followers do, to turn the timelessly projected assertion that 'the number of the wealthy increases' into the generalized *model of socialist emancipation*.

However, it is the *international* dimension of the reformist claim which reveals its complete vacuity. For even if one could argue – keeping in mind the inescapable limits – that in *some* capitalist countries *certain sections* of the working class greatly benefit from the growth of wealth (and they do so only for *as long* as such developments can be sustained out of the margins of profitable capital-expansion), the same line of reasoning would be an obvious absurdity if applied to the world as a whole in which the privileges of the imperialistically or neo-colonially dominant few are obtained at the expense of the overwhelming majority. This is why the neglect of this problem happens to be in fact so complete within the confines of the reformist perspective (all the way down to Habermas and others). It is either kept under *total silence* (which speaks loud enough for itself, so long as we are willing to listen), or, in more recent times, it is simply postulated that the same kind of 'development' and 'modernization' which characterized the history of the dominant capitalist countries will do its 'good work' if we wait long enough for its coming or, at best, if we adopt an 'enlightened self-interested' posture (like the *Brandt Reports*, for instance) in order to hasten its arrival.

8.5.5
Bernstein's ideological blind alley acquired its representative significance precisely because it offered a conceptual framework in which the complicity of silence could predominate with the greatest ease and the (for socialists highly embarrassing) questions concerning the *generalizability* or otherwise of the search for privileges at the expense of the overwhelming majority of humankind could not even be asked. The chapter of *Capital* which Bernstein openly and categorically rejected had to be rejected because in it Marx pushed into the foreground the absolutely vital concern of the socialist movement – inasmuch as it really wanted to make advances towards its proclaimed aim – with 'the entanglement of *all peoples* in the net of the *world market*, and with this, the *international character* of the capitalist regime'.[727]

In the sharpest possible contrast to the Marxian conception, Bernstein idealized the anticipated developments as confined to the given *national* setting, totally ignoring the ways in which capital's global determinations were bound to overrule them sooner or later. Accordingly, he metamorphosed the wishful and next to meaningless projections of a 'general social progress' (self-contradictorily limited in his discourse to a particular national setting) into the model of rationality in order to be able to dismiss the stragetic necessity of a revolutionary socialist transformation as utterly meaningless. These were his words:

> As soon as a *nation* has attained a position where the *rights of the propertied minority* have ceased to be a serious obstacle to *social progress*, where the negative tasks of political action are less pressing than the positive, then the appeal to a revolution by force becomes a *meaningless phrase*.[728]

Typically, an element of hypocritical mystification was added here to Bernstein's argumentative arsenal, suggesting that the author's objections concerned revolution *by force*, and not revolution as such, when in fact the *whole* of *Evolutionary Socialism* was dedicated to the task of discrediting the 'emotionalism' of revolution, in favour of the 'intellectualism' and rational adequacy of piecemeal legislation through 'democracy in politics'.

Two basic truths were obscured by this method. *First*, that whether a revolution had to assert itself predominantly 'by force' – athough it must be pointed out here that in any case the bourgeoisie would consider the prospect of even the most straightforward and non-violent legislative measures against its domination of society nothing but 'force' and 'lawlessness' – or could achieve its objectives without resorting to repressive methods, depended on the sociohistorical *relation of forces*. Consequently the issue had to be concretely assessed in its given historical setting rather than aprioristically condemned. And *second*, that envisaging a socialist – i.e. a radical structural – transformation of society while renouncing revolution was a contradiction in terms, because to be radical means, literally, to 'grasp things at their roots' and act accordingly, as Marx had rightly stressed. Naturally, the function of disregarding such fairly elementary considerations was to make people subscribe to Bernstein's absurd and, as usual, totally unsubstantiated proposition that 'the rights of the propertied minority *have [actually] ceased to be* a serious obstacle to social progress'.

Given such reasoning – which predicated the realization of general social progress out of the crumbs that could be secured while 'positively' safeguarding 'the rights of the propertied minority' – the open capitulation of social democracy to bourgeois chauvinism, and its active support of imperialist adventures, was only a question of time and opportunity, as the outbreak of the first world war in the end painfully demonstrated.

By the time of the initiation of the military hostilities in 1914, the openly advocated revisionist line – which was still under fire in the party press and at party conferences when Bernstein first published his *Evolutionary Socialism* – became almost completely dominant in the German Social Democratic Party as well as in the Second International in general, thanks in no mean degree to Bernstein's own rising influence.

However, the really significant aspect of these developments was that the seeds he was sowing, in the company of others like him, met with an exceptionally fertile ground. For already at the height of the debates surrounding the publication of Bernstein's work, the German Party hierarchy behaved with utmost cynicism and duplicity in these matters, pretending one thing in public and doing something completely different behind stage. Thus Ignaz Auer, not a minor provincial functionary but the general secretary of the German Social Democratic Party, wrote to Bernstein in 1899, at the time when the revisionist line championed by *Evolutionary Socialism* was strongly criticized at Party conferences: 'My dear Ede, one does not formally make a decision to do the things you suggest, one doesn't *say* such things, one simply *does* them.'[729] This is how Bernstein's intellectually less than mediocre but politically and ideologically representative conception came to occupy its still far from eclipsed place as a 'classic' in the social democratic movement.

To be sure, the strategy advocated by Bernstein represented a blind alley for the working-class movement right from the beginning. Yet, to be fair to him, he was not the sovereign maker of that blind alley. Rather, he reflected and energetically propagandized an objective trend of development which continued to gather strength – no matter how problematical and ultimately destructive its implications had to be with respect to the original aspirations of the socialist movement – ever since Marx's 'dominant peoples', setting out from the European 'little corner of the world', embarked, in the last quarter of the nineteenth century, on their fateful imperial drive, in order to subject the rest of the world to the service of their capitalistically circumscribed self-interests.

With this the chances of an early socialist breakthrough in the Western world suffered a tragic historical setback, thereby rendering unavoidable the radical redefinition of the material and ideological conditions of emancipation one day, in accordance with the new determinations of the epoch, within capital's now truly global terrain. But before such redefinition of the conditions of socialist emancipation – corresponding to the objective characteristics and human needs of the fundamentally altered historical circumstances – could become possible, the actualization of capital's qualitatively expanded potentialities through the development of underdevelopment on one side, and the accumulation of enormous privileges on the other, had to unfold with all its bewildering twists and confounding ideological/political consequences.

Thus, the constant reproduction of labour's antagonistic dual perspectives of emancipation (first consolidated at the turn of the century) had to remain the iron rule, despite all attempts at 'organizational unity' and 'political reconciliation', for as long as the *global* system of capital could sustain itself without reaching its point of *saturation* and the *structural crisis* implicit in the latter. This is why the reformist approach first popularized by Bernstein – and enthusiastically embraced at once, as their natural creed by all surplus-Tories like him who came to dominate the top echelon of all social democratic parties – could maintain its tragically mystifying but historically representative hold on the Western working-class movement to our own days.

8.6 THE MEANING OF ROSA LUXEMBURG'S TRAGEDY

8.6.1
However, tragedy by no means ended there. Far from it. For the radical wing of the working-class movement produced three major tragic figures among its leaders in the twentieth century; all three with statures of

Shakespearean proportions. They were: in Western Europe, Antonio Gramsci; in the East, Lenin; and bridging the East with Western Europe, Rosa Luxemburg.

Gramsci's tragedy was not simply what is obvious about his personal history: namely that he had to suffer extreme hardship for 11 years of his life and then prematurely perish in Mussolini's jail. More than that, his tragic cofinement meant that a revolutionary leader of immense practical gifts, in his real element when he could organize and directly communicate with the masses of working people, had to spend his potentially most fruitful years, cruelly cut off from his companions of struggle, as a philosopher of the vanguard party, deprived of the necessary tools of intellectual work and often condemned to use obscure and Aesopic language in order to outwit his jailers. And worse still, in the end he was even subjected to the indignity of sectarian excommunication for the capital sin of remaining true to his non-fractional principles.

By contrast, Lenin could remain active as the formally uncontested leader of a successful revolutionary movement to the end of his life. And yet, the cruel irony in his destiny was that, totally dedicated as he was to the cause of the socialist revolution, he helped to paralyse the self-same forces of the working-class base to which he tried to turn towards the end of his life for help, when he perceived the awesome danger of those developments in Russia which were to culminate in Stalinism. As I have argued elsewhere,[730] Lenin, a genius of realistic strategy, had to behave like a desperate utopian from early 1923 to the moment of his death: insistently putting forward hopeless schemes – like the proposal to create a majority in the Central Committee from working-class cadres, in order to neutralize the Party bureaucrats, with Stalin at their head – in the hope of reversing the dangerous trend, by then far too advanced. His great tragedy was that his incomparable, instrumentally concrete, intensely practical strategy in the end defeated him. In the last years of his life, there was no way out of his bleak predicament of isolation. The developments he himself, far more than anybody else, had helped to set in motion had made him historically superfluous. The specific form in which he lived the unity of theory and practice proved to be the fateful limit even of his greatness.

But the most intensely tragic figure in the history of the working-class movement was Rosa Luxemburg. For, like the heroes and heroines of some classic tragedies – reflecting the destiny of great historical forces and their collisions – she arrived too early and had to suffer the consequences for being so far ahead of her conflict-torn age.

8.6.2
For one thing, Rosa Luxemburg arrived too early in the sense that she could write with utmost clarity and far-sightedness the epitaph of 'Eurocommunism' half a century in advance of its birth, without any hope of

reversing an objective tendency which in the end had to engulf even the radical political wing of the Western working-class movement before it could be fully consummated. Situating the issue of reformism within the framework of world economic and political/military developments,[731] Rosa Luxemburg painted with daunting accuracy the portrait of the political accommodator, past and present:

> He advises the proletariat to disavow its socialist aim, so that the mortally frightened liberals might come out of the mousehole of reaction. Making the suppression of the socialist labour movement an essential condition for the preservation of bourgeois democracy, he proves in a striking manner that this democracy is in complete contradiction with the inner tendency of development of the present society. . . . By making the renouncement of the socialist aim an essential condition of the resurrection of bourgeois democracy, he shows how inexact is the claim that bourgeois democracy is an indispensable condition of the socialist movement and the victory of socialism. . . . We must conclude that the socialist movement is not bound to bourgeois democracy, but that, on the contrary, the fate of democracy is bound with the socialist movement. We must conclude from this that democracy does not acquire greater chances of life in the measure that the working class renounces the struggle for its emancipation, but that, on the contrary, democracy acquires greater chances of survival as the socialist movement becomes sufficiently strong to struggle against the reactionary consequences of world politics and the bourgeois desertion of democracy. He who would strengthen democracy should want to strengthen and not weaken the socialist movement. He who renounces the struggle for socialism renounces both the labour movement and democracy.[732] And he who tries to apply the home-made wisdom derived from parliamentary battles between frogs and mice to the field of revolutionary tactics only shows thereby that the very psychology and laws of existence of revolution are alien to him and that all historical experience is to him a book sealed with seven seals.[733]

Thus, she clearly perceived that democracy itself as actually constituted was becoming more and more problematical, requiring for its revitalization the firmest possible socialist commitment and corresponding class action, instead of the latter being subordinated to the abstract and vacuous notion of 'democracy in politics' that had been repeatedly opposed to radical socialist strategies in the twentieth century not only by the enemies of socialism but also by its social democratic advocates. Moreover, Rosa Luxemburg realized with equal clarity that while the socialist movement itself was heavily constrained by the parliamentarian institutional setting of bourgeois democracy, its class adversary did not hesitate for a moment to break its own rules of political conduct whenever the circumstances required it to do so in the interest of its continued domination of society, however *undemocratic*.

8.6.3
The parliamentary institutional framework in fact had been fully established well before the working class appeared on the historical stage as an

autonomous political force. Hence it completely failed to reflect the interests of labour as against capital even in its basic constitutional articulation and formal rules of operation.

Nor was it conceivable, according to Rosa Luxemburg, to alter radically the prevailing state of affairs. For the given legislative framework of parliamentary democracy could never transcend the all-important material circumstance that

> What distinguishes bourgeois society from other class societies – from ancient society and from the social order of the Middle Ages – . . . [is] precisely the fact that class domination does not rest on 'acquired rights' but on *real economic relations*; the fact that wage labour is *not a juridical relation* but purely an *economic relation*. In our juridical system there is not a single legal formula for the class domination of today. [Thus] how can wage slavery be suppressed the 'legislative way', if wage slavery is not expressed in laws? Bernstein, who would do away with capitalism by means of legislative reform, finds himself in the same situation as Uspensky's Russian policeman who tells: 'Quickly I seized the rascal by the collar! But what do I see? The confounded fellow has no collar!' And that is precisely Bernstein's difficulty.[734]

Nor was indeed the difficulty here indicated by Rosa Luxemburg confined to Bernstein. On the contrary, it became the apparently inescapable predicament of the social democratic movement in all capitalistically advanced countries, looking for legislatively effective 'collars' where none could be found, in view of the immanent nature of the relationships at issue. Consequently, as Luxemburg put it, 'no *law* in the world could give to the proletariat the means of production while it remained in the framework of bourgeois society, for not laws but *economic development* have torn the means of production from the producers' possession.'[735]

This is why the revisionist abandonment of the Marxian guiding principle – namely that 'the economic emancipation of the working classes is the great end to which every political movement ought to be subordinate as a means' – proved to be so fateful in the twentieth century. Understandably therefore, against the historical background of the up to the sudden post-war explosions overwhelmingly dominant reformist/opportunist trend of Western working-class action, Rosa Luxemburg was attempting to revive the original spirit of the Marxian First International when she insisted in the middle of the German revolutionary upheavals, in her evaluation of what was happening, that

> It was typical of the first period of the revolution down to December 24th that the revolution remained *exclusively political*. Hence the infantile character, the inadequacy, the half-heartedness, the aimlessness, of this revolution. Such was the first stage of a revolutionary transformation whose main objective lies in the economic field, whose main purpose it is to secure a fundamental change in economic conditions. Its steps were as uncertain as those of a child groping its way without knowing whither it is going; for at this stage, I repeat, the revolution had a purely political stamp. But within the last two or three

weeks a number of strikes have broken out quite spontaneously. Now, I regard it as the very essence of this revolution that strikes will become more and more extensive, until they constitute at last the focus of the revolution. Thus we shall have an *economic revolution*, and therewith a *socialist revolution*.[736]

8.6.4

From this vision of the socialist revolution followed the necessary definition of the organizational tasks as befitting a highly principled mass movement. This is how Luxemburg articulated it already in her critique of Bernstein in 1899:

> The union of the broad popular masses with an aim reaching beyond the existing social order, the union of the daily struggle with the great world transformation, this is the task of the social democratic movement, which must logically grope on its road of development between the following two rocks: abandoning the *mass character* of the party or abandoning its *final aim*, falling into bourgeois reformism or into sectarianism, anarchism or opportunism.[737]

And this is how the same concerns appeared in her critical assessment of the 'Organizational questions of the Russian Social Democracy':

> On the one hand, we have the mass; on the other, its historic goal, located outside of existing society. On the one hand, we have the day-to-day struggle; on the other, the social revolution. Such are the terms of the *dialectical contradiction* through which the socialist movement makes its way. It follows that this movement can best advance by tacking betwixt and between the two dangers by which it is constantly being threatened. One is the loss of its *mass character*; the other the abandonment of its *goal*. One is the danger of sinking back to the condition of a *sect*; the other, the danger of becoming a movement of *bourgeois social reform*. That is why it is illusory, and contrary to historic experience, to hope to fix, once for always, the direction of the revolutionary socialist struggle with the aid of *formal means*, which are expected to secure the labour movement against all possibilities of opportunist digression.[738]

Naturally, this conception of the socialist movement as a genuine *mass movement* – one firmly oriented towards socialist goals, in the same spirit in which Marx himself spoke many years earlier of the need to constitute a socialist *mass consciousness* – carried with it a corresponding conceptualization of real *power*. In this sense, while Luxemburg was fully aware of the necessity to conquer and retain state power (in a fundamentally altered form, that is; for the purpose and duration of the *radical restructuring* of the socioeconomic order), she conceived the task in terms of the *transfer* of all power to the social body, coupled with the elimination of the cleavage between *legislative and executive* powers through their effective embodiment in the masses of working people. This is how she argued her case:

> We have to seize power, and the problem of the seizure of power assumes this aspect: what, throughout Germany, can each workers' and soldiers' council achieve? There lies the source of power. We must mine the bourgeois state and we must do so by putting an end everywhere to the cleavage in public

powers, to the cleavage between legislative and executive powers. These powers must be united in the hands of the workers' and soldiers' councils. . . . For us the conquest of power will not be effected at one blow. It will be a progressive act, for we shall progressively occupy all the positions of the capitalist state, defending tooth and nail each one that we seize. Moreover, in my view and in that of my most intimate associates in the party, the *economic struggle*, likewise, will be carried on by the workers' councils. The settlement of economic affairs, and the continued expansion of the area of this settlement, must be in the hands of the workers' councils.

The councils must have all power in the state. To these ends must we direct our activities in the immediate future, and it is obvious that, if we pursue this line, there cannot fail to be an enormous and immediate intensification of the struggle. For step by step, by hand to hand fighting, in every province, in every town, in every village, in every commune, *all the powers of the state* have to be *transferred* bit by bit from the bourgeoisie to the workers' and soldiers' councils. . . .

History is not going to make our revolution an easy matter like the bourgeois revolutions. In those revolutions its sufficed to overthrow that official power at the centre and to replace a dozen or so of persons in authority. But we have to work from beneath. Therein is displayed the *mass character* of our revolution, one which aims at transforming the *whole structure* of society. It is thus characteristic of the modern proletarian revolution, that we must effect the conquest of political power, *not from above, but from beneath.*[739]

Thus, on all major issues of vital practical importance to the movement, Rosa Luxemburg put forward a coherent, profoundly dialectical, yet, despite the complexities with striking clarity argued and – with regard to the *long-term perspectives* of the coming socialist transformation – quite unsurpassable set of ideas.

8.6.5

The tragedy was that under the prevailing historical circumstances, notwithstanding the clarity of Rosa Luxemburg's vision and the depth of her revolutionary socialist commitment, the course of action which she was advocating with exemplary consistency throughout her life could not be successfully accomplished.

In this sense one could truly witness in Luxemburg's predicament 'the tragic collision between the *historically necessary* postulate and the *practical impossibility* of putting it into effect.'[740] This is what gave her life its tragic intensity, and not simply the brutal murder which she could have avoided by going into hiding. But she rejected the advice of her friends and comrades who repeatedly urged her to do so; not out of bravado but out of a heightened (and decidedly not 'romantic') 'sense of responsibility, a feeling that she simply had to share every danger with the ordinary fighters of the revolution.'[741] And even when it was already quite obvious that the forces of 'law and order' were looking for her, and 'a woman comrade, sent out to discover what was happening in the *Rote Fahne* offices' was mistakenly arrested in place of Luxemburg and 'subjected to long hours of frightful treatment before she finally managed to escape', describing to Rosa the death threats which she received in captivity on her behalf and 'warned her to flee, she emphatically rejected the idea, explaining that she and Karl [Liebknecht] had to remain in Berlin to prevent the defeat of the workers from leading to their demoralization.'[742]

As Lukács had pointed out in his early essay on 'The Marxism of Rosa Luxemburg':

> Her death at the hands of her bitterest enemies, Noske and Scheidemann, is, logically, the crowning pinnacle of her thought and life. Theoretically she had predicted the defeat of the January rising years before it took place; tactically she foresaw it at the moment of action. Yet she remained consistently on the side of the masses and shared their fate. That is to say, the unity of theory and practice was preserved in her actions with exactly the same consistency and with exactly the same logic as that which earned her the enmity of her murderers: the opportunists of Social Democracy.[743]

In this sense, she had to live the raging historical conflicts all the way to their bitter end, even if personally to her this meant perishing in the course of the struggle. For she knew full well (and firmly said so in her polemics against Kautsky and others) that the pioneering socialist revolutions could not be other than 'unripe' and 'premature', and therefore inevitably burdened with the risk of defeat. And she knew equally well what that risk meant for the people who took part in such revolutions, consciously and defiantly accepting the fateful implications of their active involvement in the 'tragic collision between the historically necessary postulate and the practical impossibility of putting it into effect'.

The same tragic intensity which we could witness in Rosa Luxemburg's actions was characteristic also of her theoretical work. For just as she pursued her calling as a militant to its utmost limits – not only at the time when the ring of her murderers was visibly closing around her, but throughout her life when she refused the offer of exceptional treatment and accepted, instead, imprisonment as a matter of course – in the same way she carried the investigation of the subjects under her critical scrutiny to their farthest implications, refusing to make any concession whatsoever to tactical considerations even in the midst of the war when the threat of being sentenced for a 'treasonable offence' was hanging over her head for her uncompromising views. Thus, during the war, in a German prison, she could find the strength not only for denouncing 'the world-wide conflagration and chaos of the imperialist mass slaughter' but also for something much more difficult: she could simultaneously summon up her inner resources for underlining, in the same sentence, with the anguished instransigence of a true revolutionary, 'the completest failure on the part of the international working class'[744] to prevent the consummation of its own slaughter and the realization of the most absurd irony of history: '*dividends are rising – proletarians falling*',[745] as she graphically expressed it in another pamphlet.

Furthermore, Rosa Luxemburg could apply the same uncompromising and principled criticism to the Russian revolution, which she acknowledged to be struggling under the shadow of 'the failure of the German proletariat and the occupation of Russia by German imperialism'.[746] This is how she formulated her 'immanent critique' of the revolution in continuation of the last quoted sentence, objecting to the use which its leaders made of the force of circumstance and of the limitations of tactics forced upon them:

> It would be demanding something superhuman from Lenin and his comrades if we should expect of them that under such circumstances they should conjure forth the finest democracy, the most exemplary dictatorship of the proletariat and a flourishing socialist economy. By their revolutionary stand, their exemplary strength in action, and their unbreakable loyalty to international socialism, they have contributed whatever could possibly be contributed under such devilishly hard conditions. The danger begins only when they make a *virtue of necessity* and want to freeze into a complete theoretical system all the *tactics forced upon them* by these fatal circumstances, and want to recommend them to the international proletariat as a *model* of socialist tactics.[747]

Thus, perceiving the world from the broadest historical perspectives of socialism and articulating her vision of the fundamental social antagonism as an inextricably global challenge in her references to the necessary 'settlement of the score between *capital and labour* in the *entire world*',[748] Rosa Luxemburg had to conclude that 'in Russia the problem could only be posed. It could not be solved in Russia.'[749] The same approach characterized, throughout her life, Luxemburg's assessment of *all* major issues. She always presented her ideas with the stark authenticity of what she called clear, blunt, unenigmatic and unreservedly embraced 'naked truth', with its *epochal* frame of reference, utterly defiant of 'the force of circumstance'. Given the 'unripe' historical circumstances under which she had to live and work, the outcome, understandably, could not be other than a 'tragic collision between the historically necessary postulate and the practical impossibility of putting it into effect'.

In one of her rousing speeches she quoted a passage from Lessing, representing one of her dearest maxims. This is how it read:

> I do not know whether it be a duty to sacrifice happiness and life to truth. But this much I know, that it is our duty, if we desire to teach truth, to teach it *wholly* or not at all, to teach it clearly and bluntly, unenigmatically, unreservedly, inspired with full confidence in its powers. The cruder an error, the shorter and more direct is the path leading to truth. But a highly refined error is likely to keep us permanently estranged from truth, and will do so all the more readily in proportion as we find it difficult to realize that it is an error. One who thinks of conveying to mankind truths masked and rouged, may be truth's pimp, but has never been truth's lover.[750]

The enduring relevance of Rosa Luxemburg's writing has a great deal to do with living up to this maxim as one of the key orienting principles of her theory and practice. It is therefore doubly mystifying to read a pronouncement made in the spirit of Merleau-Ponty's 'league of abandoned hope' by one of her 'sympathetic' commentators. In the concluding paragraph of the introduction to the Ann Arbor paperback edition of *The Russian Revolution* by Rosa Luxemburg, the author of this introduction, Bertram D. Wolfe, declared – as usual in the writings of this curious League, without bothering to prove anything or even of giving some illustrative examples that might point in the direction of the required proof – that 'much of what Rosa Luxemburg wrote in this little pamphlet is now *hopelessly dated*, for much of it stems from *dogmas* which would not bear examination and have not resisted the passage of time.'[751]

Nothing could be wider of its mark than such a judgement. On both counts. For whatever the historical limits of Rosa Luxemburg's achievements, the last thing one could rightfully say about her work is that it suffered from being 'dogmatic' and 'hopelessly dated'. Quite the opposite. For, as regards the first accusation, she spent much of her life in fighting dogmatism and sectarianism in her tireless advocacy of socialism as a genuine *mass movement*, constantly warning against the danger to be avoided which she described as 'the danger of sinking back to the condition of a sect', as we have seen in several passages of her writings quoted above. And with regard to the second count against her, the only sense in which she could be considered 'out of phase' with her time – and even with ours – is not on account of being 'hopelessly *dated*' but, on the contrary, in that in some important respects her time has *not yet* come.

8.6.6

To understand the meaning of Rosa Luxemburg's tragedy we have to turn to her uneasy political relationship with Lenin.

On the face of it, the constant tension in this relationship was all the more surprising since Lenin and Luxemburg were the two outstanding revolutionary figures of their age who, despite their repeated disagreements, had so much in common. Yet, what made it difficult (if not altogether impossible) for them to bring to a common denominator their major differences was the fact that the strategic perspectives of *both* had their well founded historical justifications.

After her murder, on the occasion of the much disputed publication by the dissident Paul Levi[752] of Rosa Luxemburg's critical assessment of the Russian revolution, Lenin wrote:

> We shall reply to this by quoting two lines from a good old Russian fable: 'Eagles may at times fly lower than hens, but hens can never rise to the height of eagles.' Rosa Luxemburg was mistaken on the question of the independence of Poland; she was mistaken on the theory of the accumulation of capital; she was mistaken in July 1914 when, together with Plekhanov, Vandervelde, Kautsky and others, she advocated unity between the Bolsheviks and Mensheviks; she was mistaken in what she wrote in prison in 1918 . . . But in spite of her mistakes she was – and remains for us – an eagle.[753]

Similarly, Lenin was on the whole highly appreciative of *The Junius Pamphlet* by Rosa Luxemburg when he stated in his review article that this work (written in April 1915 and published in defiance of the censor in 1916) was 'a splendid Marxist work'.[754]

Yet, the difference in perspective between the two was also strongly highlighted in the same article when Lenin emphasized that 'a very great defect in revolutionary Marxism in Germany as a whole is its *lack of compact illegal organization* that would systematically pursue its own line and educate the masses in the spirit of the new tasks.'[755] And Lenin not only repeated the same concern but further reinforced it in his concluding remarks by insisting that:

> Junius's pamphlet conjures up in our mind the picture of a lone man who has no comrades in an *illegal organization* accustomed to thinking out revolutionary slogans to their conclusion and systematically educating the masses in their spirit. But this shortcoming – it would be a grave error to forget this – is not Junius's personal failing, but the result of the weakness of all the German Leftists ... Junius's adherents have managed, in spite of their isolation, to begin the publication of *illegal leaflets* and to start the war against Kautskyism. They will succeed in going further along the right road.[756]

As he made it quite clear on numerous occasions, the right road for Lenin was the road of illegality. As such, this road precluded the possibility of pursuing several of Rosa Luxemburg's fundamental concerns. Thus, the revolutionary paths of these great socialist figures *had* to diverge in significant ways.

In terms of its negative determination, the road adopted by Lenin was forced upon the Bolsheviks by the extreme repressive measures of the Tsarist regime. But that alone would not have been enough to make it viable. It had to be sustained positively as well, as indeed it was by the dramatic growth of the Russian revolutionary movement during the first two decades of the twentieth century.

No one saw this more clearly than the author of *The Junius Pamphlet* herself. For she considered the outbreak of this first world war as an act capable of merely postponing the eruption of the Russian revolution whose arrival and victory was in her view on the order of the day.[757]

However, Rosa Luxemburg also knew that the conditions favouring the successful accomplishment of a mass supported revolution were not present in Germany: the country in which this outstanding socialist theoretician and political militant of Polish origin happened to live. Consequently, according to her, other strategies had to be pursued in order to lay the foundations of a victoriously self-asserting socialist *mass movement*, given the parliamentary entrapment of the unquestionably mass supported German Social Democratic Party and of the similarly oriented working-class parties in the capitalistically advanced countries of the West with which German social democracy was closely associated.

In this sense, the major difference in perspective between Lenin and Rosa Luxemburg happened to be the accurate reflection of the sharply contrasting objective characteristics of their countries within the strategic framework of global capital.

Irrespective of differences of interest among themselves, the 'metropolitan' or 'core' countries of the global capitalist system were objectively opposed to (as well as directly and indirectly benefiting from their dominant relationship with) the 'periphery' from the very beginning of the late nineteenth-century imperialist expansionary phase. Inevitably, this circumstance carried with it far-reaching consequences on the plane of the feasible sociopolitical movements of labour as well, resulting in the separation (and indeed irreconcilable clash) of the reformist and revolutionary wings of the original international working-class movement.

In the final analysis, their separation and opposition (both in strategic objectives and corresponding organizational forms) tended to coincide with the country boundaries of 'developed' and 'backward' regions. Since, however, the radical socialist transformation of the capitalist social order – envisaged by Rosa Luxemburg no less than by Lenin himself – was inconceivable within isolated country boundaries, it was necessary to demonstrate that the sociohistorical specificities and limitations of the very different labour movements could be transcended towards the overall objectives of the desired socialist change on a global scale. Thus, the question of how to make *generally valid* one rather than the other of the alternative roads could not be avoided.

As we have seen above, the reformists of the Second International (from Bernstein and his friends all the way down to their distant followers in our own days) bypasssed the issue in a characteristically evasive fashion. They declared the importance of the 'movement' as such, abandoning at the same time its socialist aims either explicitly or by watering them down beyond recognition. And given the structurally dominant and privileged position of the countries to which they belonged *vis à vis* the capitalistically underdeveloped regions, there could be absolutely no question of *generalizing* in a tenable way their approach to 'social reform'. For their conception of 'general social advancement' was objectively premised – explicitly or by implication – on the continued subordination of the rest of the world to the interests of the societies of 'advanced capitalism'. Thus, it was by no means accidental that the reformist trends of the labour movement became dominant in the structurally privileged part of the global capital system. Only the revolutionary currents – those which consciously rejected the prevailing capitalist social order, with all its acquisitions as well as structural inequalities – attempted to face up to the challenge of establishing the general validity of the course of action which they pursued.

Understandably, the requirement to demonstrate the general viability of the advocated strategies presented the revolutionaries both in the West and on the 'periphery' with some major difficulties. In the West, the difficulties were due primarily to the dominance of the reformist trends themselves and to the marginalization of the revolutionary currents (and with regard to both, to the underlying material determinations, of course). On the other hand, the revolutionary movements of the backward regions had to come to terms with the problem that the socialist project, in presenting itself as the only viable alternative to the rule of capital, explicitly stated the necessity of the highest degree of productive developments as a way of avoiding 'the generalization of misery' (Marx) and therewith the failure of the socialist enterprise. Naturally, this consideration could not help underlining the limitations and deficiencies of their predicament from the point of view of the necessary global transformations which had to represent a fundamental social advancement even with regard to the circumstances of the capitalistically most advanced societies.

In truth, Lenin was well aware of the fact that there was something very problematical about having to turn the strategies based on the socio-economic realities of a backward country like Russia into the model of action for the international socialist movement as a whole. This is why he did not hesitate to concede that 'soon after the victory of the proletarian revolution in at least one of the advanced countries, a sharp change will probably come about: Russia will cease to be the *model* and will once again become a backward country (in the "Soviet" and the socialist sense).'[758] And yet, in order to be able to sustain his line of argument under the circumstances, he had to add in the next sentence:

> At the present moment in history, however, it is the *Russian model* that reveals to *all countries* something – and something highly significant – of their *near and inevitable future*. Advanced workers in all lands have long realized this; more often than not, they have grasped it with their revolutionary class *instinct* rather than realised it. Herein lies the international 'significance' (in the narrow sense of the word) of Soviet power, and of *the fundamentals of Bolshevik theory and tactics.*[759]

Since the crucial question for Lenin was how to conquer and retain state power as the vehicle of socialist transformations in an extremely backward country, expecting with hope and optimism the victory of the socialist revolution in 'at least one of the advanced countries' in the *'near and inevitable future'* as a way of strengthening the precarious position of his own forces, he could see absolutely no alternative to such a solution, notwithstanding his totally honest and clear acknowledgement of its paradoxical, indeed problematical, character.

'Things turned out differently',[760] as Lenin himself often used to say. The Russian revolution could not fulfil its role as the model of action – the 'near and inevitable future' – of the privileged societies of the West. The failure of the attempted socialist revolutions in capitalistically advanced countries (including Rosa Luxemburg's Germany) brought home the painfully sobering truth that one had to face up to the almost forbidding complications of significantly different types of development (and 'underdevelopment') in different parts of the world, despite their common global socioeconomic framework. This required the elaboration of the strategic solutions and organizational forms appropriate to the specific social setting of each radical movement, while remaining faithful to the international animating principle of the socialist movement as a whole. For without the latter the particular socialist movements could not succeed even in their most limited partial objectives.

8.6.7
Rosa Luxemburg, more than anybody else since Marx, had constantly in the forefront of her attention the importance of global connections as well as constraints that inevitably arise from the reciprocal determinations of interdependence.

Methodologically Lenin's greatest asset was his unrivalled perception of the given historical and social specificities and of the immediate practical possibilities that could be derived from them. Rosa Luxemburg, by contrast, oriented herself towards the signposts of the broadest historical tendencies, often defiant of the given historical realities.

As an example, we may think of her assessment (and forceful assertion) of the fundamental identity of the strategic interests of all national working classes, no matter how deeply divided they might find themselves under the conditions of imperialist rivalries:

> The modern labour movement, its laborious daily struggle in the industries of the world, its mass organization, are based upon the cooperation of the workers in all capitalistically producing countries. If the truism that the cause of labour can thrive only upon a virile, pulsating industrial life applies, then it is true not only for Germany, but for France, England, Belgium, Russia, and Italy as well. And if the labour movement in all of the capitalist states of Europe becomes stagnant, if industrial conditions there result in low wages, weakened labour unions, and a diminished power of resistance on the part of labour, labour unionism in Germany cannot possibly flourish. From this point of view the loss sustained by the working class in its industrial struggle is in the last analysis identical, whether German capital be strengthened at the expense of the French or English capital at the expense of the German.[761]

What Rosa Luxemburg was asserting in this passage of *The Junius Pamphlet*, right in the middle of the global conflagration that set one nation's working class dead against the other, was absolutely true under its general theoretical aspects. It was also *epochally* valid in all its vital practical implications, notwithstanding the fact that she consciously rejected the confounding realities of the moment that carried a very different message.

Clearly, there is much that the labour movements of the capitalistically advanced societies could learn from her perspective even today. If it was 'practically impossible to put into effect' – not only then but today as well – 'the historically necessary postulate' of which she spoke with so much passion and insight, that was decidedly not Rosa Luxemburg's fault, only her tragedy.

The self-same radical global perspective from which she castigated the capitulation of Western Social Democracy and asserted the inevitable interdependence and concomitant mutal interests of the various labour movements also made impossible for her to yield to the temptation of turning the partial validity of any particular historical experience, no matter how important, into a *general model*.

The truth for her could not be other than the *whole*, in its contradictory unfolding.[762] On the one hand, this meant according to her that the historical adversary had to be identified as the closely interlocking and imperialistically articulated system of global capital. For:

> Imperialism is not the creation of any one or of any group of states. It is the product of a particular state of ripeness in the *world development of capital*, an innately international condition, an *indivisible whole*, that is recognizable only in *all its relations*, and from which no nation can hold aloof at will. From this point of view only is it possible to understand correctly the question of 'national defence' in the present war.... Capitalism is incompatible with economic and political divisions, with the accompanying splitting up into small states. It needs for its development large, united territories, and a state of mental and intellectual development in the nation that will lift the demands and needs of society to a plane corresponding to the prevailing stage of capitalist production, and to the mechanism of modern capitalist class rule.[763]

In the same spirit, on the other hand, her vision, in its orientation towards the 'indivisible whole', stipulated the strategic axiom that no single part (in view of its unavoidable sociohistorical limitedness) could stand for the complex and constantly changing whole. We have already seen in this respect her anguished critique of Lenin and his comrades who in her view tried to make from the force of 'fatal circumstances' a complete theoretical system which they could recommend to the international proletariat 'as a *model* of socialist tactics'.[764] And we have also seen that, despite Clara Zetkin's assurances, according to which Rosa Luxemburg considered her critique 'erroneous',[765] the concerns and reservations which she expressed (with regard to the Bolshevik political vanguard's conceptualization of the necessary constraints under which the Russian revolution had to address itself to the problems of the day) were in fact by no means unfounded. For, in the passages quoted above,[766] Lenin explicitly claimed the status of a *model* for the Russian experience as the 'near and inevitable future' of the advanced capitalist societies of the West, notwithstanding his severe reservations about the extreme backwardness of his own country.

8.6.8

Yet, it would be quite wrong to set Luxemburg against Lenin and idealize her perspective in that way. Indeed, to do so would do injustice not only to Lenin but also to Rosa Luxemburg herself, depriving her predicament of its tragic intensity and true historical significance.

As mentioned before, the strategic perspectives of both Lenin and Rosa Luxemburg had their well founded historical justifications. For it was precisely the essential *complementarity* of their contrasting perspectives – i.e. the objective necessity of simultaneously sustaining *both*, with equal authenticity and integrity, without the possibility of reconciling the differences – that provided us with the true measure of the obstacles facing the international socialist movement in its historic mandate to go beyond the rule of capital.

This contrast in perspective clearly displayed the fundamental dilemmas encountered in attempting to produce strategically valid as well as tactically viable solutions to the practical challenges that divided not simply the working-class movement as a whole, resulting in its fracture into reformist and revolutionary approaches, but created further divisions even within its revolutionary wing. This tragedy of the outstanding revolutionary figures – Lenin and Rosa Luxemburg – acquired its historical significance through being representative of the tragedy of the movement itself.

The profound tragedy of the divided socialist movement as such (which continues to haunt the practical possibilities of the required radical structural change even today), could be summed up in this, that the global strategic interests and the tactically viable avenues of the revolutionary currents themselves could not be brought together under the historically prevailing conditions and relation of forces.

It was in this important sense that it proved to be practically impossible so far to put into effect the 'historically necessary postulate' that animated both Lenin and Luxemburg. Without this weighty circumstance, the recurrent polemics between even such major historical figures could be reduced to purely theoretical/intellectual disputes, enabling us to side with one or the other (or sometimes with one while on other occasions with the other), and consequently could not retain our attention any further.

However, in view of the fundamental complementarity of the two perspectives in question which representatively reflected the objective separation of the global strategic interests and the tactically viable avenues of the revolutionary socialist movement, the issues that divided Lenin and Rosa Luxemburg could not be confined to the realm of political and intellectual history. On the contrary, they preserve their direct practical relevance and vitality for us in the sense that it is impossible to envisage a way out of the present impasse of the international socialist movement without historically resolving the dilemmas that, as a matter of objective necessity (and not as a result of 'subjective failure' and inability to recognize or acknowledge their 'errors'), polarized for so long the strategic perspectives of its best representatives.

Thus, it would be hopelessly one-sided to identify oneself with the perspectives of Lenin *or* Luxemburg, one against the other, without recognizing at the same time the historically determined – problematical aspects of *both*. For only the two together, in their complementarity as reciprocal correctives to one another, could add up to a fully adequate strategic vision. One that transcends the immediacy of sociohistorical constraints, in the spirit of Luxemburg, and at the same time provides the necessary practical correctives from Lenin's standpoint, in accordance with the 'force of circumstance', to the most fundamental socialist principles and corresponding material determinations (constantly reiterated in Rosa Luxemburg's writings) which can only prevail in the long run.

8.6.9
To hold on to these two perspectives together, in a *unified vision*, is by no means an easy matter. It is possible only if we bear in mind the specific (i.e. not only historically *necessary* but – representing the core of the meaning of 'historical necessity' – also *transcendable*) circumstances that separated them, together with the unfolding dynamic of *global* transformations that produces the framework of their necessary *complementarity*.

Although attempting to decide the relative historical merits of Lenin and Luxemburg in terms of who was 'right' and who was 'wrong' would be hopelessly one-sided, as mentioned before, nevertheless, the contrast between the two perspectives could be temporarily summed up by a double paradox: Rosa Luxemburg was right in being *wrong* and Lenin was wrong in being *right*.

A few instances of their controversy should be able to illustrate the complicated, inextricably intertwined issues at stake. Unhappily, they were embodiments of a tragic conjuncture, because they have arisen in such a way that precluded the possibility of being disentangled under the given historical and political circumstances.

The dilemma which the leaders of the revolutionary forces had to face concerned the possibility of *initiating* a socialist assault on the established order at a time when the latter seemed to be able to expand and consolidate its positions all over the world, despite its inner antagonisms. Thus, if the revolutionary forces wanted to make a *breakthrough* in the direction of an eventual socialist transformation, they had to exploit whatever opportunities they could see arising from the contradictions of imperialist rivalry. At the same time, there could be no guarantee that the processes set in motion by the very attempt at a first breakthrough would lead to the realization of the envisaged socialist objectives, since so much had to remain, under the prevailing relation of forces, well beyond the control of the revolutionary social agency. The possibility of relapses, and even of major defeats, could not be removed from the horizon. Yet, without attempting the necessary historical breakthrough, no matter how unfavourable the circumstances, there could be no hope for carrying the socialist project even one step nearer to its successful completion.

Lenin, concentrating with an extraordinary sense of timing on the historically specific and both tactically and organizationally viable determinations, articulated his fundamental philosophical principles by putting the emphasis firmly on the *concrete*, so as to be able to secure the maximum practical impact of conscious political intervention by seizing the 'next link of the chain', as he liked to put it. Thus, it comes as no surprise that in one of his confrontations with Rosa Luxemburg Lenin took her to task, accusing her of being incapable of understanding the ABC of the dialectic. He summed up his emphatic rejection of Luxemburg's approach to the subject of their dispute by saying that:

> There is no such thing as *abstract truth*, truth is always *concrete*. Comrade Rosa Luxemburg loftily ignores the *concrete facts* of our Party struggle and engages in grandiloquent declamation about matters which it is impossible to discuss seriously.[767]

A careful examination of the political controversies between Lenin and Luxemburg shows that in most cases the circumstances required Lenin's unsurpassable grasp of the concrete if one wanted to prevail against the powerful historical adversary. Indeed, to make things even more paradoxical, at times we find that Rosa Luxemburg herself, in a concrete historical situation of great adversity, was *forced* to modify her general position and come to much the same conclusions as Lenin. As an example, we may think of her critical – and self-critical – rejection of the 'illusion of unity', abandoned in the aftermath of a 'bitter awakening from our dreams', as quoted above.[768] This sounded perfectly in tune with Lenin's position which she could not accept at the time of their sharp disagreements over the question of organizational reform and party unity. These were Lenin's words:

> Unity is a great thing and a great slogan. But what the workers' cause needs is the unity of Marxists, not unity between Marxists, and opponents and distorters of Marxism.[769]

However, to admit the correctness of Lenin's position under the constraints of 'fateful circumstances' would by no means resolve the underlying historical dilemma. On the contrary, it could only put even more sharply into relief the tragedy of the movement – and of its outstanding representatives – who were forced to come to such conclusions.

We can illustrate the same dilemma with reference to another major controversy, perhaps the sharpest. This is how Rosa Luxemburg put her perception of the fundamental historical stakes:

The working class demands the right to make its mistakes and learn in the dialectic of history. Let us speak plainly. *Historically*, the errors committed by a truly revolutionary movement are infinitely more fruitful than the infallibility of the cleverest Central Committee.[770]

Lenin could never consent to upholding such 'abstract truths' for which Rosa Luxemburg herself had to pay with nothing less than her own life. For the 'infinitely fruitful errors' of the revolutionary movement are not made on a terrian that historically favours the socialist forces. They are committed (or more or less successfully avoided) under 'necessarily premature' conditions – as Rosa Luxemburg rightly observed in her critique of Kautsky – which were in fact bound to favour the ruthless adversary.

And yet, the historical truth, in its broadest *epochal* determination, could only be on the side of Rosa Luxemburg's 'unwise' – and truly premature – insistence on the working class's 'right to make its mistakes and learn in the dialectic of history'. For, in the final analysis, without learning the lessons that can and must be derived from the dialectical interaction and feedback between the constantly renewed results of the adopted policies and the collective *mass agency* consciously involved in, as well as responsible for, making the policies themselves – no matter how painful at first the lessons that must be learned in the course of such a feedback – there can be no question of mastering, by the working people, 'how to use power by using power': an absolute necessity if one is to realize the fundamental socialist objective of transforming, by the popular masses themselves, 'from top to bottom the conditions of their industrial and political existence, and consequently their whole manner of being'.

It was for the same reason that the frequently 'derailing' rule of the *concrete* had to be corrected – not simply as a philosophical principle but as the practical reality of historical development, corrected by historical development itself – in the direction of the *general*, and not the 'abstract'. For while Lenin was right in his insistence that under the prevailing circumstances a politically viable unity between Marxists and opponents and distorters of Marxism was impossible to achieve, the 'concrete truth' of this proposition (a thoroughly negative truth, however necessary) had a very limited historical significance. It had a strictly limited significance because it left the monumental issue of how to bring together the relatively small vanguard of Marxists and the broad masses of non-Marxists, in the course of the difficult transition towards the desired socialist society, almost totally out of account.

To be sure, at first the necessary corrective to the rule of the concrete could only be articulated as a theoretical anticipation, in the form of an alternative strategic perspective. In part this anticipation took the form of an important methodological orienting principle. In its spirit, Rosa Luxemburg laid the emphasis firmly on the *global* connections and global determinations of the historical antagonism between capital and labour, situating the concrete socioeconomic and political events and trends of development within their general perspective by underlining not only their historical specificity but simultaneously also their unavoidable *limitations* as regards their potential impact on the major *epochal* issues themselves. And she did this irrespective of where the concrete instances of the struggle were located, be that on the side of capital or labour.

At the same time, the adoption of Rosa Luxemburg's methodological orienting principle – which denied that 'truth is always concrete', since 'truth in its historical process of becoming' could not claim to itself the concreteness and corresponding validity that only its full articulation could aspire to, although it was absolutely vital to hold on to it, in whichever shape it could assume, from the very moment when it first became visible on the historical horizon – enabled her to pinpoint from its perspective both the general direction of the journey, and some of the worst dangers that had to be avoided if one wanted to complete it successfully.

This is how Rosa Luxemburg's diagnoses could turn out to be *right* on a *long-term* historical basis, despite being often highly questionable (and in that sense *wrong*) as practical policies and viable tactics for the *immediate* future. Just as, by the same token, Lenin's orienting principle – which in a negative way identified *general truth* (the necessary overall framework of *concrete truths*) with, dismissively treated, '*abstract truth*' – in the end had to turn out to be wanting as a truly generalizable, and thereby epochally valid, strategy, i.e. as the 'model' representing even if not the 'near future' but nonetheless the '*inevitable future*' of the various capitalist societies. Being the result of the unfavourable sociohistorical specificities and constraints, it had to turn out to be wanting as the generalization of the ungeneralizable 'concrete truth', even if it had to be pursued with single-minded dedication and self-sacrifice under the given historical circumstances. For while being pursued as the only tactically viable course of action, necessary for breaking the stranglehold of global capital 'at the weakest link of the chain', it could not help bequeathing at the same time – due to the inherent limitations of the given historical concreteness, problematically generalized under the force of 'fatal circumstances' – enormous problems to the future.

8.6.10

Rosa Luxemburg's 'grandiloquent declamations', which Lenin rejected as a totally irrelevant 'lecture on opportunism in the parliamentary countries',[771] concerned her attempt at finding remedies against the dangers facing the socialist movement. Her answer saw the solution in a genuine *mass* articulation of the working-class movement, as against *formal* measures and regulations codified in party statutes. This is how she voiced her concerns:

It is illusory, and contrary to historical experience, to hope to fix, once for always, the direction of the revolutionary socialist struggle with the aid of formal means, which are expected to secure the labour movement against all possibilities of opportunist digression. Marxist theory offers us a reliable instrument enabling us to recognize and combat typical manifestations of opportunism. But the socialist movement is a *mass movement*. Its perils are not the product of the insidious machinations of individuals and groups. They arise out of unavoidable social conditions. We cannot secure ourselves *in advance* against all possibilities of opportunist deviation. Such dangers can be overcome only by the *movement itself* – certainly with the aid of Marxist theory, but only after the dangers in question have taken tangible form in practice.

Looked at from this angle, opportunism appears to be a product and an *inevitable phase* of the historic development of the labour movement.... In view of this, we find most astonishing the claim that it is possible to avoid any possibility of opportunism in the Russian movement by writing down certain words, instead of others, in the party constitution. Such an attempt to exorcise opportunism by means of a scrap of paper may turn out to be extremely harmful – not to opportunism but to the socialist movement.

Stop the natural pulsation of a living organism, and you weaken it, and you diminish its resistance and combative spirit – in this instance, not only against opportunism but also (and that is certainly of great importance) against the existing social order. The proposed *means* turn against the *end* they are supposed to serve.

In Lenin's overanxious desire to establish the guardianship of an omniscient and *omnipotent Central Committee* in order to protect so promising and vigorous a labour movement against any misstep, we recognize the symptoms of the same *subjectivism* that has already played more than one trick on socialist thinking in Russia.[772]

Holding the perspective from which these lines were conceived, in 1904, also enabled Rosa Luxemburg to identify later, at the time of the October Revolution of 1917, a number of major threats to socialist developments in the future. While her practical recommendations were, again, of dubious viability under the prevailing circumstances, which prescribed tactical accommodations fully recognized by Lenin, her vision of the strategic implications, for the more distant future, of the measures adopted by the Bolsheviks, turned out to be of the greatest importance. Tragically, however, by the time when the negative and ultimately destructive consequences of the force of 'fatal circumstances' became clearly visible, it was impossible to undo them.

One example out of a whole series of far-reaching critical remarks – which ranged from the nationalities question to the assessment of the Constituent Assembly and to a challenging discussion of the relationship between democracy and dictatorship in the construction of socialism – should suffice here to illustrate the point at issue. It concerned Rosa Luxemburg's 'maximalist' approach to the question of land, sharply opposed to Lenin's policy that favoured the immediate seizure and distribution of the land by the peasants. This is how she argued her case:

As a political measure to fortify the proletarian socialist government, it was an *excellent tactical move*. Unfortunately, however, it had two sides to it; and the reverse side consisted in the fact that the direct seizure of the land by the peasants has in general nothing at all in common with socialist economy.

A socialist transformation of economic relationships presupposes two things so far as agrarian relationships are concerned:

In the first place, only the *nationalization* of the large landed estates, as the technically most advanced and most concentrated means and methods of agrarian production, can serve as the point of departure for the socialist mode of production on the land.... Moreover, in the second place, it is one of the prerequisites of this transformation, that the separation between rural economy and industry which is so characteristic of bourgeois society, should be ended in such a way as to bring about a mutual interpenetration and fusion of both, to clear the way for the planning of both agrarian and industrial production according to a unified point of view.... The nationalization of the large and middle-sized estates and the union of industry and agriculture – these are two fundamental requirements of any socialist economic reform, without which there is no socialism....

Now the slogan launched by the Bolsheviks, immediate seizure and distribution of the land by the peasants, necessarily tended in the opposite direction. Not only is it not a socialist measure; it even cuts off the way to such measures; it *piles up insurmountable obstacles to the socialist transformation of agrarian relations*.... What was created is not social property but a new form of private property, namely, the breaking up of large estates into medium and small estates, or relatively advanced large units of production into primitive small units which operate with technical means from the time of the Pharaohs.

Nor is that all! Through these measures and the chaotic and purely arbitrary manner of their execution, *differentiation* in landed property, [between rich and poor peasants] far from being eliminated, was even further sharpened.... now, after the 'seizure', as an opponent of any attempt at socialization of agrarian production, there is an enormous, newly developed and powerful mass of *owning peasants who will defend their newly won property with tooth and nail against every socialist attack*. The question of the future socialization of agrarian economy – that is, any socialization of production in general in Russia – has now become a question of opposition and of struggle between the urban proletariat and the mass of the peasantry. How sharp this antagonism has already become is shown by the *peasant boycott of the cities* ... now that the Russian peasant has seized the land with his own fist, he does not even dream of defending Russia and the revolution to which he owes the land. He has dug obstinately into his new possessions and abandoned the revolution to its enemies, the state to decay, the urban population to famine.

The Leninist agrarian reform has created a new and powerful layer of popular enemies of socialism in the countryside, enemies whose resistance will be much more dangerous and stubborn than that of the noble large landowners.[773]

In the light of the Stalinist collectivization of Soviet agriculture and the ensuing upheavals whose consequences reach down to our own days, reproducing the chronic inadequacy of agricultural production more than seven decades after the revolution, it would be hard to deny the far-sightedness of this diagnosis. The tragedy – both for Rosa Luxemburg personally and for the international socialist movement as a whole – was that the perspective from which such a diagnosis (on this issue as well as on many others) became possible had to remain marginal and ineffective under the pressure of 'fatal circumstances'.

8.6.11
Here, again, it is important to stress the need to bring together the two contrasting perspectives of revolutionary socialism, recognizing their fundamental complementarity despite their tragic irreconcilability at the time of the eruption of the various controversies between Lenin and Luxemburg. For even if Lenin's judgement over Rosa Luxemburg's analysis of opportunism as a 'grandiloquent declamation' can only be considered a harsh and untenable instance of misplaced polemics, he had some very good reasons indeed for combating in the way in which he did, the opportunists in his own party. For he had to face and defeat constantly renewed forms of opportunism as the necessary precondition for turning the Russian movement into a coherent, disciplined and effective fighting force under the conditions imposed on him by the Tsarist regime.

A critical footnote addressed to Kautsky well before their clamorous political break gave us in this respect a graphic example of Lenin's meticulous attention to detail and incomparable grasp of the concrete historical situation without which the political achievements of the Bolsheviks could hardly have been conceivable. This is what he had to say:

> Comrade Kautsky has sided with Martov's formulation [in the debate over party organization], and the argument he pleads is *expediency*. In the first place, at our Party Congress this point was not discussed from the standpoint of expediency, but of *principle*. That was the way the question was put by Axelrod. Secondly, Comrade Kautsky is mistaken if he thinks that under the *Russian police regime* there is such a big difference between *belonging* to a Party organization and simply *working under its control*. Thirdly, it is particularly misleading to compare the position in Russia today to that in Germany under *Anti-Socialist Law*.[774]

Clearly, two out of the three points raised here by Lenin in opposition to Kautsky were, again, directly concerned with his paramount aim of overcoming the specific historical constraints of *illegality* imposed by Tsarist political/military repression, with the central objective of creating an organization capable of both overthrowing the Tsarist regime and retaining effective control over state power during the whole period of transition to a socialist society. His constant polemics against '*economism*' and '*strikeism*'[775] constituted an integral part of the same preoccupation. This approach had to put the accent on the need for a centrally organized, disciplined and tactically viable *political* action whose organizing principle Lenin described as 'democratic centralism'. The 'concrete facts' which he counterposed to what he called Rosa Luxemburg's 'abstract commonplaces and formulas'[776] were assembled by Lenin from this perspective.

Sadly, however, in this necessary insistence on the centrality of political action, forcefully asserted by Lenin against all those who (both in the Russian Party and in the Western Social Democratic movement) 'belittled the importance of political struggle',[777] some vital constituents of the original Marxian conception – well summed up in the proposition according to which 'the *economical emancipation* of the working classes is the great end to which every *political movement* ought to be subordinated as a *means*'[778] – were pushed to the margin of strategic interest. Indeed, in the mind of some of the revolutionary leaders they became wrongly subsumed under the label of 'economism' and 'strike-ism'.

This unhappy entanglement of the original Marxian terms of emancipation with the suspiciously regarded idea of 'economism' was to a large extent understandable under the prevailing 'fatal circumstances'. The 'concrete facts' of Lenin's ongoing political and ideological struggles within his own party, and the broader political context of a constant confrontation with the police force of the most reactionary capitalist state, in a backward country, left very little room for contemplating the fundamental socialist strategic issue of *economically* emancipating the working class when even the most elementary conditions of its political emancipation were missing.

Moreover, as we have seen above, the economism of the Second International, under the slogans of Bernstein's 'evolutionary socialism', made a veritable mockery out of the Marxian proposition of economic emancipation by asserting that it was already well in the process of being accomplished, without any further need for a revolutionary socialist intervention in the political arena as the necessary precondition of its realization. (We have seen how contemptuously Bernstein dismissed the advocacy of revolutionary political action as 'a meaningless phrase'.[779]) Besides, under the prevailing historical circumstances the economic dimension of the question of socialist emancipation in the context of the Russian Empire seemed to possess very little urgency. For the political and organizational difficulties of overthrowing a powerful state machinery, with all its military might and ubiquitous police force, had to be first resolved before one could consider the necessary practical moves that one day must be embarked upon within the framework of – globally interdependent – economic emancipatory action.

Naturally, Rosa Luxemburg's perspective had nothing whatsoever to do with the economism of the Second International. On the contrary, she continued to castigate it in every way from a truly revolutionary standpoint. At the same time she rightly insisted, on the one hand, that 'not laws but *economic development* have torn the means of production from the producers' possession',[780] and on the other, that the 'infantile character' of the attempted socialist revolution in Germany (at first unfolding only as a strictly political revolution) will be overcome when 'we shall have an *economic revolution*, and therewith a *socialist revolution*'.[781] Tragically, however, under the prevailing circumstances her far from 'economistic' discourse could find very little affinity with the central concerns of the other revolutionary perspective, as articulated by Lenin.

To Lenin – intensely preoccupied as he was with gaining a secure hold on the 'next link of the chain', which in his view could only be accomplished by organizationally sound *political* action – many of Rosa Luxemburg's strategic formulations sounded very much like 'economism' and 'strike-ism'. Understandably, therefore, they had to be rejected as 'grandiloquent declamations which it is impossible to discuss seriously', subjective 'errors', practically irrelevant intellectualistic 'lectures', and 'abstract common-places and formulas' devoid of any awareness of the 'concrete facts of our Party struggle'.

In truth, though, Rosa Luxemburg's perspective adopted as its centre of reference some of the most fundamental issues (and difficulties) of the socialist project of emancipation. Accordingly, Luxemburg insisted that the test of viability of any particular measure devised to resolve in favour of the working classes the global antagonism between capital and labour can only be this: does it contribute (and to what extent) to the ultimate supersession of the *social division of labour*, or, on the contrary, does it contain the seeds of new contradictions that reproduce, even if in a new form, the structural hierarchies of super- and sub-ordination and the concomitant passivity and alienation of the broad masses of people. This is why the unavoidability of the socialist *'economic* revolution' – a challenge incomparably greater than any possible anti-capitalist prolitical revolution – figured so large in her conception.

8.6.12

What Rosa Luxemburg said about the appearance of opportunism in the international socialist movement – that it was not 'the product of the insidious machinations of individuals and groups' but had 'arisen out of unavoidable social conditions', thus representing 'an *inevitable phase* of the historic development of the labour movement'[782] – must be said with equal validity about the major difference in perspective between Lenin and Luxemburg, the outstanding revolutionary leaders of their age.

It was the unavoidable tragedy of the socialist movement that the two revolutionary perspectives of twentieth-century Marxist ideology had to be articulated not only separately, but often in sharp opposition to one another. And it was Rosa Luxemburg's personal tragedy that she arrived too early, with her clear-sighted, powerful, and moving plea for firmly orienting and – whenever diverted by the force of 'fatal circumstances' – stubbornly reorienting the movement towards its fundamental aims, within the *global* and *epochal* frame of reference of the original Marxian conception.

Thus, as a result of weighty objective determinations, in Rosa Luxem-burg's predicament we had to bear witness to 'the tragic collision between the historically necessary postulate and the practical impossibility of putting it into effect', participating at the same time in the equally tragic historical necessity and insufficiency of what actually *could* be put into effect, under the given conditions, by making Lenin's perspective prevail in the interest of the *first breakthrough*, before in its turn it became subsumed under or subverted by Stalinist subjectivism.

As Rosa Luxemburg clearly perceived, the strategy geared to the objective of the first breakthrough cannot be sustained as the model of further advances aimed at a radical restructuring of the globally interconnected social system. All the less since in the aftermath of the first breakthrough the adversary can – and indeed does – adapt itself to the qualitatively changed conditions of the basic sociohistorical antagonism between capital and labour.

At the same time, however, the necessary reassertion of the overall strategic objectives of an irreversible socialist transformation on a global scale – which inevitably questions the feasibility of 'socialism in one country', no matter how immense – cannot by itself provide the required answers. For the 'general truth' of socialism in its historical unfolding needs the *practically viable material mediations* through which it can be successfully articulated, under the given constraints, by the *available* social agency – irrespective of how severe its initial fragmentation due to the inherited division of labour – as the 'concrete truth' and progressively more fulfilling everyday life of the broadest masses of people. Accordingly, it becomes possible to approximate the fundamental aim of a socialist restructuring of society in its entirety – i.e. the radical alteration of 'the conditions of industrial and political existence and consequently the whole manner of being' of its people – only to the extent to which the evolving social agency itself succeeds in superseding, with the help of those historically specific and changing material mediations, its own internal divisions.

This is why the way out of the historical tragedy of the socialist movement can only lead through the ultimate *unification* of the complementary revolutionary perspectives of Lenin and Luxemburg. Once, that is, the global development of capital's productive potentialities – as well as of its inseparable contradictions which turn the positive potentialities into devastating realities – effectively alters the historical relation of forces, so as to replace the long prevailing 'fateful circumstances' by more favourable ones as regards the general objective of socialist emancipation.

8.7 THE MATERIAL GROUND OF SOLIDARITY

8.7.1

In her attempt to explain the appearance of opportunistic tendencies in the working-class movement, Rosa Luxemburg put under her scrutiny the impact of bourgeois parliamentarism on the party itself. She argued that

This parliamentarism is the breeding place of all the opportunist tendencies now existing in the Western Social Democracy. The kind of parliamentarism we now have in France, Italy and Germany provides the soil for such illusions of current opportunism as overvaluation of social reforms, class and party collaboration, the hope of pacific development toward socialism, etc. It does so by placing intellectuals, acting in the capacity of parliamentarians, above the proletariat and by separating intellectuals from proletarians inside the socialist party itself. With the growth of the labour movement, parliamentarism becomes a springboard for political careerists. That is why so many ambitious failures from the bourgeoisie flock to the banners of the socialist parties. . . .

The party acts as a bulwark protecting the class movement against digressions in the direction of more bourgeois parliamentarism. To triumph, these tendencies must destroy the bulwark. They must dissolve the active, class conscious sector of the proletariat in the *amorphous mass of an 'electorate'*.[783]

Thus she made it quite clear that the *ideological* trend of opportunism (or, under another name, the advocacy of reformist revisionism) could not be made intelligible in *strictly ideological* terms. To understand its origin and spectacular success in the Western world, it was necessary to relate it to its 'breeding place': the material/institutional ground of bourgeois parliamentarism.

Political developments since 1904, when Rosa Luxemburg wrote these lines, amply confirmed the correctness of her analysis. For in the 85 years that have elapsed since the publication of her reflections on these issues, not only the reformist parties of Western Social Democracy have been sucked more and more deeply into the – from labour's standpoint utterly hopeless – accommodations of bourgeois parliamentarism, but several of the originally anti-reformist workers' parties of the Third International, too, followed the same road, with the *social-democratization* of nearly all Western Communist Parties.

Once the given parliamentary framework is taken for granted as the limiting horizon of all permissible political intervention, the Marxian definition of the basic socialist aim as the 'economic emancipation of labour' (to which the historically changing strategies of political action must be subordinated as a means) is necessarily discarded. For the 'economic emancipation of labour', in its Marxian sense, and the politics corresponding to it, is radically incompatible with an uncritically accepted political regulatory framework that stipulates as the criterion of 'legitimacy' and 'constitutionality' the strictest observance of the rules favouring the perpetuation of the established property relations, i.e. the continued rule of capital over society.

The perverse logic of the reformist/opportunist accommodation to the insuperable constraints of bourgeois parliamentarism progresses like this. First, it is declared (in direct opposition to the Marxian perspective while pretending to conform to its spirit) that 'political action', in the sense in which it has been practically defined by the bourgeoisie in its own favour within the framework of its long established parliamentary system, 'is the most important duty of the movement',[784] restricting thereby the great historical task of the socialist movement to the election of 'representatives' totally unaccountable to the working-class base itself. Next, the objectives of political action are tendentiously divided into 'negative tasks' and 'positive' ones. Those which *cannot* be subsumed under the limited practices of parliamentary action (as necessarily constrained by the structural interests of capital) are classified as the 'negative tasks', and they are declared to be 'no longer pressing'.[785] At the same time, and by decree of the same circular logic of capital's parliamentary apriorism that assumes itself, by definition, as the absolute horizon of all legitimate politics, those objectives that *can* be accommodated within the given boundaries of (marginally effective) sociopolitical adjustments are promoted to the noble status of 'the positive tasks'.[786] And finally – representing the circular 'conclusion' of what has been presupposed from the very beginning by the willing acceptance of curtailing the objectives and stifling the agencies of emancipatory political action, so as to fit the limits prescribed by the capitalist parliamentary setting – it is proclaimed that pressing for a radical alternative to the established order by organized socialist action is a 'meaningless phrase'[787] (or 'mere posturing', in more recent Labourite parlance).

Whatever might be the partial differences among the various reformist trends of Western Social Democracy, on the whole they all seem to have adopted the same approach with regard to the feasible strategic objectives of the working-class movement within the parliamentary framework. Their ideologies are thus not the result of 'insidious machinations' and 'subjective betrayals'. Nor could they be considered simply the 'erroneous conceptions' of particular individuals who, however unlikely, in principle could be persuaded to acknowledge their mistakes and change their views accordingly. They are the *necessary* articulation of a historical '*short circuit*' in which the parliamentary wing of the Western working-class movement finds itself at a determinate time in its development.

8.7.2

The nature of this 'short circuit' can be understood if we remind ourselves that the 'dialectic of history' from which a truly significant social movement can and must learn, involves, in Rosa Luxemburg's sense, participating with total commitment in the vicissitudes of the unfolding sociohistorical development, interacting with its diverse forces and absorbing the fruits that can be derived from such interaction, in accordance with the intrinsic potentialities of the movement in question. By contrast, the 'short circuit' of Western Social Democracy, caused by partaking in the capital/labour antagonism through the restrictive instrumentality of bourgeois parliamentarism (which inevitably prejudges the contested issues in capital's favour), leads to the impoverishment of the movement instead of its enrichment. For the *contingent* and challengeable constraints of the capital-istically restrictive – yet by Western labour not *under protest* temporarily accepted but, on the contrary, permanently embraced and idealized – political framework are *internalized* in the course of their uncritical adop-tion as *absolute* limits, generating thereby the self-paralysing ideologies of reformist accommodation with which we are all familiar.

It is therefore by no means accidental that *90 years* of reformist theoriza-tion in the *whole* of Western Social Democracy could not produce any significant advance over Bernstein's original formulations. The repeated claims according to which every new compromise with the class adversary is made in order to bring the political strategy of the movement 'up to date' and more fitting to its task, in line with the changed historical circumst-ances, in reality amounts to no more than the blatant rationalization and justification of the short-circuited manipulatory practices of the parliamen-tary wing, in its separation and alienation from the social class base which once brought it into being.

The post-Bernsteinian ideology of Western Social Democracy consists in commending as the only viable strategy for the working-class movement the already adopted 'short circuit' of reformist accommodation. This is the only real object of its 'theory', and this is why it cannot offer any significant innovation as compared to the original Bernsteinian formulas. Indeed, this is why the vacuous postulates and arbitrary generalizations of Eduard Bernstein are never considered with the necessary qualifications, as the questionable product of a determinate historical conjuncture. Rather, they must be credited with the status of a 'classic', no matter how obviously and conclusively the confident anticipations of *evolutionary socialism* are refuted by subsequent historical developments, as we could witness in the case of Bernstein's wishful denial of the inexorable *concentration* and *centralization* of capital, for instance.

As far as Western Social Democracy is concerned, perceiving the world from within the parameters of its self-imposed 'short circuit', not even the greatest revolutionary upheavals (including the Russian and the Chinese revolutions) can make the slightest difference *vis à vis* the righteously presumed and therefore unchallengeable virtues of its own parliamentary accommodation (described with self-congratulating unreality as 'democracy in politics'). The real 'dialectic of history' does not and cannot enter its preconceived picture. No new event or development can affect in a mean-ingful way the strategic perspective of Western Social Democracy, oriented towards the apologetic justification of its original choice – the road of *strictly gradual reform* and the categorical rejection of the possibility of *revolutionary* change – and towards the *aprioristic* confirmation of the rightfulness of the adopted strategy. Thus, the last thing which this per-spective needs or could take on board without undermining itself would be some really new theoretical tenets and radically reorienting signposts. For the inherently defensive object of its theoretical enterprise (in its necessary linkage to the practical strategies that could be derived from the professed theory) remains unchanged – and, of necessity, *unchangeable* – for as long as the parliamentary framework itself, with all its severely constraining structural limitations for labour (but not for capital) remains effectively in control of the political interchanges of the contending social agencies.

There can be no advancement in matters of social and political theory without an adequate interaction with the objective dynamic of the unfolding historical development itself. Thus, the absence of genuine innovation in the domain of theory at a determinate time in history is either the manifestation of socioeconomic stagnation, or of the failure of the theoreticians associated with the principal social movements to give adequate expression to the actual historical dynamics of their age. And in the second case the failure is due principally to the intrinsic limitations and contradictions of the institutionally circumscribed sphere of operation of the social agency itself, whose material interests and corresponding ideological standpoint the representative theoreticians of a particular social class or group share, and try to translate into an intellectual vantage point from which the ongoing events and developments can be coherently conceptualized.

In this sense, the intellectual poverty of Western social democratic theory – from Bernstein to Anthony Crosland and to the recently converted former Stalinists of 'Eurocommunist' social-democratism – is not simply a theoretical failure. Rather, it is the unavoidable consequence of trying to turn into a comprehensive theory an object which in its short-circuited constitution necessarily resists all such attempts. For the elementary condition of producing a truly comprehensive strategic vision is that the latter must be open to *questioning everything*, including the instruments and institutional parameters of the struggle, instead of restricting its view of the world to what may be visible through the obfuscating conjunctural matrix of parliamentary compromises. However, in the monotonously repetitive social democratic theorizations of labour's potentialities for change within the confines of the established order – theorizations determined with regard to their internal conceptual structure by the imperative of taking for granted the parliamentary framework itself as the unchallengeable arbiter over what *may* and what *may not* be contested – all the substantive issues of a 'feasible' socialist transformation are *ipso facto* defined in terms of *maintaining as it is* the established *structure* of society, and thereby allowing even for 'gradual' changes only insofar as they can be accommodated within the given structure.

In truth, therefore, the legitimized 'gradual changes' of social democratic theory are not even *gradual* in any meaningful sense of the term (i.e. changes fit to secure, no matter how slowly, the promised transition to a very different – *socialist* – society), but merely *accommodatory*. For their more or less openly admitted premiss is the *necessary exclusion* of all radical *structural change*, by whatever means (no matter how repressive) at the disposal of the established 'constitutional order'.

The so-called 'gradual changes' of reformist social democracy, introduced through legislative measures at the snail's pace over *many decades*, can be 'constitutionally' overthrown almost *overnight*, as the savage anti-union laws of the recent past, coupled with the wholesale 'de-nationalization' of the 'family silver' (the pride not only of postwar Labourite governments but also of consensually inclined Tories), amply testify. In the real world of politics the comforting philosophical paradox of the tortoise beating the hare quite simply does not work. Yet, clinging to such fictions – because of the aprioristic rejection of any idea of a radical structural change, together with the scathing dismissal of the need for practical revolutionary interventions in the economic order of society – means accepting full complicity with the forces of 'constitutional' repression, in order to maintain a rather impotent position as the potentially governing (but never really *ruling*) part of the system. The role of German Social Democracy not only in the murder of Rosa Luxemburg but also in Hitler's 'constitutional' rise to power should be a cautionary tale to all in this respect.

Thus, the strategic framework of orientation of Western Social Democracy suffers from a fateful ideological blindspot. For the insuperable limitations of parliamentary politics as such to gain mastery over the fundamental controlling forces of the capitalist social metabolism are never even raised, let alone seriously challenged on the basis of, and in response to, the unfolding changes and the emerging new possibilities. On the contrary, as a result of its paralysing institutional integument, social democratic theory itself is transformed into a manipulative *public relations exercise* whose object is, either, how to get elected, or, how to remain in office.

This is why the working class as the social agency of the necessary socialist alternative in the end becomes *superfluous*, and indeed in terms of its radical aspirations thoroughly *embarrassing* for the parliamentary party. For this reason, it must be ideologically diluted beyond recognition in all Western social democratic conceptualizations of 'what is to be done'. Naturally, in this diluted 'updating' of the required social agency of transformation the 'active' contribution of the working class can amount to no more than delivering itself as *electoral fodder* to those who claim to act on its behalf. Even its existence as a political factor is acknowledged by the party leaderships only for a few weeks, while the electoral campaigns last. Not surprisingly, therefore, even in 1987–88 we were still offered – as the great 'innovation' promising to remedy the painfully obvious historical failure of Western Social Democracy – nothing more original (nor indeed more realistic) than Bernstein's strategy, scorned by Rosa Luxemburg as far back as 1904. That is to say, the dissolution of the *'active, class conscious sector of the proletariat in the amorphous mass of an "electorate".'*

8.7.3
The acquisition of their formally/numerically quite impressive parliamentary position by Western social democratic parties is usually hailed as a great victory of the working-class movement. To say the least, this is a tendentiously one-sided presentation of the complex, and under several aspects very problematical, determinations at the roots of 'the forward march of labour', which is now supposed to have come to a major compromise-commanding (and, of course, for all intents and purposes totally capitulatory) end not only in the 'advanced capitalist' societies of the West but all over the world. For, as a matter of great historical irony, one can find some – once upon a time radical – political parties now wedded to the accommodatory, and even in its original context rather vacuous, 'Eurocommunist' perspective in several countries of Latin America as well, however unbelievable this may sound, given the potentially explosive social predicament of the countries concerned.

Two important factors are left out of consideration by those who offer us such idealization of social democratic parliamentary involvement and accommodation.

First, that the originally *repressive* posture of the major Western capitalist governments towards their indigenous working classes was historically altered largely as a result of the material imperatives emanating from their *imperial drive*, in the last third of the nineteenth century. The objective requirements of this drive made it *necessary* for them to make their peace with their national working classes, so as to be able to expand their operations overseas with that much greater effectiveness.

From the point of view of the ruling classes it made a great deal of sense to secure the full cooperation of the national labour force, instead of continuing to antagonize it by enforcing the rather outdated repressive measures, and thereby jeopardizing (or indeed completely undermining) the imperialist expansionary enterprise itself.

The material imperatives here referred to were so fundamental that in the end they sealed the fate of even such shrewd and powerful representatives of the German ruling class, for instance, as 'Iron Chancellor' Bismarck himself. They turned his anti-socialist laws into a hopeless, and by the 'enlightened' (i.e. imperialistically aspiring) members of the ruling class no longer tolerable, historical anachronism. The collapse of these laws, coupled with the politically compromised Bismarck's departure from the political stage, threw the door wide open to the spectacular parliamentary success (and remarkably speedy integration) of the German Social Democratic Party into the sociopolitical system of the country. Ironically, though, Bismarck himself tried to integrate them much earlier (to his misfortune rather prematurely), with the same imperialist expansionary objectives in mind, dreaming even about Dr Marx's 'orderly' return to

Germany in the service of his 'great plan'. He resorted to the notorious anti-socialist laws only when his 'scheming' (with Lassalle and others) failed, as it had to, under the prevailing historical circumstances.

The second factor was a corollary of the First. For, to a most significant extent as a result of the imperial expansion of Western capitalist countries towards the end of the nineteenth century, their earlier greatly constrained economies (which experienced some severe crises between the 1850s and 1880s) gained a new lease of life. As a consequence, they continued to expand at a formerly unimaginable rate, enabling imperialistically successful and more than ever dynamic Western capital to concede to the particular national labour forces a much larger real income from the margins of inflated super-profit than in the previous historical period. At the same time, the working peoples of the subjected countries had to experience and endure levels of material and human degradation quite unimaginable in the West. For only the most intense form of capitalist exploitation could secure for the dominant 'metropolitan' countries the ruthlessly extracted rates of super-profit for the sake of which they embarked in the first place on their imperial venture.

The impact of this relationship became cumulative and produced the crippled 'development' – that is to say, the *structural* dependency and chronic *underdevelopment* – of the subjugated countries. But this was by no means the end of the matter. For the new imperialist system of globally articulated capital simultaneously also produced the fundamental restructuring of the socioeconomic relations *everywhere*, in the form of a closely intertwined network of dependencies and hierarchies in which *all* countries participated, whatever their degree of development and strategic position in the imperialist pecking order.

In fact, the particular 'developed capitalist' societies could only secure for themselves the conditions of their further development by becoming heavily involved, as irreconcilable antagonists, in the global system of twentieth-century imperialism, in accordance with their relative weight in relation to one another under the constantly (and ever more sharply) contested relation of forces. And they *had* to adjust their *internal* structures of socioeconomic metabolism in tune with the changing conditions of worldwide competition and confrontation. As Harry Magdoff stressed in his book, *The Age of Imperialism*:

> The same type of thinking that approaches the concept of economic imperialism in the restricted balance-sheet sense usually also confines the term to control (direct or indirect) by an industrial power over an underdeveloped country. Such a limitation ignores the essential feature of the new imperialism that arises in the late nineteenth century: the competitive struggle among the industrial nations for dominant positions with respect to the *world* market and raw material sources.
>
> The structural difference which distinguishes the new imperialism from the old is the replacement of an economy in which many firms compete by one

in which a handful of giant corporations in each industry compete. Further, during this period, the advance of transportation and communication technology and the challenge to England by the newer industrial nations [like Germany] brought two additional features to the imperialist stage: the intensification of competitive struggle in the world arena and the maturation of a truly international capitalist system. Under these circumstances, the competition among groups of giant corporations and their governments takes place over the entire globe: in the markets of the advanced nations as well as in those of the semi-industrialized and non-industrialized nations.[788]

The combined effect of the developments here surveyed – the consolidation of global capital as a result of its imperial drive, and the manifold internal division of labour arising from the new hierarchies and dependencies both in the underdeveloped and in the metropolitan countries – was that *international solidarity*, which was and remains vital for the advancement and eventual victory of the socialist forces, suffered a tragic setback.

What was at issue here was not a so-called 'ideological crisis' that could be satisfactorily resolved within the domain of ideology itself, by persuading (through the right kind of political agitation) the international popular masses to adopt the 'correct' ideological position. For what had fundamentally changed, and indeed very much for the worse since the days of the First International, was the *material ground of solidarity* as such, making the discourse of internationalism itself rather problematical in the eyes of precisely those to whom it was meant to appeal. Moreover, the discourse of socialist internationalism (readily adopted by the earlier, even though in their size much more limited, working-class organizations) became problematical not only for the duration of a limited political conjuncture. Its doubtful viability extended over an entire historical epoch in which the new material structures of imperialistically articulated capital – as well as the various ideological edifices arising on the ground of such material structures – could dominate the lives of the broadest masses of people relatively undisturbed.

8.7.4

The painful legacy of these developments is still with us, although the possibility of a positive change in this respect is *objectively* much greater today than for a whole century before. This contradicts sharply the reformist misconception according to which the 'forward march of labour' had been halted and only the abandonment of the working class in favour of a 'broad electoral alliance' could put things right. For what is strikingly amiss today is, on the contrary, an adequate strategic conception and corresponding organizational articulation of the materially well grounded objective possibilities of international working-class action which appeared in the course of postwar capitalist developments and, particularly, with the unfolding structural crisis of capital.

As to the alleged end of labour's forward march, this thesis is a complete travesty of the truth, both with regard to the past (the more distant past as well as the quite recent) and in relation to the emerging trends. For, as a matter of historical record, the much idealized electoral success of Western social democratic parties in the past has been accomplished in direct proportion to their transformation into 'responsible', and from capital's point of view 'well educated'[789] (i.e. perfectly *safe*), managers of the capitalist socioeconomic order.

They were allowed by capital to remain in *government* (while clinging to the illusion that they *rule* the country) precisely to the extent to which they could not interfere with the material and political imperatives of the system, in virtue of their more or less openly proclaimed abandonment of all radical socialist objectives. Numerous German, French, British, Austrian, etc. social democratic governments in Europe, including several decades of uninterrupted social democratic 'rule' in some Scandinavian countries, failed to bring about the slightest structural change in the capitalist socioeconomic order. At the same time, and by the same logic fully in tune with the requirements of capital's continued rule, the Italian Socialist Party of Pietro Nenni – which had a radical past and assumed a most remarkable position not only during the first world war but also at the time of the dissolution of the Second International and the foundation of the Third – was never allowed to get involved in government until it threw out all its once cherished radical socialist aims. Even more revealing, the socialist government of Salvador Allende was brutally overthrown in Chile, because it dared even to *contemplate* the introduction of some potentially far-reaching and meaningful social reforms 'in the American hemisphere'.

Thus, with regard to the recent events and developments, the real problem is that the structural crisis of capital is simultaneously also the crisis of Western Social Democracy. For the latter actively sustained capital for almost a century, even under the conditions of world conflagration in the first world war and during the revolutionary upheavals in its aftermath.

The electoral setbacks of the recent past, in all major European countries, acquire a much clearer significance in this light. For its structural crisis presents new problems and new challenges to capital, under circumstances when the margin of manoeuvre is shrinking while the contradictions are intensifying. Consequently, the social democratic promise of continued 'responsible' behaviour (even the Labourite adoption of the wishful perspective of 'popular capitalism') can mean very little, if anything. For capital needs something much more reliable than undeliverable promises. Especially since the recent collapse of social democratic governments in the major European countries followed a period of great disappointments from capital's standpoint ('the winter of discontent', etc.) in that under the circumstances we were witnessing the eruption of social conflict potentially dangerous to the established order.

Thus, the traditional usefulness of social democracy as such for managing the system for capital and containing the conflicts within the boundaries of the established system is being questioned under the *severity* of the deepening *structural crisis*. That the remedy proposed by reformist politicians and theorists is nothing more realistic than the postulated 'broad electoral alliance', fits in perfectly well with the traditional social democratic logic, even if it necessarily implies diluting not only the working-class base but simultaneously also its own aspirations to 'rule'. But all this cannot be considered an adequate response to the erupting tensions and contradictions which in the end will have to be fought out also among the diverse political factions of the Western social democratic movement itself, in response to the renewed ferment in their social base.

However, to conclude the point concerning the massive setback suffered by the cause of international solidarity as a result of the successful imperialist articulation and consolidation of global capital, it is important to stress the role of the *differential rate of exploitation*. For the global capital system, notwithstanding the never abated inter-capitalist rivalries, could derive benefits from the differential rate of exploitation on a monumental scale, both in the metropolitan centres and in the imperialistically controlled (or structurally dependent) territories, without having to pay anything for it. On the contrary, capital could take advantage of the materially imposed differentials not only in strictly economic terms, on which its own survival as a dynamically self-expanding productive system depended, but also as one of its most powerful weapons against socialist aspirations.

Thus, thanks to the successful institution and operation of the differential rate of exploitation *everywhere*, the workers of the metropolitan centres could be *objectively* set against the incomparably more exploited workers of the imperialistically dominated countries. As a revealing example, we may quote Renato Constantino:

> Ford Philippines, Inc., established only in 1967, is now [four years later] 37th in the roster of 1,000 biggest corporations in the Philippines. In 1971, it reported a return on equity of 121.32 per cent, whereas its overall return of equity in 133 countries in the same year was only 11.8 per cent. Aside from all the incentives extracted from the government, Ford's high profits were mainly due to cheap labour. While the US hourly rate for skilled labour in 1971 was almost $7.50, the rate for similar work in the Philippines was only $0.30.[790]

The relative privileges of the metropolitan working classes depended, to a far from negligible extent, on such super-exploitation. This happened to be the case even when they were not *conscious* of the real state of affairs – largely as a result of the deliberate obfuscating role of their parliamentary leaders. Yet, the moment of truth occasionally presented itself, when it became very difficult to plead ignorance as an excuse. Thus, the ignominious role of Harold Wilson's 'socialist' government in sabotaging the economic sanctions of the United Nations against Ian Smith's Rhodesia could not be indefinitely hidden away. Likewise, when the need for disinvestment and economic sanctions was raised by those who advocated effective measures against the super-exploitative Apartheid system of South Africa, some major dilemmas had to be faced in the open. Yet, again, the proposals were quietly shelved on the ground that their implementation would worsen the condition of the working class in England by causing more unemployment. Both instances clearly displayed the vested interests built upon the successful operation of the differential rate of exploitation, heavily weighed down in capital's favour both with regard to its lucrative economic dividends and in terms of its efficacy for dividing the working class even in matters of elementary human rights.

On another plane, thanks to the efficacy of the differential rate of exploitation, workers have been set against other workers within every single country, dividing them from one another by powerful discriminatory material incentives, strengthening thereby at the same time capital's control over them. Futhermore, there was always the promise of additional rewards at the expense of an 'outside enemy', which could temporarily unite at times of extreme crises the otherwise deeply divided national working classes. This is how it could come about that Rosa Luxemburg had to cry out in anguish and sorrow in the middle of the first world war, lamenting the total failure of international working-class solidarity: 'dividends are rising, proletarians falling'. They were falling as a result of the willing participation of other proletarians.

8.7.5

Through the consolidation of the 'new imperialism', reproducing itself in an altered form when its direct political/military control over the subjected countries has become historically obsolete, the material ground of international solidarity has been shattered. The broken pieces could not be put together by way of an ideological counter-offensive. For even the most deeply felt and eloquent words of ideological exhortation are powerless if they are not sustained by dynamic material forces and objective tendencies of development.

Solidarity is viable only as a three-dimensional concept. It must have its socially/materially constituted roots in the past, maintain itself in the present, and branch out with enduring ramifications towards the future. The radical Greens, who today underline the hopeless predicament of future generations if the ongoing destruction of the environment is allowed to continue much longer, are compelled to enquire into the injurious causal determinations emanating from the established socioeconomic order as it has been constituted through history. In the same way, all talk of socialist international solidarity could only amount to empty rhetorics in a one-dimensional present if its spokesmen lost their awareness of its other temporal dimensions by turning their back, for whatever reason, to the past, and closing their eyes to the future.

As is well known, this is precisely what happened through the emergence and consolidation of reformist social democracy, parallel to the materially effective historical transformations and differential rewards of the 'new imperialism'. Thus, it became necessary to sever the links with the past of the movement by claiming that its socialist concerns, which called for class solidarity, did not apply any longer. For, according to the reformist claim, the issue that really mattered was no longer the conflict between capital and labour, but simply the following: how quickly the 'poor' might become 'rich' by way of expanding the national wealth and thereby automatically transferring more and more poor people into the category of the ever-increasing number of the rich (as evidenced by the proceedings of our tax-inspectors). At the same time, the door towards the future was just as firmly bolted by declaring that 'the movement was everything, the final aim nothing'. For the original aim of a radical socialist transformation of our fetishistic conditions of living had to be discarded and labelled at best as a 'utopian dream', and at worst as a sinister conspiracy and subversion directed by an 'outside enemy', in order to justify the accommodatory involvement of the 'movement' in the perpetuation of 'reformed' capitalism, with its allegedly generous scope for 'democracy in politics' and 'democracy in industry'.

Naturally, this kind of disengagement from both the past and the future had to take the greatest liberties also with the interpretation of the *eternalized* present. The actual trends of the unfolding socioeconomic development had to be twisted beyond recognition, in order to deduce from them the wishfully postulated happy commodity existence for everyone, in a 'popular' capitalist social order. In this respect, again, we can see how little any particular variety of contemporary social-democratism succeeded in improving on Bernstein's fallacious categorizations, exposed by Rosa Luxemburg 90 years ago:

> Bernstein hoped to show the existence of a *counter-Marxian tendency* for the retransformation of large enterprises into small ones. The obvious answer to his attempt is the following. If you are to prove anything at all by means of your statistics, you must first show that they refer to the *same* branches of industry. You must show that small enterprises really replace large ones, that they do not, instead, appear only where small enterprises or even artisan industry were the rule before. This, however, you cannot show to be true. The statistical passage of immense shareholding societies to middle-sized and small enterprises can be explained only by referring to the fact that the system of shareholding societies continues to penetrate new branches of production....
>
> What is the meaning, therefore, of the statistics cited by Bernstein, according to which an ever greater number of shareholders participate in capitalist enterprises? These statistics go to demonstrate precisely the following: at present a capitalist enterprise does not correspond, as before, to a single

proprietor of capital but a number of capitalists. Consequently, the economic notion of 'capitalist' no longer signifies an *isolated individual*. The industrial capitalist of today is a *collective person*, composed of hundreds and even of thousands of individuals. The category 'capitalist' has itself become a social category. It has become 'socialized' – *within* the framework of *capitalist* society.

In that case, how shall we explain Bernstein's belief that the phenomenon of shareholding societies stands for the dispersion and not the concentration of capital? . . . This is a simple economic error. By 'capitalist', Bernstein does not mean a *category of production* but the *right to property*. To him, 'capitalist' is not an *economic* unit but a *fiscal unit*. And 'capital' is for him not a *factor of production* but simply a certain *quantity of money*. That is why in his English sewing thread trust he does not see the fusion of 12,300 persons with money into a single capitalist unit but 12,300 different capitalists. . . . That is why for Bernstein the *entire world seems to swarm with capitalists*.

Here, too, the theoretic base of his economic error is his *'popularization' of socialism*. For this is what he does. By transporting the concept of capitalism from its *productive* relations to *property* relations, and by speaking of simple individuals instead of speaking of entrepreneurs, he moves the question of socialism from the domain of *production* into the domain of relations of *fortune* – that is, from the relation between *capital and labour* to the relation between *poor and rich*. . . . Bernstein locates the realization of socialism in the possibility of *making the poor rich*. That is, he locates it in the *attenuation of class antagonisms* and, therefore, in the petty bourgeoisie.[791]

That the poor of the subjugated countries had to be *excluded* from the relative improvements that could be obtained in the conditions of living of the metropolitan working classes, at the expense of others, this sobering fact had to remain unmentioned (and unmentionable) in the reformist conceptualizations of the changes in progress. Only the worst apologists of the system – like Walt Rostow – could go on, during the postwar euphoria of consensus and expansion, propagandizing the ideal condition of capitalist 'modernization' that was supposed to remedy absolutely everything even in the poorest countries of the 'Third World'.

The mystifying Bernsteinian shift in the meaning of 'capital' (perpetuated in a suitably cerebralized form by people like Habermas even today, as we have seen above) served a dual purpose. On the one hand, by transforming 'capital' from a category of *production* into a *fiscal unit* (or a category of *fortune*), it obfuscated the fact that *exploitation* is intrinsic to the established *structure of production* both in the metropolitan centres and in the subjected countries.[792] At the same time, on the other hand, while the shift in question had the primary function of 'attenuating class antagonism' in general, in all capitalistically advanced as well as underdeveloped countries, in addition it had a specific function, too. It consisted in dangling the carrot of becoming 'rich' before the capitalistically exploited masses of the dominant countries. As a result, it not only helped to obliterate the consciousness of solidarity of the metropolitan working classes with the subjected working classes, but also made acceptable the differential rate of exploitation (no matter how extreme) *inside* the dominant countries themselves, by denying the fact of exploitation and metamorphosing its *structurally necessary* manifestations into *temporary fiscal differences.*

8.7.6
Characteristically, the reformist discourse had to concentrate on '*distribution*', hypostatizing with predictable unreality the realization of 'fairer distribution' while ignoring its objective preconditions. Above all, it consistently failed to question the capitalist *structure of production* as the necessary material ground and *limit* of the postulated improvements in distribution.

Naturally, Marx had to be, again, 'superseded' (or declared to be dead) because he forcefully argued that 'distribution is itself a product of production, not only in its object, in that only the results of production can be distributed, but also in its form, in that *the specific kind of participation in production determines the specific forms of distribution*, i.e. the pattern of participation in distribution.'[793]

By contrast, the reformist conceptualizations of 'distribution', thanks to the taboo which they imposed upon themselves by declining to question the prevailing structure of production, could go no further in understanding the problems at stake than what appeared on the surface. Thus they confined their attention to arguing over the relative share of the particular social groups in the *products* to be distributed, thereby implicitly or explicitly accepting the productive parameters of the established order and the material imperatives emanating from them. For the latter must ultimately overrule all those demands for a 'fairer distribution' that cannot be reconciled with the drive for the maximization of profit, once the given structure of production is taken for granted. Marx called this approach 'the shallowest conception' in which:

> distribution appears as the distribution of *products*, and hence as further removed from and *quasi-independent of production*. But before distribution can be the distribution of products, it is: (1) the distribution of the *instruments* of production, and (2), which is a further specification of the same relation, the distribution of the members of the society among the different kinds of production. (*Subsumption of the individuals* under specific relations of production.) The distribution of products is evidently only a result of this distribution, which is comprised within the process of production itself and determines the *structure of production*. To examine production while disregarding this internal distribution within it is obviously an empty abstraction; while conversely, the distribution of products follows by itself from this distribution which forms an original moment of production.[794]

Thus, it is quite impossible to gain a strategic hold, in isolation, over any particular constituent of the complex whole under discussion. Only a dialectical grasp of the mutual determinations between production, distribution, exchange and consumption can yield an adequate understanding of each of these moments – which in reality are inextricably bound together – when considered separately in theoretical analysis. As Marx put it:

> The conclusion we reach is not that production, distribution, exchange and consumption are identical, but that they all form the members of a *totality*, distinctions within a *unity*. Production *predominates* not only over itself, in the antithetical definition of production, but *over the other moments as well*. The process always returns to production to begin anew. That exchange and consumption cannot be predominant is self-evident. Likewise, distribution as distribution of *products*; while as distribution of the *agents* of production it is itself a *moment of production*. A definite production thus determines a definite consumption, distribution and exchange as well as definite relations between these different moments. Admittedly, however, in its one-sided form, production is itself determined by the other moments. For example if the market, i.e. the sphere of exchange, expands, then production grows in quantity and the division between its different branches becomes deeper. A change in distribution changes production, e.g. concentration of capital, different distribution of the population between town and country, etc. Finally, the needs of consumption determine production. *Mutual interaction* takes place between the different moments. This is the case with every *organic whole*.[795]

Production is, therefore, not only inseparable from distribution, etc. but in fact constitutes the *übergreifendes Moment* of the whole complex of dialectical interrelations and reciprocal determinations. This is why the reformist postulate of resolving the contradictions of capital's profoundly iniquitous socioeconomic system by intervening in the sphere of product-distribution – through 'progressive taxation' and more or less easily reversible social security legislation – while leaving the given structure of production intact, *had* to fail.

Transforming the 'poor' into 'rich' while condemning them to remain in their (socially predetermined and legally safeguarded) subordinate position in the *command structure of capital* – which in the end always determines also the relative share of the various groups in the iniquitously distributed social product – turned out to be a pipe-dream everywhere. Contrary to the great postulate of distributory miracles, to be squeezed out of the conjuncturally available product, many millions of people continued to live in abject poverty even in the richest and capitalistically most advanced countries. At the same time, 'progressive taxation' turned out to be a sham even in the judgement of its honest social democratic advocates, as we have seen above.[796] And, moreover, even the basic social security provisions were constantly under threat, as they had to be, whenever the capitalist process of expansion ran into serious difficulties and 'dysfunctions'.

In any case, a theory that claims for itself *general validity* while refusing even to consider whether its propositions and postulates are *generalizable* in terms of the *global* socioeconomic interrelations whose development and permanence its particular tenets presuppose, is a *contradiction in terms*. For if one of the basic preconditions for maintaining the relative privileges of the working classes in the capitalistically advanced countries is the continued super-exploitation of their counterparts in the 'under-developed world', in that case it is not only a theoretical absurdity but also an obscenity to predicate the general proposition that, as a result of the beneficial workings of 'reformed capitalism', the 'poor' are going to become 'rich' in due course. All the more since even in the capitalistically advanced countries the real improvement in the popular masses' conditions of living is highly *selective* (i.e. differential), strictly *conjunctural* (in that it depends on the capitalist system's undisturbed functioning), and subject to qualifications necessarily arising from the particular 'advanced' country's *relative position* within the global hierarchical system of neo-imperialism.

In this sense, it was very far from accidental that reformist social democracy became oblivious to the earlier firmly held *international* concerns of the working-class movement. As Engels bitterly complained already in 1875, in the debates over the Gotha Programme, 'the principle that the workers' movement is an *international* movement is, to all intents and purposes, *completely disavowed.*'[797] As time went by, the practical disavowal of socialist internationalism became so firmly rooted that the 'internationalism' of the Second International could be only skin-deep. Thus, the consequences of the imperial venture for a long period of development of the Western working-class movement had to be quite devastating.

8.7.7
To be sure, under the new conditions the earlier, rather small, socialist groups and organizations could become *mass* parties, in their *national* setting, as Lenin had pointed out. But the price they had to pay for such growth was the loss of their global perspective and radical stance. For the two were (and will remain) inextricably tied together. Socialist radicalism was feasible only if the antagonist of capital could assess the potentialities as well as the inescapable structural limitations of its adversary from a global standpoint.

Under the historical conditions of the new imperial drive, however, nationalistic reformism constituted the general trend in the working-class movement to which there were only very few exceptions. As to the exceptions themselves, they could arise mainly as a result of the complicating circumstance of *dependent development*, as in the case of Russia, for instance. Russia's dependent capitalist development – in conjunction with the repressive political anachronism of the Tsarist regime that, unlike its Western counterparts, offered no peace and parliamentary accommodation to the working classes – provided a more favourable ground for a radical socialist movement. But precisely on account of these rather special circumstances the roads had to be divided for a long time to come.

The Russian socialist movement, as the revolutionary movement of a mass-oriented but tightly organized political *vanguard*, inevitably had to adapt itself to the specificities of its sociohistorical setting; just as the legalized and mass-vote-oriented parliamentary parties of Western Social Democracy articulated their strategic tenets in accordance with the political demands arising from the complicated, indeed contradictory material interests of their economically much more advanced and imperialistically poised national predicament.

Ideology alone could not bridge the cleavage that objectively separated these movements in terms of the different *degrees* of development of their countries; of their relatively privileged or dependent *type* of development; of the more or less favoured *position* which the particular countries concerned occupied in the global system of imperialist hierarchies; of the character of the respective *states* as developed over a long historical period; and of the feasible *organizational* structures of the socioeconomic and political/cultural transformation that could be envisaged within the framework of the established (or inherited) material base and its complex superstructure in each particular country. This is why Lenin's remarks in the aftermath of the Russian revolution, depicting the latter as the model and as the 'inevitable and near future' of the capitalistically advanced Western countries, had to turn out to be so hopelessly optimistic, whereas Rosa Luxemburg's words that 'in Russia the problem could only be posed; it could not be solved in Russia' stood the test of time.

The difficulties became particularly acute a few years after the first world war, following the defeat of the uprisings outside Russia. For once the 'revolutionary wave' receded and the capitalist regimes on the losing side of the war became relatively stable again, the cleavage mentioned above – which in the immediate after-war situation not only *seemed to be*, but for the brief historical moment of the end-of-the-war collapse of the defeated regimes (though decidedly not of the victors who could count on the spoils of the war) *actually was* much narrower – widened enormously, resulting in a breach much greater than ever before.

The temptation to bridge it through *ideology* in the newly formed Communist Parties of the Third International became irresistible. All the more since the material structures of *development* and *underdevelopment* asserted themselves in the world with increasing severity, rather than diminishing in importance. Western capitalist countries had some objective possibilities open to them through which they were able – for a relatively long historical period – to *displace* (though by no means to *resolve*) their contradictions. This in its turn made the revolutionary discourse of the leading left intellectuals of the Third International in the West very problematical, as Lukács later self-critically admitted, characterizing his own position, together with that of his comrades associated with the periodical *Communism*, as 'messianic utopianism'.[798] For they tended to ignore the objective possibilities at the disposal of their historical antagonist, greatly underrating capital's 'staying power' in their insistence that 'the actual strength of capitalism has been so greatly weakened that . . . *Only ideology stands in the way*'.[799]

Lenin's own discourse was quite distinct even when in the fight against reformist opportunism he laid the stress on ideology, in that he addressed himself to people who had to cope with the problems and contradictions of a very different setting. The two basic factors of his socioeconomic and political predicament mentioned above – the burden of dependent capitalist development in Russia and the extreme repressive measures of the Tsarist police state – made his strategy viable under the circumstances. Yet, even in his case the advocacy of the *clandestine* form of party organization as the universally valid guarantor of the correct ideology and strategy, to be applied also in Germany and elsewhere in the West, and later his direct ideological appeal to the model character of the Russian revolution, had their insuperable dilemmas. Once the strategic orientation of '*socialism in one country*' prevailed in Russia after Lenin's death, the general line of the Third International – which continued to insist on the model character of Soviet developments – was in fact a contradiction in terms. It was therefore not in the least surprising that the Third International should come to the sorry end which it eventually reached.

8.7.8

The failure to engage in a thorough analysis of Western capitalist developments, adopting instead the proposition according to which the Russian model represented the 'near and inevitable future' of capitalism in general, brought with it some truly peculiar conclusions even in the case of such outstanding and profoundly committed revolutionary intellectuals as Lukács. With regard to the question of legal or illgal forms of action he asserted in *History and Class Consciousness* that:

> The question of legality or illegality reduces itself for the Communist Party to *a mere question of tactics*, even to a question to be resolved on the *spur of the moment*, one for which it is scarely possible to lay down general rules as decisions have to be taken on the basis of *immediate expediencies*.[800]

At the same time, Lukács revised his earlier enthusiasm for Rosa Luxemburg's position and reinterpreted some of her views in such a way that they bore no resemblance to her actual statements. Thus, concerning the possible change of capitalistic structures into socialist ones, he attributed to her the view that capitalism is 'amenable to such change "through legal devices" within the framework of capitalist society'.[801] In fact she had only scorn for such an idea, putting into relief in the most graphic way the absurdity of *Bernstein* looking for legislatively effective 'collars' where none could be found.[802] Worse still, Lukács also asserted – and to give it greater weight he even italicized – the most surprising proposition of all, according to which Rosa Luxemburg '*imagines the proletarian revolution as having the structural forms of bourgeois revolutions*'.[803] Yet, as a matter of fact, she repeated again and again that 'history is not going to make our revolution an easy matter like the bourgeois revolutions. In those revolutions it sufficed to overthrow that official power at the centre and to replace a dozen or so of persons in authority. But we have to work from beneath. Therein is displayed the mass character of our revolution, one which aims at transforming the *whole structure of society*.'[804]

This was not an accidental misreading on Lukács's part; nor indeed the result of 'opportunistic capitulation to party orthodoxy', as often claimed. It was, rather, the consequence of not giving sufficient weight to the fact that the *material ground of solidarity* had been shattered at the turn of the century. No *ideological* counter-moves could put things right in this respect while leaving the material ground itself intact.

Nor was it really feasible to remedy the situation by political *organizational* efforts alone. Not even by the best possible ones. For the great difficulty which the socialist movement had to face concerned the fundamental socioeconomic metabolism of the global capitalist system and the *organic* determinations involved in it. ('Organic' in the sense in which Marx used the term in our quotation above from the *Grundrisse*.) No direct ideological appeal to the consciousness of the proletariat could, so to speak, 'jump the gun' of such objective developments, nullifying or overruling thereby the organic character of the developments in question, when capital could still find vast outlets for displacing its contradictions on the basis of its *global ascendancy*, notwithstanding the setbacks it suffered through the victory of the Russian revolution.

Characteristically, therefore, even the *organizational* questions tended to be reduced to *ideological* concerns. The Party was defined as the carrier of the purely 'ascribed' or 'imputed class consciousness of the proletariat', and the latter was described as follows:

> By relating consciousness to the whole of society it becomes possible to *infer* the thoughts and feelings which men *would have* in a particular situation if they were *able* to assess both it and the interests arising from it in their impact on immediate action and on the whole structure of society. That is to say, it would be possible to *infer* the thoughts and feelings *appropriate* to their objective situation.... Class consciousness consists in fact of the *appropriate and rational* reactions '*imputed*' [*zugerechnet*] to a particular *typical position* in the process of production.[805]

Accordingly, the Party was idealized like this:

> the Party is *assigned* the sublime role of bearer of the class consciousness of the proletariat and the conscience of its historical vocation.... Class consciousness is the 'ethics' of the proletariat ... the Party is the historical em-

bodiment and the *active incarnation* of class consciousness . . . the visible and *organized incarnation* of [proletarian] class consciousness.[806]

In the same way, Lukács's attempt to ascribe to ideology the crucial role everywhere, dominated his diagnosis of the unfolding socioeconomic processes as well:

> With the crises of the War and the postwar period . . . the idea of a 'planned' economy has gained ground at least among the more progressive elements of the bourgeoisie. . . . When capitalism was *still expanding* it rejected every sort of social organization . . . If we compare that with current attempts to harmonize a 'planned' economy with the class interests of the bourgeoisie, we are forced to admit that what we are witnessing is the *capitulation of the class consciousness of the bourgeoisie before that of the proletariat*. Of course, the section of the bourgeoisie that accepts the notion of a 'planned' economy does not mean by it the same as does the proletariat; it regards it as a *last attempt to save capitalism* by driving its internal contradictions to breaking-point. Nevertheless this means *jettisoning the last theoretical line of defence*. (As a strange counterpart to this we may note that at just this point in time certain sectors of the proletariat *capitulate before the bourgeoisie* and adopt this, the most problematical form of bourgeois [party] organization.) With this the whole existence of the bourgeoisie and its culture is plunged into *the most terrible crisis*. . . . This *ideological crisis* is an unfailing sign of decay. The bourgeoisie has already been thrown on the defensive; however aggressive its weapons may be, it is fighting for self-preservation. *Its power to dominate has vanished beyond recall.*[807]

The historical fact that the 'strange counterpart' to the 'capitulation of the class consciousness of the bourgeoisie before that of the proletariat' had arisen not 'at just this point in time' but at least three decades before the 'postwar period' did not seem to matter to Lukács's diagnosis. Nor did he attempt to explain what caused it.

Similarly, he did not feel the need to undertake a serious analysis of the global capitalist economy and its recent trends of development within their own terms of reference. His ideology-oriented discourse provided both the diagnosis and the solutions in strictly ideological/theoretical terms: as the 'jettisoning of the last line of *theoretical defence*' and the '*ideological crisis*' resulting from it.

However, since the paradoxical 'strange counterpart' to the ideological crisis of the bourgeoisie was conceptualized in the same way, the solution to this paradox was theorized in the same spirit, within ideology. It was asserted that:

> The stratifications within the proletariat that lead to the formation of the various labour parties and of the Communist Party are *no objective*, economic stratifications in the proletariat but simply stages in the development of its class consciousness.[808]

Consequently, the possible solution to the identified problems could only be defined by Lukács in ideological/organizational terms, as 'the *conscious*, *free action* of the *conscious vanguard* itself ... the overcoming of the *ideological crisis*, the struggle to acquire the correct proletarian class consciousness.'[809]

As to the paradox of the 'strange counterpart' itself, Lukács's answer conformed to the same pattern. It was given in the form of assigning to political organization the *ideological mission* of rescuing 'the great mass of the proletariat which is instinctively revolutionary but has not reached the stage of clear consciousness'[810] from the hands of its opportunistic leadership.

Thus, the importance of the objective factors was consistently minimized by Lukács in order to enhance the plausibility of his direct ideological appeal to an idealized proletarian class consciousness and its 'active, visible and organized incarnation' in the party. The crisis of the capitalist system was exaggerated out of all proportion so as to suggest that, had it not been for the 'minds of the workers', the established order could not sustain itself any longer. This is how Lukács himself put it:

> The crisis-ridden condition of capitalism makes it increasingly difficult to relieve the pressure coming from the proletariat by making minute concessions. Escape from the crisis, the 'economic' solution to the crisis can only come through the intensified exploitation of the proletariat. For this reason the tactical theses of the Third Congress very rightly emphasise that 'every mass strike tends to translate itself into a civil war and a direct struggle for power.'
>   But it only tends to do. And the fact that this tendency has not yet become reality even though *the economic and social preconditions were often fulfilled,* that precisely is the *ideological crisis of the proletariat.* This ideological crisis manifests itself on the one hand in the fact that the *objectively extremely precarious position of bourgeois society* is endowed, *in the minds of the workers* with all its erstwhile stability; in many respects the proletariat is still caught up in the old capitalist forms of thought and feeling. On the other hand, the *bourgeoisification of the proletariat* becomes institutionalized in the Menshevik workers' parties and in the unions they control.[811]

In this way, the neglect of the material factors gave the illusion to Lukács that the economic and social preconditions of revolutionary transformation were '*often fulfilled*' and only the 'minds of the workers' had to be modified by the 'active and visible incarnation of their class consciousness' in order to gain victory over the '*objectively extremely precarious* condition of bourgeois society'. The historically produced and objectively sustained stability (i.e. the successful pre-war imperial drive and the post-1919 re-stabilization and expansion) of Western capitalist society was brushed aside by Lukács as devoid of real existence, in that allegedly it existed only 'in the minds of the workers'. Likewise, the manifold objective stratifications within the working class were denied an objective status and were described, instead, (somewhat mysteriously, on the model of Weberian 'typology'), as 'stages' in the self-development of proletarian class consciousness. As a result of this approach, the historical task of 'what is to be done' had to be de-

fined as the work of consciousness upon consciousness. This is how Lukács
– one of the most original and truly dialectical thinkers of the century –
ended up arguing with undialectical one-sideness that the 'ideological
crisis' of the proletariat 'must be solved *before* a practical solution to the
world's economic crisis can be found'.[812]

8.7.9
In our own age, the reconstitution of international solidarity, in accordance
with its fundamentally altered material ground, is one of the greatest challenges facing the socialist movement everywhere. For, to take a recent
example, the difficulties which the British miners had to cope with during
their one-year-long strike could not be entirely divorced even from the
indifferent attitude of the Polish Solidarnosc movement.[813] Similar interconnections can be identified in virtually every field of production and
exchange. Thus, if super-exploitatively produced and therefore highly
profitable South African coal exports cause unemployment in Europe
(including Britain), or if Japanese steel imports from South Korea result
in the closure of major steel plants in Japan, all this shows that the international connections and operations of global capital can produce extremely problematical consequences even for the working class of the up
until quite recently relatively well protected and privileged metropolitan
countries.

Many years ago Rosa Luxemburg pointed out that 'in refuting the existence of the *class struggle*, the Social Democracy has denied the very basis
of its own existence.'[814] While for several decades the reformist attenuation
of the class struggle objectively suited the strategies of Western capital-
expansion in the world arena, and thus the social democratic denial of the
very basis of its own existence could remain *latent*, the structural crisis of
capital brings with it very unpleasant surprises for the 'forward march of
social democratic labour'. It *activates* the innermost contradiction of social
democratic existence which for so long could remain latent. For the class
struggle – in a multiplicity of its forms – simply refuses to go away and
thereby conform to the wishful strategies of reformist parliamentarism.
This is why the structural crisis of capital is simultaneously and inseparably
also the crisis of Western Social Democracy.

With this, the question of how to make decisions, in the interest of the
working class as the *effectively ruling majority* of the country – a question
that earlier seemed to be automatically settled by way of uncritical references to the parliamentary framework as such – suddenly reappeared
again on the horizon, in view of the growing difficulties of global capital-
expansion and the inevitable repercussions of the latter for labour even
in the capitalistically most advanced countries. In this respect, too, Rosa
Luxemburg characterized the self-imposed difficulties of the social democratic movement, together with their feasible solution, in a striking way:

The party of Lenin was the only one which grasped the mandate and duty of a truly revolutionary party and which, by the slogan – 'All power in the hands of the proletariat and peasantry' – insured the continued development of the revolution.

Thereby the Bolsheviks solved the famous problem of 'winning a majority of the people,' which problem has ever weighed on the German Social-Democracy like a nightmare. As bred-in-the-bone disciples of parliamentary cretinism,[815] these German Social-Democrats have sought to apply to revolutions the home-made wisdom of the *parliamentary nursery:* in order to carry anything, you must first have a majority. The same, they say, applies to revolution: first let's become a 'majority'.

The true *dialectic of revolutions*, however, stands this wisdom of parliamentary moles on its head: *not through a majority to revolutionary tactics, but through revolutionary tactics to a majority* – that is the way the road runs.[816]

Naturally, this answer implied the existence of *objectively favourable* conditions, even if a dialectical thinker would never make a fetish out of 'objectivity' in human affairs. For the seminal importance of conscious strategic interventions in the course of social developments cannot be overstated as regards the 'dialectic of revolutions' and the 'dialectic of history'. Indeed, without such interventions the hopes of progressive historical forces invariably turn out to be disappointed expectations, as they are dashed by the – mechanically conceived – 'force of circumstance' to which they believe simply to submit in the absence of viable alternatives, while in fact they themselves actively contribute to the triumph of 'bad objectivity' through their submission to it.

Nevertheless, only voluntaristic subjectivism can ignore the real weight of objectivity, usually with disastrous consequences, as the still far from wholly superseded Stalinist violations of the 'dialectic of history' abundantly testify.

The social democratic 'derailment' of the early trends of international socialism had the strength of immense material forces and corresponding vested interests behind it, even if the benefits were on the whole confined to the 'metropole of capital' (Marx), i.e. England at the time, and to a few other capitalistically advanced countries. As we have seen, the 'principle that the workers' movement is an international movement was completely disavowed', and with it the perspective of international solidarity abandoned. Yet, this fateful development came about not as a matter of the irrational arbitrariness of reformist/opportunist leaders, but in close conjunction with the emerging material changes.

We have also seen Marx's complaint that although English capitalist developments represented a very high degree of '*maturity and universality*', and therefore 'the English possess all the necessary *material conditions* of the revolution', nevertheless, 'what they are lacking in is the *spirit of generalization* and revolutionary passion'.[817] Again, this circumstance could not be explained by something like the influence of *philosophical empiricism* (with which the English workers had very little contact) but by two other, fundamentally different, factors.

First, by the circumstance that from the 'maturity and universality' of capital no straight line follows to the 'maturity and universality' (i.e. the international socialist consciousness and corresponding institutional/ organizational articulation) of the working-class movement itself. On the contrary, so long as the necessarily contradictory 'maturity and universality' of capital – this 'living contradiction' (Marx) – can offer significant material rewards to the national working classes of the 'metropoles of capital', at the expense of their brothers in other countries, the ideological parameters of emancipation become extremely confused. Under such circumstances the *partial* interests of self-oriented immediacy prevail over against the *general* interests of the working class as a whole, considered in its capacity as the historical agency of socialist emancipation.

And second, by the fact that – as a matter of powerful historical determinations – England's 'maturity and universality' (on account of being the dominant capitalist country at the time of Marx's complaints) was inseparable from her leading (indeed over-powering) role in the global expansion of the 'new imperialism'. Thus, the missing 'spirit of generalization' in the English workers, and the likewise missing socialist/internationalist 'revolutionary passion' that would have been appropriate to such spirit, were in fact well in keeping with the scope provided for their movement by the contradictory 'maturity and universality' of imperialistically expanding English capital. Indeed, the latter succeeded in welding the destiny of its national labour force – for the entire historical period of the undisturbed imperial drive – to the dynamics of its own needs and interests.

If, therefore, one takes seriously the idea of reconstituting the much needed international solidarity of the socialist movement on the globally changed material ground of postwar capitalism, it is necessary to take note of and respond to the objective material transformations that have actually taken place within the international framework of capital. For the far-reaching material changes of the postwar period offer a new margin of action for the people on the radical wing of the movement who maintain their interest in the potentialities of socialist emancipation.

8.7.10
One of the thorniest issues in this respect concerns the relationship between nationalism and internationalism. It also illustrates how the perverse 'universality' of capital can directly contradict and undermine the solidarity of the exploited and oppressed, preventing thereby the emergence of the rival universality of socialist internationalism which is of necessity diametrically opposed to capital's interests.

Clearly, the idea of socialism without internationalism is a contradiction in terms. At the same time, it would be very naive to postulate the easy resolution of the objective conflicts of interest that favour the acceptance of capital's perverse 'universality' – and phoney 'internationalism' – by the metropolitan working classes.

Those who in the 'Third World' find themselves at the receiving end of capital's global system of hierarchies and dependencies, have a much more direct stake in this matter than their counterparts in the capitalistically advanced countries. They are forced to fight for genuine *national* emancipation – in contrast to the rather vacuous formal/political devices of the 'post-colonial' arrangements that leave the formerly established material structures of domination intact – whenever they raise the issue of *economic* emancipation. However, to question the substantive power relations of the 'post-colonial' arrangements is extremely difficult, both in political and in cultural/ideological terms. For, as Constantino rightly argues:

> The advanced nations of the world naturally do not view with favour the growth of nationalism in a Third World country although, shrewdly, they encourage its more neutral or harmless manifestations in the cultural field as an escape valve for the discontent of dominated peoples. What the powerful capitalist states are encouraging is the concept of *internationalism*, the idea that they and the Third World nations are economically interdependent in a mutually beneficial way and must therefore stand together politically. Just as the generations of Filipinos under American rule were brainwashed into believing that their status as an agricultural, raw-material exporting country was the only proper one for them, the Filipinos of today are beguiled into believing that the only path to progress open for them is that of modernization through a dependent industrialization. Western cultural institutions and mass media generally reinforce all these concepts as they continue Westernizing the cultures of the Third World.
>
> Subtly, the idea of nationalism is downgraded as no longer relevant, or it is associated with its past jingoistic manifestations in other countries such as Germany and Japan.
>
> There are Filipinos who think they must make a choice between nationalism and internationalism or that one should be subordinated to the other. It is necessary to know the correct interconnection of the two. Internationalism is a feeling of kinship with the peoples of the world, not with their rulers or their governments. Nationalism is the Filipinos' consciousness of their interests. To be a good nationalist one must share the goals of other peoples for a better life, in effect making one a *real internationalist*. But before one can be a good internationalist, one must be a nationalist first, taking into consideration the welfare of one's own people before being able to help others – but ever conscious of the fact that the larger goals of a whole people *preclude the exploitation of others*. In other words, the internationalist content of nationalism lies in the *egalitarian aspect of world brotherhood*, and the nationalist content of internationalism lies in the concept of *national sovereignty* within the present system of world states and in its defence against imperialist onslaughts.[818]

Thus, the real issue is not nationalism *or* internationalism, but *what kind* of nationalism *and* internationalism can – *together* – advance the cause of socialist emancipation. For the dialectic of their interrelations makes it

CONSTITUTION OF SOLIDARITY 363

impossible to fill with content the demand for socialist internationalism without taking care of the vital needs of the national working classes; and vice versa, the pursuit of nationalistic objectives at the expense of other peoples can only generate (ultimately self-destructive) antagonisms, even if its immediate results happen to be favourable to the forces that embark on such ventures.

The point is that 'nationalism' and 'internationalism' are not disembodied values or abstract imperatives of impotent 'ought', but materially anchored *categories of social being*, just like 'capital' and 'labour' are. They are not the subjective invention of more or less enlightened individuals, set before the rest of society for the purpose of emulation, but the necessary products of social being, made possible only at a certain stage of its historical development.

Nationalism as an elemental political/ideological force capable of mobilizing (for better or worse) vast numbers of people, first appears with the bourgeoisie in its ascendancy. As such it greatly contributes to the successful breakthrough and progressive completion of the capitalist socioeconomic order. In this original bourgeois form, nationalism has no meaningful, materially grounded connection with internationalism. Thus, given its inescapably conflict-ridden structural setting, determined by the imperatives of capital-expansion, it can lead to the most extreme forms of destructive conflagration, as the annals of modern history – particularly in the twentieth century – testify.

By contrast, attempts at articulating the principle of socialist internationalism first appear in the turmoil of the French Revolution and in the aftermath of the Napoleonic wars, emanating from the social being of the rising working classes. In this case, again, we are not dealing merely with an 'idea', discovered by some exceptional individuals, to which reality is supposed to conform as a matter of abstract moral imperative. Socialist internationalism is very different from ideas like the religiously advocated but in reality never even approximated 'universal brotherhood of men', or the loudly proclaimed but with regard to their content vacuous 'Rights of Man' to which the real world of capital quite simply refuses to pay other than purely rhetorical lip-service. For internationalism is the categorial reflection of fundamental material determinations in the innermost structure of capitalist production which *tends*, in a most *antagonistic* way, towards its *global integration*.

Thus, precisely because the necessary modality of such integration is *antagonistic*, bringing with it the prospect of ever-escalating conflicts and disasters – hence the stark alternative of 'socialism or barbarism' – the category of *internationalism* as rooted in the reality of social being *cannot* be conceptualized from the standpoint of the bourgeoisie. For no social class whose existence and privileges depend on the antagonistic exploitation of the other classes in its society can acknowledge the resolution of the antagonisms that sustain it, and thereby the end of its own social order. This is so irrespective of whether we have in mind the ruling classes of slavery, or the aristocracy of the feudal order, or the bourgeoisie of the capitalist system. Their representatives, from Menenius Agrippa to the present, can recognize the antagonisms of their society – antagonisms that of necessity point *beyond* their society – only to the extent to which they can be *attenuated*, so as to be successfully *contained* within the existing socioeconomic parameters. This is why, given the structural limitations intrinsic to the dominant material interests, the standpoint of capital can only produce the bastardized concepts of pseudo-internationalism at the roots of which one finds the reality of *imperialist expansionism* (in one form or another) and the most callous economic exploitation – nay, if need be, even the most brutal political/military repression – of other peoples.

By contrast, from the historical vantage point of labour – to be sure, not in its particularistic immediacy, but in the sense in which the potentialities of labour represent the *hegemonic alternative* to capital's structural order – the category of internationalism can be adequately conceptualized. For internationalism becomes visible from the standpoint of labour not as a '*desideratum*', however desirable, but as an objective tendency of socioeconomic and cultural/political development towards cooperatively run global production and interchange. As such, this category of social being both *reflects* the *objective reality* of the self-assertive and inexorably expanding capitalist forces, with all their dynamism wedded to internal antagonisms, and at the same time *envisages* the necessary *transcendence* of the given order, as the potential resolution of the destructive antagonisms.

The problems facing the historically given forces of labour are, accordingly, twofold. Inasmuch as these forces are located, in more or less privileged positions, at determinate points in the established structures of globally articulated capital, they themselves reflect (and as a rule also internalize) the constraints and contradictions of their predicament, as tied to the fortunes of their national capital. (Social democratism as a historical phenomenon is the objective manifestation of such contradictions and constraints.) At the same time, however, inasmuch as they find themselves, of necessity, at the receiving end of capital's adaptive measures and irrepressible contradictions, they are forced to look in the direction of the potential resolution of the prevailing antagonisms, i.e. in the direction not of their temporary *attenuation* but of their practically viable *transcendence* that lies beyond the perimeters of the established order.

The evidence required for the historical viability of labour's quest to go beyond capital is partly only implicit, in a negative way, in the constantly erupting contradictions and disturbances of the given productive system. More importantly, however, it is also provided – in a tangible, and in that sense 'positive' way – by the emerging structures of global capital, such as the ever-more dominant monopolistic formations of the 'advanced capitalistic' transnational corporations, for instance. To be sure, developments of this kind are still very far from being fully accomplished, and their further extension may bring with it additional problems for labour. Nevertheless, by their very nature they also open up new possibilities for emancipatory action, including the necessary, even if difficult and painful reconstitution of the material ground of solidarity.

We shall return to this problem presently. But before we do, it is necessary to say a few concluding words about the social democratic derailment of the socialist movement.

What needs stressing in the present context concerns the question of *what kind* of nationalism and internationalism can contribute to the realization of socialist aims. For as soon as Western Social Democracy capitulates to bourgeois nationalism, and thereby simultaneously loses its own international dimension in exchange for the benefits conferred upon it by the imperial venture (as it happened, in fact, at the outbreak of the first world war), the condition of 'denying the very basis of its own existence' – by abandoning the class struggle – is further aggravated. From that moment on, no matter for how long the self-destructive implications of this condition may remain hidden, Western Social Democracy plays its role in the political arena by courtesy of capital of which it ceased to be a historical antagonist. This is so irrespective of how often Western Social Democratic parties are allowed to form the government, from Ramsay Macdonald to Harold Wilson (not to mention Giuseppe Saragat and Bettino Craxi), tangibly demonstrating on every occasion the wisdom of Rosa Luxemburg's assertion about the only meaningful sense of 'majority' for socialists. Namely, that 'not through a majority to revolutionary tactics, but through revolutionary tactics to a majority – that is the way the road runs.'

It is, therefore, quite logical on the part of the British Prime Minister, Margaret Thatcher, to boast openly after her last electoral victory about her design and ability to get rid of socialism forever, under circumstances when the ruling class sees little use for indulging in parliamentary compromises with social democratic parties even over matters of secondary or marginal importance, just as she and her colleagues boasted about 'seeing the miners off' three years ago. However, given the standpoint of the class which she represents, she fails to perceive the total contradiction between the two statements. For the one-year-long British miners' strike itself (and many others beside, both before and since) demonstrate that 'seeing the social democratic parties off' is not the same thing as suppressing the inner antagonisms of the capital system and eliminating the historical agencies involved in the drive for socialist emancipation.

The periodic eruption of class conflicts is with us more than ever before, even if by the nature of such struggles, and the sacrifices involved in the actions of those who challenge the established order, they can seldom assume the dramatic form of a one-year-long mass strike. Nevertheless, the fact is that even defiant working-class actions of such magnitude – quite unimaginable in the distant and not so distant past – take place *90 years* after Western Social Democracy first denied the existence of class struggle, and with it also the basis of its own existence.

Likewise, the need for international solidarity in the socialist movement today is greater than ever, 113 years after Engels complained that with the emerging trends of social democratic accommodation 'the principle that the workers' movement is an international movement is, to all intents and purposes, completely disavowed'.

Nor are we facing here the opposition between impotent moralistic 'desiderata' and the 'hard realities' of capital's insuperable socioeconomic order in the face of which the only sensible thing to do is to adopt the 'new realism' of (100-year-old) social-democratic accommodation. For both the class struggle and the demand for international solidarity are *materially* sustained. They are grounded in and reproduced by not only the irrepressible antagonisms of the capital system, but also by the tangible productive and organizational structures through which that system *is* already, as well as is still in the process of *being*, globally articulated, and without which it cannot possibly function. Thus, capital as 'the living contradiction' sees to it that, for as long as the capital system itself survives, neither the class struggle as such, nor the globally diffused and still reinforced productive structures of the system – which on the one hand make the class struggle constantly erupt, and on the other increase its historical chances of success – can 'go away' in order to suit the convenience of *'conflict-attenuation'*.

8.7.11

Two centuries ago Immanuel Kant made a heroic attempt to come to terms with the contradictions of the emerging – in his view globally interconnected – new social order and superimpose upon them the dimension of morality. This is how he argued his conception of a purposeful and benevolent 'nature' (one of his terms for 'providence' in human affairs) which he saw at work in the natural and historical world around him:

> The narrower or wider community of *all nations* on earth has in fact progressed so far that a violation of law and right in *one* place is felt in *all* others. Hence the *idea of a cosmopolitan or world law* is not a fantastic and utopian way of looking at law, but a necessary completion of the unwritten code of constitutional and international law to make it a *public law of mankind*. Only under this condition can we flatter ourselves that we are continually approaching *eternal peace*.
>
> No one less than the great artist nature (*natura daedala rerum*) offers such a guarantee. Nature's mechanical course evidently reveals a *teleology:* to *produce harmony from the very disharmony of men even against their will*. If this teleology ... is considered in the light of its usefulness for the evolution of the world, it will be called *providence* ... The relation and integration of

these factors into the end (the moral one) which *reason directly prescribes* is very sublime in theory, but is axiomatic and well founded in practice, e.g. in regard to the concept of a *duty toward eternal peace* which that mechanism promotes.[819]

Appealing to the idea that divine teleology was inherent in the mechanism of 'provident' nature was a necessary step in the Kantian philosophy. For it enabled the author both to retain the bourgeois conception of unalterably disharmony- and war-provoking 'human nature' (Kant's version of the Hobbesian *bellum omnium contra omnes*), and to reconcile it with his moral postulate of a harmonious and eternally peaceful 'cosmopolitan' world order.

Kant knew full well that without such 'evidence' and materially sustaining power – to which one could point in the world of 'nature' – all discourse on the 'higher goal' of human existence would be appropriate only to a 'state of angels', and totally impotent as regards real human beings who are 'incapable of so sublime a constitution'.[820] This is why he had to insist in his reflections on the paradoxical relationship between 'incorrigible human nature' and the 'gradually unfolding' as well as morally commendable cosmopolitan world order that:

> Nature comes to the aid of this revered, but *practically ineffectual general will* which is founded in reason. It does this by the *selfish propensities* themselves, so that it is only necessary to *organize the state well* (which is indeed within the ability of man), and to direct these forces *against each other* in such wise that *one balances the other* in its devastating effect, or even suspends it. Consequently the result for reason is as if both selfish forces were *non-existent*. Thus man, although not a morally good man, is compelled to be a *good citizen*.[821]

Kant viewed – and welcomed – the promise of the English industrial revolution, together with the anticipated benefits of Adam Smith's 'commercial spirit', from a great geographic distance and from the highly abstract vantage point of his transcendental philosophy. Not surprisingly, therefore, his evaluation of the emerging trends of development and the forces behind them had to turn out to be rather problematical in the light of actual historical changes. He perceived with real insight that the 'trading nations ... simply identify visiting with *conquest*. ... In East India (Hindustan) they brought in foreign mercenaries, under the pretense of merely establishing trading posts. These mercenary troops brought suppression of the natives, inciting the several states of India to extended wars against each other.'[822] Yet, from the standpoint that produced his idealist moral postulate in the spirit of which he could anticipate the establishment of the realm of the 'eternal peace', he had to fail in his attempt to grasp the real dynamism of the socioeconomic forces whose 'evil' manifestations he was so eager to leave behind in the course of historical development. In

368 THE POWER OF IDEOLOGY

accordance with his morally inspired wishful thinking, Kant minimized their power and chances of success, arguing that

> The *worst* (or viewed from the standpoint of a *moral* judge the *best*) is that the European nations are not even able to enjoy this violence. All these trading companies are on the point of an *approaching collapse*; the sugar islands, which are the seat of the most cruel and systematic slavery, *do not produce a yield.*[823]

If 'the worst' was really 'the best' when viewed from the vantage point of a 'moral judge', then from the same standpoint provident nature itself could be counted upon to rectify the impact of the fundamental destructive contradictions in and through the lawfully ordered global relationship between states, while leaving the bourgeois propensities of 'human nature' in charge of everyday matters in 'civil society'. For 'nature's care' was said to have sent even *driftwood* to the inhospitable arctic regions with a provident purposefulness behind it, 'since without this material the inhabitants could neither build boats and weapons, nor huts in which to dwell.'[824] Indeed, provident nature, according to Kant, arranged things right from the beginning in such a way that it provided, most appropriately, the agile *horse* for men to tame and to domesticate as 'the first instrument of warfare among all the animals', keeping the much less mobile *elephant* wisely in reserve for a later time, 'when established states made greater luxury possible'.[825]

This conception had more than a touch of Dr Pangloss about it, even if it was infinitely more subtle in the characterization of the conditions under which the postulated realm of the 'eternal peace' should be realized. Besides, after the French Revolution it was possible to hold such views, for a while, with relatively greater historical justification than the target of Voltaire's irony could do so before it.

Nevertheless, the Kantian approach had to climax in the totally idealistic harmonization of Adam Smith's benevolent 'commercial spirit' and the destructive tendencies of the unfolding global development. Accordingly, Kant offered the following solution to his own paradox:

> *Nature unites nations* which the concept of a cosmopolitan or world law would not have protected from violence and war, and it does this by *mutual self-interest*. It is the *spirit of commerce* which *cannot coexist with war*, and which sooner or later takes hold of every nation. For, since the *money power* is perhaps the most reliable among all the powers subordinate to the state's power, states find themselves impelled (though hardly by moral compulsion) to promote the noble peace and to try to avert war by mediation whenever it threatens to break out anywhere in the world. It is *as if* states were *constantly leagued for this purpose* ... In this way *nature guarantees lasting peace by the mechanism of human inclinations* ... for practical purposes the certainty [that this will come to pass] suffices and makes it *one's duty* to work toward this (not simply chimerical) state.[826]

Thus, from the standpoint of political economy shared by Kant, the 'spirit of commerce' had to be exempted from all responsibility and blame for the bitter fruits of its necessary manifestations in the exploitative practices of the 'trading nations'. Moreover, it had to be elevated to the lofty status of being the active promoter of 'eternal peace', on the purely fictitious ground that the 'spirit of commerce cannot coexist with war', when in reality it could (and did) provide both the *means* and the *motivation* for the most extreme forms of war and destruction, advancing not to Kant's morally commendable 'cosmopolitan world order' but, on the contrary, to the point where it can threaten the very survival of mankind.

Yet, despite the limitations of his standpoint, Kant's solutions possessed a representative significance. For he conceptualized the unfolding trend of global integration at an early stage of capitalistic developments, when the material structures at the roots of the emerging trend were still in a most flexible state, without any firm indication as to how subsequently they might be restructured and consolidated. After all, the French Revolution, for a considerable time in its turbulent history, saw the bourgeoisie and the proletariat fight side by side, on the inherited common social ground of the 'Third Estate'.

Remaining anchored to the individualistic stance of his 'practical reason', and viewing the French Revolution, just as he contemplated the English industrial revolution, from a distant land, Kant made no attempt at grasping theoretically the nettle of internal class contradictions between the bourgeoisie and labour which surfaced and intensified in France in the course of the revolution itself. Even less did he attempt to ascribe to the category of class antagonism as such a generalizable theoretical importance. At the same time and in the same way, in his assessment of the prevailing and lawfully developing relationship between states, he could see no use for the obvious alternative hypothesis to his own; namely that what the future might in fact have in store for humankind was the sharpening of national rivalries and antagonisms between states, rather than their harmonious progress towards the realm of the 'eternal peace' as prescribed by reason, sustained by one's moral duty, and guaranteed by provident nature itself through the mechanism of human inclinations.

What gave to the Kantian approach its unique character was the circumstance that the German philosopher found himself in a 'no man's land' in virtue of the not-yet-consolidated character of both the nascent material structures and the trend towards global integration. It seemed, then, that one may – indeed, that one must – opt for a solution whereby the contradictions and irrationalities of the 'old world' should be superseded for good, unblocking thereby the path of Reason so as to enable it to give proper direction to human pursuits, in a harmonious alliance with provident nature's helpful mechanism. To opt for the solution of *nationalistic particularism* had to be, thus, quite inadmissible under the circumstances.

For such a solution would have preserved the irrationality of past contradictions and forms of exploitation. The idea that the old colonialism or
imperialism of the dominant 'trading nations' might nevertheless survive,
or worse still, renew itself in an even more ruthless and all-embracing form
in the more or less distant future, seemed at the time totally inconceivable.
This is why the Kantian vision of 'eternal peace' could appear at the time
when it did, in conjunction with the postulated idea of a *cosmopolitan/
international* world order.

However, Kant's 'heroic bourgeois' ideal of the future cosmopolitan/
international world order could only be an abstract moral imperative to
which reality *had* to conform, but it refused to do so. By the time Hegel
was writing his *Philosophy of Right*, the Kantian 'no man's land' completely disappeared from the horizon. The new structures of the bourgeois
world have sufficiently consolidated themselves to make Hegel scorn the
idea that the relationship between the existing states could ever be envisaged as part of a cosmopolitan/international world order and its 'eternal
peace'. The regular eruption of conflicts and antagonisms was in evidence
everywhere. Accordingly, Hegel defined the *nation state* as the 'absolute
power on earth' which could not tolerate any infringement of – or even any
check on – its absoute sovereignty. He considered the relationship between
states by analogy with being '*in a state of nature*'. At the same time, he
characterized any attempt at regulating the relationship of autonomous
nation states, given the insuperable sovereignty of each, as being 'infected
with contingency'. No wonder, therefore, that he had to conclude that if the
particular wills of the states cannot be harmonized, 'the matter can only
be settled by *war*'.[827]

With a sense of realism verging on cynicism, Hegel could even acknowledge the organic link between the internal repressive functions of the
state and its external military enterprises, underlining that '*successful wars*
have checked *domestic unrest* and consolidated the power of the state at
home.'[828] Moreover, he was well aware of the existence of classes 'in civil
society', as well as of the need to keep the lower classes in their proper
place, in the interest of '*universal permanent capital*' and of its increase as
'the general capital'.[829]

But even this kind of 'realism' represented only another hypostatized
ideality to which reality *had* to conform but could not. For in the idealist
Hegelian conception the state as the 'ethical whole' was supposed to
subsume under itself (and thereby supersede) the contradictions of civil
society, providing us, in objectivity, with 'the true reconciliation which
discloses the state as the image and actuality of reason'.[830] Judging by
actual historical developments, there is nothing to substantiate the obliging
conformity of the antagonistic real world to the Hegelian postulate of 'the
true reconciliation'.

Thus, although both Kant and Hegel were conscious of the emerging trend of global integration under the sway of the 'commercial spirit', neither of them could conceptualize it adequately. More than three decades before Hegel, Kant could still project the vision of a cosmopolitan/ international world order, but only at the price of depriving it of its national content and real substance. By contrast, Hegel could acknowledge the facticity and substantiveness of the state's national determinations, but only at the cost of fatally infecting his characterization of the state and of its relations to other states, as well as his conception of 'world history', with extreme contingency, notwithstanding his original aspirations.[831]

Grasping the dialectical relationship between the national and the international dimension of capital's world order proved to be elusive even to these great thinkers. Focusing on one side inevitably meant emptying of content the other, or even denying its legitimate existence, and vice-versa.

The two dimensions could not be held together in a dialectical unity even in the greatest bourgeois conceptualizations, because they cannot be envisaged as harmoniously coexisting in social practice itself from the standpoint of political economy. Taken together in capitalist society, they constitute an inherently *contradictory* unity. The standpoint of political economy cannot transform the latter into a *dialectical* – i.e. practical transcendence-positing – unity. For by its very nature such a standpoint internalizes the structural constraints of the given society which objectively define the national and international dimensions of capital's world order in their irreconcilable contradictoriness. At determinate historical conjunctures one of the two sides pushes itself into the foreground, while at different times it is the other that can become dominant, depending on the prevailing conditions of socioeconomic development and the more or less accomplished state of capital's global articulation. Only the prospect of a *real* transcendence of the material antagonisms that are intrinsic to this contradictory unity can remove the undialectical one-sidedness which we have seen manifest in the conceptions of both Kant and Hegel.

8.7.12

In sharp contrast to Hegel's ideal construct according to which 'Philosophy concerns itself only with the glory of the Idea mirroring itself in the History of the World', so that it can 'reconcile Spirit with the History of the World',[832] Marx offered a perfectly straightforward definition of history. He pointed out that 'history is nothing but the succession of the separate generations, each of which uses the materials, the capital funds, the productive forces handed down to it by all preceding generations, and thus, on the one hand, *continues* the traditional activity in completely changed circumstances and, on the other, *modifies* the old circumstances with a completely changed activity.'[833]

By taking the same conception another step forward, 'world history', too, ceased to be a mysterious entity. It was made intelligible in the context of the capitalistically structured global productive and distributive processes of large-scale industry. For, according to Marx, 'large-scale industry universalized competition, established means of communication and the modern world market, subordinated trade to itself, transformed all capital into industrial capital, and thus produced the rapid circulation (development of the financial system) and the centralization of capital.... It produced *world history* for the first time, insofar as it made all civilized nations and every individual member of them *dependent* for the satisfaction of their wants on the *whole world*, thus destroying the former natural exclusiveness of separate nations.'[834]

Thus it became possible to assess the global trend of integration and its often painful consequences in a tangible way, with the aim of practically intervening in the process of development in order to bring under control its destructive dimension. For the new reality of 'world history' tended to affect directly the lives of the individuals everywhere through its material and organizational structures, and it did so in a most disconcerting way. Against this background – just as the categories of 'capital' and 'labour', or 'nationalism' and 'internationalism' – the category of 'world history' acquired its very precise meaning in terms of the clearly identifiable transformations of social being. Marx expressed the world-historical character and tangible impact of the transformations in question with a strikingly simple example:

> If in England a machine is invented which deprives countless workers of bread in India and China, and overturns the whole form of existence of these empires, this invention becomes a *world-historical fact*.[835]

All this was most important for understanding the real processes of world history and the violent 'tearing away' of the individuals all over the world from their earlier social setting through the irresistible power of globally expanding capital.

However, when Marx touched upon the question of nationalities, his discourse became problematical. For he insisted that:

> Generally speaking, large-scale industry created *everywhere the same relations between the classes* of society, and thus destroyed the peculiar features of the various *nationalities*.... While the *bourgeoisie* of each nation still retained separate national interests, large-scale industry created *a class which in all nations has the same interest* and for which *nationality is already dead*; a class which is really rid of all the old world and at the same time stands pitted against it.[836]

In truth, this judgement jumped to a conclusion that could not be sustained on the basis of material evidence. It turned a *potentiality* into *actuality* while disregarding some important aspects of its own terms of reference, as illustrated by Marx's own example of English productive developments directly affecting the social metabolism of India and China.

Our necessary departure from Marx on this issue could not be considered a matter of hindsight, since the missing qualifications concern Marx's own object of analysis. This is so because the question of the claimed identical class interests of all workers all over the world, as well as its corollary, the postulated transcendence of nationality and nationalism by the working class everywhere, necessarily involve the consideration of *reciprocity* or its absence. Clearly, however, the materially and politically effective reciprocity of fully shared interests cannot be asserted about the social reality of the working class as a whole even today, let alone under the conditions to which Marx's analysis applies.

Today the theorists of 'farewell to the working class' deny even the potentiality of fully shared class interests, not only its historically effective actuality. This is quite unjustifiable. For the potentiality in question can only be judged in terms of its proper frame of reference – i.e. the fully developed global system of capital – and not on the limited ground of a few privileged and exploitative 'advanced capitalist societies'. Nevertheless, the difficulties concerning the relationship between potentiality and actuality with regard to the historically changing predicament of the working class as a whole cannot be bypassed.

Taking Marx's own example, it is clear that there can be no question of reciprocity as regards the relevant material structures themselves. Inventions made in productively underdeveloped India and China, at the time of Marx's analysis, could not have an even remotely comparable impact on the socioeconomic metabolism of capitalistically advanced countries. In other words, they could not become 'world-historical facts' but must remain confined to the local circumstances. For, in order to assert themselves as world-historical facts, they would have to be inserted into the material setting of the countries with the highest level of productivity and prevail there successfully. The chances of success of such an enterprise are, of course, totally non-existent under the circumstances, in that even the most attractive *isolated* invention is condemned to powerlessness against the combined forces of a much more advanced *system*.

These considerations are directly relevant to understanding the relationship between solidarity and internationalism as motivating forces arising on a material ground that sustains them in an enduring way. For without its sustaining material ground socialist internationalism and solidarity could only be considered abstract 'ideals' (no matter how positively commendable) to which reality itself would have to conform as a result of the presumed power of persuasion of the advocated moral imperatives.

The genuine *potentiality* of shared values and strategic objectives by the working class as a whole can become *actuality* only when the feeling of reciprocity required for the promotion of lasting and practically viable international solidarity arises from meaningfully shared experience as far as labour's relationship to capital is concerned. This means:

First, that the material ground of solidarity itself is already (or, at least, is demonstrably in the process of becoming) so structured – through the irrepressible global articulation of capital – that *reciprocity* (in the form of capital's contradictory *reciprocal determinations*, objectively affecting all countries involved, irrespective of how privileged happens to be their position in the hierarchically interrelated neo-imperialist system) can be truly operative at the level of the fundamental productive and distributive structures and practices themselves.

Second, that the prevailing state of affairs, with all its negative implications for the dependency and structural subordination of labour, both in the 'underdeveloped' and in the 'advanced capitalist countries', is recognizable as such by social consciousness.

To illustrate the first aspect, we may think of our earlier example of Ford Philippines. Unlike the prevailing power relationships in productivity between England on the one hand, and India and China on the other, in Marx's lifetime (power relations that were later further strengthened by the political/military arrangements of the late nineteenth century colonial empires), the productive structures established by the US transnational company in the Philippines are objectively capable of producing a far from negligible economic impact not only locally, but even in the capitalistically most advanced countries, including the United States of America. The condition of *reciprocity* is, thus, very real, and sooner or later is bound to assert itself in accordance with its objective possibilities, however problematical might be its impact on the 'metropole of capital'.

However, viewed under the second aspect, the same example is far less reassuring. For so long as the US Ford worker can continue to receive for the same work *25 times* the wages of his counterpart in the factory of Ford Philippines, or wherever else (i.e. $7.50 as against 30 cents per hour), the chances of social consciousness recognizing the real state of affairs in the US are not very good. Instead, given the undisturbed functioning of the differential rate of exploitation and the corresponding vested interests, the shutter of self-complacent blindness is likely to descend in front of the American car-worker, so as to black out from his vision the possibility of perceiving the actual relations of exploitation and domination both at home (since he is, too, a victim of capital's material imperatives and reified determinations) and abroad.

Yet, it would be quite absurd to take for granted not only the absolute permanence of the differential rate of exploitation, but on top of it also the gratuitous assumption that the material structures of expatriate transnational capital, established in the former colonies on the basis of cheap labour, will always remain benevolent *vis à vis parts* of their country of origin in which some of the least profitable enterprises of the controlling transnational corporations are located.

It used to be said that 'what is good for General Motors is good for

America'. This cannot sound convincing any longer to all those parts of the United States in which the destructive impact of capital's contradictory reciprocity is being felt with increasing frequency. To take one example only, at the time of writing the city of Norwood, Ohio, is suing General Motors for the fairly large sum of 380 million dollars for 'breaking its promises' to the city. For General Motors, following its own imperatives of profit maximization, decided to pull out from Norwood, abandoning a 59-acre industrial plant to dereliction, the totality of the large workforce to the misery of unemployment, and the city finances to disaster.

Naturally, it would be very naive to expect that the capitalist state and its judiciary should rectify such grievances in the interest of the workers, whatever the outcome of this particular law-suit. What is extremely important, however, is the fact that the global expansion of capital and the integrated material structures which it produces should misfire in this – by the guardians of capital's interests totally unexpected and unwelcome – form. The material determinations of reciprocity, thus, become tangible and direct in their negative impact on the livelihood of the workers even in the most privileged capitalist countries. Workers who can no longer blame the Japanese, or the Brazilians, or someone else, for being forced to join the end of a long dole queue, are also compelled to *begin* to reflect on their 'very own' General Motors and on the acute contradiction between *its* interests and their own. No one should underrate the critical potential of such reflection. Theoreticians who have written off the 'integrated' working class in the past, might have to wake up to some major surprises as a result.

What makes things paradoxically hopeless and hopeful at the same time is that any 'negotiated settlement' of the particular kind of disputes witnessed in Norwood can only be envisaged to take place *within* (and to be constrained by) the existing structural parameters of the system itself. The outcome can amount, at best, only to a temporary palliative. For the real issue at stake concerns the underlying contradictions of the – irreconcilable – conflicts of interest. Such contradictions cannot be resolved without radically challenging, and in the last analysis replacing, capital's highly effective local rationality and global irrationality.

What is utterly hopeless in all such cases is the attempt to remedy, *post festum*, whether 'at the negotiating table' or by means of some occasional legal procedure, capital's decisions (whose extreme consequences are of necessity imposed on the workforce in one form or another, whatever the outcome of the 'negotiated settlement' or legal ruling), while at the same time accepting its *framework* (and corresponding – in unquestionable economic terms sanctioned and rationalized – *despotic rights*) of decision making. What is hopeful, nevertheless, is first, the fact itself that such formerly quite unimaginable contradictions of reciprocity should erupt with increasing frequency and intensity within the sphere of operation of advanced capital; and second, that the material ground of the workers' solidarity – on the basis of which the structural parameters of capital *can* be challenged – is being objectively reconstituted by the global integrative processes themselves. For without the latter capital cannot fulfil its controlling functions at the present juncture of history.

International solidarity, in this sense, is not an ideological imperative addressed to politically alert groups of workers. It could not be defined simply as 'the work of consciousness upon consciousness', even if the appropriate reconstitution of social consciousness is, of course, an integral part of the overall process. It is the necessary response to the objective challenge posed by the global articulation and integration of capital that in the course of twentieth-century developments (and particularly in the last few decades) acquired a most effective transnational dimension against its workforce. At the same time, it is a response made not only necessary but also materially feasible by the selfsame material structures of capital's transnational articulation which – in the absence of international solidarity – can be easily and with great efficacy used against the workers.

An example describing the complex mode of operation of a giant transnational corporation can illustrate both aspects. To quote the words of a former head of General Motors:

> If the South African assembly operation and its recently added manufacturing facilities are to function smoothly and efficiently, they must today receive a *carefully controlled and coordinated* flow of vehicle parts and components from West Germany, England, Canada, the United States, and even Australia. These must reach General Motors South Africa in the *right volume* and at the *right time* to allow an orderly scheduling of assembly without accumulation of *excessive inventories*. This is a challenging assignment which must be made to work if the investment is to be a profitable one.[837]

No doubt, the former head of General Motors is interested in stressing (and exaggerating) the heroic managerial functions of his 'challenging assignment', described in terms of pure organizational rationality and corporate profitability, which would seem to justify his annual salary – counted in millions of dollars – not only against the miserable income of those who receive only 30 cents per hour, but even against the US carworkers who might earn an hourly wage of $7.50, if not more. The class controlling function of the self-same 'challenging assignment' is left unmentioned. Yet, it happens to be of an enormous importance to the globally articulated capitalist productive system, and the real justification of the astronomic managerial salaries.

The vital class-controlling function of capital's transnationally organized productive structures consists in *minimizing the power of the workforce* in such a way that its traditional weapons – above all the *strike* weapon – lose their cutting edge, or even become totally inapplicable. Productive linkages and supply routes are consciously so designed and organized by the management of the transnational corporation that in the event of a 'local dispute' (and even of a national one) *alternative* sources can be brought into play for the purpose of strike-breaking, so as to 'bring back to its senses' the protesting labour force. Besides, in view of the fact that the productive structures and supply routes are coordinated in this eminently 'rational' way, of which the various trade union bureaucracies are made well aware in their dealings with management, 'common sense can prevail' in many cases in advance, before even contemplating the initiation of a dispute, given the uphill struggle which the workers would have to undertake on their own, in the absence of an adequate organizational framework in which they could counteract capital's transnationally extended power.

Here we must also notice the *objective complementarity* of, and the conscious *division of labour* between, private capital and the contemporary bourgeois state. For the state intervenes in the overall process with the kind of labour legislation that suits the convenience of the – changing – capitalist system. This is why the repressive anti-union laws of the recent past are far from accidental. Significantly, their principal objective is to outlaw *solidarity strikes*, which happen to be of crucial importance to big capital, both within the boundaries of any particular country and with regard to the international operations and supply-route safeguards of the transnational corporations.

Furthermore, the capitalist state can undertake, out of the pocket of the idealized general 'tax-payer', anti-labour ventures that would make bankrupt even the largest transnational companies. In this respect, the advantages of the state's intervention on the side of capital are threefold.

First, it can secure the funds necessary to sustain, over a very long period, a labour dispute that would be quite prohibitive to private corporations.

Second, it can mobilize the political/repressive apparatus of the state, including the 'objective' judiciary, to fix the odds in its own favour against the working class.

Third, it can intervene at a level of conflict beyond the reach of any particular private enterprise, and even beyond the combined capitalist forces of a whole branch of industry.

Thus, the state can heighten the chosen dispute to the point where it involves and implicates the whole of the radical wing of the socialist movement, for the purpose of undermining the combativity of the working class in its entirety.

As we have seen, the former head of General Motors excluded, in the name of pure business rationality and profitability, the practice of amassing 'excessive inventories'. In reality, of course, the managers of the transnational corporations indulge a great deal in this sin, in the interest of the class-controlling function mentioned above. In this respect, however, there is an obvious limit beyond which they cannot go, since they cannot risk 'biting off the hand that feeds them' by making their corporations bankrupt. Not even in the service of the noble cause of beating strikes.

This is where the material and political power of the capitalist state is activated with great effectiveness. The transnational corporations do not hesitate to intervene directly in the political process, both in their home countries and abroad, telling the state legislators with unashamed arrogance what kind of labour legislation they want. To quote an editorial article of the *Guardian:*

> Mr Bob Lutz, chairman of Ford of Europe, recently told the *Financial Times:* 'If we find we have major assembly facilities regardless of the country involved, which for one reason or another – perhaps *uneducated government action (giving longer holidays, a shorter working week)* or *union intransigence* – cannot be competitive, we would not shy away from a decision to *close them.*'
>
> Ford UK ... is also a substantial drain on the balance of payments, amounting to £1.3 billion in 1983 as it (quite properly from its own self interest) sourced from the cheaper imports.
>
> The Government claims not to have an industrial strategy. In fact, of course, it has one. *Privatize everything that moves and sell what you can to foreign buyers.* You don't have to be a Little Englander to realise that this is an *abdication of responsibility* which could make the *terminal decline of industry* in this country a self-fulfilling prophesy.[838]

All such talk, however, is condemned to remain a cry in the wilderness. For notwithstanding the fact that undisguised political intervention of the US Ford Corporation (even if it is called 'Ford of Europe') represents a blatantly obvious *unconstitutional blackmail*, there can be no question of making an issue of it. Rather, capitalist governments *oblige* and behave in a truly *'educated'* fashion, giving minimal holidays and trying to extend the working week (from five days to six in the case of British Coal, acting under direct government instruction), and in general by doing their very best to break *'union intransigence'*. At the same time, the transnational corporations can do whatever they please. They can blackmail with great efficacy their own labour force, compelling it by the threat of redundancy to accept settlements that maximize their profits; or, alternatively, they can indeed close down their 'unprofitable plants' whenever they are able to secure higher profitability elsewhere, as closures of car and other plants in the recent past amply demonstrate this not only in Europe (including Britain) but even in the United States.

The British Government's role in the miners' strike provides a very clear example of how the state can intervene in capital's favour. Contrary to the elementary rules of good business practice praised by the former head of General Motors, the capitalist state in Britain could plan its anti-labour action in the way of a 'carefully controlled and coordinated amassing of *excessive inventories*', with the obvious (and hardly even concealed) purpose of provoking the miners into a strike action which – given the total resources of the state – they could not win. At the same time, various measures were adopted, with considerable success, in order to divide both the miners and the working-class movement as a whole. Also, the state authorities, with the full cooperation of the judiciary, intervened in the dispute in every possible way, depriving the strikers of their legitimate claims and the National Union of Mineworkers of all its funds. In addition, massive sums were expended by the state during the one-year-long dispute – estimated at around five to six billion pounds sterling – in order to defeat the strike. And perhaps most important of all, by mobilizing the forces of international capital as well as the British state's international connections (including its ability to secure supplies of coal even from Poland), the confrontation was organized in such a way that it should put an end to 'intransigent unionism' in general, and not simply to bring a particular industrial dispute to its conclusion. Calling the miners 'the enemy within' and boasting about 'seeing them off' served the purpose of *deterrence* against radical unionism in general, whenever it might appear with unintegrable claims.

It is important to stress all this, in order to have a realistic assessment of the forces lined up against the cause of socialist emancipation. Yet, it would be quite wrong to forget the obverse side of these material power relations, and conclude that the objective chances of international solidarity are hopelessly weak today. For even if the obstacles to the reconstitution of socialist solidarity are enormous, both in strictly material and in legal/political terms, it is not too difficult to identify some powerful material and political determinations that point in the opposite direction.

First, one must stress the importance of the fact that the *international* 'harmony' of capital's diverse forces is very far from being an unproblematical one. Although 'when the chips are down' the discordant particularistic interests of the various sections of any national capital tend to coalesce around the central interest of maintaining their combined rule over society, this cannot suspend – let alone completely eliminate – the fundamental contradictions that exist between the different national (and nationally anchored transnational) capitals. It is in this respect quite telling that even the greatest bourgeois theories of the state could not succeed in going beyond the insoluble dichotomy between the noble but utterly wishful Kantian '*cosmopolitan world order*' and its idealist postulate of 'eternal peace' on the one hand, and the 'realistic' Hegelian rationalization of the 'absolute sovereignty' – as well as of the inescapably war-oriented ultimate determination – of 'universal permanent capital's' *national state*, on the other. Postwar trends towards the regional attenuation of capital's national conflicts of interest – through the European Economic Community and other cosmopolitan/international formations – can undoubtedly make some of the contradictions *latent*, without however really transcending them. At the same time, the complicated inter-state relations of the regional complexes themselves – both *within* each and in their external manifestations *vis à vis* one another – add a new dimension to the traditional capitalistic national antagonisms, even if the machinery of conflict-attenuation is constantly brought into play in order to reconcile (or, more realistically, in order to keep in a state of latency) the existing regional contradictions of interest, under the ever more contested hegemony of the dominant postwar imperialist power, the United States of America.

As far as the emerging material structures of transnational integration are concerned, the potentialities inherent in them for the constitution of international solidarity are considerable. For the '*carefully controlled and coordinated flow*' of supplies necessary for the undisturbed functioning of the various transnational corporations is in its objective determination extremely vulnerable to conscious working-class action. The imperative of securing the '*right volume*' of the required parts and materials at the '*right time*', in order to avoid the major penalty of holding '*excessive inventories*' and thereby undermining the profitability of the capitalistic transnational enterprise, is not an easy one to satisfy. This is not because of the technical and purely organizational complexities of transnational capitalist coordination, but on account of the *social conflictuality* inherent in the capital/labour relationship at all levels. Determined and adequately coordinated working-class action on an international scale can obviously have an immense impact in this respect, strategically interfering in furtherance of its own interests with the capitalistically undisturbed functioning of the global productive and distributive processes.

To be sure, what we can clearly identify here is a *potentiality* that cannot be turned into *actuality* without the articulation of the necessary *organizational* framework of international working-class solidarity. Nevertheless, this is a potentiality sustained by the *material structures* themselves which *objectively* facilitate the necessary countermoves to the 'carefully controlled and coordinated' domination of labour by capital at the present juncture of history.

For a long time, the forces of socialist emancipation were greatly handicapped by capital's ability to assume a conflict-attenuating transnational mode of functioning while denying its equivalent to its labour force trapped within the confines of various particularistic determinations and divisions. The necessity to overcome such determinations and divisions through the reconstitution of materially anchored international solidarity represents the greatest challenge to labour for the foreseeable future.

9 · IDEOLOGY AND AUTONOMY

9.1 CONCEPTIONS OF INDIVIDUAL AUTONOMY AND HUMAN EMANCIPATION

9.1.1

It is customary to treat ideology as the prime obstacle in consciousness to autonomy and emancipation. In such view, ideology becomes synonymous with self-deceiving 'false consciousness', or even with downright lies, behind which the 'truth' is concealed by seven veils, allowing access to its secrets only to the privileged 'experts' who know how to decipher the complicated meaning of tell-tale signs. As to the 'duped masses' (to use Adorno's self-pleasing expression), they are left to their own fate, condemned to remain hopelessly captive of ideology.

The dominant discourse on ideology thus becomes utterly *negative*, and the once seriously pursued quest for emancipation is abandoned altogether. The idea of 'autonomy' is kept alive only as a purely theoretical concern, addressed in an élitistic spirit to the chosen individuals. In this way it is postulated that the qualifying (supra-ideological) intellectuals can 'understand' – by adopting a strictly contemplative stance – what goes on in more or less gloomily described society, while rejecting the possibility of engaging with others in a practical enterprise designed to alter the historically unfolding course of events. It is hardly surprising, therefore, that unrelieved *cultural pessimism* should pervade all such advocacy of intellectual detachment and 'understanding', from Max Weber to Merleau-Ponty and Lévi-Strauss, and from the founding fathers of German Critical Theory to the various trends of post-structuralism.

To proclaim, as Lévi-Strauss does, that 'social consciousness always lies to itself',[839] is not only disheartening but also intellectually self-defeating. Conceptualizing in this spirit the relationship between ideology and social consciousness – i.e. depicting the latter as the incurable producer of self-deceiving ideological 'false consciousness' (in other words, as the perverse totalizing Subject that 'feels at home in unreason as unreason') – can only lead to the most depressing conclusions. For even if the self-distancing intellectual could as rightfully claim as he cannot, that he is in a privileged position to reveal the truth hidden beneath the mystifying veil of constantly reproduced collective lies, this would be of no real help for solving the problems at stake. No help at all because in virtue of the fact that he defines the conditions of unearthing the concealed truth in such a way that he simultaneously also puts himself *outside* and *above* social consciousness, he has no guarantee whatsoever that his understanding and enlightening discourse on truth would be listened to even for a moment. As a result, he condemns to futility – and to the concomitant world-castigating pessimism (as we have witnessed among others in Lévi-Strauss's *weltschmerzliche* tirades against 'humanity which reveals itself to be its own worst enemy and at the same time also the worst enemy of the rest of the creation'[840]) – his own enterprise.

Ironically, this is how the purely theoretical and contemplative stance of 'understanding' turns against those who adopt it. It is therefore by no means surprising that the people concerned invariably end up, at times against their original intentions, with deeply pessimistic conceptualizations of the social world. For they try to understand that world and render it intelligible to the addressees of their message in terms of a theoretical discourse – concerned, in Weber's words, 'strictly with *meanings*, not with *forces*' – which aims at disclosing to the 'unhappy consciousness' of fellow intellectuals (unhappy, because trapped without hope in what they themselves describe as a 'disenchanted world') the truth buried beneath the 'false consciousness' of social consciousness.

9.1.2

In view of such inescapably contemplative determination of the intellectual stance of Weber's *Verstehen* and Merleau-Ponty's *entendement* (shared by many others as well), it is all the more baffling that Lévi-Strauss should try to credit Marx with originating the curious idea that 'social consciousness always lies to itself'. For nothing could be more alien to the Marxian account of the relationship between ideology and social consciousness than self-defeating notions like this. In fact Marx held the view from a very early age that:

> The question whether objective truth can be attributed to human thinking is not a question of theory but is a *practical* question. Man must prove the truth, i.e. the *reality and power*, the *this-worldliness* of his thinking in practice. The dispute over the reality or non-reality of thinking which is isolated from practice is a purely *scholastic* question.
>
> Feuerbach starts out from the fact of religious self-estrangement, of the duplication of the world into a religious world and a secular one. His work consists in resolving the religious world into its secular basis. But that the secular basis lifts off from itself and establishes itself as an independent realm in the clouds can only be explained by the inner strife and *intrinsic contradictoriness* of this secular basis. The latter must, therefore, itself be both understood in its *contradiction* and *revolutionized in practice*.[841]

Clearly, then, Marx sees the root cause of the trouble in the '*intrinsic contradictoriness*' of the practically alienating secular basis itself, recommending, as the only feasible solution, not an abstract theoretical understanding, but one directly geared to the demands of *revolutionizing practice*. Thus, he cannot conceivably indict – nor indeed rescue from its allegedly disastrous inclinations – the pseudo-subject of 'social consciousness' as such, taken in its abstract generality.

Marx's discourse is concerned with dialectically grasping the concrete articulation of *social being* in its '*intrinsic contradictoriness*'. This is what he wants to 'understand' in a socially meaningful as well as practically effective way. For only the concrete determinations of social being, manifesting under the prevailing historical circumstances in the form of antagonistically opposed *social forces* (and not disembodied 'ideal typical *meanings*'), can provide the *practical* solution also to the apparently insoluble dilemmas and 'mysteries' of the mutually opposed *social standpoints*, namely, the 'standpoint of capital' (or the 'standpoint of political economy') set against the 'standpoint of labour'. The irreconcilable opposition between these two standpoints corresponds, in Marx's view, to the historically contingent but very real *split* in social being itself, bringing to the fore in the fundamental antagonism of the principal social agencies the 'intrinsic contradictoriness of the secular basis' of capitalist society as a mode of production and social reproduction. Accordingly, the 'standpoint of social humanity' – which anticipates the resolution of this antagonism – cannot be formulated as a traditional *theoretical* concern, appealing to 'reason' and 'understanding' for its triumph, in the spirit of bourgeois Enlightenment. It must be conceived as an intensely *practical* enterprise, pursuing *truth* in terms of the '*reality* and *power*, the *this-worldliness* of thinking'.

This is why the *critique of ideology* becomes inseparable from – indeed, to a very large extent *identical* with – the quest for *autonomy* and *emancipation*. And this is why it cannot exhaust itself in the one-sided and utterly idealistic denunciation of ideology as bewildering 'false consciousness' in the production of which that compulsive and incurable liar and self-deceiver – 'social consciousness' – indulges as its favourite pastime. For by denouncing ideology as such, the socialist forces would achieve nothing besides condemning themselves to impotence, handing over the power of ideology – without which it is inconceivable to prove the 'reality and this-worldliness' of emancipatory thought in the domain of hegemonic (i.e. overall social control-contesting) confrontations – exclusively to the social adversary. As we have seen above, the representatives of the ruling ideology of capitalist society did not hesitate to appropriate (at times quite cynically) the power of ideology to themselves, denouncing only the *other* side as reprehensibly 'ideological'. At the same time, revealing the true meaning of their anti-ideological crusade, they have also dismissed any serious concern with *emancipation* as utterly delusory, decreeing (in the words of Raymond Aron) that 'anti-ideology means being *resigned* to the endless renewal of *alienation* in some form or other',[842] after admitting that 'states are *built by violence* and are *maintained by force* that has become an institution, a *camouflage of violence* that is henceforth unperceived even by those who suffer it'.[843] This is why their self-serving general denunciation of ideology is devoid of all credibility.

9.1.3

In complete contrast, the ideology of the Enlightenment was originally articulated as a great intellectual search for the emancipation of humanity. It postulated that the removal of the 'artificial' obstacles from the path of Reason – including, in a prominent place, the kind of obstacles for the erection of which the priestly arsenal of obscurantism and intolerance was said to be directly responsible – would bring about an ideally rewarding social order, since the autonomously self-determining *individuals* could from then on follow unhindered, as eminently commendable dictates of their own intellectual and moral faculties, 'what Reason demands', instead of submitting to 'false prophets' and tyrannical rulers. There could be no question, in such a vision, of a serious contradiction between the autonomous *individual* and the *whole*. For in the liberal/Enlightenment conception of the individual as a 'species-individual' (whose society-shaping innermost 'nature' was claimed to be formed by the deepest determinations of the species itself) a direct line was drawn between the particular individuals and humanity in general. The positive/emancipatory solution of the identified problems was optimistically anticipated on these grounds, both in terms of attainable *knowledge* and of the feasible *moral improvement* of the parts as well as the whole.

However, things started to go sour when – in the aftermath of the French Revolution – it became transparent that the great expectations of the Enlightenment strategy of human emancipation had failed to materialize. Instead, the most acute forms of social antagonism erupted into the open not only between the forces that appealed to Reason and the defenders of the ancien régime but, with rather more serious implications for the viability of the originally envisaged solutions, more and more also among the formerly quite cohesive constituents of the Third Estate.

Thus, as a result of the newly surfaced inner antagonism of the Third Estate, the liberal myth of aggregative individuality that would directly and harmoniously coalesce in the world order of Reason into the collective subject of humanity, had been blown to pieces never to be reassembled again. For now, manifesting the 'revolution within the revolution' that had to be bloodily suppressed by executing its principal figures, two irreconcilable collective subjects – the bourgeoisie preaching the virtues of egotistic individualism as against communistically inclined labour – appeared on the historical stage locked into struggle, offering radically different conceptions of the right and proper social order in accordance with their mutually exclusive interests. The *'Society of the Equals'* (headed by the eventually guillotined François Babeuf) was fighting for what its members called '*real equality*', formulating from the standpoint of labour the communist slogan 'from each according to their ability, to each according to their need'. And they showed a great subtlety in defining equality in *qualitative* terms, saying that in the social order which they advocated:

> Equality must be measured by the *capacity* of the worker and the *need* of the consumer, not by the intensity of the labour and the quantity of things consumed. A man endowed with a certain degree of strength, when he lifts a weight of ten pounds, labours as much as another man with five times the strength when he lifts *fifty* pounds. He who, to satisfy a burning thirst, swallows a pitcher of water, enjoys no more than his comrade who, but slightly thirsty, sips a cupful. The aim of the communism in question is *equality of pains and pleasures*, not of *consumable things* and *workers' tasks*.[844]

This was indeed a striking formulation, emerging with the 'this-worldliness' of its truth and clarity from the thick of the struggle. Not surprisingly, therefore, when nearly *eight decades* after Babeuf's conspiracy and execution, in 1875, Marx wrote his *Critique of the Gotha Programme*, pinpointing in it also the major differences in the orienting principles of the lower and higher phases of a feasible communist society, he adopted exactly the same criteria we have just seen for the regulation of production and distribution in the higher phase. For it would be very difficult to put with greater precision the radical differences that separate the world order corresponding to the standpoint of capital from that of emancipated humanity. Differences which for the first time in history became visible in the course of the revolutionary upheavals from the standpoint of labour. Even a cursory comparison of the Babeuf/Buonarroti conception of communism with the representative 'managerial' views of a Frederic Winslow Taylor quoted in Chapter 3 – the latter expressing in fact what is generally practised in the authoritarian capitalist organization of the labour process and in the iniquitous distribution of its fruits – makes it amply clear that the bloody conflict between the constituents of the Third Estate that surfaced in the turmoil of the French Revolution was nothing short of a *hegemonic confrontation*. The contestants were literally worlds apart. Their hegemonic confrontation defined itself through the adoption of *irreconcilable* aims and objectives which called for the mobilization of the practical power of ideology '*to fight out*' the differences as the necessary condition of their realization.

9.1.4
Significantly, the first direct theorizations of ideology (explicitly under the name of ideology) appeared in response to this new historical situation and crisis, attempting to harmonize the contesting forces of the emerging post-revolutionary social order, in tune with the material and political interests of the bourgeoisie.

In this spirit, the originator of the new 'science' of ideology, Destutt de

Tracy, tried to articulate in his *Éléments d'idéologie* a theory of ideas matching in soundness and exactness (he claimed) the natural sciences, so as to be able to ground firmly the education of the individuals destined to fit unproblematically into the consolidating social framework of the bourgeois order. In much the same way as later in the philosophy of Feuerbach and others, society was thereby divided into those who were considered to be in need of 'education' in the above sense, and those – the self-appointed 'ideologues' – who would 'soundly' educate them.

Thus, harking back to the illusions of the Enlightenment well after the violent destruction of their relative historical justification in the great French bourgeois revolution, the solution to the problems arising in the social world from *collective*, materially rooted, conflicts and ever more entrenched *class* confrontations was envisaged in terms of *individualistic/educational* remedies. But from now on there could be no question of reasserting the Enlightenment ideal of instituting a rational order fit for *all* individuals without discrimination as *autonomous* individuals. For the vast majority of individuals had to be *practically* denied the possibility of reaching such a status, in the interest of maintaining a system of domination in which capital – as a matter of objective necessity – had to assign them a subordinate position.

Ideology itself was defined as a strictly scientific enterprise, idealistically postulating its ability to achieve the desired objective of unchallengeable social stability by making the individuals *conform* to the structural imperatives of society through a dubious mind-shaping practice, based on characteristically bourgeois ideological preconceptions. What was put forward with the claim of being a scientifically grounded system of education was in fact no more than an idealistic metaphysics wedded to the methods of *positivistic manipulation*. The defeated and dispirited Napoleon was therefore quite right in criticizing the 'ideologues' for their abstract metaphysical projections and utter failure to take into consideration in their theories 'the human heart and the lessons of history'.

This is how the 'positivist rot' (to which Marx later referred with well justified sarcasm) originated on the ruins of bourgeois Enlightenment. The new intellectual trend emerged in a post-revolutionary society in which there could be no more room for keeping alive the idea of universal human emancipation – in any meaningful sense of the term – on the original class basis of the Enlightenment movement.

Positivism, true to the spirit of its 'uncritical positivism' towards the capitalistic socioeconomic and political order, had for its ideal the educational imposition of conservative *accommodation*, envisaging only the possibility of marginal improvements for the overwhelming majority of the people. At the same time it eagerly and categorically rejected the idea of introducing structural changes which by their very nature would, of course, undermine the established system of class domination in 'modern society'.

As Auguste Comte, the most prominent figure in this line of political and cultural/ideological development in France put it, with cynical bluntness:

> As it is the *inevitable lot* of the majority of men to live on the more or less precarious fruits of daily labour, the great social problem is to ameliorate the condition of this majority, without destroying *its classification*, and *disturbing the general economy*; and this is the function of the positive polity, regarded as regulating the *final classification of modern society*.[845]

Thus, making a veritable mockery of the meaning of 'positive' for the overwhelming majority of humankind on a *permanent* basis, by talking of its 'final classification', the founder of positivism provided the theoretically rather crude but from the standpoint of the status quo ideologically most attractive model for the uncritical ideological defence of the established order. A model which, understandably, remained popular in its numerous neo-positivistic and neo-liberal variants ever since.

9.1.5

Hegel's ideological reconciliation and accommodation followed a much more complicated course. He never subscribed to the unproblematical Enlightenment vision which wishfully exiled all contradiction from the path of Reason. Nor was he willing to ascribe the power of victoriously advancing Reason to the limited consciousness of particular individuals. On the contrary, he described even the 'world historical individuals' – like Napoleon Bonaparte – as *tools* in the hands of Reason proper, the 'world mind'. The latter alone could be considered in Hegel's view the true agent of the unfolding world history. This is how he put it:

> In the course of this work of the world mind, states, nations, and individuals arise animated by their particular determinate principle which has its interpretation and actuality in their constitutions and in the whole range of their life and condition. While their consciousness is limited to these and they are absorbed in their mundane interests, they are all the time the *unconscious tools and organs* of the world mind at work within them. The shapes which they take pass away, while the *absolute mind* prepares and works out its transition to its next higher stage.[846]

Thus Hegel, by adopting this line of reasoning, did not have to face the dilemmas of extricating himself from the failure of the Enlightenment to live up to its promise of bringing about a social order in accordance with the demands of Reason and run autonomously by the particular individuals who would constitute the rational society. Instead, he could argue for what he considered to be the only viable – '*dialectical*' – conception of the relationship between the particular and the universal, insisting that:

> The principles of the *national minds* are wholly restricted on account of their *particularity*, for it is in this particularity that, as existent individuals, they have their objective actuality and their self-consciousness. Their deeds and destinies in their reciprocal relations to one another are the *dialectic* of the

finitude of these minds, and out of it arises the *universal mind*, the mind of the world, free from all restriction.[847]

Nevertheless, the interests of accommodation and reconciliation to the existing power relation prevailed, despite the high-sounding phrases about the unrestricted freedom of the 'universal mind' contrasted by Hegel with the limited particularity of the 'national minds', conveniently reversing in the end everything in favour of the latter in *actuality*, where it really mattered. Accordingly, we were told by Hegel that 'The *nation state* is mind in its substantive rationality and immediate actuality and is therefore the *absolute power on earth*.'[848]

As a corollary to this reversal, the universality of international law was given the status of a mere '*ought-to-be*', characterizing at the same time the relationship between necessarily competing and warring states – despite their exalted location at the pinnacle of the Hegelian progression of Reason's self-realization – as remaining in a *state of nature*:

> The fundamental proposition of international law (i.e. the universal law which *ought to be* absolutely valid between states, as distinguished from the particular content of positive treaties) is that treaties, as the ground of obligations between states, *ought to be* kept. But since the sovereignty of a state is the principle of its relations to others, states are to that extent in a *state of nature* in relation to each other. Their rights are actualized only in their *particular* wills and not in a *universal* will with constitutional powers over them. This universal proviso of international law therefore does not go beyond an *ought-to-be*, and what really happens is that international relations in accordance with treaty alternate with the *severance* of these relations.[849]

Nor did Hegel's accommodation end there. He also provided the ideological justification for the imperialist world dominance of the 'Germanic state', even though he could only do this by violating his own, explicitly stated, principle of the historical dialectic, directly contradicting himself on the stipulated inexorable transition of the 'universal mind' to its 'next higher stage'. For once the ideological interests of the European capitalist order effectively prevailed, there could be no further development envisaging – from the standpoint of political economy with which Hegel uncritically identified himself – a transition to a 'next higher stage'. There could be no question of a higher stage; neither next time nor ever after. Instead, it had to be arbitrarily decreed that: 'The History of the World travels from East to West, for *Europe is absolutely the end of History*.'[850] In this way Hegel could claim that with the realization of the Germanic world order (which embraced the colonizing power of England, said to be driven by its 'commercial spirit'[851]) the 'world mind' comes to its full realization in that it 'receives in its inner life its truth and concrete essence, while in *objectivity* it is *at home* and *reconciled* with itself'.[852]

Naturally, within the confines of this frozen 'historical dialectic' there could be no possibility of real human emancipation. The individuals had to be subsumed in its terms of reference under an abstract entity – the self-disclosing and self-comprehending world mind – which used them for its own purposes, without granting them even the consolation prize of a vague intuition of what they were preordained to accomplish. For, in the Hegelian scheme of things:

> All actions, including world-historical actions, culminate with individuals as subjects giving actuality to the substantial. They are *living instruments* of what is in substance the *deed of the world mind* and they are therefore directly at one with that deed though it is *concealed* from them and is *not their aim* and object.[853]

Thus, since the individuals could only be considered unconscious tools and instruments of the world mind, hopelessly at the mercy of the '*List der Vernunft*' (cunning of Reason), the dialectic of their 'reciprocal relations' among themselves could not conceivably amount to an open-ended real dialectic. For the 'outcome' of this dialectic – the Hegelian reconciliation with the existent, in the name of the 'world mind's reconciliation with itself' in the false positivity and dubious rationality of the historically emerged 'objectivity and actuality' – was aprioristically prefabricated, presenting as a 'conclusion' what was in fact anticipated right from the beginning. Namely, that the objectivity in which the world mind 'feels at home' and reconciled with itself is 'the *true reconciliation* which discloses the *state* as the *image and actuality of reason*.'[854]

Nor could the 'mediations' enunciated by Hegel be real mediations through which the individuals – in accordance with the objective potentialities of their enlarged margin of action due to their combination into representative collective forces – could shape their own history. Distancing himself from the Enlightenment illusion of human emancipation as defined in terms of the liberating power of Reason, Hegel conceptualized the historical movement itself not as the course of (socially no longer credible) actual emancipation, but as a somewhat mystically transfigured version of it: i.e. as the world mind's progression towards the hypostatized realization of the 'essential destiny of Reason'.[855]

This theoretical shift, fully in accord with the intrinsic requirements of the 'commercial spirit's' newly consolidated mode of domination in the real world, brought with it the characteristic determination of the 'transcending' historical movement as the Spirit '*returning* into itself', together with the definition of – pseudo-historical – temporality as nothing but the '*eternally present*'. Reaching such a conclusion was justified by Hegel on the ideologically most convenient ground that:

> Spirit is immortal; with it there is *no past, no future*, but an *essentially now*. This necessarily implies that ... what Spirit is it has *always been* essentially; distinctions are only the development of this essential nature.[856]

Since the 'rationality of the actual' could not be subjected to critical scrutiny from the standpoint of political economy even in its most sophisticated Hegelian version, ideology itself had to assume the function of blatant rationalization and eternalization, defending the established sociopolitical order as one in which 'self-consciousness finds in an organic development the actuality of its substantive knowing and willing'.[857] Hegelian ideology, thus, irremediably parted company with the long-standing philosophical concern with actual *human* emancipation, even if it retained the abstract/idealist skeleton of the latter under the categories of the 'self-realization of the *Spirit*' and the 'development of the *Idea* of Freedom'.[858] Inevitably, therefore, if Marx wanted to reopen the issue of how to emancipate the *real individuals* in a practically feasible society, he could not do so without 'settling the accounts' with the rationalizing and mystificatory functions of the ruling ideology as the vitally important first step. Only after accomplishing this negative task could he begin to focus attention on the even more important *positive* functions of socialist ideology in the advocated cause of actual human emancipation.

9.1.6

In sharp contrast to Hegel, Marx argued that emancipation was inconceivable within the framework of the Hegelian 'Absolute on earth', the national state. Indeed, the recognition of the profound interconnections and reciprocal determinations between existing states – whose contradictions Hegel bypassed by arbitrarily decreeing the absoluteness of the sovereign national states, quite cynically accepting at the same time the necessary implications of this class-determined idealization of *particularity* (notwithstanding his cult of *universality*) for the inevitability of periodic *wars*[859] – compelled Marx to conclude that the capitalist state formation in its entirety (i.e. the Hegelian 'modern Germanic state') had to be the subject of materially secured 'practical criticism', precluding at the same time the reconstitution of the old contradictions in some other form. For in Marx's view the *state as such* represented the alienation of the most comprehensive power of decision making from the social individuals, complementing and enforcing in the contemporary world the globally intertwined exploitative practices of the capitalist productive system at the level of society's legal and political superstructure.

Naturally, this conception of the practical transcendence of the state (spelled out with regard to its historically feasible mode of realization not as the state's 'abolition' but as its 'withering away') had far-reaching implications also for ideology. For the acknowledgement of the necessary limitations of ideology – as arising from the role it was called upon to play in the preservation of deeply divided societies – meant that the question of radical human emancipation could not be contemplated without envisaging the eventual supersession of the distorting forms of social consciousness as well. Nevertheless, Marx also had to stress that it was unthinkable to go *beyond ideology* by postulating the possibility of an effective critical position somewhere *outside* ideology itself.

Again, the analogy with the envisaged transcendence/withering away of the state's various repressive institutions was directly relevant to assessing the future of ideology. For just as it was inconceivable to get 'outside' the established legal and political superstructure and 'abolish' the state from the imaginary vantage point of sheer voluntarism (as the anarchists conceived the task), in the same way, the ultimate transcendence of ideology as the inescapable practical consciousness of class societies could only be projected in the form of the progressive elimination of the *causes* of antagonistic conflicts which the class individuals had to 'fight out' under the prevailing historical circumstances. In other words, the Marxian realization – in opposition to voluntarism – that the 'withering away' of the state had to take place through the radical *restructuring* of its existing institutions and the progressive transfer of their manifold functions to the social individuals: the 'associated producers', imposed the same consideration of objective constraints also on one's attitude to ideology in general. As Marx's assertion (of which, characteristically, a small fragment is frequently quoted, while the rest, which confers on the quoted judgement its true meaning, is tendentiously ignored[860]) made it amply clear: the only relevant practical critique of the most problematical ideological form of counsciousness, *religion* – called by Marx in the same breath not only the 'opium of the people' but also 'the *heart of a heartless world*' – has for its object not the sterility of abstract theoretical disputes over theological niceties, nor indeed over the imaginary merits or drawbacks of militant 'atheism' (be that in its variety of Feuerbachian 'humanism'), but the creation of a world which no longer could be described as *heartless*.

In this sense, the critique of ideology was, strictly speaking, not at all an '*Ideologiekritik*'. For what was really at stake in the critical assessment of both the state and ideology was the long established and apparently insurmountable *structural/hierarchical social division of labour*. Accordingly, the immense practical difficulties implicit in the task of emancipating the real individuals from their subjection to the material imperatives of the hierarchical social division of labour had to be faced – and *countered* at the appropriate level of *materially effective transformative mediations* – if one wanted to take seriously the project of setting into motion the complex process (of which the *political* revolution was only the *precondition*, but not even the first step[861]) whereby the state as such could begin to 'wither away', carrying with it also the simultaneous transcendence of the distorting forms of social consciousness.

The advocacy of this strategy was by no means unproblematical as far as its feasible instruments of realization were concerned. For the 'end of ideology' (in any meaningful sense of the term) necessarily implied going beyond *class society* as such (in that only then would the need for 'fighting out' the constantly reproduced conflicts from the pre-set positions of opposing class-interests disappear), just as the 'withering away of the state' implied the radical supersession of the alienating social division of labour. Paradoxically, however, in the same way as the supersession of the state could only come about through the progressively '*self-transcending*' material agency of the state itself, in the form of the genuine appropriation of its vital control functions by the increasingly self-activating and self-controlling social body, likewise, the *practical mediations* (and not just ideological disputes) required for going 'beyond ideology' could only be conceived by envisaging the realization of the immediate, socio-historically constrained, tasks (which had to be faced in the everyday life of the given community) as organically linked to the long-term objectives of *emancipatory ideology*.

The idea of breaking the *hegemony* of the ruling ideology through the forceful articulation of a critical ideology, in tune with the standpoint of labour, was an integral part of this conception. The whole approach emerged in response to the regressive change we could witness in the attitude of the liberal/Enlightenment tradition to the question of emancipation in the aftermath of the French Revolution. The openly pessimistic trends that in more recent times summarily rejected all concern with emancipation, dismissing at the same time social consciousness in general for its allegedly incorrigible ideological self-deception, emanated from the same crisis of conscience, due to the once sincerely believed but socially undeliverable promises of the Enlightenment. The qualitative difference in the orientation of the representative figures of liberal/bourgeois thought which we have seen becoming dominant in the twentieth century was due to the fact that while Hegel – in the absence of globally manifest class antagonisms and their material embodiments in the 'rational actuality' of self-asserting national states – could still redefine his terms of reference from the standpoint of political economy without having to abandon at least the abstract '*Idea*' of emancipation, such a consoling retreat into the realm of the 'Absolute Idea' was no longer feasible for his ideological comrades in arms in the contemporary world. This is why ideology in general had to acquire for them the kind of *negative* connotation which we are all familiar with, despite their active participation in securing – with all means at their disposal – the continued hegemony of the ruling ideology.

9.1.7

The Marxian conception of ideology was worked out against the background of this apparently irreversible retreat of the bourgeois Enlightenment ideals. Many of the original tenets of the Marxian conception, therefore, had to bear the marks of its connection with the problematics of its consciously superseded historical predecessors. This became manifest both in the way in which Marx's negative critical evaluation of the retreat itself was concerned, and as regards his attempt to rescue the positive features and aspirations of the Enlightenment tradition.

The twentieth century, however, added a qualitatively new dimension to socialist conceptions of ideology. Now – for the first time ever in history – it became both possible and necessary to be practically critical of the actual conditions (and contradictions) of the *post-capitalist states* which emerged from the social turmoil that followed two devastating world wars. It became possible and necessary to engage in such criticism not in narrowly political terms, but by making intelligible the contradictions of the political dimension itself in terms of the *social division of labour* that continued to rule the metabolism of post-capitalist 'civil societies', without abandoning thereby the earlier announced project of radical socialist transformation. For a failure to maintain commitment to the all-comprehensive radical project of structural change would expose even the most limited achievements of post-capitalist societies to the threat of insecurity, given the continued material and ideological power as well as the historically well known recovery-potential of the social adversary.

The principal lesson that emerged from the painful historical experience of 'actually existing socialist societies' was that the objective constraints of global interdependence could not be wished out of existence by Stalinist type political appeals, arbitrarily enunciated and ruthlessly enforced as they were in the name of 'socialism in one country'. For these constraints continued to exercise their power of inertia everywhere, partly through the facticity of the inescapable global interdependence itself, and partly on account of the inherited metabolic structures which have been shaped in the last two or three centuries all over the world by capital: by far the most dynamic force of productive interchange known to human beings throughout history.

In the light of twentieth-century historical experience it became clear that the objective constraints in question could not be counteracted in the interest of emancipation by voluntaristic strategies and administrative measures. Just as the pessimistic denunciation of 'social consciousness lying to itself' proved to be utterly futile, in the same way, even if formulated with very different social premises and objectives in mind, the Stalinist direct appeals to ideology could make no positive impact on the real issues. For the problems of ideology, be they large or small, cannot conceivably be solved *within* ideology itself.

Both the problematical features and the positive characteristics of ideology find their rational explanation in the objective requirements of the social reproduction process of which ideology itself is an organic constituent. Thus, on the one hand, so long as the established system of societal reproduction is dense with material antagonisms, it would be nothing short of a miracle if the corresponding forms of social consciousness – which actively participate in the formation and more or less undisturbed functioning of the basic reproductive structures themselves – could be free from their impact. At the same time, on the other hand, the emancipatory power of ideology arises from the same dialectic of reciprocity through which social consciousness can significantly contribute to the autonomy-enhancing transformation of the basic material reproductive structures under favourable historical circumstances. In this sense, the 'self-determining activity of the associated producers' is bound to remain a frustrated ideal so long as it is *practically negated* by the material constraints of the dominant reproductive structures. Yet, without the forceful intervention of emancipatory ideology – capable of demonstrating *ad hominem* both the feasibility of, and the historically alive need for, such practical ideals – there can be no hope for overcoming the destructive antagonisms of these structures.

9.2 PRACTICAL AND IDEOLOGICAL INVERSIONS

9.2.1

The power of the dominant ideology is as great as undoubtedly it is not simply because of the overwhelming material might and commensurate political/cultural arsenal at the disposal of the ruling classes. For such ideological power itself can only prevail thanks to the positional advantage of *mystification* through which the people at the receiving end can be induced to endorse, 'consensually', the values and practical policies which are in fact quite inimical to their vital interests.

In this respect, as in several others, the situation of the contending ideologies is decidedly *non-symmetrical*. The critical ideologies which attempt to negate the established order cannot mystify their adversaries for the simple reason that they have nothing to offer – in the way of bribes and rewards for accommodation – to those who are already well established in their positions of command, conscious of their tangible immediate interests. Accordingly, the power of mystification over the adversary is a privilege of the ruling ideology only.

This circumstance, already on its own, shows how self-defeating it is to try to explain ideology simply under the heading of 'false consciousness'. For what defines ideology as ideology is not its alleged defiance of 'reason', nor its departure from the preconceived rules of an imaginary 'scientific discourse', but its very real situation in a determinate type of society. The complex functions of ideology arise precisely from such – materially grounded – situation, and they are not in the least made intelligible in terms of abstract rationalistic and scientistic criteria counterposed to them, which merely beg the question.

What is particularly important to stress here is that the material and ideological determinations which we are concerned with affect not only the more or less systematic intellectual articulations of the established social relations, but the *totality* of social consciousness in all its practically feasible varieties. Irrespective of whether one has in mind the 'sophisticated' or the 'popular' ideological conceptualizations of any particular epoch, in order to be able to find the key to understanding their common structuring core one must focus attention on the vital practical requirements of the established social reproductive system.

One can in fact point to a most remarkable *affinity* between the practical/operational determinations of a given socioeconomic order and the dominant ideological characteristics of the epoch to which that order belongs. If we consider in this regard the distinctive features of post-Cartesian ideological developments, it transpires that the *'formal rationality'* which is idealized (and fetishized) in various conceptualizations of theoretical discourse as a 'self-generating' intellectual advancement, closely matches, in fact, the *material processes* of abstraction, reduction, compartmentalization, formal equalization and 'dehistorization' which characterize the establishment and consolidation of the capitalistic socioeconomic metabolism in its entirety. It is thanks to these formalizing/reductive material processes that *generalized commodity production* can articulate itself in the first place. Nor is it conceivable to envisage subsequently the successful functioning of the capitalist system even for a moment without the material processes mentioned above. For they happen to constitute the essential requirements of the *universal exchange relations* under which everything must be firmly subsumed in globally developing and expanding capitalist society.

Thus, the philosophers who try to deduce the social structure and institutional/administrative machinery of modern capitalism from the 'spirit of rational calculation', etc. put the cart before the horse and represent the world of capital upside-down. Nor is it accidental that they proceed in this way. On the contrary, their room for manoeuvre is circumscribed by what can or cannot be brought into agreement with the 'eternalizing' ideological standpoint of political economy. For the methodology of the latter *must* treat the historical *outcome* (labour's 'self-alienation' and conversion into capital) as the self-evident and unalterable (i.e. characteristically 'dehistorized') point of *departure*. The paramount *ideological interest* of safeguarding the *legitimacy of capital* as the permanent controlling force of society thus receives its *material* underpinning from the 'rational actuality' of the already accomplished *end-result* which the intellectual defenders of the ruling order find at hand not only as the ideal presupposition of their thinking, but simultaneously also the necessary *practical premiss* and *materially effective regulator* of the established metabolic interchange of society with nature.

Here we can see, again, the complete untenability of equating ideology with 'false consciousness', simply to discard it. For the various theoretical transformations and inversions which we encounter in the course of bourgeois intellectual/ideological development, no matter how bewildering they must appear at first sight, are in fact perfectly in accord with their socioeconomic ground.

In this sense, however paradoxical this may sound, the contradictory characteristics of this intellectual/ideological development must be grasped and explained in terms of the *peculiar rationality* of their objective contradictoriness, as arising from their sociohistorically determined real ground, instead of being 'explained away' and 'dissolved', as formal/theoretical 'inconsistencies', from the imaginary height of a timeless, self-complacent, and completely circular 'pure rationality'. After all, the reason why Hegel's magisterial attempt to elucidate the interconnection between 'rationality' and 'actuality' had to run into insurmountable difficulties was not that in reality the relationship itself does not exist. Indeed it does and, moreover, it happens to be of a very great theoretical and practical importance. Hegel had to fail in the end on account of grossly violating his own principle of historicity when he made *congeal* the dynamic rationality of the historically unfolding actuality into the static pseudo-rationality of a structurally prejudged and closed present. Significantly for our present context, Hegel did this in accordance with the standpoint of political economy which makes the '*rationality* of the actual' synonymous with the antagonistically *divided* (hence by its very nature inherently unstable) yet in a baffling way unproblematically eternalized actuality of the *established* order.

In the various theories which conceptualize the world from the standpoint of political economy (irrespective of how great are the thinkers who produce the theories in question), the material determinations and the historical *genesis* of capitalistic rationality are characteristically ignored. Moreover, the nearer we come to the present the more evident becomes the wanton disregard for the devastating irrationality of capital's reified rationality under many of its self-contradictory, destructive, and ultimately even self-destructive practical aspects. It is therefore quite bizarre to misrepresent the *end-result* of ubiquitous capitalistic 'rational calculation' as a *self-generating 'principle'*, so as to be able to treat it both as a quasi-theological *causa sui* and as the necessary point of departure and inner cause of all subsequent development.

The problem here is not the idealism *per se* of these approaches, but the *reason* for their idealism which arises from their revealing ideological substance. For the kind of idealist ideological bias we are presented with in such conceptions – which locate the structural determinants of fundamental social transformations in mysteriously emerging 'spirits of the age' and in self-generating 'formal principles', etc. – can only serve to undermine (and ultimately to disqualify as utterly utopian) all belief in the viability of radical interventions in the socioeconomic sphere for the purpose of instituting a meaningful alternative to the established order.

Nevertheless, all these socially specific irrationalities, notwithstanding the obvious ideological bias of their originators, are in their own rather peculiar way both rational and representative. This is because they *necessarily* arise from a socioeconomic (material/existential) ground whose fundamental *structural determinations* are *shared*, and perceived in a characteristically – but by no means haphazardly – distorted form, by all concerned, be they leading philosophers, economists, 'political scientists', etc. or only spontaneous participants in the prevailing 'common sense' of capitalist everyday life.

Indeed, the 'hegemony' of the ruling ideology cannot be made intelligible at all in terms of its claimed 'autonomous power'; not even if one is willing to ascribe to it a materially unlimited and diabolically perfected range of instruments. Rather, the normally preponderant rule of the dominant ideology must be explained in terms of the *shared existential ground* just referred to. For the constantly reproduced *practical inversions* of the given socioeconomic system – to which the various theoretical and instrumental manifestations of the ruling ideology actively contribute at the appropriate level – constitute, in the paralysing immediacy of their inescapable materiality, the most fundamental determination in this respect.

One cannot stress often enough that it is impossible to explain the power of ideology (effectively exercised despite all identifiable distortions) in self-referential ideological terms. Only the profound *structural affinity* between the *practical/material* and *intellectual/ideological inversions* can make intelligible the massive impact of the ruling ideology on social life. An impact which is incomparably more extensive than what could be expected from the relative size of its directly controlled resources, displaying the dominant ideology's unimpeded influence on the broad masses of the people in the form of an ability to '*preach to the converted*', as it were, under normal circumstances. For the great masses of the 'converted' not only *recognize* the fundamental characteristics of the prevailing social intercourse in the discourse of the ruling ideology, but also *acknowledge* that such characteristics constitute the *limits* of their own practically feasible action under the *stable* conditions of successfully self-asserting capitalist normality.

9.2.2

The 'autonomy' and 'self-sustaining power' of the ideological forms is often greatly exaggerated, at times to the point of assuming their complete *independence* from the underlying material determinations.

In truth, the plausibility of such explanations is extremely weak. What gives rise to interpretations of this kind is a twofold '*optical illusion*' under which the relationship of the various ideological forms to their socioeconomic ground, on the one hand, and to the rest of the superstructure (particularly the state), on the other, appears to the theoreticians concerned.

To put it in a different way, the adoption of such an unrealistic view of 'autonomous ideology' is due to:

1. The attribution of the spontaneous consequences of the objective *structural affinity* mentioned above – i.e. the disheartening but

perfectly intelligible ability of the ruling ideology 'to preach to the converted' under normal circumstances – to the *immanent* resources of the specific ideological manifestations themselves.
2. A predilection to treat the ideological forms of social consciousness in a way which mechanically subsumes them under the characteristics of various *state* institutions.

Apart from the need to stress that often the 'autonomy of the state' is also greatly overstated, it is equally necessary to underline that the state-institutions and the ideological forms of social consciousness cannot be simply merged into one another for the purpose of theoretical analysis. There are some vital differences that must be constantly kept in mind. Thus, while undoubtedly there is an area of close reciprocal integration between the two, one can also identify some sharp contrasts and divergences in their intrinsic constitution and mode of operation.

Here we should note a paradoxical correlation with regard to the question of 'autonomy'. For inasmuch as the specific *ideological forms* (philosophies, legal and social theories, theological systems, aesthetic ideas, etc.) can be considered truly autonomous – in that they define their respective positions within their own field of interest, in relation to various sets of historically transmitted ideas and rules of discourse – they are *least* likely to exercise a direct influence on the *masses*. This is because it is a necessary precondition for the exercise of such influence that the ideas in question should find a theoretically suitable and practically effective *material articulation*. Naturally, the latter in its turn requires the constitution of well sustained and practically viable carriers, instruments, institutions, administrative networks, etc. without which the desired influence would remain at the level of mere wishful thinking. Thus *religious discourse*, for instance, cannot exercise its potential power simply through the proclamation of its *ideas*. It must find a *practical/material intermediary* of some sort – i.e. the various rule-enforcing Church institutions, however rudimentary at first, as in the case of small sects – through which the ideas themselves can become materially effective.

The same consideration applies also the other way round. For, paradoxically, inasmuch as the ideological forms proper are *least autonomous* – since they greatly depend on the just mentioned material factors which remain, of necessity, outside their direct control (hence the frequently lamented 'corruption of the original ideas and ideals' once the necessary material instruments and institutions are truly activated) – their impact on society happens to be the *most powerful* and influential.

Such considerations do not apply, of course, to the state and its complex network of institutions. The problematical 'autonomy' of the various state institutions (ranging from juridical organs to educational establishments) stands in a much more *direct relationship* to the state's effectively controlled material power.

9.2.3

We must bear in mind the above-mentioned structural affinity on which so much depends also in relation to the historically more than once experienced (though by no means necessarily permanent or even long-lasting) '*sudden collapse*' of formerly dominant ideological forms and institutional practices, under the circumstances of a major structural crisis. For such a collapse can only find its explanation in the effective *paralysis* of the otherwise materially sustained and spontaneously reproduced ideological processes (with all their underlying practical inversions), as a result of the crisis in question. (We may recall in this respect the revolutionary upheavals – and their defeats – in 1918–19, in the aftermath of a lost war and the ensuing socioeconomic crisis, in Germany and Hungary; and to some extent even the ideological turmoil of 1968 – emanating from the crisis generated above all by the unsuccessful involvement of the United States and its allies in Vietnam – in the capitalistically advanced countries.)

What is highly relevant here is that the *reconstitution* of the ruling ideology after its earlier 'collapse' normally does not require major investment in new ideological enterprises and instruments, as historical experience shows. It comes about on the whole *spontaneously*, as the material and corresponding legal/political structures themselves recover from the crisis. This fact reinforces the point made earlier about the fundamental importance of the objective *structural affinity* between the given ideological forms and the material reproductive framework of society.

The successful recovery of the material structures in the normal course of events happens to be also the main reason why the periodically experienced 'sudden collapse' of the power of the ruling ideology cannot be considered permanent or long-lasting.

The trajectory of the *ideological crisis* and the subsequent reconstitution of the ruling ideology in due course must be made intelligible in terms of the relative 'recovery-potential' of the fundamental metabolic structures of the established social order. For the issue is ultimately decided by the intrinsic nature of the crisis of the material reproductive framework itself, and not by the unsuspected vitality (or, for that matter, simply the force of inertia) of the ideological forms as such. The outcome depends on how deep and how widespread is the crisis of the material foundation of society; to what extent can it be considered a truly *structural*, as opposed to a cyclic-conjunctural crisis, etc.

As an example we may think of the so-called 'world economic crisis' of 1929–33, dramatically inaugurated by the collapse of the New York Stock Exchange. Although this crisis reverberated across the entire capitalist world, it did not result at all in a major ideological collapse of the system. For, notwithstanding the rather romantic colours with which some intellectuals like to paint the 'pink thirties', the established social order was not significantly affected in its basic metabolic functions by the limited – in its character cyclic and primarily financial – economic crisis of the private enterprise system. Nor did the alleged 'pinkness' of the ideological forms themselves extend over much more than a very narrow intellectual stratum, affecting thereby for a brief historical moment only the periphery of global capitalist society.

9.2.4

In order to better understand the intricate relationship and structural affinity between the mystifying *practical* inversions, abstract/reductive transformations, and absurd formal equations which assert themselves in reality, on the one hand, and their *conceptualizations* both by 'ordinary common sense' and by sophisticated theoretical/ideological syntheses, on the other, we must focus attention on the materially effective spontaneous regulators of the capitalistic socioeconomic metabolism.

Perhaps nowhere is the *practical irrationality* which we are concerned with more striking in this respect than in the materially articulated determination of spurious (but at the level of society's metabolic interchanges fully operative) connections of formal equality between qualitatively different entities that, *prima facie*, have absolutely nothing to do with one another. As Marx puts it in a very important section of *Capital*:

> The relation of a portion of the surplus-value, of money rent . . . to the land is in itself *absurd* and *irrational*; for the magnitudes which are here measured by one another are *incommensurable* – a *particular use-value*, a piece of land of so many and so many square feet, on the one hand, and *value*, especially *surplus-value*, on the other. This expresses in fact nothing more than that, under the given conditions, the ownership of so many square feet of land enables the landowner to wrest a certain quantity of unpaid labour, which the capital wallowing in these square feet, like a hog in potatoes, has realized. But prima facie the expression is the same as if one desired to speak of the relation of a five-pound note to the diameter of the earth.
>
> However, the *reconciliation of irrational forms* in which certain economic relations appear and *assert themselves in practice* does not concern the active agents of these relations in their *everyday life*. And since they are *accustomed* to move about in such relations, they find nothing strange therein. A *complete contradiction* offers not the *least mystery* to them. They feel as much *at home* as a fish in water among manifestations which are separated from their internal connections and *absurd* when isolated by themselves. What Hegel says with reference to certain mathematical formulas applies here: that which *seems irrational* to ordinary common sense is rational, and that which *seems rational* to it is itself irrational.[862]

Thus, the irrationality of 'common sense' (to which systematic ideological mystifications can readily attach themselves and use as their vehicle of diffusion) grows out of the same soil as the 'sophisticated' conceptualizations which constantly reinforce everyday consciousness in its 'absurd' prejudices.

More important still, in the present context, is to stress that the *practical absurdity* – which constitutes their common ground – simultaneously also corresponds to the only feasible 'rationality' and 'normality' of the given order, as manifest in the most vital regulators of its socioeconomic metabolism as a whole.

Of necessity, the practical irrationality of separating manifestations from their internal connections is an important aspect of the capital system. But key material factors cannot and do not remain for long suspended in their irrational separateness. For if they did so, it would be quite impossible to exercise society's essential metabolic functions, and therefore the whole structure erected on them would collapse.

This is why the successful '*reconciliation of irrational forms*' mentioned by Marx is an elementary requirement of the capitalist socioeconomic metabolism from the very beginning, and it remains so throughout its long history. In other words, capital's dynamic but inherently problematical and irrational regulatory system is viable only so long as its 'irrational forms' can be *successfully reconciled* with one another in the practicality of the social reproduction process itself.

This is where the most varied manifestations of the ruling ideology organically fit into the picture. For it happens to be one of their most important functions to contribute actively – through mobilizing the practically effective arsenal of ideological inversion and 'uncritical positivism' – to the reconciliation of the materially operative irrational forms. It is therefore quite ironical that one of the most sophisticated and influential of twentieth-century ideologies, the Weberian conception, should formulate its principal theoretical tenets – while curiously also enunciating its claim to the status of the most advanced critical theory of society – in terms of the open glorification of the allegedly untranscendable system of capitalist 'rational calculation'.

9.3 THE ACTIVE ROLE OF 'COMMON SENSE'

9.3.1

There is an unfortunate tendency – at times even in Gramsci – to characterize the 'common sense' of the subaltern classes in strictly ideological terms, with reference to the inherited conceptions of the world, religious beliefs, etc. While no one should deny the importance of such factors, they do not really explain the persistence of distorted conceptualizations of the world which, however distorted, nonetheless acquire the status of 'common sense'. For, contrary to voluntaristic notions, the continued grip of direct ideological determinations cannot be considered the self-sustaining *cause* of such persistence.

To be sure, if the identifiable causes of ideological mystification were primarily ideological, they could be counteracted and reversed in the sphere of ideology itself. Hence comes the great temptation to offer voluntaristic explanations and solutions.

However, as we have seen already, the massive impact of the ruling ideology on social life as a whole can only be made intelligible in terms of the profound *structural affinity* that exists between the practical mystifications and inversions on the one hand, and their intellectual/ideological conceptualizations on the other. If the latter become 'sedimented' in the prevailing form of 'common sense' the way in which they do, this is thanks to the self-same structural affinity that arises from the ground of material determinations shared by *all* modalities of ideology, whether they are produced by relatively few specialized intellectuals, or by innumerable particular individuals who are both active contributors to the formation of 'common sense' and its bearers.

If we do not recognize the existence and the practical importance of this objective structural affinity, we are forced to accept Gramsci's depressing conclusion that 'in the masses as such, philosophy can only be experienced as a *faith*'.[863]

Inevitably, from such diagnosis of the situation, corresponding to a strangely passive conception of what Gramsci elsewhere calls 'the amorphous mass element', an equally problematical remedy follows. Since the 'common sense' of the 'amorphous mass element' seems to be merely the depository of rather chaotic ideological influences, the active role of changing the situation must be assigned to 'intellectual *élites*' (and their 'political *vanguard*') whose task is defined as the modification of the 'ideological panorama of the age'. As Gramsci puts it in his discussion of the 'specific necessities for any cultural movement which aimed to replace common sense and old conceptions of the world in general':

1. Never to tire of repeating its own arguments ... repetition is the best *didactic* means for *working on the popular mentality*.
2. To work incessantly ... to give a personality to the amorphous mass element. This means working to produce *élites* of intellectuals of a new type which arise directly out of the masses, but remain in contact with them to become, as it were, the whalebone in the corset.

This second necessity, if satisfied, is what really modifies the 'ideological panorama' of the age. But these *élites* cannot be formed or developed without a hierarchy of authority and intellectual competence growing up within them. The culmination of this process can be a great individual philosopher. But he must be capable of reliving concretely the demands of the massive ideological community and of understanding that this cannot have the flexibility of movement proper to an individual brain ...[864]

Thus, given its terms of reference, Gramsci's solution can merely stipulate how the envisaged '*élites* of intellectuals of a new type' ought to behave under the circumstances, paradoxically and unrealistically anticipating a form of discipline that expects the new intellectuals to deny themselves even 'the flexibility of movement proper to an individual brain'.

9.3.2

Gramsci is, of course, well aware of the dilemmas involved in the postulated remedy. This is how he pursues his line of reasoning, ending up with a number of very difficult questions:

> *Mass adhesion* or non-adhesion to an ideology is the real critical test of the rationality and historicity of modes of thinking.... These developments pose many problems, the most important of which can be subsumed in the form and the quality of the relations between the various *intellectually qualified strata*; that is, the importance and the function which the *creative* contribution of *superior groups* must and can have in connection with the organic capacity of the *intellectually subordinate strata* to discuss and develop new critical concepts. It is a question, in other words, of *fixing the limits* of freedom of discussion and propaganda, a freedom which should not be conceived of in the administrative and police sense, but in the sense of a *self-limitation* which the leaders impose on their own activity, or, more strictly, in the sense of fixing the direction of cultural policy. In other words – *who is to fix the 'rights of knowledge'* and the limits of the pursuit of knowledge? And *can these rights and limits indeed be fixed?*[865]

The trouble is, though, that even if one can find answers to these questions which prove to be acceptable to a large number of intellectuals under favourable circumstances (as indeed Togliatti tried to do in the postwar period within the framework of the Italian Communist Party's highly successful cultural policy), that would still not resolve the difficulty of 'mass adhesion or non-adhesion', nor, in more general terms, the underlying problem of 'common sense'.

Gramsci's dilemma is in part self-imposed, in the sense that he ascribes too passive a role, and grants an excessively small amount of rationality, to the 'amorphous mass element' and its 'common sense'. As a result, the constitution and transmission of an overall view of the world by 'common sense' – in the framework of which the particular individuals as 'average individuals' define their own position while they take part also in its constitution – cannot be visualized as a creative process. Rather, it must be considered as no more than directly subsumed under the dominant ideology, from which follows that the masses can experience philosophy 'only as a *faith*'.

In truth, they need not experience philosophy either as a faith or as anything else. They can simply ignore it under the conditions of capitalist 'normality': when, that is, nothing compels them to reexamine the ruling practical premises of the given social order. Nor would it follow from acknowledging this state of affairs that as a matter of course they are condemned to an essentially passive role, and thus to acting merely as the depository of heterogeneous and chaotic ideological influences which originate 'above their heads', so to speak. For the 'sophisticated' ideological systems express in their own way the same conditions of practical reification which 'common sense' also finds at hand and *actively confirms for itself* on a daily basis. (As Marx put it, people are 'accustomed to move about' within the established relations of capitalist everyday life, no matter how irrational and absurd the practical equations imposed upon them by the dominant metabolic processes of the given system.)

Inasmuch as the various specialized constructs of the ruling ideology and the more straightforward, seemingly 'spontaneous', responses of 'common sense' are supported by the same objective structures of practical mystification and inversion – which happen to be ubiquitous in the societies of generalized commodity production – the view according to which 'common sense' is characterized by an unproblematical adhesion to, and absorption of, the systematically articulated ideological beliefs, ascribes much more credit to the latter than they really deserve. For in reality 'common sense' can actively evaluate and confirm on its own account the dominance of the basic structural determinations of commodity society which *also* find their way into the systematic ideological conceptualizations. The alternative hypothesis, namely that the actively produced ideological beliefs are one-sidedly deposited by the 'intellectually qualified strata' into the 'amorphous mass element', is not a very plausible explanation of the objective limits within which the various ideological conceptions are articulated and relate to one another.

9.3.3

Naturally, no great comfort can be directly derived from the active role of 'common sense' in constituting its overall view of the world, since its relationship to *critical ideology* is not the same as that to the *ruling ideology*. Again, nothing is symmetrical in this respect. Far from it. Indeed, the necessarily *'uphill struggle'* of all critical ideology – in contrast to the ruling ideology's earlier mentioned ability to 'preach to the converted' – is itself a clear confirmation of the overwhelming importance of the objective structural affinity discussed in Section 9.2.

Only under the conditions of a major crisis – as, for instance, during the first world war and its aftermath of revolutions not only in Russia but in several other European countries as well, or during the second world war which was followed by the victory of the Chinese Revolution and by a significant leftward shift of the political spectrum, practically all over the world, for a few years at least – can critical systems of thought dramatically affect the 'ideological panorama of the age'. For under normal circumstances they must contend not only with their specialized ideological adversaries, but, in a rather more disheartening way, with the 'unholy alliance' between 'common sense' and the ruling ideology as sustained by the *practical evidence* of the established material structures within which people have to reproduce the material and cultural conditions of their existence and 'feel at home as a fish in water'.

Understandably, therefore, Gramsci – whose primary concern is always how to maximize the impact of the 'philosophy of praxis' (one of his codenames for Marxism) under the given circumstances – tends to underrate the weight of the material structural determinations. He counterposes to them an approach that wants to change 'the ideological panorama of the age' through direct ideological intervention, in complete defiance of the objectively prevailing affinity between the material structures and the ideological images of 'common sense'.

Thus, although acknowledging the importance of the first world war for preparing the ground for the October Revolution ('In Russia the war helped to spur on the wills. Through three years of suffering, they very quickly found themselves in unison. Famine was imminent, hunger, dying of hunger, could hit everyone, exterminate in one blow tens of millions of people. The wills aligned themselves in unison.'[866]), nevertheless he reaches voluntaristic conclusions, counterposing 'ideologies' to 'facts' (thus contradicting his own insights about the significance of the brute facticity of the war) in his insistence that:

> The Bolshevik Revolution emerged from ideologies more than from facts. (Thus in the end it is of little importance to us that we should learn about it more than what we already know.) It is the Revolution against Karl Marx's *Capital*. . . . Marxist thought is the continuation of Italian and German idealist thought, which in Marx had become contaminated with positivistic and naturalistic incrustations. . . . Socialist preaching created the social will of the Russian people. . . . The Russian proletariat, educated in socialism, will begin its history at the highest level of production that England has reached today. For, as it must begin, it will set out from the stage brought to perfection elsewhere; and from that it will receive the impulse to reach that economic maturity which, according to Marx, is the necessary condition of collectivism. . . . One has the impression that the maximalists were, at this point, the spontaneous expression, *biologically* necessary, lest the Russian humanity should fall in a most horrible disintegration.[867]

It must be also pointed out that although Gramsci later introduces some correctives to his overemphasis on '*la volontà*' (the will) as such, yet even in his later years he retains a voluntaristic bias, despite the fact that the viability of the latter becomes plausible only under the historically very rare circumstances of massive revolutionary explosions, when everything happens to be in a state of flux, and therefore the forceful intervention of the will can more readily push things in the desired direction than under stable conditions. Here, adopting a position based on his unqualified belief in the power of the will, Gramsci suggests that:

> With regard to the historical role played by the fatalistic conception of the philosophy of praxis one might perhaps prepare its funeral oration, emphasising its usefulness for a certain period of history, but precisely for this reason underlining the need to bury it with all due honours.[868]

What renders extremely problematical Gramsci's conclusions on the recommended burial of the 'fatalistic conception of the philosophy of praxis'

– of which not only the mechanistic 'vulgar Marxists' but Marx himself is
supposed to be guilty, on account of the alleged 'contamination of positivistic and naturalistic incrustations' in his theory – is his twofold assumption
according to which:

1. The *actual experience of material developments* can be successfully
   replaced and superseded by the *'thought-experience'* (Gramsci's expression) of a politically conscious *minority.*
2. The belief that the socialist transformation of post-revolutionary
   society can *start* at the *highest level* of Western capitalist developments, just like North American capitalism could build on all the
   accomplishments of England as its point of departure.

This is how Gramsci spells out these assumptions in the article on 'La
rivoluzione contro il *Capitale*' quoted above:

> The Russian people has gone through these experiences by thought, be that
> *the thought of a minority*. It has *superseded these experiences*. It uses them to
> assert itself in the present as it will make use of Western capitalistic experi-
> ences to raise itself, in a short time, to the *highest level of production of the
> Western world*. North America is capitalistically more advanced than England
> because in North America the Anglosaxons have started, *with one leap*, at the
> stage reached by England after a long evolution.[869]

Given such assumptions, the immense material constraints under which all
anti-capitalist revolutions – as well as the societies arising from them – must
operate, can be 'superseded *col pensiero*' ('by thought'), by the work of
politically active minority consciousness upon passive 'common sense'
consciousness. Yet in reality there is no symmetry in the respective relationships of critical and established ideology to 'common sense'. Nor in
the way in which North American capitalism can indeed unproblematically
follow on from the highest point reached by England (with the active involvement and positively disposed contribution of British capital), whereas
post-capitalist societies decidedly cannot. They cannot do so partly because
of their relative (and in some cases even extremely pronounced) economic
backwardness, coupled with the obvious hostility of the capitalist outside
world; but even more importantly, because of the total inadequacy of the
capitalist inheritance as a viable material foundation for truly socialist
interchanges.

   This is why the Russian Revolution could not be – nor, for that matter,
can any other anti-capitalist revolution conceivably be in the foreseeable
future – a 'revolution against Karl Marx's *Capital*', and even less so against
capital as such. For, unlike *capitalism*, capital cannot be 'overthrown' (or
suddenly 'abolished') through the *negations* of a revolutionary upheaval,
no matter how radical those negations might be in political terms. It must
be progressively *displaced* (and ultimately *replaced* in all its aspects) by the
laborious and *positive* constitution of a new social metabolism, with its

qualitatively different objective presuppositions and orienting principles that define it as an *organic whole*. (Just as capital could rightfully claim for itself, in its own terms, a solid organic foundation in the sense in which Marx indicated this in a most important passage of the *Grundrisse*.[870])

9.3.4

The great obstacles that 'common sense' puts before critical ideology, thereby actively resisting the modification of the 'ideological panorama of the age', arise from its inherent relationship to the given socioeconomic framework. Since the long drawn out and in its historical dynamics highly contradictory genesis of the established order is hidden behind the veils of the past and the practical mystifications of the present, the individuals who share the 'common sense of the age' can only find at hand, as their *common* frame of reference, the relatively *stable* features of the capitalist social organism as it is already constituted in reality. Normally, against the background of the relative stability and undisturbed functioning of the system that 'delivers the goods' for which it is organically constituted, common sense '*internalizes*' the forbidding difficulties of embarking on the road to a veritable structural change – one that would present a radical alternative to the established system in its entirety – not merely as difficulties but as a practical '*impossibility*'.

Thus, the 'recognition' and (often even openly resigned) 'acknowledgement' of this 'impossibility' – whose measure and orienting framework is the stability of the given order – becomes one of the principal defining characteristics of 'common sense' as (common) sense that 'makes sense'. Nevertheless, it would be quite wrong to consider 'common sense' as passive and devoid of a potentially critical stance. For unless its basic expectations – oriented towards the undisturbed functioning of the given social metabolism – are *actually confirmed* by the ongoing societal reproduction process, its allegiance can evaporate with surprising speed. As indeed happens under the conditions of truly structural crises which also provide a favourable terrain for the exercise of Gramsci's *volontà* and for conscious political intervention on the ground of formerly unimaginable *mass-involvement* (and not simply '*mass-adhesion*').

But even in this respect we need a note of caution. For, in view of the primary constitution of 'common sense' through its orientation towards stability and relatively undisturbed societal reproduction, even in periods of persistent crisis the first reaction tends to be to follow 'the line of least resistance'. This is because the latter promises to bring about the desired objective with greater probability than the adoption of more radical (and in the light of the 'normality' of the past by definition more unpredictable) alternative courses of action.

Only when the crisis deepens (instead of 'blowing itself out' like a minor hurricane) and expands over the whole of society – as, for instance, between

February and October 1917 in Russia – only then can we witness a massive shift of allegiance, reoriented towards the newly arisen alternative. And even then, the basic expectation of 'common sense' in crisis will inevitably remain the reconstitution of social stability and the establishment of a new normality as soon as feasible. At the same time, as historical experience teaches us, the continued disappointment of its expectations with regard to the productive stabilization of the new order tends to make 'common sense' revert to its earlier position. Not simply on account of 'enemy ideological influences' but, above all, because it is impossible to reconcile the objective structural determinations of 'common sense' – as rooted in its relationship to the fundamental social metabolism of which it is itself an organic part – with the perspective of living in a permanent 'state of emergency'.

9.3.5

Admittedly, from all this it clearly follows that genuine mass-involvement in a revolutionary enterprise is unthinkable without the profound crisis of the dominant material structures of society. However, this unequivocal rejection of the voluntarist and élitist perspective does not imply the advocacy of a 'fatalist conception of the philosophy of praxis' which calls for *waiting* until the crisis itself has done the necessary work on its own. It only means that the radical transformation of the 'ideological panorama of the age' cannot be defined within strictly ideological terms, as the *work of consciousness upon consciousness*. Rather, it must contain, as an organizationally articulated constituent of the overall strategy, the *materially effective practical negation* of the dominant reproductive structures, instead of strengthening them through the 'mixed economy' and through various forms of 'participation' in the socioeconomic and political *restabilization* of capital in crisis.

Without such constituents of radical negation and practical contestation, not only 100 years of so-called 'parliamentary socialism' but also 45 years of the 'Italian road to socialism' can only lead to the social-democratization of the Western working-class movement, including its formerly radical wing, and to the blind alley of the 'great historical compromise': great only in the measure of defeat which it signals for the socialist movement.

It must be stressed here that the materially effective practical negation of the dominant reproductive structures does not imply lawlessness or even an aprioristic rejection of the parliamentary framework as such. It involves, nevertheless, an organizationally sustained challenge to the crippling constraints which the parliamentary 'rules of the game' *one-sidedly* impose on the subaltern classes only. What concerns us in the present context is that while the parliamentary representatives of the ruling classes heavily rely, as a matter of course, on the *extra-parliamentary forces of capital* – which not only completely dominate the material foundations of society, but also happen to be rigorously organized in the political and cultural sphere, with immense resources at their disposal – the idea of *extra-parliamentary opposition and action* on the other side of the sociopolitical confrontation counts as absolute blasphemy.

A telling example of how things really stand was supplied by a television interview with Sir Campbell Adamson: the former Director General of the Confederation of British Industry. He revealed in this interview that he had actually threatened Harold Wilson – now appropriately Lord Wilson, but at the time Labour Prime Minister of the British Government – with a *general investment strike* if Wilson failed to respond positively to the ultimatum of his Confederation. Adamson candidly admitted that the threatened action would have been *unconstitutional* (in his words), adding that 'fortunately' in the end there was no need to proceed with the planned investment strike because 'the Prime Minister agreed to our demands'.

Thus, while the *extra-parliamentary* forces of *capital* can and *do*, without the slightest inhibition and scruples even as regards the blatantly *unconstitutional* character of their actions,[871] profoundly affect what happens in the political sphere, the corresponding extra-parliamentary potential of the working class – above all of its Trade Union movement – is heavily constrained, and ultimately paralysed, not only by repressive anti-Trade Union legislation, but even more so by the exigency to subordinate working-class demands to hypothetical or real electoral considerations.

This happens irrespective of whether the mass party of the working class is in opposition or in government. Thus the working-class movement, instead of making a radical impact on politics as its entrance into the parliamentary framework of constitutional contest had originally promised, is forced to suffer constant defeats through the discriminatory – and even cynically unconstitutional – operation of the 'liberal/democratic' legal and political rules, in the absence of an adequate assertion of its interests against the methods and actions of its adversary. This is why the proper articulation of the *socialist extra-parliamentary forces* as a self-asserting *mass* movement – in conjunction with the traditional parliamentary forms of political organization which badly need the *radicalizing support* of such extra-parliamentary forces – must be an integral part of the Gramscian strategy to transform 'the ideological panorama of the age'.

9.4 AUTHORITY IN THE LABOUR PROCESS AND IN SOCIETY AT LARGE

9.4.1

'Liberation', Marx argues, 'is a *historical* and not a *mental* act.'[872] This is so because the great obstacles, that must be overcome in order to make feasible in real historical terms the advocated autonomous action of the social individuals, happen to be located not in the realm of self-generating ideas but at the level of society's most vital reproductive structures. Moreover, what makes the realization of the conditions of genuine individual autonomy even more difficult to envisage is the fact that the reproductive structures in question have been articulated in the course of historical development in conjunction with deeply divisive and iniquitous forms of decision making. For these reasons, any attempt to offer a solution to such apparently insurmountable problems in the form of the World Spirit's resignatory reconciliation with itself (which we find in Hegel's monumental system), leaving the real individuals 'out in the cold' by condemning them to remain forever 'unconscious tools' in the hands of the Cunning of Reason, can only amount to an idealist glorification of the historically given material constraints. Within the framework of such a philosophy – no matter how great as an intellectual enterprise – the social contradictions that systematically frustrate the conscious aspirations of the individuals are amenable only to a pseudo-transcendence which leaves their antagonistic terms of reference in actuality standing.

The most challenging problem for socialists is how to turn the personal freedom of *each* individual into a tangible reality without which the antagonisms characteristic of hierarchical social orders are bound to be reproduced in one form or another. This is why the socialist historical project, as originally conceived by Marx, requires the formulation of strategies for action which do not wishfully abstract in their diagnoses of the individuals' predicament from the objective exigencies of the social reproduction process; nor do they tendentiously transubstantiate the changeable *historical* determinations of social intercourse into the *unalterable* pseudo-natural (or metaphysical) attributes of a preordained socioeconomic and political order, be that the one claimed by Hegel to correspond in its unfolding to 'the true *Theodicaea*'[873] or its less lofty but just as eternalized counterpart benevolently ruled by Adam Smith's 'invisible hand'.

To be sure, in their very different ways both the well intentioned but totally ineffective 'ought-to-be' of the Enlightenment, and the Hegelian hypostatization of the 'World Spirit', admit that there is a striking contradiction between the stubbornly persistent human aspirations for self-fulfilment and the prosaic constraints to which the individuals are compelled to accommodate themselves in the real world. However, given the standpoint of political economy that circumscribes the horizon of these thinkers, they are unable to point their finger at the structural antagonisms of the class-exploitative social metabolism itself as the culprit. For they themselves must take for granted as *insurmountable* the social parameters of class domination and subordination as the practical premiss of their own conceptualizations of the right and proper socioeconomic order.

Marx's conscious rejection of the standpoint of political economy makes it possible for him to offer a radically different diagnosis of the issues at stake, together with a solution that defines the question of *autonomy* in terms of the socially necessary productive life-activity of the *particular individuals*, instead of ascribing the power of autonomous action to some abstract *supra-individual* entity.[874]

This is how Marx argues the inseparability of individual autonomy and social emancipation:

> The transformation, through the division of labour, of personal powers (relations) into *material powers*, cannot be dispelled by dismissing the general idea of it from *one's mind*, but can only be abolished by the *individuals* again *subjecting these material powers to themselves* and abolishing the *division of labour*. This is not possible without the community. Only within the community has *each individual* the means of cultivating his gifts in all directions; hence *personal freedom* becomes possible only *within the community*. In the previous substitutes for the community, in the state, etc., personal freedom has existed only for the individuals who developed under the conditions of the ruling class, and only insofar as they were *individuals of this class*. The illusory community in which individuals have up till now combined always took on an *independent existence* in relation to them, and since it was the combination of one class over against another, it was at the same time for the oppressed class not only a completely illusory community, but a new fetter as well. In the *real community* the individuals obtain their *freedom* through their *association*.[875]

In the light of passages like this it is almost incomprehensible that Marx should be so often accused of superimposing the interests of 'abstract collectivism' on the individuals. As we can see, nothing could be further from the truth. In fact it is precisely the approach of his liberal castigators that remains inseparably tied to postulating some kind of supra-individual entity – like the earlier mentioned 'invisible hand' – under which the 'nature-determined' (hence by definition at their roots insurmountable) conflicts between egotistically self-oriented *individuals* are supposed to be not only constantly renewed but also conveniently reconciled within the framework of a market-dominated socioeconomic order.

Naturally, in such a conception it cannot be acknowledged that capitalist society is torn by irreconcilable *class* antagonisms, even if a curiously repressed awareness of the fundamental social confrontation constitutes the structuring core of the theories formulated from the standpoint of political economy. A meaningful share in the power of decision making cannot be conceded by theories of this kind to all individuals, since the prevailing class relations of super- and sub-ordination (which forcibly *exclude* the overwhelming majority of people from all decision making that really counts) must be considered absolutely 'non-negotiable'. Accordingly, the last thing they could envisage would be the realization of personal freedom and autonomy through the productive association of equals in a self-determining community. Instead, they must conceptualize as the only viable socioeconomic and political order one that reduces the question of class relations and determinations to utter irrelevance by hypostatizing in their place nature's iron determinations over instinctively quarrelsome individuals. In this way the absolute permanence of conflict in 'civil society' can be positively embraced by these theories in a tendentiously transfigured form.

Understandably, then, the contrast between the Marxian and the liberal approach to these problems could not be greater. In the case of the former, we find the acknowledgement that real personal freedom and autonomy (just like Babeuf's and Buonarroti's *'real equality'*) are possible only within the community that successfully emancipated itself from the internal antagonism of contending classes. On the other side, by contrast, the necessity to retain an unavoidably conflict-torn system of socioeconomic and political interchanges through which capital can enforce the 'final classification' (Comte) and domination of labour, rules out the idea of a harmonious association of the individuals as a *conceptual impossibility*.

This is why the concept of the *social individuals' productive association* cannot play any role whatsoever in liberal theories. Only the *isolated individual* – abstracted from all class relations so as to be subjected with unchallengeable finality to the supra-individual 'power of things' – can fulfil the necessary ideological legitimating function assumed by such theories. For the realization of genuine personal freedom and autonomy through the voluntary association of individuals, in a community of meaningful self-activity, necessarily presupposes the historical supersession of class antagonism and class exploitation. Clearly, however, from the standpoint of political economy – which, representing the interests of the beneficiary, must assume an affirmative attitude towards the perpetuation of the prevailing structural antagonisms without which the real creator of wealth, labour, could not be kept in subjection – the voluntary association of social individuals in a dynamically changing society is totally out of the question. Hence in theories formulated from the standpoint of political economy the individuals can only be brought together – in a mechanical/aggregative fashion – in an *abstract 'community'*, where their specific social determinations (inseparable from the given class divisions) do not really matter. And by the same token, only the isolated *abstract individuals* can fit into – or rather: be unproblematically subsumed under – this abstract 'community' of idealized market relations and their corresponding state formation.

Thus, thanks to the adoption of the isolated individual as the model in terms of which both the problems and the 'natural' solutions of capitalist society are made intelligible, *class* antagonisms are turned into – commendably 'competitive' and 'enterprising' – *individual* conflicts, and even the classes themselves appear on the stage as some sort of liberal/individualist afterthought. As a result of such, ideologically motivated, conceptual transformations, it is then stipulated that what is truly relevant about classes in capitalist society is not that people are *born* into them (which makes the constraining determinations of the contending classes *vis à vis* the individuals inherently problematical), but the absurdly exaggerated claim according to which the individuals can freely raise themselves to the higher ranks of society, or sink into the lower ones, as the case might be, on account of purely *personal* merit or failure (which is meant to *legitimize* the perpetuation of class exploitation, fully in accordance with the 'principle of justice', of course).

The repressive impact of the division of labour on the individuals is, therefore, not only not questioned in these theories. Worse than that, it is perversely metamorphosed into a fundamental virtue. For from the standpoint of political economy the structural hierarchies of the established division of labour must be taken for granted as absolutely permanent, even at the price of completely abandoning the once cherished ideal of individual autonomy to be appropriated by all. What is substituted for the latter is the advocacy of conferring rewards on a limited number of privileged individuals for their 'enterprising spirit', on the basis of the position they assume in the service of the 'power of things' through which *capital* asserts its control over society as a whole while conceding the *illusion* of autonomous action to its willing 'personifications'.

9.4.2
Since the individuals cannot emancipate themselves from the 'power of things' without subjecting the alienated material forces that dominate their lives to their consciously chosen aims, the question of individual autonomy becomes inseparable from radically altering the fundamental social metabolism on which everything else depends. This is why Marx talks about 'abolishing the division of labour'.

Once, however, this imperative is unequivocally stated, the enormity of the task itself must be acknowledged as well. For, given the intrinsic nature and ubiquitous diffusion of the division of labour, it is inconceivable to master the objective and subjective conditions of its 'abolition' in other than (a) only *global* terms; and (b) through a most *extensive* historical period. Indeed, strictly speaking, one cannot envisage at all the *abolition* of the division of labour; only its progressive 'withering away' through the radical transformation of the labour process itself and the simultaneous restructuring of the complex institutional framework within which the fundamental metabolic process of individual and social reproduction must be carried on. There can be no short cuts in this respect, just as with regard to the advocated historical supersession of the state – with which the task of overcoming the division of labour is inextricably intertwined – one can only have the *illusion* of shortcuts.

Two sets of problems arise in this context.

The first concerns the question of *necessary material mediations* by means of which a socialist society can extricate itself from the power of capital. The problematic of such mediations does not belong to this study but calls for an adequately detailed investigation, in conjunction with other important issues of a theory of transition. Nevertheless, it must be mentioned in passing that these problems appear only peripherally (if at all) in Marx's theory. However regrettable this may sound, Marx had to operate under the theoretical constraints of having to oppose in his confrontations with the adversary the 'eternalizing' tendency of bourgeois political economy, which constituted one of the most important and ideologically most revealing characteristics of the latter. In this way the stress had to be put on capital's historical *transience*. Thus Marx repeatedly underlined that 'capital is posited as a *mere point of transition*',[876] adding that the antithetical form in which capital as alienated labour counterposes itself to 'the working individual' is itself only '*fleeting* and produces the real conditions of its own suspension'.[877]

Another obvious reason behind the unfortunate theoretical omission of concern with the unavoidable material mediations imposed on all feasible transitional societies, on an extensive temporal scale, was that Marx did not have before him the weighty historical evidence that the power of capital survives, even if in a significantly altered form, in post-capitalist societies. At the same time, what was abundantly clear was that in the writings of Marx's theoretical adversaries:

> The aim is to present production – see e.g. Mill – as distinct from distribution etc., as encased in eternal natural laws independent of history, at which opportunity *bourgeois relations are quietly smuggled in* as the *inviolable natural laws* on which society in the abstract is founded. This is the more or less conscious purpose of the whole proceeding.[878]

Understandably, therefore, under the given circumstances, when Marx had to insist time and again on the inherently historical constitution and transient character of capital as a mode of socioeconomic interchange and control, he could not help understating the awesome magnitude of its stubborn historical persistence, together with its far-reaching negative implications for the prospects of socialist developments in the future.

The second set of problems indicated above is directly relevant to us in the assessment of ideology and social consciousness. For it concerns the question of social control in all spheres of life – from the management of the material reproductive processes and structures to the regulation of the manifold different kinds of interchanges in which the individuals engage in their everyday life – whatever their scope and complexity.

There is a long-standing tradition – going back in its liberal version all the way to the earliest theories of 'social contract' – which tendentiously (and fallaciously) equates the necessary control of the social processes (unavoidable in all conceivable forms of society) with the preponderant role of the state (characteristic of our own). 'Control' thus becomes synonymous with the power 'rightfully' assumed by the state, and any challenge to it is summarily dismissed as 'unconstitutional', 'irrational', and 'anarchistic'. As a result, the margin of legitimate action conceded to the individuals is defined in such a way that they are forced to accommodate themselves (not merely *de facto* – which could be challeged in principle – but on the ground of claimed *de jure* considerations) within the established boundaries of the dominant reproductive structures.

Moreover, in this way the state itself becomes a mysterious entity. It is depicted as the embodiment of the principle of legitimacy as such, coupled with the claim that this legitimacy directly emanates from the 'rational' individuals' properly self-interested interdeterminations. The prosaic truth, that the state in fact is not the embodiment of the 'principle of legitimacy' but of the prevailing *power relations*, and that it is constituted not on the basis of sovereign *individual* decisions but in response to the ongoing *class* antagonisms, remains hidden behind the impressive theoretical façade of the ruling ideology.

In reality the state's power is neither self-generated, nor is it the depository of individual determinations on which its claims to legitimacy rest. Its institutional constituents – from the cultural/ideological establishments to the judiciary and to the various repressive apparatuses – cannot account by themselves for the massive power which the state effectively exercises (while it does). Nor could they explain the periodic sudden collapse of state power and its subsequent reconstitution, at times in a significantly altered form. To attempt to make historical formations and developments of this kind intelligible in terms of the individuals' fictitious 'sovereignty' (in class societies), coupled with the projection of their equally fictitious 'contractual' inclinations, is even less plausible than the role assigned by Christian theologians to Pontius Pilate by dragging him into the Credo. For state power can only be sustained for as long as – and also, only to the extent to which – its symbiotic relationship to the material power structures of 'civil society' remains historically viable.

9.4.3

The state is essentially a *hierarchical command structure*. As such, it derives its problematical legitimacy not from its claimed 'constitutionality' (which invariably happens to be 'unconstitutional' in its original constitution), but from its ability to *enforce* the demands placed upon it.

Only marginally is the state itself the source of such demands, inasmuch as they are considered necessary for the continued exercise of the functions assigned to the state by the prevailing social order. Indeed, only under the conditions of a profound structural crisis and 'historical emergency' of the given socioeconomic order is the state able to superimpose itself, for a relatively short period of time, on the normal decision making structures and processes of 'civil society', with the implicit or explicit mandate to *reconstitute* 'at the earliest possible moment' (as it is often stated) the temporarily lost conditions of normality.

As a general rule, the normative requirements which the state is called upon to enforce by means of its hierarchical command structure are spontaneously generated, as objective determinations, by the fundamental material reproductive processes themselves. The state's suitability to meet such requirements, in virtue of its intrinsic nature as the hierarchical political command structure of society, becomes intelligible only if we bear in mind the dialectical 'correspondence' of the state's institutional articulation to the equally *hierarchical material command structure* of the established socioeconomic order itself.

Only because the particular members of society are distributed within the hierarchically organized productive structures of the ongoing labour process the way they are – in that the individuals are directly determined with regard to their very survival by the spontaneously enforced[879] structural relationship of super- and sub-ordination, equivalent to production-controlling command and its unquestionable execution – only on this ground can the state and its *relative* autonomy arise and sustain itself. As the blood-soaked history of the so-called 'primitive accumulation' – the necessary material premiss of the capitalist state's very existence, as well as of its hallowed 'rule of the law' – testifies, the violent expropriation of the means of production by the few at the expense of the overwhelming majority of the people first exists as a brute relation of forces and as the corresponding material command structure of society, however unruly. Only subsequently can the 'defence of property' be enshrined in endlessly multiplying (and in accordance with the changing circumstances of bourgeois rule more or less refined) legal statutes, so that in the end it can be idealized even by radical thinkers – like Rousseau – who proclaim that 'the right of property is the most sacred of all the rights of citizenship, and even more important in some respects than liberty itself'.[880]

In this sense, we may indeed assert that there is an objective *homology* of structures and modes of decision making between the state and the sphere of material reproduction, even if the functions fulfilled by the two are significantly different. The differences themselves become meaningful only if assessed in terms of the *historical specificity* of the overall division of labour characteristic of the given social formation. After all, it should not be forgotten that the state itself is the tangible manifestation – and one of the most important dimensions – of the social division of labour as such, and consequently it can only 'wither away' with the historical transcendence of the latter.

The homology between the power structures and modes of decision making of the state, on the one hand, and those articulated in the sphere of material reproduction, on the other, means neither the *identity* of the two (as depicted by eternalizing bourgeois thought which thereby sets up an 'iron cage' from which, veritably, there can be no escape), nor the *one-sided determination* of the state's functions by the material structures and reproductive processes of capitalist 'civil society' (as 'vulgar Marxists' would have it). It amounts, instead, to a genuine *interdependence* between the functioning of the state and the objective requirements of material reproduction within the framework of the prevailing social division of labour.

The neglect of this vital relationship of – historically qualified – interdependence tends to lead either to the wild exaggeration, or to the mechanistic denial of the state's relative autonomy. Since the latter arises from the facticity of the historically prevailing division of labour, it can amount neither to *less* nor to *more* 'independence' than the state's intrinsic determination as the materially generated – and therefore not only very real but simultaneously also objectively well defined and circumscribed – margin for essential co-ordinative, legitimatory, and repressive action which no other constituent of the overall social system can bring to effective realization. And by the same token, the restitution of this overall co-ordinative function to the no longer antagonistically torn social body should remove the need for setting up a separate organ for its repressively guaranteed implementation and concomitant sham legitimation in an antagonistic world.

To put it in another way, the state's relative autonomy exists because the material reproductive structures and functions of society are so constituted – in the form of historically specific systems of super- and sub-ordination – that they are incapable of fulfilling the necessary function of overall co-ordination without conferring its ultimate guarantee on an alienated, external body; so that the latter should put the seal of approval on the materially exercized, spontaneous enforcement of a totally unjustifiable – since profoundly *exploitative* – modality of production and distribution in and through the labour process, *legitimating* the latter in its own name against all rival claims that may arise in antagonistic societies.

Again, we can see that the alienation of labour and its conversion into a self-perpetuating controlling power, capital, precedes, as a socioeconomic facticity, the need for a guarantee of its antagonism-minimizing – i.e. allegedly 'legitimate', though by no means necessarily 'consensual' – continuation in existence. Moreover, one of the most important characteristics of the state's functional determination arises from the circumstance that the alienation of labour and its domination by capital cannot conceivably be justified at the level of the socioeconomic facticity itself which embraces only the naked relation of forces. Considered in its materiality, the world of capital has no ground for self-legitimation. Quite the contrary. For inasmuch as at the level of the basic metabolic structures and processes of society capital is compatible with one principle only – that of letting the naked relation of forces prevail not only in its hegemonic confrontation with labour but also *vis-à-vis* those of its own units which prove to be less viable in the relentless process of capital concentration and centralization – the principle of legitimation can only be tolerated to apply *outside* the sphere of capital's unchallengeable material authority, in the domain of the alienated political body.

This is why the need for a legitimatory 'communality' can only arise in a most abstract form, defining the conditions of its 'shared' membership in such a way that the justificatory formal/legal determination of 'equality before the law' (in terms of which everybody is 'equally forbidden to sleep under the bridges') should leave the material power relations absolutely intact. Understandably, therefore, although the capitalist state can introduce *partial* correctives to the deficiencies of the prevailing material processes, in the interest of fulfilling its necessary legitimatory functions, it is quite incapable of producing basic *structural* alterations even in a situation of major crisis. This is why the necessity to sweep aside the institutional articulation of the state in its entirety must be envisaged by the forces which aim at a radical structural change.

What makes it impossible for the capitalist state to produce fundamental changes at the level of the historically established socioeconomic metabolism itself is precisely the earlier mentioned objective homology in structures and modes of decision making between the legal/political sphere and 'civil society'. A homology which, paradoxically, both enhances the state's autonomy in some respects and strictly circumscribes it in others. Accordingly, the state can exercise its important controlling/coordinating functions only up to the point that remains compatible with the structural parameters of the capitalist socioeconomic metabolism, but not beyond.

To take an example directly relevant in the present context, given the objective homology of the material/reproductive and the legal/political structures, the *institutional articulation* of the *liberal/democratic state* as such is inseparable from, and totally unviable without, the *material reproductive articulation* of the capitalist *market* as a historically specific network of *distributive* interchanges deeply embedded in the *productive* structures of the given socioeconomic system. In this sense, a significant shift in the productive and distributive framework of capital in favour of *monopolistic* structures and processes – a shift which becomes visible both in the increasingly centralized control of the particular units of total social *production* and in the operation of the ever more globally intertwined network of commodity, labour, and financial *markets* – carries with it the far-reaching practical implication in accordance with which the relevant state institutions must be adjusted on the same lines, in order to match up to the altered requirements of the new conditions.

It is, therefore, by no means accidental that in the last decades the 'advanced' capitalist state had more and more assumed a 'facilitating' or 'enabling' role in the service of such transformations. It not only unceremoniously removed the obstacles – once erected in the name of 'free competition' by the liberal/democratic state – from the path of the monopolistic concentration of economic power, but took the most active initiative for the acceleration of the whole process, in harmony with the demands emanating from the changing material ground.

The part played by the state in pushing through the notorious monopolistic 'denationalizations' (or 'privatizations') of the recent period is quite revealing in this respect. All the more so, since the appropriate adjustments in the *ideological* rationalization of the unfolding monopolistic developments could not keep pace with the 'radical' squandering of the 'family silver' (condemned as such by no less an authority than former Conservative Prime Minister Harold Macmillan) which characterized the actual transformations themselves. For under the pressure of the apparently irresistible monopolistic tendencies, a noticeable distancing from the heritage of the paternalistic liberal/democratic past had to take place not only at the level of the material reproductive structures but also in the correspondingly modified state institutions and practices. This had to be done despite the fact that the – often embarrassing – old forms of ideological rationalization could not be for the time being dispensed with.

Thus, in recent years, under the banners of liberal/democratic ideology and its claimed defence of 'individual freedom', we have been presented in the field of politics with some truly peculiar *faits accomplis*. In this way, we had to witness the savage curtailment of 'local democracy' (in England through the abolition of the Greater London Council, the imposition of 'rate capping' and the 'poll tax' by central government, the frequent overruling of the planning decisions of local councils by the central authorities in the interest of big business, etc., etc.) as well as the conversion of the 'mother of democracy', Parliament itself, into a glorified rubber stamp. Even the traditional functions of the Cabinet have been unashamedly nullified, thanks to the now prevailing authoritarian practice of short circuiting the earlier decision making processes by the deliberations of cosy 'Cabinet Committees' in which less than a mere handful of people monopolize the power of political control, in unison with the 'captains of industry' at the head of the dominant monopolistic corporations.

Some years ago the Secretary of State of the US Administration declared with undisguised cynicism that 'The business of the United States Government is to protect the interests of American Business.' Naturally, the same ethos animates the governments of the other 'liberal democracies' too, subject only to the qualification made necessary by their more or less prominent position in the international pecking order of monopoly capital. This is how the complementary command structures of capital fulfil the functions assigned to them by the historically prevailing social division of labour.

9.4.4

One of the most paradoxical characteristics of the state's objective determination is that it is called upon to fulfil some all-embracing coordinating functions without possessing its own material infrastructure adequate to the task. For the existence of a (no matter how powerful) repressive apparatus – which itself must be materially sustained by the productive efforts of 'civil society' – should not be confused with the substantive material infrastructure necessary for the realization of the state's mandate. In this sense we may speak of the precarious nature and inherent fragility of the state's material foundations.

Indeed, the exercise of the necessary state functions would be threatened by permanent instability – which would be quite intolerable from the point of view of the societal reproduction process – if the material factors themselves spontaneously did not make their impact on the side of the state, reinforcing its claims on society's relatively limited resources. Without this, the state could not become the generally acknowledged arbitrator over the allocation of the pooled funds of society. On the contrary, it would be compelled to fight tooth and nail, against rival claims, for the successful expropriation of its own – bitterly resented – share from the social product (as in fact often happens with military dictatorships).

The point is that the overall controlling and coordinating functions exercised by the state represent a *structural necessity* without which the capitalist formation could not maintain itself in existence. This is why the state's ultimate arbitrating role is accepted without serious contest. At the same time, however, neither the content of state arbitration and control, nor its material instruments of implementation originate in the legal and political sphere.

The state itself could not effectively control the undisturbed and economically viable distribution of commodities in capitalist society, let alone the distribution of the people in stable structures of super- and subordination (the social classes) adequately matching the demands that arise from the most varied (and, moreover, constantly changing) branches of production on a daily basis. Instead, it must confine its activities to the functions more or less directly relevant to the defence (and legitimation) of the *structural parameters* of the given socioeconomic order. Consequently the state cannot help in the end 'acknowledging' the 'rational actuality' of the unfolding *monopolistic* tendencies, so as to facilitate unquestioningly their 'legitimate' rise to dominance, irrespective of how much the original *anti-monopolistic* legal statutes and their ideological justification – as conditioned by the structural demands of an earlier phase of development – must be contradicted in the course of such readjustments.

It is the spontaneous regulatory self-determination of capitalism as a system of production and distribution – with its specific mode of controlling the vital metabolic processes of society through the reified second order mediations of the labour, commodity, and financial markets – which makes it possible for the state to fulfil on such foundations *its own* controlling/ coordinating functions. It is because the spontaneous material regulatory structures and processes of the capitalist system are *ubiquitous*, as well as *successful* in the particular domains concerned with securing the material requirements of societal reproduction; it is because of this circumstance that the capitalist state formation does not have to over-extend itself into areas over which its power would turn out to be hollow. Instead, the state can become effective in its specific role of defending and legitimating the structural parameters of the established order against external and internal challenge. The material and human resources needed for the fulfilment of its coordinating/defensive/legitimatory role are readily made available to the state even under the circumstances of great hardship; but only for the fulfilment of that role. For this reason alone, if for no others, the idea of transforming the capitalist system of production and distribution into a socialist one through the adoption of gradual political measures must be a non-starter. The notorious capitulation of German Social Democracy to the dominant class and state interests at the outbreak of the first world war graphically demonstrated that the entire institutional network of the capitalist political system, including its parliamentary opposition, is firmly locked into the structural parameters of the ruling socioeconomic order.

The capitalist state is quite incapable of assuming the substantive reproductive functions of the material regulatory structures, except to a minimal extent in an extreme situation of emergency. But neither is it expected to do so under normal circumstances. In view of its intrinsic constitution, the state could not control the labour process even if its resources were multiplied by a hundredfold, given the *ubiquitousness* of the particular productive structures which would have to be brought under its necessarily limited power of control. Tragically, in this respect, the failure of post-capitalist societies in the sphere of production must be attributed to a very large extent to their attempt to assign such metabolic controlling functions to a centralized political state, when in reality the *state as such* is not suitable to the realization of the task that involves, one way or another, the everyday life-activity of each individual.

Nor could the capitalist state act as the global coordinator of social interchange in and through the legal and political sphere if it had to impose a *separate* global matrix – one uniquely of its own – upon society. Not only would it chronically lack the prohibitive material and human resources needed for such a task, but it would also constantly clash with those forces of 'civil society' which, for whatever reason, would fail to conform to the preconceived requirements of its arbitrarily totalizing matrix. Again the case of military dictatorships is instructive in this regard. For as a rule in our age they manage to survive (so long as they do) only by the grace of the dominant imperialist power – the list of such dictatorships and military client regimes of the United States is extensive, from the Greece of the Colonels to Pinochet's Chile, and from South Vietnam in the 1960s and early 1970s to El Salvador today – imposing an utterly *alien* totalizing matrix on their country, together with the destructive burden of permanent instability and constant turmoil.

The totalizing legal/political forms of control exercised by the capitalist state possess a much more secure material foundation. They are not superimposed from the outside on a recalcitrant framework of socioeconomic control, as an alien matrix, but faithfully transpose to the legal and political sphere the objective requirements of the latter, readjusting themselves, as the circumstances demand, parallel to the shift in favour of monopoly in the substantive metabolic structures and processes of capitalist society. Thus, the issue of recalcitrance or willingness does not hinge on the personnel involved but above all on the objective affinity between the controlling structures of the historically prevailing social division of labour. The officials occupying the top echelons of the state as a command structure are no *less* the 'personifications of capital' than the 'captains of industry'; only in a *different* way. Neither should one fallaciously misdescribe the impact emanating from the objective *homology of structures* as the manifestation of genuine *popular consent*. To be sure, it is in the interest of the ruling ideology to present matters in that light, and its representatives do not miss a single opportunity to do so. Regrettably, however, at times also theories which profess critical intent adopt the self-same assessment as the key premiss of their confused and hopelessly self-defeating discourse on 'hegemony' in the 'post-Marxian' mould.

The global controlling and coordinating authority of the capitalist state arises from, and is constantly reproduced by, the ubiquitous network of substantive metabolic structures which spontaneously control in their partiality and specificity every single unit constitutive of the capitalist labour process, together with its corresponding distributive determinations. Thus, a spontaneous mode of aggregative totalization – call it 'the invisible hand' or whatever else – is operative at the level of the fundamental reproductive structures themselves. Without the latter the legal and political form of totalization exercised by the capitalist state would be utterly vulnerable, if feasible at all.

The state itself only supplies the legitimatory framework of the noncontestable totalizer, the 'invisible hand', but not its substance. This is why the ruling class's ever-repeated assertion that 'there is no alternative' does not rebound against the state itself, despite the fact that its spokesmen (and women) at the apex of the state organs of control utter such words of unmitigated capitalist wisdom on behalf of the 'invisible hand'. Indeed, the capitalist state as such is the tangible embodiment – as well as the active guarantor – that there can be no alternative to the given socioeconomic and political system so long as its complementary command structures reciprocally sustain one another, 'delivering the goods' on the ground of the relatively undisturbed functioning of the overall reproduction process. This is what appears through the refractive lens of the ruling ideology as deservedly legitimatory 'popular consent'. Through this distorting lens the actual order in which the *a posteriori* and more or less resigned acknowledgement, by 'common sense', of the system's alternative-denying stability (notwithstanding its contradictions and inhumanities) is completely reversed, and projected onto the screen of ideological apologetics as *positive approval* freely exercised by the sovereign popular will from which the 'democratic order' derives its strength and proper *justification*.

9.4.5
To be sure, no social order can escape the imperative of gaining adequate mastery over the conditions necessary for its successful reproduction on a continuing basis. This involves, on the one hand, the task of securing the undisturbed internal functioning of the *particular units* whose combined activity constitutes the characteristic labour process of the socioeconomic order in question. At the same time, on the other hand, the necessity of *integrating* (loosely or firmly, as the historical conditions require) the great multiplicity of productive units into a viable overall *system*, must also be satisfied. For neither of the two vital tasks could be successfully fulfilled for a prolonged period of time without the other.

The historical specificity of any particular socioeconomic order is defined by the constitutive relationship between its manifold '*micro-structures*' and its synthesizing '*macro-structure*'. This relationship is inherently dialectical as well as historical. Dialectical, in that the nature of the relationship between the parts and the whole can only be grasped in terms of genuine *reciprocal determinations* that result in a *dynamic unity*. Accordingly, the micro-structures bear the indelible marks of the macro-structure to which they belong; and vice versa, the macro-structure of the particular socioeconomic formation represents the overall configuration of its multifaceted constituents. As to the question of inexorable historical determinations, the macro-structure of any social formation is itself made of historically determinate micro-structures which cannot escape the necessary limitations – and corresponding life-span – of their social specificity. In other words, the historical character of the overall social complex is practically defined and constantly redefined by the *changing overall configuration* of the particular complexes among themselves within the objective dynamics of the unfolding transformations.

In this sense, the particular socioeconomic formation is bound to disintegrate, in due course, whether its cementing overall structure suffers a major breach, or in case its constitutive micro-structures are internally undermined for some reason. As a paradigm example of the first, we may recall the way in which colonial/imperalist penetration superimposed the macro-structure of the capitalist 'metropolitan' countries over the conquered territories, destroying in the end their mode of production in its entirety by making the indigenous productive units (i.e. the original microstructures of the countries in question) economically unsustainable within the new synthesizing framework. With regard to the second case – concerning the internally caused disruption and ultimate disintegration of a productive system – it is enough to think of the final phase in the development of the guild system. We must remember in this respect above all the disruptive penetration of merchant capital into the formerly well protected productive units and the increasing domination of exchange-value over use-value (which used to orient firmly and with great success the productive practices of the guild system) resulting from such penetration.

We should not ignore, however, the *system-strengthening* aspect of this dialectical relationship between the overall socioeconomic complex and its micro-structures. It asserts itself in such a way that so long as the latter are economically viable in their internal constitution – i.e. in the case of the capitalist system, so long as they are capable not only of securing the necessary material resources, but also of generating the appropriate scientific and technological know-how, together with the required productive and organizational/managerial skills, for successfully reproducing themselves on an *ever-expanding* scale – the power of the system as a whole is correspondingly reinforced thereby, enabling it to react back in its own turn, with a strengthening/expansionary impact, on the particular production units. This happens irrespective of how problematical the whole process might turn out to be in its global and historical implications, extracting in the end a prohibitive price from the people involved for the tragic circumstance that the system and its constitutive parts can self-expansively renew themselves only on condition that the long-term consequences of such destructive self-renewal are disregarded (and, of course, the forces of critical concern swept aside), for as long as the productive order as a whole does not reach its ultimate limits and suffers an irreversible structural breakdown.

This is the 'tendency of *things*'.[881] Its harmful effects cannot be countered unless the social individuals consciously assume control over the *whole* network of objective interconnections within which their productive life-activity evolves. The reason why they cannot do so under the prevailing conditions is because the *social antagonisms* inseparable from the historically established division of labour disrupt the link between the parts and the whole at the level of potential social control by making the iniquitous *partial* interests prevail in 'civil society', complementing them only by the rationalizing/legitimatory façade of an illusory 'common interest' in the sphere of legal and political relations. The latter by itself cannot act as a substantive corrective. For it merely acknowledges as an abstract *desideratum* the need for harmonizing the parts with the whole while, of necessity, it allows (and indeed actively helps) the dominant forces of the antagonistic social complex to follow their objective tendency of short-sighted self-assertion.

9.4.6
Naturally, the more complex the productive system becomes in its entirety, the greater will be the imperative to secure the undisturbed functioning of the fundamental social metabolism by means of some unchallengable material mechanisms; if, that is, the social individuals – for whatever reason – are not in a position of consciously controlling the structural relations of the established socioeconomic order. Since the effects of the breakdown or blockage that may occur in the parts of a closely intertwined complex are bound to reverberate in an amplified form over the system as a whole, the modality of the cementing/integrating overall control must be articulated in such a way that it should be able to minimize the potentially harmful impact of troubles arising in the partial complexes. This means, in the case of the capitalist system, the imposition of *objective* ('thing-like') forms of control, which operate *within* the subordinate structures themselves as the *unquestioned* (and, without overturning the ruling socioeconomic and political order, also unquestionable) *premises* of their productive and distributive practices, thereby obliterating in most instances the need for spelling them out as legally enforceable *formal* rules of operation.

In this way the overall requirements of the capitalist mode of production can be secured, while also maintaining the – no matter how problematical, yet by no means merely illusory – *autonomy* of the particular enterprise, so long as the latter can effectively sustain itself (in accordance with the practical premises which it considers to be its own intrinsic values) in the economic arena. For thanks to the type of totalizing interconnection through which the 'thing-like' rules are *materially* (even if not formally/legally) superimposed on all particular productive and distributive enterprises – namely, through the impersonal intermediary of the *rewarding or destructive market* itself, which objectively favours the strong against the weak – the tyrannical operative rules can be embraced by them as their own inherent 'rationality' and 'freely' orienting principles, as if they originated *inside* the particular firms, rather than at their 'grow or perish' interface.

At the same time, this cohesive and reciprocally sustaining interrelationship between the system as a whole and its economically viable parts is further strengthened by the circumstance that the 'personifications of capital' (i.e. the 'captains of industry' who are in charge of the partial complexes) are given an unchallengeable position within their own domain. For they can – indeed, to be more precise, they must – exercise the same kind of tyrannical authority internally (over the labour force, in all matters of substance) which they accept as perfectly natural from the market at large. This must be the case even when the unalterable economic dictates are rendered more palatable either by the soothing words of paternalistic 'understanding' or by the 'soft-selling' public relations expertise of manipulative 'managerial science'. In this respect, at least, the autonomy of the particular enterprise is quite genuine, however perverse, in view of its authoritarian domination of the real producers. Only when a major disaster strikes (whether at Bhopal in India or on some North Sea oil platform), only then is the fatefully inhuman, anti-labour substance of enterpreneurial autonomy – as exercised from the sole material premiss of profitability – revealed for a brief moment, underlining the gross violation of elementary safety requirements, with the full complicity of the capitalist state, and at times even with the 'free cooperation' of the labour force itself – which is in fact compelled to put up with such scandalous conditions under the threat of losing its livelihood.

9.4.7

What is at issue here concerns the most vital dimension of any society's socioeconomic metabolism, namely the control of the *operating conditions of production*.

The conditions here referred to embrace the *means* (or instruments) as well as the *material* of labour, together with the *rules* governing their employment. Considered under all three aspects, it is fairly obvious that in the course of historical development enormous changes take place with regard to the operating conditions of production. For in the case of primitive man, the self-made instruments of labour are not divorced from and set against him but constitute the '*inorganic extension*' of his organic body. At the same time, the material of labour confronts him as external *nature*, but not as the *alien man* who rules over his own society, conceding to him the possibility of self-reproduction only on condition that he accepts total dependency (for his very survival) on an alienated power of control. And even much later, when the social division of labour is already firmly consolidated in the form of class exploitation, the power of alien control ultimately sanctioned by the threat or actual exercise of *violence* is far less mystifying than under capitalist conditions. For what is external and forced in the exercise of controlling authority appears as *external* and *forced*, rather than as the 'just' consummation of a 'freely entered' and 'fair' contractual relationship.

The worst aspect of 'commodity fetishism' is precisely the way in which it affects the control of the operating conditions of production. For one thing, it creates the illusion that the authority which prevails in determining the nature, objectives, distributory shares, etc., of production is 'reason' itself, emanating directly from the objective conditions themselves as faithfully adhered to both by productivity-enhancing natural *science* and by '*efficiency-oriented*' (hence fully justified) entrepreneurial/managerial concern. Thus, the prevailing naked material power relations, as ruled by capital and its imperative of *profitable* (and only in that sense 'efficiency-oriented') *self-expansion*, are metamorphosed in the broadly diffused ideological reflections of capitalist authority into pure rationality and incontestable objectivity.

Moreover, this fetishistic misrepresentation of the commanding authority is complemented by its corresponding juridical image. Thus, the claims of pure rationality and unsurpassable economic viability are extended also to the sphere of political relations, depicting the inherently exploitative and – whenever the exploitative structural framework is practically challenged even openly repressive – capitalist order as the paradigm of economically beneficial civilized life itself. As Marx noted in his critique of such self-complacent ideological images:

> All the bourgeois economists are aware of is that production can be carried on better under the modern police than e.g. on the principle of might makes right. They forget only that this principle is also a legal relation, and that the right of the stronger prevails in their 'constitutional republics' as well, only in another form.[882]

Clearly, then, the claimed ideal realization of the equitable and universally rewarding 'rule of the law' is just as false an appearance as the pure rationality and objectivity of generalized commodity production in which the legitimacy of human need can only be recognized to the extent to which the production of use-value can be subordinated to the material dictates of self-expanding exchange-value.

In truth, these relations are much more confounding than it transpires even after identifying the complicated material determinants and vested interests behind the successfully prevailing practical mystifications. At the level of the dominant productive and distributive practices one's ability to bring to light the fundamental irrationality of a system of *profit-seeking at all costs* – which in the everyday life of the people asserts itself as incontestable rationality and ideally productive (i.e. truly 'efficient') objectivity – does not remove the paradoxical 'rationality of actuality' conceptualized by Hegel. For as a matter of fact, under the circumstances of capital's globally ever more dominant actuality the pursuit of profit truly *is* the one and only practically feasible rationality, arising from the innermost determinations of this mode of production. This is so no matter how *irrational* the capitalist cost-accountancy turns out to be in its long-term implications, as viewed not from the standpoint of political economy (reflecting the alienated and class divided structural power relations of present-day actuality), but from the historical perspective of 'socialized' (i.e. with regard to its fundamental social objectives united) humanity.

Furthermore, the way in which the relationship between the parts and the whole is objectively articulated, within the capitalist framework of structural interdeterminations, greatly reinforces the perverse 'rationality of the actual'. As we have seen above, the micro-structures (partial complexes) of the historically established socioeconomic formation act as a vital *system-strengthening* factor. Nowhere is this correlation more important than in the case of the capitalist system. For – in view of the fact that through the reciprocity of dialectical interchanges the macro-structure reflects itself into the micro-structures, which in their turn are also reflected in the changing configuration of the overall complex – the more truly all-embracing/integrated the system happens to be, the more difficult it becomes to modify it structurally by means of limited interventions in some of its constitutive parts.

Thus, the 'curse of interdependence', which frustrates the attempted partial negations of capital's power of domination, stems from one of the most dynamic aspects of this metabolic system. For only with the unfolding of capital's mode of production does 'global' become *truly global*, in the planetary sense. This means, on the one hand, that the possibility of assuming an effective *external* vantage point of negation against it is practically denied; and on the other hand, that using the levers made available by the *partial* manifestations of capitalist crisis by no means guarantees success over the closely intertwined and forcefully resistant whole.

Capital's 'staying power' is often depicted as emanating from the 'psychological' circumstance in terms of which the working people are, necessarily or contingently, tied to the partial complexes of society in which their productive and distributive practices take place and within which they have to reproduce themselves. Consequently, as argued by those who assert the necessary unbreakability of such ties (from the standpoint of the established order), on the basis of the claimed fact that they are animated by the rationality of self-interest and personal ambition, they cannot possibly contemplate attacking the very conditions of their own reproduction, except in an utterly irrational – 'Luddite' fashion; or, as the same consideration is expressed from the opposite viewpoint, proclaiming (in the spirit of one-sided theories of 'false consciousness') the mere 'psychological contingency' of the prevailing inertia, it is hypothesized that the members of the working class fail to overthrow the capitalist system because they are in the midst of an 'ideological crisis', and this alone prevents them from fulfilling their 'historic mission' for the realization of which the objective conditions themselves are fully ripe.

In reality what is at stake here is not a 'psychological' (or purely 'ideological') circumstance but an objective structural determination which, understandably, makes its impact *also* on the consciousness of the people concerned. If we need proof of the paralysing objective interdependencies and structural constraints that prevail in this respect, we should remind ourselves of the sad history of the *cooperative* movement; practically destroyed by the imperative to conform to the operational rules of the capitalist framework, notwithstanding the profound ideological commitment of many individuals and groups of workers to the idea of gradually extending the power of socialist forces by establishing such 'bridge-heads' over enemy territory. Similarly, the reality of postwar '*nationalizations*' within capitalist parameters, set against the optimistic original expectations, proved to be most disconcerting. For, far from conquering the 'commanding heights of the economy' in the interest of the promised gradual socialist transformation, they were in fact used to subsidize and revitalize profit-seeking private enterprise, excluding all the time the producers themselves from running the nationalized concerns, in conformity to the reifying requirements of commodity society.

All this shows quite clearly that blaming for the failures of the past and the present the 'undeveloped political consciousness' of the working people is totally beside the point. For the measure of objective difficulties encountered by all attempts at making *partial inroads* into the capitalist system, in the absence of a *structural* crisis, cannot be overstated.

9.4.8

Returning to the question of juridical fetishism in commodity society, it is important to stress that the demystification of the legally protected and idealized material power relations – i.e. the demonstration of the unacknowleged 'right of the mighty' in the capitalist 'constitutional republics' – is very far from being able to produce the necessary structural change. As Marx makes the same point with striking modesty, putting the significance of his own work of critical clarification in perspective: after the discovery of the component parts of the air the atmosphere itself remained unchanged.

Indeed, the problem in the present context is considerably more difficult and sobering than that. For even if the work of theoretical demystification is coupled with the practical negation of the capitalist juridical power relations (through the abolition of the exploitative private ownership of the means of production and the corresponding networks of exchange), we are still very far from the implementation of the required structural change, despite the dramatic shift accomplished in the legal/political sphere. It is in fact one of the most disheartening aspects of juridical fetishism that it creates the illusion of its own overdetermining importance – and that is precisely how it fulfils its functions in capitalist society – diverting thereby attention from the real target.

Unfortunately, however, by practically negating the specific capitalist juridical form of private ownership through its transformation into state ownership, many of the substantive conditions of the socioeconomic metabolism – at the level of the labour process and its identifiable productive structures, from the inherited plant and machinery to the material organization of the economic enterprise in accordance with the prevailing division of labour – remain basically unchanged, even if the 'personification of capital' on a hereditary basis is now rendered impossible.

Again, what is of overriding importance here concerns directly the practical levers available in a given society for effectively controlling the operating conditions of production. Commodity fetishism, and the doubly mystifying juridical form in which the material determinations of capital's rule over the social metabolism are articulated in the legal and political sphere, obfuscate these matters beyond belief. For in reality capital is *itself* essentially a *mode of control*, and not merely a – legally codified – *entitlement* to it.

This is true irrespective of the fact that under the specific historical conditions of capitalist society the entitlement to exercise control over production and distribution is 'constitutionally' assigned, in the form of hereditary *property rights*, to a limited number of individuals. For what really matters is the necessity of an *accumulation-securing* expropriation of surplus-value, and not its contingent form. The latter is bound to be modified anyway – even within strictly capitalistic social parameters – in the course of capital's inexorable self-expansion, in accordance with the changing intensity and scope of its practically feasible accumulation.

Accordingly, the question of *directing purpose and authority* must be made intelligible in terms of the material structural determinations upon which the varying possibilities of effective personal intervention in the societal reproduction process arise. For, paradoxical as it may sound, the objective power of decision making, and the corresponding unwritten (or non-formalized) authority of capital, *precedes* the strictly mandated authority of the capitalists themselves. This explains the apparent contradiction between the *individualistic ethos* and the *total conformism* with regard to *purpose* that characterizes the activity of the individual capitalists.

To be sure, the contradiction is obvious enough at the level of ideology, which turns into a mythical virtue the individualistic aspect of the actual correlation, obliterating at the same time the necessary connection of profit-seeking individualism with the underlying imperative of total conformity to the objective requirements of the system. In reality, though, this ideological contradiction is of very little practical importance. For inasmuch as the private capitalists represent the historically specific personifications of capital, they have to exercise an *economic* form of control over the social metabolism from the material premiss of inherited, or acquired (and henceforth inheritable) property, which defines them as more or less prominent individuals, in accordance with the controlling power of their tangible material possessions. Furthermore, the untranscendable *competitive* dimension of the capitalist mode of socioeconomic reproduction – i.e. the ongoing competition not only among capitalists but, much more importantly, between capital and labour – confers upon the particular agents of 'economic enterprise' a self-assertive individualist role (no matter how class-mandated) in which they can excel or fail to varying degrees. This makes the ethos of their 'possessive individualism' quite genuine, no matter how misconceived with regard to its real ground of determination.

On the other hand, the total conformity of purpose which fuels the single-minded activity of the individual capitalists is not their own making. In fact it would be quite impossible to explain such uniformity (and slavish conformity) of purpose in individualistic terms, be that even with the help of the most ingenious 'parallelogrammatic' models. By contrast, however, the historical specificity of the capitalist mode of socioeconomic control makes it perfectly intelligible. For the objective structural imperative of *self-expansion* inseparable from capital as a mode of control (under all its historically known as well as in principle feasible forms of existence) makes it an absolute requirement for its personifications, under the prevailing circumstances, to define the necessary *expansion of exchange-value* of which they are the custodians as their own rational objective, summed up in the maxim: 'succeed by growth or perish'.

We have to take note of two important and frequently misrepresented traits of development in the present context.

First, that despite the well known attempts by vested interests to 'eternalize' the capitalist system of metabolic control, no other mode of production was ever characterized by the structural imperative of self-expansion in the course of human history. Thus, contrary to much apologetic wishful thinking, there can be no a priori ground for anticipating the permanence of this system of control in the future. What needs explaining (and countering) is precisely the alienating preponderance of capital's power of domination *despite its uniqueness* in history, instead of being fallaciously metamorphosed into a *universal* rule.

The second point is that the dehumanizing pursuit of wealth-expansion by the individual capitalists is not the result of some *distorting* ideological determination (which, therefore, in principle could be done away with by reform-minded 'caring capitalists' and their Bernsteinian social democratic brethren) but corresponds to a highly *rational* design. For the individual capitalists who might like to challenge the structural imperatives of the system (expressing by deeds, not by words only, their misgivings about the 'unacceptable face of capitalism'), or, much more representatively, all those who simply fail to live up in an economically viable way to capital's ruthless demands for properly 'entrepreneurial' competitive behaviour, will soon enough find out that by their non-conformity (whatever the reasons) they *objectively* expel themselves at once from the domain of control. They really have no alternative.

This is how the required match between capital, as the reified mode of control of the established social order, and its willing personifications – including the few 'grudging' ones – is actually produced and, through the competitive struggle over very real stakes, constantly reproduced. As a result, the blind and naked power emanating from capital's material being is transformed into the individualized controlling authority of property-owners and into the uniform directing purpose 'freely' adopted and consciously pursued by them. Nevertheless, the real controlling power remains deeply embedded in the material structures themselves. Personalized authority can only *conform* to the dictates emanating from this material power which 'lends', so to speak, the entitlement to control the reproductive processes of capitalist society on condition that *its* demands are fully implemented. It is quite revealing in this respect that the responsibility for the greatest oil industry disaster the world has ever known – amidst bitter accusations, by the relevant trade union, directed at the company's gross negligence in providing the necessary (and rather costly) safety measures and at its disregard for the warnings provided by smaller past accidents on the same platform – should be with a firm (Occidental Petroleum) whose owner had the reputation of being an enlightened and caring capitalist.

9.4.9

Given these determinations, the real target of socialist critique obviously cannot be the mystifying capitalist juridical form itself. It must be, rather, the objective power that creates and continues to sustain the individualized and with regard to some of its major aspects also formally institutionalized controlling authority.

Naturally, the difficulties facing post-capitalist societies in this respect are enormous. For the legally instituted removal of the juridical entitlement as such from the formerly exclusive property of the 'personifications of capital' leaves the question of capital's real mode of existence – as the *materially* and not merely *juridically* controlling force of the social metabolism – fundamentally unresolved. Indeed, the objective constraints which prevent the abolition of the inherited social division of labour, under circumstances when it becomes necessary to do away with the earlier personifications of capital in 'civil society' through the agency of the state, creates a *vacuum* that sooner or later must be filled in some form.

It is one of the most unexpected 'ironies of history' that the persistence of the inherited material structures in post-capitalist societies, coupled with the forcefully accomplished legal and political changes, calls into being new and extremely problematical forms of 'socialist *personification*'. In fact the aspect of personification is much more prominent in the reproductive processes of all known post-capitalist societies than under capitalism, where many of the necessary regulative functions of socioeconomic interchange are automatically (and unchallengeably) exercised by impersonal market forces and other depersonalized institutions of capitalist reification. To put the contrast as sharply as possible into relief, whereas under the conditions of generalized commodity production even the worst *man-made disasters* can be excused in the name of the 'power of things' (described by the mouthpieces of capital as 'forces beyond our control'), in post-capitalist societies the personified and allegedly omnipotent authority in charge of decision making takes not only the credit for the achievements of the people under its control, but can be blamed just as soundly even for *natural calamities*.

This new phenomenon of personification is often dismissed by concerned critics – under the term of *'bureaucratization'* – as a 'political degeneration' and, consequently, as a *politically corrigible* condition. Two circumstances of seminal importance seem to be overlooked by such a diagnosis. First, that – far from being a post-capitalist phenomenon – a massive growth in bureaucratism characterizes capitalistic developments. This happens to be the case not only in the legal and political sphere but also in the domain of material production and distribution, especially in the twentieth century, as even the most class-conscious defenders of commodity society are forced to acknowledge it.[883] And second, that what is summarily described as 'bureaucratism' in post-capitalist societies covers both the traditional bureaucratic functions, and those which under capitalism are carried out by the 'personifications of capital' in the economy in fulfilment of genuinely productive tasks.

The material imperatives intrinsic to a given system, however overwhelming, cannot impose themselves over society without the intervention of human agency. Their objective structural determinations and material limits can only assert themselves by exercising a determinate – more or less sharply corrective – impact on the actions of the individuals and groups at work in the historically constituted social complex. The people who carry out the tasks of coordination and control conceptualize the objective characteristics of the established institutional and instrumental framework as the margin of viable productive and distributive activity, anticipating certain results and instituting the necessary adjustments if they encounter major resistances. This is how even the most voluntaristic decision making is bound to be humbled in due course by the 'force of circumstance', though usually only after the imposition of enormous human costs, as the tragic history of Stalinist mismanagement testifies. And by the same token, correct evaluation of the prevailing constraints and their objective potentialities for adjustment in line with the desired objectives can significantly enlarge the originally available margin of action.

Thus, no social system can function without its specific form of 'personification' through which strategic anticipations can be formulated and practically tested by the intervention of corrective feed-back. The problem, though, in post-capitalist societies is that although the *nominal* power of personified decision-making authority is extended beyond comparison, it cannot match even remotely the need for an *effective* power of control over the recalcitrant material structures. The vacuum created by the necessary juridical intervention – which not only abolishes the private property of the means of production but simultaneously also puts out of commission the capitalist market and the formerly unquestioned normative authority of the 'invisible hand' – must be filled through the *political* agency of 'visible hands' badly suited to carry out the necessary *economic* task.

Moreover, since the 'invisible hand' at work in the capitalist market is also the *'invisible totalizer'* of the fragmentarily constituted overall productive and distributive complex, a new and equally powerful totalizer must be found to take over the vital coordinating and integrative functions of its abolished predecessor. Also, *'socialist accumulation'* remains for a long time as pressing an imperative in post-capitalist societies as *capital accumulation* used to be in the inherited system, if not more so. Consequently on both counts – i.e. both as regards the necessity to find an alternative to the 'invisible totalizer' and the need for an authority capable of imposing on the producers a forced rate of 'socialist accumulation', on the ground of the existing 'state of emergency' – the post-capitalist state, under the prevailing historical circumstances, has to assume the role of a *centralized* political controlling authority. As a result, new resistances are created through the structural mismatch between the post-capitalist state's objective constitution and the task of economically managing the everyday functions of production and distribution. To add insult to injury, for the new material and human resistances (and for the failures caused primarily by the state's inadequacies to deal successfully, as promised, with the task of improving socioeconomic reproduction) the blame is put on a mythical 'internal enemy'. At the same time, the vicious circle of instituting more centralized control in order to compensate for the economic failures of centralized political control is further strengthened, setting into motion a process of state-bureaucratic development which has its self-sustaining logic and inertia.

Clearly, then, bureaucratization is quite prominent in post-capitalist societies. But, just as clearly, it is not simply the consequence of 'political degeneration'. Nor could it be rectified by the adoption of even the most radical set of political measures. For its causes arise in the first place from the inherited material structures and from the corresponding social division of labour to which the unavoidable juridical intervention against capitalist private property adds its further complications. There is no way of avoiding the severe practical dilemma which, on the one hand, calls for a most powerful centralized political intervention (both for abolishing the exploitative socioeconomic relations wedded to the old property system and for protecting the new juridical form against internal and external subversion) while, on the other hand, also anticipates the necessary failure of political centralism as regards the much more difficult task of genuinely *decentralizing* and profoundly restructuring the instrumental and institutional complexes of societal reproduction in their entirety.

It is fairly obvious that capitalist private property cannot be abolished without the power of a centralized political authority. For even its *partial* (and completely *reversible*) curtailment, in the form of the well known postwar 'nationalizations', needed the intervention of the centralized capitalist state. What is less obvious though, because of the impersonal character of the spontaneously imposed capitalistic decision making processes and structures, is that the system of generalized commodity production is *authoritarian* to the core; and that it could not function at all without remaining authoritarian at the level of 'civil society', i.e. where the hierarchically ordered material reproductive structures of society are complemented by an equally hierarchical authority of decision making from which the producers themselves are categorically excluded.

This is the material reproductive framework which the post-capitalistic society of necessity inherits. Changing the juridical form of entitlement to control does not *ipso facto* change the materially embedded hierarchical structure of metabolic control itself to which the system, as it stands, is successfully amenable. For in the form in which it is taken over from the capitalist order, it is in tune only with authoritarian modes of decision making. Thus, also under this latter aspect, the post-capitalist state cannot help being authoritarian (and correspondingly bureaucratic) for as long as the inherited reproductive framework itself is not effectively *restructured* and profoundly *democratized*, in a way totally unimaginable under the conditions of capitalist market society. No amount of political goodwill can be a substitute for that. Thus, the fate of '*glasnost*' itself surely depends on the successful implementation of '*perestroika*' in the above sense, and not simply on the – however necessary – improvement in the 'economic efficiency' of the country.

It is one of the most bewildering aspects of capital's rule over society that under its system of control the operating conditions of production assume the fetishistic character of 'pure *materiality*'. They are conceptualized as nothing but the means and the material of production to which (as regards their conditions of exercise) only the rationally uncontestable considerations of 'technical efficiency' – said to arise directly from the nature of the material factors themselves – must be added.

This misrepresentation of the operating conditions successfully conceals the *tyrannical normativity* intrinsic to their objective constitution, both as material *preconditions* of production – according to which the very possibility of production (and survival for the workers) is premised by the 'constitutionally' safeguarded, and in its origins utterly violent, divorce of the means of production from the real producers – and as *functional/operational rules* exercised on a daily basis by the despotic controlling authority in charge of the particular capitalistic enterprises. Yet, on the face of it, everything seems to be ordered and decided by 'rational procedures', claimed to arise directly from concentrating with utmost objectivity on the realization of 'maximum efficiency' – from which the system can derive its ground of justification. In fact this fetishistic semblance of 'rationality', 'objectivity' and 'efficiency' – which hides the underlying despotic normativity – is so powerful that (as a matter of ultimate irony) even 'market socialists' are captivated by it.

Naturally, the success of any mode of production, including the socialist one, is inconceivable without a rational and efficient system of resource-management. The primary meaning of the term 'economy' is in fact precisely this proposition summed up in one word. However, what all those who are charmed by the siren song of market-determined 'efficiency' seem to forget is that by far the most important resource for economic and social development is none other than the human being itself.

This is why there can be no question of adopting even partially the methods and procedures of capitalistic market society as models for socialist productive advancement. On the contrary, in comparing the guiding principles of the two systems we are confronted by fundamental *incompatibilities*. For capital *must* treat human resources, just like everything else, as '*costs of production*' to be minimized – and eliminated as much as possible from the labour process, as the perilous growth of 'structural unemployment' testifies – through the application of its ruthless 'rationalizing efficiency', irrespective of the *human costs*. The reified authority of capital can only be exercised to this end.

The line of demarcation between socialist conceptions and the various ideologies representing the 'standpoint of political economy' is sharply drawn in relation to this vital issue. For the former continue to insist on the objective viability of the autonomous self-definition and action of the social individuals in a new social order, whereas the latter cannot help treating the producers in a way that degrades them to the level at which they can enter capital's horizon as the disposable 'costs of production'.

Inevitably, therefore, the role of authority, both in the constitutive units of the labour process and in society at large, is conceptualized in radically different ways by the representatives of the opposing social forces. On one side, voicing the interests of the ruling class with claims that there can be no other order than the established 'natural order', it is stipulated that the labour process ought to be managed under the iron discipline of capital, eulogizing the success of the recently instituted Draconian anti-trade union laws in these words, 'The greatest single achievement of Mrs Thatcher's government has been to pioneer a return to industrial discipline.'[884] At the same time, the role of authority in society at large is visualized as the necessary extension of capital's hierarchy-enforcing power, lamenting that in contemporary society, 'Where there was once a *natural social order*, there has grown up a *disrespect for authority* and a mindless wish to flout the rules, and defy both law and convention.'[885] The lost golden age of unquestioned submission to authority is idealized in the same vein:

The old, extended families of grandparents, aunts and uncles, cousins, brothers and sisters were *powerful organisms and bulwarks of social order*.

Children were given a sense of continuity and *their place in the natural order*. Family *hierarchy* and respect for one's elders was matched by *hierarchies* and a sense of purpose and *order* elsewhere – in the school, in the churches, the public life at local and national level.[886]

Not surprisingly, therefore, it is advocated by the same ideologists that the old order should be reconstituted both through the forceful exercise of repressive laws by the state organs of control, and by mobilizing the cultural/ideological institutions of society for the realization of the same objective. Thus, they pontificate that:

The church, for example, needs to stop arguing over the virgin birth and women priests and return to its *basic role in society* as a moral guide.[887] [Meaning, of course, 'as a bulwark of the natural social order'.]

In complete contrast, on the other side of the social divide, socialists argue that the only authority appropriate to the task of managing human beings as the vital resources of social and economic advancement is the self-constituting authority of the associated producers themselves. *Self-management* is considered by them not only practically feasible but historically necessary as well, in view of the growing internal contradictions of the capitalist reproductive system and the crisis of authority now openly admitted even by its most aggressive defenders.

Obviously, then, the gap between these two conceptions of authority is quite unbridgeable, indicating the persistence of objective antagonisms as their ground of determination. This and related issues need to be discussed on the concluding pages.

9.5 AUTHORITY AND AUTONOMY: SELF-ACTIVITY OF THE ASSOCIATED PRODUCERS

9.5.1

In the final analysis, what makes it imperative for socialist aspirations to envisage progressively doing away with *capital as such* is not the strictly economic or technical inflexibility of the latter (which can be adjusted to a considerable extent within its own structural limits, as twentieth-century developments amply prove). Rather, it is that capital is totally incompatible with the necessary *autonomous* mode of action of the social individuals. For it cannot conceivably hand over even *partially* its mode of – alienated, aprioristically determined, and by its very nature *unrestrainably totalizing* – control to human beings without abolishing itself.

Capital's only feasible mode of control emanates from its innermost *ontological* determination as a reified self-expanding mechanism to which everything in the sphere of social reproduction must be subordinated. Accordingly, the capitalist processes of control within the particular units of the established productive system must be complemented in society as a whole by the kind of social arrangements which secure and enhance the power of capital everywhere. The function of the latter is to facilitate capital's unquestionable domination of the producers in the interest of maintaining the only kind of social reproduction with which its mode of – dynamic, despotic, and reified – control is compatible. As Marx forcefully argues,

> The *a priori* system on which the division of labour, within the *workshop*, is regularly carried out, becomes in the division of labour within the *society*, an a posteriori, *nature-imposed* necessity ... Division of labour within the workshop implies the *undisputed authority of the capitalist* over men, that are but *parts of a mechanism* that belongs to him. The division of labour within the society brings into contact independent commodity-producers, who acknowledge no other authority but that of competition, of the *coercion* exerted by the pressure of their mutual interests; just as in the animal kingdom, the *bellum omnium contra omnes* more or less preserves the conditions of existence of every species. The same bourgeois mind which praises division of labour in the workshop, life-long annexation of the labourer to a partial operation, and his *complete subjection to capital*, as being an organization of labour that increases its productiveness – that same bourgeois mind denounces with equal vigour every conscious attempt to *socially control* and regulate the process of production, as an inroad upon such sacred things as the rights of property, freedom and unrestricted play for the bent of the individual capitalist. It is very characteristic that the enthusiastic apologists of the factory system have nothing more damning to urge against a general organization of the labour of society, than that it would turn all society into one immense factory.... In a society with capitalist production, *anarchy* in the social division of labour [in society as a whole] and *despotism* in that of the workshop are mutual conditions the one of the other...[888]

Understandably, thus, the social control *of* capital is an a priori impossibility in a social system which is itself controlled *by* capital.

In fact the most openly committed ideologists of the capitalist system, like Raymond Aron, do not hesitate to admit defiantly – from a position of strength – that:

> All modern firms are organized on an *authoritarian* basis.... As regards the *techno-bureaucratic* direction of industries, it is at present *authoritarian* rather than *democratic* under all types of systems.[889]

As we can see, an automatic justification is given here for the despotic character of the capitalist system by asserting (a) that it arises from the 'techno-bureaucratic' determinations of 'modern' production as such, and (b) that authoritarianism is a necessary characteristic of 'all types of systems'. Significantly, however, several important questions are left not only unanswered but even unasked. Thus, we are not offered any explanation at all as to how it is possible to maintain the *democratic* pretences of a social system which is based for its reproduction on a mode of production (and distribution) wedded to a profoundly *anti-democratic, authoritarian* command structure, nor what happens if major conflicts erupt into the open with regard to the legitimacy and viability of the authoritarian command structure itself.

In the view of the ideologists of the ruling order, this is quite inconceivable. For its uncontested and incontestable viability – as the supremely efficient modern 'techno-bureaucratic' system – automatically legitimates the capitalist mode of production and control well beyond its historical boundaries. The system is secure, the self-reassuring tale goes on, because the 'modern firm' delivers the goods 'in ever-increasing abundance'. But what if the capitalist system fails to live up to this myth of 'ever-increasing abundance' – which is in any case highly questionable as the allegedly automatic legitimatory ground of a hierarchical system of domination and subordination – even in the most privileged 'metropolitan' countries? And what about the countless millions of people – very nearly *90 per cent* of the world's population – who could never even dream about, let alone effectively enjoy, the fruits of 'ever-increasing abundance' so iniquitously distributed in capital's global system? And perhaps the most disturbing of all the unasked questions: how can one consider 'sound' and 'viable' an authoritarian socioeconomic system which practically postulates as the unproblematical ground of its *permanence* the continued *exclusion* from the benefits of society's growing wealth the exploited 90 per cent?

In reality the authoritarian character of the system is not the result of rationally incontestable and beneficial '*techno*-bureaucratic' demands, but the manifestation of primarily *social* determinations through which the capitalist socioeconomic and political order asserts and defends itself. Just as one cannot fundamentally alter capital's rule over society as a whole without envisaging at the same time the internal democratization of the '*despotic workshop*', in the same way it is inconceivable to render the latter responsive to the needs and initiatives of the producers without eliminating the now prevailing *anarchy in the social division of labour* in society as a whole and the *tyranny of the market* that goes with it. To suggest otherwise, in the name of some hypostatized rules and mechanisms of 'rational efficiency' (however authoritarian they are admitted to be), is sheer mystification.

In addition to the capitalist way of articulating the interdeterminations between the parts and the whole of the social complex – whereby the despotism in the workshop is complemented by the market-determined resolution of the untenable anarchy in society as a whole – there could be in principle two other ways of effecting a workable relationship.

First, the despotism practised in the various units of society's labour process could be enveloped by a form of overall social integration which is itself openly despotic; as indeed it happens in societies whose mode of reproduction rests on the ownership and politically unrestrained exploitation of slaves. Obviously, however, in view of the fact that under capitalism the producers play a vital role in the overall reproduction process also in their capacity as consumers, the adoption of an unconstrained variant of political despotism as the overall cementing force of the social complex, in preference to the good offices of the 'invisible hand', would create enormous complications at the core of the given structures. The system of 'wage slavery' is a much more adequate way of satisfying the internal needs of the capitalist system than resorting to corporatist political tyranny as the unchallengeable overall integrator, even if at times of major crises the wishful thinking for the latter can assume frightening actual forms, as twentieth-century history – above all Hitler's Nazi order in the service of consolidating again capitalist control over a society torn by explosive antagonisms – clearly demonstrated. Nevertheless, under normal conditions capital's 'constitutional republics' are considered preferable to its Hitlers, at least in the 'metropolitan countries'.

The second alternative to the prevailing system of despotism in the workshop and anarchy in the market-oriented division of labour in society at large is even less compatible with the capitalistic mode of control than the first one. For it would require capital's complete uprooting both from the micro-structures within which society's productive and distributive practices are carried on and from the way in which they are combined into a coherent whole. Without this the *consciously planned self-activity* of the associated producers at the level of their comprehensive interchanges would be rendered impossible, which in its turn would inevitably undermine also their efforts to institute *autonomous self-management* in the productive activity of the workshop.

This radical uprooting of capital by the self-emancipating individuals from its present domination of the social metabolism is precisely what the socialist project is all about. In opposition to the way in which capital's rule over society is exercised, the socialist conception envisages, in Marx's fitting words, 'a *general plan of freely combined individuals*',[890] on the basis of their recognition that 'modern universal intercourse cannot be controlled by individuals, unless it is controlled by all'.[891] This is what is meant by the advocated 'transformation of *labour* into *self-activity*'[892] on the material premiss of regaining control over the social division of labour (instead of being subjected to its dictates) and making the instruments of production in a *substantive* sense, not only juridically, 'subject to *each* individual, and *property to all*'.[893]

9.5.2

To be sure, the obstacles to translating this vision into reality are immense. For the inherited labour process and long established social division of labour – both in the workshop and in society at large – bear the marks of 'despotism and anarchy' which cannot be abolished by the decree of any government, no matter how 'admirably socialistic', as Rosa Luxemburg put it. The issue remains, as before, how to break the chains of capital 'where the chains are forged', replacing them in a positive sense by consciously adopted – reciprocally connecting and strengthening, as well as mutually entitling and obliging – *cooperative ties* through which the necessary changes can be implemented by the associated producers.

The problems and difficulties that must be faced can be identified in precise terms, for the purpose of practical intervention, in the context of historically specific socioeconomic developments. By contrast the transcendental vacuities recommended by those who deny the feasibility of *substantive* changes in the name of an evasive '*procedural utopianism*' can only blur the lines of demarcation between oppression and emancipation, diverting critical negation from its tangible targets. For Marx the real issue was – and it remains more than ever today – the effective exercise of *control* over the reproductive processes of society, and not simply how to counter the negative effects of technical advancement and complexity. For both 'technics' and 'complexity' are always socially incorporated and, consequently, can only be controlled by taking firm hold on their historically changing social leverage. As Raniero Panzieri argues in a deservedly influential article:

> The process of industrialization, as it achieves more and more advanced levels of technological progress, coincides with a continual growth of the capitalist's *authority*. As the means of production, counterposed to the worker, grow in volume, the necessity grows for the capitalist to exercise an absolute control. The *capitalist's plan* is the ideal shape in which 'the interconnection between their various labours' confronts the wage-labourers, while it presents itself 'in practice, as his authority, as the powerful will of a being outside them.' Hence the development of capitalist planning is something closely related to that of the capitalist use of machines. To the development of cooperation, of the social labour process, there corresponds – under capitalist management – the development of the plan as *despotism*. In the factory, capital to an ever-increasing extent asserts its power 'like a private legislator'. Its despotism is its planning, a 'capitalist caricature of the social regulation of the labour process' (Marx). . . . It is obvious [therefore] that simply to ratify rationalization processes (taken as the totality of productive techniques evolved within the framework of capitalism) is to forget that it is precisely capitalist 'despotism' which takes the form of technological rationality. In capitalist usage, not just machines, but also 'methods', organizational techniques, etc., are incorporated into capital and confront the workers as capital: as an extraneous 'rationality'. Capitalist 'planning' presupposes the planning of living labour, and the more it strives to present itself as a closed and perfectly rational system of rules, the more it is abstract and partial, ready to be utilized solely in a *hierarchical* type of organization. Not 'rationality', but *control*, not *technical* programming, but a *plan for power* of the associated producers, can ensure an adequate relation to the global techno-economic processes.[894]

In view of these determinations and their highly realistic conceptualizations by Marx and his followers, like Panzieri, it is truly astonishing to see some 'critical theorists' trying to discredit the demand for a substantive socialist control of the labour process by counterposing to their approach the socially unqualified 'technical conditions' of 'our world', rejecting at the same time Marx's so-called 'aestheticist' and 'expressivist model' (which he never had) by declaring that:

> It becomes increasingly difficult to imagine how under current *technical conditions*, or even humanized versions of them with *smaller-scale* plant and equipment, work processes could ever be reintroduced that would bring with them the type of fulfilment originally derived from the exemplar of the artistic genius, who objectifies his most essential nature into his artefact and then contemplates and re-appropriates what he has externalized. I just don't think that *our world* affords a foothold for that *any longer*.[895]

This line of reasoning, which turns Marx into a caricature, is questionable not only in its general assessment of the rejected adversary but in every one of its particular steps as well. First, because the alleged 'technical conditions' are not simply *technical* but inseparably – and perniciously – also class-determined, in the sense of being articulated within the confines of capital's hierarchical and despotic structure of authority and social control. Second, because the rhetorical/mechanistic equation of 'smaller scale' with 'humanized' (a straw-man devised for the purpose of being shot down immediately) has no bearing whatsoever on the subject. By becoming 'smaller scale' an enterprise is by no means *ipso facto* humanized. For a 'small-scale' capitalist (and, of course, not only capitalist) enterprise can just as despotically dominate the lives of those who work in it as its 'large-scale' counterparts. Third, because no serious socialist – least of all Marx himself – ever imagined that bringing back an idealized archaic mode of production, based on the model of the 'artistic genius', could be even an infinitesimal part of the answer. And fourth, because not only 'our world' does not afford such a return to that polemically hypostatized fictitious/ archaic condition, but no world *ever* really did so – which makes the concluding assertion '*no longer*' utterly vacuous.

Likewise, it is a travesty of Marx to suggest that he 'spoke of *neutral forces of production*'.[896] As we have seen in several contexts, including Panzieri's analysis of capitalist machinery and 'rationality', Marx knew very well that 'in capitalist usage, not just machines, but also "methods", organizational techniques, etc. are incorporated into capital and confront the worker *as capital*: as an *extraneous "rationality"*.' Consequently the whole system is 'abstract and partial, ready to be utilized solely in a *hierarchical type* of organization'. Marx could never consider the *forces* of production neutral for the simple reason of their organic links with the *relations* of production; which implied that a radical change in the latter, in the societies which aim at uprooting capital from its dominant position, necessitates a fundamental restructuring and a qualitatively new way of embedding the forces of production into the socialist relations of production.

In the same sense, it is not enough to notice that 'complexity' is not neutral, since doing so can cut both ways. One must also be able to grasp the real *causal relationship* between 'complexity' and the social order, instead of presenting it *upside down*, so as to justify its continuation. Besides, in the event the causal order is reversed, the confused reasoning based on such tendentious reversal is bound to end up in a blind alley where it is impossible to understand what might have been the point of the whole intellectual exercise (apart from trying to 'supersede' Marx by Luhmann and Popper). The following quotation illustrates this very well:

> I wonder whether there are neutral *increases in complexity*, or whether this higher level of system differentiation which we have reached in the *modern age* was achieved only at the cost of some form of *class domination*. If the latter were the case, then there could be only *regressive* solutions for socialism. That doesn't necessarily make socialism less *attractive*, but it does leave it more or less *without a future*. What kind of condition would we be in if the majority of the population, in order to achieve more humane forms of collective life, were ready to pay the heavy price of a *regressive economic system*? But there are no a priori arguments for the pessimistic premiss underlying that question.[897]

As before, in the dismissive hypostatization of the archaic mode of production (said to be illusorily modelled by socialists on the 'artistic genius'), we find here, again, an attempt to link the project of socialism to a quixotically pursued *regressive* condition, which could only discredit it. To say, as a matter of lip-service to the effectively discredited idea, that the desperate regressiveness of socialism would not necessarily make it 'less attractive' – notwithstanding the fact that it would be 'without a future' – is entirely gratuitous. For a 'regressive economic system', which is anyway 'without a future', can be attractive only to the deluded or the insane. It is as 'attractive' as the suggestion that – instead of undertaking the dangerous job of getting through the encountered minefield inch by inch, disarming or by-passing the located mines the best one can under such unavoidable constraints – one should jump, in defiance of the law of gravity, from one end of the field to the other in one go.

The curious arguments displayed in this quotation are formulated in order to enable the author to commend a Popperian 'fallibilist' process of 'socialization',[898] as against the Marxian project concerned with the radical socialist transformation of the established social order. Linked to the idea of Luhmann's 'system-differentiation' (which is supposed to be inseparable from the 'modern age' as such), the advocacy of this fallacious fallibilism appears to be an inescapable conclusion. In the course of reaching it, we are also expected to embrace uncritically a most apologetic corollary. Namely, that the capitalist system – with its technology ('our technology', as the author puts it), rationality, and complexity befitting the necessary system-differentiation of the modern age – is *ipso facto progressive*. The fact that even in strictly *economic* terms – and, moreover, that even if confined to such narrowly economic terms, only with the most sobering *historical* qualifications, with a dark shadow on the future, concerning the very survival of humankind[899] – the capitalist system is '*progressive*' only as regards the material standard of living of the *small minority* of the world's population, is completely disregarded. Since it would undermine the self-complacent 'Eurocentric' premises of the advocated 'gradual/fallibilist socialization' of the privileged and relatively well-off, there can be no room in this framework of thought for taking on board the most disconcerting fact, that the 'progressive economic system' of capital leaves the *over-whelming majority* of humankind in conditions of utter deprivation; indeed, that it drags them at times even into an *economically regressive condition* (not to mention regression in other respects), compared to their previous mode of existence. This is why concern for the problems of the 'Third World' cannot appear in such a conception even marginally.

It is quite undialectical – and with regard to its socioeconomic terms of reference also totally uncritical – to suggest that 'some form of class domination' is the necessary consequence of a 'modern increase' in complexity. There can be no such thing as a socially unqualified 'complexity' which could be somehow derived from the 'ideal-typical' paradigm of the 'modern age'. Class domination and exploitation did not appear in history in the aftermath of 'unavoidable modern complexity' and 'system-differentiation'. On the contrary, 'some form of class domination' predates the modern age by thousands of years.

Thus, all those who maintain their concern for the cause of human emancipation must face the threat of complexity – as well as the degrading actuality of class domination – not as a disembodied ideal-typical abstraction, but in its tangible sociohistorical specificity. What is objectionable to socialists is a certain *type* of complexity, which precludes the possibility of autonomous action, and not 'complexity' as such. To use the Weber-inspired and socially unqualified category of 'complexity' as an aprioristic argument against the possibility of autonomous action – as Habermas, Colletti and others do – is to side with the ideologists of the established order in their effort to 'eternalize' it.

Under the capitalist system the overriding characteristic of 'complexity' – which emanates from the innermost nature of capital itself – concerns the question of *social control*. 'Complexity' in the course of capitalist development has been articulated for the fundamental purpose of institutionally *excluding* the producers not only from the *effective* control of the reproductive process but even from its remote *possibility*.

The sociohistorically unique kind of capitalist complexity originates in a most peculiar – indeed inherently contradictory – double complication of the system. On the one hand, as a matter of intrinsic structural determination without which capital would not be viable as the effective controller of society's productive and distributive practices, the producers themselves must be prevented from taking decisions over matters affecting the labour process as a *whole*, despite the fact that they must be able to control adequately all the *specific* productive functions assigned to them, no matter how complicated they might be. At the same time, on the other hand, in virtue of the fact that the producers are 'free labourers' who cannot be compelled by *political* means (i.e. by the direct exercise or threat of violence) to lend their services to the cause of capital expansion, they must nevertheless be brought somehow – through *economic* compulsion, that is – into the workshop, *and retained* (as a matter of economic imperative) within it on a *continuing* basis – without which, again, the system would inevitably lose its viability. The subsequent unfolding of the capitalistic *technical/technological* division of labour remains always subordinated to this double complication peculiar to the fundamental requirement of *social control* as feasible within the special constraints (and paradoxical 'freedoms') of capital's reproductive framework. Understandably, therefore, the self-expansive reproductive and valorizing system of generalized commodity production built on such foundations could not avoid the most bewildering 'complexity' progressively resulting from its complicated inner determinations and contradictions. For every additional major step in the course of capital's tendentially global expansion and integration must reproduce the original structural complications at an increasingly more complicated level of rather pernicious – not simply productivity – but primarily social domination-oriented – complexity, adding new layers of control to the expanding capitalist edifice, together with the inescapable necessity to monitor the growing number of controllers in the interest of maintaining the ever more bureaucratized system's viability.

Given such *social* premises (and structural imperatives), which arise from capital's objective determination as a unique mode of metabolic interchange and control, there can be no alternative to excluding the real producers from the possibility of control from the very outset of capital's historical consolidation as a dynamic and comprehensive reproductive system. They must be practically and categorically denied the power of *decision making* in the capitalistically organized productive and distributive units even at their *simplest*, on the ground of *class-incompatibility*, and not on the basis of a presumed inability to grasp the 'complexity' of the given tasks. It is therefore a theoretical *non sequitur* (as well as a somewhat disingenuous position) to predicate the impossibility of the autonomous productive life-activity of the associated producers in the name of 'increasing complexity'.

Complex or simple, over the issue of *control* there can be no compromise within the capitalistic socioeconomic and political framework. Nor is the problem automatically resolved by the political/juridical abolition of the capitalist relations of production. The obstacles to autonomous productive activity remain for as long as the power of capital survives in and through the inherited reproductive structures.

Much of the 'complexity' in the capitalist system is due to the need to hide – not only from the competing capitalists but, much more imperatively, from the social antagonist: labour (who might put forward, as a minimal consequence of the gained insights, some inadmissible wage claims) – what should not be hidden at all in a rationally organized reproductive system. This fact, too, makes it quite clear that the real issue is *control* and not socially unqualified 'complexity'.

Obviously, there are many aspects of 'capitalist complexity' – due, as already mentioned, not to intrinsically productive determinations but to the imperative to maintain the established system of class domination in existence – which could be eliminated with relative ease, whereas the remaining ones would have to be brought under a much more effective control than the way in which capital can deal with the complexities arising within its system.

In fact it is one of the most contradictory aspects of the position of those who use the argument of 'complexity' in capital's favour that they refuse to notice the established system's increasing failure to deal with the negative impact of growing complexity even at the ecological level directly affecting the conditions of human survival. At the time when Weber first introduced this apologetic argument, the capitalist system and its idealized bureaucracy (commendably likened to the 'virtuoso' by Weber himself)[900] seemed to be able to meet the challenge of increasing complexity. Significantly, however, already Weber's own argument, with its categorically asserted but never demonstrated claims, was spelled out not as an objective assessment of the established system's questionable long-term viability, but quite unashamedly as an ideological weapon against the prospects of ('non-virtuoso' bureaucratic) socialist development. Besides, what makes the recent emulations of the Weberian line of reasoning even more problematical is that they quietly disregard the fact that things have greatly deteriorated in this respect since Weber's reassuring reflections. Thus, by all tenable account the argument of complexity should be used exactly the other way round to what we are repeatedly offered. For the increasing complexity generated by a system which cannot productively control its escalating complications is a serious liability, not an asset, despite the curious logic of Weber-inspired systems-theory and its various transplants.

The combined resources of the associated producers are in principle much more adequate for mastering the complexity proper to the genuine productive requirements of the social reproduction process – as a whole and in its parts – than the relatively few privileged 'personifications of capital' to whom the power of decision making is assigned in the established system, be they 'captains of industry' or state bureaucrats. It stands to reason that a labour process organized so that its controlling functions need not be transferred to a separate system and, worse still, *hidden away* in an 'adversary way' from the producers themselves who are called upon to carry out the necessary productive tasks but that, on the contrary, offers ample scope for their conscious participation and creative invention at all levels, is an inherently less complex one than its capitalist alternative.

The possibility of progress in this respect hinges on the producers' determination and ability to alter quite drastically the structural conditions of production and distribution as articulated in the prevailing division of labour. 'Mastering complexity' is thus synonymous with *regaining control* over the labour process as a whole, with the ultimate aim of establishing a relationship of *'transparency'* between the parts and the whole, above all in terms of the relationship between the self-determining individuals and the overall productive framework of society which they autonomously constitute and consciously modify in accordance with their changing needs. Contrary to fetishistic appearances, this is not a question of 'instrumental rationality' but of establishing a fundamentally altered relationship among themselves as a result of which their instrumental and institutional complexes lose the *abstract* and *partial* character they have at present, which makes them suitable 'to be utilized solely in a *hierarchical type* of organization'. Accordingly, failure in attacking the inherited division of labour and the corresponding system of control – which denies the power of decision making in the labour process to the producers – could only mean that even the most sustained 'technical simplification' of the existing tasks, as well as of the formal/organizational linkages among the productive units, would leave the underlying substantive problems unresolved.

This is the radical meaning of the overall socialist strategy – concerned with changing 'from top to bottom the conditions of industrial and political existence, and consequently the whole manner of being of the associated producers' – as formulated by Marx. Naturally, its implementation is feasible only through the historically changing strategies which focus on the specific mediatory steps required for the process of restructuring. This implies no less the realistic acknowledgement and flexible practical mastery of the encountered material, political and cultural/ideological constraints than the firm refusal to abandon the fundamental objectives.

9.5.3

It must be stressed in the present context that what makes things particularly difficult for the articulation of viable socialist strategies is that the capitalist division of labour, and the hierarchy-oriented 'technological rationalization' and 'complexity' that go with it, deeply affect the internal composition and organization of labour as well. For:

> In manufacture, as well as in simple cooperation, the *collective working organism* is a form of existence of *capital*. The mechanism that is made up of numerous individual detail labourers belongs to the capitalist. Hence, the productive power resulting from a combination of labours appears to be the *productive power of capital*. Manufacture proper not only *subjects* the

previously independent workman to the *discipline and command of capital*, but, in addition, creates a *hierarchic gradation of the workmen themselves.*[901]

Since Marx wrote these lines, more than 120 years ago, this dimension of the capitalist reproduction process has become greatly extended. This is partly because the staggering expansion and global integration of the capitalist system made the imposition of capital's 'despotic discipline', with the active involvement of certain sections of wage-labour, that much more imperative and widespread. What is immediately at issue here is the fact that capital:

> Hands over the work of *direct and constant supervision* of the individual workmen to a special kind of wage-labourer. An industrial army of workmen, under the command of a capitalist, requires, like a real army, *officers* (managers), and *sergeants* (foremen, overlookers) who, *while the work is being done, command* in the name of the capitalist.[902]

We may note here in passing that, in contrast to the mythologies of 'the managerial revolution', even so-called chief executives – who are often presented with the brute fact of being sacked without as much as one day's notice, even if with a large 'golden handshake' – exercise capital's command functions in a rather limited context, and strictly *on behalf* of capital, 'while the work is being done'. They do not determine on their own account even the overall strategy of their particular firms, let alone of the capitalist system as a whole.

However, the internal stratification and hierarchization of the totality of labour (as a *global* class, in confrontation with its antagonist: the *totality* of capital, on a *global* scale) is further affected by a number of other powerful factors and circumstances. We can clearly identify the most important of them as:

1. The *territorial division of labour*, creating *zones* of relative privilege coupled with crying 'underdevelopment'. This is manifest in *international* relations first through colonialism and imperialism, and more recently by way of instituting the system of 'neo-capitalist' (and 'neo-colonial') exploitation, and *internally* by developing some parts of the territory under the control of a national capital at the expense of others. The tendency here referred to is so overpowering in fact that every major capitalist country has its own 'North' and 'South', though of course at times – as in the case of Great Britain – the economic 'North' corresponds to the geographic 'South', and vice versa.
2. The impact of the law of *uneven development* and its concomitant *differential rates of exploitation*, prevailing both internally, in every single country, and internationally in the relations of the dominant capitalist powers to the rest of the world capitalist system.
3. The growing *centralization and concentration* of capital, as linked to

its rising *technical composition* and worsening *organic composition*, with far-reaching consequences for the structure of employment in the capitalist socioeconomic framework as a whole.

Naturally, all these factors directly affect not only the internal composition and stratification of labour but simultaneously also its capacity for organizing itself in its strategic confrontation with capital. It is for this reason that the severe problems arising from the necessary internal hierarchization of labour under the rule of capital are bound to occupy in the future a much more important role in the elaboration of socialist strategies than they did in the past.

Given the conditions of neo-colonial exploitation, uneven development, and the prevailing differential rates of exploitation, there can be, of course, no question of formulating a uniform strategy. In some areas (e.g. South Africa today) the struggle against exploitation inevitably assumes the form of violent confrontations with the repressive (state terrorist) class adversary – just as it did in the postwar liberation wars of Vietnam, Algeria and Rhodesia/Zimbabwe, among others – whereas in other places it can advance its objectives by more peaceful means. Nevertheless, whatever the political circumstances and the relative degree of socioeconomic development of the particular countries concerned, the condition of lasting success remains everywhere the objective requirement to insert the partial strategies – with their mediatory specificities, in response to the class composition of the forces participating in the struggle and their available means of emancipatory action – into the overall *hegemonic* confrontation between capital and labour. For capital and labour are the *only* classes in contemporary society whose social being can constitute the foundation of alternative, globally viable reproductive systems.

In the last six decades it was Mao Tse-tung who provided us with the historically most significant example of theoretical analysis and practical strategy in this respect. In one of his earliest works – the 'Analysis of the Classes in Chinese Society'[903] – he appraised with great care and subtlety the specific socioeconomic determinations for over 30 different social strata in contemporary China, relating them to the ongoing struggle and to the prospects of radical social transformation. At the same time he made it quite clear that not even *three* (let alone *30*), but only *two* viable strategic alternatives were feasible under the globally unfolding conditions of twentieth-century historical confrontation between capital and labour. And he did this despite the fact (strongly underlined by Mao Tse-tung himself) that the *peasantry* constituted the overwhelming majority of the Chinese population, numbering more than *500* million people as compared to less than *two* million industrial workers.

Thus, although he forcefully stressed against the then prevailing sectarian Party-line[904] the key importance of basing the revolutionary struggle on the elemental force of the awakening peasantry (which in his view absolutely no power on earth could subdue), at the same time he did not hesitate to link this prophetic vision to the equally far-sighted strategic assertion that 'The leading force in our revolution is the *industrial proletariat.*'[905] As Mao Tse-tung clearly perceived it, the sociological specificities of the given sociohistorical context, no matter how monumental in proportion, could not radically alter the fundamental hegemonic antagonism between capital and labour in global historical terms, even if they called for the most realistic appraisal of the formerly unforeseen, but under the emerging new circumstances uniquely appropriate, mediatory forms and instruments for the successful realization of the chosen objectives. For it was quite impossible to *generalize* the peasant mode of production even at its most dynamic as a *global alternative* to the dominant capitalist system.[906]

It is this latter condition of generalizability or its absence that ultimately decides the issue in favour of or against emancipatory aspirations. For although the particular forms of stratification and hierarchization of the labour force vary enormously from one place to another and from one type of development to another, nevertheless the different sociological strata happen to be everywhere grouped, most tellingly, under structurally very similar hierarchical institutions of subordination and superordination, dependency and domination. In other words, the fairly easily identifiable characteristics of *class exploitation* are in evidence everywhere, notwithstanding all fashionable talk about 'variety', 'system-differentiation', 'upward mobility', and similar categories of theoretical obfuscation in the service of the dominant ideological interests. Moreover, it is also fairly obvious that despite the greatly overstated claims of 'variety', 'differentiation', etc., the real stakes are arranged, with monotonous repetitiveness, in a perfectly straightforward pattern – i.e. for or against indefinitely maintaining the rule of capital and its problematical market mechanism as the overall controller and 'invisible totalizer' of the multifaceted processes of societal reproduction – thereby underlining again the inescapability of the hegemonic confrontation not between numerous historically novel social agencies and corresponding strategies, but quite simply between capital and labour. It is therefore by no means accidental that the idealization and eternalization of capital's allegedly unsurpassable 'rational efficiency' goes hand in hand with constantly renewed attempts to discredit the idea that the associated producers could institute an economically viable and at all levels of decision making truly self-regulating alternative to the established social order.

That the idea of the associated producers' autonomous self-activity is dismissed by the ideologists of the ruling order, should come, of course, as no surprise to anybody. What is much more baffling, however, is when we see the same position – namely, the acceptance of the established structural parameters of society – theorized and advocated in the name of critical emancipatory claims.

At the political level, we find this in the strategic orientation of the long-established social democratic tradition, going back all the way to the Bernsteinian reformist programme, as we have seen in Chapter 8. The failure of this strategy over a period of nearly 100 years speaks for itself. For it is impossible to emancipate the structurally subordinated class of the capitalist socioeconomic and political order by starting out from the false premiss, that even if social classes still exist (which is also wishfully put in doubt quite often, on the basis of the puniest available 'evidence'), *class exploitation* and the resulting *class struggle* between the major classes of contemporary society have been historically (and irretrievably) left behind by the development of 'modern industrial society'.

Thus the whole movement, which had been originally constituted for the purpose of asserting in a combative way the claims of the subordinate class against the capitalistically unavoidable reality of class exploitation – from which it necessarily followed that it *had* to challenge the established structural order *as such* from the standpoint of a qualitatively different social order – lost not only its former identity but the very basis of its existence and *raison d'être*, as Rosa Luxemburg put it so many years ago; a judgement whose correctness has been abundantly confirmed by the practical failure of the 'reformed' movement in all these intervening decades. Taking refuge behind the slogan of a 'broad electoral alliance' does nothing to remedy the situation. Nor does it indicate in the slightest what would follow in substantive terms from the electoral success of the advocated strategy. For both *exploitation* and the continuing – even if unmentioned – *class struggle* remain *unmentionable* taboos, since admitting their existence would 'rock the boat' of the advocated 'broad electoral alliance' itself.

The theoretical literature linked to such political strategies has been for a long time doing the same thing: denying the existence of the class struggle and often even the existence of social classes, in the name of a wishfully anticipated and never really seen 'merging of the classes into one another'. It predicated the necessary *'embourgeoisement* of the proletariat', and announced a radical change in class relations in terms of the *changing colours of the collars* of the working people.

In truth, however, what decides the class position of people in our societies is not the colour of their collars but their location in the *command structure of capital*. Many sociological changes can be identified in this respect with precision, and no political movement can ignore them without suffering the consequences. Also, parallel to the changes that take place in the labour process itself, the strategic position of various groups of workers is altered accordingly. Thus, to take only one example, the relative strategic position of the electricians and the miners in the last 30 years has been significantly modified in favour of the former, not only by greatly reducing the number of the miners but, much more importantly, by weakening in other ways as well the potential impact of their strike action on the capitalist economy. (Obviously, 30 years ago it would have been quite inconceivable that the capitalist economy should be able to counter successfully the consequences of a one-year-long miners' strike.) Also, in the course of productive developments the occupational structure of capitalist society undergoes important changes which are bound to exercise their impact on forms of political organization earlier taken for granted.

All this, however, does not eliminate the fundamental hegemonic confrontation between capital and labour. Nor does it radically change the command structure of capital either in 'civil society' or on the terrain of the capitalist state. By changing the colour of the workers' collars from 'black' to 'blue' – and even to 'white' – their position in the command structure of capital is not really altered. Not to mention the fact that the colour of the collars of the overwhelming majority of the people under the rule of capital particularly in the Third World – those, that is, who are lucky enough to have a collar at all – remains as dark a shade of black as ever before.

9.5.4

Paradoxically, the necessity of domination arises partly from the *cooperative* nature of the capitalist production process itself. For:

> All *combined labour on a large scale* requires, more or less, a *directing authority*, in order to secure the harmonious working of the *individual activities*, and to perform the *general functions* that have their origin in the action of the *combined organism*, as distinguished from the action of its separate organs. A single violin player is his own conductor, an orchestra requires a separate one. The work of *directing, superintending and adjusting*, becomes one of the *functions of capital*, from the moment that the labour, under the control of capital, becomes *cooperative*.[907]

However, the inescapable need for a directing authority does not explain the *specific form* of the given authority. For in principle all such authority could be constituted in a number of very *different* ways, including and not precluding the possibility of autonomous action.

The particular form in which any given form of controlling authority happens to be *actually* constituted under a historically given set of circumstances requires a materially sound explanation, instead of being aprioristically assumed. Yet we are offered precisely such aprioristic (and circular) assumptions in the self-mythology of the capitalist system which tries to deduce the established authority from the concept of 'rationality' as intrinsic to the undeniable need for superintending coordination. This is all the more problematical, since the most obvious direct line that one could draw between 'rationality' and cooperative production, as far as the nature of the directing authority itself is concerned, would be to bring the mode of direction as such – in the form of the *cooperative self-direction of the associated producers* – in line with the *necessarily cooperative* character of the capitalist production process itself.

Thus, all talk about the alleged 'rationality' of the capitalist system of production and distribution which fails to indicate the *objective motive* that underpins the abstractly rational 'need for a directing authority' (thereby transforming it from a vague and generic imperative into its materially viable and actually existing particular form) is totally vacuous even in terms of the limited rationality ascribable to the capitalist organization of production. In reality:

> The *directing motive*, the *determining purpose* (*bestimmender Zweck*) of capitalist production, is to *extract* the greatest possible amount of *surplus-value* ['Profits . . . is the sole end of trade.'[908]] and consequently to *exploit labour-power* to the greatest possible extent. As the number of the cooperative labourers increases, so too does their resistance to the domination of capital, and with it, *the necessity for capital* to overcome this resistance by counter-pressure. The *control* exercised by the capitalist is not only a special function, due to the nature of the social labour-process, but it is, at the same time, *a function of the exploitation of a social labour-process*, and is consequently rooted in the *unavoidable antagonism* between the exploiter and the living and labouring raw material he exploits.[909]

What is important to stress here is that insofar as the concept of 'directing motive' and 'determining purpose' appears at all in the academically respectable fairy-tales of 'capitalistic rationality' (Weber included), it is completely distorted and fallaciously transmuted into a purely *subjective motivation*. It ceases to be an *objective necessity for capital* – without which capital as a specific mode of social control, in the just quoted sense, could not conceivably function at all – and becomes the individual capitalist's '*entrepreneurial motivation*' (for which the enterprising 'captains of industry' fully deserve, *of course*, even the most generous rewards, counted not unfrequently in millions of dollars per annum), circularly derived, as we have already seen, from the mysterious 'spirit of capitalism'. Yet:

> It is not because he is a *leader* of industry that a man is a capitalist; on the contrary, he is a leader of industry because he is a *capitalist*. The leadership of industry is an *attribute of capital*, just as in feudal times the functions of general and judge were attributes of landed property.[910]

Naturally, the same mystifying subjectivism prevails in conceptualizing the situation of labour as well. In this respect we find that the *objective determinations* at work are turned into the alleged *subjective motivations* of particular workers who are supposed to choose the higher values of '*embourgeoisement*' as a matter of '*sovereign individual choice*'. For if the latter could be considered a generalizable condition (even if its realization might take a long time), instead of being confined to a limited number of relatively privileged workers, that would seem to absolve the dehumanizing social system itself of all blame with regard to the actual conditions of existence of the working class as a whole.

The combined rationalizing and legitimating effect of this arbitrary subjectivization of the '*determining purpose*' of both capital and labour is that the capitalist socioeconomic system appears not only to originate but also to be constantly sustained and reproduced in virtue of *conscious individual choices* at all points of the social spectrum, excepting only the 'few zealous trouble-makers', 'agitators', and 'misfits', who could be safely disregarded, of course. At the same time, the *class exploitative* character of the established socioeconomic and political order conveniently disappears by definition, since *choosing to be exploited* is a priori incompatible with the concept of '*rational choice*'.

In the real world, however, we have to face the pressure of *objective determinations* which become '*internalized*' – and thus *also* transformed into *motives*, without losing thereby their character as objective determinations – on both sides of the exploitative relationship of super- and subordination. For the advancement of the capitalistic division of labour:

> creates new conditions for the *lordship of capital* over labour. If, therefore, on the one hand, it presents itself historically as a *progress* and as a necessary *phase* in the economic development of society, on the other hand, it is a *refined and civilized method of exploitation.*[911]

Moreover, the refined and highly perfected exploitative system of capital is a *global* one, which is precisely one of the fundamental reasons for its incomparable efficacy and 'staying power'. For its ability to penetrate even into the most distant corners of the world, across a multiplicity of national and local barriers, provides it not only with an immense scope for expansion – first as an *extensive*/colonial/imperialist and later as an *intensive*/neo-capitalist/neo-colonial totality – but also with a formerly unimaginable ability to *displace its contradictions* from one level and mode of exploitation to another[912] and from one region to another,[913] parallel to its historical advancement and saturation which go hand in hand with the intensification of its inner contradictions.[914]

The disarming internalization of the encountered objective constraints is perhaps the most important function of the ruling ideology. It is accomplished – in the form of *conflating* and confusing the necessity of *some* form of *directing authority* with the effectively (but contingently) *ruling authority*, as well as *outside coercion* with *internal motivation* – by preaching the accommodatory wisdom of 'there is no alternative'. For, once it is accepted that 'there is no alternative' either to the established directing authority, or to the 'rational choices' made by such authority (in politics no less than in the economy) under the 'force of circumstance', the brutish necessity to submit to the power of *coercive competition* is mystifyingly metamorphosed into something that can claim to itself the elevated status of consciously and freely adopted *inner motivation*, which no rational being could (nor should) question even in their thoughts, let alone actively oppose.

Understandably, therefore, socialist ideology at first cannot be other than '*counter-consciousness*', so as to be able to negate the dominant material and ideological practices of the established order. Under the circumstances of capital's ideological hegemony, the fundamental premisses of the socialist alternative cannot help being articulated as a defiant counter-consciousness to *internalized coerciveness* and as a clear – even if necessarily qualified – rejection of the fallaciously absolutized alternative-denying power of the given, sociohistorically contingent constraints, no matter how real they might be within their own terms of reference.

To be sure, in its time and place the emancipatory belief of the Enlightenment was also articulated as a combative counter-consciousness to the ruling ideology. There was, however, a major difference then, as compared to the Marxian theorization of its socialist counterpart. For the *material ground* of the Enlightenment's ideological negation was itself *positive*, even if in its long-term perspective very problematical.

It was positive in the sense that the ideology of the Enlightenment could directly relate itself to, and rely upon, the structural change in productive practices which was taking place under the impact of capital's growing power; a process that reached almost its full consummation at the height of the Enlightenment movement. That the socioeconomic order of this spontaneously advancing and positively/successfully self-assertive – i.e. historically tangible and apparently limitless – material force became idealized in the various Enlightenment conceptions as the natural order corresponding to the dictates of Reason itself, thereby transforming the new ideology into an '*uncritical positivism*' (from Adam Smith's vision of the capitalistic 'natural propensity to exchange and barter' under the benevolent guidance of the 'invisible hand', to Kant's idealization of the 'commercial spirit' and its hypostatized 'eternal peace'), does not alter the fact itself that the theorists concerned could base their reflections on the historical reality of the victoriously unfolding power of capital all over Europe. Indeed, the capitalist system was beginning to make its inroads by then also in other parts of the world.

Socialist counter-consciousness could not derive the necessary evidence for the validity of its critique from a comparable advancement of a new productive order. It could only point to the destructive inner antagonisms and disintegrating tendencies of the system in power which endanger even those positive potentialities contained within it which could be, in principle, turned to the benefit of all in the aftermath of a successful socialist negation and overthrow of the capitalist social formation. This is why socialist ideology had to put the stress right from the beginning on being the necessary *counter-consciousness* to that *internalized coerciveness* –

whether directly material/economic or politically mediated – through which the prevailing relations of domination could be legitimated and made acceptable to the exploited and oppressed.

It is a matter of great importance that in the socialist perspective the *individuals* had to be brought into the forefront of ideological debate, *challenging* at the same time the *class determinations* of their existence, instead of *ignoring* or transubstantiating them into a fictitious, generic, 'individual sovereignty', or 'consumer sovereignty', corresponding to the vested interests of the prevailing order. For the ideology of internalized coerciveness operated with categories which either dissolved the real individuals in the postulated (and, again, largely fictitious) 'natural' determinations of their species (like the earlier mentioned 'natural propensity to exchange and barter'), in order to 'prove' the full concordance of human inclinations with the dominant characteristics of the established 'natural order'; or submerged them in an abstract/aggregative pseudo-individuality (by extinguishing both their class-attributes and personal characteristics) from which the various stereotypes of capitalist 'civil society' (and later, of 'consumer society', the 'lonely crowd', and even of so-called 'popular capitalism') could be constructed.

Against this kind of legitimation of the given socioeconomic and political order it became necessary to orient the possibility of autonomous productive life-activity towards the developing powers of the *social individuals* under the 'new historic form'. This view sharply contrasted the blind acceptance of society's objective constraints in the form of *internalized coerciveness* with the reassertion of the need for genuine *subjective motivation* at the roots of the individuals' autonomous action, within the framework of fully shared decision making.

This is how the initially unavoidable negativity of socialist counter-consciousness had been transformed into an intrinsically *positive* vision. For the socialist conception of productive activity as 'not only a means of life but life's prime want'[915] (in other words: work in which the individuals freely engage in order to realize themselves *as particular individuals*, as real persons) is compatible only with its corresponding form of authority. That is to say, with the *freely self-constituted directing authority* of the associated producers themselves.[916]

Adopting this conception means that one cannot take seriously the idea that in post-capitalist societies the individuals can acquire substantive freedom unless the latter is demonstrably and organically linked to their own – freely *self-constituting* – authority in the realm of *productive and distributive practices*, rather than having one superimposed upon them either by the severe material constraints of the social metabolism, or by an outside state-organ, or indeed by a combination of the two. The need to transform the directing authority into one which is self-constituting persists, but the impossibility of its realization makes the freedoms feasible under the rule of capital extremely limited for the overwhelming majority. To turn the possibility of substantive freedom into a tangible social condition under which work can be embraced by the individuals themselves as 'life's prime want' implies the practical overcoming of the dual authoritarianism of controlling authority, manifest, on the one hand, in the *despotism of the workshop* and, on the other, in the *tyranny of the market*.

9.5.5
Post-capitalist societies, in their attempts to overcome the power of capital, must cope with the survival of grave material constraints – as well as with their institutionally articulated cultural/ideological corollaries – for a long historical period of transition after the political overthrow of the capitalist system. Such constraints are bound to exert their negative impact even if the *directing authority* itself is adequately *decentralized* and *democratized*.

This circumstance highlights the one-sidedness of those theories which try to reduce the encountered difficulties and contradictions of post-capitalist societies to the issue of democratization. Naturally, it would be quite wrong to diminish the importance of democratization in its proper context. However, the provision of so-called 'democratic guarantees' – especially when they are conceptualized in the form of 'market socialism' – does not remove the burden of 'socialist accumulation'; nor does it dispose of the other structural problems which arise from the intrinsic limits of the inherited productive forces and practices. Indeed, the danger is that too much reliance on the advocated 'market mechanism' might tend towards the reinstatement of the *tyranny of the market* and the ultimately unwelcome power of other blind material structures – linked to the 'rational' *despotism of the workshop*' – in affinity with the market, even if such practices are under the new circumstances rationalized in the name of 'socialist efficiency'.

Notwithstanding this caveat, though, the issue itself cannot be avoided, in view of the historical experience of post-capitalist societies. For given their failure in bringing about a genuine socialist democratization of the decision making institutions and processes of society on the one hand, and in realizing the promised productive achievements of the new system of reproduction on the other, it remains a major problem for all post-capitalist formations, how to break the historically experienced unhappy connection between democratization and productivity. For even without a demonstrable causal link between the two, failure in achieving the required level of productivity can be used – and as we all know, *has been used*, with enormous human cost – to deny the legitimacy of democratization as such.

But even so, from this contingent and corrigible historical fact it does not follow (as 'market socialists' seem to argue) that the remedy lies in instituting the *incorrigible control mechanism* of the capitalist market to take care of the problem. For the market mechanism can properly function only if it is allowed to take away the power of decision making from the associated producers, or, more precisely, if it is allowed to assume again its traditional role as a straitjacket that makes it impossible for them to become, in the Marxian sense, truly associated producers who are in charge of their own life-activity.

It is not an accidental and easily surmountable feature of post-capitalist societies that rather peculiar forms of 'economic inefficiency' and 'indiscipline' – for instance the well known phenomenon of 'moonlighting' – appeared on a considerable scale in the course of their development, once the imediate post-revolutionary state of emergency (due to Western military intervention and the civil war) had been successfully left behind. Such practices are often attributed to the 'survival of the past', in the sense that the motivational force of individual material incentives is said to persist in the workers, but the centrally controlled socioeconomic framework prevents its productive manifestations.

Whatever might be the relative weight of this factor, one should not forget that a quite fundamental change does indeed take place in society's reproductive processes with the political/juridical overthrow of the capitalist system. For with the removal of the private property-owning 'personifications of capital', the potential *despotism of the workshop* – whose legitimacy was established in the past through measures which at the same time forcefully safeguarded the unchallengeable authority of the particular capitalists and their managerial representatives – is itself severely curtailed. Furthermore, due to the nature of the changes that actually take place through the overthrow of private capitalism, it becomes quite impossible to replace the *unquestioning* discipline in the particular economic enterprises – with the desired 'economic efficiency' – by a 'socialist' (politically controlling/controlled) despotic equivalent.

The failure of Stalinism in its claim to represent a more advanced socioeconomic reproductive system than that of the capitalist antagonist (which it was meant to supersede) is as clear and painful a demonstration as one can possibly have, that the authoritarian political domination of the producers in the particular economic enterprises, instituted for the purpose of securing the maximal extraction and accumulation of surplus-labour, is totally unviable as an alternative to the economically grounded despotism of the workshop under capitalism. Nor should this failure of the Stalinist-type control of the economy be considered surprising. For, as we have seen above, the micro-structures of the capitalist system in which the *economically grounded* despotism of the workshop is both practicable and unavoidable, cannot be separated from – but have their *rationale* in – the macro-structure of the overall reproductive system in which the 'invisible hand' (through the *tyranny of the market* without a Court of Appeal) can reward or punish the participants who submit to its authority.

The cementing force of this relationship between the parts and the whole under capitalism is underlined at times in rather bewildering ways. Thus, for instance, when at the time of crises arising from the weakened competitive position of a *particular* firm, which is threatened with bankruptcy and liquidation, the labour force 'freely' accepts significant wage cuts in order to secure the enterprise's continued profitability. (Periodic appeals, usually by Labourite Governments, to a return to the so-called 'Dunkirk spirit' – and its equivalents in other capitalist countries – depicting thereby the *general* interest of capital as 'the national interest', represent, of course, a very different proposition.)

One can find no such motivating and cementing *rationale* at work in the productive and distributive enterprises of the various post-capitalist societies. On the contrary, the responsibility for the failures of the local units can be quite easily deposited at the door of the central controlling authority. It would be, therefore, an ideal solution from the standpoint of the bureaucratic controlling authority if it could be exempted from its responsibility for the actual and potential failures by ascribing them to local managers and to the 'unavoidable dysfunctions' of the revitalized market mechanisms, while also retaining the power of central control over them.

However, the problems are much more complicated than such a wishful scenario could indicate. In fact we have to face here some forbidding structural difficulties, with far-reaching implications for the possible solution of the persistent, nay deepening, complications in accordance with the objectively available margin of action. For the various post-capitalist socioeconomic systems (as we know them, the way in which they were actually constituted, under the historically prevailing relation of forces and corresponding material as well as political constraints) are characterized by the absence of a reciprocally supportive relationship between *politically* determined and enforced central decision making over the economy – local as well as country-wide – and the (far from incontestable) tangible *economic* justification of the adopted decisions. This type of structural articulation is in sharp contrast to the *mutually reinforcing* and inherently *economic* interconnection between the particular productive and distributive units and the totalizing market under the capitalist socioeconomic formation.

It is this missing link of reciprocal support and reinforcement between local and central as well as political and economic modes of decision making that happens to be wrongly conceptualized as a fateful disregard for individual material incentives – and for the market as their self-asserting vehicle of management – in the post-capitalist economic system. It is wrongly conceptualized because the key issue here concerns the intrinsic relationship between the micro-structures and the totalizing macro-structure of capitalist and post-capitalist societies. What is most appropriate for one may be an intolerable force of disruption in the other. In this sense, reinstating a mechanism brought to its optimal efficiency under the conditions of generalized commodity production would not make more coherent – as well as, in a socialist sense, productively viable – the relationship between the micro-structures and the overall integrating framework of post-capitalist societies. Nor would the strategy of strengthening the role of individual material incentives at the local level solve this problem, no matter how extensively it might be backed up by a 'controlled' market mechanism. Rather, if it were feasible at all on the necessary scale, the reinstatement of the market mechanism would tend to intensify the existing problems of post-capitalist societies by creating a dangerous mismatch between the newly generated expectations and what the system could actually deliver.

For one thing, in the strategies that advocate this solution it is by no means even vaguely indicated what would be the workable criteria by which enforceable limits could be set to the 'controlled' market mechanism without undermining its usefulness. The inner logic of the totalizing market would tend towards the *restoration of capitalism* and its authoritarianism both in the workshop and in the ruthlessly 'efficiency-oriented' accumulation process of society at large; a line of development which, obviously, cannot be allowed to run its course. Thus, the only concrete meaning that one can properly ascribe to the anticipated 'control' of the market mechanism is that the latter must be put out of action at the point where it would become fully effective. It is far from surprising, therefore, that there are some 'reform-minded' theoreticians in the various post-capitalist societies who take the objective implications of the advocated remedies to their logical conclusion and argue in favour of allowing the system of 'market socialism' to run its full course. No doubt, such solutions will be rejected, at least in those countries where the anti-capitalist revolution had deep roots. At the same time, however, in case the strategy of the 'controlled' variety is chosen, the necessary and understandable denial of its (restoratory) totalizing logic to the ultimately uncontrollable market mechanism would inevitably deprive the adopted system of its *rationale*, and thereby make the motivational framework of the particular productive and distributive enterprises – in which the new expectations are generated – quite unworkable.

It is by no means accidental that these problems have surfaced at the present juncture of history. For not only the capitalist system and the 'Third World' but the 'Second World', too, is confronted today by a dual crisis: the *crisis of development* and the *crisis of authority*. The old forms of control do not seem to work any longer, and the attempted new strategies bring with them many unanswered questions and practical difficulties.

Considering the much canvassed 'market socialist' solution, it is necessary to underline that the suggestion, according to which in post-capitalist societies the role of individual material incentives is disregarded, is a complete misdiagnosis of the actual state of affairs. Failure to meet the expectations associated with individual material incentives does not mean at all that the expectations themselves, as well as the legitimated mechanism of their incentives, are not already present in the given socioeconomic system. At the same time, the idea that they must be further enhanced and anchored to the market, in order to make the productive efficiency of post-capitalist societies greater, is itself a rather problematical proposition. For there is no available evidence to prove that reorienting social production in that way would make it more viable with regard to the realization of its tasks taken in their entirety, which must include several other objectives in addition to the production of goods for direct individual consumption even in capitalist society, let alone if one wants to make progress in the direction of a socialist transformation.

The failures of the past could not be attributed to the repression of the mechanism of individual material incentives but, rather, to the refusal to face up to the difficult practical question of their status and role in the process of the necessary socialist restructuring of society. They were left in a limbo; for addressing this issue would only be possible if simultaneously the inherited *hierarchical/structural division of labour* – with all its subsequent modifications – could be forcefully tackled. It was much easier to leave the inherited structures – and the associated motivational mechanism of *differential* material incentives legitimating the given hierarchical structure – in their place, even if the expectations of the individuals concerned could not be adequately satisfied. For the same reasons, it is quite understandable that the 'market socialist' remedy to the experienced problems and contradictions has arisen with relative ease from the same soil, representing in its own way the 'line of least resistance'.

However, due to the nature of the problems at stake, following the 'line of least resistance' is not very likely to succeed. For inasmuch as they are directly affected both by the present state of affairs and by any practical alternative to it, only the associated producers could face up to the great difficulties involved in restructuring the productive and motivational framework of post-capitalist society, radically challenging the established division of labour.

Inevitably, therefore, the road to a possible solution of these problems is a *two-way street*. It requires profound commitment – even continued sacrifices – on the part of the associated producers if they are to secure the rewards which they can produce for themselves, leading to conditions when they are fully in charge of their life-activity.

No doubt, the starting point of this transformative enterprise cannot be other than the conditions in which the post-capitalist societies find themselves today. For no one would dispute any longer that they have to face with real urgency the task of satisfying the long neglected needs and demands of their individual members. At the same time the question also arises, how can they make sure that they avoid the danger of overturning

462 THE POWER OF IDEOLOGY

both their actual achievements and their original commitment to the socialist cause.

To cope successfully with these essentially structural challenges requires the adoption of some major structural remedies. This means that the now both necessary and feasible individual material incentives – which, to a large extent, are inevitably *divisive*, and not positively *associative* – must be part of a coherent strategy in which they fulfil a *mediatory* function towards the envisaged aim of radical restructuring, instead of being considered a *corrective ideal*, to be embraced as an *end in itself*.

In this sense, the Marxian programme of transferring the control of the social metabolism to the associated producers has lost none of its validity in all those years since the time of its first formulation. On the contrary, it has appeared again, stronger than ever, on the historical agenda of our own days. For only the associated producers can work out, for themselves, the practical modalities through which the now ubiquitous dual crisis of authority and development can be resolved.

9.5.6

The question of 'universality' appeared in the philosophy of the Enlightenment in a most emphatic form, reaching its climax in the monumental synthesis produced by Hegel. This turn of events in intellectual history was understandable, in that the philosophers concerned expressed through their categories, however abstractly, the social being of their time in its growing complexity and contradictoriness.

The social being in question was inseparable from the dynamic power of capital, advancing objectively – and in fact for the first time ever in history – towards the problematical universality of its global domination. Theorizing, more or less systematically, and (at least with regard to the philosophers' openly announced intentions) in a *secular* framework – in contrast to the earlier theological attempts to write ahistorical accounts of history merely to illustrate the eternal validity of the divine message through earthly events – about the course of unfolding 'world history' thus became feasible. This was true notwithstanding the fact that the limitations of the thinkers' social standpoint left their indelible mark on their historical conceptions, which had to be brought to an 'eternalizing' culmination in the focal point of the present.

The universalizing tendency of capital was indeed very real, no matter how contradictory. Given the intrinsic character of capital, its practically dominant universality could only prevail through internal and external antagonisms, making possible to assert an ultimate positive outcome – which was always implicitly assumed, and often rendered even explicit, in the philosophies of history here referred to – only as a pure '*act of faith*'. For this reason Hegel himself (who pushed the question of universality most forcefully and fruitfully into the forefront of philosophical interest) could not come to terms with the underlying contradictions. He too, despite his usually magisterial grasp of the encountered problems, had to adopt as 'solutions', at key points in his synthesizing attempt, mere declarations of faith as a way out of the difficulties.

Thus, on the one hand, when he had to consider in his *Philosophy of History* the potentially devastating implications of the antagonisms intrinsic to bourgeois individualism (the latter defined by him as one of the most fundamental 'principles' of the modern age), he could only *decree* the future arrival of their positive resolution, in the context of his poetic summing up of world history as *Theodicaea*.[917] This was his way of wishfully attempting to rule the *internal* antagonisms of 'eternal universal capital' out of court.

On the other hand, neither could the destructive implications of all the uncontrollable *external* antagonisms, generated by the capital system and its state formation, be brought to a more satisfactory solution within the Hegelian conceptual framework. Again, as we have seen in Section 9.1.5, Hegel could only *decree* the absolute primacy and unconstrainable sovereignty of the particularistic and necessarily warring national states, opposing this view with contemptuous disdain to the advocacy of a universally adopted and peaceful solution as an alternative. Thus, despite his general devotion to the 'principle of universality', Hegel embraced in his act of faith with uncritical enthusiasm the position that in the relations between states ultimately the *'state of nature'* prevails (and, according to him, rightfully so), adopting thereby a position which is particularly problematical – and with regard to its class determinations most revealing – in the case of an idealist philosopher.

Since Hegel's days the destructive aspects of capital's antagonistic universality have become much more pronounced. What could be considered only latent in the more distant past, came to the fore with a vengeance in the form of two devastating global wars and in the ravages of imperialism. At the same time, both in the field of military weaponry and on the ecological plane the means and methods of destruction have advanced to such an extent that capital's unconstrainable drive towards universal domination can now threaten the very survival of humanity.

If, on account of the earlier latency of capital's most destructive contradictions, Hegel could still be forgiven for his starry-eyed view of universality, there could be no such excuses today for the ideologists who continue to idealize 'Western universalism' against the emancipatory aspirations of all those who are exploited and oppressed by it. Thus, to claim that 'a *universal* society is coming into being. . . . The West is dying as a separate "culture", but it has a future as the *centre of a universal society*',[918] instead of submitting to a searching critique the deeply divisive and exploitative character of this alleged 'universality', shows that the ideological defence of the ruling *class* interests does not hesitate to reject even the most obvious factual evidence – the domination of the overwhelming majority of humankind by a tiny minority – in order to legitimize itself by maintaining the fiction of its own 'universality'. No wonder, therefore, that we could witness in the debates of the last 20 years a great disenchantment with the very idea of universality, due to a considerable extent (but by no means entirely) to such transparent ideological practices.

And yet, it would be quite wrong to follow the sceptical or pessimistic advice of those who want to persuade us to abandon these concerns. For the destructive universality of capital cannot be countered by a withdrawal into the 'little world' of local skirmishes. Like it or not, there is no getting away from the historical predicament in terms of which only *global solutions* are conceivable to get to grips with our *global problems*.

The socialist conception was envisaged right from the beginning as an alternative to the antagonistic universality of the capital system. As such, however, the socialist mode of control could not constitute a viable alternative to *universality* – which represents a dynamic historical condition and attainment from which there can be no way back either to the past or to some form of idealized localism – but only to the destructive (and ultimately self-destructive) inner *antagonism* of capital as the regulator of social reproduction.

In the end the great historical issue of our epoch is bound to be decided precisely in terms of the universal – i.e. *globally* defined – viability (or failure) of these two systems of control in an inescapably intertwined world tending towards its full integration. For there are too many problems – some absolutely vital for securing the elementary conditions of human survival on this planet – to which other than literally global solutions are quite unthinkable.

For a long time now the principal line of the ruling ideology, in its attempts to minimize the significance of the socialist alternative, was to confine the latter to conditions of underdevelopment. As we have seen in an earlier chapter, this took the form of arguing – even if not alway in this crude form – that socialism is:

> A kind of disease which can befall a transitional society if it fails to organize effectively those elements within it which are prepared to get on with the job of modernization.[919]

Accordingly, the remedy was conceived as 'rolling back' the boundaries of socialism, so as to make prevail the claimed naturalness and universality of the capitalist system, prophesying that:

> As the Revolution recedes into the past, revisionism gains ground, along with a more middle-class mode of life. The more men enjoy possession of a world they are in danger of losing, the less impatient they are to change that world.[920]

It was thus categorically denied that the socialist alternative was applicable to the circumstances of 'advanced industrial societies', proclaiming that it had no chance to compete with, let alone to supplant, the social order of 'Western universalism'.

To make such a view plausible, the actual state of affairs in 'advanced industrial societies' had to be grossly misrepresented, so that the validity of the categories in terms of which the socialist critique of capitalist society had been articulated – above all the categories of 'class' and 'exploitation' – could be declared no longer applicable to the conditions of 'modern industrial societies'. Yet, as a recent article rightly argued with regard to the severe problems experienced by the Western labour movement:

> The decline of the unions in the US cannot be explained by the shrinkage of the working class, not even of its manufacturing sector. In fact, while union membership in goods-producing sectors declined in the US by 1.9 million between 1980 and 1984, these sectors had an increase of 1.1 million new jobs. If US unions are declining it is not because they have run out of workers to be organized. Among industrial production non-supervisory workers alone, 12 million are unorganized. Moreover, 50 per cent of the metal, machine and electrical workers; 69 per cent of the chemical, oil, rubber, plastic and glass workers; 69 per cent of all garment and textile workers; 64 per cent of all wood, paper and furniture workers; and 67 per cent of all food processing workers are unorganized in the US.... The decline of some socialist and progressive forces in the last few years cannot be attributed to the sudden collapse or shrinkage of the working class but is explained by the behaviour of the unions, of the parties themselves and by the correlation of class forces. The decline of the US union movement and of the Democratic Party has to be explained by the behaviour of those instruments. Canada and the US have similar class structures, but while the Canadian unions and the Social Democratic Party of Canada (NDP) are growing, the US unions are declining and the Democratic Party is losing presidential election after presidential election.... Their decline is caused by distancing themselves from class practices and by the increasingly aggressive class policies of the US Establishment. This last point bears repeating in the light of the thesis that we are living in disorganized capitalism with great diffusion of power: the US capitalist class has not for a long time been as organized, cohesive and aggressive as it is today. We have witnessed a most dramatic move to the right by US establishment institutions – political, media, academic and foundations – showing a remarkable cohesiveness in ideological position. The loss of diversity within these establishments has been facilitated by the virtual disappearance of the liberal alternative to the conservative message. The capitalist class is indeed very well organized, with an enormous (and growing) concentration of political, economic and social power. A symptom of that power is the class ability to disaggregate the dominated (i.e. working) class, facilitated by its great racial and ethnic diversity.[921]

Thus, instead of being 'no longer applicable', as it is claimed, the Marxian categories help to throw light on the far from uniform economic and political conditions of the capitalistically most advanced countries, explaining also some of the most baffling setbacks of their governmental oppositions in the last few decades.

The idealization of 'advanced' capitalist countries as the insurmountable (natural) social order is pursued with all means at the disposal of the ruling ideology. If the class-interested 'economical use', or blatant misrepresentation, of the facts is not enough, other methods are adopted to discredit the social adversary. While the ideologists of the 'end of ideology' sing the praises of 'detached objectivity' and proper theoretical 'neutrality', in reality every ideological weapon is sharpened and deployed in order to defeat and bury the historical opponent.

One of the favourite stratagems is to mobilize the ideological army of those who once belonged to the 'other side' and have 'seen the light'. Consequently their regular announcement of the inevitable doom of socialism – which is described by them at best as a utopian dream – is supposed to be most authoritative. Thus, in an article by a prominent former Labour Member of Parliament we are presented with the following insights into the predicament of the respective oppositions in Great Britain and in the United States:

> Dukakis mania has broken out in the newspapers and intellectual journals of the left. It is not that Dukakis is regarded with affection or approval, but he does seem to have found a way of winning the votes of the gullible. The British left is in the same business and is open to any suggestion of what it could say – whether it believes it or not – to get back into power.... Nor has the strange record of socialist parties in power passed unnoticed. In France, Spain, Australia and New Zealand the ruling so-called socialist parties are pursuing policies which to the layman are not easily distinguishable in many spheres from those of Margaret Thatcher.... Dukakis oozes moderation and Thatcherite financial rectitude from every pore and, in Lloyd Bentsen, has selected a running mate who is more conservative than George Bush. Never mind that the whole thing is a miserable fraud which, if Dukakis wins, will disappoint both Jackson's army of the dispossessed and the reactionary hard-hats who dislike blacks. What concerns the Labour party is not how Dukakis will perform in office, but whether he can win the election.... If Labour, however insincerely, accepts modern capitalism, then the gravest cause of national uncertainty will have been removed. The gains of recent years will be preserved and *socialism will become a harmless eccentricity*, celebrated in books and theatrical performances, trotted out occasionally for the reverent worship of a diminishing band of believers.[922]

The establishment belief in the universality and eternal permanence of capitalism is thus reaffirmed with the characteristic ideological zeal of the converted. However, if the readers look for some theoretical substance behind this declaration of faith, they will be disappointed. For one can find only the confused (and confusing) platitudes of the 'radical Right'. In the spirit of the latter the author of the quoted article offers us, in explanation of what motivates the rival systems of capitalism and socialism, his watered down version of the 'radical Right's self-serving opposition between *'equality of opportunity'* and *'equality of outcome'*. After asserting that Dukakis 'has to fool Jackson and Jackson has to pretend to be fooled if the

Democrats are to win', he adds, on the basis of 'inside knowledge', that 'in the days of its power the Labour party operated in exactly this way. Its leadership did not believe in equality of outcome, but declared it was an interesting issue for the distant future. Many activists in the party bewailed the leadership's lack of socialist conviction, but hardly expected anything better.'

We are also told that: 'Put bluntly, equality of opportunity is a *capitalist* concept, whereas equality of outcome is the basic tenet of *socialism*.' In truth, however, while 'equality of opportunity' is indeed one of the most frequently and loudly advertised propaganda tenets of bourgeois ideology, the socialist concern with equality is much more real and subtle than the crude 'equality of outcome' image would suggest. As we have seen above, it was defined nearly 200 years ago in these terms:

> Equality must be measured by the *capacity* of the worker and the *need* of the consumer, not by the intensity of the labour and the quantity of things consumed. . . . The aim is equality of pains and pleasures, not of consumable things and workers' tasks.[923]

But even in its own terms of reference the 'capitalist concept' of equality is completely untenable. For the so-called 'equality of opportunity', as far as the overwhelming majority of the people even in the most privileged countries are concerned, is at best a fantasy, confined to the equal right to put a piece of paper into the ballot box, in order to reaffirm the legitimacy of the ruling order of capital to carry on exploiting and dominating the producers as before.

Moreover, 'equality of opportunity', without actually offering the prospect to lead to *substantive* equality, defined in qualitative terms (as already Babeuf and Buonarroti tried to define it), is entirely vacuous, if not a complete fraud. For it says absolutely nothing about the *starting point* of the contestants, although no one could deny that the starting point has a vital bearing on the *outcome* of any race.

Characteristically, bourgeois ideology – especially in its right wing variety which wants to execute socialism on the stake of its 'equality of outcome' – refuses to consider this all-important aspect of the question of equality. It prefers to stay silent about the embarrassing truth that under capitalism a *structurally articulated and enforced inequality* constitutes the necessary starting point in the race between the 'haves' and the 'have-nots'. It is therefore quite *obscene* to talk about 'equality of opportunity' so long as the starting point itself remains *incorrigibly unequal*. The dice are *heavily loaded* against the vast majority of the contestants, making any meaningful advance in this respect quite impossible even in the capitalistically most developed (and privileged) countries, not to mention their underdeveloped dependencies in the 'Third World'. The categorical refusal to consider this circumstance reveals the true meaning of capital's 'Western universalism'.

The irrelevance of the Marxian alternative has been announced with monotonous regularity in the last few decades – particularly in relation to the problems of the capitalistically most advanced country, the United States – and continues to inspire countless books and articles even today. Yet the theoretical arsenal of the dominant ideology which produces these books and articles is not very impressive, even if its institutional domination is overpowering. As Paul Baran – the author of the path-breaking *Political Economy of Growth* and, with Paul Sweezy, co-author of an equally important book on the development of *Monopoly Capital*[924] – poignantly characterized the arbitrary method and precarious intellectual credentials of a much publicized 'alternative to Marxism':

> We are told that we have to re-do our price structure, refashion our wages, redeploy our profits, revamp our entrepreneurship, reapportion our resources, with all of these categories being treated as if they referred to marbles which can be pushed around at pleasure. But a price is not only paid but also received; profit is not only an accounting concept but income; entrepreneurship not only a term most useful these days in drafting applications for research grants but the actual management of corporate business; and productive resources are not free gifts of nature but private property. All of these concrete elements and relations which constitute the basis of economic and social life appear in Professor Rostow's theorizing as disembodied entities obeying mysterious laws of movement. Although it is the outstanding characteristic of capitalism that people do not control the economic system but that the economic system controls people, Professor Rostow finds the 'root cause' of our difficulties, not in the nature of our economic and social order, but in 'certain American habits of mind.' Accordingly, the explanation of the way in which our productive resources are used is not sought in the prevailing system of ownership, not in the working principles of a market- and profit-determined economy, but in our 'concepts,' which in turn are produced by an 'interplay of intellectual and political features of the American scene.' Thus the impetus of the spirit takes over from the drive for profits, the interplay of concepts substitutes for the competition in the market, and habits of thought take the place of regularities of the historical process. This kind of social science from which society is abstracted and this kind of economic history in which there is no longer room for economic interests was recommended in one of Professor Rostow's recent publications[925] as an alternative to Marxism and an alternative indeed it is. But not one which would tempt me to make the switch.[926]

Let those make the switch who like to be carried afloat by the fashionable ideological/intellectual currents. And let the Panglosses of 'modernity' and 'postmodernity' wait for the transcendental miracle, or cultivate the little corners of their well manicured gardens, as they please. In the meantime, the real problems of our world continue to press for tangible solutions. They could hardly be found by abstracting from the globally intertwined conditions and contradictions of 'modern industrial society', no matter what kind of variations are introduced into the intellectual game of marbles with disembodied categories.

To be sure, insisting on the continued validity and universality of the socialist solution, as the only feasible alternative to the antagonistic reality and all-engulfing destructive tendency of capital's 'Western universalism', cannot be intended as an easy reassurance. For an alternative mode of regulating the social metabolism can claim universality for itself only if it is suitable to solve the emerging problems and difficulties of societal reproduction *everywhere*, irrespective of how advanced or undeveloped the conditions from which they arise.

This means that the potential universality of the socialist alternative to capital's mode of control can only prevail if it succeeds in fully embracing the now highly privileged societies of the capitalistically advanced countries, including the United States of America, overcoming the obstacles presented by the prevalent vested interests in significant sections of the working classes as well. Short of the realization of this condition, there can be very little hope indeed for the future of socialism – or, for that matter, for the survival of humanity. This is because it is unthinkable to project the perpetuation of the present stalemate between the two rival systems far ahead into the future, in view of the perils and prohibitive material and human waste that go with their continued confrontation.

There are many who argued in the past and continue to assert today that socialism is doomed because it will never break through in the United States and in other 'advanced' countries, given the irreversible 'integration' of their working classes. However, we can find a completely different view as well. It is quite significant that this alternative view, notwithstanding all adversity, has been sustained with great vitality and commitment – in the case of the major intellectuals grouped around *Monthly Review* now for *40 years* – precisely in the United States.

The words of the late Harry Braverman – the author of a seminal study on *Labour and Monopoly Capital: The Degradation of Work in the Twentieth Century* – sum up with moving authenticity this 'longer view':

> I have every confidence in the revolutionary potential of the working classes of the so-called developed capitalist countries. Capitalism will not, over the long run, leave any choice to these classes, but will force upon them the fulfillment of the task which they alone can perform. This presupposes an enormous intensification of the pressures which have only just begun to bear upon the working class, but I think there is no question that it will happen. I have long tended to agree with those who think it will still be a long time in coming. But time is a social and historical concept, not a purely chronological one. When I look at the great changes that have occurred during the past ten or fifteen years, I believe I see this time passing rather more quickly than I used to think would be the case. In any event, historical time is difficult to forecast, and may be measured out in generations; it sets its own pace and not a pace to satisfy our wishes. But pass it will, whether rapidly or slowly, and bring in its train those explosive developments which for the past few decades have appeared limited to 'other' parts of the world.[927]

There is very little that needs to be added to these words. Perhaps two things. First, the obvious, that today we are somewhat nearer to the maturation of the fruits of that 'social and historical time' to which Harry Braverman attached his hopes when he wrote these lines. And second – what *should be* obvious, if it was not for the demobilizing ideological fog generated by the ruling interests among the members of the subordinate classes, with the active participation of many of their leaders and theorists – that it is inconceivable to realize the socialist potentialities with which our historical time is pregnant without activating the power of emancipatory ideology. For without the latter the working classes of the capitalistically advanced countries cannot become 'conscious of their interests', let alone 'fight them out' – in solidarity and effective cooperation with the working classes in those 'other' parts of the one and only real world – to a positive conclusion.

NOTES

Throughout the book, italics in quoted material are the author's own, unless otherwise stated.

1. 'Word Finder' – an electronic Thesaurus made by Microlytics, Inc., of East Rochester, New York – is bundled with Version 4 of MicroPro's best selling 'WordStar Professional'. It can be used with other word processor programmes as well.
2. Quoted by Harry Magdoff in his book on *Imperialism: From the Colonial Age to the Present*, Monthly Review Press, New York, 1978, p. 148.
   The scholar in question is David K. Fieldhouse, Beit Lecturer at the time in the History of the Commonwealth at Oxford University.
3. Magdoff, *ibid.*, pp. 148–9.
4. Keynes, 'A short view of Russia' (1925), republished in *Essays in Persuasion*, Norton & Co., New York, 1963, p. 300.
5. Keynes, 'Am I a Liberal?' (1925), *Essays in Persuasion*, p. 324.
6. Keynes, 'The end of laissez-faire' (1926), *Essays in Persuasion*, p. 319.
7. Keynes presents an almost unbelievable rationalization of even British colonial plundering in terms of 'compound interest'. This is how he argues his case:

   > The value of British foreign investments today is estimated at about £4,000,000,000. This yields us an income at the rate of about 6 and ½ per cent. Half of this we bring home and enjoy; the other half, namely 3 and ¼ per cent, we leave to accumulate abroad at compound interest. Something of this sort has now been going on for about 250 years. For I trace the beginnings of British foreign investment to the treasure which Drake stole from Spain in 1580. [Which is fine, of course, since Spain stole it from *her* colonies.] ... Queen Elizabeth found herself with about £40,000 in hand. This she invested in the Levant Company – which prospered. Out of the profits of the Levant Company, the East India Company was founded; and the profits of this great enterprise were the foundation of England's subsequent foreign investment. Now it happens that £40,000 accumulating at 3 and ¼ per cent compound interest approximately corresponds to the actual volume of England's foreign investments at various dates, and would actually amount today to the total of £4,000,000,000 which I have already quoted as being what our foreign investments now are. Thus every £1 which Drake brought home in 1580 has now become £100,000. *Such is the power of compound interest.*
   > ('Economic possibilities for our grandchildren' (1930), *Essays in Persuasion*, pp. 361–2)

   Reading such 'arguments' and the 'evidence' devised to support them, one does not quite know whether to laugh at their level of 'scientific' penetration, or to cry over the fact that some people can actually take them seriously. The self-reassured ideological blindness of a major bourgeois intellectual could hardly find a more blatant form of manifestation.

8. *Ibid.*, p. 373.
9. *Ibid.*, p. 359.
10. *Ibid.*, p. 364. 'Mankind is solving its economic problem' is italicized by Keynes.
11. *Ibid.*
12. *Ibid.*, p. 366.
13. *Ibid.*, pp. 369–70.
14. *Ibid.*, p. 372.
15. *Ibid.*, p. 373.
16. *Ibid.*
17. Marx, Preface to *A Contribution to the Critique of Political Economy*.
18. Hegel, *The Philosophy of Right*, Clarendon Press, Oxford, 1942, p. 212.
19. As Hegel puts it:

> We have, in traversing the past – however extensive its periods – only to do with what is *present*; for philosophy, as occupying itself with the True, has to do with the *eternally present*. Nothing in the past is lost for it, for the Idea is *ever present*; Spirit is immortal; with it there is *no past, no future*, but an *essentially now*. This necessarily implies that the present form of Spirit comprehends within it all earlier steps. These have indeed unfolded themselves in succession independently: but what Spirit is it has *always been* essentially; distinctions are only the development of this essential nature. The life of the ever present Spirit is a *circle* of progressive embodiments, which looked at from another point of view *appear* as past. The grades which Spirit *seems* to have left behind it, it still possesses in the *depth of its present*.
> (Hegel, *The Philosophy of History*, Dover Publications, New York, 1956, p. 79)

20. Hegel, *The Science of Logic*, Allen & Unwin, London, 1929, Vol. 2, p. 484.
21. Hegel, *The Philosophy of History*, p. 39.
22. *Ibid.*, p. 103.
23. Characteristically, Hegel weds 'the principle of modernity' to the 'principle of the north, the principle of the Germanic peoples' in his *Philosophy of Right*.
24. See, for instance, 'The Lost Paradise of regionalism: the crisis of postmodernity in France' by Claude Karnoouh, *Telos*, No. 67, Spring 1986.
25. Max Weber, *The Theory of Social and Economic Organization*, edited with an introduction by Talcott Parsons, The Free Press, New York, 1964, p. 92.
26. *Ibid.*, p. 342.
27. *Ibid.*, p. 328.
28. Weber, *General Economic History*, Collier Books, London, 1961, p. 207.
29. *Ibid.*
30. Weber, *The Theory of Social and Economic Organization*, p. 92.
31. *Ibid.*, p. 139.
32. *Ibid.*, p. 354.
33. H.H. Gerth and C. Wright Mills (eds), *From Max Weber: Essays in Sociology*, Routledge & Kegan Paul, London, 1948, p. 299.
34. Weber, 'Objectivity', published in E. A. Shils and H. A. Finch (eds), *The Methodology of the Social Sciences*, The Free Press, New York, 1949, p. 91.
    Weber's definition of capitalism as a culture in which 'the governing

principle is the investment or private capital' is supposed to be a neutral 'ideal type'. However, as I argued some time ago:

> The choice of such defining characteristics is far from being 'value free', although on the surface it seems to express a self-evident truth: namely that capitalism and the investment of private capital are linked together. But this is, of course, merely a tautological truth, and by no means a very accurate one at that. What goes in Weber's definition beyond sheer tautology is either blatantly ideological and 'value bound', or false – or indeed both ideologically biased and false.

> Weber's definition is formulated from a definite standpoint: not that of 'pure logic' but one which very conveniently blocks out the possibility of rival definitions, without establishing itself on other than purely *assumptional* grounds. The adoption of this ideal type as the principle of selection of all available data necessarily carries with it that 'scientifically self-controlled' research (Weber) is confined to data which easily fit into the ideological framework of Weber's definitional assumptions.

> Let us see, briefly, how the Weberian definition of capitalism fulfils its ideological functions under the appearance of a 'non-ideological' and 'descriptive' formulation.

> The *first* thing we have to notice is the choice of the term *'culture'* (in place of available alternatives, such as 'social formation', or 'mode of production', etc.): a term which anticipates a determinate type of interpretation as to the development of the capitalistic social formation. (See in this respect his approach to *The Protestant Ethic and the Spirit of Capitalism*.)

> *Secondly*, Weber's capitalism is characterized by the assumption of a *'governing principle'*, without any attempt at explaining the grounds – if any – of this strange metaphysical entity. The methodological consequences of this assumption are extremely serious. For its adoption nullifies the possibility of a comprehensive historical enquiry into the actual grounds of the development of capitalism. In its place, we find an ahistorical projection of the developed form backwards into the past, since the 'governing principle' must be exhibited at all stages. (This is why in the last analysis it must be identified with the somewhat mysterious 'spirit of capitalism'). And Weber's qualifications concerning the relationship between the 'ideal type' and empirical reality are, in this respect, nothing more than an ideological *escape clause* to provide blanket coverage against possible objections to his general model.

> *Thirdly*, the definitional assumption of the *'investment of private capital'* as the governing principle of capitalism conveniently blocks out the absolutely crucial question of structural interrelationship between capital and *labour*. The term which is conspicuously absent from the Weberian type of discourse is, of course, 'labour'. And since no 'spirit' – not even 'the spirit of capitalism' – can explain the *actual* constitution of capital (the 'mechanism' of its constitution, so to speak), such questions must be either disregarded or relegated to the intellectually secondary realm of describing a determinate stage of empiria. It is, thus, ideologically highly significant that 'labour' does not appear in the general model. Why bother with the thorny issues of *'the extraction of surplus-value'* if you have the 'investment of private capital' conveniently at your disposal in a ready-made form as the 'governing principle' of capitalism?

> *Fourth*, while 'labour' is conspicuously absent from Weber's social

equation, the definition of the governing principle of capitalism as the '*investment* of private capital' conveniently supplies the necessary justification for and legitimation of the continued existence of the capitalist mode of production against the counter-claims of appropriated labour. That private capital is invested only when it anticipates *profit* – i.e. that the underlying 'governing principle' is *profit* and not *investment* as such – this vital fact is quietly and significantly hidden from sight by Weber's definitional assumption.

Fifth, it is by no means true that capitalism is characterized by the '*investment* of private capital'. As is well known, capitalism is, equally, characterized by the *failure to invest* overproduced capital and, thus, by periodic *crises* and social upheavals. By taking the 'investment of private capital' for granted as the 'governing principle' of capitalism, Weber successfully blocks out a fundamental area of enquiry: namely, a critical questioning of the extremely *problematic* character of the capitalistic type of investment insofar as it is *necessarily* associated with crises and upheavals.

Sixth, it is quite inaccurate to describe capitalism in general as characterized by the 'investment of *private* capital'. Such a characterization is valid – with the qualifications made above – only of a determinate historical phase of capitalistic development, and by no means as an 'ideal type' in its Weberian sense. By stressing the investment of *private* capital Weber uncritically champions the subjective standpoint of the individual capitalist, disregarding at the same time one of the most important objective trends of development of the capitalist mode of production: namely the ever-increasing involvement of *state-capital* in the continued reproduction of the capitalist system. *In principle* the outer limit of this development is nothing less than the transformation of the prevailing form of capitalism into an all-comprehensive system of *state-capitalism*, which theoretically implies the complete abolition of the specific phase of capitalism idealized by Weber. But precisely because of such implications, this crucial trend of development must be excluded from the ideological framework of Weber's 'ideal type'.

And last but not least, the definition taken as a whole constitutes a completely *static* model.... the elimination of the fundamental structural interrelationship between capital and labour and its replacement by the frozen metaphysical entity, 'governing principle', excludes all dynamism from the picture. Thus, not only can there be no room for a dynamic account of the actual genesis and development of the capitalist social formation, as we have already seen; equally – and this is the point at which the ideological function of the static model becomes obvious – there can be no question of a possible dissolution and ultimate replacement of capitalism by a new type of social formation. There are no traces of dynamic contradictions in the model; consequently it can only comprehend the stable features of continuity – completely disregarding the dialectic of discontinuity – of a prevailing *status quo*. Such continuity is simply assumed, in the form of an already prevailing 'principle', and once it exists it cannot be altered in terms of the Weberian static model. (The same static approach is used to assess the strategically important question of the bureaucratic administrative system of capitalist society.)

These are then, roughly, the ideological features we can detect in *one single line* of Weber's voluminous writings, provided that we do not simply accept his claims at their face value.

('Ideology and social science', *The Socialist Register*, ed. Ralph Miliband and John Saville, Merlin Press, London, 1972; reprinted in I. Mészáros, *Philosophy, Ideology and Social Science*, Harvester Wheatsheaf, Hemel Hempstead, 1986. Quoted from pp. 6–9 of the latter.)

35. More about this and related issues in Chapter 3.2, 3.3, 3.4, 3.6, 3.7 and 3.8.
36. See in this respect Chapters 6 and 8, particularly 6.8, 8.1, 8.4, 8.6 and 8.7.
37. Habermas, 'The dialectic of rationalization: an interview with Jürgen Habermas' by Axel Honneth, Eberhard Knoedler-Bonte and Arno Widmann, *Telos*, No. 49, Fall 1981, p. 7.
38. Weber, *General Economic History*, p. 223.
39. Habermas, *Autonomy and Solidarity*, Interviews edited and introduced by Peter Dews, Verso, London, 1986, p. 187.
40. *Ibid*.
41. Such claims are developed in Habermas, *The Theory of Communicative Action*, of which the first volume – *Reason and the Rationalization of Society*, translated by Thomas McCarthy – has been published by Heinemann, London, in 1984. For an earlier version of this theory see Habermas, *Knowledge and Human Interests*, Heinemann, London, 1972.
42. See in this respect Chapter 3.4.
43. Habermas, *Toward a Rational Society*, Heinemann, London, 1971, p. 113.
44. Habermas, *Autonomy and Solidarity*, p. 82.
45. Habermas, *Toward a Rational Society*, p. 110.
46. Richard J. Bernstein, Introduction to *Habermas and Modernity*, edited and introduced by R.J. Bernstein, Polity Press, Cambridge, 1985, p. 17.
47. See Richard J. Bernstein, *The Restructuring of Social and Political Theory*, Basil Blackwell, Oxford, 1976, particularly pp. 185–225.
48. See Raymond Geuss, *The Idea of a Critical Theory: Habermas and the Frankfurt School*, Oxford, 1976.
49. See two essays by Thomas McCarthy, 'Rationality and relativism: Habermas's "overcoming" of hermeneutics', in John B. Thompson and David Held (eds), *Habermas: Critical Debates*, Macmillan Press, London, 1982, pp. 57–78, and 'Reflections on rationalization in the *Theory of Communicative Action*', in R. J. Bernstein (ed.), *Habermas and Modernity*, pp. 176–92.
50. Richard Rorty, 'Habermas and Lyotard on postmodernity', in R. J. Bernstein (ed.), *Habermas and Modernity*, p. 164.
51. *Ibid*., pp. 165–6.
52. As Habermas puts it in an interview:

> In the Federal Republic of Germany, too, a stronger Eurocommunist Party could be in many ways a *liberalizing* factor. Many things would be *normalized*. For instance, in this country you can't be a professor or a director of the Max Planck Institute and at the same time a Marxist. As long as that's the case, the basis of political culture is not *liberal*.
> (Habermas, *Autonomy and Solidarity*, p. 85)

53. Hans-Jürgen Krahl (a radical pupil of Adorno) remarked with irony about Habermas's opportunistic 'flexibility' that: 'A year ago Habermas denounced as *Left-Fascism* what he today praises as "fantasy-rich invention of *new techniques* of demonstration".' And he added that 'Habermas's tactic was to isolate the radical vanguard'. See Hans-Jürgen Krahl, 'Antwort auf Jürgen Habermas', in Krahl, *Konstitution und Klassenkampf: Zur historischen Dialektik von bürgerlicher Emanzipation und proletarischer Revolution*, Verlag Neue Kritik, Frankfurt, 1971. Quotations from pp. 244–5.

54. As Adorno put it: 'When I made my theoretical model I could not have guessed that people would want to realize it with Molotov cocktails.' Quoted from Martin Jay, *Adorno*, Fontana Paperbacks, London, 1984, p. 55. Originally appeared in *Die Süddeutsche Zeitung*, 26–27 April 1969, p. 10.

Of course, there was no question of the radical movement adopting the strategy of throwing 'Molotov cocktails'. What happened, in fact, was that the question of how to make some *practical sense* of 'critical theory' was put on the agenda under the circumstances of the first major postwar social crisis in capitalistically advanced countries of the West, after decades of 'economic miracles' and corresponding political consensus. Since, however, Adorno's 'theoretical model' categorically rejected the possibility of a meaningful, collectively articulated practical intervention in the 'totally reified' social world, any radical movement that represented a practice-oriented departure from his self-enclosed theorization had to be dismissed and denounced as 'Left-Fascism' and the threat of 'Molotov cocktails'.

55. R. J. Bernstein (ed.), *Habermas and Modernity*, p. 169.

56. In this context we should remind ourselves of the relationship between a society's 'ruling ideas' and its 'ruling classes', discussed by Marx already in *The German Ideology*.

57. 'Incorporability' does not mean here the alleged 'integrability' of the working class even for a limited period. It refers to the ability of the capitalist system to compensate for the negotiated wage increases and other material concessions by transforming them into its own expansionary gains, partly through the reabsorption of the enlarged overall wage fund of society (i.e. the dynamic role of productive consumption in the capitalistic reproduction process as a whole), and partly through the improved level of productivity secured within the particular industrial enterprises themselves: a productivity increase as a rule directly linked to the negotiated wage settlements.

58. See in this respect Habermas, 'Neo-conservative culture criticism in the United States and West Germany: an intellectual movement in two political cultures', in R.J. Bernstein (ed.), *Habermas and Modernity*, pp. 78–94.

Typically, even under the new circumstances Habermas is prevented by his idealist discourse from seeing (or acknowledging) the antagonistic *material* grounding of this intellectual movement.

59. See below, with regard to Habermas's critique of Marx's alleged non-procedural utopianism.

60. See in this respect Chapter I, 'Approaches to the problem of rationality', in Habermas, *The Theory of Communicative Action*, Vol. 1, pp. 1–142.

61. For Adorno's treatment of potentiality, see Chapter 3.4.7.

62. Habermas, *The Theory of Communicative Action*, Vol. 1, p. 239.

63. *Ibid.*

64. *Ibid.*

65. Habermas, 'A Reply to my critics', in *Habermas: Critical Debates*, edited by John B. Thompson and David Held, Macmillan Press, London, 1982, p. 221.

66. *Ibid.*, p. 225.

67. The strategy pursued by British Coal – inspired by an aggressively privatizing government of the radical Right – is by no means untypical. The British Seamen's Union had to declare an official strike in 1988 against private capitalist employers for the same reason of lengthening workloads. (In fact the ship-owners want to *add 50 days per annum* to the existing contractual commitments of seamen.) Similar examples could be found quite easily among the recent labour disputes of every 'advanced capitalist country'.

The double irony of the British Seamen's action was that – in compliance to the present, blatantly anti-union, labour legislation – they wanted to have a postal ballot, in order to receive a mandate from their members for future eventualities. Since, however, the outcome of the ballot was most likely to go against the employers, in view of the enormity of their demand, they applied for a High Court injunction to get the ballot itself forbidden. And – surprise, surprise! – the fearlessly independent judiciary of the capitalist state came down on the side of the employers, against the workers, declaring that the proposed ballot, on account of the *intentions* that might be read into them from the 'objective' vantage point of the ship-owners, was unlawful. Hence all the assets of the British Seamen's Union would be confiscated if they dared to proceed with it.

The British Government's anti-trade-union legislation hoped that the postal ballot would bring the triumph of the 'moderates' and the end of militant trade unionism. Instead, the results were as a rule deeply disappointing, producing massive majorities – at times in excess of 80 per cent – even in traditionally not very militant unions, like the various teachers' unions, for instance. It seemed, thus, that there could be no foolproof way of having both the ballot and the desired results, in conformity to the interests of capital. But only until the Seamen's case. For the learned judiciary, it appears, has cut with a brilliant single stroke the Gordian knot of the employers' insoluble dilemma in 'modern', 'post-capitalist' and 'post-industrial' industrial disputes.

68. I have discussed some related issues in an essay on 'Customs, tradition, legality: a key problem in the dialectic of base and superstructure', published in *Social Theory and Social Criticism: Essays for Tom Bottomore*, edited by William Outhwaite and Michael Mulkay, Basil Blackwell, Oxford, 1987, pp. 53–82.
69. Cf. Chapter 3.4.11 on the categorial changes proposed by Habermas.
70. Habermas, *Autonomy and Solidarity*, pp. 206–7.
71. *Ibid.*, p. 212.
72. John B. Thompson, 'Universal pragmatics', in *Habermas: Critical Debates*, p. 126.
73. *Ibid.*, p. 129.
74. Habermas, 'Wahrheitstheorien', in *Wirklichkeit und Reflexion: Walter Schulz zum 60. Geburtstag*, ed. by Helmut Fahrenbach, Neske, Pfullingen, 1973, pp. 255–6.
75. John B. Thompson, 'Universal pragmatics', p. 298.
76. Habermas, *The Theory of Communicative Action*, Vol. 1, p. 42.
77. Habermas, 'Vorbereitende Bemerkungen zu einer Theorie der kommunikativen Kompetenz', in Habermas and Niklas Luhmann, *Theorie der Gesellschaft oder Sozialtechnologie – Was Leistet die Systemforschung?*, Suhrkamp, Frankfurt, 1971, p. 140. Quoted in John B. Thompson, 'Universal pragmatics', p. 125.
78. Marx and Engels, *Collected Works*, Lawrence & Wishart, London, 1975ff, henceforth referred to as MECW. Quotation is from Vol. 5, p. 52.
79. *Ibid.*, p. 73.
80. *Ibid.*, p. 87.
81. Habermas, *Autonomy and Solidarity*, p. 213. The word 'just' is italicized by Habermas.
82. *Habermas: Critical Debates*, pp. 222–3.
83. Habermas, *The Theory of Communicative Action*, Vol. 1, p. 74.
84. *Ibid.* The words 'possible' and 'successful' are italicized by Habermas.

85. *Habermas: Critical Debates*, pp. 227–8. The words 'only' and 'possible' are italicized by Habermas.

The same idea is put forward in another essay where Habermas argues, after praising the *sensitivization potential* of modern art and the *enlightenment potential* of the sciences that:

> A morality is *universalistic* if it permits only norms of which all those con-cerned *could* approve on the basis of *full consideration* and without *duress*. No one would object to that – the *basic rights* and the principles of our *constitutions* are norms which we may *assume* everyone *could* affirm. I do not want to treat the problems which result when such *abstract principles* are applied to *concrete* life situations.
> (Habermas, 'Neoconservative culture criticism', in *Habermas and Modernity*, p. 90)

The problem here is not only that Habermas *assumes* again too much on behalf of the illusory 'universality' of established legal/political order, exempting thereby from critical scrutiny the 'basic rights' enshrined in 'our constitutions'. Equally problematical is the fact that he shies away from dis-cussing the problems which result when his 'abstract principles' are tested in the light of '*concrete situations*'. But, of course, this is by no means accidental. For, as we have seen above, he has to admit that his theory – confined to constructing a quasi-transcendental vision of 'the communicative infrastruc-ture of *possible* forms of life' – is completely at a loss when it comes to judging 'the value of competing forms of life' – as they assert themselves in the real world, in *concrete historical* situations.

86. See Habermas, 'Walter Benjamin: consciousness-raising or rescuing criti-que?', *Philosophical-Political Profiles*, Cambridge, MA, 1983.
87. *Habermas: Critical Debates*, p. 227.
88. Richard Rorty, 'Habermas and Lyotard on postmodernity', p. 171.
89. *Ibid.*, pp. 172–3.

In contrast to Rorty's critical treatment of 'modernity' and 'postmodernity', commentators often accept the self-characterizations of the contending theor-ists at their face value. To take an example, Gerard Raulet offers the following characterization of 'modernity':

> Compared with traditional, pre-industrial societies characterized by an organic cohesion of the life-world, modern industrial societies are ruptured by the differentiation of autonomous spheres and the polariza-tion of class antagonisms. ... Modernity is the historical state in which the relation to history is no longer one of *homogeneous continuity*, for the history of modernity is full of ruptures.
> (Raulet, 'Marxism and the post-modern condition', *Telos*, No. 67, Spring 1986, pp. 148 and 154)

As we can see, this description takes for granted the view of 'modernity' propounded by its champions, diffusing thereby the myth of 'homogeneous continuity' (which never existed), instead of critically challenging the undialectical nature of such claims and assumptions.

For a discussion of various aspects of 'modernity' and 'postmodernity' see Stuart Sim, 'Lyotard and the politics of antifoundationalism', *Radical Philosophy*, No. 44, Autumn 1986; Hilary Lawson, *Reflexivity: The Post-Modern Predicament*, Hutchinson, London, 1985; David Frisby, *Fragments of Modernity*, Polity Press, Oxford, 1985; Mark Poster, *Foucault, Marxism and*

History: Mode of Production versus Mode of Information, Polity Press, Oxford, 1984; Peter Dews, *Logics of Disintegration: Post-Structuralist Thought and the Claims of Critical Theory*, Verso, London, 1987. On the problems of modern art and literature, discussed in their proper sociopolitical setting, see also the fine volumes of critical essays by Franco Fortini, *Insistenze: Cinquanta scritti 1976–1984*, Garzanti, Milan, 1985, and *Saggi Italiani* (2 vols., the second entitled *Nuovi Saggi Italiani*), Garzanti, Milan, 1987.

90. Jean-François Lyotard, *The Postmodern Condition: A Report on Knowledge*, Manchester University Press, 1979, p. xxiii.
91. *Ibid.*, p. xxv.
92. *Ibid.*, p. 60.
93. See Note 85.
94. Lyotard, *The Postmodern Condition*, p. 66.
95. See Note 82.
96. Habermas, *The Theory of Communicative Action*, Vol. 1, p. 398.
97. Lyotard, *Ibid.*, p. 64.
98. To make things even more baffling, in one of the notes attached to *The Postmodern Condition* Lyotard writes: 'After the separation of Church and State, Paul Feyerabend (*Against Method*), demands in the same 'lay' spirit the separation of Science and State. But what about Science and Money?' *Ibid.*, p. 102.

It is very difficult to make out what meaning should one ascribe to this remark. For even Feyerabend's idea of separating Science and State without doing away with the State itself is highly questionable. Indeed, one could strongly argue that the separation of Church and State – which happens to be in principle a much more feasible enterprise than the separation of State and Science – is in all its historically known varieties a rather limited accomplishment. The problems arising from the separation of Science and State would be incomparably greater. For while the Church plays an important role in the process of cultural/ideological reproduction, its role in the material reproduction process is basically that of a collective *consumer* taking its share from the overall social product. By contrast, Science is a vital *productive force* of society. Consequently, its radical separation from the State would have far-reaching implications for the material foundation and practical viability of the State itself. Thus, to envisage, on top of this unresolved structural difficulty, the materially effective sovereign implementation of its ideal determinations by 'separated' Science – purely on the ground of the 'pragmatics of science itself', in an abstract/rhetorical opposition to the 'socioeconomic system' and to 'money' – while accepting the political authority of the State and the material imperatives of the capital system (for radically questioning them would require the articulation of a practically viable 'grand narrative'), seems to be a contradiction in terms.
99. Lyotard, *ibid.*, p. 64.
100. *Ibid.*, p. 66
101. *Ibid.*
102. *Ibid.*
103. Lyotard rightly resents such characterization. See in this respect his sarcastic reply to Habermas on p. 73 of *The Postmodern Condition*.
104. Lyotard, *ibid.*, p. 67
105. The case referred to by Lyotard is described as follows:

The municipality of Yverdon (Canton of Vaud), having voted to buy a computer (operational in 1981), enacted a certain number of rules: exclusive authority of the municipal council to decide which data are collected, to whom and under what conditions they are communicated; access for all citizens to all data (on payment); the right of every citizen to see the entries on his file (about 50), to correct them and address a complaint about them to the municipal council and if need be to the Council of State; the right of all citizens to know (on request) which data concerning them is communicated and to whom. (*Ibid.*, p. 103).

What is missing here, again, is an awareness of the forbidding difficulties involved in transforming into a *general social practice* – extended over not only the jealously guarded secrets of the capitalist state but also over those of the all-powerful transnational corporations structurally wedded to the military/industrial complex – what seems to be admissible strictly as a *local* measure, confined to issues of relatively limited importance. A far cry indeed from the idealized condition of the 'games of perfect information'.

106. Lyotard, *ibid.*, p. 82.
107. *Ibid.*, p. xxiii.
108. If they abandoned altogether such emancipatory concerns, that would undoubtedly remove some of the difficulties here referred to. However, doing so would by no means make things any better. Rather the opposite. For the radical elimination of all emancipatory concern, indirect or polemical though it might be, would inevitably undermine the theoretical edifices of both 'modernity' and 'post-modernity' which depend entirely on being parasitic on (or, if one prefers, negatively determined by) past discourses on emancipation. It would also make them ideologically quite useless, in that the old theories of emancipation – above all the Marxian conception – would remain uncontested.
109. Lyotard, *ibid.*, p. 79.
110. Habermas, *The Theory of Communicative Action*, Vol. 1, p. 388.
111. Marx, 'Theses on Feuerbach', MECW, Vol. 5, p. 4.
112. To use Mannheim's characteristic expression that ascribed an imaginary power of supra-class arbitration to the '*freischwebender Intelligenz*' (i.e. the 'free-floating' or unattached intelligentsia).
113. The title of Daniel Bell's book, published by Basic Books, New York, in 1976.
114. Habermas, 'Neoconservative culture criticism', p. 93.
115. Adorno *et al.*, *Aesthetics and Politics: Debates between Ernst Bloch, Georg Lukács, Bertolt Brecht, Walter Benjamin, Theodor Adorno*, NLB, London, 1977, pp. 105–6.
116. See Chapter 3.4.3 in this respect.
117. *Dialectic der Aufklärung* by Adorno and Horkheimer was written during the war and first published by Querido of Amsterdam in 1947. First English edition by Herder and Herder, New York, 1972.
118. According to the published testimony of one of Einaudi's closest advisers, Cesare Cases ('La "mauvaise époque" e i suoi tagli', *Belfagor*, Anno xxxii, No. 6, November 1977, pp. 701–15), 'i tagli della *Dialettica dell'illuminismo* sono dovuti all'intervento di Horkheimer, cioè investono il problema dei tagli d'autore (p. 702). See also his article on the Correspondence of Walter Benjamin with Gershom Scholem (*Studi Germanici*, nuova serie, Anno vi, No. 2, pp. 168–77) in which he discusses – among other matters – the relationship between Benjamin and Adorno and the notorious alteration of Benjamin's posthumously published texts by Adorno.
119. See the literature quoted in Chapter 3.4.3.

120. See Chapter 3, sections 3.2, 3.3, 3.6, 3.7, and 3.8 on these issues.
121. See Note 454.
122. See Note 463.
123. See Note 464.
124. See in this respect 'A critique of analytical philosophy' in my book: *Philosophy, Ideology and Social Science: Essays in Negation and Affirmation*, Harvester Wheatsheaf, Hemel Hempstead, 1986.
125. Daniel Bell, *The End of Ideology*, The Free Press, New York, 1965, pp. 405–6.
126. This was the title of the *epilogue* to Daniel Bell's book on *The End of Ideology*. But well beyond that, many other thinkers too – Raymond Aron, for instance – mesmerized themselves and others into believing that the traditional 'ideological' line of demarcation between 'left' and 'right' had totally lost its meaning in the West, together with the nowadays allegedly just as meaningless distinction between 'market economy' and 'planning', 'capitalism' and 'socialism', etc., not to mention 'the nationalist ideology' which was said to be irreprievably 'condemned in Western Europe'. (See Raymond Aron's celebrated book, *The Opium of the Intellectuals*, Secker & Warburg, London, 1957, written in 1954 and originally published in Paris in 1955.)
127. MECW, Vol. 5, pp. 36–7.
128. *Ibid.*, p. 30.
129. *Ibid.*, p. 37.
130. *Ibid.*, p. 56.
131. Sartre, *The Problem of Method*, Methuen, London, 1963, pp. 7–8.
132. See Daniel Singer's illuminating book, *Is Socialism Doomed?: The Meaning of Mitterrand*, Oxford University Press, 1988.
133. See Sartre, 'Le réformisme et les fétiches', *Les Temps Modernes*, No. 122, February 1956, pp. 1153–64.
134. *Ibid.*, p. 1155. In the same article Sartre contrasted with the deplorable state of Marxism in the French C. P. the positive achievements of two communist intellectuals, Tran Duc Tao and Lukács. He wrote:

> Le seul, en France, qui ait tenté de combattre l'adversaire, sur son propre terrain, c'est Tran Duc Tao, un membre du P.C. vietnamien; le seul qui tente en Europe, d'expliquer par leurs causes les mouvements de pensées contemporains, c'est un communiste hongrois, Lukács, dont le dernier livre n'est même pas traduit.
> (*Ibid.*, p. 1159)

135. See Chapter 7, concerned with the thorny issues of the 'Social Revolution' advocated by Marx and his followers, and the painful actuality of the Division of Labour.
136. See Chapter 8, 'The constitution of solidarity'.
137. Sartre, *ibid.*, p. 1159.
138. *Ibid.*, p. 1158.
139. See Sartre, *The Problem of Method*, as well as his *Critique of Dialectical Reason*, NLB, London, 1976. A key passage in this respect is quoted from *The Problem of Method* in Chapter 6.2.
140. Claude Lévi-Strauss, *The Savage Mind*, Weidenfeld and Nicolson, London, 1966, p. 246.
141. See the long and wide-ranging interview, 'Plus loin avec Claude Lévi-Strauss', *L'Express*, No. 1027, 15–21 March, 1971, pp. 60–6.
142. This is one of the most important passages discussing Lévi-Strauss's relationship to Marx in this interview:

L'Express: Il y a une époque où le marxisme a marqué votre vie.
Lévi-Strauss: Il continue. L'idée que la conscience sociale se ment toujours à elle-même et que, derrière le mensonge, la vérité se dévoile par la manière même dont le mensonge s'affirme, c'est déjà un enseignement de Marx. C'en est un aussi que l'idéologie d'une société quelconque ne devient compréhensible qu'à la lumière des rapports concrets que les hommes de cette société entretiennent entre eux, et qu'ils entretiennent avec le monde où ils vivrent et oeuvrent.

Marx, à qui nous sommes redevables de la distinction entre *infrastructures et superstructures*, s'est surtout occupé des premières, et il n'a fait qu'esquisser, par moments, la façon dont on pourrait formuler leurs rapports. C'est à cette *théorie de superstructures*, dont Marx a réservé la place plus qu'il ne l'a vraiment élaborée, que j'essaie d'apporter une contribution.
(*Ibid.*, p. 63)

143. *Ibid.*, p. 66.
144. *Ibid.*, p. 61.
145. Michel Foucault, *The Order of Things*, Tavistock Publications, London, 1970, p. 385.
146. *Ibid.*, p. 387.
147. *Farewell to the Working Class: An Essay on Post-Industrial Socialism* is the title of a celebrated booklet by André Gorz (once a radical activist and a close collaborator of Sartre), published in England by Pluto Press, London, in 1982.
148. Sartre, Interview by Simon Blumenthal and Gérard Spitzer, *La Voie Communiste*, new series, June–July, 1962.
149. See Note 278.
150. See Chapter 6.2 on this question.
151. F.W. Taylor, *Scientific Management*, Harper and Row, New York, 1947, p. 29. This postwar popularization of Taylor's major writings comprises his *Shop Management, The Principles of Scientific Management* and *Testimony before the Special House Committee*. These works were written between 1901 and 1914, but Taylor tried out his ideas in several factories, rather unsuccessfully, a few years earlier.
152. Taylor, *ibid.*, p. 30.
153. *Ibid.*, p. 60.
154. Adam Ferguson, *Essay on the History of Civil Society* (1767), edited with an Introduction by Duncan Forbes, University Press, Edinburgh, 1966, pp. 181–3.
155. Lucien Goldmann, Preface to the new edition (1966) of *The Human Sciences and Philosophy*, Jonathan Cape, London, 1969, pp. 10–11.

In a note appended to this passage Goldmann accurately described the ideological changes that went with this transition to 'organized capitalism' as follows:

The more a given theory eliminates, by its very structure and by the methods it elaborates, the problem of meaning and that of history, the less it needs to become explicitly involved in the defence of the existing social order. As formalistic structuralism is completely divorced from social and political problems, its implicit value-judgements arise on the methodological level. Raymond Aron, who retains many of the traits of the liberal rationalism of the Enlightenment, takes a much more explicit position in favour of organized capitalism. At the end of the line are to be found certain former Marxists who, having scarcely assimilated the intellectual methods and structure of contemporary sociological thought, finish by becoming direct and almost crude apologists for technocratic society.

(*Ibid.*, p. 142)

156. C.B. Macpherson, 'A political theory of property', in Macpherson, *Democratic Theory: Essays in Retrieval*, Clarendon Press, Oxford, 1973, p. 138.
157. *Ibid.*, p. 139.
158. *Ibid.*, p. 131.
159. Talcott Parsons, 'Social class and class conflict in the light of recent sociological theory', *American Economic Review*, Vol. 39 (1949), reprinted in Parsons, *Essays in Sociological Theory*, The Free Press, New York, 1954, p. 326.
160. See in this respect 'The ideology of Parsonian "General Theory"' in my *Philosophy, Ideology and Social Science*.
161. 'Convergence between the two ostensibly different industrial systems occurs at all fundamental points. This is an exceedingly fortunate thing. In time, and perhaps in less time than may be imagined, it will dispose of the notion of inevitable conflict based on irreconcilable difference.' (John Kenneth Galbraith, *The New Industrial State*, Revised and Updated Edition, The New American Library, New York, 1971, p. 376.)

From the distance of the long persistent economic crisis and the 'new cold war', the relevance of such reasoning appears rather remote.
162. See, for instance, Serge Mallet's trend-setting book, *La nouvelle classe ouvrière*, Paris, 1963; in English: *The New Working Class*, Spokesman Books, Nottingham, 1975.
163. According to Galbraith, 'the industrial system absorbs the class interests. It does so partly by minimizing the reality of conflict and partly by exploiting the resulting malleability of attitude to win control of belief. The goals of the industrial system, in this process, become the goals of all who are associated with it and thus, by slight extension, the goals of the society itself.' *The New Industrial State*, p. 313.
164. *Ibid.*, p. 233. Galbraith added to the lines quoted above, with his customarily exuberant self-confidence, that 'The view of the system in the preceding chapters makes these tendencies predictable; and the statistics, which in this case are good, affirm the expectation or are consistent with it.'

To be sure, Galbraith's ' view of the system' makes the claimed tendencies of unemployment 'predictable', in a thoroughly circular fashion. One wonders, however, what kind of data or statistics he was talking about when the *actual* trends of development were already unmistakably pointing in a very different direction, and were clamorously confirmed by the crises of the 1970s and 1980s.

Nor should one imagine that insisting on a view radically different from that expressed by Galbraith and others is supported only by 'hindsight'. The use to which data and statistics are put is inseparable from the *social standpoint* one adopts, circumscribing what becomes 'visible' or 'invisible' from among the great multiplicity of social facts and trends available to all to see or close their eyes to, in accordance with the far from 'value-neutral' procedure of all social enquiry. As a matter of fact, at the same time when Galbraith's book was published, the present writer tried to approach these problems in a totally different way. To quote:

Equally important is the newly emerging pattern of unemployment. For in recent decades unemployment in the highly developed capitalist countries was largely confined to 'pockets of underdevelopment'; and the millions of people affected by it used to be optimistically written off in the grand style of neo-capitalist self-complacency as the 'inevitable costs of modernization', without too much – if any – worry about the social-economic repercussions of the trend itself.

Insofar as the prevailing movement was from *unskilled* to *skilled* jobs, involving large sums of capital outlay in industrial development, the matter could be ignored with relative safety, in the midst of the euphoria of 'expansion'. Under such circumstances the human misery necessarily associated with all types of unemployment – including the one produced in the interest of 'modernization – could be capitalistically justified in the name of a bright commodity-future for everyone. In those days the unfortunate millions of apathetic, 'underprivileged' people could be easily relegated to the periphery of society. Isolated as a social phenomenon from the rest of the 'Great Society' of affluence, they were supposed to blame only their own 'uselessness' (want of skill, lack of 'drive', etc.) for their predicament ... What was systematically ignored, however, was the fact that the trend of capitalist 'modernization' and the displacement of large amounts of unskilled labour in preference to a much smaller amount of skilled labour ultimately implied the *reversal* of the trend itself: namely the breakdown of 'modernization', coupled with massive unemployment. This fact of the utmost gravity simply *had* to be ignored, in that its recognition is radically incompatible with the continued acceptance of the capitalist perspectives of social control. For the underlying dynamic contradiction which leads to the drastic reversal of the trend is by no means inherent in the *technology* employed, but in the blind subordination of both *labour and technology* to the devastatingly narrow limits of capital as the supreme arbiter of social development and control.

To acknowledge, though, the social embeddedness of the given technology would have amounted to admitting the socioeconomic limitations of the capitalist applications of technology. This is why the apologists of the capitalist relations of production had to theorize about 'growth' and 'development' and 'modernization' *as such*, instead of assessing the sobering *limits* of *capitalist* growth and development. And this is why they had to talk about the 'affluent', 'modern industrial' – or indeed 'post-industrial' (!) – and 'consumer' society *as such*, instead of the artificial, contradictory affluence of *waste-producing commodity society* which relies for its 'modern industrial' cycle of reproduction not only on the most cynical manipulation of 'consumer demand' but also on the most callous exploitation of the 'have-nots'.

Although there is no reason why *in principle* the trend of modernization and the displacement of unskilled by skilled labour should not go on indefinitely, as far as *technology itself* is concerned, there is a very good reason indeed why this trend must be reversed under capitalist relations of production: namely the catastrophically restricting criteria of profitability and expansion of *exchange-value* to which such 'modernization' is necessarily subordinated. Thus, the newly emerging pattern of unemployment as a social-economic trend is, again, indicative of the deepening structural crisis of present-day capitalism.

In accordance with this trend, the problem is no longer just the plight of unskilled labourers but also that of large numbers of *highly skilled* workers who are now chasing, in addition to the earlier pool of unemployed, the depressingly few available jobs. Also, the trend of 'rationalizing' amputation is no longer confined to the 'peripheral branches of ageing industry' but embraces some of the *most developed* and modernized sectors of production – from ship-building and aviation to electronics, and from engineering to space technology.

Thus, we are no longer concerned with the 'normal', and willingly accepted, by-products of 'growth and development' but with their driving to a halt; nor indeed with the peripheral problems of 'pockets of under-development' but with a fundamental contradiction of the capitalist mode of production as a whole which turns even the latest achievements of 'development', 'rationalization' and 'modernization' into paralysing burdens of chronic underdevelopment. And, most important of all, the human agency which finds itself at the receiving end is no longer the socially powerless, apathetic and fragmented multitude of 'underprivileged' people but *all* categories of skilled and unskilled labour: i.e. objectively, the *total labour force* of Society.

(István Mészáros, *The Necessity of Social Control*, Isaac Deutscher Memorial Lecture, delivered at the London School of Economics and Political Science on 26 January 1971, published by Merlin Press, London, 1971, pp. 51–5)

165. W.W. Rostow, *The Stages of Economic Growth*, Cambridge University Press, 1960, p. 155.
166. *Ibid.*
167. Walt Rostow subtitled *The Stages of Economic Growth:* 'A *Non*-Communist Manifesto'. Readers of his book can readily testify that – given its extreme ideological zeal – this was a modest understatement.
168. John Kenneth Galbraith, *The Affluent Society*, Pelican Books, Harmondsworth, 1962, (first ed. 1958), pp. 260–1.
169. *Ibid.*, p. 262.
170. *Ibid.*, p. 263.
171. *Ibid.*
172. First published in 1952, in the aftermath of the Korean war which left its heavy imprint on the first edition; now circulated in a substantially revised version, made in 1956.
173. Galbraith, *The Affluent Society*, p. 264.
174. Galbraith, *American Capitalism: The Concept of Countervailing Power*, Penguin Books, Harmondsworth, 1963, p. 129.
175. Galbraith, *The Great Crash 1929*, Penguin Books, Harmondsworth, 1961, p. 209.
176. Galbraith, *American Capitalism*, p. 214.
177. *Ibid.*, p. 151.
178. *Ibid.*, p. 164.
179. *Ibid.*, pp. 165–7.
180. This is how Galbraith summed up in *American Capitalism* what looked to him the supreme merits of the Keynesian approach:

> The essence of the Keynesian formula consists in leaving private decisions over production, including those involving prices and wages, to the men who now make them. The businessman's apparent area of discretion is in nowise narrowed. *Centralized decision* is brought to bear only on the *climate* in which those decisions are made; it insures only that

the factors influencing *free and intelligent decision* will lead to a *private action* that contributes to *economic stability*. Thus, in times of depression, increased government expenditures or decreased taxation will cause or allow an increase in demand. The resulting business decisions on production and investment, though quite uncontrolled, will result in *increased production and employment*.
(*Ibid.*, p. 192)

All this sounded a little bit too good to be true on a permanent basis. Such doubts, however, could be brushed aside with relative ease in the name of applying the right 'regulatory measures' – or, in Walt Rostow's terminology, 'the technical tricks of the trade' – to the allegedly well understood problems.

181. *Ibid.*, p. 187.
182. *Ibid.*, p. 188.
183. *Ibid.*
184. *Ibid.*, p. 189.
185. *Ibid.*, p. 210. The introduction of the category of 'reasonable luck' into Galbraith's economic theory was, no doubt, yet another proof of the 'scientific rigour' with which he tackled the problems of unemployment.
186. *Ibid.*
187. *Ibid.*, p. 130.
188. As a deepening corollary and embellishment of the claimed law, Galbraith also argued that:

Where markets are regulated by countervailing power, a net increase in demand at any time when the labour force and plant are being used to approximate capacity brings a further train of consequences. As noted, both labour and management are in a position to seek and obtain increases in prices or wages. It makes little difference which takes the initiative; one forces the other to follow. ... In the *nature of man*, if for no other reason, both labour and management will normally seek something more than mere compensation for the last change to their disadvantage. Thus, as has been well demonstrated by modern experience, management after paying a wage increase ordinarily recoups something more than the resulting cost increase in prices. The result is an increase in profits which, along with the further increase in living costs, remains a kind of residual incentive to labour to start the next round.
(*Ibid.*, pp. 205–6)

189. Galbraith, *The Affluent Society*, pp. 272–3.
190. *Ibid.*, p. 273.
191. *Ibid.*, pp. 273–9.
192. Galbraith, *The New Industrial State*, p. xvii.
193. *Ibid.*, p. 258.
194. *Ibid.*
195. *Ibid.*, p. 261.
196. *Ibid.*, p. 268.
197. *Ibid.*, p. 258.
198. *Ibid.*, p. 274.
199. *Ibid.*, p. 275.
200. W.W. Rostow, *op. cit.*, p. 167.
201. *Ibid.*, p. 164.
202. Three years after the mass tragedy the surviving victims were still waiting, in vain, for compensation from the US transnational company which could suc-

cessfully use (and abuse) all the tricks of the law in its own favour.
203. Renato Constantino, *The Nationalist Alternative*, revised edition, Foundation for Nationalist Studies, Quezon City, 1986, pp. 28–30.
204. M.R. Bhagavan, 'A critique of India's economic policies and strategies', *Monthly Review*, July-August 1987, pp. 63–4.
205. *Ibid.*, pp. 65–6.
206. See in this respect Harry Magdoff's rightly famous study: *The Age of Imperialism: The Economics of U.S. Foreign Policy*, Monthly Review Press, New York and London, 1966. See also Michael Barratt Brown, *After Imperialism*, Merlin Press, London, 1963; R. Rhodes (ed.), *Imperialism and Underdevelopment*, Monthly Review Press, New York, 1970; Samir Amin, *Imperialism and Unequal Development*, Harvester Press, Hassocks, 1977; and Giovanni Arrighi, *The Geometry of Imperialism*, NLB, London, 1978.
207. From the First Inaugural Address of Franklin Delano Roosevelt, in *Nothing Fear: The Selected Addresses of F.D. Roosevelt 1932–1945*, Hodder & Stoughton, London, 1947, p. 16.
208. See Arghiri Emmanuel, *Unequal Exchange: A Study of the Imperialism of Trade*, Monthly Review Press, New York, 1972. Emmanuel's more recent book – *Appropriate or Underdeveloped Technology?*, John Wiley, Chichester, 1982 – puts forward a much more problematical approach.
209. F.W. Taylor, *op. cit.*, p. 142.
210. Just how powerful the direct state interventions must or might not be, depends to a large extent on the temporary viability of trying to resolve the structural contradictions of the material base by means of superstructural manipulation. Authoritarian tendencies, like the aggressive monetarism of the 'radical Right', gain the upper hand at times when more limited 'papering over the cracks' or 'band-aid' type state-interventions are no longer effective. However, since the more centralized and authoritarian trends themselves operate within the same sphere of manipulative state-interventions, it is a delusion to expect major structural remedies from them.
211. Even Taylor himself had to admit that the anticipated results would be available 'particularly for those who adopt it *first*'. Naturally, he rationalized the inherent limitations of the whole approach by adding at once that 'the manufacturer and the workman will be far more interested in the especial local gain that comes to them and to the people immediately around them'. (Taylor, *op. cit.*, p. 142.)
212. See sections 2, 3 and 4 of the essay on 'Ideology and social science' in my volume: *Philosophy, Ideology and Social Science*.
213. Max Weber, *Collected Political Works*, Munich, 1921, pp. 258ff.
214. Georg Lukács, *The Destruction of Reason*, Merlin Press, London, 1980, pp. 608–9.
215. Marianne Weber, *Max Weber*, Tübingen, 1926, p. 665. Quoted by Lukács, *The Destruction of Reason*, p. 610.
216. Raymond Aron, *The Industrial Society*, Weidenfeld and Nicolson, London, 1967, p. 101.
217. *Ibid.*, pp. 148–9.
218. *Ibid.*, p. 107.
219. Reference to Marcuse's *One-Dimensional Man*.
220. R. Aron, *The Industrial Society*, p. 175.
   Again it should be noted that the realization of a society's 'full potentiality' is crudely reduced to the technological dimension: to the more or less complete application of its technological advances.
221. *Ibid.*, pp. 175–6.

222. *Ibid.*, p. 160. And elsewhere, talking about the substance that unites the various 'post-ideological' approaches, we find this admission: 'What we have in common is our opposition to Marxism-Leninism and to the type of ideology of which it is the perfect embodiment.' *Ibid.*, pp. 143–4.
223. *Ibid.*, p. 147.
224. *Ibid.*, p. 121.
225. *Ibid.*, p. 158.
226. Benjamin was close to Bertolt Brecht and Karl Korsch.
227. *'Alles was gut und teuer'* ('all that is good and precious', i.e. highly acclaimed), as they say in German. See a fine critical review of Habermas's *Legitimation Crisis* by James Miller, *Telos*, No. 25, Fall 1975, pp. 210–20. The same issue of *Telos* contains a very interesting debate between Wolfgang Müller, Christel Neusüss, Jürgen Habermas and Claus Offe which is relevant for understanding Habermas's political posture. The articles in question are: W. Müller and C. Neusüss, 'The illusion of state socialism and the contradiction between wage labour and capital', pp. 13–91; J. Habermas, 'A reply to Müller and Neusüss', pp. 91–8; Claus Offe, 'Further comments on Müller and Neusüss', pp. 99–111.
228. Hans Bunge, *Fragen Sie mehr über Brecht: Hanns Eisler in Gespräch*, Rogner and Bernhard, Munich, 1970, p. 30.
229. Susan Buck-Morss, *The Origin of Negative Dialectics: Theodor W. Adorno, Walter Benjamin, and the Frankfurt Institute*, Harvester Press, Hassocks, 1977, p. 42. For a thoughtful analysis of Adorno and Marcuse, see Joseph McCarney, 'What makes critical theory "critical"?', *Radical Philosophy*, No. 42, Winter/ Spring 1986.
230. He tried to persuade Arnold Hauser – who was far less proficient at reading musical scores than Adorno himself, hence remained thoroughly sceptical – of the soundness of this judgement.
231. Theodor W. Adorno, *Prisms*, Nevile Spearman, London, 1967 (from 'Perennial fashion – jazz', pp. 119–32), p. 125.
232. *Ibid.*, p. 127.
233. *Ibid.*, p. 129.
234. *Ibid.*, p. 132.
235. *Ibid.*, pp. 129–30.
236. *Ibid.*, p. 130.
237. Lukács, *The Theory of the Novel*, Merlin Press, London, 1978, p. 22.
238. *Ibid.*, p. 12.
239. *Ibid.*, p. 18.
240. See for instance Adorno, *Aesthetic Theory*, Routledge & Kegan Paul, London, 1984, p. 336.
241. Cf. Adorno, *Prisms*, p. 34.
242. Lukács, *The Theory of the Novel*, p. 22.
243. Adorno, *Prisms* (from 'A portrait of Walter Benjamin', pp. 227–42), p. 237. And Adorno added in another context:

> As far as the late *Benjamin* himself is concerned, his refusal to take the aesthetic avant-garde seriously unless it subscribed to the programme of the Communist Party may have been influenced by *Brecht's enmity to Tui intellectuals*. The *élitist segregation of the avant-garde is not art's fault but society's*. The unconscious aesthetic standards of the *masses* are precisely those that *society needs* in order to perpetuate itself and its hold on the masses.
> (*Aesthetic Theory*, p. 360)

244. *Ibid.*, p. 362.
245. *Ibid.*, p. 344.
246. *Ibid.*, p. 362.
247. *Ibid.*, p. 440.
248. *Ibid.*, p. 324.
249. *Ibid.*, p. 328.
250. *Ibid.*, p. 333.
251. *Ibid.*, p. 334.
252. *Ibid.*, p. 362.
253. *Ibid.*, p. 339.
254. *Ibid.*, p. 362.
255. *Ibid.*, p. 325.
256. Adorno, Introduction to *The Positivist Dispute in German Sociology*, Heinemann, London, 1976, p. 12.
257. Adorno, *Prisms* (from 'Cultural criticism and society', pp. 17–34), p. 24.
258. *Ibid.*, p. 25.
259. *Ibid.*, p. 26.
260. *Ibid.*, p. 30.
261. *Ibid.*, p. 34.
262. Adorno, *Aesthetic Theory*, p. 2.
263. *Ibid.*, p. 27.
264. *Ibid.*, p. 336.
265. *Ibid.*, p. 362.
266. *Ibid.*, p. 468.
267. Adorno, *Negative Dialectics*, The Seabury Press, New York, 1973, pp. 404–5.
268. Adorno, *Aesthetic Theory*, p. 331.
269. Martin Jay, *Adorno*, Fontana Paperbacks, London, 1984, p. 162.
270. *Ibid.*
271. Adorno, *Prisms* (from 'The sociology of knowledge and its consciousness', pp. 35–49), p. 41.
272. Martin Jay, *Ibid.*, pp. 46–7.
    Jay also reports that 'Supported in part by *funds from the American High Commissioner* John J. McCloy, the Institute officially reopened its doors in 1951. . . . the Institute established a specifically empirical branch in 1956 under the direction of Rudolf Gunzert.' (*Ibid.*, pp. 44–5.)
    That a decade later Adorno started to have misgivings about the wisdom of the Institute's wholehearted commitment to diffusing in Germany the methods and techniques of American social science, does not alter the fact that he was himself heavily implicated in that enterprise from the very beginning.
273. Martin Jay sees as evidence for the '*radical dimension*' of Adorno's work that he maintained the continued existence of classes in contemporary society. (Jay, *ibid.*, p. 50.) To read such a judgement in this perceptive study is all the more surprising since Jay himself acknowledges that 'Fredric Jameson mistranslated *Klassengesellschaft* as "class struggle", when Adorno's point was that *struggle had ended*, but classes remained.' (*Ibid.*, pp. 171–2.)
274. Adorno, Introduction to *The Positivist Dispute in German Sociology*, p. 7.
275. Hans-Jürgen Krahl, 'The political contradictions in Adorno's critical theory' *Telos*, No. 21, Fall 1974, p. 165.
276. *Ibid.*
277. Adorno, *Minima Moralia: Reflections from Damaged Life*, London, 1974, p. 50.
278. Krahl, *op. cit.*, p. 166. See Note 275 and also Krahl's remarkable collection of essays and articles, referred to in Note 53.

279. Adorno, *Prisms* pp. 20–1.
280. *Ibid.*, p. 34.
281. '*Generaltunken*' is a 'universal sauce' which bad German cooks pour on top of almost everything.
282. Martin Jay, 'The Frankfurt School's critique of Karl Mannheim and the sociology of knowledge', *Telos*, No. 20, Summer 1974, p. 82. Adorno is quoted from p. 41 of his *Negative Dialectics*.
283. Adorno, Introduction to *The Positivism Dispute in German Sociology*, p. 3.
284. Adorno, *Prisms*, p. 31.
285. *Ibid.*, p. 28.
286. Adorno, *Aesthetic Theory*, p. 171.
287. Marx, 'Contribution to critique of Hegel's *Philosophy of Law*. Introduction', MECW, Vol. 3, pp. 182–7.
288. Adorno, *Prisms*, pp. 28–30.
289. As Adorno put it: 'To advocate art is to advocate ideology, if not to reduce art to an ideology.' (Adorno, *Aesthetic Theory*, p. 27).
290. In Adorno's words:

> *The material process of production* finally unveils itself as that which it *always was*, from its origin in the exchange relationship as the false consciousness which the two contracting parties have of each other: *ideology*. (Adorno, *Prisms*, pp. 30–1)

291. Adorno, *Negative Dialectics*, p. 203.
292. Adorno, 'Lyric poetry and society', *Telos*, No. 20, summer 1974, p. 63.
293. *Ibid.*, p. 58.
294. *Ibid.*
295. 'Duped by the culture industry and hungry for its commodities, the masses find themselves in a condition this side of art.' Adorno, *Aesthetic Theory*, p. 24.
296. *Ibid.*, p. 343.
297. *Ibid.*, p. 469.
298. See Adorno, *Prisms*, p. 135.
299. Adorno, *Aesthetic Theory*, p. 31.
300. *Ibid.*, p. 323.
301. Marx, *The Poverty of Philosophy*, MECW, Vol. 6, p. 134.
302. Adorno, *Aesthetic Theory*, p. 493.
303. *Ibid.*, p. 494.
304. *Ibid.*, p. 493.
305. We learn from the 'epilogue' of the editors that 'a quotation from Friedrich Schlegel was to have served as a motto for *Aesthetic Theory*. It reads: "What is called philosophy of art usually lacks one of two things: either the philosophy or the art".' (*Ibid.*, p. 498.)

    Curiously, Adorno seemed to be convinced, not only in his letters but also in various passages of his work, that his own work provided, the first time in history, an adequate synthesis of both philosophy and art, inasmuch as it was achievable at all.
306. *Ibid.*, p. 496.
307. Adorno's biassed definition of the task, and his characterization of his own achievement as the only viable procedure as well as obtainable result, were accepted by his surroundings as the self-evident truth. Thus, the editors of *Aesthetic Theory* commended the 'torso' of this work to the reader in the following terms:

> A theory that takes off from the *individuum ineffabile*, wanting to make restitution to the unique, the non-identical, for the mutilations wrought by identifying thought – such a theory is *necessarily in conflict with its aim*, for *qua* theory it cannot help but be *abstract*. Adorno's aesthetics is driven, by its philosophical content, to embrace a *paratactical form* of presentation. This form is an aporia. Adorno had no doubts about that at all. He knew that aesthetic demands a solution to a problem which *cannot be delivered in the medium of a theory*. What validity aesthetic theory has is predicated on the philosopher's dogged determination *not to give up* in the face of an *insoluble dilemma*. This *paradox* might be a *good model* for the appropriation of this work, too.
> (*Ibid.*, p. 497)

That something might be inherently problematical about the theoretical enterprise itself which consisted in pursuing 'an insoluble dilemma' that, in principle, 'could not be delivered in the medium of a theory', did not seem to occur to them.

308. Adorno, *Aesthetic Theory*, p. 48.
309. Adorno, 'Commitment', in Adorno, Benjamin, Bloch, Brecht, Lukács, with an afterword by Fredric Jameson and presentations by Perry Anderson, Rodney Livingstone and Francis Mulhern (subsequently Adorno *et al.*) *Aesthetics and Politics*, NLB, London, 1977, p. 191.
310. *Ibid.*, p. 193.
311. *Ibid.*, p. 194.
312. *Ibid.*, p. 147.
313. Adorno, *Aesthetic Theory*, p. 36.
314. Adorno frequently returned to Hitler's Germany – after leaving it in 1934 – almost until the war broke out. His essay 'On jazz':

> Was written under the pseudonym Hektor Rottweiler, which perhaps expressed Adorno's still flickering hope to find a position back in Germany. In fact, his decision during those years to drop his patronymic Wiesengrund in favour of his mother's name was interpreted by another refugee, Hannah Arendt, as evidence of an almost collaborationist mentality.
> (Martin Jay, *Adorno*, p. 34)

   Arendt's judgement is reported in Elizabeth Young-Bruehl, *Hannah Arendt: the Love of the World*, New Haven, 1982, p. 109.
315. Adorno, 'Commitment', in Adorno *et al.*, *Aesthetics and Politics*, p. 192.
316. Adorno, *Aesthetic Theory*, p. 40.
317. Adorno *et al.*, *Aesthetics and Politics*, p. 143.
318. Fredric Jameson, 'Reflections in conclusion', in Adorno *et al.*, *Aesthetics and Politics*, p. 208.
319. 'Presentation iv', in Adorno *et al.*, *Aesthetics and Politics*, p. 142.
320. All these quotations are from a relatively short article by Adorno, 'Reconciliation under duress'. See Adorno *et al.*, *Aesthetics and Politics*, pp. 151–76. The German original, under the title 'Erpresste Versoehnung', appeared in *Der Monat*, in November 1958.
321. See for instance Adorno, *Aesthetic Theory*, pp. 24–5.
322. Adorno *et al.*, *Aesthetics and Politics*, p. 171.
323. Adorno, *Aesthetic Theory*, p. 27.
324. *Ibid.*, p. 48.
325. Adorno *et al.*, *Aesthetics and Politics*, p. 188.

326. Adorno, *Aesthetic Theory*, p. 65.
327. *Ibid.*, p. 64.
328. *Ibid.*
329. *Ibid.*, p. 49.
330. *Ibid.*, p. 28.
331. *Ibid.*, p. 29.
332. *Ibid.*, p. 274.
333. *Ibid.*, p. 58.
334. *Ibid.*, p. 59.
335. *Ibid.*, p. 33.
336. Hegel, *Logic: Part One of the Encyclopaedia of the Philosophical Sciences*, Clarendon Press, Oxford, 1975, p. 291.
337. Adorno, *Aesthetic Theory*, p. 50.
338. 'By relating consciousness to the whole of society it becomes possible to infer the thoughts and feelings which men would have in a particular situation if they were able to assess both it and the interests arising from it in their impact on immediate action and on the whole structure of society. That is to say, it would be possible to infer the thoughts and feelings appropriate to their objective situation.... Now class consciousness consists in fact of the appropriate and rational reactions "imputed" [*zugerechnet*] to a *particular typical position in the process of production*.' (Lukács, *History and Class Consciousness*, Merlin Press, London, 1971, p. 51.)
339. According to Habermas, the relevant question for critical social theory was:

 > How would the *members of a social system*, at a given state in the development of productive forces, have *collectively and bindingly* interpreted their needs ... if they could and would have decided on organization of social intercourse through discursive will-formation, with adequate knowledge of the *limiting conditions and functional imperatives of their society*?
 > (Habermas, *Legitimation Crisis*, Beacon Press, Boston, 1975, p. 113)

340. For a sympathetic critique of Luhmann's systems theory, see Cesare Luporini, 'Marx/Luhmann: trasformare il mondo o governarlo?', *Problemi del Socialismo*, Anno XXII, May–August 1981, pp. 57–70. The most representative volume by Niklas Luhmann available in English is *A Sociological Theory of Law*, Routledge, London, 1985.
341. Habermas, *Legitimation Crisis*, p. 15.
342. 'The formal anticipation of idealized discussion guarantees the final supporting *contra-factual consensus* which must previously connect the potential speakers-hearers.' Habermas, 'Summation and response', *Continuum*, Vol. 8, No. 1–2, Spring – Summer 1970, p. 132.
343. 'If, first of all, each conversation has as its meaning that at least two subjects come to an *agreement* about something; if secondly, agreement means the inducement of a *true consensus*; if, thirdly, the *true consensus* can be distinguished from a *false* one only through a reference to an *ideal speaking situation*, i.e. through recourse to an *agreement* which is *contra-factually* thought of as if it had come to pass under ideal *conditions* – then, in this idealization of the speaking situation, an anticipation is being considered which we (a) must undertake in every empirical speaking situation if we want to communicate at all, and (b) which we can undertake with the help of the means of construction which every speaker has at his disposal by virtue of his *communicative competency*.' (*Ibid.*, p. 131.)

In other words, if we assume agreement, 'true consensus', the 'ideal speaking situation', and 'communicative competency', we can deduce from them the true-consensus-generating communicative-competency of Habermas' ideal-speaking-situation in the strictly contra-factual world of the ideal-communications-community.

344. *Ibid.*, p. 132.
345. Habermas, *Toward a Rational Society*, Heinemann, London, 1971, p. 105.
346. *Ibid.*, p. 110.
347. *Ibid.*, p. 100.
348. *Ibid.*, p. 104.
349. The next few quotations, until otherwise stated, are all from p. 104 of the same work.
350. W. Müller and C. Neusüss, 'The illusion of state socialism', *Telos*, No. 25, pp. 23–4. Rosa Luxemburg's words quoted in the last few lines are from 'Reform or revolution?', *Selected Political Essays*, ed. Dick Howard, New York, 1971, pp. 115–16.
351. Marx, *Grundrisse*, Penguin ed., Harmondsworth, 1973, p. 831.
352. *Ibid.*, p. 705.
353. *Ibid.*, p. 709.
354. *Ibid.*, p. 694–5.
355. *Ibid.*, p. 699.
356. *Ibid.*, p. 700.
357. *Ibid.*, p. 706.
358. *Ibid.*, p. 708.
359. *Ibid.*, p. 706.
   There has been so much talk in the recent past about the 'obsolescence' – thanks to the development of science and technology – of *absolute surplus value* and, with it, of the exploitation of the 'immediate producers'. Such talk, however, is extremely premature not only in relation to the 'Third World' but even with regard to the most advanced capitalist countries. The point is that the development of science and technology as interlocked with the structural relationship between capital and labour can only be realistically assessed in its *global* setting, in the context of the contradictorily unfolding tension between *total* social capital (which includes both 'advanced' and 'underdeveloped' constituents), and the *totality* of labour. An irreconcilable conflictual relationship involving both *absolute* and *relative* surplus value, as well as their corollaries of *exploitation* and *oppression*, instead of the wishfully predicated consensus.
   It is this kind of assessment of the potentialities and structural constraints of the development of science and technology which Habermas not only fails to achieve, but even to consider.
360. Daniel Bell, *The Coming of Post-Industrial Society: A Venture in Social Forecasting*, Basic Books, New York, 1976, (first ed. 1973), p. xiv.
   Habermas, of course, fully returned the compliment. He wrote in his essay on 'Neoconservative culture criticism': 'Bell has a complex mind and is a good social theorist'. *Habermas and Modernity*, p. 82.
361. Habermas, *Toward a Rational Society*, p. 107.
362. *Ibid.*, p. 112.
363. *Ibid.*, p. 113.
364. *Ibid.*, p. 101.
365. *Ibid.*, pp. 111–12.
366. *Ibid.*, p. 110.
367. At a demonstration during the long-drawn-out miners' strike the president of

the British miners' union (the NUM), Arthur Scargill, told the Labour leader, Neil Kinnock, in front of a mass audience, that 'when the miners have paved the way for the next election "you have only one lesson to learn from Mrs Thatcher – when you become the Government of the day, show us the same loyalty to *our class* that she has shown to *their class*".' (*The Observer*, 15 July 1984.) And the British Prime Minister put things in even stronger terms. For, talking about the strikers in her end-of-term address, 'Mrs Thatcher told Tory MPs that her government had fought the *enemy without* in the Falklands conflict and now had to face the *enemy within*.' (*The Guardian*, 20 July, 1984.)

368. Habermas, *Toward a Rational Society*, p. 110.
369. *Ibid.*, p. 112.
370. *Ibid.*, p. 108. It is worth noting that even this residual conflict – which is said to have 'the greatest probability of remaining latent' – is concerned only with the 'private mode of capital utilization' (elsewhere: 'private form of capital utilization', p. 105), i.e. not with the antagonisms of the social order itself. In other words, *capital* remains society's absolute frame of reference, be it utilized (not possessed and exploitatively imposed upon the totality of producers, etc.) 'privately' or 'non-privately'.
371. *Ibid.*, p. 111.
372. *Ibid.*, p. 105.
373. 'It is true that social [and not the primarily capitalist class] interests still determine the direction, functions, and pace of technical progress. But these interests define the *social system* so much as a *whole* that they coincide with the interest in maintaining the *system*.' *Ibid.*
374. *Ibid.*, p. 88.
375. *Ibid.*, p. 87. (The word 'our' italicized by Habermas.)
376. Marcuse, *The Permanence of Art*, published in English under the title: *The Aesthetic Dimension* by Macmillan, London, 1979; see also Note 398.
377. Marcuse, *An Essay on Liberation*, Alen Lane/The Penguin Press, London, 1969.
378. *Ibid.*, p. 48.
379. *Ibid.*, p. 52.
380. *Ibid.*, p. 49.
381. *Ibid.*, p. 52.
382. *Ibid.*, p. 91.
383. *Ibid.*, p. 13.
384. *Ibid.*, p. 16.
385. *Ibid.*, p. 18. Marcuse's italics.
386. *Ibid.*, p. 10.
387. *Ibid.*, p. 22.
388. *Ibid.*, p. 32.
389. *Ibid.*, p. 14.
390. *Ibid.*, p. 17.
391. *Ibid.*, p. 4.
392. *Ibid.*
393. *Ibid.*, p. 5.
394. *Ibid.*, p. 4.
395. *Ibid.*, p. 5.
396. *Ibid.*, p. 4.
397. *Ibid.*, p. 10.
398. Marcuse, *Die Permanenz der Kunst*, Carl Hanser Verlag, München 1977. See also Note 376.

399. *Ibid.*, p. 23.
400. Even in Marcuse's generous description 'the movement of the sixties' only 'tended toward the transformation of subjectivity in its sensitivity, imagination and reason, and to a new vision of things: the irruption of the superstructure into the basis', without actually producing a lasting impact and on the necessary scale. (*Ibid.*, p. 41.)
401. *Ibid.*, p. 73.
402. *Ibid.*, p. 74.
403. *Ibid.*
404. *Ibid.*, p. 46.
405. *Ibid.*, p. 77.
406. *Ibid.*, p. 76.
407. *Ibid.*, p. 53.
408. Marcuse, *One-Dimensional Man*, p. 257.
409. Aron, *The Industrial Society*, pp. 174–5.
410. Aron, *History and the Dialectic of Violence*, Basil Blackwell, Oxford, 1975, p. 191. (Originally published in Paris in 1973.)
411. Aron, *The Industrial Society*, p. 179.
412. Lukács, *The Destruction of Reason*, p. 618.
413. Weber, *Gesammelte Aufsätze zur Wissenschaftslehre*, Tübingen, 1922, p. 555. Quoted by Lukács, *The Destruction of Reason*, p. 618.
414. Weber, *Gesammelte Aufsätze zur Wissenschaftslehre*, p. 545. Lukács, *Ibid.*, p. 616. For an English translation of 'Science as a vocation' – to which the last two quotes belong – see H. H. Gerth and C. Wright Mills (eds), *From Max Weber: Essays in Sociology* Routledge & Kegan Paul, London, 1948, pp. 129–56.
415. Weber, 'Science as a vocation', *op. cit.*, p. 147.
416. Weber, *Gesammelte Aufsätze zur Wissenschaftslehre*, p. 154. Quoted in Maurice Merleau-Ponty, *Adventures of the Dialectic*, Heinemann, London, 1974, p. 26.
417. 'In terms of its meanings, such and such a practical stand can be derived ... from this or that ultimate *weltanschauliche* position. Perhaps it can only be derived from one such *fundamental position*, or maybe from several, but it cannot be derived from these or those other positions. Figuratively speaking, you serve this god and you offend the other god when you decide to adhere to this position. And if you remain faithful to yourself, you will necessarily come to certain final conclusions that *subjectively* make sense.' (Weber, 'Science as a vocation', p. 151.)
418. 'Today the routines of everyday life challenge religion. Many old gods ascend from their graves; they are *disenchanted* and hence take the form of *impersonal forces*. They strive to gain power over our lives and again they resume *their eternal struggle* with one another.... so long as life remains immanent and is interpreted in its own terms, it knows only of an unceasing struggle of these gods with one another. Or speaking directly, the ultimately possible attitudes toward life are *irreconcilable*.' (*Ibid.*, pp. 149–52.)
419. *Ibid.*, p. 152.
420. Or 'value freedom', '*Wertfreiheit*'. As to how Weber himself succeeded in living up to this ideal, see the discussion of his definitions of 'capitalism' and 'bureaucracy' in Sections 2 and 3 of the essay on 'Ideology and social science', in *Philosophy, Ideology and Social Science*. Part of Section 2 is quoted in Note 34.
421. Weber, 'Science as a vocation', p. 155.
422. *Ibid.*

423. See the passage quoted in Note 417 above.
424. Raymond Aron, for instance, who claimed that he had been 'excommunicated' by the Left because he had argued his case against 'Marxist-Leninists' and 'progressives' from an Atlanticist political perspective. See Aron, *The Industrial Society*, p. 145.
425. Indeed, Merleau-Ponty gave the title: 'The crisis of understanding' to the first chapter of his book, *Adventures of the Dialectic*; and he proposed the resolution of this crisis within the framework of the Weberian conception.
426. 'Raymond Aron writes that his politics is, like that of Alain, a "politics of the understanding". Only, from Alain to Weber, the understanding has learned to doubt itself.' (Merleau-Ponty, *op. cit.*, p. 25.)
427. Merleau-Ponty strongly stressed this aspect of Weber's reasonableness. He wrote: 'Though he rejects nationalism, communism, and pacifism, he does not want to *outlaw* them; he does not want to renounce the attempt to *understand* them.' *Ibid.*, p. 26.

   Thus, the criterion of *understanding* one's ideological/intellectual adversaries is reduced to a formal/legal sense, defined as supporting the state practices which abstain from *outlawing* them, in the interest of preserving the ideological rationalization of the 'democratic state'. There could be no question of entering into a *substantive dialogue* with the other side. The same attitude – formulated from the point of view of an abstract and formalistic 'universalism' that merely wants to *subsume* the interlocutor under its own, preconceptions – is reflected in Merleau-Ponty's clash with Sartre at the Conference referred to in Note 436 below.

428. The Italian historian, Franco Venturi, told me at the time of General De Gaulle's recall to power, in the midst of the Algerian war: 'One day we ought to erect a statue to Mussolini and engrave on its base: "This was a very stupid man, with one great achievement: he lost the Empire for us".'

   Admittedly, the Italian Empire was a very different proposition from the French one. Nevertheless, the astonishing stability of governmental rule in Italy – a country where the Marxist party was considerably stronger than even in France, and yet remained under the domination of Christian Democratic governments, notwithstanding some purely cosmetic changes, now for more than four decades without interruption – was to a more than negligible degree due to the absence of the bitterly divisive issues of 'disengagement from Empire'.

429. Merleau-Ponty, *Adventures of the Dialectic*, p. 25. The words 'meanings' and 'forces' italicized by Merleau-Ponty.
430. *Ibid.*, p. 27.
431. *Ibid.*, p. 29
432. Raymond Aron never tired of reiterating that 'all modern firms are organized on an authoritarian basis.... As regards the techno-bureaucratic direction of industries, it is at present authoritarian rather than democratic under all types of systems.' (*The Industrial Society*, pp. 117–18.) How such an inherently authoritarian socioeconomic structure could institutionally articulate itself in a truly democratic political system, remained a mystery.
433. See in particular Weber, *The Theory of Social and Economic Organization* (Part I of *Wirtschaft und Gesellschaft*), The Free Press, New York, 1947, and *The Protestant Ethic and the Spirit of Capitalism*, Unwin University Books, London, 1965.
434. His principal theoretical work, *The Social System* (Routledge & Kegan Paul, London, 1951) deals with the subject, more or less extensively, in virtually every chapter.

435. Aron, 'Development theory and evolutionism', *The Industrial Society*, p. 74.
436. See the exchange between Sartre and Merleau-Ponty at a conference organized by the 'Société Européenne de Culture' at Venice, between 25–31 March 1956, published in *Comprendre*, September 1956; partially reprinted in Michel Contat and Michel Rybalka, *Les Ecrits de Sartre: Chronologie, bibliographie commentée*, Gallimard, Paris, 1970, pp. 299–304. Quotations from pp. 301–2.
437. Aron, 'Development theory and ideology', *The Industrial Society*, p. 40.
438. '*Measurement* – of working hours or output – is basic to that form of procedure which *used to be termed capitalist* but is now recognized as being *characteristic of all modern societies*. Measurement leads to the endeavour to produce more in the same time, or to spend less time on producing the same amount, or to produce a more valuable output in less time. But to achieve this ambition quantitatively, it is also necessary to replace the usual *methods* of work and *organization* by *reflection or calculation*, that is, to adopt what Max Weber calls a *"rational attitude"* or what is also known as *rationalization*.' *Ibid.*, p. 14.
439. *Ibid.*, p. 24.
440. *Ibid.*, pp. 1–2.
441. *Ibid.*, p. 25.
442. *Ibid.*, p. 13.
443. *Ibid.*, p. 29.
    Thus, *social* problems are transmuted into *technical* ones. The highly contested issue of development is reduced to that of 'modernization' through the application of science and technology. This approach shows great affinity with Walt Rostow – one of the chief architects of the US policy of 'modernization' in Vietnam by way of saturation bombing – who is often quoted by Aron with approval.
444. *Ibid.*, pp. 24–5.
445. Literally from page 1, as we have seen in Note 440.
446. See Caio Prado Júnior's classic *História económica do Brasil*, Editora Brasiliense, Saó Paulo, 28th edition, 1983; first published in 1945.
447. *Ibid.*, p. 26.
448. *Ibid.*
449. *Ibid.*, p. 181.
450. *Ibid.*, p. 182.
451. Addressing himself to the question, 'Is North America to blame for the fact that Latin America has lagged behind in the nineteenth and twentieth centuries? Can it be said that American corporations prevented industrialization in areas where they were established?', Aron produces another characteristic line of argument which runs like this:

> Nowadays, the advanced countries vie with each other in proclaiming their intention to come to the aid of the less favoured countries – to which the representatives of the latter reply, *sometimes* with justification, that deeds do *not always* accord with words and that the terms of trade often result in the exploitation of the producers of raw materials to the advantage of the industrialized economies; that is, *in the last resort*, exploitation of the underdeveloped by the advanced. I do not underestimate the importance of the phenomenon, *but it is a mistake*, I think, to believe it to be a *deliberate policy* on the part of *governments* or *corporations*.
> (*Ibid.*, p. 27)

The first impression of 'reasonableness' quickly disappears if we pay a closer attention to what is being said. For the acknowledgement of even the most obvious grievances is immediately watered down by Aron's carefully studied qualifications, like 'sometimes', 'not always', 'in the last resort', etc. And that is by no means the end of the matter. Far from it. For the last sentence sweepingly takes back *everything* that has been half-heartedly admitted before, by denying – on the irrefutable evidence of 'it would be a mistake to believe, *I think*' – that there was some 'deliberate policy' behind the actions of Western governments and corporations.

Let us suppose, for the sake of the argument – without granting in the slightest its dubious substance – that American and other Western governments and corporations pursued their vested interests, at the expense of the countries which they unquestionably dominated and exploited, 'in the last resort' or not, without 'deliberate policies' in mind (if that was conceivable). Would that *in any way* diminish the painful burden of twisted development and structural dependency? 'Obviously not', as Aron put it in an argument asserting the opposite, as we have seen above. Such diversionary 'red herrings', therefore, can only serve an apologetic ideological function, even if they are presented in the guise of the 'politics of the understanding'.

452. Aron, 'The end of the ideological age?', in Chaim I. Waxman (ed.), *The End of Ideology Debate*, Simon and Schuster, New York, 1968, p. 27.
453. *Ibid.*, p. 29
454. Merleau-Ponty, 'Paranoid politics', *Signs*, Northwestern University Press, 1964, p. 250.
455. *Ibid.*, p. 252.
456. In the Sulzberger interview quoted by Merleau-Ponty, Malraux claimed that 'had Leon Trotsky won his party battle with Joseph Stalin, he himself would today be a Trotskyist Communist' (p. 247). Merleau-Ponty's ironical references to the implications of such claims for General de Gaulle and his movement were meant to demystify the attempt to give the semblance of left-wing concern to a fundamentally conservative movement. The 'wave' mentioned by Merleau-Ponty refers to the 'development of anti-Communist fronts in Europe', using the Marshall plan and American advisers 'to bring workers into pale' while keeping socialism – 'even including western Socialism' – out of the new labour federations and alliances. (Quotations from Sulzberger's article.)
457. Merluea-Ponty, 'Paranoid politics', p. 252.
458. Merluea-Ponty, 'Tomorrow ...', an interview given in July, 1958, *Signs*, p. 349.
459. *Ibid.*, p. 348.
460. *Ibid.*, pp. 348–9.
461. Hegel, *The Philosophy of Right*, Clarendon Press, Oxford, 1942, p. 13.
462. Merleau-Ponty, 'Tomorrow ...', p. 350.
463. Merleau-Ponty, 'Paranoid politics', p. 260.
464. Merleau-Ponty, 'The USSR and the Camps', *Signs*, pp. 269–70.
465. *Ibid.*, p. 272.
466. 'Their rebellion against us is not *intellectual*, they *love conversation in the French manner* and practice it admirably; it is wholly *emotional* and *moral*.' Reading sentences like this from the pen of an intellectual of Merleau-Ponty's stature, it is hard to decide whether to laugh or despair. Merleau-Ponty, 'On Madagascar', an interview based on Merleau-Ponty's stay in Madagascar in October-November 1957, published in *l'Express* not on 3 July, as originally intended, but on 21 August 1958; *Signs*, p. 331.

467. *Ibid.*, p. 329.
468. *Ibid.*, p. 331.
469. *Ibid.*, p. 329.
470. Merleau-Ponty, 'On Indo-China', *Signs*, p. 324.
471. *Ibid.*, p. 325.
472. *Ibid.*
473. Merleau-Ponty, 'On Madagascar', *Signs*, p. 332.
474. *Ibid.*, p. 333.
475. *Ibid.*, pp. 334–5.
476. *Ibid.*, p. 335.
477. *Ibid.*
478. *Ibid.*
479. *Ibid.*, p. 332
480. *Ibid.*, p. 336
481. Hegel, *Philosophy of Right*, p. 10.
482. Merleau-Ponty, 'On Madagascar', *Signs*, p. 336.
483. Hegel, *Philosophy of Right*, p. 11.
484. This 'science' was meant to provide the philosophical proof for the identity of 'actuality' and 'rationality' in the state which itself was supposed to constitute 'the ethical universe'. In Hegel's words, '*the science of the state* is to be nothing other than the endeavour to apprehend and portray the state as something *inherently rational*' (*ibid.*). The resignatory apologetics of this '*philosophical science of the state*' became clear a few lines later when Hegel described its purpose in the following terms: 'To recognize reason as the rose in the cross of the present and thereby *to enjoy the present*, this is the *rational insight* which *reconciles us to the actual*, the reconciliation which philosophy affords to those in whom there has once arisen an inner voice bidding them to comprehend, not only to dwell in what is *substantive* while still retaining subjective freedom, but also to possess subjective freedom while standing not in anything *particular* and *accidental* but in what exists *absolutely*' (*ibid.*, p. 12). Merleau-Ponty's appeal to 'something substantial, requiring the State' with its 'strength and personality' – as against 'particularity and accidentality' attached to the contemptuously dismissed 'submission to each shiver of opinion' (i.e. to '*criticism*' to which Merleau-Ponty opposed, despite the lip-service which he paid to it, the overriding need to 'reorganize the power' of the state) – revealed his ultimate submission to a conservative and thoroughly ahistorical conception of the state as both the *absolute* precondition and the final arbiter of freedom.
485. 'In Western societies, to reject a *total synthesis* . . . is simply to state that no one (apart from the Marxist-Leninists) conceives of a social order *radically different from the established one*.' (Aron, *The Industrial Society*, p. 163.)
486. *Ibid.*, p. 176. Naturally, the defenders of the established order always want to have it both ways. Thus, Aron first castigates the 'utopianism' of individualistic solutions by adding to his condemnation of 'the impulses of anarchistic individualism' the following declaration of establishment faith: 'For the administration of material things to cease to be the government of people – and this seems to be one of the utopian ideals Marcuse advances – people would have to lead leisurely and solitary existences.' At this point, however, he realizes that the mainstream of socialist critical tradition – in its *collectivist* inspiration and aspirations – is very far from being oriented towards 'solitary' practices. He therefore inserts a footnote, dismissing the collectivist approach too by peremptorily enunciating yet another article of establishment faith, without the slightest attempt at offering proofs in its support: 'Another

utopian idea is to make the workers themselves responsible for the administration of industry.' (*Ibid.*, pp. 176–7.)

487. On some related issues, see 'Contingent and necessary class consciousness' in
Philosophy, Ideology and Social Science.

488. A few years ago *Time* magazine had on its front cover Marx's bust with the
caption: 'Marx is dead', signed 'The New French Philosophers'. It reminded
me of what happened many years earlier in Vienna University's Hall of Fame
where Nietzsche's bust carried the caption: 'God is dead', signed 'Nietzsche'.
For one day another caption appeared beneath the original one. It read:
'Nietzsche is dead. God.' As they say in Italian: 'Se non è vero, è ben trovato.'

489. As Sánchez Vázquez rightly stressed: 'Through technics, science – once
constituted – penetrates in modern times into production. However, only in
our times – with technology – does the real, transforming, productive action
acquire a fully rational dimension which it receives precisely through the
unification of science and technology.' (Adolfo Sánchez Vázquez, 'Racionalismo tecnologico, ideologia y politica', *Dialéctica*, June 1983, p. 13.) See
also pp. 185–205 of Adolfo Sánchez Vázquez, *Ensayos marxistas sobre
filosofia e ideologia*, Océano, Barcelona, 1983.

490. 'It is, in a word, the development of the social individual which appears as
the great foundation-stone of production and of wealth.... The free development of individualities, and hence not the reduction of the necessary
labour time so as to posit surplus labour, but rather the general reduction of
the necessary labour of society to a minimum, which then corresponds to the
artistic, scientific, etc. development of the individuals in the time set free, and
with the means created, for all of them.' (Marx, *Grundrisse*, pp. 705–6.)

491. *Ibid.*, pp. 540–2.

492. The interested reader can find a voluminous documentation in this respect in
my book on *Marx's Theory of Alienation*, Merlin Press, London, 1970, 4th ed.
1975, pp. 217–53 and 328–36.

493. Significantly, in his radical diagnosis of the ongoing developments Rousseau
even hinted at 'a revolution which I regard as inevitable. Indeed, all the kings
of Europe are working in concert to hasten its coming.' (Rousseau, *The Social
Contract*, Everyman Edition, p. 37.) Yet, in his own defence later on he also
asserted that he 'always insisted on the preservation of the existing institutions.' (Rousseau, *Troisième Dialogue, Oeuvres Complètes*, Ed. du Seuil,
Paris, 1967, Vol. 1, p. 474.)

The fundamental contradiction in Rousseau's thought lies in his incomparably sharp perception of the *manifestations* of alienation and the glorification of their *ultimate cause*. The fundamental premisses of his system are:
the assumption of *private property* as the sacred foundation of civil society
on the one hand, and the '*middle condition*' as the only adequate *form of
distribution* of property on the other. He writes:

> It is certain that *the right of property is the most sacred of all the rights* of
> citizenship, and even *more important* in some respects than *liberty itself*;
> ... property is the true foundation of civil society, and the real guarantee
> of the undertakings of citizens: for if property were not answerable for
> personal actions, nothing would be easier than to evade duties and laugh
> at the laws.
> (Rousseau, *A Discourse on Political Economy*, Everyman Edition,
> p. 254)

As to the 'middle condition', according to Rousseau, its necessity arises out of
the inherent requirements of social life itself. As he puts it:

Under bad governments equality is only apparent and illusory; it serves only to keep the pauper in his poverty and the rich man in the position he has usurped. In fact, laws are always of use to those who possess and harmful to those who have nothing: from which it follows that the social state is advantageous to men *only when all have something and none too much*.

(Rousseau, *The Social Contract*, p. 19)

Accordingly, to remedy the situation, one must positively encourage the general diffusion of this 'middle condition' which 'constitutes the genuine strength of the State' (Rousseau, *A Discourse on Political Economy*, p. 268). For 'nothing is more fatal to morality and to the Republic than the continual shifting of rank and fortune among the citizens'. (*Ibid.*, p. 255.)

Rousseau recognizes that the law is made for the protection of private property and that everything else in the order of 'civil society' – including 'civil liberty' – rests on such foundation. Since, however, he cannot go beyond the horizon of this idealized civil society, he must maintain not only that the law is made for the benefit of private property but also that private property is made for the benefit of the law as its sole guarantor. Thus the circle is irrevocably closed: there can be no escape from it. And precisely because Rousseau operates from the standpoint of the same material base of society whose manifestations he denounces – the social order of private property and 'fair and advantageous exchange' – the terms of his social criticism must be intensely and abstractly moralizing. Capitalistic alienation as perceived by Rousseau in its particular manifestations – those, that is, which are harmful to the 'middle condition' – is considered by him contingent, not necessary; and his radical moral discourse is supposed to provide the non-contingent alternative so that the people, enlightened by his unmasking of all that is merely 'apparent and illusory', should turn their back on the artificial and alienated practices of social life.

These moralizing illusions of Rousseau's system, rooted in the idealization of a way of life allegedly appropriate to the 'middle condition', in opposition to the actuality of dynamically advancing and universally alienating large-scale capitalist production, are necessary illusions. For if the critical enquiry is confined to devising alternatives merely to the dehumanizing effects of a given system of production while leaving its basic premises unchallenged, there remains nothing but the weapon of moralizing – 'educational' – appeal to individuals. Such an appeal directly invites them to oppose the trends denounced, to 'resist corruption', to give up 'calculating', to show 'moderation', to resist the temptations of 'illusory wealth', to follow the 'natural course', to restrict their 'useless desires', to stop 'chasing profit', to refuse 'selling themselves', etc., etc. Whether or not they *can* do all this, is a different matter; in any case they *ought* to do it. (I have discussed these problems in much greater detail in *Marx's Theory of Alienation*, pp. 48–61, 80–4, 105–7, and 317–19.)

494. Marx's expression.
495. To quote Lukács:

It would be to simplify and falsify history to assume that a certain changing of the terms would suffice to get from Hegel's idealist to Marx's materialist dialectics.... [For] even those progressive elements in Hegel's dialectic with which Marx could associate himself had to be thoroughly transformed, as regards both form and content, and critically re-worked

THE POWER OF IDEOLOGY

in the materialistic dialectic. Little though this procedure was understood by bourgeois philosophy, its presence must have likewise become a co-determining reason for bourgeois thought's turning away from Hegel. Bernstein, a blind adherent of bourgeois philosophical tendencies and the founder of revisionism, expressed this state of things the most clearly when he simultaneously sought to make Kant the philosopher of 'seasonable' Marxism and attacked Marx on account of his 'Hegelianism', because of the dialectical (revolutionary, not evolutionary) character of his doctrine.

(Lukács, *The Destruction of Reason*, pp. 547–8)

In broad terms the same approach is recognizable in the writings of Galvano della Volpe and his school, including Colletti.

496. See, for instance, Otto Liebmann's book, *Kant und die Epigonen* (Leipzig, 1865) which glorified Kantian agnosticism as the only scientific way to proceed while curtly dismissing Hegel as an insignificant epigone and the trendsetter of 'unscientific metaphysics'.

497. This Kantian way of doing away with the thorniest philosophical problems by 'dissolving' them became the model for the neo-positivist method of agnostically 'explaining away' major theoretical and practical issues and persistent ideological conflicts as really non-existent – as having merely the existential status of 'conceptual confusions' – from the early Wittgenstein to the Viennese school of logical positivists and to the followers of the later Wittgenstein among the 'analytical' school of linguistic philosophy.

498. Raymond Aron, *The Industrial Society*, pp. 56–7.

499. As Marx puts it in *The German Ideology*: 'The satisfaction of the first need, the action of satisfying and the instrument of satisfaction which has been acquired, leads to *new needs*; and this *creation of new needs is the first historical act*' (MECW, Vol. 5, p. 42). And he develops the complex dialectical interrelationship between production, consumption and needs in a seminally important passage of the *Grundrisse*:

Hunger is hunger, but the hunger gratified by cooked meat eaten with a knife and fork is a different hunger from that which bolts down raw meat with the aid of hand, nail and tooth. Production thus produces not only the object but also the manner of consumption, not only objectively but also subjectively. Production not only supplies a material for the need, but it also supplies a need for the material. As soon as consumption emerges from its initial state of natural crudity and immediacy – and, if it remained at that stage, this would be because production itself had been arrested there – it becomes itself mediated as a drive by the object. The need which consumption feels for the object is created by the perception of it. The object of art – like every other product – creates a public which is sensitive to art and enjoys beauty. Production thus not only creates an object for the subject, but also a subject for the object. Thus production produces consumption (1) by creating the material for it; (2) by determining the manner of consumption; and (3) by creating the products, initially posited by it as objects, in the form of a need felt by the consumer. It thus produces the object of consumption, the manner of consumption and the motive of consumption. Consumption likewise produces the producer's inclination by beckoning to him as an aim-determining need.

(Marx, *Grundrisse*, p. 92)

500. Aron, *The Industrial Society*, p. 57.
501. All this is, of course, conveniently circular. As usual with such theories, the ideologically motivated circularity operates with unsustained assumptions from which it can easily deduce the desired conclusions of rationalization and legitimation.
502. Marx, *Capital*, Foreign Languages Publishing House, Moscow, 1958, Vol. I, pp. 72–6. Some of the key ideas of this section on *The Fetishism of Commodity* are anticipated in the following passage from *The German Ideology:* 'The transformation, through the division of labour, of *personal* powers (relations) into *material* powers, cannot be dispelled by dismissing the general idea of it from one's mind, but can only be abolished by the individuals again *subjecting these material powers to themselves* and *abolishing the division of labour*.' (MECW, Vol. 5, pp. 77–8.)
503. The apologetic substance of this conflation becomes clear if we remind ourselves of the potentially explosive fact that '*Division of labour and private property are, after all, identical expressions:* in the one the same thing is affirmed with reference to *activity* as is affirmed in the other with reference to the *product* of the activity.' (MECW, Vol. 5, p. 46.)
504. 'New culture or new politics', *Comunità*, August–September 1958, pp. 71–4.
505. See Althusser's 'Ideology and the state', written in 1969 and reprinted in the volume: *Lenin and Philosophy and Other Essays*, NLB, London, 1971, pp. 123–73, as well as his discussion of 'the category of a process without a subject' in his paper on 'Marx's Relation to Hegel', written in 1968, pp. 163–86 of the English volume: *Montesquieu, Rousseau, Marx*, Verso Editions, London, 1982.
506. See Cesare Cases, *Marxismo e neopositivismo*, Einaudi, Turin, 1958, pp. 95–6.
507. Della Volpe remained a Stalinist and a follower of Zhdanov to the end, unlike some of his pupils whose intellectual and political trajectory, from the sectarian left to the 'radical Right', tells a very sad story indeed.
508. For a forceful critique of Althusser from a socialist perspective, see E. P. Thompson, *The Poverty of Theory*, Merlin Press, London, 1978, and Adolfo Sánchez Vázquez, *Ciencia y revolución: El marxismo de Althusser*, Alianza Editorial, Madrid, 1978.
   Another writer who formulates his criticism from the same perspective, Simon Clarke (see his 'Althusserian Marxism' in the volume: *One-Dimensional Marxism: Althusser and the Politics of Culture* by S. Clarke *et al.*, Allison & Busby, London, 1980) relates the Stalinist intolerance with which the Althusserian coterie advising publishers wanted to prevent the appearance of his study. To quote him:

> The response from Althusserians was one of outrage.... The paper was described in the following terms by anonymous readers: 'almost entirely inadequate ... incoherent ... a bald series of assertions ... crude distortions ... misrepresentations ... grotesque misreading ... a form of intellectual dishonesty ... pathetic'. A rather less sympathetic Althusserian reader considered it 'the worst article I have ever read on Althusser ... the very worst kind of dogmatic, ill-informed polemic ... absolutely appalling ... a series of totally unsubstantiated attacks ... the article is worthless ... nothing short of scandalous ... nonsense ... the most philistine and philosophically naive epistemology ... absolutely breathtaking'.
> (*Ibid.*, p. 8)

A recent study (John Hoffman, *The Gramscian Challenge: Coercion and Consent in Marxist Political Theory*, Basil Blackwell, Oxford, 1984) rightly stresses the similarities between some of Althusser's propositions and Bernstein's original revisionist arguments. On the face of it, this would seem difficult to reconcile with Althusser's Stalinism. In fact, however, the connection is very close. For one should not forget that by far the most extensive (and damaging) revision of the Marxian approach in the twentieth century – in the name of the one and only admissible interpretation of Marxism-Leninism – was theoretically accomplished and administratively imposed on the international Communist movement by none other than Stalin himself.

509. Sadly, Colletti – once upon a time one of della Volpe's closest associates and followers – is in the forefront of those who intellectually turned against Marx and politically moved a long way to the right. See, for instance, his collection of essays: *Tra marxismo e no* (Laterza, Bari, 1979), not to mention some of his more recent articles.

Typically, Colletti's anti-Marxist recantations – 'The breach is irreparable; it came about as a consequence of the *historical exhaustion of Marxism*.... One cannot make *science* with the *dialectic*. If this is positivism, I am a positivist.... My difficulties started when I realized – and, to tell the truth, it shouldn't take long; but the fact is that it took a long time for me – that the dialectic is there also in *Capital*.... The model of *self-government* is impracticable.' etc. (Lucio Colletti, 'La crisi del marxismo', *Mondoperaio*, November 1977) – exhibit the same logical circularity which characterizes the 'scientific' ideological constructs of capital's apologists which we have seen above in various contexts. 'Complexity', likewise, in the hallowed tradition of bourgeois social science from Max Weber onwards, becomes the magic centre of reference and self-justificatory assumption in terms of which all radical criticism can be curtly dismissed, without any further discussion, as self-evidently 'impracticable', or whatever else. Thus we are told that 'The Commune *does not exist* because it *cannot* exist; because there is *no society* – no matter how *little developed and complex* – which could be ruled by such *simplistic* and vague principles as that of *self-government*.' (*Ibid.*) What is the 'proof' that the Marxian principles are 'simplistic'? Nothing more than the – theoretically empty but ideologically dense – *assumption* that *all* societies are *complex* to the point of a priori invalidating the Marxian concept of *self-government*, even the most *underdeveloped* ones.

This is, then, the claimed 'science' which Colletti produces through his liquidation of the dialectic in favour of Galvano della Volpe's 'Aristotelian' principle of 'non-contradiction'. It has been argued that:

> These undialectical conceptions of dialectic within Western Marxism, and the general survival of Enlightenment materialism, reflect the twin pressures of working-class defeat and the success of bourgeois technology and natural science, and more specifically at the theoretical level the academic rebirth of formal logic through Frege and Russell, with its self-reflective philosophy of logic echoing unmistakably in the work of Althusser and the school of della Volpe.'

(Roy Edgley, 'Marx's revolutionary science', in *Issues in Marxist Philosophy*, edited by John Mepham and David-Hillel Ruben, Harvester Press, Brighton, 1979, Vol. III, p. 22. See also Roy Edgley's fine essay, 'Dialectic: the contradiction of Colletti', *Critique*, No. VII, Winter 1976–7)

There is a great deal of truth in this analysis. However, one must also remember that a long time before the lines just quoted were published, Colletti had already abandoned all pretences to belong to Marxism, 'Western' or otherwise, and wholeheartedly joined the other side. Besides, 'Western Marxism' is itself an extremely problematical concept. It has been invented by Merleau-Ponty, in his *Adventures of the Dialectic*, with an openly *anti-Marxist* intent and corresponding ideological/intellectual plausibility (opposing so-called 'Western Marxism' to 'the Marxism of *Pravda*' which was supposed to have swallowed up the post-*History and Class Consciousness* Lukács as well), and later uncritically adopted by some theoreticians of the New Left, from Perry Anderson's *Considerations on Western Marxism* (NLB, London, 1976) to several contributors to the three volumes of *Issues in Marxist Philosophy*.

In truth, though, the social and political substance of Colletti's circular logic and anti-Marxist 'science' has been visible for a very long time. Moreover, far from being 'otherwise exemplary' (Ted Benton, 'Natural science and cultural struggle: Engels on philosophy and the natural sciences', *Issues in Marxist Philosophy*, Vol. II, p. 138.), the relationship of his inherently positivistic neo-Kantianism to Marx has been a most uneasy one right from the beginning, as the Italian edition of the first part of *Il marxismo e Hegel* – originally published in 1958 as the Introduction to Lenin's *Philosophical Notebooks* – already testified. Once the political ties with the Italian socialist movement were loosened, and eventually broken, there remained no reason whatsoever why Colletti should not take his neo-positivistic scientism to its uninhibited conclusion and throw out Marx altogether, even if only by instalments.

In this sense Colletti is philosophically more consistent today than when he at first embarked, with complicated political ambitions and inhibitions, on his journey of 'critical revision'. As a result of Colletti's rejection of Marx, many of the earlier ambiguities have been removed. Accordingly, the now for a good many years more or less openly confessed ideological function of his philosophy has become (and remains) to discredit and dismiss as born enemies of the – by Colletti idealized – 'liberal-democratic institutions' (*op. cit.*) all those socialists who argued or still maintain that 'Asiatic backwardness' (Lenin) and desperately distorted 'underdevelopment' had something to do with the kind of socioeconomic and political developments which we have witnessed in the post-revolutionary societies. For, according to Colletti, we have to give up all hope that it could be otherwise in the future, because the failures are the necessary consequence of the 'simplistic principles' themselves which cannot possibly fit the 'complex' realities of *any* society. Thus, the sociohistorically conditioned (and by all socialists firmly condemned) *violations* of the vital principle of '*self-government by the associated producers*' become the convenient (as well as transparent) excuse for the categorical rejection of even the possibility of socialism. At the same time, the established order receives an *a priori* justification and permanent legitimation in Colletti's theoretically vacuous and logically fallacious defence of 'insurmountable complexity'.

510. Cases, *Su Lukács: Vicende di un'interpretazione*, pp. 76–7.
511. Althusser, *Montesquieu, Rousseau, Marx*, p. 165.
512. *Ibid.*, p. 181.
513. Galvano della Volpe joined the Italian Communist Party after the liberation of Sicily, at the age of 50, after 15 years of undisturbed university career under Mussolini, seven years of which he spent as Head of Department in Messina. Indeed, he contributed a curious piece of 'aesthetic' writing to the periodical *Primato*, founded by the fascist Minister of Culture Bottai in 1940. As reported in a letter of Cases to Lukács (dated 9 January 1959): 'our friend

Della Volpe published in *Primato* an article with the strange title of *The Aesthetics of the Tank* (*L'estetica del carro armato*).' (See Cesare Cases, *Su Lukács: Vicende di un'interpretazione*, Einaudi, Turin, 1985, p. 172.)

Naturally, the philosophical transformation of a thinker in his 50s is a much more complicated business than his joining the Communist Party. In fact, even the last versions of Galvano della Volpe's *Logic as a Positive Science* (NLB, London, 1980; Italian edition of 1960) remained heavily dominated by his original neo-Kantian formation.

514. See, for instance, Bertrand Russell's book, *The Impact of Science on Society*, Allen & Unwin, London, 1968. For two classic works, written from a perspective radically different from Russell's approach, see J.D. Bernal, *The Social Function of Science*, Routledge & Kegan Paul, London, 1939, and Joseph Needham, *Science and Civilization in Ancient China*, Cambridge University Press, 1954–65.

515. From the Introduction to a collection of essays – by Daniel Bell, Irene Taviss, Robert Nisbet, Karl Mannheim, David Riesman, Norbert Wiener, Carl R. Rogers, B. F. Skinner, C. Wright Mills, Lawrence K. Frank and Edward T. Chase – characteristically entitled: *The Technological Threat*, edited by Jack D. Douglas, Prentice Hall, Englewood Cliffs, New Jersey, 1971, p. 2.

516. *Ibid.*

517. Edward T. Chase, 'Politics and technology', in Jack D. Douglas, ed., *op. cit.*, p. 170.

518. *Ibid.*

519. *Ibid.*, p. 171. The '*exponential* rate of change' is the favourite myth of all those gloom-mongers who metamorphose their conservative social preferences into purely technological formulas, attempting the 'scientific' authentication of their curious notions – in the absence of any supporting evidence, other than fictitious 'computer-projections' – with reference to what is supposed to be by definition scientifically persuasive 'non-ideological' phraseology.

520. *Ibid.*

521. An editorial in *The Sunday Times* (21 October 1984), carrying the sonorous title: 'It's time to get a grip', makes unexpectedly clear the class character of the connection between established politics and technology. Referring to the eight months long mining dispute, it insists that:

> There should be no hesitation in using *all the power at the government's disposal* to defeat Scargill and end his strike. That means paying out redundancy money, pushing ahead with the closure programme and making it clear that *the full force of the state* will be used to move pit-head stocks to the power stations. There is no time to lose. When the Commons held its last major debate in July, Nigel Lawson [the Chancellor of the Exchequer] pointed to the American economy as the way forward – its greater freedom and dynamism, lower taxes, lower public spending and 'the absence of Luddite trade unionism'.

Naturally, what is meant by the last phrase in plain language is *the absence of trade unionism tout court*. For all trade unionism willing to fight in defence of the interests of its members is '*Luddite*' by definition, and must be defeated as such, in the name of the supposedly self-evident virtues of 'technological advance' and of its fully desirable imperatives for the 'rational allocation of resources'. This is why on the 'positive' side of the Chancellor's equation we find 'lower taxes, lower public spending and greater freedom *for business*', while the 'negative' side is represented by the intolerable obstacles to the realization of the first in the form of (Luddite) trade unionism. And this is why the British Government has been and is pursuing anti-trade-union legislation (and practices), modelled on American realities and advice, as the centre-piece of its strategy. Understandably, more of the same remedy is advocated by the editorial of *The Sunday Times* quoted above, talking about a so-called 'revolution' and asking for the use of the 'full force of the state' while presenting the hesitant politicians with the dramatic warning:

> The *Thatcherite revolution*, if it is not to end up as yet another failed attempt to reverse Britain's decline, has to infuse this country with the *sense of realism* that pervades the American economy ... At the same time *radical steps* are needed to *encourage enterprise* and *revolutionize our arthritic labour market*.

The socially 'neutral' yet for the whole of society highly beneficial nature of 'advanced technology' is supposed to speak 'loud and clear' for itself. So much so, in fact, that only the 'Luddites' of an 'arthritic labour market' can remain insensitive to it. However, the disturbing truth is that Lawson's parliamentary public relations exercise is absurd even in its own terms. For it fails to acknowledge the apparently 'minor details' that the much advertized dynamism of the American economy is inseparable from the *structurally dominant position* of American capital in the global capitalist system, coupled with the *astronomical budget and international trade deficits* of the American Government in the last few years (which every self-respecting monetarist should notice and abhor as the *diametrical opposite* of the idealized 'sense of realism'). Obviously, however, such prosaic (and perhaps also too embarrassing) matters are unworthy of the attention of lofty leader writers.

522. Jack D. Douglas, 'The impact of technology on political values', *op. cit.*, p. 152.
523. C. Wright Mills, 'Liberal values in the modern world', in Jack D. Douglas, ed., *op. cit.*, pp. 154–61.
524. From an excellent study by Hilary and Steven Rose, *Science and Society*, Penguin Books, Harmondsworth, 1970, pp. 243–5.
525. The fact that human beings belong to the order of *nature*, and consequently they must satisfy the objective conditions of their self-reproduction as beings of nature, means that the ongoing process of *mediation between men and nature* through productive activity is an absolute necessity. However, an alienated *second order* 'mediation of the mediation' is superimposed on the fundamental one, deeply affecting all facets of human life. As a result, the capitalistically institutionalized second order mediations – *private property* (capital) – *exchange* (market) – *hierarchical social* (not simply technological) *division of labour* – interpose themselves as an 'alienated mediation' ('*entäusserte Vermittlung*', Marx) between the natural order and essential productivity, totally subordinating the latter to their own dictates. Science, just as much as any other form of productive activity, inevitably suffers the far-reaching negative consequences of being subjected to the reified material and social/institutional imperatives of these alienated second order mediations.
526. Norbert Wiener, 'Some moral and technical consequences of automation', first published in 1960, reprinted in Jack D. Douglas, ed., *op. cit.*, pp. 92–101.
527. *Ibid.*, pp. 100–1.
528. Otto Nathan and Heinz Norden, eds, *Einstein on Peace*, Schocken Books, New York, 1960, p. 343.
529. From a letter by Daniel Q. Posin to Einstein, dated 21 October 1945, published in *Einstein on Peace*, pp. 340–1.

530. *Ibid.*, p. 401.

531. *Ibid.*, pp. 520–1.

532. *Ibid.*, p. 554. (From a letter to the Queen Mother of Belgium, dated 6 January, 1951.)

533. *Ibid.*, p. 616. (Letter dated 2 January, 1955.)

534. He wrote in an article published in the first issue of *Monthly Review*: 'The *economic anarchy* of capitalist society as it exists today is, in my opinion, the real source of the evil.... The result of these developments is an oligarchy of private capital the enormous power of which cannot be effectively checked even by a democratically organized political society.... Moreover, under existing conditions, private capitalists inevitably control, directly or indirectly, the main sources of information (press, radio, education). It is thus extremely difficult and indeed in most cases quite impossible, for the individual citizen to come to objective conclusions and to make intelligent use of his political rights.... I am convinced there is only one way to eliminate these grave evils, namely through the establishment of a *socialist economy*, accompanied by an *educational system* which would be oriented towards *social goals*.... A *planned economy*, which adjusts production to the *needs of the community*, would distribute the work to be done among all those able to work and would guarantee a livelihood to every man, woman, and child. The education of the individual, in addition to promoting his own innate abilities, would attempt to develop in him a *sense of responsibility for his fellow men* in place of the glorification of power and success in our present society.' (Einstein, 'Why socialism?', *Monthly Review*, May 1949.)

535. *Einstein on Peace*, p. 613.

536. J.L.Austin, Contribution to 'Cahiers de Royaumont', *Philosophie No. IV: La Philosophie Analytique*, p. 350. For a detailed discussion of Austin's fetishistic conception of science as the only viable model for 'non-ideological' philosophy, see my 'Critique of analytical philosophy' in *Philosophy, Ideology and Social Science*.

537. On 25 October 1945, 'Congressman John Rankin, a Mississippi politician of ultraconservative views, strongly attacked Einstein in the House of Representatives for allegedly supporting an anti-Franco organization. "This *foreign-born agitator* would have us plunge into another European war in order to further *the spread of Communism throughout the world*," he claimed. "It is about time the American people got wise to Einstein".' (Ronald W. Clark, *Einstein: The Life and Times*, Hodder and Stoughton, London, 1973, p. 552.) What the author omits is *how* this Congressman, well known for his racist views, wanted to make the American people 'get wise to Einstein'. He insinuated that Einstein was 'violating the law', adding that he '*ought to be prosecuted*' forthwith. (*Einstein on Peace*, p. 344.)

538. *Einstein on Peace*, p. 533.

539. *Ibid.*, p. 107.

540. *Ibid.*, p. 116.

541. *Ibid.*, p. 514.

542. *Ibid.*, p. 124.

543. Commenting on Leo Szilárd's projected organization of intellectuals to work for peace and disarmament, Einstein wrote in a letter to H. Noel Brailsford (on 24 April 1930): 'I consider Szilárd a fine and intelligent man who is ordinarily not given to illusions. Like many people of that type, he may be *inclined to exaggerate the significance of reason in human affairs*.' (*Ibid.*, pp. 103–4.)

544. Following his bitter disappointment with the *Bulletin of the Atomic Scientists* – which betrayed its mission in his eyes by devoting an issue to 'civil defence', abandoning the principle of opposing war, in preference to considerations of how best to prepare for it – he rejected (on 5 January 1951) the editor's invitation to submit 'a presentation of the pacifist point of view'. Einstein replied to Eugene Rabinowitch, the *Bulletin's* editor: 'I do not intend to write the article which you suggest; I believe *an appeal to reason would be utterly futile* in the present polluted atmosphere.' (*Ibid.*, p. 553.)

545. On 3 July 1930, less than three months after his somewhat sceptical remark on Szilárd's inclination to exaggerate the significance of reason in human affairs, in a letter expressing his solidarity with the militant pacifist Rozika Schwimmer, Einstein wrote: 'World peace, so urgently needed, will never be achieved unless the *best minds* actively oppose the organs of authority and the real forces behind authority.... Success will come only when a sufficient number of *influential people* have the moral courage to adopt such an attitude.' (*Ibid.*, pp. 106–7.)

546. *Ibid.*, p. 404, for instance.

547. See *Einstein on Peace*, pp. 116–19.

548. Einstein in *The Born-Einstein Letters*, Macmillan, London, 1971, p. 231.

549. *Einstein on Peace*, p. 402.

550. In his address to the students of the California Institute of Technology, delivered on 16 February 1931, Einstein stressed that: 'Concern for man himself must always constitute the chief objective of all technological effort, concern for the big, unsolved problems of how to organize human work and the distribution of commodities in such a manner as *to assure that the results of our scientific thinking may be a blessing to mankind*, and not a curse. Never forget this when you are pondering over your *diagrams and equations!*' (*Ibid.*, p. 122.)

In the same spirit, when he criticized 'applied science' for the way it actually contributed to human misery, instead of fulfilling its great positive potential, he made it clear that what was to be opposed was the enslaving social application of applied science and the insecurity of the workers' existence going with it. For, as he put it:

> In times of war, applied science has given men the means to poison and mutilate one another. In time of peace, science has made our lives hurried and uncertain. Instead of liberating us from much of the monotonous work that has to be done, it has enslaved men to machines; men who work long, wearisome hours mostly without joy in their labor and with the continual fear of losing their pitiful income.
> (*Ibid.*)

551. *Ibid.*, p. 621.

552. The wishful title of a chapter in Daniel Bell's book: *The Coming of Post-Industrial Society*. For Bell's arguments see pp. 165–266 as well as the related concluding sections of his book on 'The future of science' and on 'Meritocracy and equality' (pp. 378–455).

553. David Walker, 'The pure and applied scientist', *The Times*, 8 November 1984.

554. *Ibid.*

555. *Ibid.*

556. *Ibid.*

557. *Ibid.* And yet the article, curiously, after absolving Chilver of all possible accusations of adhesion to Tory ideology, concludes:

He would even, one suspects, like to have a go at applying [the Cranfield lessons] as the vice-chancellor of one of the big universities, perhaps, or *as a politican in the Thatcher Government.* . . . Sir Henry Chilver is waiting for a call to other things. Is there not a nationalized industry which would respond to his radical conviction that we need to 'break out' of the 1940s-style pattern of ownership and organization? Isn't there an institution on the Prime Minister's list that needs Chilver's managerial philosophy? Mrs. Thatcher's resources of personnel are surely not so deep that she can afford to *leave this kindred spirit relatively underemployed.*

558. T. Durham, 'Fifth generation fever', *Practical Computing*, Vol. 7, October 1984, p. 115.

559. *Ibid.* A sinister aspect of the growing trend of subordinating scientific research – and even the much cherished 'democratic freedom of publication' – to the interests of the military/industrial complex has come to public attention with the suppression of a book by Richard Ennals, who earlier resigned in protest from the prestigious government sponsored Alvey Programme and as Research Manager at Imperial College Department of Computing. His book: *Star Wars: A Question of Initiative*, proved to be too embarrassing to the powerful political/military establishment which has a finger in every pie. As reported in *Computer Weekly* (25 September, 1986), the book was 'withdrawn a few days before it should have been published by John Wiley. . . . The picture he presents in his book is of a UK government cynically selling out to the American military machine. "Since March 1985, behind closed doors, the UK government has assembled a plan to sell off UK advanced technology for US military use", he claims . . . It could be statements such as this which led Wiley to withdraw the book before publication.'

560. *Einstein on Peace*, p. 122.

561. Norman Moss, *Men Who Play God. The Story of the Hydrogen Bomb*, Penguin Books, Harmondsworth, 1968, pp. 55–6.

562. Karl Popper, 'Reason or revolution?', in T. W. Adorno *et al.*, *The Positivist Dispute in German Sociology*, Heinemann, London, 1976, pp. 295–6.

563. *Einstein on Peace*, pp. 464–5.

564. Naturally, very different rules apply in their international relations with the countries of the 'Third World' where the destabilization and violent overthrow of democratically elected governments, and the establishment of 'friendly' military dictatorships are actively promoted.

565. Quoted by E. T. Chase, *op. cit.*, p. 174.

566. Marx, *Grundrisse*, p. 270.

567. *Ibid.*, p. 411.

568. Sartre, *The Problem of Method*, Methuen, London, 1963, p. 7.

569. *Ibid.*, p. 8.

570. At this point Sartre adds a clarifying footnote: 'In the case of Cartesianism, the action of "philosophy" remains *negative*; it clears the ground, it destroys, and it enables men, across the infinite complexities and particularisms of the feudal system, to *catch a glimpse of the abstract universality of bourgeois property*. But under different circumstances, when the social struggle itself assumes other forms, the theory's contribution can be *positive*.' (*Ibid.*, p. 5.)

571. *Ibid.*

572. *Ibid.*, p. 3.

573. *Ibid.*

574. Kant, *Critique of Pure Reason*, Dent & Sons, London, 1934, p. 474.

575. *Ibid.*, p. 475.
576. Marx, *Letter to Kugelmann*, 9 October 1866.
577. *Ibid.*
578. Marx, *Letter to Engels*, 11 March 1865.
579. Marx, *Letter to Kugelmann*, 27 January 1870.
580. Engels, *Anti-Dühring: Herr Eugen Dühring's Revolution in Science*, Lawrence & Wishart, London, 1975, p. 9.
581. MECW, Vol. 5, pp. 50–1.
582. *Ibid.*, p. 49. And a little further on Marx adds in the same spirit: 'the real intellectual wealth of the individual depends entirely on the wealth of his real connections. Only this will liberate the separate individuals from the various national and local barriers, bring them into practical connection with the production (including intellectual production) of the *whole world* and make it possible for them to acquire the capacity to enjoy this *all-sided production of the whole earth* (the creations of man). *All-round dependence*, this primary 'natural' form of the *world-historical co-operation* of individuals, will be transformed by this communist revolution into the *control and conscious mastery* of these powers, which, born of the action of men on one another, have till now overawed and ruled men as *powers completely alien to them.*' (*Ibid.*, pp. 51–2.)
583. Here is a selection of the relevant passages from his letters, confined to the years 1857–8:

> In England, things will at last be brought to a head.
> (*Letter to Engels*, 18 March 1857)
> The American crisis – its outbreak in New York was forecast by us in the November 1850 *Revue* – is beautiful and has had immediate repercussions on French industry, since silk goods are now being sold in New York more cheaply than they are produced in Lyons.
> (*Letter to Engels*, 20 October 1857)
> The monetary panic in London has subsided to some extent during the past few days but will soon begin afresh ... As for America, it seems almost certain that the protectionists will prevail as a result of the crisis. This will have lasting and disagreeable repercussions so far as the worthy English are concerned.... Jones is playing a very inane role. As you know, long before the crisis and with no particular end in view unless to provide a pretext for agitation during the lull, he proposed to hold a Chartist conference to which bourgeois radicals (not just Bright, but even men like Cunningham) were to be invited.... Now, instead of making use of the crisis and substituting genuine agitation for an ill-chosen pretext for agitation, he clings to his nonsense; he shocks the working-men by preaching co-operation with the bourgeois ...
> (*Letter to Engels*, 24 November 1857)
> The police measures against bullion exports, now pretty well in full vigour in France, ... have put off for a week or two the drain of bullion from the Bank of France. Nevertheless, the drain will set in and even if, as in 1856 (October), it gets no further than the gutter, the catastrophe will be complete. Meanwhile French manufacturers are treating their workers as ruthlessly as though there had never been a revolution. This will do good.... I am working like mad all night and every night collating my economic studies so that I at least get the outlines [the *Grundrisse*] clear before the *déluge*. Since Lupus [Wilhelm Wolff, a revolutionary worker and close friend] keeps a regular record of our *crisis forecasts*, tell

him that last Saturday's *Economist* maintains that, during the final
months of 1853, throughout 1854, the autumn of 1855 and 'the sudden
changes of 1856', Europe has never had more than a hair-breadth escape
from the *impending crash*.
(*Letter to Engels*, 8 December 1857. To the last sentence Engels replied
in a *Letter to Marx*, dated 17 December 1857: 'Lupus is eating humble
pie; we were right.')
    I am working enormously, as a rule until 4 o'clock in the morning. I
am engaged on a twofold task: 1. Elaborating the outlines of political
economy.... 2. The present crisis. Apart from the articles for the
Tribune, all I do is keep records of it, which, however, takes up a
considerable amount of time. I think that, somewhere about the spring,
we ought to do a pamphlet together about the affair as a reminder to the
German public that we are still there as always, and *always the same*.
[Marx's italics.] I have started 3 large record books – England, Germany,
France. All the material on the American affair is available in the
Tribune, and can be collated subsequently.... Write to me whenever
you have the time, for later on you are sure to forget all the 'chronique
scandaleuse' of the crisis which is so invaluable to us.
(*Letter to Engels*, 18 December 1857)
    The present commercial crisis has impelled me to set to work seriously
on my outlines of political economy, and also to prepare something on
the present crisis.
(*Letter to Ferdinand Lassalle*, 21 December 1857)
    The French crisis proper does not break out until the *general crisis* has
attained a certain level in Holland, Belgium, the Zollverein [customs
union], Italy (including Trieste), the Levant and Russia ... When the
French crisis proper breaks out, it will play the very devil both with the
security market and the security of that market, the *State*.... The whole
rotten old structure is falling to pieces and the ludicrously rash surge
hitherto manifested by the security market in England, etc., will likewise
end in disaster.
(*Letter to Engels*, 25 December 1857)
    Now that I am at last ready to set to work after 15 years of study, I
have an uncomfortable feeling that *turbulent movements* from without
will probably interfere after all. Never mind. If I finish too late and thus
find *the world no longer attentive to such subjects*, the fault is clearly my
own.... There are turbulent times in the offing. If I were merely to
consult my own private inclinations, I would wish for another few years
of superficial calm. There could, at any rate, be no better time for
scholarly undertakings ... However all these are themselves philistine
ruminations which will be swept away by the first storm.
(*Letter to Lassalle*, 22 February 1858)
    There is no doubt, there will be a crash in France, answered by crashes
in Belgium, Holland, Rhenish Prussia, etc. In Italy the situation is truly
frightful.... Taken all in all, the crisis has been burrowing away like the
good old mole it is.
(*Letter to Engels*, 22 February 1858)
    History is about to take a *new start*, and the signs of dissolution
everywhere are delightful for every mind not bent upon the conservation
of things as they are.
(*Letter to Lassalle*, 31 May 1858)

584. He wrote to Engels in February 1857: 'Since, in the midst of *my own crisis*, it is very edifying for me to hear about *crises*, drop me a few lines telling me how things are in the industrial districts. Not at all well, according to the reports in the London papers.' (*Letter to Engels*, 24 February 1857.)

Nine months later he returned to the subject in the same vein: 'Though my own financial distress may be dire indeed, never, since 1849, have I felt so cosy as during this outbreak.' (*Letter to Engels*, 13 November 1857.) And his attitude remained the same even when he had to make clear his perception of the bitter irony inherent in the situation, in his confession to Engels: 'I personally can bury myself in my work and escape the *misère* by devoting my attention to *universalities*. My wife, of course, has no such refuge.' (*Letter to Engels*, 28 January 1858.)

585. Marx, *Letter to S. Meyer*, 30 April 1867.
586. See Marx's *Letter to Engels*, 8 October 1858.
587. 'In my opinion, the biggest things that are happening in the world today are on the one hand the movement of the slaves in America, started by the death of John Brown, and on the other the movement of the serfs in Russia. You will have seen that the Russian aristocracy have thrown themselves directly into agitation for a constitution and that two or three people from the chief families have already found their way to Siberia. At the same time Alexander has spoilt things with the peasants by the latest Manifesto, which declares in so many words that the "communistic principle" must cease with emancipation. Thus the "social" movement has started in the West and in the East. This, added to the prospective downbreak in Central Europe, will be grandiose.' (*Letter to Engels*, 11 January 1860.)
588. Marx, *Letter to Kugelmann*, 13 October 1866.
589. Marx, *Letter to Engels*, 20 June 1866.
590. *Ibid*. With reference to 'Proudhonist socialism now fashionable in France' Marx insists that 'Communism must above all rid itself of this false brother.' (*Letter to Weydemeyer*, 1 February 1859.) He follows the fortunes of Proudhon and his followers with keen interest, reporting to Engels in 1856 that 'Proudhon has become a director of the royal imperial railways' (*Letter to Engels*, 29 February 1856), and to Lassalle in 1859 that 'Proudhon is said to have gone out of his mind and been put in a lunatic asylum in Brussels.' (*Letter to Lassalle*, 10 June 1859.)
591. Engels, *Anti-Dühring*, Lawrence & Wishart, London, 1975, p. 15.
592. See Marx's *Letter to Engels* in which he talked about this 'positivist rot' and described Comte's writings as 'miserable compared to Hegel', 7 July 1866.
593. Marx, *Letter to Engels*, 22 June 1867.

Incidentally, the same letter, written on the occasion of *Capital's* first publication, also contains the sentence in which Marx says that 'I hope the bourgeoisie will remember my carbuncles all the rest of their lives.' Showing the inextricable ideological passion and commitment of Marx's 'proletarian science', he speaks in this letter in the same breath of scientific proofs and dialectical laws as of 'the vampires of home work', of the fight in which he is personally involved (through his position in the International) for 'abolishing the torture of one and a half million human beings', of 'another proof of what swine [the bourgeoisie] are', etc.
594. I have discussed some related problems in an essay entitled 'Il rinnovamento del marxismo e l'attualità storica dell' offensiva socialista', *Problemi del Socialismo*, No. 23, January-April 1982, pp. 5–141. See in particular sections I/1 ('L'incompiuto progetto di Marx: scopo, metodo e risultati', pp. 7–13) and

II/6 ('Ambiguità temporali e mediazioni mancanti', pp. 92–9).
595. Lukács, *History and Class Consciousness*, Merlin Press, London, 1971, p. 41.
596. *Ibid.*, p. 43.
597. *Ibid.*, p. 74.
598. *Ibid.*, p. 43.
599. *Ibid.*, p. 219.
600. *Ibid.*, p. 1. Lukács's italics.
601. In *Aspects of History and Class Consciousness*, ed. I. Mészáros, Routledge & Kegan Paul, London, 1971, p. 55.
602. *La lotta fra progresso e reazione nella cultura d'oggi*, Feltrinelli, Milan, 1957.
603. *Ibid.*, p. 18.
604. *Ibid.*, p. 34.
605. *Ibid.*, p. 46.
606. *Ibid.*, p. 44.
607. *Ibid.*, p. 34.
608. *Ibid.*, p. 5.
609. *Ibid.*, p. 7.
610. *Ibid.*, p. 9.
611. *Ibid.*, p. 10.
612. *Ibid.*, p. 36.
613. *Ibid.*, p. 45.
614. *Ibid.*, p. 25.
615. Lukács, *History and Class Consciousness*, p. xxv.
616. MECW, Vol. 5, p. 77.
617. *Ibid.*
618. Lenin, *Collected Works*, Vol. 25, p. 492.
619. Marx, *Letter to Joseph Weydemeyer*, 5 March 1852.
620. See MECW, Vol. 28, p. 508.
621. Marx, *Grundrisse*, p. 108.
622. Lukács, 'Az erkölcs szerepe a kommunista termelésben' (The role of morality in Communist production), first published in Hungarian in *Szocialista Termelés* in 1919.
623. See a most challenging series of articles by Norberto Bobbio (written between 1973–6 and collected in a volume under the title: *Quale socialismo? Discussione di un'alternativa*, Einaudi, Turin, 1976) which generated a wide-ranging discussion in Italy on the relationship between socialism and democracy at a time when these problems dramatically reappeared on the political agenda under the impact of some grave international developments (like the coup in Chile) and the deepening internal crisis of Italian society itself. As Bobbio rightly remarked, with a touch of irony, after being presented with an enthusiastic approval by the leader of the Italian Socialist Party, Pietro Nenni:

> I have been writing studies on political theory for thirty years but I am not aware of as much as a single word of them being quoted by a politician of so high an authority at a party congress! *O tempora o mores!*
> (*Ibid.*, p. 68)

624. See 'The role of morality in Communist production', in Georg Lukács, *Political Writings 1919–1929*, NLB, London, 1968, pp. 48–52.
625. Sections 2–7 of this chapter first appeared in *Praxis y Filosofia: Ensayos en homenaje a Adolfo Sánchez Vázquez* (ed. Juliana González, Carlos Pereyra and Gabriel Vargas Lozano, Grijalbo, Mexico/Barcelona/Buenos Aires 1985, pp. 57–94), and subsequently in *Radical Philosophy* (No. 44, Autumn 1986,

pp. 14–32), in *Monthly Review* (July–August 1987, pp. 80–108), and in *Meenyaya Epitheorese* (December 1987, pp. 3–38).

626. Marx, 'The eighteenth brumaire of Louis Bonaparte', Marx and Engels, *Selected Works*, Foreign Languages Publishing House, Moscow, 1958, Vol. 1, p. 340.
627. The term used by Marx to characterize the tasks of the socialist revolution from 1843 onwards, sharply contrasting the *'social* revolution' with the narrowly *political* horizons of the revolutions of the past.
628. 'Empirically, communism is only possible as the act of the dominant peoples "all at once" and simultaneously, which presupposes the universal development of productive forces and the world intercourse bound up with them.' (MECW, Vol. 5, p. 49.)
629. Marx, 'The class struggles in France 1848–1850', *Selected Works*, Vol. 1, p. 163. Marx's italics.
630. Marx, *Letter to Engels*, 8 October 1858, MECW, Vol. 29, p. 360.
631. We should recall Lenin's repeated complaints about the paralysing impact of 'Asiatic backwardness' on post-revolutionary developments.
632. This is how Lenin tried to reinsert the revolution of *'backward Russia'* – contrasted with the potentialities of the *'advanced countries of Western Europe'* – into the original perspectives:

> It would be erroneous to lose sight of the fact that, soon after the victory of the proletarian revolution in at least one of the advanced countries, a sharp change will probably come about: *Russia will cease to be the model* and will once again become a *backward country* (in the 'Soviet' and socialist sense).
> (Lenin, *Collected Works*, Lawrence & Wishart, London 1960ff, Vol. 31, p. 21)

To be sure, the relation of forces has significantly changed since Lenin wrote these lines. Nevertheless, the still unrealized proletarian revolution 'in at least one of the advanced countries' continues to maintain the 'historical dislocation' with regard to the radical transformation and ultimate 'withering away' of the state as well as to the potentialities of 'conscious collective totalization' – i.e. the self-determined comprehensive integration and conscious collective action of the social individuals – implicit in the developments anticipated by Marx.
633. Paul Mattick, *Critique of Marcuse: One-Dimensional Man in Class Society*, Merlin Press, London, 1972, p. 61. While one cannot value highly enough the genuinely Marxian perspective of Mattick's work – maintained over a period of many years, with single-minded determination and consistency, under the conditions of an almost complete isolation in the United States – the point at which one has to part company with him is where he summarily characterizes the various *post-capitalist* societies as *'state capitalist'* formations.
634. Marx, *The Civil War in France*, Foreign Languages Press, Peking, 1966, p. 166.
635. *Ibid.*, p. 167.
636. *Ibid.*, p. 237.
637. *Ibid.*, p. 227.
638. The Commune 'was essentially a *working-class* government'. *Ibid.*, p. 72.
639. *Ibid.*, p. 172.
640. *Ibid.*, p. 72.
641. *Ibid.*, p. 73.
642. '. . . to serve as a lever for uprooting the economic foundations upon which

rests the existence of classes' (*Ibid.*, p. 72.), and 'to make *individual property a truth* by transforming the means of production, land and capital, now chiefly the means of enslaving and exploiting labour, into mere instruments of *free and associated labour.*' (*Ibid.*, p. 73.)

643. *Ibid.*
644. MECW, Vol. 5, p. 52.
645. *Ibid.*, pp. 52–3.
646. *The Civil War in France*, p. 73.
647. *Ibid.*, p. 171.
648. '*The working class know* that they have to pass through different phases of class-struggle. *They know* that the superseding of the economic conditions of the slavery of labour by the conditions of free and associated labour can only be the progressive work of time, ... that they require not only a change of distribution, but a new organization of production, or rather the delivery (setting free) of the social forms of production in present organized labour, (engendered by present industry), of the trammels of slavery, of their present class character, and their harmonious national and international coordination. *They know* that this work of regeneration will be again and again relented and impeded by the resistance of vested interests and class egotism. *They know* that the present "spontaneous action of the natural laws of capital and landed property" – can only be superseded by "the spontaneous action of the laws of the social economy of free and associated labour" by a long process of development of new conditions ... But *they know* at the same time that great strides may be made at once through the Communal form of political organization and that the time has come to begin that movement for themselves and mankind.' (*Ibid.*, pp. 172–3.)
649. MECW, Vol. 5, p. 49.
650. *The Civil War in France*, p. 73.
651. In the *Communist Manifesto*, for instance.
652. *The Civil War in France*, p. 171.
653. *Ibid.*, p. 173.
654. *Ibid.*, p. 171.
655. *Ibid.*, p. 73.
656. Marx, 'Conspectus of Bakunin's book: *State and Anarchy*', in Marx, Engels, Lenin, *Anarchism and Anarcho-Syndicalism*, Progress Publishers, Moscow, 1972, p. 151. Concerning the heated debates between Marx and Bakunin, see Mauricio de Tragtenberg's illuminating article: 'Marx/Bakunin', *Nova Escrita Ensaio*, Año V., No. 11/12, 1983, pp. 279–300.
657. MECW, Vol. 5, p. 86
658. *Ibid.*, p. 210.
659. See Marx, *The Poverty of Philosophy*, MECW, Vol. 6, pp. 206–12.
660. *Ibid.*, pp. 211–12.
661. MECW, Vol. 4, p. 36.
662. Marx, 'Conspectus of Bakunin's book: *State and Anarchy*', *op. cit.*, p. 150.
663. Marx, 'The eighteenth brumaire of Louis Bonaparte', *op. cit.*, p. 334.
664. For us, in hindsight, it is enough to think of the United States to see how problematical Marx's stipulative generalization is. The 'development and growth of modern industry' and the advancement of the international division of labour which, according to the Marxian formula, should have brought with it the highest degree of 'combination' and a correspondingly high level of organized and fully conscious political militancy, failed to achieve the anticipated results. To explain the actual trend of US developments – often

described as the 'integration of the working class' – together with the possibility of its reversal, it is obviously necessary to introduce a number of important qualifying conditions which do not appear at all in Marx's original framework of assessment.

665. Marx, *The Holy Family*, MECW, Vol. 4, p. 37.
666. Marx, *Contribution to Critique of Hegel's Philosophy of Law*, MECW, Vol. 3, p. 182. (Marx's italics.) This is how Marx defines the role of the proletariat in the context of the 'categorical imperative' here referred to: 'In France partial emancipation is the basis of universal emancipation; in Germany universal emancipation is the *conditio sine qua non* of any partial emancipation. In France it is the reality of gradual liberation, in Germany the impossibility of gradual liberation, that *must* give birth to *complete freedom.*'

Starting from such premiss, Marx proceeds to ask the question, 'Where, then, is the positive possibility of a German emancipation?', and answers it as follows: 'In the formation of a class with *radical chains*, a class of civil society which is not a class of civil society, an estate which is the dissolution of all estates, a sphere which has a *universal* character by its *universal* suffering and claims to *no particular right* because no particular wrong but wrong generally is perpetrated against it; which can no longer invoke a historical but only a human title; which does not stand in any one-sided antithesis to the consequences but in an all-round antithesis to the premisses of the German state; a sphere, finally, which cannot emancipate itself without emancipating itself from all other spheres of society and *thereby emancipating all other spheres of society*, which, in a word, is the complete loss of man and hence can win itself only through the complete rewinning of man. This *dissolution* of society as a *particular* estate is the *proletariat.*'

Thus, the proletariat fits in perfectly well with the 'categorical imperative to overthrow all established relations'. While the imperatival connotations of this train of thought are later largely removed, several of its vital aspects – from explaining the development of the 'universal class' from the 'drastic dissolution of society, mainly of the middle estate', to the definition of the relationship between partiality and universality in relation to the conditions of emancipation – remain central to Marx's thought throughout his life. (Quotations from MECW, Vol. 3, pp. 186–7.)

667. MECW, Vol. 4, p. 36.
668. *Ibid.*, p. 37. (Marx's italics.) Here we can see Lukács's model of class consciousness in the Marxian contrast between 'what the proletariat at the moment regards as its aim', and what is 'ascribed to the fully-formed proletariat' by the socialist writers (i.e. the 'psychological' as opposed to the 'imputed' class consciousness in Lukács's terms). However, the fundamental difference is that while Marx expects the realization of his version of 'ascribed consciousness' in the class *as a whole*, in accordance with the transformation of its being under the compulsion of history, Lukács assigns to the Party the function of being the actual 'carrier' and 'embodiment' of the proletariat's 'imputed' class consciousness.

669. *Ibid.*
670. Marx, *The Civil War in France*, p. 72.
671. Marx, *Grundrisse*, p. 705.
672. *Ibid.*, pp. 705–6.
673. Unconsciously in the sense of operating by way of atomistic totalizations – i.e. in the form of *partial* anticipations and *expectations* more or less ruthlessly overruled by a reifying *feedback* from the unwanted consequences of the

post festum aggregative individual interactions – as implemented through the market and similar vehicles and institutional intermediaries.

674. Engels, *Letter to August Bebel*, 1–2 May 1891.
675. *Ibid.*
676. Engels, *Letter to Bebel*, 18–28 March 1875.
677. Marx, *Letter to Wilhelm Bracke*, 5 May 1875.
678. *Ibid.*
679. *Ibid.*
680. *Ibid.*
681. Rosa Luxemburg, *Spartacus*, Merlin Press, 1971, p. 15.
682. Lukács, 'Party and class', in Lukács, *Political Writings, 1919–1929*, New Left Books, London, 1972, p. 36. (First published in Hungarian under the title: 'The theoretical significance of the restoration of proletarian unity' in a pamphlet, *Documents on Unity*, Budapest, 1919.)
683. 'Due settimance prima Vilmos Böhm mi aveva chiesto di autorizzarlo a liberare il paese dai comunisti, ch'egli faceva ammontare a 1000. "Non acconsentirò mai," gli risposi.' (Mihály Károlyi, *Memorie di un Patriota*, Feltrinelli, Milan, 1958, p. 165.)
684. Rosa Luxemburg, *Spartacus*, p. 15.
685. Hugo Haase was leader of the left social democratic USPD.
686. Friedrich Ebert and Philip Scheidemann represented the right-oriented 'mainstream' of the German Social Democratic Party.
687. Luxemburg, *Spartacus*, p. 16.
688. Lukács, 'Az erkölcs szerepe a komunista termelésben' (The role of morality in Communist production). The translation here is my own, but see Lukács, *Political Writings, 1919–1929*.

Rosa Luxemburg is incomparably more realistic also in this respect. She both refuses to idealize the achievements of the revolution, and identifies the magnitude of the tasks in terms of radically transforming the structural foundations of society, instead of preaching 'labour-discipline' from above to the individual workers in the name of the abstract collective entity 'proletariat' opposed to them. These are her words:

> The revolution of November 9th was characterized by inadequacy and weakness.... What happened on November 9th was to a very small extent the victory of a new principle; it was little more than a collapse of the extant system of imperialism.... The sequel of this collapse was a more or less chaotic movement, one practically devoid of reasoned plan. The only source of union, the only persistent and saving principle, was the watchword 'Form Workers' and Soldiers' Councils'.... This was our common rallying cry, and it is through the councils alone that we can hope to realize socialism.... On the other hand, we have to recognize, comparing this splendid battle-cry with the paucity of the results practically achieved, we have to recognize that these were no more than the first childish and faltering footsteps of the revolution, which has many arduous tasks to perform and a long road to travel before the promise of the first watchwords can be fully realized.... The thoughtless had a very different picture of the course of affairs. They imagined it would merely be necessary to overthrow the old government, to set up a socialist government at the head of affairs, and then to *inaugurate socialism by decree*. Another illusion? Socialism will not be and cannot be inaugurated by decree; it cannot be established by any government, however admirably socialistic. Socialism must be created by the masses, must be made

by every proletarian. *Where the chains of capitalism are forged, there must the chains be broken.* That only is socialism, and thus only can socialism be brought into being.... *The masses must learn how to use power by using power. There is no other way....* we have to work from beneath. Therein is displayed the mass character of our revolution, one which aims at transforming the *whole structure of society.* It is thus characteristic of the modern proletarian revolution, that we must effect the *conquest of political power, not from above, but from beneath.* The 9th of November was an attempt, a weakly halfhearted, half-conscious and chaotic attempt, to overthrow the existing public authority and to put an end to ownership rule. What is now incumbent upon us is that we should deliberately concentrate all the forces of the proletariat for an attack upon the very foundations of capitalist society. There, at the root, where the individual employer confronts his wage slaves; at the root where all the executive organs of ownership rule confront the object of this rule, confront the masses; there, step by step, we must seize the means of power from the rulers, must take them into our own hands. (*Ibid.*, pp. 13–27)

689. Marx, *Capital*, Vol. 1, p. 763.
690. *Ibid.*
691. Engels forcefully stressed already in 1843, in his *Outlines of a Critique of Political Economy*, that the opposition set up by different schools of political economy between monopoly and competition was 'a quite hollow antithesis', adding that:

Competition is based on self-interest, and self-interest in turn breeds monopoly. In short, competition passes over into monopoly. On the other hand, monopoly cannot stem the tide of competition – indeed, it itself breeds competition; just as high tariffs, for instance, or a prohibition of imports positively breed the competition of smuggling.... Moreover, competition already presupposes monopoly – namely the monopoly of property (and here the hypocrisy of the liberals comes once more to light); and so long as the monopoly of property exists, for just so long the possession of monopoly is equally justified – for monopoly, once it exists, is also property. What a pitiful half-measure, therefore, to attack the small monopolies, and to leave untouched the basic monopoly.... Free competition, the key word of our present-day economists, is an impossibility.... Monopoly produces free competition, and the latter, in turn, produces monopoly. Therefore, both must fall, and these difficulties must be resolved through the transcendence of the principle which gives rise to them.

Naturally, the precise relationship between the competitive and monopolistic dimensions of the capitalist system changes historically. Thus, Lenin could rightly lay the stress on the monopolistic aspect when he defined imperialism as 'the monopoly stage of capitalism'. Equally, Baran and Sweezy powerfully argued in *Monopoly Capital* that the operation of the dominant economic system, that of US capitalism, and the future which the latter foreshadows for the 'second-echelon capitalist countries', cannot be made intelligible without centering attention on the monopolistic/oligopolistic big corporation.

However, from all this it does not follow that when the centralizing and monopolistic trends gain the upper hand, the decentralizing and competitive tendencies lose their significance. As Harry Magdoff rightly emphasized, US capitalism has found a way of decentralizing its manufacturing operations to such an extent that in 1958 only 29.7 per cent of its labour force was working in plants with 1,000 or more employees. (See H. Magdoff, 'China: contrasts with the USSR', *Monthly Review*, July-August 1975, p. 26.) Thus, the competitive dimension remains essential even in strictly productive/manufacturing terms, not to mention its importance on the plane of successfully reproducing the necessary purchasing power of the – no matter how monopolistically advanced – capitalist system.

692. Two important qualifications are needed here for a proper assessment of the way in which the dominant tendencies and counter-tendencies of capitalist development historically unfold and structurally assert themselves.

First, that since the functioning of this system throughout its history is characterized by the prevalence of the law of *uneven development*, the tendencies and counter-tendencies in question can manifest in very different ways in different parts of the world, depending on the more or less dominant position of the latter within the framework of *global* capital.

Thus, it is possible that *one side* of the objectively interlinked tendency/counter-tendency *predominates* in *one* country, whereas the *other* prevails in a *different country*. It is enough to think in this respect of the extreme hardship, 'thrift', and 'tightening of the belt' to which the Brazilian and Mexican working classes, among others, must be subjected since the evaporation of their respective 'miracles' of expansionary development, while the United States in particular, and the capitalistically advanced countries of the West in general, have to continue to waste vast amounts of resources under the pressure of the decreasing rate of utilization. Nevertheless, it must be stressed at the same time that one can only talk of the *pre*-dominance of one of the interlinked sides of this tendential law, in that – however absurd this is – even in the 'underdeveloped world' the capitalistically advanced sectors cannot escape the imperatives of waste-production at the present juncture of history, given the globally intertwined character of the capital system.

The *second* qualification is equally important. It concerns the inner determinations of the various tendencies themselves as well as their relative weight in the totality of capitalistic developments. For whatever their transformations, changes in emphasis, and shifts with regard to each other, or in relation to their specific counter-tendencies, in different places and at widely differing times in history – i.e. what we may consider their strictly transient characteristics, identifiable in terms of the *conjunctural interrelationship* of the diverse forces and determinations of which they themselves constitute a specific part in the given sociohistorical setting – they also possess an immanent logic of their own in accordance with which they unfold *across history*, and thereby objectively circumscribe the *limits* of global capitalist development.

In this sense, while the dialectical reciprocity of the manifold tendential interactions defines the characteristics of any particular tendency or counter-tendency as *relative* to the *overall* configuration of the *given* social forces and determinations, there can be no question of historical *relativism* and 'equidistance from God' in the spirit of post-Ranke-type historiography. For in each case *one* side (or one of the principal aspects) of the various tendencies mentioned above asserts itself as *dominant* – i.e. in Marx's terminology it constitutes the *'übergreifendes Moment'* of the relevant dialectical complex – across the *global trajectory* of capitalist development, notwithstanding the fact that (considered in terms of their own particular histories) they can show great variations, and even complete reversals, from one phase of global capitalist history to the other.

Thus, *monopoly* tends to prevail over *competition* in the long run, as the capital system historically progresses towards its ultimate structural limits as a productive system. Moreover, the early *monopolistic* manifestations that characterize the 'empire-building' practices of the 'large stirring Nations' (Mandeville), in due course give way – as a clear example of the possible reversals referred to a moment ago – to the predominance of forceful *competition* (and to the concomitant anti-monopolistic measures of the capitalist state) in the middle period of capitalistic expansion; but only to be reversed again with an awesome finality in the twentieth century, and particularly in the last few decades, in favour of giant monopolies, while maintaining with complete hypocrisy the resounding rhetorics of competition as the ultimate legitimation of the private enterprise system. Significantly, even the practice of 'denationalization' (or 'privatization') has undergone a major change in this respect in the postwar period. For at first the ruling class was satisfied with the restoration to competing private capitals the British steel industry, for instance, once its earlier bankruptcy had been remedied through the public funding of 'nationalization'. Soon enough, however, the troubles started all over again, necessitating not only a second round of bankruptcy-absorbing state-intervention and 'nationalization', but simultaneously also the ideologically most embarrassing admission of yet another major capitalist failure. Understandably, therefore, in recent years the *dominant form* of 'denationalization' became the establishment of *nation-wide private monopolies* – from British Telecom to British Gas – which quite cynically eliminated even the possibility of competition (and the economic risks inherent in it) within the confines legislatively controlled by the capitalist state in question. (Similar moves – or their suitable variants, aimed at retaining the bankrupt parts of a whole industry under state control while hiving off to private capital its highly profitable sectors – are now being planned in Britain for the coal industry, already renamed British Coal on the model of privatized British Telecom; for the management of water and electricity supplies, etc.)

In the same way as in the case of monopoly and competition, with regard to the historically unfolding tendency and counter-tendency of *centralization* versus *fragmentation* the '*übergreifendes Moment*' is the first. Likewise, the *internationalizing* tendency of capital quite obviously predominates in our times over against the identifiable national and regional *particularisms*, in the form of the irresistibly growing power of *transnational* corporations, in all major capitalist countries. And what is no less important, the upsetting and *breakdown of equilibrium* happens to be the ultimately dominant tendency of the capital system, and not its complementary tendency to *equilibrium*. This is so notwithstanding the countless theories and practical policies dedicated to the task of safeguarding equilibrium in the course of twentieth century capitalist developments. The ultimately overriding character of the tendency to the breakdown or equilibrium (i.e. its self-assertion as the '*übergreifendes Moment*') is evidenced in our epoch by the 'ever-diminishing return' the system receives from the ever-increasing efforts invested in reconstituting – with the help of unashamedly direct state-intervention – the periodically (but more and more frequently) lost equilibrium, whereas in the more distant past the need for the reconstitution of equilibrium seemed to be able to take care of itself.

693. Winnig belonged to the annexationist-imperialist wing of German Social Democracy, expecting the improvement of the conditions of the German working class from the conquest of the world market by German capitalists. He was nominated in November 1919 – by the 'revolutionary' Social

Democratic government – Reich Commissar for the Baltic States and also acted as adviser in the military intervention against the Russian Soviets.

This is how Rosa Luxemburg described his role under the circumstances:

You will all have read how the German troops in Riga are already marching shoulder to shoulder with the English against the Russian Bolsheviks. Comrades, I have documents in my hands which throw an interesting light upon what is now going on in Riga. The whole thing comes from the headquarters staff of the Eighth Army, which is collaborating with Herr August Winnig, the Social-Democrat and trade union leader. We have always been told that the unfortunate Ebert and Scheidemann are victims of the Allies. But for weeks past, since the very beginning of our revolution, it has been the policy of *Vorwärts* [the official organ of the German Social Democrats] to suggest that the suppression of the Russian Revolution is the earnest desire of the Allies. We have documentary evidence how all this was arranged to the detriment of the Russian proletariat and of the German revolution. In a telegram dated December 26th, Lieutenant-Colonel Burkner, chief of general staff of the Eighth Army, conveys information concerning the negotiations which led to his agreement at Riga. The telegram runs as follows:

'On December 23rd there was a conversation between the German plenipotentiary Winnig, and the British plenipotentiary Mosanquet, formerly consul-general at Riga. The interview took place on board *HMS Princess Margaret* and the commanding officer of the German troops was invited to be present.... The conversation took the following course:

From the English side: The British ships at Riga will supervise the carrying out of the armistice conditions. Upon these conditions are based the following demands:

(1) The Germans are to maintain a sufficient force in this region to hold the Bolsheviks in check and to prevent them from extending the area now occupied ...

(3) A statement of the present disposition of the troops fighting the Bolsheviks, including both the German and the Lettish soldiers, shall be sent to the British staff officer, so that the information may be available for the senior naval officer. All future dispositions of the troops carrying on the fight against the Bolsheviks must in like manner be communicated through the same officer....'

A number of additional demands follows.

Let us now turn to the answer of Herr Winnig, German plenipotentiary and trade union leader.

'Though it is unusual that a desire should be expressed to compel a government to retain occupation of a foreign state, in this case it would be our own wish to do so, since the question is one of protecting German blood.... Our endeavours would, however, be likely to be frustrated, in the first place, by the condition of the troops, for our soldiers in this region are mostly men of considerable age and comparatively unfit for service and, owing to the armistice, keen on returning home possessed of little will to fight; in the second place, owing to the attitude of the Baltic governments, by which the Germans are regarded as oppressors. But we will endeavour to provide volunteer troops, consisting of men with a fighting spirit, and indeed this has already in part been done.'

Here we see the counter-revolution at work. You will have read not long ago of the formation of the Iron Division expressly intended to fight the Bolsheviks in the Baltic provinces. At that time there was some doubt as to the attitude of the Ebert-Scheidemann government. You will now realize that the initiative in the creation of such force actually came from the government.

(Luxemburg, *Ibid.*, pp. 22–3)

694. 'Son organisation factice de secte est opposée à l'organisation historique et spontanée de la classe ouvrière.' (*Documents of the First International*, Lawrence & Wishart, London (n.d.), Vol. 3, p. 362.)

695. Marx, *Letter to Engels*, 18 February 1865.

696. Engels, *Letter to Marx*, 27 January 1865.

697. Lassalle, *Letter to Bismarck*, 8 June 1863.

698. Lassalle, *Letter to Bismarck*, beginning of February 1864. These letters were first published in *Bismarck and Lassalle* by Gustav Mayer, in Berlin 1928.

699. Marx, *Letter to Engels*, 30 October 1869.

700. 'l'Angleterre seul peut servir de levier pour une révolution sérieusement économique. . . . C'est le seul pays où la lutte des classes et l'organisation de la classe ouvrière par des Trades Unions ont acquis un certain degré d'universalité. A cause de sa domination sur le marché du monde, c'est le seul pays où chaque révolution dans les faits économiques doit immédiatement réagir sur tout le monde. . . . Les Anglais ont toute la *matière* nécessaire à la révolution sociale. Ce qui leur manque, c'est *l'esprit généralisateur et la passion révolutionnaire.*' (*Documents of the First International*, Vol. 3, p. 357.)

701. 'L'Angleterre ne doit pas être simplement traitée comme un pays après des autres pays – Elle doit être traitée comme la *métropole du capital.*' (*Ibid.*, p. 358.)

702. *Ibid.*, p. 21.

703. Lenin, *Collected Works*, Vol. 21, p. 49.

704. *Documents of the First International*, Vol. 3, p. 361. This passage is quoted from the original English statutes in the French circular; emphases by Marx.

705. I have discussed some aspects of this problem, including Bismarck's role in the conflict and of its resolution, in 'The cunning of history in reverse gear', *Radical Philosophy*, No. 42, Winter/Spring 1986, pp. 2–10.

706. Lukács, *History and Class Consciousness*, pp. 67–9.

707. *Ibid.*, p. 79.

708. Eduard Bernstein, *Evolutionary Socialism*, Schocken Books, New York, 1961, p. 216.

709. *Ibid.*, pp. 222–3.

710. *Ibid.*, p. 221.

711. *Ibid.*, p. 223.

712. *Ibid.*, p. 219.

713. *Ibid.*, p. 221.

714. *Ibid.*, p. 222.

715. The Schocken paperback edition of *Evolutionary Socialism* quoted above – with an Introduction by Sidney Hook: one of the intellectuals sarcastically criticized by Merleau-Ponty for belonging to 'The League of Abandoned Hope' – advertises Bernstein's book on its front page even today as: 'The Classic Statement of Democratic Socialism'.

716. See her *Reform or Revolution*, first published in 1898 and 1899 as two articles in the *Leipziger Volkszeitung*, and in volume form in 1900 as well as – in an updated edition – in 1908. An easily available edition, based on the 1908 version, has been published by Pathfinder Press, New York, in 1970.

717. Bernstein, *Evolutionary Socialism*, pp. 209–13.

718. See Note 419.
719. Characteristically, Bernstein's vacuous postulate of 'general social progress', which is said to arise mechanically and unproblematically from the 'growth of social wealth and of the social productive forces', is coupled with his defence of the theses of 'bourgeois harmony economists' (in the first place of his own, of course) against Marxism.
720. Luxemburg, *Reform or Revolution*, p. 58.
721. Richard Titmuss, for instance, forcefully argued in his excellent Introduction to the 1964 edition of R.H. Tawney's *Equality* that the hopes of labour's gradual emancipation simply did not work out. He pointed out that:

> Still the most striking fact about British society is the great concentration in the ownership of personal net capital. According to Professor Lydall and Mr Tipping, 1 per cent of the population owned 42 per cent in 1951–6 and 5 per cent owned 67.5 per cent. Even these proportions are underestimates, for the figures exclude pension funds and trusts (which have grown enormously in recent years), and they do not take account of the increasing tendency for large owners of property to distribute their wealth among their families, to send it abroad, and to transform it in other ways.... Long years of economic depression, a civilians' war, rationing and 'fair shares for all', so-called 'penal rates of taxation' and estate duty, and 'The Welfare State' have made little impression on the holding of great fortunes. The institution of concentrated wealth appears to be as tenacious of life as Tawney's intelligent tadpoles.... A new analysis by Professor Townsend and Dr Abel-Smith of the national surveys of income and expenditure carried out by the Ministry of Labour in 1953-4 and 1960 shows that there has been a sharp increase in the proportion of the population living at or around the official definition of subsistence – an increase which appears to have been accompanied by a rise in the incidence of malnutrition....
>
> In all these fundamental sectors of wealth, income, education, employment and the ownership of land, there are no signs that Britain has been moving towards a more classless society.
> (Quotations from pp. 16–22 of Tawney, *Equality*, Unwin Books, London, 1964. See also Richard M. Titmuss, *Income Distribution and Social Change*, Allen & Unwin, 1962.)

> Peter Townsend's monumental recent monograph on *Poverty* (Penguin Books, Harmondsworth, 1985) paints a much more desolate picture than his essay on 'The meaning of poverty' (*British Journal of Sociology*, Vol. XIII, No. 3, 1962) referred to by Titmuss.

722. Even in a country like India, where the overwhelming majority of the population is extremely poor, with 300 million people below the officially acknowledged 'absolute poverty line', the governmental policy of placing the burden of taxation in the form of indirect taxes on the shoulders of the poor is abundantly clear:

> The cuts in direct income tax are of no benefit to the poor 80 percent of the population who pay no income tax. But the poor pay *indirect taxes* on the purchase of food and a few other essential commodities which absorb 75 to 85 percent of their income. Indirect taxes are the source of the great bulk *(80 percent) of the country's tax revenue*, and they have been *increasing*. Between 1975–76 and 1984–85 when direct taxes as a proportion of GDP decreased, indirect taxes increased from 11.7 to 14.0

percent. Thus, the poor will, as usual, pay for the increased luxury consumption of the middle and upper classes, and the increased profits of the private corporate sector.

(M.R. Bhagavan, *op. cit.*, p. 73)

723. For instance, it can be adapted to the manipulative electoral requirements of the given political framework; it can be even quantified in terms of how many million 'ordinary people applied for shares' in British Telecom, or British Gas, and other ventures of state-organized bribery, as a 'proof', by the Conservative Government, that they must be considered today the true guardians of 'general social progress'; and, on the other side, in a defensive move, in order not to lose electoral ground, such figures and procedures can be quickly translated into a semantic redefinition of some varieties of private property as 'social ownership' by the Eurocommunist-inspired social democratic opposition, etc.

724. Bernstein, *Evolutionary Socialism*, p. 222.

725. *Ibid.*, p. 223. In this sense, as we can see, the vehicle of idealistic neo-Kantianism is adopted to serve a tangible ideological/political purpose in fighting the materialist adversary inside the movement.

As we could observe eailier (see Chapter 6.4), Marx prophetically perceived the danger which Lange – who understood absolutely nothing of the dialectic either in its Hegelian or in its Marxian version – represented for the German working-class movement, by putting himself forward as an unprincipled 'conciliator' who, in Marx's words, 'flirts with all sides'. Characteristically, for Bernstein this unprincipled neo-Kantian philosophical charlatan became the moral and intellectual model of socialist thought.

726. Richard Titmuss, in his essay quoted in Note 721, rightly poured scorn on those who continued to propagate the myth of taxing the rich out of existence. Characterizing the ideological climate of the period he wrote:

> By 1960 England had become a more muffled society. The condition of its people, rich, middling and poor, was concealed by a combination of myth and computer incompetence. Inequality, as a subject of political discourse, was less in evidence everywhere, and what remained of poverty in Britain was thought to be either eradicable through the 'natural' processes of growth or as constituting a permanent residue of the unfortunate and irresponsible. The rich, it was further argued, were no longer with us; they had been *taxed out of existence* by the class which had formerly revered them.
>
> (*Ibid.*, p. 11)

Thus, 60 years after Bernstein it could no longer be simply promised that *one day* the rich will be taxed out of existence. In the light of the massive evidence which proved the *exact opposite* – namely the ever-growing concentration of wealth in the hands of the few – it had to be cynically asserted, heaping lies on top of statistical and other 'scientific' distortions, that the original promise of revisionist social democracy had already been fully realized.

727. Marx, *Capital*, Foreign Languages Publishing House, Moscow, 1958, Vol. 1, p. 763.

728. Bernstein, *Evolutionary Socialism*, p. 218. And Bernstein added here in a footnote: 'Fortunately, "revolution" in this country has ceased to be anything more than an affected phrase.' – The monthly *News* of the Independent Labour Party in England, January 1899.

729. Quoted in Mary-Alice Waters' introduction to Rosa Luxemburg's *Reform or Revolution*, New York, 1970, p. 7.
730. See my essay on 'Political power and dissent in postrevolutionary societies', *New Left Review*, No. 108, March–April 1978; particularly pp. 7–14.
731. 'As a result of the development of the world economy and the aggravation and generalization of competition on the world market, *militarism* and the policy of big navies have become, as instruments of *world politics*, a decisive factor in the interior as well as in the exterior life of the great states. If it is true that world politics and militarism represent a rising tendency in the present phase of capitalism, then bourgeois democracy must logically move in a descending line.

    In Germany, the *era of great armaments*, begun in 1893, and the policy of world politics, inaugurated with the seizure of Kiao-Cheou, were paid for immediately with the following sacrificial victim: the decomposition of liberalism, the deflation of the Centre Party, which passed from opposition to government. The recent elections to the Reichstag of 1907, unrolling under the sign of the *German colonial policy*, were at the same time the historical burial of German liberalism.' (Luxemburg, *Reform or Revolution*, p. 47.)
732. *Ibid.*, pp. 47–8.
733. Luxemburg, *The Russian Revolution*, The University of Michigan Press, 1961, p. 36.
734. Luxemburg, *Reform or Revolution*, p. 50.
735. *Ibid.*, p. 51.
736. Luxemburg, *Spartacus*, p. 19.
737. Luxemburg, *Reform or Revolution*, pp. 60–1.
738. Luxemburg, 'Organizational questions of the Russian social democracy', in *The Russian Revolution*, p. 105.
739. Luxemburg, *Spartacus*, pp. 26–7.
740. Engels, *Letter to Ferdinand Lassalle*, 18 May 1859.
741. Paul Fröhlich, *Rosa Luxemburg: Her Life and Work*, Monthly Review Press, New York, 1972 (originally published in Paris in 1939), p. 294.
742. *Ibid.*, p. 295.

Luxemburg's first biographer also described the circumstances under which the 'head-hunt' in which the Social Democratic government was heavily implicated was set in motion:

> Finally, there was the spy office of the so-called Reichstag Regiment, founded by the SPD. The true colours of this institution, officially known as the 'Auxiliary Service of the SPD, Section 14', were later exposed in the libel proceedings conducted against a certain Herr Prinz. According to the findings of the court, this Section 14 of the Reichstag Regiment, in the names of Philipp Scheidemann and the regiment's financial backer, Georg Sklarz (an evil grafter and speculator), set a price of 100,000 Marks on the heads of Karl Liebknecht and Rosa Luxemburg. Hesel, the officer in charge of Section 14; Ernst Sonnefeld, the Regiment's paymaster; and Krasnik, an officer of the regiment, all declared under oath that Fritz Henck, Scheidemann's son-in-law, had expressly confirmed to them that the offer of the reward was serious and that money was available for such a purpose. A host of other members of the regiment confirmed this testimony, reiterating that *an order to murder Liebknecht and Luxemburg had been given* though it had never been put into writing, and that whoever brought in the two, *dead or alive*, was to receive a *reward of 100,000 Marks*. By acquitting Prinz of the libel charge, the

court was in effect condemning Scheidemann and Sklarz. Neither of
them ever dared to try and clear themselves of this incriminatory verdict.
(Fröhlich, *ibid.*, pp. 297–8)

743. Lukács, *History and Class Consciousness*, p. 44.

The other two essays in *History and Class Consciousness* dedicated to the
discussion of Rosa Luxemburg's ideas – 'Critical observations on Rosa
Luxemburg's *Critique of the Russian Revolution*' and 'Towards a methodology of the problem of organization' (pp. 272–342): written at a later date,
following Lukács's acceptance of Lenin's criticism of his article 'On the
question of parliamentarianism' as a manifestation of *'Left-Wing' Communism – An Infantile Disorder* – contain some very problematical judgements,
as we shall see in a moment.

744. Luxemburg, *The Russian Revolution*, p. 28.
745. Luxemburg, *The Junius Pamphlet: The Crisis in the German Social Democracy*, A Young Socialist Publication, Colombo, 1967, p. 82.
746. Luxemburg, *The Russian Revolution*, p. 78.
747. *Ibid.*, pp. 78–9.
748. *Ibid.*, p. 80.
749. *Ibid.*
750. Luxemburg, *Spartacus*, p. 17.
751. Bertram D. Wolfe's Introduction to *The Russian Revolution* by Rosa Luxemburg, *op. cit.*, p. 24.

Although the people who belong to this brand of thought had such a
predilection for castigating 'zeal', the last sentence of Wolfe's introduction
clearly revealed the author's anti-Marxist ideological zeal. For he self-contradictorily praised Luxemburg's 'dogmatic' and 'hopelessly dated little pamphlet' as a *'classic'*, just as Bernstein praised Marx as 'a great scientific spirit'
and simultaneously dismissed him as ' a slave to a doctrine'. In fact Wolfe's
left-handed compliment to Rosa Luxemburg only served the purpose of
supplying the author with a ritualistic occasion for somewhat prematurely
proclaiming the burial of everything she stood for. This is why the author
of this introduction offered to us the peculiarly contorted final judgement
according to which Luxemburg's allegedly so defective work was 'a classic of
that *now vanished Marxist socialist movement* in which she was so ardent a
crusader.' (*Ibid.*, p. 24.)

752. Even before the publication of Rosa Luxemburg's text Lenin expressed in a
letter his great concern about the way it might be used. He wrote to Zinoviev
on August 28, 1921:

In view of a number of statements made by [Clara] Zetkin, I regard the
conversation I had with her yesterday, before her departure, to be so
important that I must inform you of it.
She wants to set Levi two conditions:
1) resign his parliamentary seat;
2) close down his organ (*Soviet* or *Unser Weg*, as I believe it is now
called), issuing a statement of loyalty in respect of the decisions of the
Third Congress of the Communist International.
Furthermore, she is afraid that it could occur to some friend of Levi's
to publish Rosa Luxemburg's manuscript against the Bolsheviks (which I
think she wrote in prison in 1918). If anyone should do this, she intends
to make a statement in the press that she is quite sure such an act is
disloyal. She would say that she had known Rosa Luxemburg best of all,
and is sure that she herself admitted these views to be erroneous, that she

528 THE POWER OF IDEOLOGY

admitted, upon her release from prison, that she had been insufficiently informed.

In addition, Léon Jogiches, Rosa Luxemburg's closest friend, in a detailed talk with Zetkin, two days before he died, told her about this manuscript of Rosa Luxemburg's, and about Rosa Luxemburg herself admitting that it was wrong. Zetkin was going to write you about this at my request.
(Lenin, *Collected Works*, Vol. 45, pp. 231–2)

In fact Clara Zetkin published a book entitled *Um Rosa Luxemburg's Stellung zur russischen Revolution* (Moscow-Leningrad, 1922) in which she sharply criticized Paul Levi's presentation of Luxemburg's manuscript. Levi's publication, too, appeared in 1922, under the title: *Die russische Revolution. Eine kritische Würdigung. Aus dem Nachlass von Rosa Luxemburg.*

753. Lenin, 'Notes of a publicist', *Collected Works*, Vol. 33, p. 210. He also added that Luxemburg's 'biography and her *complete* works (the publication of which the German Communists are inordinately delaying ...) will serve as useful manuals for training many generations of Communists all over the world.' (*Ibid*. The word 'complete' is italicized by Lenin.)
754. Lenin, review of *The Junius Pamphlet*, *Collected Works*, Vol. 22, p. 306.
755. *Ibid.*, p. 307.
756. *Ibid.*, p. 319.
757. She wrote in April 1915:

Political mass strikes, protests and demonstrations comprised 1,005,000 workers in 1912, 1,272,000 in 1913. In 1914 the flood rose higher and higher. On January 22nd, the anniversary of the beginning of the Revolution [of 1905] there was a demonstration mass-strike of 200,000 workers. As in the days before the revolution of 1905, the flame broke out in June, in the Caucasus. In Baku, 40,000 workers were on a general strike. The flames leaped over to Petersburg. On the 17th of June 80,000 workers in Petersburg laid down their tools, on the 20th of July 200,000 were out; July 23rd, the general strike movement was spreading out all over Russia, barricades were being built, the revolution was on its way. A few more months and it would have come, its flags fluttering in the wind.... But German reaction checked the revolutionary movement. From Berlin and Vienna came declarations of war, and the Russian revolution was buried beneath its wreckage.... When the war broke out the Russian revolution had occurred. Its first attempt had not been victorious; but it could not be ignored; *it is on the order of the day*.
(Luxemburg, *The Junius Pamphlet*, pp. 48–9)

758. Lenin, '"Left-wing" Communism – An infantile disorder', *Collected Works*, Vol. 31, p. 21.
759. *Ibid.*, p. 22.
760. For instance, 'The right of nations to self-determination', Lenin, *Collected Works*, Vol. 20, p. 441.
761. Luxemburg, *The Junius Pamphlet*, p. 76.
762. As Rosa Luxemburg had put it in the middle of the war:

Historic development moves in *contradictions*, and for every *necessity* puts its *opposite* into the world as well. The capitalist state of society is doubtless a historic necessity, but so also is the revolt of the working class against it. Capital is a historic necessity, but in the same measure is its grave digger, the Socialist proletariat. The world rule of imperialism is a historic necessity, but likewise its overthrow by the proletarian international. Side by side the two historic necessities exist, in constant conflict with each other. And ours is the necessity of Socialism. Our necessity receives its justification with the moment when the capitalist class ceases to be the bearer of historic progress, when it becomes a hindrance, a *danger*, to the future development of society. That capitalism has reached this stage the present world war has revealed. (*Ibid.*, p. 79)

In case someone thinks that Luxemburg was thinking of mechanical necessities which excluded or even underplayed the role of human agency, it is worth reminding ourselves of the terms in which she cried out: 'a *world tragedy* has occurred; the *capitulation of Social Democracy.*' (*Ibid.*, p. 2.) And when she spoke of the stark alternative facing humanity, *socialism or barbarism*, she put the accent of 'inevitability' again on the inescapable *choice* of the progressive historical agency by insisting that 'This is the dilemma of world history, its inevitable *choice*, whose scales are trembling in the balance awaiting the *decision* of the proletariat.' (*Ibid.*, p. 9.) And she went even further in her characterization of the way in which great historical crises unfold:

Revolutions are not 'made' and great movements of the people are not produced according to technical recipes that repose in the pockets of the party leaders. Small circles of conspirators may organize a riot for a certain day and a certain hour, can give their small group of supporters the signal to begin. *Mass* movements in *great historical crises* cannot be initiated by such primitive measures. The best prepared mass strike may break down miserably at the very moment when the party leaders give the signal, may collapse completely before the first attack. The success of the great popular movements depends, aye, the very time and circumstance of their inception is decided by a number of *economic, political and psychological* factors. The existing degree of tension between the classes, the degree of intelligence of the masses and the degree of ripeness of their spirit of resistance – all these factors, which are incalculable, are premises that cannot be artificially created by any party. That is the difference between the *great historical upheavals*, and the small show-demonstrations that a well-disciplined party can carry out in times of peace, orderly, well-trained performances, responding obediently to the baton in the hands of the party leaders. The great historical hour itself creates the forms that will carry the revolutionary movements to a successful outcome, *creates and improvises* new weapons, enriches the arsenal of the people with weapons unknown and unheard of by the parties and their leaders. (*Ibid.*, p. 70)

763. *Ibid.*, p. 62.
764. See Note 747.
765. See Note 752.
766. See Notes 758 and 759.
767. Lenin, 'One step forward, two steps back: reply to Rosa Luxemburg', *Collected Works*, Vol. 7, p. 478.
768. See Note 681.
769. Lenin, 'Unity', *Collected Works*, Vol. 20, p. 232.
770. Luxemburg, 'Organizational questions of the Russian social democracy',

published under the title: 'Leninism or Marxism' in the University of Michigan/Ann Arbor Paperback edition of *The Russian Revolution, op. cit.*, p. 108.

771. Lenin, 'Reply to Rosa Luxemburg', *Collected Works*, Vol. 7, p. 478.
772. Luxemburg, 'Organizational questions of the Russian social democracy', *op. cit.*, pp. 105–7.
773. Luxemburg, *The Russian Revolution*, pp. 40–6.
774. Lenin, 'Reply to Rosa Luxemburg', *Collected Works*, Vol. 7, pp. 481–2.
775. This issue occupied an important place also in Lenin's 'Reply to Rosa Luxemburg', as we can see from the following quotation:

> Very soon after the [founding] congress [of the Russian Social-Democratic Labour Party], the Central Committee of the Party was arrested. *Rabochaya Gazeta* [the central organ of the Party] had to cease publication after its second issue. The whole Party became a shapeless conglomeration of *local* Party organizations (known as committees). The only bond between these local committees was an *ideological, purely spiritual one*. A period of disunity, vacillation, and splits was bound to set in again. The intellectuals, who in our Party made up a much larger percentage than in the West-European parties, had taken up Marxism as a new vogue. This vogue very soon gave place to slavish acceptance of the bourgeois criticism of Marx, on the one hand, and an infatuation for a *purely trade-unionist* labour movement (*strike-ism – Economism*), on the other. The divergence between the intellectual-opportunist and proletarian-revolutionary trends led to a split in the Union Abroad. The newspaper *Rabochaya Mysl*, and the *Rabocheye Dyelo* magazine published abroad, expressed (the latter in somewhat lesser degree) the standpoint of *Economism*, they *belittled the importance of political struggle* ... The 'legal' critics of Marx – Messrs. Struve, Tugan-Baranovsky, Bulgakov, Berdyaev, and the rest – swung all the way to the Right. Nowhere in Europe do we find *Bernsteinism* arriving so speedily at its logical consummation – the formation of a liberal group – as was the case in Russia. (Lenin, *Collected Works*, Vol. 7, p. 479)

776. *Ibid.*, p. 478.
777. *Ibid.*, p. 479.
778. See Note 704.
779. See Note 728.
780. See Note 735.
781. See Note 736.
782. See Note 772.
783. Luxemburg, 'Oganizational questions of the Russian social democracy', *op. cit.*, p. 98.
784. See Note 708.
785. See Note 728.
786. *Ibid.*
787. *Ibid.*
788. Harry Magdoff, *The Age of Imperialism: The Economics of US Foreign Policy*, p. 15.
    The core of this conception of imperialism was first developed by Lenin, in his *Imperialism, the Highest Stage of Capitalism*, written between January and June 1916. As Harry Magdoff pointed out in an essay entitled 'How to make a molehill out of a mountain':

Lenin is primarily concerned with explaining the major historical changes that show up toward the end of the nineteenth century when, among other things, competing empire-builders emerge among industrialized nations; England's dominant position in trade, military power, and colonial empire is challenged; and there is a marked and sudden speedup in colonial acquisitions and wars associated with empire. Lenin concluded that the underlying explanation for this concatenation of events was to be found in a major structural change in capitalism. The long-run tendency for the concentration and centralization of capital had reached a point where the leading capitalist economies were dominated by a relatively small number of large firms. With the emergence of this monopoly stage of capitalism, during which finance capital (the merger of bank and industrial interests) is in the ascendancy, capitalism becomes capitalist imperialism.

Whereas Luxemburg centers her theory on the supposed inability of capitalists at all stages of their history to make profits in a closed system, Lenin locates the nature of imperialism in the modes of behaviour of monopoly capitalism to protect and increase their profits. The context of Lenin's analysis is the uneven development of the assorted capitalist nations, the tendency to stagnation in the monopoly stage, and the special features of monopolistic competition as contrasted with 'free competition'. Under these propelling forces, certain crucially important characteristics of the imperialist stage come to the fore: capital export becomes increasingly important; the world's economic markets are divided up among international monopoly groups; the territorial division of the world by capitalist powers is completed; not only colonies but semicolonies and weaker capitalist nations become enmeshed in a net of financial and economic dependence on the centers of world finance capital; and antagonisms among imperialist powers for the redivision of the world intensify. . . .

One might well argue that Lenin was imprecise, unclear, and contradictory in some of his formulations about the export of capital (and other matters as well). But what is really significant (and merits attention by aspiring theoreticians) is how right Lenin was sixty years ago in selecting (from among many variables) the growing importance of capital exports (relative to exports of goods) as a key feature of the stage of monopoly capitalism. Thus, a recent United Nations study reports that in 1971 the sales of foreign affiliates of the world's multinational corporations (in other words, the production activity resulting from the direct investments of the imperialist powers) exceeded the total export of goods by all capitalist nations combined.

(Magdoff, *Imperialism: From the Colonial Age to the Present*, pp. 267–71)

789. The aggressively outspoken remarks of the General Manager of Ford Europe quoted below are quite telling in this respect. See Note 838.
790. Renato Constantino, *Neo-colonial Identity and Counter-Consciousness: Essays in Cultural Decolonization*, Merlin Press, London, 1978, p. 234.
791. Luxemburg, *Reform or Revolution*, pp. 36–7.
792. It was, therefore, by no means accidental that Habermas curtly dismissed the Marxian category of exploitation as no longer applicable to his 'modern industrial' society, or for that matter even to the 'Third World'. What was rather peculiar, though, was his claim that this was the result of recent

developments, when in fact his reformist/opportunist ancestor, Bernstein, made the same claim nearly a century earlier.

793. Marx, *Grundrisse*, p. 95.
794. *Ibid.*, p. 96.
795. *Ibid.*, p. 99–100.
796. See Note 721.
797. See Note 676.
798. Lukács, 'Preface to the New Edition (1967) of *History and Class Consciousness*', Merlin Press, London, 1971, p. xviii.
799. Lukács, *History and Class Consciousness*, p. 262.
800. *Ibid.*, p. 264. Lukács's italics.
801. *Ibid.*, p. 283.
802. See Note 735.
803. Lukács, *ibid.*, p. 284.
804. See Note 739.
805. Lukács, *ibid.*, p. 51.
806. *Ibid.*, pp. 41–2.
807. *Ibid.*, p. 67.
808. *Ibid.*, p. 326.
809. *Ibid.*, p. 330.
810. *Ibid.*, p. 289.
811. *Ibid.*, p. 310.
812. *Ibid.*, p. 79.
813. In connection with the expansion of Western blue jeans factories in Hungary, which resulted in the closure of some of their counterparts in Scotland, I referred in an article to the fact that:

> Western capitalism can turn its ability to exploit even the relatively under-paid East European workforce to its own advantage and use the mobility of capital – while preaching the 'need for labour mobility' as the magic remedy for unemployment – against its own labour force.
>
> Another significant, as well as extremely painful, example has been provided by the doubling of Polish coal exports to Margaret Thatcher's Britain during the miners' strike. Indeed, to make things worse, this happened under circumstances where Lech Walesa's Solidarnosc organization (in contrast to some local groups of Polish workers) failed to make so much as a verbal gesture of solidarity towards the British Miners. (István Mészáros, 'The cunning of history in reverse gear', *Radical Philosophy*, No. 42, Winter/Spring 1986, p. 7)

For an excellent book on the development of the Solidarnosc organization in Poland see Daniel Singer, *The Road to Gdansk*, Monthly Review Press, New York, 1981.

814. Luxemburg, *The Junius Pamphlet*, p. 54.
815. A term first used by Marx to characterize those parliamentarians who think that social conflicts are decided by motions, points of order and votes in parliamentary debates.
816. Luxemburg, *The Russian Revolution*, pp. 38–9.

Three years later, addressing a Western audience, Lenin argued in very similar terms that:

> To win over the *majority* of the proletariat to our side – such is the principal task ... Of course, we do not give the winning of the majority a *formal interpretation*, as do the knights of philistine 'democracy' of the

Two-and-a-Half International. When in Rome, in July 1921, the entire proletariat – the reformist proletariat of the trade unions and the Centrists of Serrati's party – *followed the Communists against the fascists*, that was winning over the majority of the working class to our side.

This was far, very far, from winning them decisively; it was doing so only *partially*, only *momentarily*, only *locally*. But it was winning over the majority, and that is possible even if, *formally*, the majority of the proletariat follow bourgeois leaders, or leaders who pursue a bourgeois policy (as do all the leaders of the Second and Two-and-a-Half Internationals), or if the majority of the proletariat are wavering. This winning over is gaining ground steadily in every way *throughout the world*. Let us make more thorough and careful preparations for it; let us not allow a single serious opportunity to slip by when the bourgeoisie compels the proletariat to undertake a struggle; let us *learn to correctly determine the moment when the masses of the proletariat cannot but rise together with us*.

Then victory will be assured, no matter how severe some of the defeats and transitions in our great campaign may be.

Our tactical and strategic methods (if we take them on an international scale) still lag behind *the excellent strategy of the bourgeoisie*, which has learned from the example of Russia and will not let itself be 'taken by surprise'. But our forces are greater, immeasurably greater; we are learning tactics and strategy; we have advanced this 'science' on the basis of the mistakes of the March 21 action. We shall completely master this 'science'.

(Lenin, 'A letter to the German Communists', *Collected Works*, Vol. 32, p. 522)

817. See Note 700.
818. Renato Constantino, *Synthetic Culture and Development*, Foundation for Nationalist Studies, Inc., Quezon City, 1985, pp. 64–5.
819. Kant, 'Eternal peace', pp. 448–9 of *Immanuel Kant's Moral and Political Writings*, ed. by Carl J. Friedrich, Random House, New York, 1949.
820. *Ibid.*, p. 452.
821. *Ibid.*, pp. 452–3.
822. *Ibid.*, p. 447.
823. *Ibid.*
824. *Ibid.*, pp. 449–50.
825. *Ibid.*, p. 450.
826. *Ibid.*, p. 454–5. The words 'spirit of commerce' were italicized by Kant.
    For a detailed discussion of Kant's philosophy of history see 'Kant, Hegel, Marx: historical necessity and the standpoint of political economy' in my book, *Philosophy, Ideology and Social Science*, pp. 143–95.
827. These are the most important passages in Hegel's work directly relevant to us in the present context:

International law springs from the relations between autonomous states. It is for this reason that what is absolute in it retains the form of an *ought-to-be*, since its actuality depends on different wills each of which is sovereign.

The *nation state* is mind in its substantive rationality and immediate actuality and is therefore the *absolute power on earth*. . . .

The fundamental proposition of international law . . . is that treaties as the ground of obligations between states *ought* to be kept. But since the sovereignty of a state is the principle of its relations to others, states are to that extent in a *state of nature* in relation to each other. Their rights are actualized only in their *particular* wills and not in a *universal* will with constitutional powers over them. This universal proviso of international law therefore does not go beyond an *ought-to-be*, and what really happens is that international relations in accordance with treaty alternate with the *severance* of these relations.

There is no Praetor to judge between states; at best there may be an arbitrator or a mediator, and even he exercizes his functions contingently only, i.e. in dependence on the particular wills of the disputants. Kant had an idea for securing 'perpetual peace' by a League of Nations to adjust every dispute. It was to be a power recognized by each individual state, and was to arbitrate in all cases of dissension in order to make it impossible for disputants to resort to war in order to settle them. This idea *presupposes* an accord between states; this would rest on moral or religious or other grounds and considerations, but in any case would always depend ultimately on a particular sovereign will and for that reason would remain *infected with contingency*.

It follows that if states disagree and their particular wills cannot be harmonized, the matter can only be *settled by war*.
(Hegel, *The Philosophy of Right*, pp. 212–14)

828. *Ibid.*, p. 210.
829. *Ibid.*, p. 131.
830. *Ibid.*, p. 222.
831. To quote Hegel:

It is as particular entities that states enter into relations with one another. Hence their relations are on the largest scale a *maelstrom of external contingency* and their inner particularity of passions, private interests and selfish ends, abilities and virtues, vices, force, and wrong. All these whirl together, and in their vortex the *ethical whole* itself, the autonomy of the state, is *exposed to contingency*. The principles of the national minds are wholly restricted on account of their particularity, for it is in this particularity that, as existent individuals, they have their objective actuality and their self-consciousness.
(*Ibid.*, p. 215.)

To remedy the situation, Hegel continues his argument by announcing some abstract postulates that transfer the whole problematic to the 'Philosophy of History':

Their [the national minds'] deeds and destinies in their reciprocal relations to one another are the dialectic of the finitude of these minds, and out of it arises the universal mind, the mind of the world, free from all restriction, producing itself as that which exercises its right – and its right is the highest right of all – over these finite minds in the 'history of the world which is the world's court of judgement'.
(*Ibid.*, pp. 215–16)

But just as *The Philosophy of Right* could not solve the problem as posed by Hegel himself, his *Philosophy of History*, too, fails in this respect and coils back in a circular fashion, towards the very end, at its climax in the modern, imperialistically expanding 'great state' – which submits to itself as a matter of right its smaller neighbours that are 'properly speaking, not independent, and have not the *fiery trial of war* to endure' (*The Philosophy of History*, p. 456) – into the Hegelian theory of the state as elaborated in *The Philosophy of Right*.

832. Hegel, *The Philosophy of History*, p. 457.
833. MECW, Vol. 5, p. 50.
834. *Ibid.*, p. 73.
835. *Ibid.*, p. 51.
836. *Ibid.*, pp. 73–4.
837. Quoted in Magdoff, *Imperialism: From the Colonial Age to the Present*, p. 180.
838. 'Selling off, and shrugging yet again' [Editorial], The *Guardian*, 5/2/86.
839. See the passage quoted in Note 142.
840. See Note 143.
841. Marx, 'Theses on Feuerbach', MECW, Vol. 5, pp. 3–4. The words 'practical' and 'scholastic' are italicized by Marx.
842. See Note 411.
843. See Note 410.
844. Philippe Buonarroti, *Conspiration pour l'égalité dite de Babeuf*, Brussels, 1828, p. 297. Buonarroti was a close collaborator and fellow-conspirator of Babeuf. His work describing their revolutionary undertaking and the social order which it anticipated was translated and published in 1836 by James Bronterre O'Brien. It had a by no means negligible impact on the Chartist movement.
845. Comte, *Cours de Philosophie Positive*, in G. Lenzer (ed.), *Auguste Comte and Positivism: The Essential Writings*, Harper & Row, New York, 1975, p. 215. Quoted in Jorge Larrain, *The Concept of Ideology*, Hutchinson, London, 1979, pp. 29–30. Larrain rightly comments:

> Comte has no inkling of the metaphysical character which this very statement may have. His main assumptions about the 'inevitable' lot of the majority of men and the need for the class structure in order to avoid disturbing the economy are not scientifically verified truths, even according to his own standards.
> (*Ibid.*, p. 30)

846. Hegel, *The Philosophy of Right*, p. 217.
847. *Ibid.*, pp. 215–16.
848. *Ibid.*, p. 212.
849. *Ibid.*, p. 213.
850. Hegel, *The Philosophy of History*, p. 103.
851. As Hegel put it:

> The material existence of England is based on *commerce and industry*, and the English have undertaken the weighty responsibility of being the *missionaries of civilization* to the world; for their *commercial spirit* urges them to traverse every sea and land, to form connections with barbarous peoples, to *create wants and stimulate industry*, and first and foremost to establish among them the conditions necessary to commerce, viz. the relinquishment of a life of lawless violence, *respect for property* and civility to strangers.
> (*Ibid.*, p. 455)

852. Hegel, *The Philosophy of Right*, p. 220.
853. *Ibid.*, p. 218.

854. *Ibid.*, p. 222.
855. Hegel, *The Philosophy of History*, p. 16.
856. *Ibid.*, pp. 78–9.
857. Hegel, *The Philosophy of Right*, p. 223.
858. Hegel, *The Philosophy of History*, p. 456.
859. The cynical class motivation at the root of Hegel's positive attitude to 'necessary wars' is clearly in view when he argues that: 'Successful wars have checked *domestic unrest* and consolidated the *power of the state at home.*' (*The Philosophy of Right*, p. 210.)
860. The sentence often quoted or paraphrased as the supporting ground of distorting interpretations is this; 'Religion is the opium of the people.' But the context in which it appears refutes such interpretations. For this is how the relevant Marxian passage reads:

> Religious distress is at the same time the expression of real distress and also the *protest* against real distress. Religion is the sigh of the oppressed, the *heart of a heartless world*, just as it is the spirit of spiritless conditions. It is the opium of the people.... The demand to give up illusions about the existing state of affairs is the demand to give up a state of affairs which *needs* illusions. The criticism of religion is therefore in embryo the *criticism of the vale of tears*, the halo of which is religion.... Thus the criticism of heaven turns into the *criticism of the earth*, the criticism of religion into the *criticism of law*, and the criticism of theology into the *criticism of politics*.
> (Marx, 'Contribution to Critique of Hegel's Philosophy of Law. Introduction', MECW, Vol. 3, pp. 175–6)

861. This is because political revolutions are notoriously exposed to the dangers of major reversals, and even to the possibility of the complete restoration of the earlier *status quo*.
862. Marx, *Capital*, Vol. 3, pp. 759–60.
863. Gramsci, *Selections from the Prison Notebooks*, Lawrence & Wishart, London, 1971, p. 339.
864. Gramsci, *ibid.*, p. 340.
865. Gramsci, *ibid.*, p. 341.
866. 'In Russia la guerra ha servito a spoltrire le volontà. Esse, attraverso le sofferenze accumulate in tre anni, si sono trovate all'unisono molto rapidamente. La carestia era imminente, la fame, la morte per fame poteva cogliere tutti, maciullare d'un colpo diecine di milioni di uomini. Le volontà si sono messe all'unisono.'
    Italian quotations from Gramsci's article: 'La rivoluzione contro il *Capitale*', first published in *Avanti*, 24 November 1917, here quoted from *2000 Pagine di Gramsci*, edited by Giansiro Ferrata and Niccolò Gallo, Casa Editrice Il Saggiatore, Milan, 1964, Vol. 1, p. 266.
867. 'La rivoluzione dei bolscevichi è materiata di ideologie più che di fatti. (Perciò, in fondo, poco ci importa sapere più di quanto sappiamo.) Essa è la rivoluzione contro il *Capitale* di Carlo Marx.... il pensiero marxista ... è la continuazione del pensiero idealistico italiano e tedesco, che in Marx si era contaminato di incrostazioni positivistiche e naturalistiche.... La predicazione socialista ha creato la volontà sociale del popolo russo.... Il proletariato russo, educato socialisticamente, incomincerà la sua storia dallo stadio massimo di produzione cui è arrivata l'Inghilterra oggi, perché dovendo incominciare, incomincerà dal perfetto altrove, e da questo perfetto riceverà l'impulso a raggiungere quella maturità economica che secondo Marx è

condizione necessaria del collettivismo.... Si ha l'impressione che i massi-
malisti siano stati in questo momento l'espressione spontanea, *biologicamente*
[Gramsci's italics] necessaria, perché l'umanità russa non cada nello sfacelo
più orribile.' (*Ibid.*, pp. 265–8.)

868. Gramsci, *Selections from the Prison Notebooks*, p. 342.
869. 'Il popolo russo è passato attraverso queste esperienze col pensiero, e sia pure
col pensiero di una minoranza. Ha superato queste esperienze. Se ne serve per
affermarsi ora, come si servirà delle esperienze capitalistiche occidentali per
mettersi in breve tempo *all'altezza di produzione del mondo occidentale.*
L'America del Nord è capitalisticamente più progredita dell'Inghilterra,
perché nell'America del Nord gli anglosassoni hanno incominciato *di un colpo*
dallo stadio cui l'Inghilterra era arrivata dopo lunga evoluzione.' (*2000 Pagine
di Gramsci, op. cit.,* p. 267.)

870. This is how the passage in question reads:

> It must be kept in mind that the new forces of production and relations of
> production do not develop out of *nothing*, nor drop from the sky, nor
> from the womb of self-positing Idea; but from within and in antithesis to
> the existing development of production and the inherited, traditional
> relations of property. While in the *completed* bourgeois system every
> economic relation *presupposes* every other in its bourgeois economic
> form, and *everything posited is also a presupposition*, this is the case with
> every *organic system*. This organic system itself, as a *totality* has *its
> presuppositions*, and its *development* to its totality consists precisely in
> subordinating all elements of society to itself, or in creating out of it the
> organs which it still lacks. This is *historically* how it *becomes a totality*.
> The process of becoming this totality forms a moment of its process, of its
> *development*.
> (Marx, *Grundrisse*, p. 278)

871. *Unconstitutionality*, notwithstanding all mythology to the contrary, is by no
means an exceptional aberration within the framework of liberal democracy.
It is extensively practised even at the highest levels of political decision
making, whenever it suits the convenience of the ruling order, without serious
consequences for those who resort to its methods. Significantly, they are
exempted from an adequate retribution for their actions even when the
revelations of a public scandal prove embarrassing and damaging with regard
to the professed aims and values of liberal ideology.

To take a recent example, the US Congressional Committee investigating
the 'Irangate Contra Affair' had concluded, with an overwhelming majority,
that the Reagan Administration was involved in *'subverting the Law and
undermining the Constitution'*. However, this judgement, despite its grave
implications for the rule of the law, did not affect in the slightest the President
himself; nor did it result in the introduction of the required constitutional
safeguards in order to prevent the re-occurrence of similar violations of the
Constitution in the future.

872. MECW, Vol. 5, p. 38.
873. This is how Hegel puts it:

> Philosophy concerns itself only with the glory of the Idea mirroring itself
> in the History of the World. Philosophy escapes from the weary strife
> of passions that agitate the surface of society into the calm region of
> contemplation; that which interests it is the recognition of the process of
> development which the Idea has passed through in realizing itself – i.e.

> the Idea of Freedom, whose reality is the consciousness of Freedom and nothing short of it.
>
> That the History of the World, with all the changing scenes which its annals present, is this process of development and the realization of Spirit – this is the *true Theodicaea*, the justification of God in History. Only this insight can reconcile Spirit with the History of the World – viz. that what has happened, and is happening every day, is not only not 'without God', but is essentially His Work.
> (Hegel, *The Philosophy of History*, p. 457)

874. See *ibid.*, pp. 78–9.
875. MECW, Vol. 5, pp. 77–8.
876. Marx, *Grundrisse*, p. 542.
877. *Ibid.*, pp. 543–4.
878. *Ibid.*, p. 87.
879. Enforced, for instance, in the form of the non-legally generated necessity to sell one's labour-power, as Rosa Luxemburg rightly emphasized in her critique of Bernstein.
880. Rousseau, *A Discourse on Political Economy*, Everyman Edition, p. 254.
881. Marx, *Wages, Price and Profit*, Progress Publishers, Moscow, 1947, p. 54.
882. Marx, *Grundrisse*, p. 88.
883. It is enough to recall the views of Max Weber on the subject.
884. 'Morals for the majority', unsigned editorial article representing the collective wisdom of Rupert Murdoch's *Sunday Times*, 17 July 1988.
885. *Ibid.*
886. *Ibid.*
887. *Ibid.*
888. Marx, *Capital*, Vol. 1, p. 356.
889. Raymond Aron, *The Industrial Society*, pp. 117–18.
890. MECW, Vol. 5, p. 83.
891. *Ibid.*, p. 88.
892. *Ibid.*
893. *Ibid.*
894. Raniero Panzieri, 'The capitalist use of machinery: Marx versus the "Objectivists"', in Phil Slater, ed., *Outlines of a Critique of Technology*, Ink Links, London, 1980, pp. 48 & 54–5, Panzieri's italics.

    In addition to the quoted article, this useful volume contains a general introduction by Monica Reinfelder, entitled 'Breaking the spell of technicism', Norbert Kapferer's essay on 'Commodity, science and technology: a critique of Sohn-Rethel', Hans-Dieter Bahr's study on 'The class structure of machinery: notes on the value form', and the editor's thoughtful presentation of each contribution.
895. Habermas, *Autonomy and Solidarity*, p. 214.
896. *Ibid.*, p. 91.
897. *Ibid.*, pp. 91–2.
898. *Ibid.*, p. 92.
899. As an Italian scholar – who is in many ways sympathetic to the position of German critical theory – puts it in his critique of the 'strictly procedural' and 'non-substantive' orientation of Habermas's work:

> Today social identity must contain at least one element of contents, or better one *substantive* finality: identity cannot be founded without guaranteeing the survival of humanity and the individuals which compose it. The fact that the lives of these individuals – civilized members of world

society – are endangered makes any possibility of communicative reason not contingent but *completely vain*.

(Furio Cerutti, 'Political rationality and security in the nuclear age', in *Philosophy and Social Criticism*, Vol. 13, No. 1, Fall 1987, p. 79. And Cerutti adds (on page 81) that for such considerations 'Habermas's *opus magnum* provides no conceptual space'.)

900. This is how Weber argues his 'eternalizing' case with characteristic ideological zeal presented as objective social science:

> The ruled, for their part, *cannot* dispense with or replace the bureaucratic apparatus of authority once it exists. For this bureaucracy rests upon *expert* training, a *functional specialization* of work, and an attitude set for habitual and *virtuoso-like mastery* of single yet methodically integrated functions. If the official stops working, or if his work is forcefully interrupted, *chaos results*, and it is difficult to improvise replacements from among the governed who are *fit to master such chaos*. This holds for public administration as well as for private economic management. More and more the material fate of the masses depends upon the steady and correct functioning of the *increasingly bureaucratic* organizations of private capitalism. *The idea of eliminating these organizations becomes more and more utopian.*
>
> (*From Max Weber: Essays in Sociology*, ed. by H.H. Gerth and C. Wright Mills, p. 229. The interested reader can find a discussion of Weber's highly tendentious theory of bureaucracy in my book, *Philosophy, Ideology and Social Science*.)

901. Marx, *Capital*, Vol. 1, p. 360.
902. *Ibid.*, p. 332.
903. This article by Mao Tse-tung was written in March 1926.
904. He wrote in March 1927:

> All talk directed against the peasant movement must be speedily set right. All the wrong measures taken by the revolutionary authorities concerning the peasant movement must be speedily changed. Only thus can the future of the revolution be benefited. For the present upsurge of the peasant movement is a colossal event. In a very short time, in China's central, southern and northern provinces, several hundred million peasants will rise like a mighty storm, like a hurricane, a force so swift and violent that no power, however, great, will be able to hold it back. They will smash all the trammels that bind them and rush forward along the road to liberation. They will sweep all the imperialists, warlords, corrupt officials, local tyrants and evil gentry into their graves. Every revolutionary party and every revolutionary comrade will be put to the test, to be accepted or rejected as they decide. There are three alternatives. To march at their head and lead them? To trail behind them, gesticulating and criticizing? Or to stand in their way and oppose them? Every Chinese is free to choose, but events will force you to make the choice quickly.
>
> (Mao Tse-tung, 'Report on an investigation of the peasant movement in Hunan', *Selected Works*, Foreign Languages Press, Peking, 1967, Vol. 1, pp. 23–4)

905. Mao Tse-tung, 'Analysis of the classes in Chinese society', *Selected Works*, Vol. 1, p. 19.
906. Even at the time of the anti-Japanese struggle, waged by a national alliance

in broad agreement over the need for a democratic revolution, with the immediate aim of liberation from the colonial rule, Mao Tse-tung never abandoned for a moment the global perspective of the socialist revolution. He wrote in May 1937:

> Many comrades have been asking questions about the nature of the democratic republic and its future. Our answer is: as to its class nature, the republic will be an alliance of all revolutionary classes, and as to its future, it may move towards socialism. Our democratic republic is to be established in the course of national armed resistance under the leadership of the proletariat and in the new international environment (with socialism victorious in the Soviet Union and the approach of a new period of world revolution). Therefore, though it will still be a bourgeois-democratic state socially and economically, yet it will be different from the general run of bourgeois republics because, in concrete political terms, it will have to be a state based on the alliance of the working class, the peasantry, the petty bourgeoisie and the bourgeoisie. Thus, as to the future of the democratic republic, though it may move in a capitalist direction, the possibility also exists that it will turn towards socialism, and the party of the Chinese proletariat should struggle hard for the latter prospect.
> (Mao Tse-tung, 'The tasks of the Chinese Communist Party in the period of resistance to Japan', *Selected Works*, Vol. 1, p. 275)

907. Marx, *Ibid.*, pp. 330–1.
908. Jacob Vanderlint, *Money Answers All Things*, London, 1734, p. 11.
909. Marx, *Capital*, Vol. 1, p. 331.
910. *Ibid.*, p. 332.
911. *Ibid.*, p. 364.
912. Cf. the relationship between 'absolute' and 'relative surplus-value', for instance.
913. See the practice of capital-exports, etc.
914. As an example of the kind of contradictory yet highly successful exploitative relations instituted under the rule of capital in all parts of the global economic system, we may think of the development of capitalism in India as described by Marx:

> In consequence of the great *demand for cotton* after 1861, the production of cotton, in some thickly populated district of India, was extended *at the expense of rice cultivation*. In consequence there arose *local famines*, the defective means of communication not permitting the failure of rice in one district to be compensated by importation from another.
> (Marx, *ibid.*, p. 353)

One hundred and twenty five years later we are still haunted by the same phenomenon. The differences are that now we must speak of '*cash-crops*' in general, not merely of 'King cotton', and that the 'local famines' occur not only in India but all over the world. Wherever, that is, the capitalistic profitability of cash-crops ruthlessly overrules even the most elementary need (and right) for survival of the local population, notwithstanding the self-congratulatory rhetoric of the 'Rights of Man' at the beneficiary centres of global exploitation.

Equally, the 'means of communication' are improved only when the conditions of capital's continued profitability require it. However, they can indeed be improved for that purpose. For the uniqueness of capital's 'refined and civilized method of exploitation' stands in the sharpest possible contrast to the earlier modalities of plunder. As is well known, the primitive and barbarian plunderers had to *move on* after accomplishing their shortsighted deed, destroying thereby, within a very short period of time, the material ground on which they could function. As against that, capital's 'civilized barbarism' resides precisely in its power to plunder and *stay on* for a sustained historical phase, compensating for a considerable period of time even for its directly lost territories in different parts of the world. Capital can do this by constantly refining and perfecting the forms and modalities of plunder under the pressure of having to displace its own contradictions. As far as the latter is concerned, of all varieties of such displacement by far the most important one for the survival of this mode of social control consists in capital's ability to restructure its originally crude '*extensive totality*' into a primarily *intensive totality* of exploitation.

915. Marx, *Critique of the Gotha Programme*.
916. This is how Marx describes the material prerequisites and productive requirements of the 'true realm of freedom' in which work becomes an 'end in itself':

> Freedom in this field can only consist in *socialized man*, the *associated producers*, rationally regulating their interchange with Nature, bringing it under their common control, instead of being ruled by it as by the blind forces of Nature; and achieving this with the least expenditure of energy and *under conditions most favourable to, and worthy of, their human nature*. But it nonetheless still remains a realm of necessity. Beyond it begins that development of human energy which is an *end in itself*, the *true realm of freedom*, which, however, can blossom forth only with this realm of necessity as its basis. The shortening of the working day is its basic prerequisite.
> (Marx, *Capital*, Vol. 3, p. 800)

917. See note no. 873. For Hegel's discussion of the principle of individuality in the modern age, see pp. 452–7 of *The Philosophy of History*.
918. See Note 435.
919. See Note 201.
920. See Note 224.
921. Vicente Navarro, 'Social movements and class politics in the US', *The Socialist Register*, ed. Ralph Miliband, Leo Panitch and John Saville, Merlin Press, London, 1988, pp. 432–3.
922. Brian Walden, 'Clues that tell why Dukakis is a Labour hero', *The Sunday Times*, 31 July 1988.
923. See Section 9.1.3.
924. This book exercised a lasting influence all over the world. See also Paul Sweezy's *Five Lectures on Marxism* which put into focus with exemplary clarity the meaning of the Marxian legacy and its continued relevance to the problems of the capitalistically advanced societies.
925. Baran is referring here to Walt Rostow's book, *The Stages of Economic Growth: A Non-Communist Manifesto*.
926. Paul Baran, 'An alternative to Marxism', first published in *Monthly Review*, March 1965; republished in Baran's posthumous volume of essays, *The Longer View: Essays Toward a Critique of Political Economy*, Monthly Review Press, New York, 1969. The quotation is from pp. 50–1 of this volume.
927. Harry Braverman, 'Two comments', in *Technology, the Labour Process and the Working Class*, Monthly Review Press, New York and London, 1976, p. 124.

BIBLIOGRAPHY

Adorno, T.W., article in *Die Süddeutsche Zeitung*, 26–7 April 1969.
  Aesthetic Theory, London, 1984.
  Minima Moralia: Reflections from Damaged Life, London, 1974.
  Negative Dialectics, New York, 1973.
  Prisms, London, 1967,
  'Commitment', in Adorno *et al.* (see Note 309), *Aesthetics and Politics*, London, 1977.
  'Lyric poetry and society', *Telos*, No. 20, Summer 1974.
  'Reconciliation under duress', in Adorno *et al.*, *Aesthetics and Politics*, London, 1977; originally in German, 'Erpresste Versoehnung', *Der Monat*, November 1958.
  Introduction to *The Positivist Dispute in German Sociology*, London, 1976.
Adorno, T.W., and Horkheimer, M., *Dialectic of Enlightenment*, New York, 1972.
Aiken, H.D., 'The revolt against ideology', *Commentary*, April 1964.
Albertini, M., 'New culture or new politics', *Comunità*, August–September 1958.
Althusser, L., *Montesquieu, Rousseau, Marx*, London, 1982.
  'Ideology and the state' (1969), in *Lenin and Philosophy and Other Essays*, London, 1971.
  'Marx's relation to Hegel' (1968), in *Montesquieu, Rousseau, Marx*, London, 1982.
Amin, S., *Imperialism and Unequal Development*, Hassocks, 1977.
Anderson, P., *Considerations on Western Marxism*, London, 1976.
Antunes, R., *Classe operária, sindicatos e partido no Brasil*, São Paulo, 1982.
Apter, D. (ed.), *Ideology and Discontent*, New York, 1964.
Aron, R., *History and the Dialectic of Violence*, Oxford, 1975, (originally published in Paris, 1973).
  18 Lectures on Industrial Society, London, 1967.
  Marxismes imaginaires, Paris, 1970.
  The Industrial Society: Three Essays on Ideology and Development, New York, 1967.
  The Opium of the Intellectuals: The End of the Ideological Age?, London, 1957.
  'Development theory and evolutionism', in Aron, *The Industrial Society*.
  'The epoch of universal technology', *Encounter*, June 1964.
  'The end of the ideological age?', in Chaim I. Waxman (ed.), *The End of Ideology Debate*, New York, 1968.
Arrighi, G., *The Geometry of Imperialism*, London, 1978.
Arthur, C., *Dialectics of Labour: Marx and His Relation to Hegel*, Oxford, 1986.
Austin, J.L., Contribution to 'Cahiers de Royaumont', *Philosophie No. IV: La Philosophie Analytique*.
Baran, P.A., *The Political Economy of Growth*, New York, 1957.
  The Longer View: Essays Toward a Critique of Political Economy, New York, 1969.
Baran, P.A. and Sweezy, P.M., *Monopoly Capital*, New York, 1966.

Barthes, R., *Selected Writings*, London, 1982.
Baudrillard, J., *Le système des objets*, Paris, 1968.
La société de consommation: ses mythes, ses structures, Paris, 1970.
Bell, D., 'Unstable America', *Encounter*, June 1970.
The Coming of Post-Industrial Society: A Venture in Social Forecasting, New York, 1976 (first edn 1973).
The End of Ideology, New York, 1965.
The Cultural Contradictions of Capitalism, New York, 1976.
Benewick, R., Berki, R.N. and Parekh, B. (eds), *Knowledge and Belief in Politics: The Problem of Ideology*, London, 1973.
Benjamin, W., *Illuminations*, London, 1970.
Bennington, G., *Writing the Event*, Manchester, 1988.
Benton, T., 'Natural science and cultural struggle: Engels on philosophy and the natural sciences', in Mepham, J. and Ruben, D.-H. (eds), *Issues in Marxist Philosophy*, Brighton, 1979.
Bernal, J.D., *The Social Function of Science*, London, 1939.
Bernstein, E., *Evolutionary Socialism*, New York, 1961.
Bernstein, R.J. (ed.), *Habermas and Modernity*, Cambridge, 1985.
The Restructuring of Social and Political Theory, Oxford, 1976.
Bhagavan, M.R., 'A critique of India's economic policies and strategies', *Monthly Review*, July–August 1987.
Blackburn, R. (ed.), *Ideology in Social Science: Readings in Critical Social Theory*, London, 1972.
Bloch, E., *Natural Law and Human Dignity*, Cambridge, Mass., 1986.
The Utopian Function of Art and Literature, Cambridge, Mass., 1988.
Bobbio, N., *Quale socialismo? Discussione di un'alternativa*, Turin, 1976.
The Future of Democracy, Cambridge, 1987.
Bottomore, T.B., *Sociology and Socialism*, Brighton, 1984.
(ed.), *A Dictionary of Marxist Thought*, Oxford, 1983.
Braverman, H., *Labor and Monopoly Capital: The Degradation of Work in the Twentieth Century*, New York, 1974.
'Two comments', in *Technology, the Labour Process and the Working Class*, New York, 1976.
Brown, M.B., *After Imperialism*, London, 1963.
Buck-Morss, S., *The Origin of Negative Dialectics: Theodor W. Adorno, Walter Benjamin, and the Frankfurt Institute*, Hassocks, 1977.
Bunge, H., *Fragen Sie mehr über Brecht: Hanns Eisler in Gespräch*, Munich, 1970.
Buonarroti, P., *Conspiration pour l'égalité dite de Babeuf*, Brussels, 1828.
Callinicos, A., *Making History: Agency, Structure and Change in Social Theory*, Oxford, 1987.
Carroll, D., *Paraesthetics: Foucault, Lyotard, Derrida*, London, 1987.
Cases, C., *Marxismo e neopositivismo*, Turin, 1958.
Su Lukács: Vicende di un'interpretazione, Turin, 1985.
'La "mauvaise époque" e i suoi tagli', Belfagor, Anno xxxii., No. 6, November 1977.
'Walter Benjamin, *Briefe*, herausgegeben und mit Anmerkungen versehen von Gershom Scholem und Theodor W. Adorno', *Studi Germanici*, nuova serie, Anno vi., No. 2.
Cerutti, F., 'Political rationality and security in the nuclear age', *Philosophy and Social Criticism*, Vol. 13, No. 1, Fall 1987.
Chase, E.T., 'Politics and technology' in Douglas, J.D. (ed.), *The Technological Threat*, New Jersey, 1971.

Chasin, J., *O integralismo de Plinio Salgado*, Sáo Paulo, 1978.

Clarke, S., 'Althusserian Marxism', in Clarke, S. *et al.*, *One-Dimensional Marxism: Althusser and the Politics of Culture*, London, 1980.

Clark, R.W., *Einstein: The Life and Times*, London, 1973.

Clegg, S. and Dunkerley, D., *Organization, Class and Control*, London, 1980.

Clegg, S., Boreham, P. and Dow, G., *Class, Politics and the Economy*, London, 1986.

Colletti, L., *Il marxismo e Hegel*, Bari, 1969.

Introduction to Lenin's *Philosophical Notebooks*, Rome, 1958.

Tra marxismo e no, Bari, 1979.

'La crisi del marxismo', *Mondoperaio*, November 1977.

Constantino, R., *Neo-colonial Identity and Counter-Consciousness: Essays in Cultural Decolonization*, London, 1978.

Synthetic Culture and Development, Quezon City, 1985.

The Nationalist Alternative, Quezon City, 1986.

Contat, M. and Rybalka, M. (eds), *Les Ecrits de Sartre: Chronologie, bibliographie commentée*, Paris, 1970.

della Volpe, G., *Rousseau and Marx and Other Writings*, London, 1978.

Critique of Taste, London, 1978, (Italian edition, 1960).

Logic as a Positive Science, London, 1980 (Italian editions, 1950 and 1969).

'L'estetica del carro armato', *Primato*, 1942.

Deleuze, G. and Guattari, F., *A Thousand Plateaus: Capitalism and Schizophrenia*, London, 1987.

Derrida, J., *Of Grammatology*, Baltimore, 1977.

Writing and Difference, London, 1978.

Spurs: Nietzsche's Styles, Chicago, 1979.

Positions, London, 1981.

The Postcard, Chicago, 1987.

The Truth in Painting, Chicago, 1987.

de Tracy, D., *Eléments d'idéologie*, Paris, 1827.

Dews, P. (ed.), *Autonomy and Solidarity*, interviews with Jürgen Habermas, London, 1986.

Logics of Disintegration: Post-Structuralist Thought and the Claims of Critical Theory, London, 1987.

Documents of the First International, London, n.d.

Douglas, J.D., 'The impact of technology on political values' in Douglas, J.D. (ed.), *The Technological Threat*, New Jersey, 1971.

Douglas, M., *In the Active Voice*, London, 1982.

How Institutions Think, London, 1987.

Dowling, W.C., *Jameson, Althusser, Marx: An Introduction to the Political Unconscious*, London, 1984.

Durham, T., 'Fifth generation fever', *Practical Computing*, Vol. 7, October 1984.

Drachkovitch, M.M. (ed.), *Marxist Ideology in the Contemporary World: Its Appeals and Paradoxes*, New York, 1966.

Drucker, H.M., *The Political Uses of Ideology*, London, 1974.

Dumont, L., *From Mandeville to Marx: The Genesis and Triumph of Economic Ideology*, Chicago, 1977.

Durkheim, E., *The Division of Labour in Society*, Chicago, 1947.

Eagleton, T., *Criticism and Ideology*, London, 1976.

Edgley, R., 'Dialectic: the contradiction of Colletti', *Critique*, No. VII, Winter 1976–7.

'Marx's revolutionary science', in Mepham, J. and Ruben, D.-H. (eds), *Issues in*

Marxist Philosophy, Brighton, 1979.
Editorial, The *Guardian*, 5 February 1986.
Editorial, *The Sunday Times*, 21 October 1984.
Editorial, *The Sunday Times*, 17 July 1988.
Einstein, A., *The Born Einstein Letters*, London, 1971.
    Einstein on Peace, eds Otto Nathan and Heinz Norden, New York, 1960.
    'Why socialism?', *Monthly Review*, May 1949.
Ellul, J., *The Technological Society*, New York, 1967.
Emmanuel, A., *Appropriate or Underdeveloped Technology*, Chichester, 1982.
    Unequal Exchange: A Study of the Imperialism of Trade, New York, 1972.
Engels, F., *Anti-Dühring: Herr Eugen Dühring's Revolution in Science*
    Dialectic of Nature
    Outlines of a Critique of Political Economy
    The Origin of the Family, Private Property and the State
Ennals, R., *Star Wars: A Question of Initiative*, (unpubl.)
Fahrenbach, H. (ed.), *Wirklichkeit und Reflexion: Walter Schulz zum 60. Geburtstag*, Pfullingen, 1973.
Ferguson, A., *Essay on the History of Civil Society* (1767), edited with an introduction by Ducan Forbes, Edinburgh, 1966.
Feyerabend, P., *Against Method: Outline of an Anarchistic Theory of Knowledge*, Lodon, 1975.
Flynn, J.R., *Humanism and Ideology: An Aristotelian View*, London, 1973.
Fortini, F., *Insistenze: Cinquanta scritti 1976–1984*, Milan, 1985.
    Saggi Italiani and *Nuovi Saggi Italiani*, Milan, 1987.
Foster, J.B., *The Theory of Monopoly Capitalism: An Elaboration of Marxian Political Economy*, New York, 1986.
Foster, J.B. and Szlajfer, H. (eds), *The Faltering Economy: The Problem of Accumulation Under Monopoly Capitalism*, New York, 1984.
Foucault, M., *The Order of Things*, London, 1970.
    Madness and Civilization: A History of Insanity in the Age of Reason, New York, 1965.
    Discipline and Punish: The Birth of the Prison, London, 1977.
Frisby, D., *Fragments of Modernity*, Oxford, 1985.
Fröhlich, P., *Rosa Luxemburg: Her Life and Work*, (Paris, 1939), New York, 1972.
Gadamer, H.-G., *Truth and Method*, London, 1979.
Galbraith, J.K., *American Capitalism: The Concept of Countervailing Power*, Harmondsworth, 1963.
    The Affluent Society, Harmondsworth, 1962, (first edn 1958).
    The Great Crash 1929, Harmondsworth, 1961.
    The New Industrial State, revised and updated edition, New York, 1971.
Gane, M. (ed.), *Towards a Critique of Foucault*, London, 1986.
Gehlen, A., *Studien zur Anthropologie und Soziologie*, Berlin, 1963.
Geiger, T., *Ideologie und Wahrheit*, Neuwied, 1968.
Gerth, H.H. and Mills, C.W. (eds), *From Max Weber: Essays in Sociology*, London, 1948.
Geuss, R., *The Idea of a Critical Theory: Habermas and the Frankfurt School*, Oxford, 1976.
Gilly, A., *Sacerdotes y burócratas*, Mexico, 1980.
Giordani, J. A., *Planificación, Ideologia y Estado: El Caso de Venezuela*, Valencia, 1986.
Goldmann, L., Preface to the New Edition (1966) of *The Human Sciences and Philosophy*, London 1969.

Recherches dialectiques, Paris, 1959.

González, J., Pereyra, C. and Vargas Lozano, G. (eds), *Praxis y Filosofia: Ensayos en homenaje a Adolfo Sánchez Vázquez*, Mexico/Barcelona/Buenos Aires, 1985.

Gorz, A., *Farewell to the Working Class: An Essay on Post-Industrial Socialism*, London, 1982.

Gouldner, A.W., *The Dialectic of Ideology and Technology: The Origins, Grammar and Future of Ideology*, New York, 1976.

Gramsci, A., *Selections from the Prison Notebooks*, London, 1971.

'La rivoluzione contro il *Capitale*', *Avanti*, 24 November 1917, in Ferrata, G. and Gallo, N., (eds), *2000 Pagine di Gramsci*, Milano, 1964.

Gromyko, A., *The Overseas Expansion of Capital, Past and Present*, Moscow, 1985.

Guariglia, O.N., *Ideologia, verdad y legitimación*, Buenos Aires, 1986.

Habermas, J., *Knowledge and Human Interests*, London, 1972.

'A reply to my critics', in Thompson, J.B. and Held, D., (eds), *Habermas: Critical Debates*, London 1982.

'Neo-conservative culture criticism in the United States and West Germany: an intellectual movement in two political cultures', in Bernstein (ed.), *Habermas and Modernity*. 'Vorbereitende Bemerkungen zu einer Theorie der kommunikativen Kompetenz', in J. Habermas and Niklas Luhmann, *Theorie der Gesellschaft oder Sozialtechnologie – Was Leistet die Systemforschung?*, Frankfurt, 1971.

'Wahrheitstheorien', in Fahrenbach, H. (ed.), *Wirklichkeit und Reflexion: Walter Schulz zum 60. Geburtstag*, Pfullingen, 1973.

Legitimation Crisis, Boston, 1975.

Philosophical-Political Profiles, Cambridge, Mass., 1983.

The Theory of Communicative Action, Vol. 1: *Reason and the Rationalization of Society*, London, 1984.

Toward a Rational Society, London, 1971.

'Summation and response', *Continuum*, Vol. 8, No. 1–2, Spring-Summer 1970.

'A Reply to Müller and Neusüss', *Telos*, No. 25, Fall 1975.

Autonomy and Solidarity, Interviews edited and introduced by Peter Dews, London, 1986.

Hacker, A., *Political Theory, Philosophy, Ideology, Science*, New York, 1961.

Hamouda, O.F. and Smithin, J.N. (eds), *Keynes and Public Policy After Fifty Years*, Aldershot, 1988.

Hegel, G.F.W., *Logic: Part One of the Encyclopaedia of the Philosophical Sciences*, Oxford, 1975.

The Philosophy of History, New York, 1956.

The Philosophy of Right, Oxford, 1942.

The Science of Logic, London, 1929.

Held, D., *Introduction to Critical Theory: Horkheimer to Habermas*, London, 1980.

Hoffman, J., *The Gramscian Challenge; Coercion and Consent in Marxist Political Theory*, Oxford, 1984.

Honneth, A., Knoedler-Bonte, E. and Widmann, A., 'The dialectic of rationalization: an interview with Jürgen Habermas', *Telos*, No. 49, Fall 1981.

Horkheimer, M., *Critical Theory: Selected Essays*, New York, 1972.

Howard, D. (ed.), *Selected Political Writings of Rosa Luxemburg*, New York, 1971.

Husserl, E., *Cartesian Meditations*, The Hague, 1969.

Jakubowski, F., *Ideology and Superstructure*, London, 1976.

Jameson, F., 'Reflections in conclusion', in Adorno *et al.*, *Aesthetics and Politics*, London, 1977.

'Postmodernism, or the cultural logic of late capitalism', *New Left Review*, No. 146, July-August 1984.

Jay, M., *Adorno*, London, 1984.

'The Frankfurt School's critique of Karl Mannheim and the Sociology of Knowledge', *Telos*, No. 20, Summer 1974.

Marxism and Totality: The Adventures of a Concept from Lukács to Habermas, Cambridge, 1984.

Károlyi, M., *Memorie di un Patriota*, Milan, 1958.

Kant, I., *Critique of Pure Reason*, London, 1934.

'Eternal peace', in Friedrich, C.J. (ed.), *Immanuel Kant's Moral and Political Writings*, New York, 1949.

Karnoouh, C., 'The Lost Paradise of regionalism: the crisis of post-modernity in France', *Telos*, No. 67, Spring 1986.

Keynes, J.M., *The General Theory of Employment, Interest and Money*, London, 1936.

'A short view of Russia' (1925); 'Am I a liberal?' (1925); 'Economic possibilities for our grandchildren' (1930); 'The end of laissez-faire' (1926), all republished in *Essays in Persuasion*, New York, 1963.

Kolko, J., *Restructuring the World Economy*, New York, 1988.

Korsch, K., *Marxism and Philosophy*, London, 1970.

Krahl, H.-J., 'Antwort an Jürgen Habermas', in Krahl, *Konstitution und Klassenkampf: Zur historischen Dialektik von bürgerlicher Emanzipation und proletarischer Revolution*, Frankfurt, 1971.

'The political contradictions in Adorno's critical theory', *Telos*, No. 21, Fall 1974.

Kroker, A. and Cook, D., *The Postmodern Scene: Excremental Culture and Hyper-Aesthetics*, London, 1988.

Kruks, S., *The Political Philosophy of Merleau-Ponty*, Brighton, 1981.

Larrain, J., *The Concept of Ideology*, London, 1979.

Lawson, H., *Reflexivity: The Post-Modern Predicament*, London, 1985.

Lévi-Strauss, C., *The Savage Mind*, London, 1966.

Structural Anthropology, New York, 1967.

'Plus loin avec C. L-S', Interview with Claude Lévi-Strauss, *L'Express*, No. 1027, 15–21 March 1971.

Lenin, V.I., *Collected Works*, London, 1960ff.

Imperialism, the Highest Stage of Capitalism
Philosophical Notebooks
'Left-Wing' Communism – An Infantile Disorder
The State and Revolution
'Notes of a publicist'
'One step forward, t⁺ steps back: reply to Rosa Luxemburg'
'The Junius pamphlet'
'The right of nations to self-determination'
'Unity'
'A letter to the German Communists'

Levi, P., *Die russische Revolution. Eine kritische Würdigung. Aus dem Nachlass von Rosa Luxemburg*, Berlin, 1922.

Lenzer, G. (ed.), *Auguste Comte and Positivism: The Essential Writings*, New York, 1975.

Lichtheim, G., *The Concept of Ideology and Other Essays*, New York, 1967.

Liebmann, O., *Kant und die Epigonen*, Leipzig, 1865.

Lockwood, D., *The Black-Coated Worker. A Study in Class Consciousness*,

London, 1958.
Luhmann, N., *A Sociological Theory of Law*, London, 1985.
Lukács, G., *History and Class Conciousness*, London, 1971.
   La lotta fra progresso e reazione nella cultural d'oggi, Milan, 1957.
   The Destruction of Reason, London, 1980.
   The Theory of the Novel, London, 1978.
   'Az erkölcs szerepe a komunista termelésben', *Szocialista Termelés*, 1919.
   'Party and class' in Lukács, *Political Writings 1919–1929*, London, 1972, first
   published in Hungarian as 'The theoretical significance of the restoration of
   proletarian unity' in a pamphlet, *Documents of Unity*, Budapest, 1919.
   'The role of morality in communist production', in Lukács, *Political Writings
   1919–1929*, London, 1972.
   The Ontology of Social Being: Hegel, Marx, Labour, London, 1978–80.
Luporini, C., 'Marx/Luhmann: trasformare il mondo o governarlo?', *Problemi del
   Socialismo*, Anno XXII, May-August 1981.
Luxemburg, R., *Reform or Revolution*, New York, 1970. First published as two
   articles in *Leipziger Volkszeitung*, 1898 and 1899.
   Spartacus, London, 1971.
   The Junius Pamphlet: The Crisis in the German Social Democracy, Colombo,
   1967.
   The Russian Revolution, Michigan, 1961.
   'Organizational questions of the Russian social democracy', published as 'Leni-
   nism or Marxism' in *The Russian Revolution*, Michigan, 1961.
   The National Question, (ed. by H.B. Davies), New York, 1976.
Lyotard, J.-F., *Just Gaming*, Manchester, 1985.
   'On Terror and the Sublime', *Telos*, No. 67, Spring 1986.
   Driftworks, New York, 1984.
   The Postmodern Condition: A Report on Knowledge, Manchester, 1986.
MacIntyre, A.C., *Against the Self-Images of the Age: Essays on Ideology and
   Philosophy*, New York, 1971.
Macpherson, C.B., 'A political theory of property', in Macpherson, *Democratic
   Theory: Essays in Retrieval*, Oxford, 1973.
McCarney, J., *The Real World of Ideology*, Brighton, 1980.
   'What makes critical theory "critical"?', *Radical Philosophy*, No. 42, Winter/
   Spring 1986.
McCarthy, T., 'Rationality and relativism: Habermas's "overcoming" of herme-
   neutics', in Thompson, J.B. and Held, D. (eds), *Habermas: Critical Debates*,
   London, 1982.
   'Reflections on rationalization in the *Theory of Communicative Action*', in
   Bernstein, R.J. (ed.), *Habermas and Modernity*, Cambridge, 1985.
Magdoff, H., *The Age of Imperialism: The Economics of U.S. Foreign Policy*,
   New York, 1969.
   'China: contrasts with the U.S.S.R.', *Monthly Review*, July–August 1975.
   Imperialism: From the Colonial Age to the Present, New York, 1978.
Mallet, Serge, *La nouvelle classe ouvrière*, Paris, 1963; in English, *The New
   Working Class*, Nottingham, 1975.
Manning, D.J. (ed.), *The Form of Ideology*, London, 1980.
Mannheim, K., *Ideology and Utopia*, London, 1936.
   Man and Society in an Age of Reconstruction, London, 1940.
   Essays on the Sociology of Knowledge, London, 1952.
   Essays on the Sociology of Culture, London, 1956.
Mao Tse-tung, 'Report on an investigation of the peasant movement in Hunan',
   Selected Works, Peking, 1967.

'The tasks of the Communist Party in the period of resistance to Japan', *Selected Works*, Peking, 1967.

Marcuse, H., *An Essay on Liberation*, London, 1969.

Die Permanenz der Kunst, Munich, 1977, ('The Permanence of Art'), published in English under the title *The Aesthetic Dimension*, London, 1979.

One Dimensional Man, London, 1964.

Studies in Critical Philosophy, London, 1972.

Marx, K., *Contribution to Critique of Hegel's Philosophy of Law*

Economic and Philosophical Manuscripts of 1844

The Holy Family

The Poverty of Philosophy

A Contribution to the Critique of Political Economy

Wages, Prices and Profit

The Class Struggles in France 1848–1850

The Eighteenth Brumaire of Louis Bonaparte

Grundrisse

Capital

The Civil War in France

'Conspectus of Bakunin's book: *State and Anarchy*', in Marx, Engels, Lenin, *Anarchism and Anarcho-Syndicalism*, Moscow, 1972.

Critique of the Gotha Programme

'Marginal notes on Wagner'

Correspondence, MECW, Vols 38ff.

Marx and Engels, *The German Ideology*

The Communist Manifesto

Mattick, P., *Critique of Marcuse: One-Dimensional Man in Class Society*, London, 1972.

Mayer, G., *Bismarck and Lassalle*, Berlin, 1928.

Mattelart, A., *Mass Media, Ideologies and the Revolutionary Movement*, Brighton, 1980.

Mepham, J., 'The theory of ideology in Capital', *Radical Philosophy*, No. 2, Summer 1972.

Mepham, J. and Ruben, D.-H. (eds), *Issues in Marxist Philosophy*, Brighton, 1979.

Merleau-Ponty, M., *Adventures of the Dialectic*, London, 1974 (first published in 1955).

'On Indo-China', *Signs*, Chicago, 1964.

'On Madagascar' (interview first published in *L'Express*, 21 August 1958), *Signs*.

'Paranoid politics', *Signs*.

'The U.S.S.R. and the camps', *Signs*.

'Tommorrow ...' (an interview given in July 1958), *Signs*.

Mészáros, I, 'Customs, tradition, legality: a key problem in the dialectic of base and superstructure', in Outhwaite, W. and Mulkay, M. (eds), *Social Theory and Social Criticism: Essays for Tom Bottomore*, Oxford, 1987.

Marx's Theory of Alienation, London, 1970.

Philosophy, Ideology and Social Science, Brighton, 1986.

The Necessity of Social Control, London, 1971.

'Il rinnovamento del marxismo e l'attualitá storica dell'offensiva socialista', *Problemi del Socialismo*, No. 23, January–April 1982.

'Political power and dissent in postrevolutionary societies', *New Left Review*, No. 108, March–April 1978.

'The cunning of history in reverse gear', *Radical Philosophy*, No. 42, Winter/Spring 1986.

Mészáros, I. (ed.), *Aspects of History and Class Consciousness*, London, 1971.

Miller, D., *Philosophy and Ideology in Hume's Political Thought*, Oxford, 1981.
Miller, J., Review of Habermas's *Legitimation Crisis*, *Telos*, No. 25, Fall 1975.
Miller, P., *Domination and Power*, London, 1987.
Mills, C.W., 'Liberal values in the modern world', in Douglas, J.D. (ed.), *The Technological Threat*, New Jersey, 1971.
White Collar: The American Middle Classes, New York, 1951.
The Power Elite, New York, 1956.
The Sociological Imagination, New York, 1959.
The Marxists, New York, 1962.
Montefiore, A., 'Fact, value and ideology', in Williams, B. and Montefiore, A. (eds), *British Analytical Philosophy*, London, 1966.
Moss, N., *Men Who Play God. The Story of the Hydrogen Bomb*, Harmondsworth, 1968.
Müller, W. and Neusüss, C., 'The illusion of state socialism and the contradiction between wage labour and capital', *Telos*, No. 25, Fall 1975.
Nathan, O. and Norden, H. (eds), *Einstein on Peace*, New York, 1960.
Navarro, V., 'Social movements and class politics in the US', *The Socialist Register*, ed. by Ralph Miliband, Leo Panitch and John Saville, London, 1988.
Needham, J., *Science and Civilization in Ancient China*, Cambridge, 1954–65.
Neto, J.P., *Capitalismo e reificação*, São Paulo, 1981.
Norman, R., *Free and Equal: A Philosophical Examination of Political Values*, Oxford, 1987.
Norris, C., *Deconstruction: Theory and Practice*, London, 1982.
The Deconstructive Turn: Essays in the Rhetoric of Philosophy, London, 1983.
Offe, C., 'Further comments on Müller and Neussüs', *Telos*, No. 25, Fall 1975.
Disorganized Capitalism: The Transformation of Work and Politics, Cambridge, 1985.
Outhwaite, W. and Mulkay, M. (eds), *Social Theory and Social Criticism: Essays for Tom Bottomore*, Oxford, 1987.
Panzieri, R., 'The capitalist use of machinery: Marx versus the "objectivists"', in Slater, P. (ed.), *Outlines of a Critique of Technology*, London, 1980.
Parekh, B., *Marx's Theory of Ideology*, London, 1982.
Parsons, T., *The Social System*, London, 1951.
'Social class and class conflict in the light of recent sociological theory', *American Economic Review*, Vol. 39, 1949, reprinted in Parsons, *Essays in Sociological Theory*, New York, 1954.
Pecheux, M., *Language, Semantics and Ideology*, New York, 1981.
Pippin, R., Feenberg, A., and Webel, C.P. (eds), *Marcuse: Critical Theory and the Promise of Utopia*, London, 1988.
Plamenatz, J., *Ideology*, London, 1970.
Popper, K., 'Reason or revolution?', in Adorno, T.W. *et al.*, *The Positivist Dispute in German Sociology*, London, 1976.
Poster, M., *Foucault, Marxism and History: Mode of Production versus Mode of Information*, Oxford, 1984.
Prado Júnior, C., *História econômica do Brazil*, São Paulo, 1983.
Rabinow, P. (ed.), *The Foucault Reader*, New York, 1984.
Rancière, J., 'On the theory of ideology: the politics of Althusser', *Radical Philosophy*, No. 7, Spring 1974.
Raulet, G., 'From modernity as one-way street to postmodernity as dead end', *New German Critique*, No. 33, Fall 1984.
'Marxism and the postmodern condition', *Telos*, No. 67, Spring 1986.
Rhodes, R. (ed.), *Imperialism and Underdevelopment*, New York, 1970.

Roosevelt, F.D., *Nothing Fear: The Selected Addresses of F.D. Roosevelt 1932–1945*, London, 1947.
Rorty, R., 'Habermas and Lyotard on postmodernity', in R.J. Bernstein (ed.), *Habermas and Modernity*, Cambridge, 1985.
Rose, G., *The Melancholy Science: An Introduction to the Thought of Theodor W. Adorno*, London, 1978.
Rose, H. and S., *Science and Society*, Harmondsworth, 1970.
Rose, H. and S. (eds), *The Political Economy of Science*, London, 1976.
Rostow, W.W., *The Stages of Economic Growth*, Cambridge, 1960.
Rousseau, J.-J., *The Social Contract*, London, 1958.
   Troisième Dialogue, Oeuvres Complètes, Paris, 1967.
   A Discourse on Political Economy, London, 1958.
Russell, B., *Power: A New Social Analysis*, London, 1962.
   The Impact of Science on Society, London, 1968.
Sánchez Vázquez, A., 'Racionalismo tecnologico, ideologia y politica', *Dialéctica*, June 1983.
   Ensayos marxistas sobre filosofia e ideologia, Barcelona, 1983.
   Ciencia y revolutión: El marxismo de Althusser, Madrid, 1978.
Sartre, J.-P., *The Problem of Method*, London, 1963.
   Critique of Dialectical Reason, London, 1976.
   'Le réformisme et les fétiches', *Les Temps Modernes*, February 1956.
Sartre, J.-P. and Merleau-Ponty, M., exchange in *Comprendre*, September 1956. (See Note 436.)
Seliger, M., *Ideology and Politics*, London, 1976.
   The Marxist Conception of Ideology: A Critical Essay, Cambridge, 1977.
Sim, S., 'Lyotard and the politics of antifoundationalism', *Radical Philosophy*, No. 44, Autumn 1986.
Singer, D., *The Road to Gdansk*, New York, 1981.
   Is Socialism Doomed?: The Meaning of Mitterrand, New York, 1988.
Slater, P. (ed.), *Outlines of a Critique of Technology*, London, 1980.
Smart, B., *Foucault, Marxism and Critique*, London, 1983.
Smart, N., *Beyond Ideology: Religion and the Future of Western Civilization*, Cambridge, 1981.
Sohn-Rethel, A., *Geistige und Körperliche Arbeit: zur Theorie der gesellschaftlichen Synthesis*, Frankfurt, 1970.
Sweezy, P.M., *The Theory of Capitalist Development*, New York, 1942.
   The Present as History, New York, 1953.
   Modern Capitalism and Other Essays, New York, 1972.
   Four Lectures on Marxism, New York, 1981.
Sweezy, P.M. and Magdoff, H., *The Dynamics of US Capitalism*, New York, 1972.
Tawney, R.H., *Equality*, London, 1931.
   The Acquisitive Society, London, 1921.
Taylor, F.W., *Scientific Management*, New York, 1947.
Thompson, E.P., *The Poverty of Theory*, London, 1978.
Thompson, J.B., *Critical Hermeneutics: A Study in the Thought of Paul Ricoeur and Jürgen Habermas*, Cambridge, 1981.
   Studies in the Theory of Ideology, Cambridge, 1984.
   'Universal pragmatics', in Thompson, J.B. and Held, D. (eds), *Habermas: Critical Debates*, London, 1982.
Titmuss, Richard M., *Income Distribution and Social Change*, London, 1962.
   'Introduction' to Tawney, R.H. *Equality*, London, 1964.
Townsend, P., *Poverty*, Harmondsworth, 1985.

'The Meaning of Poverty', *British Journal of Sociology*, Vol. XIII, No. 3, 1962.
Tragtenberg, M. de, 'Marx/Bakunin', *Nova Escrita Ensaio*, Año V., No. 11/12, 1983.
Administração, poder e ideologia, Sáo Paulo, 1980.
Vanderlint, J., *Money Answers All Things*, London, 1734.
Vargas Lozano, G. (ed.), *Ideologia, teoria y politica en el pensamiento de Marx*, Puebla, 1980.
Marx y su critica de la filosofia, Mexico, 1984.
Wainwright, H. and Elliott, D., *The Lucas Plan: A New Trade Unionism in the Making?*, London, 1982.
Walden, B., 'Clues that tell why Dukakis is a Labour hero', *The Sunday Times*, 31 July 1988.
Walker, D., 'The pure and applied scientist', *The Times*, 8 November 1984.
Waters, M.-A., Introduction to Rosa Luxemburg, *Reform or Revolution*, New York, 1970.
Watkins, F.M., *The Age of Ideology: Political Thought, 1750 to the Present*, New York, 1964.
Waxman, C.I. (ed.), *The End of Ideology Debate*, New York, 1968.
Weber, Marianne, *Max Weber*, Tübingen, 1926.
Weber, Max, *The Theory of Social and Economic Organization*, (ed. and introducted by Talcott Parsons), New York, 1964.
'Objectivity', in Shils, E.A. and Finch, H.A. (eds), *The Methodology of the Social Sciences*, New York, 1949.
Collected Political Works, Munich, 1921.
General Economic History, London, 1961.
Gesammelte Aufsätze zur Wissenschaftslehre, Tübingen, 1922.
The Protestant Ethic and the Spirit of Capitalism, London, 1965.
The Theory of Social and Economic Organization, (Part I of *Wirtschaft und Gesellschaft*), New York, 1947.
'Science as a vocation', in Gerth, H.H. and Mills, C.W. (eds), *From Max Weber: Essays in Sociology*, London, 1948.
Wiener, N., 'Some moral and technical consequences of automation', 1960, reprinted in Douglas, J.D. (ed.), *The Technological Threat*, New Jersey, 1971.
Williams, R., *Culture and Society*, London, 1980.
Problems in Materialism and Culture, London, 1980.
Wolfe, B.D. 'Introduction' to Luxemburg, R., *The Russian Revolution*, Michigan, 1961.
Wuthnow, R., Hunter, J.D., Bergesen, A. and Kurzweil, E., *Cultural Analysis: The Work of Peter L. Berger, Mary Douglas, Michel Foucault and Jürgen Habermas*, London, 1984.
Young-Bruehl, E., *Hannah Arendt: the Love of the World*, New Haven, 1982.
Zetkin, C., *Um Rosa Luxemburg's Stellung zur russischen Revolution*, Moscow-Leningrad, 1922.

INDEX